W9-CGQ-362

John,

Your contributions are a big part of this.

thanks Alan

MAKING THE ENVIRONMENT COUNT

NEW HORIZONS IN ENVIRONMENTAL ECONOMICS

General Editors: Wallace E. Oates, *Professor of Economics, University of Maryland, USA* and Henk Folmer, *Professor of Economics, Wageningen Agricultural University, The Netherlands and Professor of Environmental Economics, Tilburg University, The Netherlands*

This important series is designed to make a significant contribution to the development of the principles and practices of environmental economics. It includes both theoretical and empirical work. International in scope, it addresses issues of current and future concern in both East and West and in developed and developing countries.

The main purpose of the series is to create a forum for the publication of high quality work and to show how economic analysis can make a contribution to understanding and resolving the environmental problems confronting the world in the twenty-first century.

Recent titles in the series include:

Designing Effective Environmental Regimes
The Key Conditions
Jørgen Wettestad

Environmental Networks
A Framework for Economic Decision-Making and Policy Analysis
Kanwalroop Kathy Dhanda, Anna Nagurney and Padma Ramanujam

The International Yearbook of Environmental and Resource Economics
1999/2000
Edited by Henk Folmer and Tom Tietenberg

Valuing Environmental Benefits
Selected Essays of Maureen Cropper
Maureen Cropper

Controlling Air Pollution in China
Risk Valuation and the Definition of Environmental Policy
Therese Feng

Sustainable Agriculture in Brazil
Economic Development and Deforestation
Jill L. Caviglia

The Political Economy of Environmental Taxes
Nicolas Wallart

Trade and the Environment
Selected Essays of Alistair M. Ulph
Alistair M. Ulph

Water Management in the 21st Century
The Allocation Imperative
Terence Richard Lee

Making the Environment Count

Selected Essays of Alan Randall

Alan Randall

Professor and Chair, Department of Agricultural, Environmental, and Development Economics, The Ohio State University, USA

NEW HORIZONS IN ENVIRONMENTAL ECONOMICS

Edward Elgar

Cheltenham, UK • Northampton, MA, USA

© Alan Randall, 1999

All rights reserved. No part of this publication may be reproduced, stored in a retrieval system, or transmitted in any form or by any means, electronic, mechanical or photocopying, recording, or otherwise without the prior permission of the publisher.

Published by
Edward Elgar Publishing Limited
Glensanda House
Montpellier Parade
Cheltenham
Glos GL50 1UA
UK

Edward Elgar Publishing, Inc.
136 West Street
Suite 202
Northampton
Massachusetts 01060
USA

A catalogue record for this book is available from the British Library

Library of Congress Cataloguing in Publication Data

Randall, Alan, 1944–
    Making the environment count : selected essays of Alan Randall /
Alan Randall.
    (New horizons in environmental economics)
    A selection of 17 book chapters and journal articles previously
published 1972–1999.
    Includes bibliographical references.
    1. Environmental economics.   2. Sustainable development.
3. Biological diversity.   4. Environmental policy.   I. Title.
II. Series.
HC79.E5R354   1999
333.7 — dc21   98–17604
                                                                  CIP

ISBN 1 84064 086 3

Printed and bound in Great Britain by MPG Books Ltd, Bodmin, Cornwall

Contents

Acknowledgements

The author and publishers wish to thank the following who have kindly given permission for the use of copyright material.

Academic Press, Inc. for: 'Bidding Games for Valuation of Aesthetic Environmental Improvements', with Berry Ives and Clyde Eastman, *Journal of Environmental Economics and Management*, **1**, 1974, 132–49; 'A Satisfactory Benefit Cost Indicator from Contingent Valuation', with John P. Hoehn, *Journal of Environmental Economics and Management*, **14**, 1987, 226–47.

The American Agricultural Economics Association and the *American Journal of Agricultural Economics* for: 'Market Solutions to Externality Problems: Theory and Practice', **54** (2), May 1972, 175–83; 'Valuing Increments and Decrements in Natural Resource Service Flows', with David S. Brookshire and John R. Stoll, **62** (3), August 1980, 478–88; 'Methodology, Ideology, and the Economics of Policy: Why Resource Economists Disagree, **67** (5), December 1985, 1022–9; 'What Practicing Agricultural Economists Really Need to Know About Methodology', **75**, October 1993, 48–59.

American Economic Association for: 'Consumer's Surplus in Commodity Space', with John R. Stoll, *American Economic Review*, **70** (3), June 1980, 449–55; 'Too Many Proposals Pass the Benefit Cost Test', with John P. Hoehn, *American Economic Review*, **79** (3), June 1989, 544–51.

Cambridge University Press for: 'Thinking about the Value of Biodiversity' in *Biodiversity and Landscapes: A Paradox of Humanity*, Ke Chung Kim and Robert D. Weaver (eds), 1994, 271–85.

Elsevier Science Publishers for: 'Total and Nonuse Values' in *Measuring the Demand for Environmental Quality*, John B. Braden and Charles D. Kolstad (eds), 1991, 303–21, references.

National Academy Press for: 'What Mainstream Economists Have to Say About the Value of Biodiversity' in *Biodiversity*, E. O. Wilson (ed.), National Academy Press, 1988, 217–23.

Westview Press for: 'Existence Value in a Total Valuation Framework', with John R. Stoll in *Managing Air Quality and Scenic Resources at National Parks and Wilderness Areas*, Robert D. Rowe and Lauraine G. Chestnut (eds), 1983, 265–74.

The University of Wisconsin Press for: 'A Difficulty with the Travel Cost Method',

Land Economics, **70** (1), February 1994, 88–96; 'The Rationality of a Safe Minimum Standard', with Michael C. Farmer, *Land Economics*, **74** (3), August 1998, 287–302.

The World Bank for: 'Market Failure and the Efficiency of Irrigated Agriculture' in *Efficiency in Irrigation: The Conjunctive Use of Surface and Groundwater Resources*, Gerald T. O'Mara (ed.), 1988, 21–30.

Every effort has been made to trace all the copyright holders but if any have been inadvertently overlooked the publishers will be pleased to make the necessary arrangements at the first opportunity.

Introduction

The essays collected in this volume span 30 years of work on a consistent theme: making the environment count. In Part I, the concern is with identifying the limits of competitive markets in reflecting demands for environmental quality. In Part II, the agenda is to ensure that demands for environmental quality are fully reflected in benefit cost analysis of public projects and policies. In Part III, I turn to issues of conservation, sustainability and biodiversity, asking: to what extent can sustainability and biodiversity values be reflected in benefit cost accounts; whether good reasons exist for paying attention to benefits and costs when making policy decisions about sustainability and biodiversity; and whether good reasons can be found for adopting a safe minimum standard of conservation as a constraint on business-as-usual. The final Part, Part IV, reviews recent developments in scientific methodology and the methodology of economics, paying some attention to implications for environmental economics.

These 16 essays were selected from publications totalling well in excess of 200. In so doing, I was conscious of only two criteria: my most-cited works should be included where possible, along with some less well-known pieces that, I thought, said something important. Upon looking at my selections as a group, some patterns began to emerge. First, publication outlets have been quite eclectic, ranging from major journals such as the *American Economic Review*, *American Journal of Agricultural Economics*, *Land Economics* and *Journal of Environmental Economics and Management*, to book chapters and, in the case of Chapter 2, what can fairly be called 'fugitive literature'. In two cases (Chapters 2 and 13), I have preferred to include an obscure paper revisiting, improving and extending an argument, rather than the better-known original. Second, while I have been involved in more than my share of empirical studies over the years, the selected works are mostly conceptual. Yet this is a practical kind of conceptual work, touching upon the ethical foundations of public policy, the methodological underpinnings of environmental economics, the implica-tions of market failure for policy and institutional design, the welfare-theoretic foundations of benefit cost analysis, and the conceptual foundations for empirical methods of valuing environmental amenities. Even the two empirical studies included (Chapters 6 and 7) are deeply concerned with conceptual foundations. Third, the 1970s, '80s and '90s are all well represented, although it is true, naturally, that the citations record tends to justify including the earlier pieces, while the later ones tend to make the cut mostly on account of the author's optimism about their importance. Finally, I am delighted that, as it turns out, this collection enables me to honour by their inclusion my research colleagues Clyde Eastman and David Brookshire and my former graduate students Berry Ives, John Stoll, John Hoehn and Michael Farmer.

Market failure

In the 1960s the Coase theorem challenged the emerging field of environmental economics in a fundamental way. Those conflicts that we called externalities have a certain kind of symmetry, Coase claimed: nuisances inconvenience affected parties but, if those affected parties were able to obtain injunctions against nuisance activities, that would inconvenience those who create the nuisances. Yet, when the externality is inefficient, there exist unexploited gains from trade and, regardless of the initial assignment of rights between acting and affected parties, subsequent trade will restore efficiency. In the polar case of frictionless trade, the equilibrium amount of nuisance is unaffected by the initial assignment of liability. This result was, of course, counter-intuitive to environmental economists and the environmental community at large. If, as we had been taught, pollution is properly conceptualized as an externality, Coase was arguing that pollution would be efficiently abated regardless of whether rights favoured receptors or polluters. Chapter 1, 'Market Solutions to Externality Problems: Theory and Practice' (1972), summarizes work begun in my doctoral dissertation research at Oregon State University in 1969 and 1970. Given income effects and positive transaction costs, equilibrium pollution loads after Coasean trading will be lower when rights favour the receptors. The initial assignment of rights matters, after all.

The 1960s literature on market failure was replete also with articles worrying about the nature of public goods: is the concept of nonrivalry enough to make a good public, or must some kind of nonexclusiveness be present also? In Randall (1983), it was argued that so-called 'common property' resource problems were really problems of nonexclusiveness; the discussion of public goods had become confused because two quite separate ideas were involved, nonrivalry and nonexclusiveness; and inefficient externality will not persist unless unaccompanied by nonrivalry and/or nonexclusiveness. Therefore, externality is a redundant concept, and the useful content of the market failure idea is captured in the concepts of nonexclusiveness and nonrivalry (or congestibility, the impure case of nonrivalry).

Thus it had finally penetrated my mind that the Coase theorem, being about externality, was quite simply not a theorem in environmental economics. Those environmental problems that persist (and thus require policy solutions) involve nonrivalry and/or nonexclusiveness, and their solutions must address these root causes. Chapter 2, 'Market Failure and the Efficiency of Irrigated Agriculture' (1988), includes the 1983 argument, and extends it by considering the viability of voluntary cooperation to solve nonrivalry and nonexclusiveness problems.

My interest in solutions to market failure problems continues, with recent research on monitoring and enforcement strategies for point-source pollution control (Hentschel and Randall, 1999) and for preventing the introduction of invasive exotic species via ships' ballast water (Gollamudi and Randall, 1998); and a new project on pollution permit trading among point and nonpoint sources, involving colleague Brent Sohngen and graduate students Helen Pushkarskaya and Michael Taylor.

Benefit cost analysis

Having spent much of the 1980s and 1990s in environmental policy discussions where economists were distinctly in the minority, I became convinced that the reasons given by economists for attending to benefits and costs in environmental policy decisions were generally unconvincing to the educated public at large.

Chapter 3, 'Taking Benefits and Costs Seriously' (1999), is unequivocal: the public has a point, and economists' usual reasons for according a public role to benefits and costs are unconvincing. Returning to philosophical foundations and drawing upon an important article by my colleague Don Hubin (1994), I argue that benefit cost analysis is an account of preference satisfaction and that preference satisfaction counts for something, but cannot count for everything, in any plausible theory of the good. Taking up a theme that is prominent also in Part III, I conclude that it makes sense for society to maximize the excess of benefits over costs so long as there are no more important considerations at stake; and that it makes sense to address those more important considerations that might be relevant by imposing constraints on the domain in which benefits and costs are decisive. While people may argue at length about just what particular constraints should be imposed – and that is exactly the sort of question that should engage public discussion – the general principle should be 'don't do anything disgusting'.

Chapter 6, 'Bidding Games for Valuation of Aesthetic Environmental Improvements' (1974), presents the results of one of the early contingent valuation studies. This paper made its mark in a number of ways – including providing a rigorous welfare-theoretic basis for contingent valuation, and introducing formal experimentation and hypothesis testing into empirical contingent valuation research – and has been cited widely and reprinted in several anthologies. Apparent anomalies in contingent valuation data sets led to several conceptual explorations. In Chapter 4, 'Consumer's Surplus in Commodity Space' (1980), we show that standard theory requires that the willingness to accept (WTA) and willingness to pay (WTP) measures of welfare change be equal in absolute value, in the polar case of private goods traded in frictionless markets, but permits them to deviate when valuing environmental goods that are nonrival and have relatively few good substitutes and/or have high income elasticity of total value. This result was subsequently elaborated by Hanemann (1991). Chapter 7, 'Valuing Increments and Decrements in Natural Resource Service Flows' (1980), continues this line of conceptual development, and provides a framework for application and results of an extensive empirical study.

In Chapter 9, 'A Satisfactory Benefit Cost Indicator from Contingent Valuation' (1987), we make a radical departure from the thinking of the day concerning what is going on in the minds of contingent valuation respondents: we assume a rational, utility maximizing and risk-averse respondent, an approach that surprised even the anonymous referees, whose discomfort delayed publication for several years. Starting with these assumptions about respondent motivation, we conclude (among other things) that respondents are likely to underestimate their own WTP and overestimate their own WTA, and that the referendum method of contingent valuation has relatively trouble-free incentive properties. Carson, Groves and Machina (1998) reaffirmed this result, while providing a more complete and rigorous analysis of the incentive properties of contingent valuation. In Chapter 5, 'Too Many Proposals Pass the Benefit Cost Test' (1989), we provide a general proof of the proposition that WTP for a package of innovations valued holistically will be less than the sum of WTPs for its components valued independently and that, as the number of components in the policy agenda grows large, the procedure of evaluating each component independently will result in some false 'passes' of the benefit cost test. While this result has broad implications for benefit cost analysis, it has also provided insights essential to understanding particular issues, such as the 'embedding' and 'part–whole' problems in contingent valuation. A considerable subsequent literature has developed these implications.

Given that contingent valuation is used frequently to estimate option values, existence values and total values including use and nonuse values, Chapters 8 and 10 – 'Existence Value in a Total Valuation Framework' (1983) and 'Total and Nonuse Values' (1991) – develop the conceptual foundations of total value, nonuse value and existence value. Chapter 10 builds on insights developed in Chapter 5, distinguishing between holistic total valuation (which is valid) and independent piecewise valuation (which is not), and defining a valid sequenced piecewise valuation. The practical implication of this is to provide some rigorous caveats concerning the common practices of valuation, often using different methods to value different categories of benefits and benefits transfer.

The travel cost method of valuing recreation benefits is often called a 'revealed demand method'. In Chapter 11, 'A Difficulty with the Travel Cost Method' (1994), I point out that travel cost data sets reveal much less than is commonly supposed about demand. Specifically, the analyst observes distance travelled, travel time and on-site time, but cannot observe the cost of travel and the value of time. In contrast to standard demand data sets, the travel cost analyst observes quantity but not price. The cost of travel and time is known subjectively to the traveller, we believe, but must be inferred by the analyst, who typically uses some set of conventions for this purpose. The upshot is that the welfare measures generated by the travel cost method are ordinal at best: if the analyst had applied a different convention for transforming distance travelled into trip cost, a different welfare measure would have been generated.

If space limitations for this volume had been less constraining, I would have included three more essays to illustrate the breadth of our work on nonmarket valuation and to showcase the contributions of two more of my former graduate students. Meier and Randall (1991) clarify the roles of insurance and contingent claims markets in benefit cost analysis under uncertainty; and inclusion here of that paper on option value would have rounded out the series of essays on total value, nonuse value and existence value. While contingent valuation and the travel cost method are featured in this volume, Kriesel, Randall and Lichtkoppler (1993) provide an interesting application of hedonic price analysis to estimating benefits of shoreline protection along Lake Erie. Finally, approaches to economic assessment of environmental damage are currently moving away from welfare change measure-ment in money metric terms and towards determining the scale of environmental restoration projects that would compensate directly for the damage. In Randall (1997), a paper that also has some interesting things to say about altruism and nonuse value, I develop the rudiments of a welfare-theoretic model of exact resource compensation.

Sustainability and biodiversity
A research programme in total value and nonuse value has clear implications for the

economic value of biodiversity, and these implications are spelled out briefly in Chapter 12, 'What Mainstream Economists Have to Say About the Value of Biodiversity' (1988). In addition, that chapter is clear (some would say, subversively clear) about the limited purview of the economic approach: welfare economics implements a particular moral theory, whereas in society at large there is an ongoing contest among different moral theories. This basic insight – that welfare economics, and therefore benefit cost analysis, is an exercise in applied moral philosophy, yet it implements a moral theory that is at best one contender in an ongoing and unresolved contest among moral theories – motivates much of my recent work, including Chapters 3, 13 and 14 in this volume.

If the contest among moral theories cannot be resolved, policy must move forward on the basis of heuristics: policy rules that people can agree on even though they might offer quite different reasons in support of those rules. In Randall (1991), I argued that utilitarians, contractarians and Kantians could well agree that some attention should be paid to benefits and costs when making policy decisions about protecting biodiversity, but they might agree also to impose a safe minimum standard (SMS) of conservation. An expanded version of that argument is provided here in Chapter 13, 'Thinking about the Value of Biodiversity' (1994).

In Chapter 14, 'The Rationality of a Safe Minimum Standard' (1998), we address head-on a long-standing criticism of the SMS, inconsistency: whatever justifies business-as-usual cannot also justify a discrete switch to conservation policies when the SMS is breached. We argue, in effect, that the consistency issue is moot. Given that standard moral theories are seriously incomplete in their treatment of obligations towards future generations, and the contest among moral theories is inconclusive, why should we insist that a policy rule be completely consistent with some particular moral theory? To make progress in justifying the SMS, we address the case of a natural resource necessity, so that human suffering is certain if the resource fails to be sustained. We identify a simple set of heuristics upon which diverse moral agents might reasonably be expected to agree, and show that these heuristics support the SMS as a constraint on business-as-usual.

In addition, we resolve a long-standing problem in the SMS literature. SMS proponents agree that it is reasonable to abandon the SMS should the costs of abiding it prove intolerably large. The difficulty is that the intolerable cost loophole is usually presented as an *ad hoc* addendum to the SMS concept. We show that, in the sustainability case where there is likely to be broad agreement that substantial sacrifice should be borne to prevent depletion of an essential resource, the trigger point for the SMS and the magnitude of the intolerable cost must be determined jointly if the SMS is to be effective. A society with a low tolerance for sacrifice would need to set the trigger point relatively high, that is, to implement conservation policies well before a sustainability crisis is upon them.

The bad news is that in a class of cases where the SMS is commonly recommended, preservation of species upon which human welfare can hardly be said to depend, agreement among diverse moral agents concerning the magnitude of the intolerable cost may break down. For utilitarians impressed with the modest welfare impact of species loss, the intolerable cost might be relatively small, whereas

Kantians, impressed with the intrinsic values at stake, might insist that large costs must be incurred to protect such species.

Methodology
Among natural resource and environmental economists, there co-exist various persistent schools of thought. Natural resource economists tend to think of themselves as either neoclassical or institutionalist. Environmental economists usually consider themselves neoclassical, whereas ecological economists may readily confess institutionalist leanings. Among natural resource and environmental economists, one also finds some neo-Austrian libertarians. In Chapter 15, 'Methodology, Ideology, and the Economics of Policy: Why Resource Economists Disagree' (1985), I examine these various schools of thought and show that adherents of the various schools disagree not just about the answers, but also about what questions matter and how those questions should be framed. Since the different paradigms are noncomparable, if follows that these disagreements cannot be resolved by direct tests of competing hypotheses; instead, the prospect is for long wars of attrition among the competing paradigms.

Chapter 16, 'What Practicing Agricultural Economists Really Need to Know About Methodology' (1993), is addressed to agricultural economists and applied economists generally. It summarizes recent developments in the philosophy of science and extends Popper's critical rationalism and McCloskey's rhetoric in ways that make them less susceptible to charges of relativism. Environmental economists will be interested in the final sections of that chapter which apply the general methodological position developed earlier to the specific cases of econometrics and contingent valuation of nonmarket goods and services.

Concluding comment
In pursuing a research agenda to make the environment count there is, at least in principle, the possibility of making it count too much; and I promised myself at the beginning of my career that I would remain alert to the risk of crossing that line by design or inadvertence. Nevertheless, I doubt very much that the line has yet been crossed by myself, kindred researchers or the policy processes of the real world. In particular cases, the threat of overvaluation is taken seriously and, for example, various tests are performed, calibration of contingent valuation results is suggested and open debate about the validity of the whole undertaking ensues. That process, *per se*, has the virtue both of challenging the research community and warning the public at large not to take the experts too seriously until they have their act together. But, in the bigger picture, my intuition that the environment remains, if anything, under-valued and underrepresented in the policy process is secure. So I am still trying to do my bit, in a clear-eyed and level-headed way, to make the environment count.

References
Carson, R., T. Groves and M. Machina (1998), 'Economic responses to preference surveys', working paper, Dept of Economics, University of California, San Diego.
Gollamudi, H. and A. Randall (1998), 'A monitoring and enforcement strategy to prevent introduction of nonindigenous species via transoceanic shipping', in A. Dragun and K. Jakobsson (eds), *Frontiers of*

Environmental Economics, Swedish University of Agricultural Sciences, Uppsala, Ch. 7.

Hanemann, M. (1991), 'Willingness to pay and to accept: how much can they differ?', *American Economic Review*, **81**, 635–47.

Hentschel, E. and Alan Randall (1999), 'An integrated strategy to reduce monitoring and enforcement costs', *Environmental and Resource Economics*, (in press).

Hubin, D. (1994), 'The moral justification of benefit/cost analysis', *Economics and Philosophy*, **10**, 169–94.

Kriesel, W., A. Randall and F. Lichtkoppler (1993), 'Estimating the benefits of shoreline erosion protection in Ohio's Lake Erie housing market',*Water Resources Research*, **29**, 795–801.

Meier, C. and A. Randall (1991), 'Use value under uncertainty: is there a "correct" measure?', *Land Economics*, **67**, 379–89.

Randall, A. (1983), 'The problem of market failure', *Natural Resources Journal*, **23**, 131–48.

Randall, A. (1991), 'The economic value of biodiversity', *Ambio – A Journal of the Human Environment*, **20** (2), 64–8.

Randall, A. (1997), 'What losses count? Examining some claims about aggregation rules for natural resources damages', *Contemporary Economic Policy*, **15**, 88–97.

PART I

MARKET FAILURE

[1]

Market Solutions to Externality Problems: Theory and Practice*

ALAN RANDALL

The concept of market solution to externality problems has received the favorable attention of many economic theorists. Yet, policy practitioners and the general public seem less enthusiastic. Theoretical studies and available empirical work have effectively demolished Coase's doctrine of the allocative neutrality of liability rules. In reality, a full liability law will result in a greater degree of abatement of external diseconomies than will zero or intermediate liability laws. It is suggested that market solutions can be seriously considered in a world with pervasive externalities only if something approaching a full liability rule is established. Even then, excessive transactions costs may limit the success of market solutions.

AGRICULTURAL economists are directly and immediately concerned with externalities in agricultural settings, such as the problems of pesticide residues and animal waste disposal. But their concern with externalities is much wider than these. All forms of pollution from industrial and municipal sources in both urban and rural areas, externalities associated with consumption activities such as driving automobiles for pleasure, the whole range of externalities arising from land zoning, subdivision, and provision of utilities and community services, and so on, are of interest to the agricultural economist because they influence the geographic distribution and the urban-suburban-rural mix of the population.

An externality is said to exist wherever the utility of one or more individuals is dependent upon, among other things, one or more activities which are under the control of someone else. Buchanan and Stubblebine [2] have defined a Pareto-relevant externality as one which may be modified in such a way as to make the externally affected party better off without making the acting party worse off. A Pareto-relevant externality is characterized by the existence of potential gains from trade between the affected and acting parties. In what follows, the term externality may be taken to mean Pareto-relevant externality. An external diseconomy is an externality in which the affected party is made worse off by the activities of the acting party.

Many of society's environmental quality problems, particularly those types of problems which are referred to in the popular literature as spillover effects, are the result of external diseconomies. Improvement of environmental quality requires a modification of the behavior of acting parties who produce these external diseconomies.[1]

The Theory

Economic theory is based on the premise that if one wishes to modify the behavior of an economic unit, one must modify the incentives facing that unit so that the preferred behavior becomes more appealing to it (i.e., more pleasant, more profitable, or both). Economic literature on environmental quality externalities considers three broad classes of methods of solution of environmental quality problems, each designed to make the creation of Pareto-relevant externalities less profitable to acting parties. They are (1) market solutions, following establishment of a liability rule to serve as a starting point for negotiations; (2) systems of per unit taxes, charges, fines, or subsidies; and (3) systems of standards, enforced by the threat of fines or jail sentences. While (1) relies on private negotiation and (2) and (3) on government intervention, the three classes represent a clear progression from more to less reliance on market forces to determine the equilibrium output of externality.

The logical underpinnings of the suggestion that the market may be relied upon to achieve solutions to externality problems are presented by its supporters as follows: A Pareto-relevant externality is, by definition, characterized by the existence of potential gains from trade be-

* Journal Article 409, New Mexico Agricultural Experiment Station, Las Cruces. This article has benefited from the helpful comments of an anonymous reviewer.

ALAN RANDALL *is assistant professor of agricultural economics at New Mexico State University.*

[1] Mishan [11] and an anonymous reviewer suggest that the adverse effects of a degraded environment on people may in some cases be minimized by evasive action taken by the affected party. However, this type of solution would not strictly improve environmental quality.

tween the acting and affected parties. Surely, then, self-interest can be relied upon to ensure the realization of these potential gains through exchange between the involved parties. As always, efficient exchange requires precisely defined and rigidly enforced property rights. In the case of external diseconomies, these property rights include some specification of the laws of liability for damages associated with the diseconomy. If liability rules are specified in a particular manner—allowing a specified amount of externality to be created with impunity and that amount to be exceeded only if the affected party is willing to agree—they serve as the starting point for negotiations to realize the potential gains from trade. The two extreme examples of such liability rules are the zero liability rule, L^z, and the full liability rule, L^f; an infinite number of intermediate rules could be conceived. L^z specifies that external diseconomies in any amount may be created with impunity; under such a rule, the affected party would have an incentive to offer a bribe to induce the acting party to reduce his output of external diseconomy. L^f specifies that absolutely no externality may be created without the consent of the affected party; under such a rule, the acting party would have an incentive to offer compensation to induce the affected party to accept a positive amount of externality.

Coase [5] perceived that regardless of which liability rule is in operation one or another party has an incentive to modify a Pareto-relevant externality. Given perfect competition and zero transactions costs,[2] negotiations will continue until all gains from trade have been exhausted. Coase argued that all gains from trade will be exhausted at the same Pareto-efficient outcome, regardless of which liability rule is in operation. In other words, the market solution to a particular externality problem is

allocatively neutral with respect to the assignment of liability. Of course, the specification of liability influences the final distribution of income at the completion of the exchange, since an L^z rule would result in the affected party making payments to the acting party and an L^f rule would result in the opposite flow of payments.

It is understandable that such an approach to externalities would be attractive to academic economists. It relies upon the market to establish the price of an externality. All the society has to do is to establish a liability rule, and it does not matter too much what that rule is since any rule will result in the same Pareto-efficient equilibrium solution. If society is concerned with income distribution, it may either attempt to choose a liability rule which will lead to a satisfactory distribution of income or use any other income redistribution method to attempt to restore a situation of equity.

Of the three broad groups of methods of solving externality problems listed above, it is noticeable that academic economists usually prefer market solutions or systems of fines, charges, taxes, or subsidies. There is a group of academic economists who remain fervent supporters of the market solution method. However, politicians, administrators, and the general public seem to have more faith in systems of standards. This divergence of opinion between academic economists on the one hand and the public and its representatives on the other motivated the preparation of this paper, which focuses on market solutions in theory and practice and offers some speculations on their future.

The Coasian analysis of externality was rapidly enshrined in the economic literature. Whereas Coase's analysis concentrated entirely on the case where both the acting and the affected parties were single firms engaged in production, Davis and Whinston [7] in 1965 extended the analysis to the case where both parties were single consumers. Their results duplicated those of Coase in all respects, including the finding of allocative neutrality of liability rules. Calabresi [4] spoke for the proponents of market solutions in 1968: all externalities can be internalized and all misallocations can be remedied by the market except to the extent that transactions cost money.[3]

---

[2] It is worthwhile to define transactions costs carefully, since they play an important part in the analysis to follow. Transactions costs are the costs of making and enforcing decisions. Included are the costs of obtaining information, establishing one's bargaining position, bargaining and arriving at a group decision, and enforcing the decision made. Any method of modifying externalities will involve some transactions costs. The size of the transactions costs and the type of transactions services used are likely to vary with the use of different types of solution methods and with the actual solution obtained. Transactions costs may be so large that they become a major factor in the selection of an efficient method of solution of any particular externality problem.

[3] This line of reasoning culminated in Demsetz's argument [8] that where a market for an external diseconomy does not exist it should not exist, since the benefits from

Beginning in 1966, the Coasian analysis came under attack from at least two quarters. One group claimed that Coase's assumptions were so far removed from the real world that his analysis was irrelevant for prescriptive purposes; and another group accepted Coase's static-perfect competition assumptions for the sake of argument. Even so, they were able to demolish Coase's claim of allocative neutrality of liability rules. Dolbear [9], Randall [13, 14], and Mishan [11], using static-perfect competition analysis of two-party cases, have made varying degrees of progress toward circumscribing the claimed generality of Coase's allocative neutrality doctrine. Here summarized is the treatment in Randall [14], in which the following propositions are proven mathematically.

In an external diseconomy situation where both the acting and affected parties are consumers, a change in liability rules will change the budget constraint faced by both. Under the L^z rule, the affected party would offer the acting party a bribe. Under the L^f rule, the acting party would offer compensation to the affected party. The relevant budget constraints are under L^z, for the affected party,

$$(1) \quad \overline{Y}_1 - \bar{p}_1 q_{11} - \cdots - \bar{p}_m q_{m1} \\ - p_n^*(q_{n2}^{\,0} - q_{n2}) = 0$$

and for the acting party,

$$(2) \quad \overline{Y}_2 - \bar{p}_1 q_{12} - \cdots - \bar{p}_m q_{m2} - \bar{p}_n q_{n2} \\ + p_n^*(q_{n2}^{\,0} - q_{n2}) = 0$$

under L^f, for the affected party,

$$(3) \quad \overline{Y}_1 - \bar{p}_1 q_{11} - \cdots - \bar{p}_m q_{m1} + p_n^* q_{n2}^{\,0} \\ - p_n^*(q_{n2}^{\,0} - q_{n2}) = 0$$

and for the acting party,

$$(4) \quad \overline{Y}_2 - \bar{p}_1 q_{12} - \cdots - \bar{p}_m q_{m2} - \bar{p}_n q_{n2} \\ - p_n^* q_{n2}^{\,0} + p_n^*(q_{n2}^{\,0} - q_{n2}) = 0$$

---

such a market clearly cannot exceed the costs of its operation. The absence of an observable market is, in itself, a market solution. This argument would seem to lead to the conclusion that any externalities which are observed to exist unmodified should not be modified, since transactions costs must therefore be so high that modification is unprofitable. However, the fallacy is obvious. The unprofitability of market solution does not prove that solution by any other method must also be unprofitable. If some other method of solution involves lower transactions costs, solution by that method may be preferable to no solution at all.

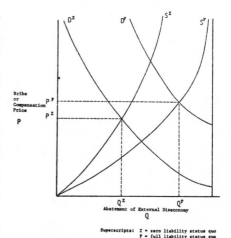

Superscripts: Z = zero liability status quo   F = full liability status quo

Figure 1. Market solutions to externality in consumption

Source: Randall [13, 14]

where the affected party suffers an external diseconomy from the acting party's consumption of the good n,

    $\overline{Y}_j$ is the income of Mr. j,

    q_{ij} is the consumption of the good i by Mr. j,

    $\bar{p}_i$ is the competitive market price of the good i,

    p_n^* is the unit bribe or compensation price,

and $q_{n2}^{\,0}$ is the amount of the good n which would be consumed by the acting party if $p_n^* = 0$.

These changes in budget constraints associated with changes in liability rules are sufficient to induce shifts in the resultant demand and supply curves for abatement of the external diseconomy. This is true for all cases, except the very special case where the affected party has an income elasticity of demand for abatement equal to zero and the acting party has a zero income elasticity of demand for the commodity associated with the externality. Figure 1 shows the situation. The L^f rule results in a greater level of abatement of an external diseconomy than does the L^z rule. Where any consumers are involved in an externality situation, the demand or supply curves of abatement associated with those consumers will shift with a change in

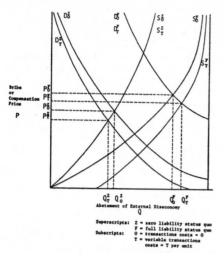

Figure 2.   Market solutions to externality in consumption: the effect of transactions costs

Source: Randall [13, 14]

may often be the case in practice, that transactions costs may be so great that movements away from the starting point defined by the liability law are impossible. In such cases, an L^z law results in zero abatement while an L^f law results in complete abatement of an external diseconomy.

In summary, allocative neutrality with respect to liability rules can be accepted only in situations where all of the involved parties are producers, the use of capital is a free good, and transactions costs are zero. In cases other than these (i.e., in almost every significant externality problem), an L^f rule will result in a market solution specifying a higher degree of abatement of external diseconomies than will an L^z rule.

Mishan [11] makes one further observation, which, although unproven in his article, seems plausible: the incentives for strategies to reduce the effects of external diseconomies are greater under a full liability law. The effects of pollution, for example, can be reduced by emission-reducing technological improvements, or by location of the externality producing business in an out-of-the-way place, or by various other means. Mishan also argues for a full liability rule on the grounds of equity. If polluters are likely to be more prosperous than the affected parties, he argues that a full liability rule would be more equitable than a zero liability rule.

If, following the arguments of Buchanan and Tullock [3] and Olson [12], transactions costs are likely to be larger when negotiations must be initiated by a large and diffuse group of individuals rather than by a much smaller group of individuals who are more vitally interested in this particular issue, it follows that in cases of pollution from industrial sources, an L^z rule is more likely than is the L^f rule to result in transactions costs too high for the achievement of a solution other than the status quo.

The current situation in the theory of market solutions to externality problems can be summarized as follows: A Pareto-relevant externality, being characterized by potential gains from trade, will generate incentives for one or the other of the involved parties to initiate negotiations aimed at modifying that externality. A solution different from the status quo situation may be achieved and, if perfect competition prevails in all relevant industries including the transactions industry, that solution may be Pareto-efficient. However, the resource allocation and income distribution characteristics of the solution achieved are not neutral to the choice of liability rules. In comparison with a

liability rules, resulting in different equilibrium levels of abatement.

In the case of externality in production, a change in liability rules will result in a change in equilibrium output of externality whenever (a) there is an inflexible capital constraint or (b) the use of capital has a positive price. The analysis is similar to that for externality in consumption: a change in liability rules changes the capital constraints affecting both parties. Again, an L^f rule will result in a greater level of abatement than an L^z rule.

Where transactions costs are greater than zero, the party who must pay makes an offer. However, the party who receives payment receives only the amount remaining after transactions costs have been subtracted. As a change in liability rules from L^z to L^f results in the former payer becoming the receiver of payment and vice versa, the assignment of liability affects the equilibrium output of externality when transactions costs are positive. In fairness, it must be noted that Coase [5] recognized that allocative neutrality is predicated upon zero transactions costs.

Figure 2 shows the effect of positive transactions costs on the equilibrium output of externality under the L^z and L^f rules. As unit transactions costs increase, the disparity between the equilibrium solutions under different liability rules increases. It is conceivable, and zero liability rule, a full liability rule will result in (1) a higher degree of abatement of an external diseconomy such as pollution, (2) a reallocation of resources toward pollution control and production of commodities which can be produced by low pollution processes, and (3) an income redistribution in favor of the affected party. The effective demolition of the doctrine of allocative neutrality of liability rules removes one of the prime advantages which has been claimed for market solutions to externality problems. The role of the body politic and the bureaucracy in setting the operative liability rule is now known to include the power to affect allocation of resources in production and allocation of budgets in consumption. In a macroeconomic sense, if externalities are as pervasive as is now believed, the power to set liability rules therefore implies the power to affect resource allocation in the whole economy, aggregate production and consumption, and relative and aggregate prices.

Economic Analyses of Observed Market Solutions

Economic analyses of market solutions to externality in practice, unfortunately, seem mostly confined to casual empiricism. As noted above, Demsetz [8] found several externality situations where no market transactions were observed. He attributed this to transactions costs so high that the operation of the market was unprofitable. Alexander [1] mentioned cases involving aluminum refining industries. In some cases market solutions have occurred where the aluminum industry pays compensation to agriculturalists and orchardists on nearby farms. In other cases, the aluminum industry has purchased the land affected by its emissions, creating a merger between acting and affected parties. However, parties less directly affected (e.g., citizens who may suffer some unpleasantness but no loss of agricultural productivity or future generations who may lose the assimilative power of the environment) may not feel that these externalities have been fully internalized.

In a notable exception to this trend of casual empiricism, Crocker [6] presented a reasonably careful regression analysis of market solutions over a time period during which the liability rule effectively changed. He examined a situation in which inorganic fertilizers were produced from locally mined phosphate rock in Polk County, Florida. Damage was observed to local citrus and beef cattle industries over an area of

approximately 400 square miles. Prior to 1957, a liability rule not very different from the zero liability rule of the theories presented here was in effect. The only recourse available to the affected parties was civil suit for damages. In such suits, the burden of proof of liability for these damages lay with the plaintiff. The burden of proof had been extremely onerous and no plaintiff had been successful in recovering any damages from the polluting fertilizer companies. Then, in 1957, an Air Pollution Control District was established. Fertilizer companies were in effect advised to buy the affected land or face the prospect of imposition of emission standards.

Crocker obtained and analyzed land sales data for a 20-year period, including 10 years before and 10 years after this effective change in the liability rule. In the earlier period there was a downward trend in land prices, correlated with the decreasing agricultural productivity of the land. However, after the establishment of the Air Pollution Control District, land prices began to rise as the fertilizer companies bought up land in order to avoid the imposition of emission standards. It was also observed that along with a rise in prices of affected land and a gradual but continuous increase in the amount of agricultural land in the ownership of the phosphate companies, the output of polluting emissions by the fertilizer companies was reduced gradually and consistently over the years. Crocker interpreted this reduction in emissions as the result of internalization of the externalities. When the companies owned most of the affected land, their optimum economic strategy was to maximize total returns from both the use of the land and the production of phosphate. No longer could they regard the land and the air above it as a cost-free waste disposal resource.

Crocker's empirical result was that the effective change in liability rules changed the allocative efficiency in the phosphate fertilizer, citrus, and beef industries. He was able to demonstrate that transactions costs were very much higher in the period when the liability situation was essentially L^z than in the later period when the fertilizer companies faced the threat of emissions standards. The change in the liability situation shifted the burden of initiating negotiations from the affected party to the acting party (which group had significantly fewer numbers). Also, the affected party was relieved of the burden of proving damage. Crocker was able to correlate a change in resource allocation with a change in liability rules and a concurrent change in transactions costs.[4] Significantly, the only detailed empirical study of market solutions to externality which has been completed has demonstrated that a change in liability rules changes resource allocation and the output of pollution emissions.

The Future of Market Solutions

What can be said, then, about market solutions to externality in practice? The theoretical and empirical demonstration that market solutions to externality problems are not allocatively neutral with respect to liability rules may provide some explanation of what has been the major practical objection to market solutions—they are very seldom observed in practice. In the past, laws with respect to externalities such as environmental pollution have been lenient, seldom and ineffectively enforced, or both. In a majority of cases, something approaching a zero liability rule has been in operation. The author's analyses have demonstrated that the zero liability rule is more likely than any positive liability rule to result in zero or low levels of abatement. If market solutions are to be used effectively to ensure environmental quality, the task seems to be that of converting liability rules to L^f, full liability, or to some intermediate position. The important policy question then becomes: are market solutions based on a full or intermediate liability rule preferable to solutions forced by systems of fines and subsidies or standards?

Kneese [10] argues vigorously against reliance upon market solutions on the grounds that market solutions are best adapted (or are adaptable only) to the two-party case, while the environmental quality problem arises from the disposal of wastes into common property resources. One, or a relatively small number of acting parties dumps wastes into a common property resource (e.g., air or water), reducing the welfare of many affected parties. This question can be considered now by briefly examining the operation of market solutions to a pollu-

tion problem under a full liability rule. The process of negotiating and enforcing a market solution can be divided into three major steps. It is possible to identify a number of alternative ways these steps can be carried out.

1. The *first step* is enforcement of recognition of the status quo established by an L^f rule. Firms polluting without having obtained the permission of the affected parties must be made to either cease polluting or obtain that permission. This could be done in several ways: **1A:** A public agency could ascertain that some emissions are being released[5] and then, **1A₁**, directly impose a very high penalty on the offender unless he ceases polluting or demonstrates he has obtained permission from the affected party, or, **1A₂**, ask a court to do the same; or, **1B:** The affected parties could initiate litigation to prove that emissions are being released and seek court enforcement of the L^f rule. Organization could occur in several ways: **1B₁**, unanimous action by the affected parties, or, **1B₂**, "unanimous" action by a leader or committee after a majority vote of the affected parties; or, **1B₃**, a class action initiated by one individual on behalf of the affected parties[6]; or, **1B₄**, a series of individual actions by affected parties.

2. The *second step:* The acting party has an incentive to initiate negotiations to induce the affected parties to accept a certain amount of emissions in exchange for compensation. The affected parties must be organized in some way in order to conduct their side of the negotiations. Possibilities are: **2A:** A public agency could bargain on behalf of the affected parties, or, **2B:** The affected parties could bargain in several ways: **2B₁**, unanimous action by the affected parties, or, **2B₂**, take a "unanimous" position and appoint a representative or committee to bargain, following a majority vote, or, **2B₃**, each individual affected could deal separately with the acting party.

3. The *third step* is the policing and enforcement of the agreement made. Compensation payments must be made as agreed and the agreed emission limit must not be exceeded. The possible types of organization of the affected party for this purpose parallel those in 1.

---

[4] Crocker interpreted this change in output of pollutants and resource allocation with the change in liability rules as being entirely attributable to the change in transactions costs. The theoretical work by Randall would suggest that the change in liability rules would result in a different solution with respect to pollution emissions and resource allocation even if transactions costs were unchanged. But this is a relatively minor quibble.

[5] Note: A full liability rule requires proof only that emissions are being released. This is a much simpler matter than proving that (a) damage is occurring and (b) the defendant is responsible.

[6] It would be necessary to change the law in most states to allow this.

It seems reasonable that different methods of organization of affected parties may lead to solutions which are different in terms of resource allocation and income distribution. The next few pages are devoted to speculation about these differences.

(a) The $1B_1$–$2B_1$–$3B_1$ procedure is most unlikely to occur widely, relying as it does on unanimity. Transactions costs required to achieve unanimity may be extremely high [3, 12].

(b) Decision procedures relying on $2B_3$, a series of bargains between the acting and the affected parties one-by-one, would suffer from the "holdout problem" familiar to urbanologists,[7] if the law required that agreement be reached with all affected parties. Also, since different affected individuals have different demand curves for abatement, while the firm has a single supply curve, individual bargains are likely to result in permission for different amounts of emission. Yet, the amount of emissions into a common property resource at any one time must necessarily be unique. So, extensive contracting and recontracting would be required to arrive at agreements with all parties allowing the same amount of emission. Transactions costs would be extremely high. The situation could conceivably be improved by a modification of the L^f rule so that once, say, 60 percent of the affected individuals had agreed upon a particular permissable amount of emissions and a unit compensation rate, the remainder must accept that agreement or go without compensation.

(c) The $1B_3$–$2B_2$–$3B_3$ and the $1B_2$–$2B_2$–$3B_2$ procedures would seem likely to involve lower transactions costs than the other procedures which rely on direct bargaining with the affected parties without the help of a governmental agency. These procedures reduce transactions costs because they allow the affected party to make decisions on the basis of less than unanimous consent. Too little is known about transactions costs to venture a guess on the relative costs of these kinds of direct bargaining methods versus bargaining by a public agency on behalf of the affected parties.

(d) The $1A$–$2A$–$3A$ pattern has been seen elsewhere. It is the system of charges advocated

by Kneese [10]. Kneese's proposal is really a type of market solution where the L^f rule is applied and a public agency bargains on behalf of the affected parties to arrive at the unit compensation price and undertakes to distribute the income from charges among the affected parties or to spend it on their behalf (e.g., on environmental projects). If the charge income simply goes into the general fund, the similarity of this type of solution to market solutions is more tenuous.

(e) It seems worthwhile to point out that any market solution relying on the help of a public or governmental agency (i.e., the $1A$–$2A$–$3A$ procedure) or on less than unanimous action by the affected parties, voluntarily organized for that purpose (i.e., the $1B_3$–$2B_2$–$3B_3$ and $1B_2$–$2B_2$–$3B_2$ procedures), would result in a unique amount of waste being dumped into a common property resource and a unique amount of compensation. This solution will not be optimal for all of the individuals and firms involved in an externality situation. (If it was optimal for all, unanimous agreement would have been reached.) So, some parties may regard the group agreement as simply a new starting point for further negotiations aimed at exhausting all possible gains from trade.

If this occurred, the group agreement would not be sabotaged. Further negotiations could not result in individual agreements to allow the quantity of emissions specified in the group agreement to be exceeded. Enforcement procedures for the group agreement would be adequate to prevent this. On the other hand, there may be some members of the affected party who feel so strongly about improvement of environmental quality that they would offer bribes to induce polluters to reduce emissions even more. The author fails to see any harm in such private agreements resulting, as they would, in reduced total emissions into the common property resource. On the other hand, the theory of common property resources does not lead him to expect such agreements to occur frequently.

(f) Decision procedures based on $2B_1$ or $2B_2$ introduce a bilateral monopoly situation. It is known that exchange in bilateral monopoly situations can achieve a unique solution in quantities but price is not uniquely determined. Rather, price depends upon relative bargaining strength. An L^f rule would give the affected parties the upper hand and therefore allow

---

[7] Once word is out, for example, that a firm is buying all houses on a block in order to demolish them and build a single large structure, one or more homeowners may hold out in order to obtain a very high price (i.e., to obtain most of the economic surplus for themselves).

them to gain the maximum possible compensation.

From this sketchy examination of the various decision and enforcement procedures which could conceivably be used to facilitate market solutions, it seems that procedures other than those which use 2A or 2B$_2$ (i.e., public agencies or committees) to facilitate the second step, the negotiations, have severe practical limitations. In cases of pollution in urban areas where there are many sources of pollution, each affecting different but overlapping geographical areas, reliance in 2B$_2$ may require a huge number of committees to be set up, each dealing with a single polluter. Alternatively, one committee would bargain with all polluters. If this latter alternative was chosen, the amount of expertise required of committee members and the amount of their time used would tend to grow so large that the committee would take on the characteristics of a public agency.

In summary, it seems that market solutions could in many cases achieve substantial improvement in environmental quality[8] if (1) the liability rules were changed to L^f or something approaching it and (2) the affected parties were legally required to either set up their own bargaining committee to make *binding* bargains or accept the help of a governmental agency to do it for them.

In the absence of institutional changes of this

----

[8] The allocative effects of a change to L^f have not received detailed consideration in this paper. In industrial pollution situations, a change to L^f would result in lower production of higher-priced commodities and lower industrial employment in a first-step adjustment. After the first stage of adjustment, a longer term adjustment may result in lower wages. Unless the practice was forbidden, some less sensitive people would move into the affected area to gain compensation; this may also drive wages down. A reduction in wages would lead to some lowering of costs of production. The final situation would lie somewhere between the initial situation and the first-stage adjustment.

nature, it seems that market solutions to externality problems are limited in practice.[9] However, market solutions based on the suggested institutional changes seem to deserve serious consideration and empirical analysis, if only because market solutions promise less institutional rigidity and inefficiency than, say, a system of nationwide emissions standards.

Conclusion

This article has attempted to examine market solutions to externality in theory and practice. It has not attempted to compare rigorously (1) market solutions with (2) systems of per unit fines, charges, taxes or subsidies, and (3) standards enforced by the threat of penalty. It is clear, nevertheless, that transactions costs are a crucial variable in the selection of suitable institutional mechanisms for the modification of externality. Unless ways can be found to reduce the transactions costs associated with market solutions, market solutions, even under an L^f rule, will remain the plaything of academic economists, largely ignored by policy makers and the general public.

Standards, although inefficient but not necessarily very inefficient, are simple decision rules, at least partially enforceable at low cost. Market solutions will be preferable to, for example, standards only if the gains in efficiency (*ceteris paribus* transactions costs) exceed the additional transactions costs of using the market solution method. The onus to develop ways in which market solutions can be made to work lies squarely on the shoulders of academic supporters of market solutions. An essential step is to generate institutional forms which minimize transactions costs.

----

[9] Crocker's paper suggests one workable method of market solution in some externality situations: a full liability rule (or something similar) and the purchase of affected property by the acting party. This "merger" solution is more likely to take place under a full liability rule.

References

[1] ALEXANDER, ROBERT M., "Social Aspects of Environmental Pollution," *Agr. Sci. Rev.* 9:9–18, 1971.

[2] BUCHANAN, JAMES M., AND WILLIAM CRAIG STUBBLEBINE, "Externality," *Economica* 29:371–384, Nov. 1962.

[3] ———, AND GORDON TULLOCK, *The Calculus of Consent. Logical Foundation of Constitutional Democracy,* Ann Arbor, University of Michigan Press, 1962.

[4] CALABRESI, G., "Transactions Costs, Resource Allocation and Liability Rules," *J. Law & Econ.* 11:66–73, 1968.

[5] COASE, R. H., "The Problem of Social Cost," *J. Law & Econ.* 3:1–44, Oct. 1960.

[6] CROCKER, T. D., "Externalities, Property Rights and Transactions Costs: An Empirical Study," Program in Environmental Economics, Working Paper No. 2, Department of Economics, University of California, Riverside, 1971.

[7] DAVIS, OTTO A., AND ANDREW B. WHINSTON, "Some Notes on Equating Private and Social Cost," *Southern Econ. J.* 32:113–126, Oct. 1965.

[8] DEMSETZ, H., "The Exchange and Enforcement of Property Rights," *J. Law & Econ.* 7:11–26, 1964.

[9] DOLBEAR, F. TRENERY, JR., "On the Theory of Optimum Externality," *Am. Econ. Rev.* 57:90–103, March 1967.

[10] Kneese, Allen V., "Environmental Pollution: Economics and Policy," *Am. Econ. Rev.* 61:153–166, May 1971.

[11] Mishan, E. J., "The Post-War Literature on Externalities: An Interpretative Essay," *J. Econ. Lit.* 9:1–28, March 1971.

[12] Olson, Mancur, Jr., *The Logic of Collective Action.*

Public Goods and the Theory of Groups, Cambridge, Harvard University Press, 1965.

[13] Randall, A., "Liability Rules, Transactions Costs and Optimum Externality," unpublished Ph.D. thesis, Oregon State University, 1971.

[14] ———, *On the Theory of Market Solutions to Externality Problems*, Oregon Agr. Exp. Sta. Special Rep. 351, 1972.

Reprinted from
American Journal of Agricultural Economics
Vol. 54, No. 2, May, 1972

[2]

Market Failure and the Efficiency of Irrigated Agriculture

Alan Randall

The efficiency of irrigated agriculture is inherently problematical. Economists have believed since Adam Smith (1776), and been able to prove since Arrow and Debreu (1954), that exchange between myriad independent buyers and sellers secured by well-specified property rights results in efficiency. There are other ways to attain efficiency, of course—a central manager with enormous capacity to assemble and process information conceivably could accomplish it—but market exchange under favorable conditions has a built-in tendency toward efficiency.

Economists are aware of a variety of circumstances in which the conditions are not favorable for attaining efficiency through unfettered exchange. Property rights may be incomplete, jointness in use may undermine the independence of individual buyers and sellers, and side effects may proliferate. Some kind of central management may seem essential. As though to reinforce their faith that in the usual scheme of things markets work for the best, economists have dubbed these unfavorable conditions "market failures."

This volume has been organized around the concept of market failures, or "externalities," in irrigated agriculture. My task is to discuss the conceptual basis for a diagnosis of market failure and the solutions that economists have suggested. In this chapter, market failure is the central theme and irrigated agriculture merely one specific area of application. Subsequent chapters focus directly on irrigation issues.

The concept of market failure has an interesting history, which is well worth exploring. As I see it, there have been three main stages: (1) a "market failure–government fix" stage, associated with Pigou (1932) and Bator (1958); (2) an "exclusive private property or disaster" stage, rooted in the writings of Coase (1960) and subsequently developed by a slew of neo-Austrian resource economists; and (3) an emerging thrust in which game theory formulations and

experimental evidence seem to be slowly but surely elucidating a vast and varied mosaic of possibilities that lie between the neo-Austrian dichotomy of private property and perdition. I consider it important to follow the argument through all three stages, because so many who would presume to offer advice on market failure issues seem to be mired in stage 1 or stage 2. Although I have made no detailed study of applications to the irrigation economy, I suspect that concepts emerging from stage 3 will be helpful in rethinking the problem of market failure in irrigated agriculture and suggesting novel solutions.

The Market Failure–Government Fix Stage

In the conventional wisdom of the market failure–government fix paradigm, there are four kinds of circumstance in which even a fundamentally competitive economy would experience market failure. These phenomena are externality, public goods, common property resources, and natural monopoly. For three of these phenomena, the conventional solutions call unambiguously for government action: to tax or regulate externalities, to raise revenue for public provision of public goods, and to regulate the pricing policies of natural monopolies. For common property resources, the range of endorsed solutions is broader. Regulation and taxation may be suggested, but it is also frequently suggested that the government specify private property rights and then stand aside as emerging markets restore efficiency.

I will argue that on close scrutiny all four concepts are wanting. All of the valid analytical content of these four terms is contained in two alternative concepts, nonexclusiveness and nonrivalry. Further, these two concepts eliminate much that is confusing and misleading in the four concepts they replace.

In 1954 Gordon introduced the notion of common property resources to the current generation of economists. Gordon's analysis and those of most subsequent authors have focused on the open access resource, that which is unowned. The analytics are basically correct in that context. The problem is that rights to the resource are *nonexclusive* and leave nobody in a position to collect the user costs that reflect increasing scarcity. If properly charged, these user costs would serve to confront current users with the costs their activities impose on future users. With nonexclusiveness, there are no incentives to ration current consumption, conserve for the future, and invest in enhancing the productivity of the resource.

A difficulty arises because the now standard analysis of common property resources is not applicable to property held in common, the *res communis* of ancient Roman law. Ownership is vested in some kind of collective, and rules of access (to some degree exclusive and enforceable, and often transferable under stated conditions) are instituted to adjudicate conflicts among the common owners. Common property organizations may be voluntary associations (corporations and clubs) or government agencies established to manage resources and provide services in the public trust. Ciriacy-Wantrup and Bishop (1975) have drawn attention to the myriad common property institutions that have been developed to handle resource management and exploitation conflicts in traditional and modern societies. They argue correctly that the conventional wisdom (which uses "common property" as a misnomer for "nonexclusiveness") is misleading in very important ways.

There is no question that persistent nonexclusiveness is a recipe for disaster. One may ask why economies based on free enterprise so often handle the nonexclusiveness problem by establishing some form of common property institutions rather than nonattenuated property rights.[1] The answer may lie in the traditional belief that private ownership is inappropriate for certain kinds of resources. More often, I suspect, the answer may be found in the high cost of establishing and enforcing private property arrangements. Where many users share a common fishery or a large oil or groundwater pool, the costs of specifying and enforcing traditional property rights may exceed any gains that might arise from market transactions thus permitted. High transactions costs are often the impediment to private property relationships. Further, it makes no sense to put the blame for high transactions costs on the large-numbers problem, as is often done. Rather, high exclusion and transactions costs are usually attributable to peculiarities in the physical nature of the resource itself.[2] For example, fencing the open sea or large underground pools of liquid resources is technologically more demanding and therefore vastly more expensive than fencing the open range.

The concept of public goods also generates confusion.

At least one, and often both, of two quite separate phenomena are involved: nonexclusiveness and nonrivalry. Nonrivalry refers to Samuelson's (1954) notion of a good which may be enjoyed (consumed) by some without diminution of the amount effectively available for others.

The literature has paid much attention to whether both of these phenomena are necessary to make a good "public," or, if one is enough, which one? The question, however, turns out to be quite pointless. Nonexclusiveness and nonrivalry have different economic interpretations and analyses, and they may occur together or separately. Accordingly, I would abandon the term "public goods," along with "common property resources," and focus instead on "nonrivalry" and "nonexclusiveness."

Nonrivalry results from some material circumstances concerning the particular good or the conditions under which the good is provided and distributed. Rationing is not a problem with nonrival goods: once the good has been produced, additional users may be added without imposing any additional costs on the system. But determining the efficient quantity to provide is a special problem for nonrival goods. If marginal willingness to pay (WTP) is determined for each individual and aggregated (vertically) across all potential users, the efficient level of provision can be identified: the level at which aggregate marginal WTP just equals the marginal cost of provision, given that aggregate total WTP exceeds total cost. So far, so good. Without exclusion, a government could use general revenues to provide the efficient quantity of nonrival goods, as long as it had good information about aggregate marginal WTP. But when aggregate WTP data must necessarily be derived at the outset from self-reported individual WTP, there is concern that individuals may indulge in false reporting for strategic reasons.

If it were possible to exclude all who did not pay the going price, revenue could be generated directly from users. Private sector provision of nonrival goods would be possible, as would public provision financed by user charges. These kinds of arrangements have some appeal and may even be second-best solutions.[3] They would not, however, be efficient solutions. Some individuals with low but positive valuations would be excluded, and this would be inefficient since their use of the nonrival good would impose no additional costs.

For complete efficiency, perfect price discrimination is necessary. Each user would have to pay his own WTP. Obviously, this would require a very special and demanding kind of exclusion. A turnstile or a tollbooth may be sufficient to exclude those who do not pay the going price, but such devices would be entirely ineffective at excluding those who did not pay their own individual marginal valuations. A technology for price-discriminatory exclusion may one day be developed. One thinks of truth serum or new developments based on the polygraph. Up to now, more progress has been made along a rather different line of

Table 2-1.   *A Classification of Goods Based on Concepts of Rivalry and Exclusiveness*

	Level of exclusion		
Type of good	*Nonexclusive*	*Exclusive*	*Price-discriminatory exclusive*
Nonrival	Private provision, or public provision financed by user charges, is impossible. Pareto-efficiency is unattainable.	Private provision and public provision financed by user charges are feasible and may permit second-best solution. Pareto-efficiency is unattainable.	Private provision and public provision financed by user charges are feasible. With perfect price discrimination, Pareto-efficiency is feasible.
Congestible	Private provision, or public provision financed by user charges, is impossible. Pareto-efficiency is unattainable.	Private provision and public provision financed by user charges are feasible. Time-variable charges may permit second-best solution. Pareto-efficiency is unattainable.	Private provision and public provision financed by user charges are feasible. With time-variable user charges and perfect price discrimination, Pareto-efficiency may be feasible.
Rival	Private provision, or public provision financed by user charges, is impossible. Pareto-efficiency is unattainable.	The ordinary private goods case. Competitive market equilibrium is Pareto-efficient.	Price discrimination leads to excess profits and violates conditions for Pareto-efficiency.

attack: incentive-compatible mechanisms. Typically, these are rather complex systems of multipart taxes carefully structured so that an individual who volunteers his true valuation will emerge better-off than someone who attempts to beat the system by strategic reporting of false values. Currently, incentive-compatible devices may be found in the realm of economic theory and experimental economics, but real-world applications are in their infancy.

While pure nonrival goods are relatively rare, so-called congestible goods characterize substantial sectors of the economy. Congestible goods have high initial capital costs and capacity constraints. When use is much less than capacity, nonrivalry is the order of the day: additional users impose only trivial costs on the system. As the capacity constraint is approached, congestion sets in and additional users impose rapidly increasing costs on the system. At full capacity it is literally impossible to add a user without simultaneously removing another. For congestible goods, the economic analysis is similar to that for nonrival goods, but an additional complication enters. Where the level of demand varies with the time of demand, appropriate prices may well be different at different times. In general, ordinary exclusion may permit second-best solutions in which revenues collected from users cover the costs of provision. Perfect price discrimination and the especially demanding form of exclusion it implies are required for complete efficiency in the provision of congestible goods.

It is possible to devise a system for categorizing goods according to three levels of exclusion (nonexclusiveness, ordinary exclusion, and price-discriminatory exclusion) and three kinds of goods (nonrival, congestible, and rival). It is possible to conceive of goods in all of the nine categories thus created. In Table 2-1 the results of economic analysis are summarized for all nine categories.

Let me review the argument to this point. The conventional concepts of common property resources and public goods are fraught with difficulty and confusion. It is more helpful to focus upon nonexclusiveness and nonrivalry, phenomena which may occur separately or together. Inefficiencies induced by nonexclusiveness may, given an adequate exclusion technology and the political-institutional will to implement it, be resolved by privatization. Where nonrivalry is the problem, ordinary exclusion is not enough; efficiency requires price-discriminatory exclusion. Finally, the existence of nonexclusiveness or nonrivalry presents a prima facie case for market failure. A conclusive case, however, requires a demonstration not only that market performance is imperfect but also that alternative institutions would do better.

Although there is nothing wrong with the economic analyses usually associated with natural monopoly, that phenomenon is entirely captured by the construct of congestible goods. Given the analytical possibilities emanating from a classification based on concepts of rivalry and exclusion, natural monopoly becomes redundant.

An externality is defined as a situation in which the welfare of one is influenced by activities under the control of someone else. In the conventional wisdom of stage 1, externalities were seen as market failures, that is, inefficient situations inviting governmental attempts at mitigation. Where the externality was harmful (that is, where the welfare of the affected party was diminished by the externality), the typical prescription was to regulate or, better yet, tax the externality into submission.

Since the writings of Coase (1960) and Buchanan and Stubblebine (1962), most authors have focused on the subset of externalities that causes inefficiency (the Pareto-relevant externalities, in the jargon). Many categories of interactions which satisfy the general definition of externality are resolved efficiently in markets; for them, no possibility of Pareto-relevance exists when markets function well. For other kinds of interactions—air pollution and water pollution are commonly cited examples—it is not immediately clear that, in the ordinary course of events, markets take care of the inefficiencies.

A Pareto-relevant externality is so defined that unrealized potential gains from trade are inherent therein. The Coase theorem states that, given nonattenuated property rights, market transactions will realize the gains from trade and thus eliminate the inefficiency. Some of the nuisance (for example, air pollution) will almost surely remain, but it will be Pareto-irrelevant: to reduce the nuisance still further would cost more than the benefits.

A special case of the Coase theorem, one of more interest to economics teachers than to policymakers, asserts that the equilibrium amount of the nuisance will be invariant with the initial specification of rights. Regardless of whether the law protects polluters or receptors at the outset, after all trading opportunities have been exploited the remaining pollution will be the same. To get this result it is necessary to assume that transactions costs are zero (specification, transfer, and enforcement of rights are costless activities) and there are no income effects. But transactions costs are always positive and income effects are significant in some important cases. Under these more realistic assumptions, initial assignment of rights *does* affect the equilibrium outcome. There will be more of the nuisance remaining at equilibrium when the law protects polluters than when it protects receptors. But the general result of the Coase theorem remains: each of these different equilibriums is efficient in its own terms. What is efficient depends on the initial distribution of endowments and rights.

The impact of the Coase theorem is that inefficient, or Pareto-relevant, externality cannot persist. The imperatives of trade make for an inherently unstable disequilibrium situation.

Pollution, for example, may persist in excessive quantities. If the initial assignment of rights favors polluters and transactions costs are so large as to preclude any trade, all of the pollution will remain at equilibrium. Excessive pollution is a persistent problem, although we have a theorem proclaiming that Pareto-relevant externality is not. There is no inconsistency here, it turns out. The high transactions costs cannot, as we have already seen, be attributed to the large-numbers problem. Rather, they must be due to other aspects of the situation: nonexclusiveness or nonrivalry or both.

In economies that maintain institutions conducive to trade and efficiency, those things called externalities cannot persist in excessive quantities unless accompanied by nonexclusiveness or nonrivalry or both. Inefficient externality is not, by itself, persistent. Further, the effects and analysis of, and recommended solutions for, externality and nonexclusiveness or externality and nonrivalry are the same as for nonexclusiveness or nonrivalry alone. The

inescapable conclusion is that externality adds nothing to the lexicon of market failure.[4]

Whereas the conventional wisdom of stage 1 offers the concepts of externality, common property resources, public goods, and natural monopoly, closer analyses find content only in the concepts addressing exclusiveness or the lack thereof and the nonrival or congestible nature of certain goods. Further, perception of the policy significance of market failure has shifted in an important way. Whereas market failure was once treated as a universal rationale for a government fix, the current approach insists that policy imperatives follow only when the diagnosis of market failure is accompanied by a demonstration that some other arrangements would actually do better.

The Exclusive Private Property or Disaster Stage

In the process of developing and critiquing stage 1 of the intellectual history of market failure, I have laid much of the groundwork for discussing stage 2. This second stage took its cue from the mid-1950s analyses of Samuelson (1954) and Gordon (1954) and the voluminous literature that followed Coase's seminal paper (1960).

Samuelson and Gordon did not merely show that rivalry and nonexclusiveness, respectively, were substantial impediments to Pareto-efficiency in a decentralized economy. Their analyses predicted the total collapse of the nonrival and nonexclusive economic sectors unless government stepped in, coercively, to save the day. Further, as we have already seen, Gordon's analysis of the open access or nonexclusive resource problem was mislabeled: the implication was that it referred to common property arrangements as a broad class.

Coase's analysis focused on nonattenuated property rights as a sufficient condition for efficiency in an economy where externality and nonexclusiveness might otherwise cause problems. The burden of proof was switched to those who would claim market failure in any particular case (Demsetz 1964 and 1969). They could now be called upon to show that what appeared to be market failure was not actually an efficient market solution. The only escape route left open, it seemed, was to argue that property rights were attenuated in some important way. An obvious prescription was for the government to establish nonattenuated property rights and then stand aside as the market took care of things. Sustained government activism—the regulation, taxation, and public provision amelioratives typically prescribed in stage 1—was unnecessary.

As the Coasian tradition developed, it was argued with increasing generality that attenuation of rights was endemic in the public sector itself. That, of course, took the argument one rather large step further. A sustained posture of government activism in control of market failure was not merely unnecessary, it was undesirable.

From this foundation developed the conventional wisdom of stage 2. So-called market failures were caused mostly by attenuated property rights, and nonexclusiveness was far and away the greatest part of that problem. Privatization was the appropriate policy response to diagnosed inefficiencies. Thus, Anderson and Hill (1976) argued, essentially, that the economic history of the United States could be encapsulated as a triumphal march of private property institutions from east to west with the predictable result of prosperity unparalleled in other times and places. Schmid (1977) raised the argument (originated by Ciriacy-Wantrup and Bishop 1975) that Anderson and Hill had ignored a whole universe of institutional possibilities, some of them quite serviceable, between the extremes of exclusive private property and open access. The Anderson and Hill (1977) response was scathing: the possibilities to which Schmid referred were essentially uninteresting, since any efficiency properties these institutions possessed must surely be attributable to some degree of exclusiveness inherent in them. Further, incomplete exclusiveness implied incomplete efficiency; why not go all the way? In this, Anderson and Hill were faithfully reflecting the mindset of stage 2: most of the issues raised by the old-fashioned notion of market failure can be addressed with a simple dichotomy between exclusive private property, which promotes efficiency, and nonexclusiveness, which leads to the collapse of the economic sectors it afflicts.

For this simple analysis, nonrivalry poses a difficulty, since ordinary exclusion is not sufficient to restore a nonrival goods sector to efficiency. Some proponents of the conventional wisdom of stage 2 (Anderson and Hill, for example) tend to play down the issue of nonrivalry. Others (Buchanan 1977, for example) confront nonrivalry directly, favoring voluntary taxation schemes in the tradition of Lindahl (1958) and Wicksell (1958) and endorsing the modern search for incentive-compatible collective decision mechanisms.

One should credit the Coasian tradition with important accomplishments in exposing the fallacies of the stage 1 concept of market failure. Nevertheless, I would argue that the stage 2 alternative—private property or perdition—is itself quite unsatisfactory. Perhaps the neo-Austrian proponents of stage 2 have simply taken the analyses of Samuelson, Gordon, and Coase too far.

New Approaches

Perhaps no long-established prediction of economics has been so thoroughly refuted as Samuelson's and Gordon's prediction of total collapse in the nonrival and nonexclusive sectors. There is evidence all around us that these sectors are seldom efficient, which supports Samuelson's and Gordon's predictions with respect to efficiency. But there is also ample evidence that, despite their predictions, these sectors have not totally collapsed.

The Samuelson-Gordon tradition left an escape route:

government could coercively regulate or tax and thereby provide what citizens will not provide through markets or other endogenous institutions. But this escape route is unsatisfactory. More contemporary analyses (reflecting the Coasian tradition and a variety of other influences) treat government itself as endogenous. From this perspective, government is not a wise external force capable of disciplining an unruly society. Rather, government emerges, warts and all, from society. How, then, can government (which is endogenous to society) impose upon society that which society cannot agree to impose on itself? Once the endogenicity of government is conceded, it is impossible to reconcile Samuelson's and Gordon's prediction of collapse with the observation that the nonrival and nonexclusive sectors seem to do no worse than limp along and often perform passably well. Clearly, Samuelson's and Gordon's theory of market failure is inadequate and misleading.

In the past two decades several novel and related approaches have emerged to shed new light on the possibilities for collective action. These approaches include game theory formulations of the nonrivalry and nonexclusiveness problems (Sen 1967; Runge 1981), resource allocation mechanisms (Hurwicz 1973), the theory of teams (Marshak and Radner 1971), incentive-compatible mechanisms (Groves and Ledyard 1980), and principal-agent models (Arrow 1986).

An early and influential game theory problem is the prisoner's dilemma. A two-person single-period prisoner's dilemma may be expressed as follows. First, we establish a minimal notation. Define:

S_i: the strategy of i ($i = 1, 2$)
$S_i = 1$: i contributes (or cooperates, and so on)
$\quad = 0$: i defects (or plays a selfish strategy, and so on)
(S_1, S_2): the strategies of 1 and 2 which together determine the outcome of the game
$F_i(S_1, S_2)$: the payoff to i, which is some function of (S_1, S_2).

Two prisoners are interrogated separately by the police, who, having little independent evidence of their guilt, are willing to bargain for confessions. The police confront each with the following individual payoffs from the various possible outcomes:

for 1, $F_1(0,1) > F_1(1,1) > F_1(0,0) > F_1(1,0)$
for 2, $F_2(1,0) > F_2(1,1) > F_2(0,0) > F_2(0,1)$.

Each is best-off if he confesses and the other does not and worst-off if he steadfastly denies the guilt of both and the other confesses. But both would prefer the "both deny" outcome to the "both confess" outcome.

Perhaps a different example may help clarify what is at stake. The disarmament game has the same structure. For country 1, the best of all worlds occurs when country 2 disarms unilaterally. Both countries are better-off when both disarm than when neither disarms.

It is clear that the outcome (0,0) is Pareto-inferior; that is, for both it is inferior to (1,1). But if the prisoners cannot communicate, each will choose his maximin strategy of 0. Thus the equilibrium outcome of the game is (0,0), a Pareto-inferior outcome.

The countries can communicate in disarmament negotiations. Nevertheless, although they may agree to the cooperative outcome (1,1), each has strong incentives to cheat subsequently in order to gain an advantage and to make sure the other does not. The noncooperative outcome (0,0) is likely to be what actually emerges.

By the 1960s it was widely held that the Samuelson-Gordon analyses of market failure could be reformulated as single-period n-person prisoner's dilemmas. Such reformulation would, of course, reconfirm Samuelson's and Gordon's prediction of total collapse in the nonrival nonexclusive sectors.

The single-period prisoner's dilemma was only the beginning, however. It was soon realized that the prisoner's dilemma is not necessarily the proper specification for nonrivalry and nonexclusiveness problems (Sen 1967; Dasgupta and Heal 1977). As Shubik (1981) observed, games of pure opposition have many uses in, for example, military tactics but relatively few applications in economics. Consider the following alternative formulations.

The assurance game:

$$F_1(1,1) > F_1(0,0) > F_1(0,1) = F_1(1,0)$$
$$F_2(1,1) > F_2(0,0) > F_2(1,0) = F_2(0,1).$$

In this game (1,1) is Pareto-optimal, but both parties prefer (0,0) to outcomes in which they play different strategies. The problem is assurance: each will play $S_i = 1$ if assured the other will, too. Once agreement is reached, there is no incentive to defect subsequently.

Runge (1981) argues for the assurance game on two grounds. First, it is the appropriate formulation for nonexclusiveness problems characterized by nonseparability among users (for example, where the cost function of one user is influenced by decisions made by others). Second, it appeals to fair-mindedness ("I will if you will"), arguably a rather common human instinct, rather than to, say, unilateral benevolence.

The unanimity game:

$$F_1(1,1) > F_1(0,0) = F_1(0,1) > F_1(1,0)$$
$$F_2(1,1) > F_2(0,0) = F_2(1,0) > F_2(0,1).$$

In this game, nothing of value is produced unless both parties contribute; successful action has to be unanimous. Thus, $F_1(0,0) = F_1(0,1)$, and $F_1(1,0)$ is the worst solution of all for 1 because 1 contributes but nothing is produced. Fairmindedness is not involved.

The cooperative solution (1,1) is Pareto-superior, but independent maximin strategies for each player will generate the (0,0) outcome. Coordination would result in the cooperative solution, and there would be no incentive for subsequent defection.

The unanimity game is characteristic of certain committee and legislative environments. It also applies to nonrival goods with high fixed costs, so that none is produced unless all players contribute.

The congestible goods game:

$$F_1(1,1) > F_1(0,1) > F_1(0,0) > F_1(1,0)$$
$$F_2(1,1) > F_2(1,0) > F_2(0,0) > F_2(0,1).$$

Benefits are nonrival, and the marginal cost of providing the good to an additional user declines as the number of users increases, as is characteristic of congestible goods operating well within the capacity constraint. The benefits from a single contribution are positive but are valued less than the cost of contributing. If both parties contribute, the nonrival benefits exceed the cost of either individual contribution, and the increment in nonrival benefits from the last-received contribution exceeds its cost. Free riding—for example, (0,1) allows 1 to free ride—is individually preferred to nonproduction (0,0). For either party, contributing while the other does not yields the worst outcome.

Again, the cooperative solution (1,1) is Pareto-superior, but independent maximin strategies by each player will generate the (0,0) outcome. With coordination, (1,1) will be chosen and there is no incentive for subsequent defection.

Although the assurance, unanimity, and congestible goods games differ a little, in all three coordinated strategies would permit stable, Pareto-optimal cooperative solutions. Further, it is argued that each of these games is a more appropriate specification than the prisoner's dilemma for a particular class of problems emanating from nonexclusiveness or nonrivalry.[5] For these problems, a more careful specification of the game theory formulation suggests that the collapse predicted by Samuelson and Gordon is by no means inevitable.

The story does not end here, but there is a fork in the road: one path of further inquiry concerns mechanisms for coordination, and the other concerns the outcomes when games, including the prisoner's dilemma, are repeated.

The demonstration that, for several relevant classes of games, coordinated strategies permit stable, Pareto-efficient cooperative solutions is not entirely comforting. Coordination is likely to be a costly activity, and complete coordination, if it requires consultation among all participants, may be prohibitively costly. Private (that is, rival and exclusive) goods markets work well because prices convey, in simple signals, sufficient information and incentives to accomplish coordination and neither centralized management nor direct consultation among all market participants is necessary. Perhaps signaling devices can be developed for adequate and cost-effective coordination so that cooperative arrangements in large organizations dealing with nonrival and nonexclusive goods are reasonably stable and efficient. This is the working hypothesis that motivates research on principal-agent models, team theory, resource allocation mechanisms, and incentive-compatible mechanisms.

For principal-agent models, the following situations are typical. Total costs of loss and damage may be reduced if insured parties have some incentives for loss-avoiding behavior; can insurance policies with appropriate incentives be designed? If the work effort of individual agents cannot be monitored directly, what incentives can the manager devise to encourage agent efficiency without incurring excessive turnover of agents? If emissions of individual polluters cannot be monitored fully, can the pollution control authority devise incentives for reasonably efficient pollution control? Given that bidders for federal oil leases have some knowledge that is unavailable to other bidders and the government, can auction rules be devised to maximize some objective, such as government receipts or some broader measure of social welfare?

Each of these problems is characterized by hidden action (the agent can take some actions unobserved by the principal) or hidden information (the agent knows some things the principal does not). An interesting variant is the problem of a single principal and many agents, where the principal can observe the combined output of all agents but not the individual output of any one of them. The relevance of this kind of thinking to nonexclusiveness and nonrivalry problems is obvious. This particular principal-agent problem is a team problem and must be formulated as a game; the example serves to illustrate the close relationships among the various approaches.

The literature on principal-agent problems is substantial and often highly mathematical. No attempt at careful review and evaluation is offered here, but some impressions can be conveyed. Considerable progress has been made in modeling information requirements and group performance, given various combinations of problems and incentives. Results about information requirements provide indirect evidence about the transactions costs associated with various arrangements. While principal-agent models reconfirm the efficiency of price signals in a neoclassical competitive economy, they offer no support for the "private property or total collapse" thesis of the neo-Austrians. A wide variety of workable arrangements, with outcomes falling between Pareto-efficiency and collapse, can be identified for diverse problems exhibiting aspects of nonexclusiveness or nonrivalry.

The literature on incentive-compatible mechanisms (Groves and Ledyard 1980) has identified the general form of a tax rule for which truthful revelation of willingness to pay for nonrival goods is the dominant strategy. The basic idea is that the individual's tax is independent of his announced WTP but depends on his message's effect on the total amount of nonrival goods collectively provided. Current theoretical results are restricted to cases in which utility functions are additively separable.

A growing literature reports the performance of experimental nonexclusive or nonrival goods economies (Smith 1980). A frequent result is that free riding is much less than universal even when incentives encourage it. Further, voluntary taxation produces near-optimal amounts of collective goods under tax rules that fall short of incentive compatibility.

Now, we take the second path and consider repeated games. Return to the prisoner's dilemma. For individual 1, the payoffs from the various outcomes are ranked:

$$F_1(0,1) > F_1(1,1) > F_1(0,0) > F_1(1,0).$$

For any i, the preferred outcome occurs when i defects while all others contribute. If the game is repeated, however, each player would learn rather quickly that playing the $S_i = 0$ strategy leads to a Pareto-inferior outcome $(0,0)$ because others would surely defect, too. For 1, $(0,1)$ is the preferred solution, but it is unstable. Since $(0,1)$ quickly degenerates to $(0,0)$, perhaps all players have an incentive to attempt to achieve the $(1,1)$ outcome. This is the basic motivation for research with repeated prisoner's dilemmas.

The first result is not helpful. A prisoner's dilemma repeated many times quickly degenerates to $(0,0)$. The reason is easy to see. For any i involved in a t-times repeated prisoner's dilemma, the preferred outcome arises when all contribute on the first $t - 1$ rounds and all but i contribute on the tth round. Each player is motivated to defect before the others. By infinite regress, the game degenerates to "all players defect" in the initial round.

Some favorable results are also evident, however. Cooperative equilibriums may be stable if the game is repeated indefinitely or stochastically many times (that is, players do not know when it will end). These results depend on various assumptions about what information is available to players and what strategies they use. Obviously, it is favorable for stable cooperative solutions if players can observe the previous-period strategy of each player. Radner (1981) and Klepper (1983) have, however, obtained favorable results with principal-agent games, indefinitely repeated, where only previous-period total group contributions are observable.

This kind of game calls for each player to announce at the outset that he will use a trigger strategy. For example, if the previous-period group output falls below some specified amount, the player will defect in the present period. The player's problem is to figure out the appropriate trigger amount. Klepper has identified a test statistic that players can use and has shown that, perhaps surprisingly, the test statistic becomes more precisely defined as the number of players increases. This result is favorable for stable cooperative solutions in repeated prisoner's dilemmas.

All of the results discussed to this point are derived with models that assume the players are unknown to one another. Results become stronger if reputation effects are considered (Akerlof 1983). If the players know one another and develop predictions about their behavior, and if the best way to earn a reputation for cooperative behavior is to cooperate repeatedly. Kreps and others (1982) have shown that cooperative solutions may be stable even for finitely repeated prisoner's dilemmas.

One rather obvious trigger strategy is the tit-for-tat: each player contributes on each round, until he believes that significant defection has occurred on the prior round, and then he defects. Axelrod (1982) has conducted computer simulations of repeated prisoner's dilemmas and reports that players using the tit-for-tat strategy regularly obtained more favorable outcomes over the long haul than players using other strategies. When all players but one use the tit-for-tat, cooperation may be restored in a repeated game that had degenerated. The defector, observing that his action was met with a tit-for-tat reaction on the following round, has a strong motivation to contribute on the next play. The tit-for-tat players would then contribute on the next round, restoring the cooperative solution, and the defector, having learned a lesson, would likely contribute thereafter.

Two final observations are in order. First, most of the favorable results cited were obtained with repeated prisoner's dilemmas. Clearly, the prospects for favorable results are more promising if the game that is repeated is not a prisoner's dilemma but one of the alternative games—the assurance, unanimity, or congestible goods game. Second, it occurs to me that a stochastically repeated game with reputation effects and opportunity for partial monitoring of individual contributions may be a sound metaphor for real life. The prospects for stable cooperative solutions for such a game are by no means trivial.

The general impression that emerges from this diverse literature is that the Samuelson and Gordon collapse thesis is refuted as convincingly by superior theoretical models as it is by observation of the real world. Again, none of this shows that the nonexclusive and nonrival sectors will achieve efficiency. Samuelson and Gordon were right about that. But total collapse is not inevitable. Theoretical and experimental results show that a wide variety of signals and incentives may result in reasonably stable, passably well-performing collective goods economies. These results mesh well with the observation by Ciriacy-Wantrup and Bishop that a wide variety of common property arrangements can be observed to operate, stably and effectively, in both traditional and modern societies.

Given the understanding that emerges from the stage 3 literature, the stage 2 "private property or perdition" argument of the neo-Austrians is seen as materially false. It may faithfully represent a particular ideological position, but the theoretical and observational basis to convert that ideological position to a valid policy prescription is lacking.

Let there be no argument: private property arrange-

ments have some demonstrable merits for handling rival and exclusive goods. Further, where exclusion is effective and inexpensive, it is a meritorious remedy for problems arising from nonexclusiveness. But private property arrangements are at a severe disadvantage when nonrivalry is the problem or when private property exclusion is technologically difficult. The mind-set that emerges from stage 3—let us explore the myriad of diverse possibilities that lie between private property and simple open access—is more helpful, and more defensible, than the stage 2 "private property or perdition" mind-set.

Many of the analyses I have grouped together and labeled stage 3 are institutionally agnostic. In a principal-agent model the principal could be a corporate boss, a Mafia capo, the head of a bureaucracy, a Soviet commandant, an elected chief executive, or society at large. A stable cooperative solution could take the form of a voluntary association, a standing committee, or a constitutional government.

That makes these models adaptable to a wide variety of collective action problems. But they all exclude at least one institutional form: a stable solution imposed on an unruly society by an all-wise exogenous government. Thus, the thinking of stage 3 rejects the precepts of stage 1 as surely as it does those of stage 2.

Market Failures and Efficiency in Irrigation Economies

Irrigation economies are typically characterized by interdependencies. Irrigators draw water from a common river, channel, or groundwater pool, and the tailwaters return to the groundwater or the river downstream. Channels are congestible, and during times of peak water demand users impose costs on one another. Groundwater may be nonexclusive, as a result of overexploitation. In the absence of effective metering of individual withdrawals, this problem would also apply to water in rivers and channels. Polluted tailwaters may be a nonexclusive discommodity, leading irrigators to pay little attention to controlling damage from that source. Principal-agent problems may bedevil any administrative attempt to resolve these problems.

Typically, these difficulties are called market failures. How would an economist diagnose these problems, and what solutions would be prescribed? As we have seen, it would depend on the economist's concept of market failure.

An economist with a stage 1 mind-set would classify these problems according to whether they are attributed to externalities, public goods, common property resources, or natural monopolies. He would recommend that the government eliminate these problems by regulation or, preferably, taxation. An exception might be made in the case of common property resources, if the economist were convinced that private property institutions could be implemented at less than prohibitive cost. In that case, he might recommend that the government establish private property rights and then stand aside as decentralized markets take care of the problem.

An economist with a stage 2 mind-set would be deeply troubled by these diagnoses and recommendations. He would maintain that externality is not a viable concept, that the absence of an observable market may itself be an efficient market solution, and that the fundamental problem is the attenuation of property rights, in which case government agencies are even more susceptible to the problem than market economies. Ever skeptical of government fixes, the economist would insist that the case for market failure be established not merely by showing the inefficiency of markets but also by demonstrating that some other arrangement would do better.

All of that is perfectly acceptable. The stage 2 economist, however, would tend to ignore nonrivalry problems and concentrate on those caused by nonexclusiveness and would tend to misspecify the latter by positing a simple dichotomy between idealized private property and nonexclusiveness. Confronted with the above-mentioned market failures in the irrigation economy, his inclination might be to suggest that all of these problems could be solved once and for all if only a single individual were empowered to collect all of the rents generated by the irrigation project. Then the rent collector would have an unambiguous incentive to maximize the efficiency of the whole project. Alternatively, the economist might seek to maximize the scope of markets within the project, so that efficient prices would coordinate withdrawals and return flows.

Strong objections would likely be raised to both proposals. The "single rent collector" proposal would violate other valid policy objectives. Although internal markets (in withdrawals and return flows, for example) may have considerable merit, it is unlikely that they would resolve all of the market failures; in some cases effective exclusion is just too expensive. The stage 2 economist, schooled in the "private property or total collapse" tradition, would be unequipped to deal with these remaining problems.

In the emerging understanding that I have labeled stage 3, the stage 1 concepts and definitions of market failure are rejected, and the focus is instead on nonexclusiveness and nonrivalry. The stage 3 economist is skeptical of the ability of a paternal government to effectively impose efficiency on an aberrant economy via regulation and taxation. At the same time, however, the stage 3 mind-set rejects the stage 2 "private property or total collapse" diagnosis for the nonexclusive and nonrival sectors. The Samuelson and Gordon predictions of total collapse are seen to be refuted by observations of the real world and by newer, more realistic theoretical models that explore the possibilities for stable cooperative action. There is no denying that exclusive private property arrangements have

desirable built-in incentives and thus are appropriate when conditions are favorable for them—that is, when exclusion costs are reasonably low and sociocultural traditions are amenable. There is, however, a willingness to consider the vast mosaic of possibilities that are now perceived to lie between the extremes of exclusive private property and uncontrolled access.

I do not bring with me prepackaged stage 3 solutions for market failure in the irrigation economy. Nevertheless, it seems clear that recent thinking allows some reformulation of more traditional analyses of market failure in irrigation and suggests some new possibilities.

Uncontrolled individual pumping of groundwater leads to excessive extraction, which lowers the water table and increases pumping costs for all irrigators. This problem is often diagnosed as a physical externality, whereas I would suggest that it is a simple case of nonexclusiveness with rivalry. The array of stage 1 and stage 2 solutions has been discussed, with pessimistic conclusions. Private control of the aquifer reduces to a prisoner's dilemma, and the stable cooperative solution invariably fails. Public ownership fails because the low-level administrators will cheat and the costs of monitoring them are prohibitive. Tax-subsidy solutions are viewed as promising in concept, but in practice they require a central government that is strong enough to impose them on a community of recalcitrant farmers.

Stage 3 thinking may be open to more alternatives and less pessimistic about those considered. It may be possible to structure private pumping as a repeated game. With reputation effects, monitoring of water tables, and partial monitoring of individual withdrawals, the chances for stable cooperative solution increase. Principal-agent models may suggest ingenious systems of incentives and signals to induce low-level public employees to better serve the objectives of the principal, the irrigation community.

Stage 3 thinking counsels us that the nonexclusive and nonrival sectors may be less vulnerable to economic collapse than economists have previously thought. It invites us to consider the myriad possibilities that exist between the extremes of exclusive private property, free-for-all, and a central government fix via manipulated prices or regulations.

Notes

1. Cheung (1970) defines nonattenuated property rights as exclusive, transferable, enforced, and in no way inconsistent with the marginal conditions for Pareto-optimality.

2. The large-numbers problem alone will never cause prohibitive transactions costs. The market for bread, with myriad buyers and sellers, works as well as any other and much better than the market for clean air, which has a similar number of potential participants.

3. See, for example, the discussion in Davis and Whinston (1967).

4. See Cheung (1970), Dahlman (1979), and Randall (1983) for elaborations of this argument.

5. Nevertheless, not all nonexclusiveness and nonrivalry problems escape the prisoner's dilemma. The n-person prisoner's dilemma seems to be the appropriate formulation for the problem concerning a nonrival and nonexclusive good with separable individual cost functions, increasing marginal costs, and decreasing marginal benefits. In that case, i would prefer an outcome in which he defects while all others contribute.

References

Akerlof, George. 1983. "Loyalty Filters." *American Economic Review* 73:54–63.

Anderson, T. L., and P. J. Hill. 1976. "The Role of Private Property in the History of American Agriculture, 1776–1976." *American Journal of Agricultural Economics* 58:937–45.

———. 1977. "The Role of Private Property in the History of American Agriculture, 1776–1976: Reply." *American Journal of Agricultural Economics* 59:590–91.

Arrow, K. J. 1986. "Agency and the Market." In K. J. Arrow and M. D. Intrilligator, eds. *Handbook of Mathematical Economics.* Amsterdam: North-Holland.

———, and Gerard Debreu. 1954. "Existence of an Equilibrium for a Competitive Economy." *Econometrica* 22:265–90.

Axelrod, Robert. 1982. "The Emergence of Cooperation among Egoists." *American Political Science Review* 75:306–18.

Bator, F. M. 1958. "The Anatomy of Market Failure." *Quarterly Journal of Economics* 72:351–79.

Buchanan, J. M. 1977. *Freedom in Constitutional Contract.* College Station, Tex.: Texas A & M University Press.

———, and W. C. Stubblebine. 1962. "Externality." *Economica* 29:371–84.

Cheung, S. N. S. 1970. "The Structure of a Contract and the Theory of a Non-Exclusive Resource." *Journal of Law and Economics* 13:49–70.

Ciriacy-Wantrup, S. von, and R. C. Bishop. 1975. "'Common Property,' as a Concept in Natural Resources Policy." *Natural Resources Journal* 15:713–27.

Coase, Ronald H. 1960. "The Problem of Social Cost." *Journal of Law and Economics* 3:1–44.

Dahlman, Carl. 1979. "The Problem of Externality." *Journal of Law and Economics* 22:141–62.

Dasgupta, P. S., and G. M. Heal. 1977. *Economic Theory and Exhaustible Resources.* Cambridge: Cambridge University Press.

Davis, O. A., and A. C. Whinston. 1967. "On the Distinction between Private and Public Goods." *American Economic Review* 57:366–73.

Demsetz, Harold. 1964. "The Exchange and Enforcement of Property Rights." *Journal of Law and Economics* 7:11–26.

———, 1969. "Information and Efficiency: Another Viewpoint." *Journal of Law and Economics* 12:1–22.

Gordon, H. S. 1954. "The Economic Theory of a Common Property Resource: The Fishery." *Journal of Political Economy* 62:124–42.

Groves, Theodore, and John Ledyard. 1980. "The Existence of Efficient and Incentive Compatible Equilibria with Public Goods." *Econometrica* 48:1487–506.

Hurwicz, Leonid. 1973. "The Design of Mechanisms for Resource Allocation." *American Economic Review* 63:1–30.

Klepper, Gernot. 1983. "Incentives for Allocating Public Goods under Incomplete Information." Ph.D. dissertation, University of Kentucky, Lexington.

Kreps, David, Paul Milgrom, John Roberts, and Robert Wilson. 1982. "Rational Cooperation in the Finitely-Repeated Prisoner's Dilemma." *Journal of Economic Theory* 27:245–52.

Lindahl, Erik. 1958. "Just Taxation: A Positive Solution." In R. A. Musgrave and A. T. Peacock, eds. *Classics in the Theory of Public Finance.* New York: St. Martin's Press.

Marshak, Jacob, and Roy Radner. 1971. *The Economic Theory of Teams.* New Haven, Conn.: Yale University Press.

Pigou, A. C. 1932. *The Economics of Welfare.* New York: Macmillan.

Radner, Roy. 1981. "Monitoring Cooperative Agreements in a Repeated Principal-Agent Relationship." *Econometrica* 49:1127–48.

Randall, Alan. 1983. "The Problem of Market Failure." *Natural Resources Journal* 23 (Jan.): 131–48.

Runge, C. F. 1981. "Common Property Externalities in Traditional Grazing." *American Journal of Agricultural Economics* 63:595–606.

Samuelson, P. A. 1954. "The Pure Theory of Public Expenditure." *Review of Economics and Statistics* 36:387–89.

Schmid, A. A. 1977. "The Role of Private Property in the History of American Agriculture, 1776–1976: Comment." *American Journal of Agricultural Economics* 59:587–89.

Sen, A. K. 1967. "Isolation, Assurance, and the Social Rate of Discount." *Quarterly Journal of Economics* 81:112–24.

Shubik, Martin. 1981. "Game Theory Models and Methods in Political Economy." In K. J. Arrow and M. D. Intrilligator, eds. *Handbook of Mathematical Economics.* Amsterdam: North-Holland.

Smith, Adam. [1776] 1977. *The Wealth of Nations.* London: J. M. Dent and Sons.

Smith, V. L. 1980. "Experiments with a Decentralized Mechanism for Public Goods Decisions." *American Economic Review* 70:584–600.

Wicksell, Knut. 1958. "New Principle of Just Taxation." In R. Musgrave and A. T. Peacock, eds. *Classics in the Theory of Public Finance.* New York: St. Martin's Press.

PART II

BENEFIT COST ANALYSIS

A

Relevance to Public Policy

[3]

Taking benefits and costs seriously

Alan Randall*

In little more than a half-century, benefit–cost analysis (BCA) has evolved from a relatively crude financial feasibility analysis for capital-intensive public works to a sophisticated and comprehensive application of the economic-theoretic principles of welfare change measurement to evaluate all manner of projects, programs, and policies. In the United States, BCA has been institutionalized for the evaluation of water resources projects (the Flood Control Act of 1937) and a broad range of regulatory initiatives (required by various Executive Orders), while well-entrenched executive practice routinely considers benefits and costs for a considerable set of activities undertaken by Federal, State, and local governments. Executive agencies in the United Kingdom have long used BCA to evaluate certain kinds of proposed investments (for example, public transportation). Similarly, BCA is well established in international development agencies, for filtering-out proposals that seem unlikely to generate benefits exceeding their costs; and British economists have played leading roles in elaborating the methodological basis for this kind of work. Continental European governments have to this point been less likely to make formal and routine use of BCA, at least in the context of environmental initiatives (Navrud and Pruckner, 1997). Nevertheless, as the large number of papers in BCA and environmental valuation submitted to the 1998 World Congress of Environmental and Resource Economists confirms, considerable research effort is being expended in this direction in many European countries; and it is reasonable to expect that much of this work plays some part, formal or informal, in the policy decision process.

JUSTIFYING A ROLE FOR BCA IN POLICY DECISIONS

None of this is to suggest that participants in public decision processes, expert informants whether from the sciences or the humanities, and concerned citizens in general have achieved a consensus welcoming an expanded public role for BCA. Instead one observes a broad range of opinion, much of it openly sceptical. Those economists whose intellectual circles are confined mostly to their fellow economists are nevertheless familiar with many of the standard criticisms of BCA. Why is valuation based on effective demand, so that the demands of the well-endowed count for more? Would it not be better to use some kind of basic needs pricing (Scandizzo and Knudsen, 1980) when evaluating the benefits of projects aimed at improving the lot of impoverished groups, or to use some set of explicit distributional weights when aggregating benefits and costs? Why do present value calculations for BCA impose positive discount rates that seem to undervalue distant future outcomes relative to those that are more immediate? What assurance can we have that intangible concerns which leave few and indistinct traces in the market place are nevertheless properly represented in BC calculations? Given that BCA involves streams of future benefits and costs, yet we can glimpse the future only dimly, what is the proper treatment in BCA of risk, uncertainty, and gross ignorance about ecological systems?

Most economists working in BCA are familiar with these questions, even if they do not have ready answers for all of them. Yet, as economists begin to engage in environmental policy discussions with the broader intellectual community, we are sometimes surprised to see how often the discussion bypasses these familiar criticisms of BCA, proceeding immediately to a question we did not expect: why should the policy process be concerned at all about benefits and costs? And it turns out that this question is exactly the right place to start. Suppose we are able to give convincing reasons why the public decision process ought to be concerned with benefits and costs, and to suggest coherent ways of dealing with conflicts that might arise between this concern and other legitimate public concerns. Then, the reasoning that justifies BCA and identifies a reasonable place for it in the public sphere should be useful also for resolving many of the controversies about BCA that are more familiar to economists. In this chapter, I will pay more attention to the first of these objectives than the second: I shall attempt a fairly complete argument that benefits and costs should be taken seriously in the public arena, and then sketch some of the implications of that argument for the way BCA should be done.

One useful way to pose the question is: does a benign and conscientious public decision maker have a duty to consult an account of benefits and costs, as economists understand the terms benefits and costs (Copp, 1985)? This question asks about a rather modest duty on the part of the decision maker: a duty to consider BC information in some way, which is much less demanding than a duty to treat it as decisive; and a duty to consult a BCA, which is less demanding than a duty to invest real resources in performing such an analysis. Nevertheless, it is by no means obvious at the outset that such a modest duty exists.

Efficiency in government

When called upon to defend the systematic use of BCA in public decision processes, economists are likely to start talking about the need to impose a market-like efficiency on the activities of government (for example, Arrow et al., 1996). However, this argument is not immediately obvious to most philosophers.

First, a case has to be made that the efficiency of markets is a good thing in the domain in which markets are permitted to operate. Perhaps we can do little better than Jules Coleman (1987) who argued that the virtues of market institutions (including, but not limited to their efficiency properties) makes them broadly acceptable for taking care of those kinds of human affairs that are not especially contentious (perhaps he meant the kinds of things that can be handled consensually by arms-length transactions), but that political institutions are required to deal with the really contentious issues of public concern. In other words, the justification for market institutions applies to a residuum of human concerns remaining after some prior assignment of the set of contentious issues to the governmental sphere.

Second, having found some virtue in market institutions for handling some appropriate set of human concerns, it is then necessary to argue that government ought to impose market-like efficiency on the remaining, and necessarily more contentious, undertakings that have been assigned to government. Mark Sagoff (1981) is most vigorous in rejecting this argument. He asserts that it is a simple category mistake to inquire about the efficiency of a governmental undertaking: government is exactly that institution that human societies invoke when they choose, for their own good reasons, not to be efficient. It is easy to play this argument for cheap laughs ('Of course! What better institution than government, if the goal is to be inefficient!'), but Sagoff's point is not entirely frivolous. Efficiency is a harsh discipline, and one that in practice tends to reinforce the distributional status quo; and it is by no means clear that society ought to impose that discipline on everything that it does.[1]

The need to impose a market-like efficiency on the activities of government is also more self-evident to economists than to the educated public at large, from whence come all manner of objections.[2] The point is that the economists' rationale is at least incomplete and requires, at a minimum, a convincing argument as to why it makes sense to apply an efficiency test to government actions.

Welfarism

When asked to defend an efficiency test for government undertakings, economists are likely to develop an argument premised on the ethic of welfarism: the goodness of an individual life is exactly the level of satisfaction of the individual's preferences, and the goodness of a society is a matter only of the level of satisfaction of its members.[3] From these premises, economists have developed, invoking various assumptions and restrictions as necessary and convenient, the whole apparatus of welfare change measurement, of which BCA is the direct practical implementation.

Welfarism is most readily understood as a kind of consequentialism: right action is whatever produces good consequences, and consequences are evaluated according to their contribution to welfare. However, the welfarist justification of an efficiency test is unlikely to be entirely satisfactory to consequentialists as a group – because many of them would insist that all manner of consequences not readily reduced to welfare are nevertheless worthy of consideration[4] – and even to many utilitarians who consider preference satisfaction an important consideration but not strictly the only concern in evaluating the goodness of a society or an individual life. Furthermore, consequentialism is itself a particular version of axiology, the theory that goodness is a matter of value (Vallentyne, 1987). Not all axiologists would want to confine considerations of value to consequences alone.

Axiology is only one of the foundational ethics in the western tradition. Philosophers frequently identify two foundational ethics, the second being deontological: goodness is whatever emerges from right action, so that the ethicist's task is to judge not value but the rightness of actions.[5] Economists often find it useful to distinguish two classes of deontological ethics: Kantianism, which defines right action as that which is obedient to moral duties derived ultimately from a set of universal moral principles; and contractarianism, in which right action respects the rights of individuals. These positions are both deontological, because the justification of Kantian moral imperatives and of individual rights requires appeal ultimately to some asserted principle.[6] Economists nevertheless distinguish Kantian from contractarian foundations, at least in part because the Paretian formulation of contractarianism has become quite familiar and congenial, for example, in the justification of voluntary exchange, while Kantian ethics – with its insistence that moral and prudential reasoning are quite distinct, and that universal moral imperatives can be found from which to deduce situational rules for action – is quite bewildering to many economists.

Many Kantians would be relatively unimpressed by the argument that welfarism justifies an efficiency test for a broad range of proposed government actions. The problem is that Kantians fall easily into associating efficiency with prudential considerations whereas, in the Kantian scheme of things, the moral high ground is occupied by the good will which acts in accord with universal duties.

Some, but not all, contractarians are comfortable with welfarism at the individual level. What is bedrock is the right of the individual to withhold consent for a proposed arrangement, or change in arrangements, for his own reasons. That a proposed change would reduce individual utility is a perfectly good reason for withholding consent, but by no means the only conceivable reason. Contractarian economists have combined the utility maximization framework with an unyielding individual rights ethic to derive strong defences of voluntary exchange for ordinary goods and voluntary taxation for public goods. Consequentialists and contractarian economists might agree that ideal markets are highly virtuous institutions, but they will have quite different reasons for that conclusion: the consequentialist endorses the market because it is efficient, the contractarian because it is free. Utilitarian or not at the individual level, contractarians are unanimous in rejecting nonconsensual changes that make some individuals worse-off.[7]

So, in offering a welfarist justification for taking benefits and costs seriously, economists seem oblivious to the insecure status of welfarism as a moral theory. Many axiologists and all deontologists would reject welfarism as at least incomplete, and seriously wrong about some important moral questions. In the context that matters most to this audience, BCA of environmental projects and policies, one glaring weakness of welfarism is its inability to take seriously the concept of intrinsic value – that some things have value independent of any satisfaction they might provide a user or observer – an idea that is unexceptional to many non-welfarists. Any justification for BCA that is grounded in pure welfarism will fail to convince many thoughtful moral agents.[8]

Pluralism

A broad acceptance seems to be emerging among philosophers that the contest among ethical theories is likely to remain inconclusive. While each contending theory has powerful appeal, each is incomplete in some important way, each remains vulnerable to some serious avenue(s) of criticism, and it seems unlikely that any one will defeat the others decisively. Each, also, is inconsistent with the others in important ways, so that a coherent synthesis is unlikely.

Among those who seek ethical grounding for policy prescriptions, two kinds of pluralism have emerged. The more traditional kind seeks to cultivate an intellectual environment in which people who hold resolutely to different foundational ethics can nevertheless find agreement on particular real world policy resolutions (Williams, 1985). Agreement might be reached – for example, that real resources should be expended to protect natural environments – among people who would give quite different reasons as to why that should be so. The task of the thoughtful moral agent in the policy arena is, then, to find heuristics – rules for action – that can command broad agreement.

The second kind of pluralism imagines thoughtful people, exposed to and familiar with several ethical traditions, each drawing upon different ethical foundations to answer different kinds of questions in their own lives (Rorty, 1992). To this way of thinking, if the search for the single true, complete, and internally consistent ethical theory is bound to be fruitless, exclusive allegiance to any particular moral theory is hardly a virtue; and it becomes coherent to argue that some questions in life are best resolved by reference to moral imperatives, some as matters of respect for rights, and for the remainder it is reasonable to go about maximizing value, perhaps even focusing on consequences and evaluating them in terms of their impact on the level of preference satisfaction.

Taking seriously both kinds of pluralism encourages us to think of the policy process as a search for heuristics we can agree upon, and to accept that these heuristics are likely to incorporate insights from various moral theories. This suggests a second formulation for the question that motivates this enquiry: would a society of thoughtful moral agents agree to take seriously an account of benefits and costs?

Benefit–Cost Moral Theory

Donald Hubin (1994) asks us to consider benefit–cost moral theory: the theory that right action is whatever maximizes the excess of benefits over costs, as economists understand the terms benefits and costs. It is hard to imagine a single supporter of such a moral theory, among philosophers or the public at large. Instead, we would find unanimity that such a moral theory is inadequate, and an enormous diversity of reasons as to exactly why. As Hubin speculates, most people probably believe that the recommendations of BCA are defeasible on any number of grounds.

Yet this is hardly an argument that BC considerations are morally irrelevant. Hubin offers the analogy of democratic moral theory: right action is whatever commands a plurality of the eligible votes. This, too, is a thoroughly unacceptable moral theory. Nevertheless, democratic institutions flourish in a wide variety of circumstances, and their justification is by no means entirely pragmatic; good reasons can be found for a society taking seriously the wishes of its citizens expressed through the ballot. So, the gross inadequacy of democratic moral theory serves to justify not the abandonment of democratic procedures but nesting them within a (written or unwritten) framework of constitutional restraints, and all of this embedded in a public life where moral and ethical issues are discussed openly and vigorously.

The claim that an inadequate moral theory might nevertheless provide some principles for institutional design is entirely consistent with the standard justification of pluralism: in a world where the unique true moral foundation for public life is bound to remain elusive, public institutions should be crafted so as to make good use of insights from a variety of ethical traditions.

The analogy with democratic moral theory hints at the possibility of a public role for BCA despite the obvious implausibility of BC moral theory. For the moment, assume that BCA is a systematic procedure for testing whether a proposal offers a potential Pareto-improvement (PPI), and thus provides a decently good (but not entirely unobjectionable) account of its potential contribution to preference satisfaction.[9] Then, the question is whether an accounting of contribution to preference satisfaction should play some systematic role in public life.

PREFERENCE SATISFACTION MATTERS

Hubin (1994) asks us to imagine a plausible moral theory in which the level of satisfaction of individual preferences counts for nothing at all. It turns out that one cannot imagine such a theory. Examining a broad array of contending moral theories, Hubin has shown that preference satisfaction counts for something, in each of them; and he argues with some confidence that a coherent moral theory in which preference satisfaction matters not at all is implausible.

Randall (1991) and Randall and Farmer (1995) have considered the two ethical theories that contend for the allegiance of mainstream economists, consequentialism and contractarianism, and the major alternative, Kantianism. They show that, while each of these ethical theories has different ways of taking preference satisfaction into consideration, each of them does consider preference satisfaction in some way. For consequentialists, one obvious way to evaluate consequences is to ask whether people prefer them; one suspects it is the natural default way, given that consequentialists have invested so much intellectual effort in identifying particular circumstances in which preference is an unreliable or inappropriate indicator of the goodness of consequences. It is natural, too, for contractarians to recommend the protection of life, liberty, and property with secure rights, in order to liberate the individual for the pursuit of happiness. Contractarians, of course, are uncomfortable with consequentialist notions of social welfare. Nevertheless, Farmer (1991) has shown that, in a world where Pareto-compensation is impeded by high transactions costs, contractarians might rationally agree to be governed by a default potential Pareto-improvement rule provided they are free to depart from it when more important concerns arise (for example, the need to protect things dear to oneself, and the need to bribe aggrieved parties to remain in the contract). In the original Kantian scheme of things, claims based on considerations of happiness were clearly morally subordinate to claims derived from universal moral imperatives. That, however, is less devastating to preference than some contemporary Kantians have made it seem. First, Kant was clear that prudential concerns matter morally.[10] Second, there may well be a broad domain of human concerns within which preference satisfaction may be pursued without violating moral strictures; and a thoughtful Kantian would concur that, within that domain, more preference satisfaction is better than less.

So the issue is not whether preference satisfaction is morally considerable; in each of these ethical theories, it is. Instead, the contest is about what sorts of considerations might trump preference satisfaction, and in what ways. What else, beyond preference satisfaction, might one want to consider, and in what manner might one want to take account of those things?

Preference Satisfaction to Inform Decisions, Rather than to Decide Issues

Since we are not convinced that right action is whatever maximizes the level of preference satisfaction, we would not want to be bound by a rule requiring us to decide every issue on the basis of preference satisfaction alone. Because the recommendations of BCA are defeasible on any number of grounds, contribution to preference satisfaction cannot be *the* decision criterion. If preference satisfaction is nevertheless a consideration under any plausible moral theory, an account of contribution to preference satisfaction might be used routinely as a component of some more comprehensive set of evidence, accounts, and moral claims to inform the decision process. An informative role for BCA does not depend on the PPI being correct as a criterion of moral value, or right action, or as a practical decision procedure. Nevertheless, for BCA to be justified as a routine component of some broader information set, it must have some moral import in general, and not just in particular cases. Hubin resolves this problem by noting that PPIs plausibly are correlated systematically with right action and good consequences.

The notion of a systematic public role for BCA within some broader information set is quite congenial to many economists: 'BCA is a tool to inform decisions, but not to decide issues' is a common assertion among us (for example, Arrow et al., 1996, p. 221). The problem is that it answers the question that motivates this inquiry only in a tentative and incomplete kind of way. Are there particular situations and circumstances in which an account of preference satisfaction should be ignored entirely, and others in which it should be decisive? How should an account of preference satisfaction be weighted relative to other kinds of information? Can the answers to these questions be principled, or must they always be circumstantial?

If we adhere closely to the initial context of this enquiry – does a public decision maker have an obligation to consult a BCA? – failure to answer these questions clearly is most worrisome. Surely we would want to say more about the additional obligations incumbent upon the public decision maker. It would not do, in the context of a serious moral enquiry about the justification of a public role for BCA, to permit the public decision maker complete latitude as to what else to consider in addition to a BCA and how to take account of these additional considerations.

This difficulty is perhaps less pressing if we take pluralism seriously: if a society of thoughtful moral agents can come to agreement to make a place for BCA in public affairs, perhaps they can also agree about what other kinds of information should be considered, and how.

Preference Satisfaction Subject to Constraints

An alternative way of coming to terms with the idea that preference satisfaction counts for something in any plausible moral theory, but cannot count for everything, is to endorse preference satisfaction as the decision rule for those issues where no overriding moral concerns are threatened. Preference satisfaction could then be decisive within some broad domain,[11] while that domain is itself bounded by constraints reflecting rights that ought to be respected and moral imperatives that ought to be obeyed. This would implement the commonsense notion that preference satisfaction is perfectly fine so long as it doesn't threaten any concerns that are more important.

The idea that, if utilitarianism is to be a plausible moral theory it requires side-constraints, turns out to be quite general. An example may help, at this point: since many individuals are able to survive comfortably with a single kidney, utilitarian moral theory could readily endorse the forcible harvest of single kidneys from healthy individuals in order to save the lives of those with incurable kidney disease. Yet, the forcible harvest of kidneys, even to increase aggregate welfare unambiguously, would be viewed widely as morally repugnant. While some would claim that this example provides sufficient reason to abandon utilitarianism, a plausible solution (given the incompleteness of all candidate moral theories) is to retain utilitarianism but embed it in a set of side-constraints. Perhaps the side-constraints can be derived from the theory itself; this is the project of rule utilitarianism, and also of Elster's (1979) 'binding behavior' argument. But is that kind of internal consistency required? Given the incompleteness of moral theories and the argument for ethical pluralism, it is entirely plausible to design the side-constraints not to implement a single moral theory but to command agreement among individuals drawing upon different theories.

As the example of forcible harvest of kidneys suggests, side-constraints securing some well-defined set of human rights seem essential. If the beneficence of reasonably free markets is to be enjoyed, a set of secure property rights is also necessary. People acting together to govern themselves need also to establish a framework of laws, statutes, regulations and policies to legitimize and also to limit the role of activist government. This approach would create a society where preference satisfaction rules, but only within a domain restricted by the rights of others and the actions of government on behalf of society. Compared to a framework in which considerations of preference satisfaction inform decisions, this present framework commits us to a stronger role for preference satisfaction, which is decisive within its domain, but also for (a perhaps smaller set of) other relevant moral considerations, the most pressing of which are installed as constraints.

To take this idea beyond the familiar protections for life, liberty, and property, consider a set of policy issues familiar to environmental economists: the protection of habitats, species and particular ecosystems. A society could adopt the practice of deciding these kinds of issues on the basis of preference satisfaction, but subject to some kind of conservation constraint. A safe minimum standard (SMS) of conservation has been suggested by a variety of authors: harvest, habitat destruction, and so on, must be restricted in order to leave a sufficient stock of the renewable resource to ensure its survival. Consider the justification for an SMS constraint. First, it makes sense to think of the SMS as a constraint adopted for good reason. Decades ago, economists were able to show readily that voluntary adoption of an SMS was inconsistent with standard assumptions of utility theory: an individual making such a choice would be exhibiting discontinuous indifference surfaces, if not some even more blatant departure from the standard model. But this argument need not detain us, because we have already conceded that an adequate resolution of the moral issues involved cannot be concerned only with preference satisfaction. As Farmer and Randall (1998) argue, the SMS constraint makes most sense when cast transparently as a discrete interruption of business-as-usual.

Now, we turn to the question of what general kinds of side-constraints might justify the SMS rule. At least three candidates have promise and we will consider briefly the sorts of justification each might provide for an SMS constraint.

Don't do anything you will regret later

Elster (1979) demonstrated that a rational utilitarian might exhibit binding behavior, i.e., choose now to constrain himself against taking later some momentarily pleasurable act that, he is reasonably sure, will be regretted eventually. Randall (1991) applied this argument to a utilitarian justification of the SMS. Because Elster's argument was not predicated on uncertainty, its most direct application is to cases where we might, on the spur of the moment, choose to pursue profitable but environmentally devastating exploitation when there is every reason to expect we will regret it later.[12] An SMS constraint would be adopted, to precommit us to avoid such foolish decisions.

Don't take inordinate risks

A tradition exemplified by Bishop (1978) maintains that an SMS constraint is simply a rational approach to a high level of uncertainty in which there is some (perhaps small) chance that loss of a species or a particular habitat might turn out to have disastrous consequences for human welfare. Rather than rely on standard utilitarian adjustments to take account of uncertainty (as does the 'extended BCA' approach), Bishop attempted to show, a risk-averse utilitarian rationally would adopt an SMS constraint: formally, the SMS is the maximin solution. However, the attempt to ground the SMS in standard versions of utilitarian decision making under risk has not proven successful: Ready and Bishop (1991) conceded that game theory did not support Bishop's earlier attempt at a utilitarian justification of a discrete interruption of business-as-usual when the SMS constraint was reached.

Don't do anything disgusting

The basic idea is that the public decision-maker should adopt – or a pluralist society would agree to be bound by – a general-form constraint to eschew actions that violate obvious limits on decent public policy. This kind of constraint is in principle broad enough to take seriously the objections to unrestrained pursuit of preference satisfaction that might be made from a wide range of coherent philosophical perspectives. Examples of such constraints might include: don't violate the rights that other people and perhaps other entities might reasonably be believed to hold; be obedient to the duties that arise from universal moral principles, or could reasonably be derived therefrom; and, do not sacrifice important intrinsic values in the service of mere instrumental ends. In each of these cases, the domain within which pursuit of preference satisfaction is permitted would be bounded by nonutilitarian constraints.

The other justifications for the SMS constraint can be collapsed into the 'don't do anything disgusting' justification. First, Elster's rational utilitarian precommitment could surely be also a coherent response to uncertainty – we would precommit not to take inordinate environmental risks in pursuit of immediate gratification. While the 'don't take inordinate risks' justification for an SMS constraint has often fallen victim to internal difficulties in utilitarian theories of decision making under risk, it does not have to. When dealing with risks it seems reasonable to allow for the possibility of sharp discontinuities in our knowledge and, therefore, our ability to perform informed quantitative analysis. We have long distinguished uncertainty from risk: with risk we can assign probabilities to the various possible outcomes while with uncertainty the probabilities are unknown. When thinking about the future performance of ecosystems we barely understand, it seems appropriate to recognize a third category, gross ignorance, in which we have great difficulty specifying the nature of possible outcomes, as well as their probabilities (see also, Dovers, 1995). Situations where we concede gross ignorance and suspect that some of the possibilities might be disastrous call for a sharp break with the practice of deciding on the basis of expected contribution to preference satisfaction.

Second, the 'don't take inordinate risks' constraint could itself be subsumed under the broader category of 'don't do anything disgusting'. The undesirability of taking inordinate risks has a utilitarian interpretation via risk-aversion – and economists' attempts to make sense of the SMS often have seized upon the 'don't take inordinate risks' interpretation for exactly that reason – but it is capable also of interpretation in contractarian terms (proposals that pass an aggregate preference satisfaction test may nevertheless expose particular individuals and groups to inordinate and nonconsensual risks), and Kantian terms (there might reasonably be a moral duty to avoid actions that would impose inordinate risks on particular individuals or groups).

The 'don't do anything disgusting' constraint is congenial to those who accept the premises of ethical pluralism. Whereas a utilitarian might object that this constraint sounds fine in principle but rather empty in practice ('OK; then, tell me exactly what kinds of things are disgusting, and why'), a pluralist might respond that defining what sorts of actions are disgusting and should therefore be ruled out by constraint is exactly the right task for public discourse. Again, the pluralist sees reason to hope and expect that reasonable people can agree on particular constraints, even as they justify those constraints in quite different ways.

THE JUSTIFICATION FOR BCA DEPENDS UPON IT BEING AN ACCEPTABLE ACCOUNT OF PREFERENCE SATISFACTION

The progress made thus far, in defining and justifying a public role for BCA, depends crucially on our heretofore undefended claim that BCA is a decently good account of contribution to aggregate preference satisfaction. Copp (1985) has put the challenge succinctly: if BCA is just any member of an arbitrary set of superficially utilitarian accounting tools, it is hard to see why a benign public decision maker would have duty to consult a BCA.

Among welfare economists, a consensus definition of BCA has at last emerged: BCA is an empirical test for potential Pareto-improvements (PPIs). The PPI test evaluates a proposed change by asking whether the amount that those who stand to gain would be willing to pay to get the change exceeds the amount of compensation that would induce those who stand to lose to consent to the change.[13]

The PPI criterion clearly surmounts the first of Copp's objections (that is, that BCA is not rigorously defined, so that we cannot know exactly what we are buying into), in that we can write down exactly what an accounting tool must do in order for it to be a valid test of PPIs. BCA according to the PPI criterion is no longer just any member of some loosely defined set of accounting tools. By defining BCA as a test for PPIs, we provide it some substantial rigour.

The next task is to consider the extent to which our various ethical theories – consequentialism, Kantianism and contractarianism – might support a PPI test. Utilitarians can recognize in the PPI a criterion that is at least admissible: it provides a measure of contribution to individual preference satisfaction, and it aggregates individual welfare changes in a way that captures the intent of 'the greatest good for the greatest number' (in terms of Copp's criticism, BCA is clearly utilitarian, not 'superficially utilitarian'). However, it cannot be claimed that utilitarianism singles out the compensating measures of welfare change as the uniquely appropriate measures. A standard utilitarian objection to the PPI criterion (and to any price-based valuation method) is familiar to economists – the valuations implied by buyer's best offer and seller's reservation price reflect not just preferences but also endowments – and is discussed in the following section. Nevertheless, it can be argued that PPI–BCA provides a more plausible account of value than do its practicable utilitarian competitors (Hubin, 1994).

Contractarianism endorses the compensating value measures, and only those measures: surely value must be based on what gainers would voluntarily pay and losers would voluntarily accept. The problem for contractarians is the aggregation rule. They reject the idea that right action could impose uncompensated (and therefore nonconsensual) harm on some people. There are those (for example, Leonard and Zeckhauser, 1988) who attempt to justify the PPI criterion as a test of hypothetical consent: since the gainers could hypothetically compensate the losers, the losers can be assumed to hypothetically consent. Hubin responds that hypothetical consent is a kind of a hypothesis, not a kind of consent (1994). That is, the very essence of consent lies in its actuality, and if real consent endows an action with real virtue imagined consent can provide only imagined virtue. Nevertheless, more subtle contractarian justifications for BCA can be developed.[14]

It is contractarian reasoning that requires the compensating welfare measures, willingness-to-pay (WTP) for gains and willingness-to-accept (WTA) for losses. This offers some nontrivial protections of a contractarian kind. Since WTA is not bounded by individual endowments, it is very difficult for a proposal that would leave its uncompensated losers inconsolably worse-off to pass a PPI-based BCA test. This contractarian virtue is likely also to have some appeal for Kantians, who would recognize a duty not to impose great harm on others.[15]

BCA implementing the PPI criterion therefore has several virtues. It is precisely defined and not just 'superficially' utilitarian, so that Copp's objection is moot; it implements a welfare change measure (compensating) and an aggregation rule (Benthamite) that are admissible, even if not uniquely so, to utilitarians; and its compensating measure of individual welfare change is exactly the measure demanded by contractarians and supported, it seems plausible, from several other ethical perspectives because it pays disproportionate attention to the nonconsensual losses of those made inconsolably worse off by public action. This amounts to a fairly strong *prima facie* case that PPI-based BCA provides an account of contribution to preference satisfaction that is acceptable from a variety of ethical perspectives.

While the above argument endorses PPI-based welfare change measurement and BCA, not all accounts presented to public decision makers and labelled as BCAs are rigorously PPI-based.[16] Some still bear evidence of BCA's roots in financial feasibility analysis, while in other cases the rules for doing BCA have themselves become the subject of policy, so that deviations from the PPI criterion are institutionalized.

If BC analysts wish to claim, based on arguments such as are provided in this chapter, that the public has a duty to take BCA seriously, then the analysts themselves have a duty to implement the PPI valuation framework rigorously and carefully. The result would be BCAs that depart from customary practice in several ways. Less attention would be paid to market prices and demands, while more attention would be paid to public preferences for public goods and the nonmarket values those preferences imply, and to WTA as the appropriate measure of costs. We found, much earlier in this chapter, that a claimed need to impose a market-like efficiency on the activities of government provides an implausible justification for taking benefits and costs seriously. Now we find that a sounder justification for BCA entails an obligation on the part of the analyst to pay more than customary attention to preferences and less than customary attention to market outcomes.

ECONOMISTS' CONCERNS ABOUT BCA

I have argued that the things that concern economists about BCA – endowment-weighted values, discounting of future benefits and costs, and the treatment of risk, very long-term commitments, and intergenerational concerns – are not the first concerns of philosophers and the public at large. This latter, and much larger, community must first be convinced that there are principled reasons for taking benefits and costs seriously before we can engage them in serious discussion about the things that worry us in the doing of BCA. My answer – that BCA provides an acceptable account of preference satisfaction, itself a valid moral concern – presents a starting point for consideration of these particular issues in doing BCA and interpreting its results.

Endowment-weighted values
Given that WTP is likely to be increasing in income and wealth, the preferences of the well off are more heavily weighted in benefit estimation. Given that the poor sell cheaply, costs to the less well off are less heavily weighted. One or another manifestation of this relationship shows up in market prices, demands and supplies, and WTP and WTA. This is the

price that utilitarian economists must pay for the improvements in data quality that they obtain from insisting that actions speak louder than words, and expressions of WTP and WTA speak louder than mere expressions of caring. To other utilitarians, the justification is by no means clear for endowment-weighting individual preferences before aggregation.

It is also the price that must be paid to bring certain important classes of nonutilitarians into a pluralist consensus in support of BCA. Contractarians, of course, insist that WTP and WTA are exactly the right measures of individual welfare change; and people reasoning from a variety of philosophical perspectives gain some comfort from the consideration that WTA is not strictly bound by endowments, so that the poor may have high WTA for things that they really hate to lose.

Discounting

The discounting of future benefits and costs is a practice introduced from financial analysis in order to account for the productivity of capital. In recent years, some environmental economists have been swayed by critics who worry that discounting implies that the concerns of the future (perhaps only a few decades hence) count only trivially in the calculations of the present. Thus we have the discounting paradox: we must discount, it is claimed, in order to avoid damaging the future by making wasteful commitments of capital to unproductive projects; and we must not discount, it is also claimed, in order to avoid trivializing future demands for present conservation.

The paradox can be resolved in the following way. We can be reasonably confident of two propositions: if the problem is simply to determine the rate of consumption from an endowment (the 'cake-eating' problem) a society with a positive discount rate will choose a consumption path relatively high at the outset and declining over time (Page, 1977); and if capital is productive and the young need to borrow it in order to produce efficiently, equilibrium interest rates will be positive and a policy of repressing the interest rate (undertaken, one imagines, in order to protect the future) will actually depress the trajectory of future welfare (Farmer and Randall, 1997).[17] That is, in a cake-eating economy, discounting is destructive of future welfare but in a productive economy it is not.

This resolution of the discounting paradox directs our attention to the real question: are we, or are we not, operating in a economy which is ultimately cake-eating? If capital accumulation is sufficiently high, renewable resources are managed carefully, capital and renewable resources are adequately substitutable for exhaustible natural resources, and technological development tends to enhance the substitutability of plentiful resources for those that are most scarce, the cake-eating problem can be avoided. In that case, concerns that discounting inherently damages the future are misplaced. It can also be argued that policy interventions such as the SMS, which address directly crucial natural resources, provide a more appropriate response to conservation crises involving essential natural resources than would discount rate repression.

Treatment of risks, uncertainty, and gross ignorance

Risk refers to situations in which each possible action has an array of possible outcomes, with probabilities assigned to each. A risk-neutral decision maker will choose the action that has the highest expected value of outcomes. Risk-averse decision makers might place more weight on avoiding unfavourable outcomes, while paying less attention to upside possibilities. Modern literature focuses on risk-management strategies, including contingent claims markets and insurance contracts. Applications to BCA (for example, Graham, 1981; Freeman, 1991; Meier and Randall, 1991) have shown how the valid conceptual measures of benefits and costs depend on assumptions concerning the completeness of contingent claims markets and the availability of fair insurance. It has been argued convincingly, I believe, that organizations with large and diverse portfolios of projects are, for that reason, efficient self-insurers, and that government is surely such an organization; therefore, government is, or ought to be, effectively risk-neutral (Arrow and Lind, 1970). Uncertainty differs from risk, according to the familiar Knightian distinction, in that it is not possible to assign objective probabilities to possible outcomes. The Bayesian tradition suggests starting with subjective probabilities, and updating them as new information emerges.

It is often claimed that these approaches to risk and uncertainty are thoroughly unsatisfactory for public decisions about projects and policies that affect, for example, ecological sustainability. The contingent claims and insurance markets approach to risk was designed to deal with private financial risks, whereas inability to know in advance the environmental outcomes of policy decisions is quite a different conceptual problem. Rather than risk, where outcomes can be defined and probabilities assigned, or uncertainty, where outcomes are defined but objective probabilities are unavailable, advance knowledge of environmental outcomes often approaches gross ignorance: we cannot even define in advance the array of possible outcomes.[18]

Economists have offered basically two kinds of responses to concerns about risk, uncertainty, and gross ignorance. First, there has emerged a tradition, now quite well-developed, of utilitarian extensions of the BC accounts: option value (Weisbrod, 1964), quasi-option value (Arrow and Fisher, 1974) and existence value (Krutilla, 1967, and Randall and Stoll,

1983). To many modern environmental economists, these categories of value are straightforward (at least in principle): they just complete the BC accounts, which began with prices multiplied by quantity changes, and gradually expanded (in recognition of the implications of the concept of preference) to include economic surplus and nonmarket use value (for example, Freeman, 1993). Nevertheless, as we move beyond the realm of risk and toward gross ignorance, fundamental difficulties of two kinds become more pressing: first, conceptual tools grounded in risk theory seem inadequate to the task; and, second, doubts multiply about the ability of ordinary citizens to absorb and interpret the necessary information and express meaningful preferences in terms of WTP and WTA.

The extended BCA approach has gained a limited degree of acceptance in policy circles, but sceptics remain to the right and to the left. Supporters of business-as-usual complain that these amendments, which move BCA ever-further from the discipline of the marketplace, are little more than 'fudge factors' to insure that the BCA generates the environmentally correct result.[19] Environmentalists, however, are concerned that, well-meant as these amendments are, they fail dismally to capture the enormity of the risks involved and the depth of human ignorance about environmental systems.

A common complaint among environmentalists – that the general public is scarcely qualified to express meaningful option, quasi-option, and existence values – raises a more general issue: to what extent is public input about policies convincing, given the highly technical nature of environmental systems and the difficulty that even the experts have in understanding them. Our model decision maker seeking policies to serve the public interest may be persuaded to put more weight on expert opinion, whereas the pluralist is likely to argue that expert opinion, once the experts themselves converge upon a convincing consensus, is quickly incorporated into the public wisdom.

A second approach with some currency in the economics literature involves the safe minimum standard of conservation (Ciriacy-Wantrup, 1968 and Bishop, 1978) discussed earlier in this chapter, in the context of the 'preference satisfaction subject to constraints' approach. Farmer and Randall (1998), arguing from existential ethical pluralism, justify the SMS as a decision heuristic, a sharp break from business-as-usual, that – given the fear of possible disastrous consequences from anthropogenic modification of environmental systems about which we know so little[20] – could earn the allegiance of people operating from quite different ethical foundations, and therefore having quite different reasons for signing on.

We should be warned, however, against premature claims of consensus. The early SMS proponents, Ciriacy-Wantrup and Bishop, recognized that a utilitarian SMS could not call for unlimited sacrifice of welfare to meet conservation objectives, so they proposed that society should be released from the conservation commitment if the costs of meeting it proved intolerably high. Randall and Farmer (1995) show that while a case can be made for a pluralistic consensus for adoption of the SMS, controversy may re-emerge concerning the magnitude of the cost that would be intolerable, especially in the case where the natural resource under threat is not essential to human welfare. Rolfe (1995) has argued that if utilitarian thinking is used to justify the SMS, it should also be applied to determining the magnitude of the intolerable cost that would justify abandoning the SMS. By the time Rolfe is done, the utilitarian SMS amounts to little more than the extended BCA approach: a warning flag raised in information-poor situations to remind the analysts to bend over backwards to give uncertainty and nonuse values their due. In contrast, Kantians and contractarians may well insist that the intolerable cost be much larger.

Very long time horizons and intergenerational concerns
While critics commonly treat very long time horizons and intergenerational concerns as a special category of problems for BCA, they are in fact extreme cases of problems already introduced under the rubrics of discounting, and risk, uncertainty and gross ignorance. Very long time horizons confront today's decision makers with responsibility for future generations that will be affected by actions taken today, and multiply exponentially the difficulties in predicting future consequences. I have argued that discounting is not *per se* a problem in a productive economy with capital accumulation and regeneration of at least some natural resources. If there is a problem, it concerns the substitutability of human-made capital for natural resources, and the SMS constraint is a coherent tool for responding to perceived problems in this respect. For fear of disastrous future consequences of actions taken today, the SMS provides a coherent response.

This is not so much an argument *for* the SMS – although I continue to believe the SMS has merit – as an argument *against* the project of perfecting BCA in response to these concerns. That project is doomed: BCA cannot be perfected. This would be quite terrible if benefit–cost moral theory was the one true moral theory, or if society had delegated without review all of its decisions to benefit–cost technocrats. But neither of these circumstances is actual or likely. Ethical pluralism will persist and benefit–cost moral theory is not even a serious candidate; and the pendulum began to swing away from technocracy long before the progressive dream of scientific government had been converted to reality. The issue is not how to perfect BCA, but how to enjoy the services it can provide for us – a reasonably good account of preference satisfaction, itself one valid moral concern among others – without according it more influence than it deserves. We could use BCA to inform decisions rather than to decide issues. Better yet, we could accord substantial influence to BCA, within a domain where preference satisfaction carries a good deal of weight, but bounded by various constraints derived from perhaps different ethical perspectives and adopted for good reason.

NOTES

*   I am grateful for the research assistance of Michael Taylor, and stimulating comments and helpful suggestions from Don Hubin, Michael Farmer, the referees and the editors of the Yearbook, and conference and seminar audiences at the Kentucky Economics Association, the University of Georgia, the Agricultural University of Norway, and Michigan State University. In particular, Hubin has struggled mightily to keep me from gross philosophical error and bears no responsibility for remaining weaknesses in this regard.

1.   This critique applies more broadly. The economists' market-failure justification for governmental action involves an implied but seldom explicitly defended premise that the market is inherently the institution of first resort, such that the institutions of government deserve consideration only in the event of a market failure.

2.   The idea that, among educated people, economists are different draws some support from the literature (Frank et al., 1993). The stylized fact has been established that economists are more likely to report that they would free-ride given the opportunity, and the literature has moved on to consider alternative explanations: is it years of instruction and mentoring within the discipline that makes economists that way, or do individuals with this proclivity self-select into specializing in economics?

3.   This definition follows Sen (1989). According to Kagan (1998), current usage among philosophers defines welfarism more narrowly, that is, as evaluating welfare by the Benthamite utilitarian welfare function, and thus ignoring distributional concerns.

4.   MacIntyre (1979) complains that BCA is committed to the commensurability of diverse values, an argument that includes but also extends beyond consequentialist values.

5.   Here, I take my cue from Rawls (1971), who – in order to contrast his approach with consequentialism – asserted flatly that justice is fairness, and fairness is whatever results from fair processes. Kagan(1998), who is concerned not with intellectual roots but with what philosophers are arguing about today, defines as deontological any ethical position that would impose constraints on the pursuit of axiological good.

6.   Thus, while Kant insisted that reason was sufficient to establish categorical imperatives (that is, universal moral duties), he was unable to defend convincingly his claim that 'not lying' should be one them. Similarly, the attempt to ground contractarian ethics in natural rights encounters difficulty in justifying these rights.

7.   Consent is what matters. For example, Harsanyi (1955) finds virtue in the Benthamite welfare function only to the extent that conditions can be defined so that individuals would agree to adopt it.

8.   For completeness, it should be noted that I have defined the ethical theories of most immediate interest – consequentialism, Kantianism and contractarianism – in strictly anthropocentric terms. In dealing with environmental policy issues, one also encounters deep ecologists, for whom ultimate intrinsic value lies in naturalness, consequentialists who are concerned with the welfare of all sentient beings, and deontologists who argue that nature and/or many of its constituents enjoy rights that human beings are bound to respect. It can be asserted safely that the economist's anthropocentric welfarist justification of BCA makes little headway with any of these people.

9. I shall return later in this chapter, to a more complete consideration of the adequacy of BCA as a test for PPIs and an account of preference satisfaction.

10. 'To secure one's own happiness is at least indirectly a duty, for discontent with one's own condition under pressure from many cares and amid unsatisfied wants could easily become a great temptation to transgress duty' (Kant, 1991, p. 66).

11. It would be plausible, also, to combine the 'BCA to inform decisions' and the 'BCA subject to constraints' approaches. Then, BCA would be informative, but not necessarily decisive, within the permitted domain.

12. In the context of environmental policy, it is natural to seek to extend this concern to the multigenerational case: 'every reason to expect future generations will regret it'. However, such an extension would need to find support elsewhere, since Elster's binding behaviour is motivated by reasoned calculations concerning the impact of precipitous action on one's own wellbeing.

13. As it happens, there is a practical objection to this definition of BCA. It requires compensating measures of welfare change and, while such measures indicate reliably whether a proposal promises a welfare improvement vis-à-vis the status quo, they do not rank reliably a slate of alternative proposals; however, a family of alternative welfare change measures, including the well-known Hicksian equivalent measure, avoids this defect (Chipman and Moore, 1980). This objection is not fatal, however, since the PPI test is reliable in pairwise comparisons; so, one can work through a sequence of pairwise tests to find the best among many alternatives, or identify the best of the challengers using the equivalent welfare measure and then apply a PPI test to the top challenger versus the status quo.

14. The previously cited justifications offered by Farmer (1991) and Harsanyi (1955) do not exhaust the possibilities.

15. Infinite WTA on the part of a single individual would be sufficient to forestall an otherwise net-beneficial project. Two issues arise at this point. The first is practical: strategic false claims of infinite WTA could deny others substantial benefits. My argument assumes implicitly that WTA can be observed accurately, and is thus a specific case of my general approach: difficulties in implementing BCA are not the topic of this essay.

    The second is more foundational: what does it mean for an individual to have an infinite WTA, and what influence should this individual position have on the collective decision? While economists seek to explain infinite WTA in terms of lexicographic preferences, I think something quite different is usually at work. Infinite WTA is an announcement not that the individual has lexicographic preferences but rather that she draws upon some nonutilitarian moral tradition to address the particular kind of issue at hand. This has an interesting implication: an individual's refusal to think of a particular issue in terms of utilitarian trade-offs (which is what I take infinite WTA to mean) is decisive if incorporated into a BCA account, but may not be in a pluralistic discourse to discover, for example, an agreed-upon set of constraints on public decisions.

16. Copp's complaint still has currency when addressed to the set of BCAs that are actually submitted for the attention of decision makers.

17. Farmer and Randall differ explicitly with Arrow et al. (1996) regarding the justification for discounting. We emphasize the productivity of capital and the need of the young to borrow it, whereas Arrow et al. motivate discounting by appeal to time preference.

18. Rather than private misfortune, environmental risk threatens collective misfortune: Bayesian approaches, which use subjective probabilities, seem not so well-adapted to public decisions because widely differing subjective expectations of outcomes and probabilities among the general public is itself often the motivation for the controversies that BCA is intended to help resolve.

19. Ironically, perhaps, Sagoff (1996) makes similar complaints, not to keep BCA safe for market values, but to bolster his charge that extended BCA is incoherent, being a futile attempt to make utilitarian sense of intrinsic values that are inherently nonutilitarian.

20.   Taken seriously, the fear of disastrous consequences, even if quite improbable, makes a mockery of the idea that BCA, even with just the right amount of tweaking to account for uncertainty and non-use values, can get the right answer.

REFERENCES

Arrow, K. and A. Fisher (1974), 'Environmental preservation, uncertainty, and irreversibility', *Quarterly Journal of Economics*, **55**, 313–19.

Arrow, K. J. and R. C. Lind (1970), 'Uncertainty and the evaluation of public investment decisions', *American Economic Review*, **60** (3), June, 364–78.

Arrow, K. J., M. L. Cropper, G. C. Eads, R. W. Hahn, L. B. Lave, R. G. Noll, P. R. Portney, M. Russell, R. Schmalensee, V. K. Smith and R. N. Stavins (1996), 'Is there a role for benefit–cost analysis in environmental, health, and safety regulation?', Science, **272** (5259), 221–2.

Bishop, R. C. (1978), 'Endangered species and uncertainty: the economics of a safe minimum standard', *American Journal of Agricultural Economics*, **60** (1), February, 10–18.

Chipman, J. S. and J. C. Moore (1980), 'Compensating variation, consumer's surplus, and welfare', *American Economic Review*, **70** (5), December, 933–49.

Ciriacy-Wantrup, S. V. (1968), *Resource Conservation: Economics and Policies*, third edn, Berkeley, CA: University of California, Division of Agricultural Science.

Coleman, J. (1987), 'Competition and cooperation', Ethics, **98**, 76–90.

Copp, D. (1985), 'Morality, Reason, and Management Science: the Rationale of Cost–Benefit Analysis', in E. Paul, J. Paul and F. Miller (eds), *Ethics and Economics*, Oxford:Blackwell, pp. 128–51.

Dovers, S. (1995), 'A framework for scaling and framing policy problems in sustainability', *Ecological Economics*, **12**, 93–106.

Elster, J. (1979), *Ulysses and the Sirens: Studies in Rationality and Irrationality*, New York: Cambridge University Press.

Farmer, M. C. (1991), 'A unanimous consent solution to the supply of public goods: getting PPI rules from a PI process', *American Journal of Agricultural Economics*, **73**, 1551.

Farmer, M. C. and A. Randall (1997), 'Policies for sustainability: lessons from an overlapping generations model', *Land Economics*, **73**, 605–22.

Farmer, M. C. and A. Randall (1998), 'The rationality of a safe minimum standard', *Land Economics*, **74** (3), August, 263.

Frank, R., T. Gilovich and D. Regan (1993), 'Does the study of economics inhibit cooperation?', *Journal of Economic Perspectives*, **7**, 159–71.

Freeman, A. M. (1991), 'Welfare measurement and the benefit–cost analysis of projects affecting risk', *Southern Economic Journal*, **58**, 65–76.

Freeman, A. M. (1993), *The Measurement of Environmental and Resource Values: Theory and Methods*, Washington DC: Resources for the Future, Inc.

Graham, D. A. (1981), 'Cost–benefit analysis under uncertainty', *American Economic Review*, **71** (4), September, 715–25.

Harsanyi, J. (1955), 'Cardinal welfare, individualistic ethics and interpersonal comparisons of utility', *Journal of Political Economy*, **73**, 309–21.

Hubin, D. C. (1994), 'The moral justification of benefit/cost analysis', *Economics and Philosophy*, **10**, 169–94.

Kagan, S. (1998), *Normative Ethics*, Boulder, CO: Westview Press.

Kant, I. (1991), *Philosophical Writings*, (ed. E. Behler) New York: Continuum.

Krutilla, J. (1967), 'Conservation reconsidered', *American Economic Review*, **57** (4), September, 777–86.

Leonard, H. B. and R. Zeckhauser (1988), 'Cost–benefit analysis applied to risks: its philosophy and legitimacy', in D. MacLean (ed.), *Values at Risk*, Maryland Studies in Public Philosophy Series, Totowa, NJ: Rowman and Allanheld, pp. 31–48.

MacIntyre, A. (1979), 'Utilitarianism and Cost–Benefit Analysis: An Essay on the Relevance of Moral Philosophy to Bureaucratic Theory', in T. Beauchamp and N. Bowie (eds), *Ethical Theory and Business*, Englewood Cliffs, NJ: Prentice-Hall, 266–76.

Meier, C. E. and A. Randall (1991), 'Use value under uncertainty: is there a "correct" measure?' *Land Economics*, **67** (4), November, 379–89.

Navrud, S. and G. J. Pruckner (1997), 'Environmental valuation – to use or not to use? A comparative study of the United States and Europe', *Environmental and Resource Economics*, **10** (1), 1–26.

Page, T. (1977), *Conservation and Economic Efficiency*, Baltimore, MD: Johns Hopkins University Press.

Randall, A. (1991), 'The economic value of biodiversity', *Ambio-A Journal of the Human Environment*, **20** (2), 64–8.

Randall, A. and M. C. Farmer (1995), 'Benefits, Costs, and the Safe Minimum Standard of Conservation', in D. W. Bromley (ed.), *Handbook of Environmental Economics*, Cambridge, MA: Basil Blackwell Ltd, pp. 26–44.

Randall, A. and J. Stoll (1983), 'Existence Value in a Total Value Framework', in, R. D. Rowe and L. G. Chestnut (eds), *Managing Air Quality and Scenic Resources at National Parks and Wilderness Areas*, Boulder, CO: Westview Press, pp. 265–74.

Rawls, J. (1971), *A Theory of Justice*, Cambridge, MA: Harvard University Press.

Ready, R. C. and R. C. Bishop (1991), 'Endangered species and the safe minimum standard', *American Journal of Agricultural Economics*, **73** (2), May, 309–12.

Rolfe, J. (1995), 'Ulysses revisited – a closer look at the safe minimum standard of conservation', *Australian Journal of Agricultural Economics*, **39**, 55–70.

Rorty, A. Oksenberg (1992), 'The Advantages of Moral Diversity', in E. Frankel, F. D. Miller Jr and J. Paul (eds), *The Good Life and the Human Good*, New York: Cambridge University Press, pp. 38–62.

Sagoff, M. (1981), 'Economic theory and environmental law', *Michigan Law Review*, **79**, 1393–419.

Sagoff, M. (1996), 'On the value of endangered and other species', *Environmental Management*, **20** (6), 897–911.

Scandizzo, P. and O. Knudsen (1980), 'The evaluation of the benefits of basic need policies', *American Journal of Agricultural Economics*, **62**, 46–57.

Sen, A. (1989), *On Ethics and Economics*, New York: Basil Blackwell Ltd.

Vallentyne, P. (1987), 'The teleological/deontological distinction', *Journal of Value Inquiry*, **21**, 21–32.

Weisbrod, B. (1964), 'Collective-consumption services of individual-consumption goods', *Quarterly Journal of Economics*, **78** (3), August, 471–7.

Williams, B. (1985), *Ethics and the Limits of Philosophy*, Cambridge, MA: Harvard University Press.

B

Theory

[4]

Consumer's Surplus in Commodity Space

By ALAN RANDALL AND JOHN R. STOLL*

In an article which is already widely quoted, Robert Willig demonstrated that observed Marshallian consumer's surplus can be rigorously utilized to estimate the (theoretically correct) Hicksian compensating and equivalent variations. Willig's analysis was confined to price space, and thus finds its application in the use of consumer's surplus to evaluate the welfare impacts of price changes.

There is another important area of empirical research in which consumer's surplus finds application: the evaluation of the benefits and costs of proposed projects and programs.[1] In benefit-cost analysis, the economist is often concerned not so much with the welfare impacts of price changes as with the welfare impacts of changes in the bundle of goods, services, and amenities possessed, used, or consumed by individuals. Proposed projects and programs may remove some goods from individual opportunity sets, while introducing new goods; and may decrease the quantities of some goods while increasing the quantities of others. Typically, these changes in individually held bundles of specific goods are not accompanied by directly related and commensurate changes in income (or the value of "all other goods").

The goods affected by proposed projects and programs may include divisible, exclusive goods whose competitive prices can be observed in well-functioning markets. They may also include recreational and environmental amenities, the existence of unique environments and endangered species, and increases or decreases in expected human mortality or morbidity, etc.: goods which may be in varying degrees indivisible, nonexclusive, and unpriced.

The concern which motivated Willig's article, in particular, that observable consumer's surplus data are usually not in the theoretically correct form, apply to an even greater extent to the estimation of the welfare impacts of changes in the bundle of goods. In the case of priced goods, only Marshallian consumer's surplus is directly observable; for unpriced goods, value data may, depending on the estimation technique used, be in the form of Marshallian consumer's surplus, the Hicksian compensating measure, the Hicksian equivalent measure, or the expenditure function. This paper identifies the conditions under which Willig's conclusion that consumer's surplus data may be rigorously used "without apology" is adaptable to situations in which it is bundles of goods, rather than prices, which are changed.

Our findings, in broad outline, are as follows. (a) For goods which are perfectly divisible and exchanged at zero transactions costs in infinitely large markets, the Hicksian compensating and equivalent variation measures of consumer's surplus are equal in absolute value and are equal to the price multiplied by the quantity change. (b) For goods which are indivisible or lumpy, the Hicksian compensating measure of welfare loss (gain) is larger (smaller) in absolute value than the Marshallian consumer's surplus measure, which in turn is larger (smaller) than the Hicksian equivalent measure.[2] Given information on the price flexibility of income for the good in question, the individual's income and the proportion of that income which is spent on the good, bounds on the difference between the

*University of Kentucky and Texas A&M University, respectively. This paper (no. 79-1-3) is published with the approval of the Director of the Kentucky Agricultural Experiment Station. We appreciate helpful comments from an anonymous reviewer.

[1]See E. J. Mishan for example.

[2]This finding is in contrast to that of Karl-Göran Mäler (pp. 131-40) which has been cited without question by such authors as Charles Cicchetti, Anthony Fisher, and V. Kerry Smith.

compensating and equivalent measures can be rigorously calculated. (c) For divisible goods traded in costly markets (i.e., those where transactions costs are positive), the difference between the compensating and equivalent measures of welfare change will lie in the range identified in the first two cases. The result of case (a) is predicated upon costless postchange adjustments in holdings while that of case (b) is predicated on the impossibility of postchange adjustments.[3] Positive transactions costs impede adjustments in holdings, whereas either prohibitive transactions costs or indivisibility is sufficient to preclude such adjustments.

In pragmatic benefit-cost analysis terms, these findings may be interpreted as follows. When one is dealing with changes in any one individual's holdings of a divisible good which is traded in reasonably competitive and reasonably low-cost markets, the error inherent in using price multiplied by the quantity change is most likely overshadowed by inaccuracies in the estimation of, for example, the technical productivity coefficients which underlie the quantity change projections.[4] For changes in the quantities of indivisible or lumpy goods where the price flexibility of income falls in the typical range and the proportion of total budget spent on the good is small, the

bounds within which the Hicksian compensating and equivalent measures must fall can be rigorously calculated from estimates of Marshallian consumer's surplus; and these bounds will be quite narrow. Thus, the theoretically correct measure can be obtained from the estimates of more readily available value indicators.

However, the analyst is on occasion confronted with the task of evaluating lumpy changes in quantities of specific goods, services, or amenities, where one or more of the following holds: the change is large; the good is highly valued; and the price flexibility of income for the good is high and rises with income. In such cases,[5] our findings offer less comfort. The compensating measure of welfare loss (gain) is likely to be much larger (smaller) in absolute value than the equivalent measure, since the latter (former) is strictly limited by individual budget constraints while the former (latter) is not. While the rigorous bounds derived below remain valid, the information needed to estimate the correct (i.e., compensating, if the welfare criterion is the potential Pareto improvement)[6] measure from other measures more readily available to the analyst is less likely to be obtainable. Thus, in such cases, there may be no good substitute for methods capable of accurately estimating the compensating measure of welfare loss.

In short, the cases that competent benefit-cost analysts consider relatively hazard free are, in fact, relatively hazard free. On the other hand, there are cases (discussed in the preceding paragraph) which, as some benefit-cost analysts have suspected, pose the threat of significant error from the use of Marshallian consumer's surplus and, at the same time, present empirical difficulties to those who seek to estimate the correct measure of welfare change from other more readily available

---

[3]The impossibility of postchange adjustments along a quantity continuum, which may be called indivisibility or lumpiness from the perspective of the individual, may arise from any of several sources: 1) the Samuelsonian public good and congestible public good situations in which the individual consumer cannot continuously adjust his holdings of the good independently of all other individuals; 2) indivisibility in production, such that the good may be produced in one or more discrete quantities and the concept of a parametric unit price is meaningless (the argument of David Bradford is helpful); 3) nonexclusiveness, such that exchange in order to effect postchange adjustment is infeasible; 4) prohibitive transactions costs; and 5) institutional restrictions upon quantity per capita, for example, in the case of hunting where regulations such as bag limitations and hunting seasons prohibit quantity adjustments following changes in these kinds of regulations.

[4]This claim is analogous to Willig's claim (p. 589) that the errors from using Marshallian consumer's surplus will often be overshadowed by errors in estimation of the demand curve.

[5]Proposed projects or programs which have the potential to significantly modify unique environments, endangered species, threatened cultures, or the life and health expectancies of human beings may, under certain circumstances, provide examples.

[6]See Mishan.

measures. Our contribution will be to demonstrate in a rigorous manner that the intuitions of many benefit-cost analysts are in fact valid, and to show that, in those cases which we have indicated are relatively simple, consumer's surplus may be used "without" apology.

I. A Diagrammatic Exposition

Our conclusions are perhaps most readily grasped, at the intuitive level, from a diagrammatic exposition. Let us consider a normal good x, which, depending on the program alternatives chosen, may be provided in two different quantities, Q' and Q'', where Q'' is greater and *ceteris paribus* preferred. The traditional pragmatic measures of value of these two bundles of goods are willingness to pay (WTP) and willingness to accept (WTA). In a market exchange situation, these correspond, respectively, to the buyer's best offer and the seller's reservation price; in a nonmarket situation, they correspond to willingness-to-pay and willingness-to-accept compensation.

If the program alternative under evaluation would reduce the quantity of x from Q'' to Q', the compensating measure of welfare loss is WTA^C, the compensation which would keep the loser at his initial welfare level; and the equivalent measure is WTP^E, the loser's willingness to pay to avoid the quantity reduction from Q'' to Q' which, if paid, would place the loser at his subsequent welfare level. If the proposed program would increase the quantity of x from Q' to Q'', the compensating measure of welfare gain is WTP^C which, if paid, would keep the gainer at his initial welfare level; and the equivalent measure is WTA^E, the compensation which would be needed to bring the potential gainer to his subsequent welfare level in the event that the proposed program is not implemented. At this point, let us emphasize that WTA is not always the compensating measure and WTP is not always the equivalent measure.

Assume x is a perfectly divisible good, traded in infinitely large markets at zero transactions costs at the unit price p. Con-

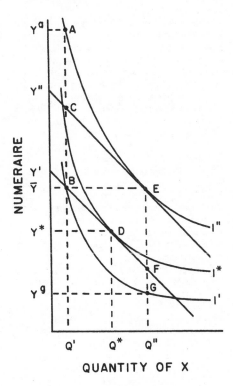

FIGURE 1. THE WELFARE IMPACT OF A CHANGE IN THE QUANTITY OF A GOOD X FROM Q'' TO Q'

sider a proposed program which if implemented would reduce an affected individual's holdings of x from Q'' to Q' while leaving his holdings of Y, a numeraire or a composite of "all other goods," at $\bar{Y}$. In Figure 1, the program would bump the individual from point E to B, lowering his welfare level from I'' to I'. However, there is no good reason for the individual to remain at B. Instead, frictionless markets will permit him to trade along his new budget line until he reaches D and achieves the welfare level I^*. Given this frictionless adjustment, his WTP^E is EF, which is equal to $Y''Y'$ while his WTA^C is BC, which is equal to $Y'Y''$. Thus, WTP^E is equal to WTA^C and both are equal to $p(Q'' - Q')$.

56   *Making the Environment Count*

THE AMERICAN ECONOMIC REVIEW

This conclusion can be grasped intuitively by considering that a good traded in infinitely large markets at a constant unit price with zero transactions costs has all the important characteristics of money (i.e., currency). Thus, the well-known result, that *WTA* compensation and permit imposition of a lump sum tax is equal to *WTP* to avoid the same tax and both are equal to the tax itself, applies to this quite restrictive case.

Now, assume that x is a lumpy good and can be held only in the amounts Q'' and Q'. Observe immediately that in the case of indivisible or lumpy goods, since intermediate adjustments in commodity holdings are not permissible, the Hicksian compensating and equivalent measures in commodity space are analogous to the Hicksian surpluses, not the variations, defined over price changes.

In this case and returning to Figure 1, the price lines become meaningless. WTP^E is *EG* which is equal to $Y^g\overline{Y}$, and WTA^C is *BA*, which is equal to $\overline{Y}Y^a$, and larger in absolute value than WTP^E. Note that this finding contrasts vividly with that of Mäler (pp. 131–140), but that Mäler's analysis is valid only if one assumes, trivially, that the individual is indifferent as to whether he holds the indivisible good or not, when its price is zero.

II. Bounds on the Difference between Compensating and Equivalent Measures, Defined in Commodity Space

Now, we derive rigorously the bounds on $WTA - WTP$ for indivisible or lumpy goods, using a formulation which proves, as a special case, that for perfectly divisible goods traded in frictionless markets, $WTA = WTP$. For the convenience of readers and to permit an otherwise unattainable brevity, our analysis at this point follows Willig. The necessary departures from Willig's treatment are explicitly highlighted and explained, while some intermediate steps analogous to those used by Willig are omitted.

Postulating the existence of the utility function $U [P(Q, Y)]$, implicit in prices p, and defined over the numeraire Y, and quantities Q of the good x, we define the

following indirect utility function

$$(1) \qquad z(Q,Y) = U[P(Q,Y)]$$

Consider an individual with $\overline{Y}$ units of the numeraire (i.e., the value of "all other goods and endowments"), who is confronted with a change in his bundle of the good x from Q'' to Q', where Q'' represents a greater quantity than Q'. His WTP^E to avoid a change from Q'' to Q' is defined by

$$(2) \qquad z(Q',\overline{Y}) = z(Q'', \overline{Y} - WTP)$$

while his WTA^C to accept a change from Q'' to Q' is defined by

$$(3) \qquad z(Q', \overline{Y} + WTA) = z(Q'', \overline{Y})$$

Using the income compensation function, $\mu(Q|Q'', \overline{Y})$ which represents the least amount of income the individual would require with quantity Q to achieve the same utility level enjoyed with quantity Q'' and $\overline{Y}$, the individual's initial income is

$$(4) \qquad \mu(Q''|Q'', \overline{Y}) = \overline{Y}$$

The *WTP* and *WTA* measures defined in (2) and (3) can be expressed

$$(5) \qquad WTP = \mu(Q'|Q', \overline{Y}) - \mu(Q''|Q', \overline{Y})$$

$$(6) \qquad WTA = \mu(Q'|Q'', \overline{Y}) - \mu(Q''|Q'', \overline{Y})$$

Now the following partial differential equation may be derived (since, although we later define x as a lumpy good, preferences are continuous over Q):

$$(7) \qquad \frac{\partial \mu(Q|Q'', Y)}{\partial Q} = P\left[Q, \mu(Q|Q'', \overline{Y})\right]$$

Equation (7) may be treated as a system of equations when x is a vector of goods.

Considering only a change in the quantity of a single good and using the fundamental theorem of calculus,

$$(8) \qquad WTP = \int_{Q'}^{Q''} P\left[Q, \mu(Q|Q', \overline{Y})\right] dQ$$

$$(9) \qquad WTA = \int_{Q'}^{Q''} P\left[Q, \mu(Q|Q'', \overline{Y})\right] dQ$$

These equations express *WTP* and *WTA* as areas under compensated demand curves. The price axis consists of a range of implicit prices which corresponds to the domain of quantities being considered.

To arrive at bounds for the difference between the Marshallian measure of welfare change, and *WTP* and *WTA*, respectively, for a quantity change which permits no subsequent adjustments in the quantity of x, we assume constant price flexibility of income, ζ, for x such that

$$(\partial P(Q,Y)/\partial Y)(Y/P(Q,Y)) \equiv \zeta$$

and follow a procedure similar to Willig's to derive the income compensation function, which is

$$(10) \quad \mu\left(Q'|Q'',\overline{Y}\right)$$

$$= \overline{Y}\left[1 + \frac{(1-\zeta)}{\overline{Y}}\int_{Q'}^{Q''} P(Q,\overline{Y})dQ\right]^{1/(1-\zeta)}$$

The expression $\int_{Q'}^{Q''} P(Q,\overline{Y})dQ$ can be interpreted as the area under an implicit Marshallian demand curve for the good x. Denoting this expression by M, it is apparent that when $\zeta = 0$ the welfare change measures will be equal to M.

Again following procedures similar to those used by Willig, we obtain

$$(11) \quad \frac{M - WTP}{M} \simeq \frac{\zeta M}{2\overline{Y}}$$

$$(12) \quad \frac{WTA - M}{M} \simeq \frac{\zeta M}{2\overline{Y}}$$

Thus,

$$(13) \quad WTA - WTP \simeq \frac{\zeta M^2}{\overline{Y}}$$

Dropping the assumption of constant price flexibility of income (see Willig, who dropped the assumption of constant income elasticity of demand) the following approximate bounds are appropriate when $\zeta M/2\overline{Y}$ is small (say, $<.05$), and are obtained for *WTP* and *WTA* for changes in the bundle of goods:

$$(14) \quad \frac{\xi^L M}{2\overline{Y}} < \frac{M - WTP}{M} < \frac{\xi^u M}{2\overline{Y}}$$

$$(15) \quad \frac{\xi^L M}{2\overline{Y}} < \frac{WTA - M}{M} < \frac{\xi^u M}{2\overline{Y}}$$

where ξ^L and ξ^u are the lower and upper bounds, respectively, on price flexibility of income for the good x. Rigorous bounds, applicable for all values of $\zeta M/2\overline{Y}$, are

$$(16) \quad \frac{\left[1 - (1-\xi^L)\dfrac{M}{\overline{Y}}\right]^{1/(1-\xi^L)} - 1 + \dfrac{M}{\overline{Y}}}{M/\overline{Y}}$$

$$< \frac{M - WTP}{M}$$

$$< \frac{\left[1 - (1-\xi^u)\dfrac{M}{\overline{Y}}\right]^{1/(1-\xi^u)} - 1 + \dfrac{M}{\overline{Y}}}{M/\overline{Y}}$$

$$(17) \quad \frac{\left[1 + (1-\xi^L)\dfrac{M}{\overline{Y}}\right]^{1/(1-\xi^L)} - 1 - \dfrac{M}{\overline{Y}}}{M/\overline{Y}}$$

$$< \frac{WTA - M}{M}$$

$$< \frac{\left[1 + (1-\xi^u)\dfrac{M}{\overline{Y}}\right]^{1/(1-\xi^L)} - 1 - \dfrac{M}{\overline{Y}}}{M/\overline{Y}}$$

The critical differences between these bounds for quantity changes and Willig's bounds for price changes are M and ζ in our bounds, and A and η in Willig's. The term A is Marshallian consumer's surplus measured as the area under a demand curve between two alternative prices for x, while M is the area under a demand curve between two quantities of x. Our ζ is the price flexibility of income for x, while Willig's η is the income elasticity of demand for x. An additional difference is that Willig's m is total income, while our $\overline{Y}$ is the amount of the numeraire held by the consumer.

Returning now to the case of a perfectly divisible good traded in frictionless markets, the expressions $P[Q, \mu(Q|Q', \bar{Y})]dQ$ (in equation (8)) and $P[Q, \mu(Q|Q'', \bar{Y})]dQ$ (in equation (9)) can both be replaced with the market price p of the good x. Thus

$$(18) \qquad WTP = \int_{Q'}^{Q''} p\,dQ = WTA$$

and it is shown that WTP and WTA are equal in value and both equal to $p(Q'' - Q')$.

For completeness, it is appropriate to note that for goods which are exchangeable and divisible, the difference between WTA and WTP becomes nonzero when transactions costs become positive and grows as transactions costs increase. It will, however, reach an upper limit at the point where transactions costs are just sufficiently great to preclude postchange quantity adjustments and will at that point be identical to the difference observed in the case of lumpy goods.[7]

III. Empirical Estimates of the Bounds

Willig presents empirical estimates of the parameters necessary to calculate the bounds on the difference between compensating, equivalent, and Marshallian consumer's surplus measures of the welfare

[7]In order to demonstrate this diagrammatically, it is possible to modify Figure 1 by introducing transactions costs, in the manner of Jürg Neihans, via a kinked budget constraint which touches the zero transactions costs budget constraint at the point denoting the individual's current holdings of x and moves progressively further away from it, always on the low side, as the quantity adjustment becomes larger. In a working paper available upon request from the authors, this diagrammatic analysis is provided, along with a method for approximating, subject to some restrictive assumptions, the bounds on the difference between WTA and WTP when transactions costs are positive but not sufficiently large to preclude any quantity adjustment. For example, if $M/\bar{Y} = 0.02$, the income elasticity of demand for the good x is 0.9 and transactions costs amount to 10 percent of p, the difference between WTA and WTP will be less than 0.36 percent of $p(Q'' - Q')$.

effects of price changes (his Table 1). That table can be adapted to permit calculation of these bounds for measures of the welfare effects of changes in the bundle of goods. If one substitutes $M/\bar{Y}$ for Willig's a in each column heading and ζ for η in each row title, the first entry in each cell of Willig's table becomes an estimate of $\zeta M/2\bar{Y}$ and may be used in empirical application of equations (11)–(13).

Making these adaptations and comparing the first entry in each cell with the second and third entries, it becomes clear that the rule of thumb for approximating WTA, M, or WTP from empirical estimates of any one of them (i.e., equations (11)–(13)) generates quite accurate results when $M/\bar{Y}$ is small, even in cases where ζ is substantially greater than 1. However, as $M/\bar{Y}$ becomes large, the error from using the rule of thumb grows; it becomes very large when both $M/\bar{Y}$ and ζ are large. In the case of a good which is indivisible and highly valued (i.e., $M/\bar{Y}$ is large) and for which the price flexibility of income rises with income, M provides only poor estimates of WTA and WTP, and the rule of thumb (equations (11)–(13)) is unreliable. The rigorous bounds, however, remain valid.

Some comment on ζ, the price flexibility of income, is appropriate. For the case of changes in the quantity of a good for which postchange quantity adjustments are impossible, ζ is the appropriate concept of income elasticity. The relevent concept is not η, which addresses the question of how changes in income affect the quantity of the good purchased at some parametric unit price, but ζ, which addresses the question of how changes in income affect the amount the consumer would spend to enjoy a given unit of the good.[8] For normal goods, $\zeta > 0$. For an especially treasured good, ζ may substantially exceed 1.

[8]The relationship of price flexibility of income, $\zeta = (\partial P(Q,Y)/\partial Y)(Y/P(Q,Y))$, to income elasticity of total value, $(\partial V/\partial Y)\cdot(Y/V)$, is obvious when one considers that $V = \int_0^Q P(Q,Y)dQ$.

REFERENCES

D. F. Bradford, "Benefit-Cost Analysis and Demand Curves for Public Goods," *Kyklos*, No. 4, 1970, *23*, 775−91.

C. J. Cicchetti, A. C. Fisher, and V. K. Smith, "An Econometric Evaluation of a Generalized Consumer's Surplus Measure: The Mineral King Controversy," *Econometrica*, Nov. 1976, *44*, 1259−76.

Karl-Göran Mäler, *Environmental Economics: A Theoretical Inquiry*, Baltimore 1974.

E. J. Mishan, *Cost-Benefit Analysis*, London 1971.

J. Neihans, "Money and Barter in General Equilibrium with Transactions Costs," *Amer. Econ. Rev.*, Dec. 1971, *61*, 773–83.

R. D. Willig, "Consumer's Surplus Without Apology," *Amer. Econ. Rev.*, Sept. 1976, *66*, 587–97.

[5]

Too Many Proposals Pass the Benefit Cost Test

By JOHN P. HOEHN AND ALAN RANDALL*

The idea of evaluating public works by submitting them to a benefit cost test has a history dating at least to Adam Smith. In the last few decades, application of benefit cost analysis has become commonplace. Federal rules require that major regulatory programs "...not be undertaken unless the potential benefits...outweigh the potential costs..." (NARA, 1985, p. 630). Numerous agencies and offices of government now apply benefit cost logic, each evaluating its own programs and policy proposals. Each evaluation typically focuses on a particular proposal and seldom takes into account what other agencies might be considering.

The current evaluation process offers little opportunity for routine evaluation of an overall policy agenda. Each agency evaluates its own proposals independently, as if each were the next increment to the existing portfolio of policies and projects. These independent evaluations stand in contrast to the optimal sequential planning procedures considered by G. M. Heal (1973). Unlike sequential procedures, current practice ignores interactions that occur between policy components. Previous research indicates some of the errors induced by the failure to consider pairwise interactions (Ronald Braeutigam and Roger G. Noll, 1984; Lester B. Lave, 1984; and Erik Lichtenberg and David Zilberman, 1986).

The net effect of these pairwise errors is not a priori clear when the analysis extends beyond a small set of impacts. One possibil-

ity is that when many policy components are evaluated, positive and negative errors tend to cancel out. If so, conventional procedures would give an unbiased assessment of the overall policy agenda. Alternatively, the expected error may not be zero and conventional procedures may result in systematic bias. If the bias is toward overstatement, wasteful policies may be misidentified as potentially beneficial.

In this paper we examine what happens to benefit cost outcomes when conventional procedures are used across a significant portion of the public sector. We consider the evaluation of a broad policy agenda that is composed of a large number of specific proposals. These proposals may be put forth by many different agencies at various levels of government. Each proposal is evaluated independently of the other changes that may occur with implementation of the overall policy agenda. To account for both technical interactions and general resource scarcity, we model an Arrow-Debreu economy composed of a single household.[1] This procedure allows us to address benefits and costs in a simple general equilibrium framework, without reference to distributional concerns.

We show that conventional benefit cost outcomes are systematically biased. First, as the number of policy proposals becomes large, conventional benefit cost procedures are certain to overstate a valid measure of net benefits. The productive capacity of an economy imposes a bound on the valid measure of net benefits whereas the conventional measure is unbounded. Thus, as the number of specific proposals becomes large, conventional procedures overstate the benefits of policy change. Second, we determine whether conventional procedures actually misstate the

*Departments of Agricultural Economics and Resource Development, Michigan State University, East Lansing, MI 48824, and Department of Agricultural Economics and Rural Sociology, Ohio State University, Columbus, OH 43210. We gratefully acknowledge support from the National Science Foundation under grant no. SES-8309157, Resources for the Future, Inc., and the Agricultural Experiment Stations of Michigan and Ohio, Michigan Agricultural Experiment Station Journal Article No. 12764.

[1] Richard W. Tresch (1981) discusses the features of a single household economy.

sign of a net benefit measure. We find that if the marginal costs of policy change are nontrivial, conventional procedures misidentify the net benefits of both the agenda and at least some of its components as positive when they are in fact negative. Too many proposals pass the benefit cost test.

These results subsume the case and sectoral studies that examine the performance of conventional procedures given pairwise interactions among a small number of policy components. The focus of this analysis is on the general error introduced by the independent analysis of a large number of proposals put forth by the numerous agencies and levels of the public sector. The identified problem is one of coordination. This is quite different from the traditional complaint about agencies' conduct of benefit cost analysis: that an agency's self-interest and technological optimism may lead to an unrealistically favorable *ex ante* evaluation. Our analysis assumes that, given their respective frames of reference, both the independent and valid valuations are conducted without error.

These findings are developed in three sections. Section I describes the structure of the economy and clarifies the relation between regulatory control, production, and consumption. Section II defines a Hicksian compensating measure of benefits and costs that is valid in a general equilibrium setting.[2] The general equilibrium setting is used in order to accommodate a large number of nonmarginal shifts in regulatory controls. Section III compares conventional and valid benefit cost outcomes in the large numbers case.

I. An Economy with Nonmarket Goods

The economy produces both market and nonmarket goods. Production and consump-

tion of market goods are guided by decentralized profit and utility maximization. Public policy controls the production and consumption of nonmarket goods. These nonmarket goods may be indivisible or non-exclusive. Allocation decisions for nonmarket goods are made on the basis of compensation tests.

The consumption sector is composed of a single household. The household consumes market commodities[3] $x \in \mathbf{R}^I$ and is exposed to the prevailing level of nonmarket services, $s \in \mathbf{R}^K$. A utility function, $u = u(x, s)$, represents household preferences across market and nonmarket goods. The utility function is strictly increasing, continuous, and strictly quasiconcave. The set of consumption bundles that yield utility equal to or greater than u at s is $X(s, u) \subset \mathbf{R}^+$. The household's salable resource endowment is $\bar{x}$, where $\bar{x}_1 > 0$.

The economy produces a netput of market goods, $y \in \mathbf{R}^I$. Efficient aggregate production opportunities are described by a convex and differentiable function, $T(y, \alpha) = 0$, that is strictly increasing in y and α and $T(0, 0) = 0$. Inputs are denoted by negative elements in y and outputs as positive elements.

The vector $\alpha \in \mathbf{R}^J$, $J \geq K$, denotes the level of nonmarket services produced by firms. The vector α is a nonmarket netput. A negative element in α represents a nonmarket input into production such as a firm's use of the waste assimilative capacities of local natural resources. A positive element indicates a nonmarket output. The background or natural endowment of nonmarket services is $\bar{\alpha} \geq 0$. The production sector's net supply of nonmarket services is $\alpha + \bar{\alpha}$.

Use of nonmarket services as inputs into production depletes the level of nonmarket services available to the household. Nonmarket services perceived by the household are $s = h(\alpha)$, where $h(\cdot)$ is continuous, one-to-one, and strictly increasing. The correspondence $h(\cdot)$ accounts for the indirect relation between nonmarket netput of firms, α, and the nonmarket perceptions of the house-

---

[2] The Hicksian compensating measure is commonly used as a measure of benefits and costs. The status of benefit cost information as means for identifying increases in social welfare is not addressed by this paper. See Robin Boadway and Neil Bruce (1984) for further discussion.

[3] Vectors are given in boldface type. Scalars are written in standard type.

hold, s. For instance, $h(\cdot)$ may represent the relation between the atmospheric disposal of hydrocarbon emissions—an element of α—and the perceived level of photochemical smog—an element of s.

The objective of public policy is to regulate the level of α in order to control the quantity of perceived nonmarket services, $s = h(\alpha)$. Policy instruments used to achieve a given α may include controls on the use of nonmarket goods, direct taxes on input or output quantities, technological constraints, or directives to produce services not sustainable by the private goods economy. However, since in this paper we are not interested in comparing different policy instruments, we define public policy solely in terms of its firm-level outcome, α. Given the nonmarket endowment $\bar{\alpha}$, only policies α with $\alpha + \bar{\alpha} \geq 0$ are feasible.

The aggregate production set for both market and nonmarket goods is

$$(1) \qquad W = \{(y, \alpha) | T(y, \alpha) \leq 0\}.$$

Production is irreversible ($W \cap (-W) = \{0\}$) and without inputs there is no output ($W \cap R^+ = \{0\}$). At an α determined by policy, the aggregate market goods production set is $Y(\alpha) = \{y | (y, \alpha) \in W\}$.

The feasible allocations of market goods play a key role in measuring the net benefits of policy change. An allocation is feasible if the net consumption of market goods, $d = x - y - \bar{x}$, lies within the bounds determined by technology, preferences, and resource scarcity; that is, if $d \leq 0$. For a given level of utility, the set of net consumption bundles that are feasible is

$$(2) \qquad \hat{D}(u) = \{d | d = x - y - \bar{x} \leq 0\},$$

where $x \in X(s, u)$, $y \in Y(\alpha)$, $s = h(\alpha)$, and $\alpha + \bar{\alpha} \geq 0$. For an α set by policy to achieve some s, the set of feasible net consumption bundles is $\hat{D}(s, u)$. A policy pair, α and $s = h(\alpha)$, is feasible if $\hat{D}(s, u)$ is nonempty. Both $\hat{D}(u)$ and $\hat{D}(s, u)$ are compact and convex.[4]

For a feasible α fixed by public policy, a competitive equilibrium exists and is conditionally Pareto efficient. For an α that results in s and an equilibrium level of utility, u, conditional Pareto efficiency means that $\hat{D}(s, u)$ contains no negative elements. That is, for a fixed level of nonmarket controls, α, markets clear and competitive exchange eliminates any surplus that would generate further gains from trade in market goods. An equilibrium market price vector is denoted p and is normalized so that p_1 is unity. At an initial α^0 and s^0 fixed by policy, p^0 sustains an allocation of market goods, x^0, and an initial utility level, u^0.[5]

II. Compensation Tests for Policy Alternatives

To examine conventional benefit estimates relative to those of a valid approach, we distinguish two types of policies. The first type of policy affects an entire subvector of s. This multiple impact policy is denoted as[6]

$$(3) \qquad s^k = \left(s_1, \ldots, s_k, s_{k+1}^0, \ldots, s_K^0\right).$$

This k-impact policy, s^k, affects perceived nonmarket services s_1 through s_k, shifting them from an initial level $(s_1^0, \ldots, s_k^0)$ to a post-change level $(s_1, \ldots, s_k)$. The change is accomplished through a vector of controls α^k. A k-impact policy shifts α^0 to α^k and s^0 to s^k.

Conventional benefit cost practice evaluates a multiple impact policy by independently evaluating each of its component elements. Toward describing this practice, we define a second type of policy that changes only a single element of s. This single impact

---

[4]See Kenneth J. Arrow and F. H. Hahn (1971).

[5]Given a fixed α, a competitive equilibrium is such that (a) $d^0 = x^0 - y^0 - \bar{x}$, (b) $p^0 y^0$ maximizes $p^0 y$ subject to $y \in Y(\alpha)$, and (c) x^0 maximizes $u(x, s^0)$ subject to $p^0 x \leq p^0 \bar{x} + p^0 y^0$.

[6]The term "multiple impact policy" is used to indicate a vector of contemporaneously proposed policy changes. Beyond contemporaneity, there is no connotation of cohesiveness. To the contrary, in a society with relatively decentralized institutions, those proposing and/or evaluating some elements of s^k may well be unaware of, or unconcerned about, other elements.

policy is denoted as a vector

$$(4) \quad \mathbf{s}_k = \left(s_1^0, \ldots, s_{k-1}^0, s_k, s_{k+1}^0, \ldots, s_K^0\right).$$

A single impact policy, $\mathbf{s}_k$, affects only the kth element of $\mathbf{s}$, s_k, and is accomplished through a vector of controls α_k. A single impact policy shifts α^0 to α_k and $\mathbf{s}^0$ to $\mathbf{s}_k$. A change in more than a single production constraint—more than a single element of α —may be required to accomplish a single impact policy.

A policy α is a potential Pareto improvement, relative to an initial α^0, if it is possible to implement α while maintaining u^0 with fewer resources than are required at α^0. The Hicksian compensating measure is a conventional metric for the surplus generated by a policy alternative α. In a general economic setting, the Hicksian compensating measure is the amount of numeraire resource removed from (added to) the economy that maintains the initial utility level at the post-change level of nonmarket goods and controls. If the economy is collectively compensated by the Hicksian measure, the initial level of utility is conditionally Pareto efficient at the post-change level of nonmarket goods.

The compensating net benefit measure is defined analytically using the net consumption bundles that are feasible at the initial level of utility and post-change level of nonmarket controls. Let commodity x_1 be the numeraire. Let $\mathbf{s}$ be either a single or multiple impact policy objective and let α be the corresponding level of policy controls. The aggregate Hicksian compensating measure is a real number $hc = hc(\mathbf{s}, \mathbf{s}^0)$ such that for the vector $\mathbf{hc}(\mathbf{s}, \mathbf{s}^0) = [hc(\mathbf{s}, \mathbf{s}^0), 0, \ldots, 0]$,

$$(5) \quad \left\{\mathbf{d} + \mathbf{hc} \mid \mathbf{d} \in \mathbf{D}(\mathbf{s}, u^0)\right\} \cap \left\{\mathbf{d} \mid \mathbf{d} \le 0\right\}$$
$$= \{\mathbf{0}\}.$$

The Hicksian measure for a single impact policy, $\mathbf{s}_k$, is denoted $hc_k = hc(\mathbf{s}_k, \mathbf{s}^0)$. For a k-impact policy, $\mathbf{s}^k$, the Hicksian measure is $hc(\mathbf{s}^k, \mathbf{s}^0)$. Given $\mathbf{s}$ and u^0, the compensating measure is unique. The Hicksian measure removes just enough of the numeraire resource so that the initial utility level is the greatest utility level feasible after the policy change occurs. Removing hc eliminates any surplus resources in the economy at u^0 and α. A policy proposal is a potential Pareto improvement if and only if $hc > 0$. A negative hc indicates that the initial utility level cannot be maintained in the post-change economy.

Equation (5) defines a valid, overall net benefit measure for either a single or multiple impact policy. At the equilibrium $\mathbf{d}$, this holistic measure of net benefit, hc, can be restated as[7]

$$(6) \quad hc(\mathbf{s}, \mathbf{s}^0) = \mathbf{p}\bar{\mathbf{x}} + \pi(\mathbf{p}, \alpha) - e(\mathbf{p}, \mathbf{s}, u^0),$$

where $\mathbf{s}$ is either a single or multiple impact policy, α is required to accomplish $\mathbf{s}$, $\mathbf{p}$ is the price vector at a post-change compensated equilibrium, $e(\cdot)$ is the household's expenditure function, and $\pi(\cdot)$ is an aggregate profit function. By (6), the net benefit of a change from $\mathbf{s}^0$ to $\mathbf{s}$ is the difference between the income produced by the economy ($\mathbf{p}\bar{\mathbf{x}} + \pi(\mathbf{p}, \alpha)$) and the minimum expenditure required to maintain the initial utility level.

A central objective of routine benefit cost analysis is the valuation of policy components. To obtain a set of valid component valuations, equation (5) imposes a single restriction: the component impacts of policy are evaluated along a sequence of changes that begins at α^0 and $\mathbf{s}^0$ and ends at α and $\mathbf{s}$. For a g-impact policy, elementwise changes from s_k^0 to s_k, $k \in \{1, \ldots, g\}$, may be ordered from first until last and then valued sequentially beginning with the change from $\mathbf{s}^0$ to $\mathbf{s}^1$ and ending with the change from $\mathbf{s}^{g-1}$ to $\mathbf{s}^g$.[8] The compensating measure for the kth component, $\mathbf{hc}(\mathbf{s}^k, \mathbf{s}^{k-1})$, is

$$(7)$$
$$\left\{\mathbf{d} + \mathbf{hc}(\mathbf{s}^k, \mathbf{s}^{k-1}) + \mathbf{hc}(\mathbf{s}^{k-1}, \mathbf{s}^0) \mid \right.$$
$$\left. \mathbf{d} \in \mathbf{D}(\mathbf{s}^k, u^0)\right\} \cap \left\{\mathbf{d} \mid \mathbf{d} \le 0\right\} = \{\mathbf{0}\}.$$

---

[7]To derive (6), note that $\mathbf{d} + \mathbf{hc} = \mathbf{x} - \mathbf{y} - \bar{\mathbf{x}} + \mathbf{hc} = \mathbf{0}$ at the post-change equilibrium. Multiplying $\mathbf{d} + \mathbf{hc}$ by $\mathbf{p}$ and substituting in the expenditure and profit functions yields equation (6) (compare Tresch, 1981, pp. 74–75).

[8]This path implicitly assumes a corresponding set of changes from α^0 to α^g.

The valuation of the kth component is conditioned upon the $k-1$ prior changes. The kth sequential valuation therefore accounts for interactions between the change from s_k^0 to s_k and the $k-1$ other dimensions of policy. Using these sequenced valuations, an aggregate valuation of a g-impact policy is

$$(8) \qquad hc(s^g, s^0) = \sum_{k=1}^{g} hc(s^k, s^{k-1}).$$

In (8), only the sum of the component valuations is unique. The kth component valuation is conditioned upon $k-1$ prior impacts. The sequenced component valuations therefore vary with the selected sequence of valuation.

In contrast to (8), the conventional approach to benefit cost analysis is one of independent valuation and summation (IVS). With IVS, the component impacts of policy are valued independently as if each were a single impact proposal. For a g-impact policy, this IVS valuation is

$$(9) \qquad \text{ivs}(s^g, s^0) = \sum_{k=1}^{g} hc(s_k, s^0).$$

Each step of the IVS approach accounts only for the kth policy impact. With IVS, there is no valid account of the incremental contribution of the kth impact and there is no valid summary account of the overall change from s^0 to s^g.

The valid and IVS procedures fail to produce the same valuation since IVS ignores policy interactions and resource scarcity. Policy interactions are easy to imagine and the evaluation errors they induce are confirmed by empirical studies (Braeutigam and Noll, 1984; Lave, 1984; Lichtenberg and Zilberman, 1986). What remains unclear is the direction of the error as the number of policy components becomes large and aggregate resource scarcity becomes more pressing.

III. Benefit Cost Outcomes in a Large Numbers Case

In a contemporary setting, benefit cost analysis is applied to a large number of policy alternatives under the authority of different, autonomous agencies. In this decentralized process, each agency has little incentive to consider the overall policy agenda. Even within a particular agency, policy proposals are customarily evaluated using IVS procedures (compare A. Myrick Freeman, 1982). Each agency evaluates its proposals as if each were the next marginal increment to the set of baseline policies.

When each component is evaluated independently as the next policy increment, a large number of policy components are likely to appear beneficial in benefit cost terms. To formalize this notion of a large number of apparently beneficial components, the policy environment is described as epsilon augmentable. A policy environment is epsilon augmentable if it is always possible to find at least one more policy component that appears to be beneficial when evaluated independently. Formally, epsilon augmentable means that for a g-impact policy and real criterion $\varepsilon > 0$ it is possible to find an additional component change from s_{g+1}^0 to s_{g+1} such that the independently evaluated net benefit of the component change, $hc(s_{g+1}, s^0)$, exceeds the criterion epsilon.

THEOREM 1: *Let the policy environment be epsilon augmentable. Let only components with independent valuations greater than epsilon be considered for implementation. Then if g is the number of policy impacts under consideration, there is a finite integer n such that for $g > n$, IVS overstates the Hicksian compensating measure associated with the policy agenda. In addition, IVS overstates the net benefits of at least some subset of components.*

PROOF:
To show that IVS overstates the compensating measure of benefits for some $g > n$ impacts, note that the IVS measure of benefits is not bounded: for each additional component change included in the policy agenda, the IVS measure of compensation increases by at least epsilon.

However, since $\hat{D}(u^0)$ is bounded and $\hat{D}(s^g, u^0)$ is a subset of $\hat{D}(u^0)$, the compensating measure is bounded above for all s^g. Let the least upper bound on hc be $\bar{a}$.

Then for $n = \bar{a}/\varepsilon$ and $g > n$ impacts, $ivs(\mathbf{s}^g, \mathbf{s}^0) > g\varepsilon > \bar{a} \geq hc(\mathbf{s}^g, \mathbf{s}^0)$. For g larger than n, IVS is certain to exceed the valid compensating measure.

Finally, the sum of the valid set of component benefits forms a bounded sequence of real numbers as g increases. As g becomes large, the valid measure of component benefits due to the gth impact must either approach zero or become negative. In contrast, each IVS measure of component benefits exceeds $\varepsilon > 0$.

Theorem 1 resolves the ambiguity left by a simple consideration of complementary and competitive effects between policy components. The economy's productive capacity imposes a bound on total benefits. Conventional procedures ignore this bound and unambiguously overstate net benefits as the number of policy components becomes large. With a large policy agenda, conventional procedures are biased and policy change appears more attractive than it actually is.

There remains an additional question: do conventional procedures actually misstate net benefits as positive when they are in fact negative? To show that the net benefits of a large policy agenda and at least some of its components actually become negative requires a further definition of policy costs. We define the marginal costs of the kth policy component as nontrivial if, at the margin, the project uses up real resources within the economy that require compensation through a nontrivial increment in the numeraire.

Algebraically, consider a change in policy controls from $\boldsymbol{\alpha}^{k-1}$ to $\boldsymbol{\alpha}^k$. Let α_j represent one of the elements of $\boldsymbol{\alpha}^{k-1}$ that takes on a different value as $\boldsymbol{\alpha}^{k-1}$ shifts to $\boldsymbol{\alpha}^k$. The marginal cost of the change from $\boldsymbol{\alpha}^{k-1}$ to $\boldsymbol{\alpha}^k$ is nontrivial if (1) there is at least one α_j that increases with the policy change, and (2) there is a $\delta > 0$ such that the marginal cost of the change in the α_j, $MC_j = (\partial T/\partial \alpha_j)/(\partial T/\partial x_1)$ evaluated at $\boldsymbol{\alpha}^{k-1}$, is greater than δ for all $\boldsymbol{\alpha}^{k-1}$.

Nontrivial marginal costs do not generally guarantee the nonzero total costs of accomplishing the change from $\mathbf{s}^{k-1}$ to $\mathbf{s}^k$. However, when combined with the convexity of

$T(\cdot)$, nontrivial marginal costs are strong enough to prove Theorem 2.

THEOREM 2: *Let the assumptions of Theorem 1 hold and suppose policy change is nontrivially costly. Then for a finite number of components, g, IVS misstates the net benefits of a g-impact policy agenda as positive when they are in fact negative.*

PROOF:
Theorem 1 indicates that the IVS measure is positive and unbounded above. It remains to be shown that a valid measure of net benefits is negative as the number of components becomes large. To show this, we distinguish possible benefits from likely costs by developing a two-stage, sequential valuation of policy that is analogous to equation (8).

The first stage of the valuation sequence evaluates impacts which may yield positive net benefits: (1) the perceived consumption effects of the overall change from $\mathbf{s}^0$ to $\mathbf{s}^g = \mathbf{h}(\boldsymbol{\alpha}^g)$, and (2) any production impacts with trivial marginal costs. Denote the production impacts of the first stage as the change from $\boldsymbol{\alpha}^0$ to $\tilde{\boldsymbol{\alpha}}^g$. First-stage net benefits, $hc(\tilde{\boldsymbol{\alpha}}^g, \mathbf{s}^0)$, are defined using the final consumption set $\mathbf{X}(\mathbf{s}^g, u^0)$, and the production set $\mathbf{Y}(\tilde{\boldsymbol{\alpha}}^g)$. As in Theorem 1, there is a positive upper bound $\bar{a}$ on first-stage benefits.

The second stage evaluates only regulatory impacts with nontrivial marginal costs. The benefits of the second stage, $hc(\mathbf{s}^g, \tilde{\boldsymbol{\alpha}}^g)$, are defined in a manner analogous to equation (7) using the consumption set, $\mathbf{X}(\mathbf{s}^g, u^0)$, the production set, $\mathbf{Y}(\boldsymbol{\alpha}^g)$, and the net consumption set, $\hat{\mathbf{D}}(\mathbf{s}^g, u^0)$.

We now show that second-stage benefits are negative and less than $-\bar{a}$ for some finite number of components. Using the convexity of preferences, we first construct a second upper bound for second-stage benefits. Let $\tilde{\mathbf{x}}^g$, $\tilde{\mathbf{y}}^g$, and $\tilde{\mathbf{p}}^g$ denote, respectively, aggregate demand, aggregate supply, and the price vector associated with the first-stage compensated equilibrium. Let $\mathbf{x}^g$ and $\mathbf{y}^g$ denote, respectively, aggregate demand and aggregate supply associated with the second-stage compensated equilibrium. By the convexity of preferences, $\tilde{\mathbf{p}}^g(\mathbf{x}^g - \tilde{\mathbf{x}}^g) \geq 0$. By definition, markets clear at compensated equilibria so that $\tilde{x}^g = \tilde{y}^g + \bar{x} - hc(\tilde{\alpha}^g, s^0)$ and $x^g = y^g + \bar{x} - hc(s^g, \tilde{\alpha}^g) - hc(\tilde{\alpha}^g, s^0)$. Substituting the market-clearing conditions into the last inequality results in

$$(10) \qquad \tilde{p}^g(y^g - \tilde{y}^g) \geq hc(s^g, \tilde{\alpha}^g).$$

Equation (10) implies that the second-stage compensating measure is bounded above by the change in the value of production associated with the second-stage change.

Using the convexity of $T(\cdot)$ and profit maximization, we show that the upper bound on second-stage benefits is negative and proportional to the number of policy components. From a Taylor-series expansion of $T(\cdot)$, we derive

$$(11) \qquad \sum_{j=1}^{r} - MC_j(\alpha_j - \tilde{\alpha}_j) \geq \tilde{p}^g(y^g - \tilde{y}^g),$$

since there are at least $r \geq g$ elements involved in the change from $\tilde{\alpha}^g$ to α^g that have nontrivial marginal costs. Since $MC_j > \delta$ and $\alpha_j - \tilde{\alpha}_j$ is finite, there is a $\sigma > 0$ such that $MC_j(\alpha_j - \tilde{\alpha}_j) > \sigma$ for all r elements. Substituting σ into (11), $-r\sigma \geq \tilde{p}^g(y^g - \tilde{y}^g)$. Combining the last inequality with (10), $-r\sigma \geq hc(s^g, \tilde{\alpha}^g)$.

Let g be no less than $\bar{a}/\sigma$. Then the valid total compensating measure for the overall change, $hc(s^g, s^0) = hc(s^g, \tilde{\alpha}^g) + hc(\tilde{\alpha}^g, s^0)$, is less than zero.   □

IV. Concluding Comments

Conventional benefit cost procedures are applied across the full spectrum of policy concerns, including public works, regulatory policy, and environmental concerns. The question is raised whether there might be some kind of "adding-up" effect that causes the customary procedures to be misleading as the number of independent applications grows large. For instance, consider only the problem of species preservation, a relatively small subset of environmental concerns. Conventional benefit cost logic demonstrates

the nontrivial benefits for each of a limited number of representative species.[9] There seems little reason to doubt that a similar level of benefits could be demonstrated for many other endangered species—at least when each is evaluated independently. Yet biologists suggest that there are literally hundreds of thousands of species in danger of extinction (Thomas E. Lovejoy, 1986). Surely, in this sort of policy environment, conventional procedures overlook some crucial element of the evaluation problem.

Our analysis indicates that the crucial elements are scarce productive capacity and the substitutions that it imposes. Our results not only demonstrate that conventional procedures systematically overstate net benefits but also define a valid benefit cost approach. However, improvements in benefit cost practice will not come easily. The structure of a valid benefit cost measure limits alternatives to either a one-shot, holistic valuation or a sequenced approach. Either approach requires coordination in policy formulation and evaluation. Technical difficulties in benefit estimation also arise. For holistic, *ex ante* valuation, the menu of techniques seems limited to those that record citizens' self-reported values, perhaps in experimental or survey contexts and with or without incentive-compatible mechanisms. Applied general equilibrium methods may be adaptable to the sequenced approach.

Interpretation of the sequenced valuations presents an additional difficulty. Component benefits are not unique and vary with the valuation sequence. Efforts to eliminate or prioritize policy components as required by Executive Order 12291 (NARA) are certainly misleading if carried out with snapshot estimates from a single sequence. For impact-by-impact analysis, selection of the sequence is as important as the choice of policy components.

---

[9]Representative studies include Richard C. Bishop, Kevin J. Boyle, and Michael P. Welsh (1987) and Karl C. Samples, John A. Dixon, and Marcia M. Gowen (1986).

REFERENCES

Arrow, Kenneth J. and Hahn, F. H., *General Competitive Analysis*, Amsterdam: North-Holland, 1971.

Bishop, Richard C., Boyle, Kevin J. and Welsh, Michael P., "Toward Total Economic Valuation of Great Lakes Fishery Resources," *Transactions of the American Fisheries Society*, May 1987, *116*, 339–45.

Boadway, Robin and Bruce, Neil, *Welfare Economics*, Oxford: Basil Blackwell, 1984.

Braeutigam, Ronald and Noll, Roger G., "The Regulation of Surface Freight Transportation: The Welfare Effects Revisited," *Review of Economics and Statistics*, February 1984, *66*, 80–7.

Freeman, A. Myrick, *Air and Water Pollution Control: A Benefit Cost Assessment*, New York: Wiley & Sons, 1982.

Heal, G. M., *The Theory of Economic Plan-ning*, Amsterdam: North-Holland, 1973.

Lave, Lester B., "Controlling Contradictions Among Regulations," *American Economic Review*, June 1984, *74*, 471–76.

Lichtenberg, Erik and Zilberman, David, "The Welfare Economics of Price Supports in U.S. Agriculture," *American Economic Review*, December 1986, *76*, 1135–141.

Lovejoy, Thomas E., "Species Leave the Ark One by One," in Bryan G. Norton, ed., *The Preservation of Species*, Princeton: Princeton University Press, 1986.

Samples, Karl C., Dixon, John A. and Gowen, Marcia M., "Information Disclosure and Endangered Species Valuation," *Land Economics*, August 1986, *62*, 306–13.

Tresch, Richard W., *Public Finance*, Georgeton, Ont: Irwin-Dorsey, 1981.

National Archives and Records Administration (NARA), *Presidential Proclamations and Executive Orders*, Washington: USGPO, 1985.

C

Methods

[6]

JOURNAL OF ENVIRONMENTAL ECONOMICS AND MANAGEMENT 1, 132–149 (1974)

Bidding Games for Valuation of Aesthetic Environmental Improvements[1]

ALAN RANDALL

Department of Agricultural Economics, University of Kentucky,
Lexington, Kentucky 40506

AND

BERRY IVES AND CLYDE EASTMAN

Department of Agricultural Economics and Agricultural Business,
New Mexico State University, Las Cruces, New Mexico 88003

Received March 19, 1974

An empirical case study of the benefits of abatement of aesthetic environmental damage associated with the Four Corners power plant and Navajo mine using the bidding game technique is presented. Bidding games were carefully designed to avoid the potential problems inherent in that technique. The results indicate the existence of substantial benefits from abatement of this aesthetic environmental damage. Aggregate bid curves, marginal bid curves, and estimates of the income elasticity of bid are presented. The effectiveness of the bidding game technique is discussed.

It has proved a difficult and often forbidding task to ascribe economic values to environmental improvements. Yet, rational and informed social decision making requires, among other things, a consideration of the economic costs and benefits of environmental improvements. The difficulties in economic evaluation are compounded in the case of environmental improvements of an aesthetic nature. This article discusses the problems inherent in the valuation of aesthetic environmental improvements and presents a case study in which bidding games were used as the valuation technique.

THE THEORY

Aesthetic damage to an outdoor environment, to the extent that it diminishes the utility of some individuals, is a discommodity and its abatement is a commodity. Abatement of this kind of external diseconomy is both a nonmarket good, since it is nonexclusive, and a public good in the sense of Davis and Whinston [6], since it is inexhaustible at least over a very substantial range. That is, additional consumers of this kind of aesthetic environmental improvement can be added without diminishing the visibility or scenic beauty available to each (at least, until crowding occurs). Additional users can be added at near zero marginal cost, over a substantial range.

Bradford [2] has presented a theoretical framework for the valuation of public goods. Traditional demand curves are inappropriate for the analysis of demand for

---

[1] Journal Article 506, New Mexico State University, Agricultural Experiment Station, Las Cruces. The authors are grateful for helpful comments from Ralph d'Arge a nd two anonymous reviewers.

Copyright © 1974 by Academic Press, Inc.
All rights of reproduction in any form reserved.

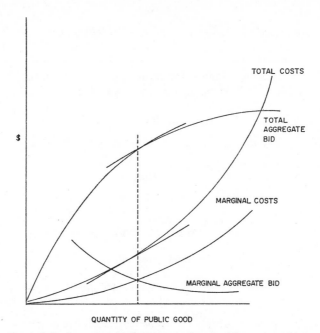

FIG. 1. Collective optimization of the quantity of public good provided.

public goods, since the situation is not one of individuals responding to a parametric price per unit by choosing an appropriate number of units. Rather, the individual directly arrives at the total value to himself of various given packages. In the case of a public good, the individual is unable to exercise any choice over the quantity provided him, except as a member of the collective which makes a collective choice. Further, the nature of a public good such as aesthetic environmental improvements is such that increases in the quantity provided are not purely quantitative increases, but are more in the nature of improvements in quality. Thus, the individual values alternative packages of a public good, which may differ in quantity and quality.

Bradford proposes the concept of an aggregate bid curve for public goods. Individual bid curves are simply indifference curves passing through a given initial state, with the numeraire good (which can be dollars) on the vertical axis and the public good on the horizontal axis.[2] The aggregate bid curve is the algebraic (or vertical, in diagrammatic analyses) summation of individual bids over the relevant population.

The aggregate bid curve is an aggregate benefit curve, as it measures precisely what an accurate benefit-cost analysis of provision of a public good would measure as benefits. Using the approach of methodological collectivism, efficiency in the provision of a public good can be achieved by maximizing the excess of aggregate bid over total cost, or equating the first derivative of aggregate bid (i.e., marginal bid)

---

[2] If different packages of a public good represented continuous quantitative increases, the individual bid curve would be smooth and would exhibit decreasing marginal utility of increasing quantities of the public good. However, Bradford's concept of different packages differing in quantity and quality logically implies that individual bid curves need be neither smooth nor of continually decreasing slope. Bradford insists that, *a priori*, nothing can be said about the slope of the "demand," or marginal bid curve, for a public good of this nature.

with the marginal cost of provision.[3] Figure 1 shows the efficient level of provision of a public good.[4]

THE BIDDING GAME TECHNIQUE

It is possible to conceive of a number of techniques for estimating the aggregate bid curve for environmental improvements. Two general classes of techniques, direct costing techniques and revealed demand techniques, have been suggested in the literature and applied in empirical studies. Each of these has its difficulties, especially when adapted for valuation of aesthetic environmental improvements. These techniques will be briefly discussed below. Then, a third type of technique, bidding games, will be proposed. Bidding game techniques are themselves not without difficulties, but we will argue that there may be applications for which they are the preferable or even the only feasible method for empirical studies. Methods of maximizing the reliability of bidding games will be discussed and an empirical study using bidding games will be presented.

Direct costing methods. Implicit in the concept of a "marginal value of damage avoided by abatement" curve, as proposed by Kneese and Bower [12], is the idea of estimating the benefits of abatement of environmental damage by directly estimating the costs attributable to that damage. Several workers have made progress along these lines. For example, Lave and Seskin [13] have had some success in relating the costs of impairment of human health to levels of air pollution. If all relevant costs of a particular incidence of environmental damage can be identified, evaluated and summed, a curve relating the value of damage avoided to levels of environmental improvements can be fitted. The first derivative of this curve is the "M.V.D.A." curve of Kneese and Bower [12].

These costing techniques are theoretically sound and may often be feasible in practice. However, difficulties may be introduced by the unavailability of information and the pricing and accounting problems inherent in this type of analysis. These techniques will have limited application in valuation of aesthetic environmental improvements, since the costs of aesthetic damages may seldom be directly reflected in the market.

Revealed demand techniques. Revealed demand techniques have been widely used for estimation of the demand for outdoor recreation, often a nonmarket good.[5] A number of applications to valuation of the benefits of air pollution abatement have been made [1, 11, 14, 16, 18]. The principle is as follows. The benefits of provision of a nonmarket good are inferred from the revealed demand for some suitable proxy. In the case of air pollution abatement, the revealed demand for residential land is related by regression analysis to air pollution concentrations. In metropolitan areas, it is possible to obtain information on the concentration of specific air pollutants in different parts of the city. If all other variables relevant to the valuation of urban residential land can be identified[6] and measured, it ought to be possible to determine by

[3] In the approach of methodological individualism, Pareto-efficiency is still not achieved since the price to the individual cannot equal the marginal cost to the individual (which is zero) and allow collection of sufficient funds to cover the total cost of provision.

[4] In Fig. 1, the aggregate and marginal bid curves are drawn as smooth curves consistent with diminishing marginal utility. As pointed out in footnote 2, this need not be even the typical case.

[5] See [4].

[6] Some appropriate variables are size and value of structures on the land, distance from places where services and employment opportunities are concentrated, proportion of park land and open space in the neighborhood, density of population, proportion of various racial and ethnic minorities in the immediate vicinity, and the incidence of violent crimes.

regression analysis the extent to which air pollution concentrations affect observed land values. In this way, a proxy measure of the benefits of air pollution abatement is obtained.

There are a number of difficulties with this type of analysis. Since the value ascribed to air pollution control is derived directly from the regression coefficient of the pollution concentration variable, accurate results require perfect and complete specification of the regression equation. In an interesting recent study, Wieand [17] claims that when such regression models are completely specified, the regression coefficient of the pollution concentration variable may not be significantly different from zero. Another difficulty, researchers in the field agree, lies in interpretation of the results. Are all of the benefits of air pollution abatement captured in residential land values? Most think not. For our purposes, the other side of that coin is of interest: Surely some benefits in addition to the aesthetic benefits are captured. Which additional benefits?

In the case study reported below, the geographical area affected by environmental damage includes urban areas, but also rural and agricultural areas, and substantial areas of Indian reservation and National Park, Monument, and Forest lands (which are typically not exchanged in the market). Thus, those revealed demand techniques currently available would seem to be inapplicable to the situation faced in our study.

Bidding games. In analysis of the demand for outdoor recreation, Davis [7] pioneered in the use of bidding games. During personal interviews, the enumerator follows on iterative questioning procedure to elicit responses which enable the fitting of a demand curve for the services offered by a recreation area. Respondents are asked to answer "yes" or "no" to the question: Would you continue to use this recreation area if the cost to you was to increase by X dollars? The amount is varied up or down in repetitive questions, and the highest positive response is recorded. Individual responses may then be aggregated to generate a demand curve for the recreation services provided by the area.

It seems reasonable that bidding games may be adapted to the estimation of the benefits from provision of an inexhaustible nonmarket good such as abatement of aesthetic environmental damage. Bidding games would seem to be the most direct method of estimating Bradford's aggregate benefit curve, which is derived from vertical summation of individual bid curves. The difficulties of interpretation which are inherent in the revealed demand techniques developed thus far do not occur when the bidding game technique is used. The data obtained with bidding games are not cost observations but individuals' perceptions of value. Thus, bidding games can be used in situations where direct costing techniques are ineffective for lack of data. These advantages of bidding games over revealed demand and direct costing techniques seem sufficient to justify attempts to adapt the bidding game technique for use in valuation of aesthetic environmental improvements.

Some General Considerations in the Design of Bidding Games

Bidding games are designed to elicit information on the hypothetical behavior of respondents when faced with hypothetical situations. In the case study presented below, the purpose of bidding games is to provide a measure of the benefits of aesthetic environmental improvements by measuring the willingness of a sample of respondents to pay for such improvements. The efficacy of bidding games used for this purpose depends on the reliability with which stated hypothetical behavior is converted to action, should the hypothetical situation posited in the game arise in actuality.

Willingness to pay is the behavioral dimension of an underlying attitude: concern for environmental quality.[7] Sociologists and public opinion researchers have built up a substantial body of literature which considers ways in which survey techniques of measuring attitudes and their behavioral component can be made as reliable as possible. Some desirable characteristics of such surveys have been identified [5, 9]. The hypothetical situation presented should be realistic and credible to respondents. Realism and credibility can be achieved by satisfying the following criteria for survey instrument design: Test items must have properties similar to those in the actual situation; situations posited must be concrete rather than symbolic; and test items should involve institutionalized or routinized behavior, where role expectations of respondents are well defined. Where the behavioral predisposition under study are affected by attitudes about a number of different things, the test instrument must be designed to focus upon those attitudes which are relevant. An example may be helpful. In the case study reported here, willingness to pay additional taxes to achieve aesthetic environmental improvement is affected by attitudes toward environmental quality, but also by attitudes toward the current tax burden and attitudes toward the idea of receptors of pollutants paying to obtain abatement of emissions. If the survey is carried out for the purpose of measuring the benefits of abatement, the test instrument must be designed to take cognizance of the various diverse attitudes which affect willingness to pay and to allow isolation of the relevant attitudinal dimensions.

Since abatement of aesthetic environmental damage is an inexhaustible, public good, bidding games intended to provide data for valuation of that good must be designed to avoid the effects of the freeloader problem, which encourages nonrevelation of preferences. One method would be to design games in which each respondent is told that all consumers of the good would pay for it on a similar basis, thus eliminating the possibility of freeloading.

With careful design of bidding games to ensure that the responses recorded are predictive of behavior, it should be possible to use the bidding technique to estimate the benefits of environmental improvements with reasonable accuracy.

AN EMPIRICAL APPLICATION:

ESTIMATION OF THE BENEFITS OF ABATEMENT OF AESTHETIC ENVIRONMENTAL DAMAGES ASSOCIATED WITH THE FOUR CORNERS STEAM ELECTRIC GENERATING PLANT

At New Mexico State University, research is under way to examine the socioeconomic impacts of development of the rapidly expanding coal strip-mining and steam electric generation industry in the Four Corners Region (southwestern United States), and to predict the impacts of alternative policies with respect to environmental management and economic development, as such policies would affect the industry. One facet of this research required estimation of the benefits of abatement of aesthetic environmental damage associated with the Four Corners power plant at Fruitland, NM, and the Navajo mine which provides its raw energy source—low energy, low sulfur, high ash, sub-bituminous coal.[8]

[7] Three dimensions of attitudes are recognized [8]: (1) a cognitive dimension, (2) an affectual dimension, and (3) a behavioral dimension.

[8] The following facts may provide some idea of the magnitude of this operation and its attendant environmental problems. In 1970, the power plant had a capacity of 2,080 MW. The mine provides

The mine–power plant complex causes several kinds of aesthetic environmental damage. Particulates, sulfur oxides and nitrous oxides are emitted into the air. The adverse effects of particulate pollutants on visibility is considered the most important aesthetic impact of the complex. The strip-mining process will create some aesthetic damage. Although the soil banks will be leveled, reclamation in the sense of re-establishing a viable plant and animal eco-system is uncertain. Transmission lines radiate from the plant in several directions, passing through the Navajo Reservation and bringing the paraphernalia of development to a landscape which is in some places very beautiful and otherwise untouched.[9]

It was decided to use bidding games to measure the benefits of abatement of the aesthetic environmental damage associated with the Four Corners power plant and the Navajo mine.[10] Considerable attention was devoted to the design and development of bidding games which provide a reliable estimator of these benefits.

Questionnaire Design

The bidding games were part of prepared schedules designed for use in a personal interview survey of samples of users of the Four Corners Interstate Air Quality Control Region environment (i.e., residents and recreational visitors to the region). In preparation for the bidding games, respondents were asked a series of questions about environmental matters, to focus their attention on that topic. Then, the subject of the coal–electricity complex in the Four Corners area was explicitly raised. The respondents were shown three sets of photographs depicting three levels of environmental damage around the Four Corners Power Plant, near Fruitland, NM.

Set A showed the plant circa 1969, prior to installation of some additional emissions control equipment, producing its historical maximum emissions of air pollutants. Another photograph depicted the spoil banks as they appear following strip-mining, but prior to leveling. A third photograph showed electricity transmission lines marring the landscape. Set A depicted the highest level of environmental damage, and accurately represented the actual situation in the early years of operation of the plant.

Set B showed an intermediate level of damage. One photograph showed the plant circa 1972, after additional controls had reduced particulate emissions (i.e., the type of emissions most destructive of visibility). Another showed the spoil banks leveled but not revegetated; a third showed the transmission lines placed less obtrusively (i.e., at some distance from major roads).

Set C was intended to depict a situation where the industries continued to operate,

---

coal at a rate of 8.5 millions tons annually. Over the 40 year projected life span of the mine, 31,000 acres will be stripped. In 1970, approximately 550 people were employed in the mine and power plant, total value of sales of electricity was $146 million, and 96,000 tons of particulates, 73,000 tons of sulfur oxides and 66,000 tons of nitrous oxides were emitted annually.

[9] To place this aesthetic environmental damage in perspective, it may be useful to point out that the Four Corners Interstate Air Quality Control Region includes the greatest concentration of National Parks and Monuments in the United States and a number of Indian reservations, the largest of which are the Navajo and Hopi reservations. The value of the region for tourism and recreation depends largely on its bizarre and unusual landscapes, the enjoyment of which requires excellent long distance visibility and depth and color perception. There exists a substantial minority of "traditional" Native Americans who have strong religious and cultural attachments to nature, and who resent the air pollution, strip-mining, and transmission lines; witness the prolonged litigation about location of the Tucson Gas and Electric Company transmission line from the San Juan power plant, which is under construction about 9 miles from the Four Corners plant.

[10] In that part of the overall study which deals with nonaesthetic environmental damage, direct costing techniques are used.

but with minimal environmental damage. One photograph showed the plant with visible emissions reduced to zero.[11] A second photograph showed a section of arid land in its natural state; it was intended to depict a situation where the transmission lines were placed underground and the strip-mined land completely reclaimed.

The interviewers pointed out the salient features of each set of photographs to each respondent. For most of the respondents (with the exception of many recreationists), the situations were rooted in real experience: the residents of the region were familiar with the plant and mine, and their operation for the previous eight years. Most remembered situation A well, for that was exactly how it was only a few years earlier. Situation B was a fairly good approximation of the real situation at the time of the interviews. With the help of the photographs, situation C would be readily visualized.

Since the fitting of bid or benefit curves requires an expression of willingness to pay for abatement of aesthetic damages, it was necessary to design games based upon appropriate vehicles of payment. The vehicles for payment were chosen so as to maximize the realism and credibility of the hypothetical situation posited to respondents. As will be discussed below, it was necessary to design and use a series of bidding games, because no one vehicle of payment was appropriate for use with all of the subpopulations sampled. First, the general format applicable to all games is discussed. Then, the particular games used for particular subpopulations are discussed.

For each bidding game played, respondents were asked to consider situation A, the highest level of environmental damage, as the starting point. The bidding games were designed to elicit the highest amount of money which the respondent, an adult speaking for his or her household, was willing to pay in order to improve the aesthetic environment to situation C, and to situation B. Answers were elicited in terms of "yes" or "no" to questions expressed in the form "would you pay amount X . . . ?" A "yes" answer would lead the enumerator to raise the amount and repeat the question, maybe several times, until a "no" answer was obtained. A "no" answer would lead the enumerator to reduce the amount until a "yes" answer was obtained. The amount which elicited the highest "yes" answer was recorded as the amount the respondent was willing to pay.

It was emphasized that the respondent was to assume that the vehicle for payment used in a particular game was the only possible way in which environmental improvements could be obtained. This stipulation was designed to minimize the incidence of zero bids as protests against either the zero liability rule implicit in "willingness to pay" games or the particular method of payment used in a particular game. If a respondent indicated that he was willing to pay nothing at all, he was asked a series of questions to find out why. A respondent indicating that he did not consider his household to be harmed in any way by the environmental damage and, therefore, saw no reason to pay for environmental improvements was recorded as bidding zero. If a respondent indicated that his zero bid was in protest against the game, his answer was analyzed as a nonresponse to the bidding game, since he had refused to play the game by the stated rules.[12]

---

[11] This feat was accomplished by photographing the plant on a day when all units were shut down.

[12] For the purpose of estimating the benefits of abatement, the treatment of "protest bids" as non-responses is legitimate. By definition, a "protest bid" recognizes that positive benefits from abatement exist, but registers a protest against a particular method of financing abatement. We recognize that the elimination of "protest bids" from analyses aimed at estimating the benefits of abatement fails to remove all downward bias from the responses to particular games: some respondents may bid low (i.e., underestimate the benefits to themselves of abatement) in conscious or subconscious protest against the method of financing assumed in a game.

The selection of appropriate vehicles for payment provided a challenge. People are not accustomed to paying for abatement of air pollution and strip-mining damage. However, they are accustomed to paying for many other types of useful goods and services, many of which, such as parks and highway beautification, have aesthetic or "quality of life" components. So selection of realistic vehicles for payment was not impossible. However, the heterogeneous nature of the affected population meant that no single vehicle was suitable for data collection among all groups. In the Four Corners Region, the affected population can be divided into three broad groups: (1) the residents of Indian reservations, primarily Navajos, but also including members of several other tribes; (2) the residents of the nonreservation sections of the region, primarily Anglo-Americans, but with a sprinkling of Spanish-Americans, Native Americans living off the reservations, and other minorities; and (3) the tourists and recreationists who visit the area to enjoy its unique natural, historical and cultural attractions. Different versions of the questionnaire, using bidding games based on different vehicles for payment, were constructed for use with the three different sub-populations of the affected population.

The particular bidding games used are described below.

The sales tax game. Members of all three subpopulations are familiar with the practice of paying sales taxes. For most, this is a frequent occurrence. It is also understood by most that income collected in sales taxes is used to provide useful public services. It does not require much imagination to conceive of a public agency collecting a sales tax from residents of the affected region and using the income to finance environmental improvements.

The sales tax bidding game was used for both the resident samples. It was not used with the recreationist sample, since that group often purchased only a few items in the region, bringing most of their equipment and supplies with them. This would make a regional sales tax largely irrelevant for that group.

Respondents were asked to assume that a regional sales tax was collected on all purchases in the Four Corners Interstate Air Quality Control Region for the purpose of financing environmental improvements.[13] All revenue from the additional tax would be used for abatement of aesthetic environmental damage associated with the power plant and mine, and all citizens would be required to pay the tax. Recreational visitors to the region would contribute to environmental improvement through payment of additional users fees for facilities.

The electricity bill game. The monthly electricity bill seemed to be a suitable vehicle for measurement of willingness to pay. It is the production of electricity which causes the environmental damage, and most people can readily comprehend that reduction of the damage may raise the cost of operating the industry and that passing these additional costs on to consumers of electricity is a not unlikely outcome. For the residents of those sections of the region outside the Indian reservations, payment of a monthly electricity bill is a routinized behavior. Therefore, a bidding game based upon the monthly electricity bill was played with the nonreservation resident sample.

This game was unsuitable for use with the other two samples. Many residents of

---

"Protest bids" were recorded and used in some other types of analyses. For example, the incidence of "protest bids" is an indicator of the relative political acceptability of various methods of financing abatement.

[13] The regional sales tax would be additional to current state and local sales taxes and would be charged on all commodities subject to existing state and local sales taxes.

Indian reservations do not have electricity available in their homes. Recreationists do not pay monthly electricity bills while vacationing away from home.

The respondent was first asked the amount of his monthly household electricity bill. He was then asked to imagine that an additional charge was added to his electricity bill, and the electricity bills of everyone who uses electricity produced in the Four Corners Region, even people as far away as southern California. All of the additional money collected would be used to repair the aesthetic environmental damage caused as a result of electricity production and transmission in the Four Corners region.

The user fees game. Measuring recreationists' willingness to pay for environmental improvements raised problems which prevented use of the electricity bill and sales tax games. For the recreationists, a satisfactory game would need to focus upon (1) the activities associated with vacationing, and (2) the collection of payments while they are in the region and using the regional environment. The payment of user fees for recreation services (i.e., campsite, utilities hook-up, boat launching), seemed to be a promising vehicle for a bidding game for the recreationists. If visitors were concerned about environmental quality in the places where they vacation, the payment of an additional sum along with their usual daily user fees would provide a suitable way to express that concern.

A sample of recreationists in the national parks, monuments and forests and state parks in the region played a bidding game based on user fees. Only recreationists who were not residents of the region were included. They were first asked the total sum of user fees they paid daily. They were then asked to suppose user fees in all the recreation areas in the Four Corners area were increased. All the additional money collected would be spent on environmental improvements. All recreators would pay and the year-round residents would pay, too, through additional regional sales taxes.

The Conduct of the Survey

The bidding games, as described above, were included in prepared schedules which also served as the instrument for collection of data for socioeconomic analysis of citizen environmental concern. Personal interviews were conducted by enumerators who were closely supervised and who had been carefully trained in formal sessions and in two separate field pre-tests of the questionnaire. Interviews were conducted during the summer of 1972.

Usable questionnaires were completed by 526 residents of nonreservation sections of the Four Corners Interstate Air Quality Control Region, 71 residents of Indian reservations and 150 recreators and tourists from outside the region who were using recreation sites within the region. The ratio of reservation residents to nonreservation residents sampled was proportional to their total numbers in the regional population; the size of the recreationist sample was chosen arbitrarily. Respondents from each subpopulation were selected by stratified random sampling. Stratification was based on concentration of air pollutants above the respondent's home or recreation site, as estimated by an atmospheric diffusion model developed as part of the larger research project. The population in higher pollution concentration zones was sampled more heavily.

Analysis and Results

For the *determination of three points on the aggregate bid curve*, corresponding to the situations, A, B, and C, the bidding game results were aggregated by methods appro-

TABLE I

AGGREGATE BIDS FOR ABATEMENT OF AESTHETIC ENVIRONMENTAL DAMAGE
ASSOCIATED WITH THE FOUR CORNERS POWER PLANT, 1972

Item	Situation		
	A	B	C
Emissions (tons of particulates per year)	96,000	26,000	0
Level of abatement (tons of particulates per year)	0	70,000	96,000
Estimated regional aggregate bid ($ millions per year)	0	15.54	24.57
Standard error ($ millions per year)	—	1.24	1.52
95% Confidence limits ($ millions per year)	—	±2.43	±2.97
Estimated consumer aggregate bid ($ millions per year)	0	11.25	19.31
Standard error ($ millions per year)	—	0.68	0.98
95% Confidence limits ($ millions per year)	—	±1.33	±1.92

priate to the stratified random sampling technique used, to provide estimates of the total bid for the relevant population. Two methods of aggregation were used, to generate two different aggregate bid curves.

(1) The results of the sales tax game with area residents (reservation and non-reservation) were added to the results of user fee games played by recreators to estimate a total regional willingness to pay for three levels of environmental improvement.

(2) The results of the electricity bill game were extrapolated over all consumers of power from the Four Corners plant to estimate consumer willingness to pay. This latter procedure involved the ethical premise that, since the production of electricity causes environmental damage, all citizens who consume Four Corners power ought to be willing to pay as much in additional electricity charges for environmental improvements as those who live in the region which suffers the damage. However appealing this ethical premise may be, our survey did not include people outside the region. Thus the consumer bid cannot be interpreted as an estimate of true "willingness to pay." It would be interesting to extend this research to include bidding games for these consumers of Four Corners electricity who do not live or recreate in the affected environment.

While both the regional and consumer aggregate bids are of interest, the authors believe that more faith may be placed in the regional bid since that bid was derived from samples of all segments of its relevant population.

Table I presents the estimated aggregate bids, standard errors, and 95% confidence limits at points A, B, and C. Regional and consumer bids are presented.

Using the estimated aggregate bids (Table I), a *regional aggregate bid curve* and a *consumer aggregate bid curve* were fitted. To fit two-dimensional aggregate bid curves, it was necessary to select a single independent variable to serve as a proxy for the total package of aesthetic environmental improvements under consideration. Situations A, B, and C were defined so that all three forms of aesthetic damage (air pollution, strip-mining, and transmission lines) were successively reduced together from their most obtrusive in situation A to virtual elimination in C. Of the three forms of damage, reduced visibility due to particulate air pollution was considered by respondents to be far and away the most serious. So, abatement of particulate air pollutant emissions (measured as the difference, in tons per year, between the level at A and the levels at

TABLE II

Tests of Hypotheses Concerning the Slopes of the Aggregate Bid Curves

Hypothesis	Confidence of rejecting H_0	
	Regional aggregate bid curve (%)	Consumer aggregate bid curve (%)
1. The aggregate bid curve is of linear positive slope[a]	99.9	99.9
2. The aggregate bid for situation B is one half of that for C[b]	99.9	94.5

[a] Rejection implies that the aggregate bid curve is of increasing positive slope.

[b] Rejection implies that the aggregate bid for B exceeds one half of that for C.

B and C, respectively) was arbitrarily chosen to serve as a single independent variable for graphical analyses.[14]

The form of the curve requires some discussion. It has already been noted [footnote 2] that the usual restraints placed on the slope of demand curves are inappropriate for the first derivatives of aggregate bid curves for public goods, due to the impossibility of separating quantity and quality factors. Here we have a case in point. It seems resonable that "consumers" of abatement of particulate emissions desire the attribute, visibility. Given the reasonable assumption that marginal utility of additional visibility is diminishing, one would expect the first derivative of the aggregate bid curve for visibility to be of negative slope.

Meteorologists have established that an inverse relationship exists between visibility and concentration of particulate pollutants. Visibility increases at an increasing rate as particulate pollution (measured in terms of weight) is abated [3, 10]. Therefore, the slope of the marginal aggregate bid curve for abatement of emissions (in tons per year) is *a priori* unpredictable, since the diminishing marginal utility of visibility and the increasing marginal visibility resulting from additional abatement influence that slope in opposite ways.

In terms of visibility, the aggregate bid curve form which provided the best fit of the three data points was

$$B = c \ln (v),$$

where B = aggregate bid in dollars, c = a constant, and v = visibility.

In terms of abatement of particulate air pollutants (measured in tons per year), the appropriate curve form was

$$B(q) = c \ln \frac{k}{k - q},$$

[14] In the case study at hand, we recognize the inelegance introduced by this procedure. We do not believe it does serious violence to the truth, since most of the aesthetic environmental damage occurring is, in fact, due to particulate air pollutants. We emphasize, however, that this problem should not typically occur in the use of aggregate bid methodology and bidding game techniques. Rather, its occurrence here was a special case and is attributable to our need to value a package of different aesthetic environmental improvements within the following constraints: (1) a limited research budget, which confined us to one personal interview survey, and (2) the need to limit the length of each interview, to avoid exhausting the patience of respondents.

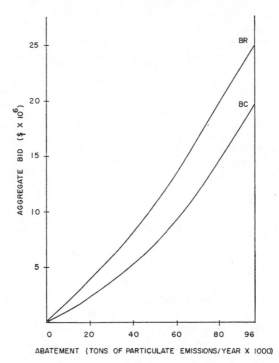

FIG. 2. Estimated aggregate bid curves for abatement of aesthetic environmental damage, Four Corners power plant, 1972. BR, Regional aggregate bid; BC, Consumer aggregate bid.

where k = a parameter relating visibility to emissions, which is determined behaviorally, and q = tons of particulate emissions abated annually.

The aggregate bid curve fitted using this equation form passes through the origin, as logically it must, given that rational citizens would bid zero for zero abatement. The first derivative of the aggregate bid curve is of positive slope.[15] Statistical tests (Table II) resulted in rejection of the hypotheses (1) that the aggregate bid curve was linear, or of decreasing positive slope, and (2) that the aggregate bid at point B was simply one-half of that at C. Regional and consumer aggregate bid curves are presented (Fig. 2).

[15] It must be emphasized that the curve form used provided the best fit, given the three data points available. It would have been desirable to have collected information adequate to generate more data points. The decision to collect data for only three points was made in recognition of limits to the patience of respondents. The multipurpose schedule was already quite lengthy, given the need to collect data relevant to the situation of the respondent, play the bidding games, and collect socio-economic, sociological and attitudinal data.

It is recognized that, if more data points had been available, a different curve form may have been appropriate. The possibility of a sigmoid aggregate bid curve is logically appealing. Such a curve would have a segment of increasing slope, where the increasing marginal visibility from particulate abatement dominates the decreasing marginal utility of additional visibility then, as complete abatement is approached (i.e., somewhere to the right of our point B), the slope may become decreasing as the diminishing marginal utility of visibility becomes dominant. Such a curve form would be consistent with theoretical considerations and with the three data points available.

The fitted aggregate bid curves were:

$$B_r = \$29{,}175{,}840 \ln \frac{168{,}890}{168{,}890 - q}, \quad \text{for the regional aggregate bid curve, and}$$

$$B_c = \$15{,}396{,}700 \ln \frac{134{,}490}{134{,}490 - q}, \quad \text{for the consumer aggregate bid curve.}$$

Marginal aggregate bid curves, or *price curves,* were generated by taking the first derivatives of the aggregate bid curves (Fig. 3). The derived price curves were:

$$P_r = \$\frac{29{,}175{,}840}{168{,}890 - q}, \quad \text{derived from the regional aggregate bid curve, and}$$

$$P_c = \$\frac{15{,}396{,}700}{134{,}490 - q}, \quad \text{derived from the consumer aggregate bid curve.}$$

These derived price curves are very useful for public policy analyses with respect to optimal environmental management policies. In Fig. 4, a hypothetical derived price curve is presented, along with a hypothetical marginal cost of abatement curve. In this hypothetical example, the optimal level of abatement is *S*. A standard allowing maxi-

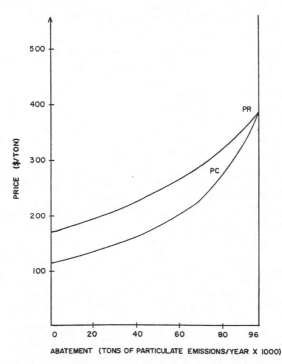

FIG. 3. Derived price curves for abatement of aesthetic environmental damage, Four Corners power plant, 1972. PR, price curve derived from regional aggregate bid; PC, price curve derived from consumer aggregate bid.

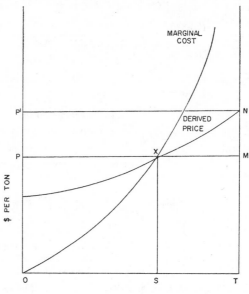

Fig. 4. Optimal standards, penalties and per unit taxes on emissions, given hypothetical marginal cost and price curves.

mum annual emissions of (*T–S*) tons of particulates would be appropriate, and the penalty for violation of that standard should be set sufficiently high that the polluter's expected penalty per ton of emissions in excess of the standard would be at least *P*. An alternative institutional framework would call for a fine or tax per ton of particulate emissions. The fine ought to be set at least as high as *P* per ton. At the level *P*, the optimal level of abatement would be achieved. A fixed fine per ton of remaining emissions would result in collection of the amount *XMTS*. However, since the derived price curve is of positive slope, the sum of the fines collected would be insufficient to compensate the receptors of the pollutants for their loss in welfare. The necessary amount would be *XNTS*. This amount could be collected, if full compensation were the accepted policy,[16] by using a sliding scale of fines, ranging from *P'* for the first ton of emissions down to *P* for all emissions in excess of *T–S*.

If the marginal costs of abatement of aesthetic environmental damage associated with the Four Corners power plant were known,[17] the derived price curves presented

[16] Under a full compensation policy, a derived price curve generated from bidding games based on the concept of willingness to pay (which implicitly places the liability with the receptor of damages) would underestimate both the optimal level of abatement and the appropriate level of fines or taxes. Randall [15] and others have demonstrated that the demand for abatement of an external diseconomy is greater in the full liability situation than in the zero liability situation implicit in willingness to pay games.

[17] We are not yet in a position to present a complete benefit/cost analysis of the abatement of the aesthetic environmental damage associated with the Four Corners power plant and Navajo mine. Preliminary and tentative calculations indicate that, *if our attribution of most of the benefits reported here to abatement of particulate air pollutants is reasonable*, 99.7% abatement of particulate emissions (the current New Mexico standard for 1975) is economically justified on the basis of aesthetic considerations alone. Some additional abatement beyond the 1975 standard may be justified. The economic benefits from that abatement which has already taken place appear to far exceed the costs.

TABLE III

INCOME ELASTICITY OF BID FOR ABATEMENT OF AESTHETIC DAMAGES
ASSOCIATED WITH THE FOUR CORNERS POWER PLANT, 1972

Subpopulation	Game	Level of abatement	Income elasticity of bid	Standard error	Significantly greater than zero[a] ?
Nonreservation residents	Sales tax	B	0.65	0.10	Yes
		C	0.65	0.08	Yes
Reservation residents	Sales tax	B	0.23	0.18	No
		C	0.24	0.18	No
Nonreservation residents	Electricity bill	B	0.54	0.09	Yes
		C	0.39	0.06	Yes
Recreators	Users fees	B	0.09	0.15	No
		C	0.16	0.11	No

[a] At the 95% level of confidence.

in Fig. 3 could be used to perform policy analyses similar to those in the hypothetical example above.

The *relationship between willingness to pay and household income* is of interest. However, the concept of income elasticity of demand is inappropriate to the public good under study. The calculation of an income elasticity of quantity of abatement demanded would require consideration of the relationship between income and quantity of homogeneous units of abatement demanded at a constant price per unit. However, in this study there were no explicit unit prices for abatement; neither were there individual variations in quantity of abatement demanded, as the quantities were fixed as defined in situations A, B, and C. These conditions result from the inherent non-exclusive nature of abatement of aesthetic environmental damage: Everyone obtains the same quantity and there is no explicit price. This situation is the inverse of the market situation for private goods; dollar bids are the response to a quantity which is given.

Since there existed no market price at which to calculate the income elasticity of demand, an "income elasticity of bid" was estimated. The income elasticity of bid was defined as:

$$e_Y = \frac{dB}{dY}\frac{Y}{B} = b_1\frac{Y}{B},$$

where Y = household income, and B = the individual's total annual bid. A linear regression model was used to determine the statistic b_1. The mean value of Y and B were used, and the calculation was made at each level of abatement.

Calculated income elasticities of bid for the various subpopulations and bidding games are presented in Table III. In all cases, income elasticity of bid was greater than zero, indicating that higher income households were willing to pay a greater amount than lower income households to achieve the same level of abatement of aesthetic damages. For the non-reservation residents, calculated income elasticity of bid

This conclusion is extremely tentative and subject to revision. It is presented in this footnote (at the request of an anonymous reviewer) to provide a "ball park" indication of the conclusions which may arise from our research.

ranged from 0.39 to 0.65, depending on the game and the level of abatement. Income elasticity of bid was significantly greater than zero at the 95% level of confidence. For the residents of Indian reservations and the recreational visitors to the region, lower positive income elasticities were recorded. These were not significantly greater than zero, at the 95% level of confidence.[18]

It was also found that willingness to pay an additional charge in the electricity bill for a particular level of abatement increased as the size of the electricity bill increased. Electric bill elasticity of bid, as defined as

$$e_b = \frac{dB}{d\text{Bill}} \frac{\text{Bill}}{B},$$

was calculated (for the nonreservation resident sample) to be 0.30 for situation B and 0.25 for situation C; at both points, it was significantly greater than zero at the 95% level of confidence. These estimates indicate that willingness to pay for a given level of environmental improvements increased as the size of the electricity bill increased, but at a lesser rate.

The Reliability of the Results

In the statistical sense, our estimates of the aggregate benefits from abatement of aesthetic environmental damage would seem to be of a high order of reliability. The 95% confidence limits of the aggregate bids are quite narrow, compared with the size of the estimated aggregate bids. Statistical estimates of the confidence which may be placed in these estimated aggregate bids are based upon the variance of the responses of the samples, and indicate the confidence with which sample results may be extrapolated to the whole population. These statistics, *per se*, are unable to give any indication of the reliability with which predispositions to behave, as measured by the bidding games, would be transmitted to actions should the hypothetical situation arise.

We argue, nevertheless, that our estimates of the benefits of abatement of aesthetic environmental damages associated with the Four Corners power plant are of a reasonable order of magnitude and, if anything, conservative. (1) We believe the design of the bidding games allows confidence in their efficacy. (2) The individual household bid for abatement, on average, is of the same order of magnitude as the estimates of the value of particulate pollution abatement obtained in revealed demand studies [1], when the latter are converted to a comparable basis. Mean individual household willingness to pay for abatement, measured by the sales tax game played with the nonreservation resident sample, was about $50 annually to achieve situation B and $85 annually to achieve situation C. (3) The estimated aggregate bids for abatement are relatively small given the scale of the operation at Four Corners, as indicated by its 1970 emissions rate and its total annual sales of $146 million [footnote 5]. (4) Theoretical analyses indicate that the demand for abatement of an externality will

---

[18] The estimates of income elasticity obtained with the nonreservation resident sample may be more reliable, for two reasons. First, the nonreservation sample was considerably larger than either of the other two samples. Second, the range of incomes encountered in the nonreservation resident sample more nearly approached that of society as a whole. The reservation resident sample was representative of its underlying population, in which incomes are concentrated at the extreme lower end of the national range. The visiting recreators had a mean household income about fifty per cent greater than the national average; very few recreators had incomes in the lower half of the national range.

be lower under a zero liability rule than under intermediate or full liability rules [15]. The bidding games used were based on zero liability rules, and they should be expected to yield conservative estimates of the benefits of abatement.

It is recognized that three data points provide an inadequate basis on which to draw conclusions with respect to the shapes and slopes of the aggregate bid curves and their first derivatives. However, it is consistent with theoretical considerations and with the limited data available that the aggregate bid curves may have at least a segment with increasing slope.

It would seem that the income elasticity of bid and the electric bill elasticity of bid fall in the range from zero to -1. This result was consistent with our prior expectations.

CONCLUDING COMMENTS

In the case study reported, bidding games were used to estimate the benefits which would accrue from abatement of the aesthetic environmental damages associated with the Four Corners power plant and the Navajo mine. The problem situation was not amenable to the use of direct costing nor revealed demand techniques.

This study has revealed that substantial benefits may be gained from abatement of aesthetic environmental damage associated with the Four Corners power plant and Navajo mine. These potential benefits have not been revealed or realized in the market place. However, the process of political and institutional change has led to the imposition of increasingly rigorous control standards for particulate emissions from the plant, indicating a recognition, in some broad sense, that benefits may be gained from emissions controls. Our contribution has been to attempt a quantification of these benefits.

We believe that the use of bidding game techniques was successful in meeting the objective, valuation of these benefits. Bidding game techniques seem amenable to use as a research tool for valuation of a wide variety of nonmarket goods. It must be understood, however, that bidding games measure the hypothetical responses of individuals faced with hypothetical situations. Thus, considerable care must be exercised in the design of bidding games and the conduct of surveys for data collection, to ensure that the results obtained are as reliable as possible.

REFERENCES

1. R. J. Anderson, Jr. and T. D. Crocker, Air pollution and housing: Some findings, Paper No. 264, Institute for Research in the Behavioral, Economic and Management Sciences (January 1970).
2. D. F. Bradford, Benefit-cost analysis and demand curves for public goods, *Kyklos* 23, 775–91 (1970).
3. R. J. Charlson, N. C. Ahlquist, and H. Horvath, On the generality of correlation of atmospheric aerosol mass concentration and light scatter, *Atmos. Environ.* 2, 455–464 (1968).
4. M. Clawson and J. L. Knetsch, "Economics of Outdoor Recreation," Johns Hopkins Press, Baltimore (1966).
5. I. Crespi, What kinds of attitude measures are predictive of behavior? *Pub. Opin. Quart.* 35, 327–34 (1971).
6. O. A. Davis and A. B. Whinston, On the Distinction Between Public and Private Goods. *Amer. Econ. Rev.* 57, 360–373 (1967).
7. R. K. Davis, Recreation planning as a economic problem, *Natural Res. J.* 3, 239–249 (1963).
8. J. F. Engel, D. T. Kollat, and R. D. Blackwell, Attitude formation and structure, *in* "Consumer Behavior," Holt, Rinehart, and Winston, New York (1968).
9. H. Erskine, The polls: Pollution and its costs, *Pub. Opin. Quart.* 36, 120–135 (1972).
10. H. Ettinger and G. W. Roger, Particle size, visibility and mass concentration in a nonurban environment, Los Alamos Scientific Laboratory, LA-DC-12197 (1971).

11. J. A. Jaksch and H. H. Stoevener, Effects of air pollution on residential property values in Toledo, Oregon, Agricultural Experiment Station Special Report 304, Oregon State University, Corvallis (1970).
12. A. V. Kneese and B. Bower, "Managing Water Quality: Economics, Technology and Institutions," Johns Hopkins Press, Baltimore (1972).
13. L. Lave and E. Seskin, Air Pollution and Human Health, *Science* **169**, 723–732 (1970).
14. H. O. Nourse, The effect of air pollution on house values, *Land Econ.* **43**, 181–189 (1967).
15. A. Randall, On the theory of market solutions to externality problems, Agricultural Experiment Station Special Report 351, Oregon State University, Corvallis (1972).
16. R. G. Ridker and J. A. Henning, The determination of residential property values with special reference to air pollution (St. Louis, Missouri), *Rev. Econ. Stat.* **49**, 246–257 (1967).
17. K. F. Weiand, Air pollution and property values: A study of the St. Louis area, *J. Reg. Sci.* **13** 91–95 (1973).
18. R. O. Zerbe, Jr., The economics of air pollution: A cost-benefit approach, Ontario Dept. of Public Health, Toronto (1969).

[7]

Valuing Increments and Decrements in Natural Resource Service Flows

David S. Brookshire, Alan Randall, and John R. Stoll

A general model for valuation of changes in natural resource service flows, entirely consistent with Hicksian concepts of consumer surplus, is developed. It is a total value model, applicable to all classes of goods: divisible and indivisible in production, divisible and indivisible in consumption, exclusive and nonexclusive. The standard result of partial equilibrium microeconomics—price is equal to value at the margin—may be derived as a special case from this model. An empirical application involving the valuation of changes in the provision of wildlife-related amenities is presented.

Key words: consumer's surplus, natural resources, valuation, wildlife.

In the course of his work, the benefit-cost analyst frequently encounters situations in which a proposed program or project would divert natural resources from their current use to some, quite different, alternative. In keeping with the "with and without" principle, he must determine "without project" benefits, which are equal to the net present value of the stream of services that would be provided by the natural resource in its current use over the life of the proposed project. For example, projects are often proposed which would drain wetlands, fill coastal marshlands for housing or resort developments, dam free-flowing streams, inundate canyons, or divert wildlife habitat for agricultural, forestry, or mineral extraction purposes. These few examples suggest that the flow of goods, services, and amenities which must be valued to determine "without project" benefits is often complex. The natural resource often provides flows of goods, services, and amenities quite diverse in

physical terms. In economic terms, too, the diversity of goods, services, and amenities produced may be awesome. There may be goods that are divisible, lumpy, or indivisible in production; divisible, congestible, or nonrival in consumption; and exclusive or nonexclusive. "With project" benefits are more likely to involve marginal increments in the supply of undifferentiated goods—e.g., agricultural commodities, electricity, and slack-water recreation—but may also include complex goods.

We propose a general conceptual model for the valuation of natural resource service flows. The model focuses on total value and, at the outset, would seem to represent a radical departure from the partial equilibrium, marginal microeconomics commonly applied in benefit-cost analysis. However, the model generates, as a special and limiting case, the traditional results of marginal analysis; and, in so doing, defines the appropriate role for marginal analysis in the benefit-cost framework.

The Total Value of Changes in the Level of Provision of a Service

Consider an individual who currently enjoys some specified level, Q, a service. In addition, he enjoys a given quantity of the Hicksian "all other goods" numeraire, Y, which for convenience is called income. Thus, his level of utility is always dependent upon his income and the quantity of the particular service upon which we focus, i.e.,

David S. Brookshire is an assistant professor of economics at the University of Wyoming; Alan Randall is a professor of agricultural economics at the University of Kentucky; and John R. Stoll is an assistant professor of agricultural economics at Texas A&M University.

This paper (79-01-117) is published with the approval of the Director, Kentucky Agricultural Experiment Station. Support from the U.S. Fish and Wildlife Service and the Resource and Environmental Economics Laboratory, University of Wyoming, is gratefully acknowledged.

Many individuals associated with the Department of Agricultural Economics at the University of Kentucky and the Resource and Environmental Economics Laboratory at the University of Wyoming assisted in various phases of the empirical study; in particular, the contribution of Larry L. Eubanks is acknowledged. David L. Debertin and an anonymous reviewer provided helpful suggestions.

Copyright 1980 American Agricultural Economics Association

$$(1) \qquad U = U(Q,Y).$$

The individual is thus at the origin (figure 1), which defines his level of welfare in the "without project" situation. Examine the axes. To the right of the origin, the level of provision of Q to the individual increases; to the left of the origin, it decreases. From the origin, a movement up the income axis indicates a decrease in income, while a movement down the vertical axis indicates an increase in income. The total value (TV) curve, or bid curve (Bradford), is of positive slope, given that the service is a commodity and the individual is not satiated in the range under consideration. For decreases in Q, the TV curve lies in the southwest quadrant; for increases in Q, it lies in the northeast quadrant. If it is possible to define the quantity of the service in unidimensional, cardinal terms, the assumption of diminishing rates of commodity substitution is sufficient to ensure the curvature shown. Alternatively, if "quantity" is multidimensional, or if it cannot be defined accurately in cardinal terms, no a priori assumption can be made concerning the curvature of the TV curve (Bradford).

The TV curve is an indifference curve, passing through the individual's initial state. That is,

$$(2) \quad U(Q,Y) = U(Q^-, Y^+) = U(Q^+, Y^-).$$

Starting at the origin, $Y^0 - Y^-$ is the individual's willingness to pay (WTP) to obtain an increment in the level of provision of the service from Q^0 to Q^+. Willingness to accept (WTA), i.e., $Y^+ - Y^0$, is the amount of money

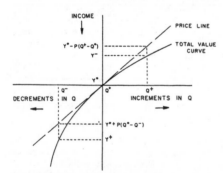

which would induce the individual to accept voluntarily a decrease in the level of provision of the service from Q^0 to Q^-. Thus, WTP is the total value to the individual of an increment from Q^0 to Q^+; WTA is the total value to the individual of a decrement from Q^0 to Q^-. Restating equation (2),

$$(3) \quad U(Q^0, Y^0) = U(Q^-, Y^0 + WTA)$$
$$= U(Q^+, Y^0 - WTP).$$

WTA and WTP bear the following relationship to the traditional market indicators of value. If $Q^+ - Q^0$ is a one-unit increment in Q, WTP is equal to the buyer's best offer for that increment. If $Q^0 - Q^-$ is a one-unit decrement, WTA is equal to the seller's reservation price for that decrement. If a market existed in which the individual could purchase the increment $Q^+ - Q^0$ for some amount less than his WTP, he would proceed with the purchase and enjoy a gain in trade. Likewise, if a market existed in which he could sell the decrement $Q^0 - Q^-$ for some amount more than WTA, he would proceed with the sale and again enjoy a gain from the transaction. If an increment would cost the individual more than his WTP, and a decrement would net the individual less than his WTA, he would eschew all trade in Q and remain at his initial situation.

WTP, WTA, and Consumer's Surplus

Following Mishan (1971, 1976), we argue that consumer's surplus is the appropriate measure of value in benefit-cost analysis; that consumer's surplus is correctly defined by the Hicksian measures, rather than the Marshallian measure; and that, unless a project or program is proposed primarily for the purpose of redistribution, the potential Pareto-improvement is the proper criterion for benefit-cost analysis and, therefore, Hicksian compensating measures are the proper measures of value. However, depending on the applied benefit-cost problem at hand, available value data may be in the form of market prices, Marshallian consumer's surplus, Hicksian compensating measures of consumer's surplus, WTP, or WTA. Our purposes in this section are to develop the relationships between these measures; to show that, in any particular benefit-cost situation, the proper measure of value can be identified on the basis of theoretical considerations; and to show that empirical estimates of the theoretically correct measure of value

Figure 1.   The total value curve for increments and decrements in the level of provision of a service, Q, for an individual who initially enjoys the level Q^0 and the income Y^0

often can be rigorously derived from estimates of other more readily available value measures.

Hicks showed that there are four measures of consumer's surplus, none of which is conceptually identical to the Marshallian measure. These are equivalent surplus, equivalent variation, compensating surplus, and compensating variation. The surpluses differ from the variations in that the latter are calculated after the consumer has made optimizing adjustments in his consumption set, while the former do not permit such adjustments. In general, the variations should be used when such optimizing adjustments are possible. However, benefit-cost analysts often encounter situations where optimizing adjustments are prohibited: once project or program specifications have been determined, the individual must take these as given. Thus there will be circumstances in which the Hicksian surpluses are appropriate.

The difference between the Hicksian compensating and equivalent measures of consumer's surplus is considerably more significant. The equivalent measure is defined as the amount of compensation, paid or received, which would bring the consumer to his subsequent welfare level if the change did not take place. The compensating measure is defined as the amount of compensation, paid or received, which would keep the consumer at his initial welfare level if the change did take place.

The Hicksian compensating and equivalent measures of consumer's surplus are both measures of the welfare impacts of changes, but they differ with respect to the reference level of welfare. The compensating measure, by using the initial welfare level as the reference level, measures the welfare impact of changes as if the individual had a right to his initial level of welfare (that is, as if he had the choice of keeping what he has or voluntarily trading for changes). The equivalent measure, by using the subsequent welfare level as the reference level, treats the individual as if he had only a right to his subsequent level of welfare (that is, as if he must accept his subsequent situation, or seek to trade his way back to his initial situation). Clearly, Hicksian compensating measures are consistent with the potential Pareto-improvement criterion, while Hicksian equivalent measures are not.

To clarify the relationship between Hicksian compensating and equivalent measures of value, *WTA* and *WTP*, and the total value

curve introduced in figure 1, consider the following example. The benefit-cost analyst is evaluating a proposed project which would, among other things, divert a specified area of wildlife habitat to some alternative use, effectively destroying its usefulness as habitat. The benefit-cost analyst needs to know, among other things, the value of the losses which would be suffered by an individual who currently enjoys the wildlife amenities provided by that habitat. In the "without project" situation, the individual has the utility level $U(Q^0, Y^0)$. To keep the example simple, assume that this individual gains no benefits from the project. Thus his "with project" utility level would be $U(Q^-, Y^0)$. The level of Q, either the "without project" level Q^0 or the "with project" level Q^-, is predetermined so that optimizing adjustments are impossible.

What is the welfare impact of the proposed change on this individual? One could determine his *WTA* to accept the proposed change. Let us call this $WTA^C_{Q^0,Y^0;Q^0,Y^0;Q^-}$. The superscript C indicates that this is a Hicksian compensating measure of value, the first subscript pair, Q^0, Y^0, indicates that the individual's reference level of welfare (or his presumed right) is Q^0, Y^0. The second subscript pair indicates that Q^0, Y^0 is also his initial welfare level. The third subscript, Q^-, indicates the level of provision of wildlife-related services the individual would enjoy after he has accepted the compensation and the change in habitat-related services; if it turned out that he were compensated with an amount exactly equal to his *WTA*, his after compensation income would equal $Y^0 + WTA^C$. This measure of *WTA* for a reduction in the quantity of wildlife-related amenities from Q^0 to Q^-, which we shall denote by the abbreviated notation WTA^C, was derived from a total value curve passing through the individual's initial state at Q^0, Y^0 (fig. 2).

However, there is another value measure sometimes used to estimate the individual wildlife amenity user's loss: the amount of money he would be willing to pay to avoid a reduction in the provision of wildlife amenities. What kind of value measure is *WTP* to avoid a less preferred situation? It assumes the individual must accept the less preferred situation, or pay to avoid it. Thus, the reference level of welfare is not the initial situation, but the proposed (or subsequent, in Hicksian terminology) welfare level. So, this second measure of the individual's welfare loss can be

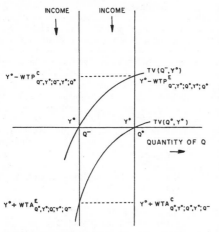

Figure 2.   The relationships between *WTP* and *WTA*, and Hicksian compensating and equivalent measures of consumer's surplus

denoted $WTP^E_{Q^-,Y^0;Q^0,Y^0;Q^0}$. The superscript indicates that it is a Hicksian equivalent measure of value. The first subscript pair indicates that the reference level of welfare (or, if you will, the individual's presumed right) is taken to be Q^-, Y^0. The second subscript pair indicates that the individual's initial state is Q^0, Y^0. The third subscript indicates that, after the individual has paid, he will be permitted to enjoy the Q^0 level of amenities; if he pays exactly his *WTP*, his final income will be $Y^0 - WTP^E$.

Notice that the initial welfare level is different from the reference welfare level. That is the distinguishing feature of Hicksian equivalent measures. Compensating measures, on the other hand, assume that the initial situation is the reference welfare level. WTP^E cannot be found using a total value curve passing through the individual's initial state. It can only be found using another total value curve, which passes through the individual's reference level of welfare (fig. 2).

At this point, it occurs to us that the pair of total value curves shown in figure 2 may also be used to estimate the value to the same individual of a different project: a project which would increase the level of provision of wildlife-related amenities from an initial level Q^- to a "with project" level Q^0. For evaluating this project, the individual's initial situa-

tion is Q^-, Y^0. His willingness to pay for the increment in wildlife-related amenities the project would provide is $WTP^C_{Q^-,Y^0;Q^-,Y^0;Q^0}$. It is a compensating measure, since the reference level of welfare is the same as the individual's initial welfare level. A *WTA* measure can also be defined: $WTA^E_{Q^0,Y^0;Q^0;Y^0,Q^-}$. This is the individual's willingness to accept compensation in lieu of a promised increment in wildlife-related amenities from Q^- to Q^0. It is an equivalent measure, since the reference level of welfare is not the same as the individual's initial welfare level. It cannot be estimated from the total value curve passing through the individual's initial welfare level, Q^-, Y^0, but must be estimated from a new total value curve passing through the individual's reference welfare level, Q^0, Y^0.

The foregoing example makes a number of points. The Hicksian compensating measures of value of alternative levels of provision of a good, service, or amenity can be determined from a single total value curve, while equivalent measures of value must be estimated using a series of different total value curves, one passing through each of the possible levels of provision under consideration. When comparing two alternative levels of provision of a good (as in fig. 2), there are four relevant Hicksian value measures: WTP^C to obtain the preferred level; WTP^E to avoid the less preferred level; WTA^C to accept the less preferred level; and WTA^E to forego a promised increment to the preferred level. There is a compensating and equivalent version of *WTP*, as there is of *WTA*. Figure 2 suggests that, when comparing any pair of alternative levels of provision of a good, service, or amenity, WTP^C is equal in value to WTP^E, while WTA^C is equal in value to WTA^E.

The Relative Magnitudes of the Compensating and Equivalent Measures of Consumer's Surplus

The concept of consumer's surplus is most commonly used, as in Currie, Murphy, and Schmitz, to analyze the welfare impacts of price changes. It generally is concluded that (in absolute value terms) for price increases, $EV \leq M \leq CV$ and, for price decreases, $CV \leq M \leq EV$ (where CV is compensating variation, EV is equivalent variation, and M is Marshallian consumer's surplus). Willig rigorously derived empirically operational bounds on the magnitude of the differences between compensating and equivalent variation measures of the welfare impact of price changes.

In benefit-cost analysis, however, the immediate concern is the evaluation of the welfare impact of changes in the levels of goods, services, or amenities provided, rather than changes in price levels. In such cases, it is convenient to work with the terms *WTP* and *WTA* (thus rendering the absolute value terminology unnecessary). A general rule can be stated: $WTP \leq M \leq WTA$ (Randall and Stoll). Returning to the specific situation of the example used in figure 2,

(4) $WTP^E = WTP^C \leq WTA^C = WTA^E$.

Two questions remain: (*a*) under what conditions are *WTP* and *WTA* equal, and (*b*) when $WTP < WTA$, can bounds on the difference be defined rigorously? The findings of Randall and Stoll, building on the work of Willig, may be summarized.

(*a*) For goods which are perfectly divisible and exchanged at zero transactions costs in infinitely large markets, *WTP* and *WTA* are equal and are equal to the price multiplied by the quantity change. In figure 1, the total value curve may be replaced with the price line. When the good whose quantity is subject to change has the characteristics of currency, and the proposed change is thus conceptually equivalent to a lump sum tax, *WTA* to permit the tax is equal to *WTP* to avoid the tax, and both are equal to the tax itself. The general total value model thus generates the primary result of partial equilibrium microeconomics (i.e., price equals unit value at the margin), as a special and limiting case. Market price is the appropriate measure of unit value lost or gained, when the good under consideration is perfectly divisible and may be exchanged at zero transactions costs in infinitely large markets.

(*b*) For goods which are indivisible or lumpy and can be held only in quantities Q^- and Q^0 (fig. 2), *WTP* is less than *WTA* (except when the income effect is zero). The difference between *WTA* and *WTP* may be approximated by $WTA - WTP = \dfrac{\zeta M^2}{Y}$,

where

$\zeta = \dfrac{\partial P(Q,Y)}{\partial Y} \dfrac{Y}{P(Q,Y)}$, i.e., the price flexibility of income for the good, Q. This approximate bound on the difference between *WTA* and *WTP* is valid when ζ is constant and $\zeta M/2Y$ is relatively small (say, equal to or less

than .05). Randall and Stoll also provide more rigorous bounds, which are appropriate when ζ is not constant and when $\zeta M/2Y$ is relatively large.

For divisible goods traded in costly markets (i.e., those where transactions costs are positive) the difference between *WTA* and *WTP* will be greater than zero, but no greater than the bounds discussed immediately above. The result of case (*a*) is predicated upon costless post-change adjustments in holdings, while that of case (*b*) is predicated upon the impossibility of post-change adjustments. Prohibitive transactions costs and indivisibility are both sufficient to preclude such adjustments. Thus, the difference between *WTP* and *WTA* in the positive transactions costs situation will never exceed the difference found in the case of indivisibility.

Annual User Values for Wildlife-Related Amenities

Consider a hunter who obtains utility from the right to hunt elk. This right is customarily granted by state agencies, in exchange for a license fee, and subject to restrictions upon hunting season, the number and type of elk taken and, often, on the region in which hunting takes place. The hunter derives utility from the environment in which he hunts; the exercise of hunting skills; the encounter with elk; and, perhaps, the taking of an elk. Frequency of encounter and probability of taking an elk vary with elk population. Enjoyment of the environment and the opportunity to exercise hunting skills may vary with the location of the hunt and, in addition, the hunter may perceive these things to be related to elk populations.

The elk is a fugitive resource which, while living, is unowned, and which may be converted to an exclusive good only at the successful completion of the hunt. Enjoyment of the environment, the opportunity to develop and display hunting skills, and the encounter with elk are all collective goods which are nonrival in consumption until the hunter population becomes so large that congestion reduces the utility of individual hunters.

The General Value Model for Elk-Hunting Amenities

Consider three levels of provision of the amenity, the annual right to hunt elk: N, nonparticipation in elk hunting; Q', participation with frequency of encounter, Q'; and Q'', participation with frequency of encounter, Q''.[1] It is conceivable that the hunter could find himself in any one of three initial situations: N, Y^0; Q', Y^0; or Q'', Y^0. Given these three initial situations, a family of three total value curves may be defined (fig. 3):

$$(5')\quad U(N,Y^0) = U(Q',Y^{-b}) = u(Q'',Y^{-c}),$$

$$(5'')\quad U(Q',Y^0) = U(N,Y^{+a}) = U(Q'',Y^{-a}),$$

$$(5''')\quad U(Q'',Y^0) = U(Q',Y^{+b}) = U(N,Y^{+c}),$$

where $N < Q' < Q''$ and $Y^{-c} < Y^{-b} < Y^{-a} < Y^0$ $< Y^{+a} < Y^{+b} < Y^{+c}$. Consider the income axis: $Y^0 - Y^{-a}$, $Y^0 - Y^{-b}$, and $Y^0 - Y^{-c}$ are measures of *WTP*, while $Y^{+a} - Y^0$, $Y^{+b} - Y^0$, and $Y^{+c} - Y^0$ are measures of *WTA*.

This family of total value curves permits estimation of the annual value of elk-hunting amenities using data provided in a wide variety of forms. For example, curve $(5')$ may be fitted, using data on *WTP* for an elk-hunting license when the hunter expects frequency of encounter Q' and Q''. Curve $(5'')$ permits the analysis of data indicating WTP^C for an increment in frequency of encounter from Q' to Q'', and WTA^C of a hunter currently enjoying participation with frequency of encounter Q' to accept nonparticipation. Curve $(5''')$ permits analysis of data for WTA^C of a hunter currently enjoying participation with frequency of encounter Q'' for a reduction in elk populations such as that his frequency would become Q', and WTA^C to accept nonparticipation in hunting. Empirical estimates of Hicksian equivalent value measures also may be used to derive this family of curves. Equivalent measures simply assume that the reference level of welfare (or presumed right) is different from the initial situation. For example, $Y^0 - Y^{-c}$ is equal to the WTP^E of a hunter currently enjoying Q'', Y^0 to avoid nonparticipation in hunting.

Data Collection

In 1977 and 1978, an extensive pilot study was conducted in the vicinity of Laramie, Wyoming, for the purposes of (*a*) testing the general value model in application and (*b*) field testing a variety of contingent valuation methods for collecting value data for a considerable variety of wildlife-related amenities. The two purposes are logically distinguishable. That is, the general valuation model provides a conceptual framework for organization of empirical data obtained using any acceptable technique. The terms, *WTP* and *WTA*, do not per se imply data collection via contingent valuation. As a part of this study, 108 licensed elk hunters were interviewed.[2]

The "good" to be valued was the right to hunt elk, for one annual season, at various levels of hunting amenities. The amenities related to elk hunting were quantified in two dimensions: the terrain in which elk hunting takes place (A. foothills; B. plains; C. mountains); and the population of elk in the hunt area, which was indicated by the frequency of encounter with elk (0.1, 1, 5, or 10 elk encountered per day of hunting). These dimensions are sufficient to permit variation in the contributions of hunting environment and elk

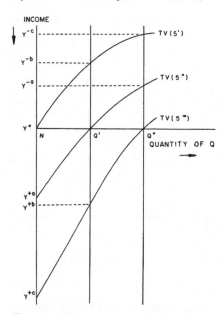

Figure 3. Total value curves for wildlife-related amenities, Q

---

[1] Compare our approach with that of Cocheba and Langford. They distinguished between an exclusive good aspect (game taken) and a collective good aspect (missed shots) of the hunting experience. We emphasize the collective good aspect, which we quantify in terms of "frequency of encounter" with elk.

[2] The pilot study was supported by the U.S. Fish and Wildlife Service (under Grant 14-16-0009-002), the Kentucky Agricultural Experiment Station and the Resource and Environmental Economics Laboratory of the University of Wyoming.

Amer. J. Agr. Econ.

population levels to the various sources of utility which the individual derives from the elk hunting experience.

The raw value data were collected using the iterative bidding technique (Randall, Ives, Eastman; Brookshire, Ives, Schulze; Randall et al.). Each iterative bidding format established a contingent market (a scenario which includes a complete description of the good to be "traded," the institutional structure within which "trade" takes place, and the subject's assumed initial situation and reference level of welfare), posited a starting level of total value, and conducted an iterative bidding process until the subject's actual total value (i.e., maximum WTP, or minimum WTA) was identified. Formats were designed to obtain estimates of WTP^C for increments in the quality of wildlife-related amenities, WTP^E to avoid decrements, and WTA^C to permit decrements.

Each survey schedule included two iterative bidding formats, a record of the subject's hunting activity, various questions designed to elicit information on the subject's attitudes relevant to hunting, and a confidential "feedback" section in which the subject could express his reaction to the interview and the contingent valuation exercise.

Analysis and Results

Previous studies (e.g., Brookshire, Ives, Schulze) have identified several sources of potential bias in value data collected with iterative bidding methods. Thus, preliminary analysis of the data collected in this case study included statistical tests for bias. The hypotheses that final value data were influenced by the initial bids posited to respondents, or by the particular interviewer who collected the data, were rejected at the .05 level of significance. The hypothesis that final bids (i.e., estimates of TV) were influenced by the choice of bidding vehicle (a component of the bidding scenario) was rejected at the 0.1 level of significance. Nevertheless, it was observed that refusal to bid, with WTP formats, occurred in six of fifty cases with a "utility bill" vehicle, but in none of fifty-eight cases with a "hunting license fee" vehicle. Negative comments in the "feedback" section occurred more frequently with the "utility bill" vehicle.[3]

---

[3] "Utility bill" vehicles were used because the sponsor expressed an interest in attempting to estimate directly preferences with respect to the trade-off between energy production and wildlife habitat in certain western states.

Although three terrains were included in the research design, no hunter in the sample typically hunted in terrain B. Thus, since the survey format collected a complete set of information for each subject's "typical" terrain and encounter frequency but only a subset of the possible information for "atypical" terrains, the data set for terrain B was incomplete. Therefore, further analyses consider frequency of encounter 0.1, 1, 5, and 10, and terrain A and C.

Using WTP^E data provided by fifty-eight subjects working with the "hunting license fee" bidding vehicle, the mean bid curve (or, mean total value curve) corresponding to curve 5' in figure 3 was estimated, using two functional forms:

$$(6) \quad Meanbid = \beta_0 + \beta_1 \, Enc + \beta_2 \, Enc^2 + \beta_3 \, Environ + \epsilon, \text{ and}$$

$$(7) \quad \ln(Meanbid) = \beta_0 + \beta_1 \ln(Enc) + \beta_2 \, Environ + \epsilon,$$

where Meanbid is the mean of fifty-eight respondents' total value bids for each of the eight Enc/Environ combinations, in dollars per year; Enc is the frequency of encounters with elk on a typical day of hunting (0.1, 1, 5, 10), and Environ is a qualitative variable taking the value 1 for terrain C and the value 0 for terrain A.

The results of estimation are shown in table 1 and figure 4. Coefficients for Enc and ln(Enc) [equations (6) and (7)] and Enc^2 [equation (6)] were statistically significant at the .01 and .10 levels, respectively, while the coefficients for Environ were insignificant. The F-statistics led to rejection of the hypothesis that all parameters are equal to zero at the .01 level of significance. To determine the aggregate sample bid for each Enc/Environ combination, Meanbid may be multiplied by the sample size (i.e., 58). To estimate the aggregate bid for the population, Meanbid may be multiplied by population size.

The "income effect". The price flexibility of income for the good, ζ, was identified as the key variable permitting rigorous calculation of the empirical value of WTA from WTP data or vice-versa (i.e., permitting correction for the "income effect"). To calculate ζ for elk-hunting amenities, equation (8) was estimated,

$$(8) \quad \ln(Bid) = \beta_0 + \beta_1 \ln(Enc) + \beta_2 \ln(Income) + \beta_3 \, Environ + \epsilon,$$

where Bid is the mean of the total value bids of respondents in each income category for each

Table 1. Estimated Bid Equations

Equation	Dependent Variable	Intercept	ENC	ENC²	ln(ENC)	ENVIRON	ln (INCOME)	R̄² / N / F
(6)	Meanbid for each ENC/ENVIRON combination.	63.251** (2.421)	8.750** (1.268)	−.284* (.112)		−3.550 (2.505)		.98 / 8ᵃ / 117.21
(7)	ln(Meanbid) for each ENC/ENVIRON combination	4.395** (.059)			.142** (.023)	−.033 (.082)		.83 / 8ᵃ / 18.71
(8)	ln(Bid) for each ENC/ENVIRON combination, for each income group	1.189 (1.125)			.188** (.047)	.107 (.167)	.306** (.115)	.40 / 32ᵇ / 7.79
	Principal diagonal (X'X)⁻¹	5.652			.010	.125	.060	MSE = .224
(9)	ln(Indbid) for each ENC/ENVIRON combination	2.916** (1.020)			.253** (.046)	.008 (.170)	.082 (.104)	.09 / 290ᶜ / 10.12
	Principal diagonal (X'X)⁻¹	.577			.001	.016	.006	MSE = 1.80

Note: * indicates significant at the .1 level of confidence; ** is significant at the .01 level of confidence.
ᵃ Eight combinations of 4 levels of ENC, and 2 ENVIRONs.
ᵇ Thirty-two combinations of 4 levels of ENC, 2 ENVIRONs, and 4 income groups.
ᶜ Five bids (4 levels of ENC at typical ENVIRON, plus 1 level of ENC at atypical ENVIRON) for 58 respondents.

Enc/Environ combination, and *Income* is mean income ($/year) for each income category.

In estimating equation (8), the sample was divided into these four income categories:

tional variables (sex of subject, subject did/did not kill an elk last season, and two variables indicating the respondent's degree of acceptance of the contingent valuation procedure) a marked increase in R^2 was noted, while the

Income Category	Income Range ($/year)	Number of Observations	Mean Income ($/year)
1	Income ≤ 10,000	12	5,592
2	10,001 ≤ Income ≤ 18,000	17	14,500
3	18,001 ≤ Income ≤ 26,000	15	21,433
4	26,001 ≤ Income	14	41,508

Because the number of observations in each category is similar, this procedure should not introduce serious heteroskedasticity problems. Coefficients for ln(*Enc*) and ln(*Income*) were highly significant, while the coefficient for *Environ* was again insignificant (table 1). Note that, when an equation such as (8) is estimated, the coefficient for ln(*Income*) is an estimate of ζ. The adjusted R^2 was 0.4. Again, the *F*-statistic for the entire equation was significant at the .01 level. When the model of equation (8) was re-estimated with four addi-

coefficient for *Enc* and *Income* changed only slightly, in each case becoming a little larger and more significant statistically.[4]

---

[4] The estimated equation was

$$\ln(Bid) = 1.563 + .197 \ln(Enc) + .369 \ln(Income) + .727\, Kill$$
$$ (.026) (.096) (.296)$$
$$- 1.017\, Sex - .697\, Acc\ 1 - 3.096\, Acc\ 2,$$
$$ (.654) (.349) (.383)$$
$$\bar{R}^2 = .83,\ N = 32,\ F = 27.10$$

where *Kill* is probability that a randomly selected member of the income category killed an elk in the previous hunting season; *Sex* is probability . . . is a female; *Acc* 1 is probability . . . thought, in

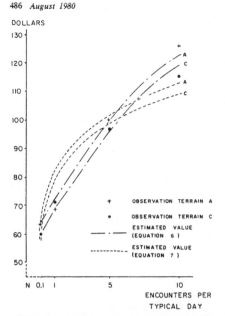

DOLLARS

OBSERVATION   TERRAIN A

OBSERVATION   TERRAIN C

ESTIMATED   VALUE
(EQUATION 6)

ESTIMATED   VALUE
(EQUATION 7)

ENCOUNTERS PER
TYPICAL DAY

Figure 4.   Mean (per hunter) annual value of the right to hunt elk, Laramie, Wyoming, 1977–78, as influenced by hunting environment and frequency of encounter with elk

An additional equation (9), which differed from (8) only in that the dependent variable was *Indbid* (i.e., individual bid for each *Encl Environ* combination) was also estimated. For equation (9), the R^2 was only .09 and the coefficient for ln(*Income*) was insignificant. The procedure of using mean bids for income groups as the dependent variable [equation (8)] results in a substantial reduction in mean square error, MSE [.224 for equation (8), as opposed to 1.80 for equation (9)], at the expense of increased magnitudes of the principle diagonal elements of the inverse transpose matrix (table 1).

Comparison of results obtained with WTP^C, WTP^E and WTA^C formats. The results of valuation exercises for the same good using WTP^C, WTP^E, and WTA^C formats may be dif-

ferent for two reasons: (*a*) as a result of "income effects," the different measures of consumer's surplus are empirically different, and (*b*) subjects may react differently to different contingent market formats. Subjects may take offense at WTP^E formats, which face the subject with an inferior reference level of welfare. Subjects who are not accustomed to being offered compensation for losses in natural and environmental amenities may find WTA^C formats incredible and unrealistic, or they could interpret WTA^C formats as providing an opportunity for making strong statements about a set of rights which seems fairer than the rights which actually exist ("If the choice were mine, I would not let them decimate elk populations for anything!"). Because WTP^C formats are based on correspondence between the subject's initial and reference welfare levels without relying on the notion of compensation payments, there seems little reason to expect WTP^C formats to encounter the resistance and difficulties which may confront WTP^E and WTA^C formats.

The bounds on the difference between *WTA* and *WTP* (Randall and Stoll) permit the precise calculation of the differences in results which may be attributed to income effects. Once these differences are accounted for, any remaining differences in results must be attributable to differential efficacy of WTP^C, WTP^E, and WTA^C formats as data collection devices.

From the raw data set used to estimate equations (6)–(9), estimates of WTP^C for increments in elk populations such that frequency of encounter would increase from 0.1 to 1, 1 to 5, and 5 to 10, and WTA^C for decrements across the same ranges, were derived, using

the formula, $WTA - WTP = \frac{\zeta M^2}{Y}$. In order to

test the following two hypotheses:

H_1: observed WTP^E = derived WTP^C, and
H_2: observed WTA^C = derived WTA^C,

observations of WTP^E and WTA^C for decrements across these three ranges were obtained using subsamples and iterative bidding formats which were different from those which provided the data used to estimate derived WTP^C and WTA^C.

The results of the tests of H_1 and H_2 are presented in tables 2 and 3, respectively.[5] Ob-

retrospect, that the iterative bidding procedure was a "waste of time" and "hard to take seriously"; and *Acc* 2 is probability . . . thought, in retrospect, that his own response to the iterative bidding procedure was "a poor guide for game management policy." The coefficient for each of these additional variables had the expected sign. *Acc* 1 and *Acc* 2 enable identification of the proportion, in each income category, of individuals whose acceptance of the contingent valuation procedure was poor.

[5] Examination of tables 2 and 3 indicates that derived WTP^C and derived WTA^C (both of which were derived from the same data

Table 2. Observed WTP^E and Derived WTP^C

Segment (# of Encounters)		WTP^E (Observed)	WTP^C (Derived)	Not Significantly Different at[a]
0.1,1	Mean ($)	43.64	12.74	
	N	11	55	
	S	42.55	54.95	.05
	$S_{\bar{x}}$	12.83	7.41	
1,5	Mean ($)	54.06	33.48	
	N	16	58	
	S	69.05	75.63	.20
	$S_{\bar{x}}$	17.26	9.93	
5,10	Mean ($)	32.00	19.47	
	N	15	58	
	S	21.28	58.33	.40
	$S_{\bar{x}}$	5.49	7.66	

Note: N is the number of observations, S is the standard deviation, and $S_{\bar{x}}$ is the standard error of the mean.

[a] The hypothesis test was $H_0: \mu_1 = \mu_2$; $H_1: \mu_1 \neq \mu_2$. If the calculated $|t^*|$ was greater than the critical value $t_{n_1+n_2-2}, 1 - \frac{\alpha}{2}$, H_0 was rejected. Thus, by failing to reject H_0, we infer that the two means are not significantly different at the chosen level of confidence.

served WTP^E was not significantly different from derived WTP^C. However, observed WTA^C was significantly different from, and up to an order of magnitude greater than, derived WTA^C. In addition, 54% of the subjects confronted with formats to obtain observed WTA^C refused to accept any finite amount of compensation, and were eliminated from the analysis to test H_2.

---

set) are of similar empirical magnitude. As Willig and Randall and Stoll demonstrate, *WTP* and *WTA* are of similar magnitude when the "income effect" is small and the total value of the good represents only a small proportion of the total budget. Where these conditions do not hold, one can expect larger differences between *WTP* and *WTA*.

Conclusions

We have derived the theoretical relationships between various measures of value and shown that, in any particular situation, the proper measure of value can be identified on the basis of theoretical considerations. Of particular importance, to implement the benefit-cost criterion (i.e., the potential Pareto-improvement) estimates of *WTA* for decrements in goods, services, and amenities are required.

While the total value model places no restrictions on the methods by which data may be collected, the iterative bidding method of contingent valuation has been found to be an effective data collection mechanism. Of the

Table 3. Observed and Derived WTA^C

Segment (# of Encounters)		WTA^C (Observed)	WTA^C (Derived)	Significantly Different at[a]
0.1,1	Mean ($)	68.52	12.74	
	N	10	55	
	S	95.08	54.95	.02
	$S_{\bar{x}}$	30.07	7.41	
1,5	Mean ($)	142.60	33.49	
	N	12	58	
	S	142.68	75.63	.01
	$S_{\bar{x}}$	41.19	9.93	
5,10	Mean ($)	207.07	19.48	
	N	9	58	
	S	121.51	58.33	.01
	$S_{\bar{x}}$	40.50	7.66	

Note: N is the number of observations; S is the standard deviation; and $S_{\bar{x}}$ is the standard error of the mean.

[a] The hypothesis test was $H_0: \mu_1 = \mu_2$; $H_1: \mu_1 \neq \mu_2$. If the calculated $|t^*|$ was greater than the critical value $t_{n_1+n_2-2}, 1 - \frac{\alpha}{2}$, H_0 was rejected.

Amer. J. Agr. Econ.

various formats which may be used for iterative bidding, it seems that formats which directly observe WTP are most effective. There are reasons to expect that WTP^C formats usually would be most effective of all because they assume correspondence between the subject's initial welfare level and his reference welfare level, without relying on the notion of compensation payments.

The results of our hypothesis tests suggest that, in contexts where compensation is not customarily paid to those who experience decrements in natural and environmental amenities, iterative bidding formats for the direct observation of WTA^C do not appear to collect reliable value data. In such contexts, it remains possible to estimate WTA^C by collecting data in the form of WTP (preferably, WTP^C) and using the theoretical relationships developed by Randall and Stoll to derive WTA^C.

[Received June 1979; revision accepted December 1979.]

References

Bradford, D. F. "Benefit-cost Analysis and the Demand for Public Goods." *Kyklos* 23(1970):775–91.

Brookshire, D. S., B. Ives, and W. Schulze. "The Valuation of Aesthetic Preferences." *J. Environ. Econ. Manage.* 3(1976):325–46.

Cocheba, D. J., and W. A. Langford. "Wildlife Valuation: The Collective Good Aspect of Hunting." *Land Econ.* 54(1978):490–504.

Currie, J. M., J. A. Murphy, and A. Schmitz. "The Concept of Economic Surplus and Its Use in Economic Analysis." *Econ. J.* 81(1971):741–99.

Hicks, J. R. "The Four Consumer's Surpluses." *Rev. Econ. Stud.* 11(1943):31–41.

Mishan, E. J. *Cost-Benefit Analysis: An Introduction.* New York: Praeger Publishers, 1971.

———. "The Use of Compensating and Equivalent Variations in Cost-Benefit Analysis." *Economica* 43(1976):185–97.

Randall, A., B. C. Ives, and E. Eastman. "Bidding Games for Valuation of Aesthetic Environmental Improvements." *J. Environ. Econ. Manage.* 1(1974):132–49.

Randall, A., O. Grunewald, S. Johnson, R. Ausness, and A. Pagoulatos. "Reclaiming Coal Surface Mines in Central Appalachia: A Case Study of the Benefits and Costs." *Land Econ.* 54(1978):472–89.

Randall, A., and J. Stoll. "Consumer's Surplus in Commodity Space." *Amer. Econ. Review* in press.

Willig, R. D. "Consumer's Surplus without Apology." *Amer. Econ. Rev.* 66(1976):587–97.

Reprinted from
AMERICAN JOURNAL OF AGRICULTURAL ECONOMICS
Vol. 62, No. 3, August 1980

23. Existence Value in a Total Valuation Framework

Alan Randall
John R. Stoll

In the last two decades, the range of resource value concepts recognized by economists has been considerably expanded. Traditionally, it was those values recorded from exchange of resource commodities in the marketplace that were recognized as legitimate measures of economic value. Some time ago, direct demands for in situ resources (eg., recreation sites, and ambient air and water of acceptable quality) were recognized and estimated. Later, as awareness spread of the potential for wholesale modification of natural environments and the accelerated extinction of species, the adequacy of traditional concepts of economic value became a frequent topic of discussion (Weisbrod 1964, Krutilla 1967, Schmalensee 1972, Arrow and Fisher 1974). It was frequently argued that legitimate economic values may be derived from maintaining the option for future use, or from simply knowing that continued existence of the resource in its current state is assured.

While considerable ingenuity and analytical rigor have been devoted to this reconsideration of resource value concepts, the task is not yet complete and some of the inevitable false starts have left a legacy of confusion. Value concepts have proliferated--use value, option price, option value, expected consumer's surplus, quasi-option value, existence value, preservation value, bequest value, etc.--but some of these are overlapping in concept while many are empirically elusive so that validation of estimates is difficult and often incomplete. Thus, confusion in some quarters is matched by skepticism in others.

In this paper, we attempt clarification of the relevant resource valuation concepts. Starting with total value, a categorization of value concepts is developed. Existence value is emphasized and the conditions influencing existence demand, supply, and value, in total and at the margin, are considered. Some estimates of existence value and option price, gleaned from previous empirical research, are presented and briefly discussed. Finally, we draw attention to some aggregation problems which arise in the transition from partial to more encompassing analyses. Our focus is, for the most part, quite general. Nevertheless, some observations on application

Alan Randall is a Professor of agricultural economics at the University of Kentucky. John Stoll is an Assistant Professor of agricultural economics at Texas A&M University. Support by the Electric Power Research Institute for the presentation of this paper is acknowledged.

to visual values are provided, and some of the empirical results concern visual values.

A BASIC CONCEPTUAL FRAMEWORK

Individuals engage in activities because they derive satisfaction from them. In economics a state of satisfaction is described by a utility function in which the activities are arguments within the function. When the arguments are assigned specific values, a level of utility or satisfaction is defined by the function. That is,

$$U = f(Z) \tag{1}$$

where U represents utility or satisfaction and Z is a vector of activities consumed by the household.

The concept of activity is broadly defined, and includes work and other income generating activities, formal educational activities, reading and watching television and movies (which may have an educational or informational component), eating, household maintenance, hobbies, and recreational activities (including sports, physical exercise, hiking, nature study, sightseeing, etc.).

These activities are produced by the household, in a process which combines purchased goods and services, environmental amenities and other public goods, and the household's time and effort. This production process is governed by the household's activity production technology.

A household production function for activities using a natural resource amenity is represented as

$$Z = z(X, Q \mid T) \tag{2}$$

where

Q = a specific natural resource amenity, eg., a scenic vista;
X = a vector of goods and services other than the specific natural resource Q; and
T = the household's production technology.

The household's production technology at any given time is a function of the activities produced during previous time periods. Thus, it may be represented as

$$T_t = h\left[z_{t_0}(X,Q \mid T_{t_0}), ..., z_{t-1}(X,Q \mid T_{t-1}) \right] \tag{3}$$

where

t_0 = the initial time period;
t = the current time period; and
$t-1$ = the time period preceding t.

This formulation explicitly recognizes the development of skill in activity production through conscious acquisition of information and instruction and through the less deliberate process of "learning by doing." Past activity production influences the capacity to achieve satisfaction from current activities. Given the nature of the processes by which activity production technology is acquired, it is immediately clear that T may differ substantially, across households, as well as across time periods in a given household.[1]

Finally, it must be noted that these processes of household activity production are constrained. Clearly, the household has a limited budget and must also allocate a fixed amount of time among alternative activities.

TOTAL VALUE AND ITS COMPONENTS

The total value of Q is determined by the quantity provided (i.e., supply) and the various demands for Q as an input in household production processes. For the individual household, total value is the <u>consumer's surplus</u> from all Q-using activities, where consumer's surplus is defined as the net benefits remaining after all household production costs have been incurred.

To consider the components of total value, we focus on the various kinds of demands for Q. Two major components of value are use value and existence value.

<u>Use Value.</u> In general, any activity produced in a process such as that defined in Equation 2 may generate use values. Activity production may take place on-site (which generates visitor values, on-site use values, recreation values, etc.), but that is not essential. Use value occurs anytime Q is combined with one or more elements of the X vector. Thus, we consider the values generated by reading about Q in a book or magazine, looking at it in photographic representations, for example, to be use values. Clearly, our definition of use includes vicarious consumption.

Several kinds of use values may be defined. The most frequently observed and measured kind is <u>current use value,</u> which is generated by use in the present time period. Use values may also be generated by anticipation of future use. In the absence of risk preferences (positive or negative), the value of future use is <u>expected consumer's surplus</u> (E). The household may be willing to pay for an option for future use, if that would assure availability in the event that future use was demanded. The value of such an option is called <u>option price</u> (OP). There is another concept, <u>option value</u> (OV), defined so that OP = E+OV, where OV is a risk premium which would be paid by risk averse households.[2] There has been considerable controversy as to whether OV may take positive or neative signs (Schmalensee 1972). The problem is that there are two kinds of risk: demand risk, in which a purchased option would prove useless if future demand did not eventuate; and supply risk, in which future availability is not assured unless the option is purchased. In buying an option, one may encounter demand risk as a result of an act taken to avoid supply risk. Only in the case where demand is certain and supply uncertain can we be assured that, for a risk averse household, OV>0 and OP>E (Bishop 1982).

An additional type of use value is termed <u>quasi-option value.</u> It is defined as the value gained by delaying a decision until a future time period when more information may be available (Arrow and Fisher 1974, Conrad 1980). While not confined to such cases, quasi-option value is often invoked in the case of destructible resources: if such resources were destroyed now, the possibility is eliminated that new technologies developed in future times may render them increasingly valuable. Quasi-option value is the value attributable to avoiding such a risk.

<u>Existence Value.</u> It is possible that value may be generated by simply knowing Q exists. Instead of the activity production function (Equation 2),

the production function for pure existence activities is

$$Z = g(Q \mid T). \qquad (4)$$

That is, existence values for Q are generated by Q alone, subject to an activity production technology (T) which permits an understanding and appreciation of Q. No elements of the X vector are involved, in the current time period. However, activities combining Q and X in some previous time periods seem essential to the acquisition of the kinds of T which permit existence activities (Equation 3).

Pure existence value excludes any values which arise from current use or anticipated future use. We defined vicarious consumption, above, as a kind of use. Thus, it seems that all pure existence demands must be altruistically motivated. One can conceive of <u>interpersonal altruism</u> which would generate existence values from knowing Q was available for others to use; <u>intergenerational altruism</u> from knowing Q will be available for future generations; and <u>Q-altruism,</u> in which the household enjoys the feeling that Q itself is benefiting from being undisturbed. These latter two kinds of altruism generate <u>bequest values</u> and <u>intrinsic values,</u> respectively, which are (of course) categories of existence value.

UNIQUENESS AND IRREVERSIBILITY: ARE THEY ESSENTIAL TO THE GENERATION OF OPTION AND EXISTENCE VALUE?

The early literature conveyed the impression that option and existence values were rather specialized phenomena, confined to unique natural objects threatened with irreversible destruction at the hands of humankind. Weisbrod (1964) assigned a key role to irreversibility in his conceptualization of option demand, while Krutilla (1967) argued that irreversibility and uniqueness were both essential to existence value. While these claims seem to have gained considerable acceptance, we believe that option and existence values have much more general application. Our argument will be addressed to existence value, although much of it is obviously adaptable to option value as well.

We conceptualize demand and supply curves for existence as in Figure 23.1. For resource amenities with many close substitutes, existence demand will be weak; for amenities in great supply, marginal existence value will be low; and if the project under evaluation will cause only a small reduction in existence supply, the aggregate loss of existence value will be small. Thus, even commonplace artifacts of human civilization (e.g., drink cans) may have existence value, although the circumstances which would make it large are unlikely. Empirically significant existence values are not confined to natural objects; we believe they occur for human artifacts and cultural manifestations, from historic buildings to grand opera. Nor are existence values confined to "the last few ___ s on earth." We would expect to find positive existence values for local amenities, local subpopulations of flora and fauna, and for local cultural amenities. Opera buffs may place genuine value on knowing that grand opera is performed live in medium-sized cities like Des Moines. Irreversibility is not essential. Although it is true that visibility at the Grand Canyon could be rapidly restored following a decision to eliminate emissions, we have no conceptual difficulties with the Schulze et al. (1981) finding of substantial existence value for good visibility at the canyon. Since it is hard to conceptualize visibility impairment as strictly irreversible, our argument that irreversibility is not a nec-

FIGURE 23.1
Existence Value and Relative Scarcity

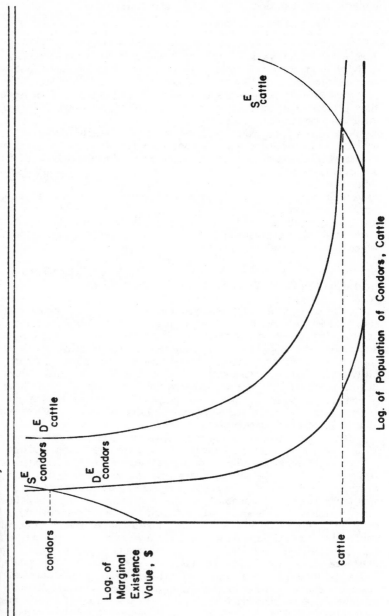

Log. of Population of Condors, Cattle

essary condition for existence value has important implications for the economics of visibility.

Consider the existence values of California condors and ordinary cattle (Figure 23.1). Given the world-wide range of cattle and their significance in many cultures, it may well be that the existence demand for cattle lies to the right of that for condors. However, the existence supply of cattle is enormous while that for condors is very limited. The existence value of the marginal condor surely exceeds that of the marginal cow. The loss of forty condors would eliminate their supply (irreversibly, in this example), while the loss of forty cattle would involve a trivial loss of existence value. However, the existence value of the whole cattle population may well exceed that for condors, and an event which destroyed all cattle would cause a greater existence loss than the destruction of the last remaining condors.

INFORMATION AND THE VOLATILITY OF EXISTENCE VALUE

Existence demands depend on T, which is itself influenced by Xs in previous time periods. Many relevant Xs are in some sense informational. The more one knows about the merits of some Q (and, perhaps, the precariousness of its circumstances), the larger existence value one may place on it.[3] Consider the snail darter. Until its discovery in 1973, its existence demand was zero. Its existence demand rose rapidly as it was accepted as a separate species and listed as endangered, and as knowledge of its existence and its plight spread rapidly among the public. Given its limited supply, it acquired a substantial marginal existence value. More recently, snail darter populations have been found in some streams where they were previously unknown, shifting the (known) supply to the right and, presumably, reducing the existence value of the marginal snail darter.

The general principle underlying this example is that, starting from an initial state of little or no information, small increments to the information base may produce large shifts in existence value, in total or at the margin. Existence value is, therefore, quite volatile in the face of new information. It is important to realize that this volatility has nothing to do with measurement error or bias. It is not that the "estimates" are volatile; the problem is that the perceived reality of existence value is volatile, especially when (relatively) large increments may be forthcoming anytime, to a small initial information base.

ESTIMATES OF OPTION AND EXISTENCE VALUES

There have been several reported attempts to empirically estimate option and existence values for resources. In each case, contingent valuation methods were used in survey situations. The results of four of these studies will be briefly reported here.

Brookshire et al. (1978) estimated option prices for grizzly bear and bighorn sheep hunting in Wyoming. These are the first researchers we know to have attempted to undertake this type of estimation. Their respective estimates were $22 and $30 per year.[4] They also estimated existence values for preserving three alternative local or regional habitats (estimates ranged from $77 to $89 per year) and prevention of 50 percent declines in several species type (estimates were in terms of annual utility bills and ranged from 25 to 47 percent). This study utilized a very small sample and was viewed as a pretest.

The South Platte River Basin in Colorado was used to study values associated with preserving water quality (Greenley, et al. 1981). Option prices associated with future recreational uses were estimated to be $23 per year, existence value to be $42 per year (interpersonal altruism and Q-altruism were $25 per year and intergenerational altruism was $17 per year). Aggregation of these values and other use values resulted in a total value of sixty-one million dollars for maintaining present water quality in a river basin. 57 percent of this value estimate was attributable to current recreational users.

Schulze et al. (1981) interviewed residents of four major metropolitan areas (Albuquerque, Chicago, Denver, and Los Angeles) to obtain information for estimating the existence value of clean air in the Grand Canyon. Their estimates ranged from $34.08 to $51.84 across the four cities (including current users of the Grand Canyon). When aggregated for the entire nation, the total value of clean air in the Grand Canyon was estimated to be about six billion dollars. The contribution of current user value to this total value was a very small proportion ("on the order of tens of millions of dollars," p. 12).

The fourth study to estimate option prices and existence values was again conducted by Brookshire et al. (forthcoming). Using a mail survey of Wyoming hunters they again estimated both option prices and existence values for grizzly bear and bighorn sheep hunting. The conditions under which these values were estimated considered variations in the probability of supply and probability of demand, and accounted for whether the individual was a hunter or wildlife observer of these species. Option price estimates range from $10 to $20 and existence values from $7 to $24 on an annual basis.

Clearly, all four studies represent preliminary estimates of option prices and existence values. Yet, they are important because they present evidence that these theoretical categories of value are measurable and generate empirically significant values. In some cases, the amounts involved are large relative to the more traditionally measured current use value.

COMPLEX PROGRAMS AND NON-MARKET VALUES

Customary benefit estimation procedures implicitly treat each project or program as the marginal increment to the existing package of goods, services, and amenities. If a non-marketed good is involved and a shadow-price is placed thereon, it is implicitly treated as the marginal addition to the vector of priced goods. But, in a world where many complex programs are under consideration at any time, each program cannot be the marginal program. In a world with many kinds of non-marketed and unpriced amenities, it makes little sense to value each, one-by-one, as though it were the only addition to the set of priced, or economically valued, goods.

Two recent studies have demonstrated the problems which arise when overly simple methods are used in truly complex situations. Schulze et al. (1981) estimated the annual value to Chicago residents of one particular increment in visibility at the Grand Canyon at $86 for a typical household. Randall et al. (1981) also working with Chicago residents, considered a sequence of air quality programs in which the affected region was incrementally expanded. Starting with the immediate Chicago region, the visibility increment was valued at about $325 per household annually. When the region was expanded to include all of the U.S. east of the Mississippi, the program was valued at about $355. When a visibility improvement program for the Grand Canyon was added, the whole package was valued at about $373. The incremental value of the Grand Canyon program was eighteen dollars, compared to $86 when that program was considered alone.

Majid et al. (forthcoming) considering proposals to add certain designated areas of land to a park system, found that the estimated benefits of proposed parks considered in isolation were much larger than the benefits of the same proposed parks explicitly treated as increments to an existing system of established parks.

These two empirical studies are merely examples of a general problem. Suppose we categorize all goods, services, and amenities into two groups, priced and unpriced. A little reflection is enough to establish that the unpriced category is surprisingly large: consider for example, how many kinds of services are produced within the household or provided by the open-access environment, and therefore unpriced. Now imagine we were to start pricing, or economically valuing, all of the unpriced goods, one-by-one. Before long, all prices (those for priced goods and those for previously unpriced goods now included in the priced category) would start changing. In principle, one could calculate the new vector of prices which would apply after all goods, services, and amenities had been shifted into the priced category. But we can be sure that no current price would be unchanged.

This problem has attracted little research, but will gain more attention as the complexities of programs to augment unpriced goods are recognized. If our argument that option and existence value concepts apply to quite a broad array of goods and amenities is correct, attempts to adequately represent these values in benefit cost analyses would rather quickly encounter this problem.

CONCLUSION

We have identified four categories of use value and three sources of demands for existence. While buoyant existence demand, uniqueness, and the threat of irreversible damage are together sufficient to generate substantial existence values, it is not true that strict uniqueness or irreversibility is necessary. Large existence values may be associated with, for example, visibility at certain scenic locations, even though strict irreversibility is not involved. In the case of scenic values, however, the possibility of irreversible scenic change does nothing to reduce existence value.

Several exploratory studies have estimated option price and existence value, in some cases for visual and scenic resources. In every case, contingent valuation methods were used. These methods are readily applied and are based on sound theory. However, they are sometimes susceptible to various data quality problems, and adequate validation is not always possible. Thus, the state of the empirical art indicates that estimation of option price and existence value is feasible, but validation problems have not yet been completely resolved. As observed in the preceding section, difficulties emerge as one moves from partial analysis of the benefits and costs of individual program components to a more general analysis of the multitude of complex programs being considered by various agencies.

The crucial role of information in generating existence values is recognized, along with its implication that existence values will often be quite volatile in the face of emerging information. It seems clear that the concepts of information and discovery, substitution possibilities, and relative scarcity (rather than strict irreversibility) will eventually make important contributions to a more complete theory of the values attributable to future use and existence.

NOTES

1. Stigler and Becker (1977) have argued that the concept of activity production technology is of great potential fruitfulness in explaining differences in activity choice among households. If, as they claim, T is analytically more tractable than the process of preference formation, an appropriate research strategy would focus on T while essentially ignoring tastes and preferences.

2. OP, E, and OV are all "sure payment" concepts. Building on the literature on the economics of insurance, Graham (1981) has shown that some schemes of contingent payments may generate values greater than the larger of OP and E. This recent, promising contribution may add new terms to the already crowded language of value categories.

3. The informational programs of many "nature lobby" organizations are clearly designed to increase existence value for particular natural amenities.

4. Unless otherwise indicated, dollar values reported here and below are annual values for a typical household.

BIBLIOGRAPHY

Arrow, K.J., and A.C. Fisher. 1974. "Environmental Preservation, Uncertainty, and Irreversibility." Quarterly Journal of Economics 55(2):313-319.

Bishop, R.C. 1982. "Option Value: An Exposition and Extension." Land Economics 58(1):1-15.

Brookshire, D.S., L.S. Eubanks and A. Randall. 1978. "Valuing Wildlife Resources: An Experiment." Transactions of the Forty-Third North American Wildlife and Natural Resources Conference

Brookshire, D.S., L.S. Eubanks and A. Randall. Forthcoming. "Estimating Option Prices and Existence Values for Wildlife Resources." Land Economics.

Conrad, J.M. 1980. "Quasi-Option Value and the Expected Value of Information." Quarterly Journal of Economics 95(2):812-820.

Graham, D.A. 1981. "Cost Benefit Analysis Under Uncertainty." American Economic Review 71(3):715-725.

Greenley, D.A., R.G. Walsh and R.A. Young. 1981. "Option Value: Empirical Evidence from a Case Study of Recreation and Water Quality." Quarterly Journal of Economics 97(4):657-673.

Krutilla, J.V. 1967. "Conservation Reconsidered." American Economic Review 57(4):777-786.

Majid, I., J. Sinden, and A. Randall. Forthcoming. "Benefit Evaluation of Increments to Existing Systems of Public Facilities." Land Economics.

Randall, A., J. Hoehn, and G.S. Tolley. 1981. "The Structure of Contingent Markets: Some Results of a Recent Experiment." Presented at the American Economic Association Annual Meeting, Washington, D.C.

Schmalensee, R. 1972. "Option Demand and Consumer's Surplus: Valuing Price Changes Under Uncertainty." American Economic Review 62(5):813-824.

Schulze, W.D., D.S. Brookshire, and M.A. Thayer. 1981. "National Parks and Beauty: A Test of Existence Values." Paper presented at the American Economic Association Annual Meeting, Washington, D.C.

Stigler, G.J., and S. Becker. 1977. "De gustibus Non Est Disputandum." American Economic Review 67(2):76-90.

Weisrod, B.A. 1964. "Collective-Consumption Goods." Quarterly Journal of Economics 78(3):471-477.

[9]

JOURNAL OF ENVIRONMENTAL ECONOMICS AND MANAGEMENT 14, 226–247 (1987)

A Satisfactory Benefit Cost Indicator from Contingent Valuation[1]

JOHN P. HOEHN

Michigan State University, East Lansing, Michigan 48824-1039

AND

ALAN RANDALL

The Ohio State University, Columbus, Ohio 43210-1099

Received July 5, 1983; revised January 9, 1986

Standard economic concepts are used to develop a model of individual behavior when subject to the constraints of the contingent valuation choice context. The model yields refutable consequences that are consistent with previously reported empirical findings, including some that have been thought to be anomalous. The model is used to show that different contingent valuation formats have predictably different performance characteristics. Notably, the Hicksian compensating measures are satisfactory benefit cost indicators when elicited using any one of several formats identified in the text. Of the formats examined, one form of a policy referendum appears to have the most satisfactory characteristics. Overall, we conclude that contingent valuation is a progressing research program. © 1987 Academic Press, Inc.

The contingent valuation method (CVM) denotes a set of procedures used to generate, through direct questioning, estimates of the Hicksian measures of welfare change [6, 27, 30]. From rather tentative beginnings in Davis [11] and Randall *et al.* [27], there has been a steady increase in the number of CVM applications. Procedures introduced in Randall *et al.* [27] have been refined and alternative procedures have been introduced [2, 14, 22, 26, 32]. Initial linkages to standard economic theory have been explored [6]. Finally, empirical evidence has been accumulated and subjected to a variety of tests. These developments establish the CVM as a research program as characterized by Lakatos [20].

The CVM is one of several alternative valuation approaches. Primary alternatives to the CVM are the weak complementarily (WC) approaches such as the travel cost method and variants of the implicit price (IP) approach discussed by Rosen [29]. The CVM and its alternatives share many conceptual underpinnings and use closely related empirical methods. Overall, the use and development of these approaches may be considered a single research program in nonmarket valuation.

Nevertheless, there is a tendency to treat CVM and the WC–IP approaches as rival research programs, in Lakatos' [20] sense. The notion of rival research programs can, at best, be applied within a limited domain of valuation problems. This domain is characterized by the following conditions: (1) the subject of valuation is an amenity that is weakly complementary to the set of market goods

[1] This research was supported in part by the U.S. Environmental Protection Agency, the Kentucky Agricultural Experiment Station, and Michigan State University. The authors are grateful for insightful comments from Richard Bishop, Gernot Klepper, John R. Stoll, and an anonymous reviewer of a previous draft.

0095-0696/87 $3.00
Copyright © 1987 by Academic Press, Inc.
All rights of reproduction in any form reserved.

and (2) there exists a historical record of market transactions that provide observations on the amenity over the full range of policy interest. Since each of the primary valuation methods may be applied to this domain, the CVM and the WC–IP approaches may be treated as rivals, if one wishes, or as complementary approaches that permit some independent replication of results.

For a second domain set of valuation problems, the WC–IP methods offer no operational alternatives to the CVM. This domain of problems includes cases where (1) markets suitable for WC–IP analysis do not exist;[2] (2) the policy options under consideration lie outside the range of available amenity data; or (3) past market transactions fail to reflect current information regarding environmental quality, substitutes, or hazards. For this domain of valuation problems, CVM has no Lakatosian rival but stands as the only option. To deny its usefulness here, it is necessary to make a case that CVM is strictly unreliable.

However, several types of evidence tend to corroborate the reliability of CVM results. First, CVM results are consistent with preferences revealed by actual choice behavior [37]. Second, numerous studies have shown CVM results to be systematically related to individual demographic characteristics as well as to the availability of substitutes and complements [6, 10, 22, 26]. Third, CVM results are consistent with valuations estimated via other applied methods [7, 16, 19, 37]. Finally, where theory is sufficiently developed to suggest a qualitative relationship between the outcomes of CVM and alternative methods, empirical results exhibit the predicted effect [7].

While the supportive evidence is substantial, several apparent anomalies do occur in empirical work. First, modest but non-trivial proportions of zero valuations for desired commodities show up in most applications with willingness to pay (WTP) formats. Second, unexpectedly large valuations often occur with willingness to accept (WTA) formats. Third, estimates of WTP and WTA may diverge to a greater degree [2, 6, 13, 30] than suggested by the theoretical analyses of Willig [38] and Randall and Stoll [28]. Finally, several studies [9, 26] have found that CVM values are sensitive to changes in the payment rules established in CVM formats.

In the absence of an adequate explanatory theory, these perceived anomalies sustain doubts regarding the performance of CVM. Some critics, borrowing from Samuelson's notion of "false signals" [31, p. 388], argue that strategic behavior obviates reliable value revelation with the CVM. Others argue that the hypothetical aspect of contingent markets may induce respondents to respond carelessly. Both concepts, however, remain incompletely specified and poorly linked to CVM value outcomes. On one hand, empirical evidence appears inconsistent with conventional models of strategic misstatement (e.g., the strong free-rider hypothesis discussed by Smith [34] and the strategic bidding model of Brookshire *et al.* [5]). On the other hand, no adequate empirical tests have been developed for hypothetical effects, perhaps because no consensus has been achieved as to the expected empirical effects. Feenburg and Mills [12] expect the purported hypothetical effects to lead to high levels of pure noise while Bishop and Heberlein [2] expect a systematic understatement of WTP. Further, Feenburg and Mills [12] treat strategic and hypothetical bias as simple antagonists (more of one strictly implies less of the

---

[2] Such cases include, but are not limited to: use values for amenities that are uniformly distributed as opposed to those for which the level of provision varies among sites or neighborhoods; vicarious use values; and existence value.

other) while Mitchell and Carson [22] claim the possibility of simultaneously reducing both.

Disagreements regarding the reliability of the CVM data are not surprising when viewed from the perspective of Lakatos' [20] methodology. Lakatos [20] argues that as research programs develop, anomalies arise. Anomalies are observations that cannot be explained by the existing body of theory and experience. A research program progresses insofar as it develops in ways that systematically explain various anomalies, subsuming them together with results that are considered compatible with the existing research program into a modified program capable of predicting novel consequences that withstand refutation tests. Such favorable progress is by no means assured. If anomalies can be explained only by stratagems that reduce the generality of predictive power of the research program, the program itself may be considered degenerating rather than progressing.

The general objective of this paper is to suggest that CVM is a progressing research program. The paper is organized in four sections. In the first section, standard economic concepts are used to develop a systematic model of CVM respondent behavior. The resulting model links the CVM more firmly to the well-established research program of mainstream microeconomics and provides an explicit framework for the development of refutation tests. In the second section, the behavioral consequences of the model are examined. Importantly, these consequences are consistent with both the regularities and the more puzzling anomalies that have appeared in previous research. The third section considers the a priori adequacy of the CVM when used in benefit cost analysis. It is shown that not all CVM procedures yield reliable benefit cost indicators. However, an important subset of CVM designs is shown to be entirely satisfactory in terms of the conventional benefit cost objective of identifying potential Pareto-improvements. A final section reviews the theoretical results for procedures that may improve the performance of the CVM in estimating policy-related benefits and costs.

INCENTIVES AND PERFORMANCE IN CONTINGENT VALUATION

The essential purpose of CVM is to elicit an ex ante valuation of policy impacts. In a survey or experimental setting, a valuation questionnaire is administered to a sample of individuals who are potentially affected by a change in public policy. The CVM format describes the physical change (e.g., in amenity levels) to be delivered by the proposed policy and defines the contingent market or policy choice mechanism. This market or choice mechanism consists of rules specifying the conditions that would lead to policy implementation and the payment to be exacted from the respondent (or his/her household) in the event of policy implementation. Given the change in amenity levels, the implementation rule and the payment rule, CVM respondents make contingent choices in a carefully structured context. These choices are interpreted as stating or reflecting the respondent's valuation of the change in amenities.

In developing an economic model of CVM respondent behavior, we consider an individual whose utility is positively associated with the amenity level and disposable income. Certainly, an amenity increasing policy would always be desired if costless to the individual. However, it is assumed that the respondent believes that the benefit information generated by CVM will have some influence on the eventual policy decision.[3] Therefore, since citizens can be expected to contribute, in one way or another, toward the costs of policy, the respondent trades off the prospect of an amenity improvement against the prospect of a reduction in disposable income. Overall, the respondent has an incentive (1) to formulate a valuation and (2) to report a valuation to influence the aggregate benefit estimate, and thus the policy decision, in a direction that he/she desires.

The structure of the typical CVM exercise requires the respondent to solve two decision problems: a value formulation problem and a value statement problem. Neither problem is unique to contingent valuation. The value formulation problem arises with any budget-constrained choice. The value statement problem arises in any situation where the individual perceives an opportunity for gain from strategic misstatement of the individually formulated valuation. Such opportunities for misstatement may be absent from competitive markets in private goods, but may be present in some other kinds of "real" markets (e.g., those with few participants and public goods markets that are not incentive-compatible) as well as in some contingent markets. If any rigorous content can be attached to the notion of hypothetical bias, it would be at the stage of value formulation. If strategic behavior were to influence stated values, it would be at the stage of value statement.

The Value Formulation Problem

Given the argument that routine market tradeoffs are based on prospects rather than experience [3, 8], there appears to be little to distinguish, in principle, the contingent valuation context from the valuation problem posed by ordinary markets. In routine market exchange, an individual evaluates alternative market prospects given previous experience and market information. In contingent valuation, an individual formulates a valuation given experience and the information provided by the contingent market.

Nevertheless, elements of the CVM choice context may make the CVM value formulation problem more difficult relative to ordinary market decisions. For instance, the CVM is more likely to be applied to policy alternatives that are unfamiliar to citizens. These are precisely the cases where the dearth of public value information for policy choice is greatest. Additionally, time and other resources devoted to contingent choices may be more limited than in market choice situations. These resource limitations could occur for two reasons. First, research strategy may seek to reduce data collection costs by limiting the time devoted to gathering each set of observations. Second, the respondent may voluntarily choose to limit the resources devoted to value formulation in the CVM context.

The time and resource constraints of the CVM context may introduce two sources of error into the value formulation process. First, information errors may arise as complex policy information is communicated to the respondent by the CVM format. Errors may be left uncorrected due to time constraints on repetition and review. Thus, the time constrained process of communicating complex information may introduce an additional source of uncertainty into the policy scenario as perceived by the respondent. Second, once policy information is assimilated, the

---

[3] This is perhaps the key assumption in the analysis. We argue that this assumption is consistent with a broad range of observed behavior in the domains of collective choice and politics. Those who find our assumption implausible may choose to analyze the implications of a contrary assumption.

process of evaluation—of selecting a bid—may also be cut short by limited time and decision resources.

To determine how a contingent valuation may differ from a valuation elicited under ideal circumstances, we analyze the impact of information errors and the constrained evaluation process. For both the ideal and the contingent choice context, we assume that the respondent is familiar with the initial policy setting and knows his/her initial level of well being, u^0.

Analytically, the initial situation perceived by the respondent is described by $(p, q^0, m) \in R^n$, where p is a vector of market price prospects, q^0 is a vector representing the pre-policy or initial amenity level, and m is initial income. Given the initial set of parameters, (p, q^0, m), the individual enjoys or suffers an initial level of utility $u^0 = v(p, q^0, m)$, where

$$v(p, q, m) = \max_{x} \{ u(x, q) ; px \leqslant m \}, \tag{1}$$

x is a vector of market goods, and $u(\cdot)$ is concave and increasing in x and q.[4]

Under ideal circumstances, a standard CVM compensating format would present a post-policy level of environmental quality, q^1, and elicit the ideal Hicksian compensating (HC) measure defined by

$$\text{HC}(q^0, q^1, u^0) = m - e(p, q^1, u^0), \tag{2}$$

where

$$e(p, q^1, u^0) = \min_{x} \{ px ; u(x, q^1) \geqslant u^0 \} \tag{3}$$

is a point on the expenditure function. With compensation HC and an expenditure bundle $m - \text{HC}$, the individual attains utility level u^0 from the post-policy situation. Specifically,

$$v(p, q^1, m - \text{HC}) = u^0. \tag{4}$$

The ideal compensating measure is free from the effects of communication error and any constraints on the evaluation process.

In a contingent choice context, the compensating measure actually formulated by the respondent, fHC, may be subject to both communication error and time constraints on evaluation. Below, we first consider the effect of the additional uncertainty imposed by the imperfect communication.

To model the impact of communication error, we suppose that imperfect communication causes the individual to view the effect of the policy proposal as a random function[5] of the described impacts, $d^1 = d(q^1)$ with $E[d^1] = q^1$, where E is

---

[4] The analysis could be placed in a fully random environment with p, q^0, and m specified as random variables. However, the qualitative impact of the constraints discussed below would remain unaffected. Therefore, to avoid additional notational complexity, we outline our results with a prepolicy environment described by a single point, $(p, q^0, m) \in R^n$.

[5] Thus, we examine the effect of pure noise in the communication of information. Miscommunication effects are confined to random noise since proper research procedures would seek to eliminate any systematic miscommunication bias.

an individual's subjective expectation operator. Letting x^* be the optimal bundle under the ideal conditions of Eq. (3), $px^* = e(p, q^1, u^0)$. However, with the effect of policy uncertain, the utility obtained from x^* must either remain the same or decrease ($u^0 = u(x^*, q^1) \geqslant E\{u[x^*, d(q^1)]\}$ by the concavity of u).

Because px^* is the minimum expenditure that maintains u^0 in the absence of communication error, expenditure to attain u^0 must either remain the same or increase in the presence of such error. That is,

$$e(p, q^1, u^0; D) \geqslant e(p, q^1, u^0), \tag{5}$$

where D denotes the uncertain case and

$$e(p, q^1, u^0; D) = \min_x \left[px | E\{u[x, d(q^1)]\} \geqslant u^0 \right]. \tag{6}$$

The valuation formulated in the uncertain case is thus

$$\mathrm{fHC}(q^0, q^1; D) = m - e(p, q^1, u^0; D) \leqslant \mathrm{HC}(q^0, q^1, u^0). \tag{7}$$

Therefore, the net result of imperfect communication is to shift the formulated valuation downward from the valuation formulated under ideal circumstances. If HC is in terms of willingness to pay, imperfect information shifts fHC downward in the positive range. If HC is a willingness to accept measure, fHC becomes more negative.

The second process in value formulation is evaluation. As is clear from Eqs. (3) and (6), evaluation (i.e., the process of valuing) involves an optimization process. If time (or, by extension, other resources) allocated to the decision process is constrained, individuals may fail to complete the ideal evaluation described by Eqs. (3) and (6).

The effect of time-constrained evaluation[6] can be analyzed directly in terms of the optimization problem posed in Eqs. (3) and (6). By standard assumptions, there is only one expenditure bundle, say px^*, that minimizes expenditure subject to the utility constraint. An individual faced with the contingent opportunity to acquire an unfamiliar amenity must search out the elements of the "with proposed policy" feasible set and select, at time t, the minimum expenditure bundle from among the identified feasible bundles. Individuals failing to identify px^* will settle for some x^0 that satisfies the constraint but with $px^0 > px^*$. Furthermore, the minimum expenditure bundle will be non-increasing in t—after identifying a bundle px^0 at t, the individual will not select a bundle $px^1 > px^0$ after an elapsed time $t^1 > t$. Thus, a time-constrained search and decision process implies that

$$e(p, q^1, t, u^0) \geqslant e(p, q^1, u^0) \quad \text{and} \quad e(p, q^1, t, u^0; D) \geqslant e(p, q^1, u^0; D), \tag{8}$$

where t denotes a time-constrained search. The valuations formulated in the

[6]A more complex formulation would treat the amount of time or decision resource as endogenous. However, for our purposes, the important point is that decision resources or time are constrained—whether by endogenous choice or by the interview context.

time-constrained search process are

$$\text{fHC}(q^0, q^1, t) = m - e(p, q^1, t, u^0) \leqslant \text{HC}(q^0, q^1, u^0) \tag{9}$$

with ideal or perfect communication and

$$\text{fHC}(q^0, q^1, t, D) = m - e(p, q^1, t, u^0; D) \leqslant \text{HC}(q^0, q^1, u^0) \tag{10}$$

in the case where policy impact is communicated with noise.

The effects of imperfect communication and incomplete optimization on the Hicksian compensating value measure are consistent and mutually reinforcing. With communication noise $d(q^1)$, a time constraint t, compensation fHC $\leqslant$ HC, and an expenditure bundle $m - \text{fHC}$, the individual anticipates a level of post-policy utility, $v(p, q^1, t, m - \text{fHC}; D)$, equal to u^0. Specifically, only if fHC $\leqslant$ HC does

$$v(p, q^1, t, m - \text{fHC}; D) = u^0 \tag{11}$$

when information is imperfectly communicated and decision time is constrained in the process of value formulation.

A further influence often claimed to be present in CVM exercises is reluctance to participate in markets for goods traditionally provided by extra-market institutions. Beliefs about the proper domains of market and non-market institutions may be involved. Where this influence is operative the initial response to a contingent market may be refusal to use it. If this occurred, fHC would be zero for increments and minus infinity for decrements. Upon further consideration—with investment of decision making resources—fHC may increase and approach HC from below. This reluctance effect is therefore mutually reinforcing with the effects summarized in Eq. (11). The finding seems quite robust, then, that fHC $\leqslant$ HC.

If the valuation problem is framed in Hicksian equivalent terms, the relationship between the formulated and ideal measures is a priori less predictable. The ideal Hicksian equivalent (HE) measure is defined as

$$\text{HE}(q^0, q^1, u^1) = m - e(p, q^0, u^1) \tag{12}$$

where

$$u^1 = v(p, q^1, m) = \max_x \{ u(x, q^1); px \leqslant m \} \tag{13}$$

and

$$e(p, q^0, u^1) = \min_x \{ px; u(x, q^0) \geqslant u^1 \}. \tag{14}$$

The quantity $\text{HE}(q^0, q^1, u^1)$ is such that

$$v(p, q^0, m - \text{HE}) = u^1. \tag{15}$$

To formulate the Hicksian equivalent measure of value, the respondent must solve two problems. First, the respondent must anticipate the with-policy level of utility as in Eq. (13). Second, as suggested by Eq. (14), the respondent must discover the minimum expenditure required to attain that utility level at the initial level of environmental quality. In anticipating u^1, imperfect communication and incomplete evaluation would result in identification of some $\tilde{u}^1$ less than the maximum with-policy utility level, u^1. With ideal expenditure minimization but substituting $\tilde{u}^1$ for u^1, the individual would underestimate the minimum expenditure required to attain u^1 at q^0 since $e(p, q^0, \tilde{u}^1) \leqslant e(p, q^0, u^1)$. The individual would therefore formulate a Hicksian equivalent measure, fHE, greater than the ideal measure HE.

However, as in the compensating case, expenditure minimization is likely to be less than ideal when decision resources are constrained. Constrained by limited time, the individual would identify a $p\tilde{x}^0 \geqslant e(p, q^0, \tilde{u}^1)$. The formulated Hicksian equivalent measure is therefore

$$\text{fHE} = m - p\tilde{x}^0. \tag{16}$$

Paying fHE and retaining q^0, the individual would anticipate a level of utility equal to that with the post-policy level of environmental amenities and initial income

$$\tilde{u}^1 = v(p, q^1, t, m; D)$$
$$= v(p, q^0, t, m - \text{fHE}). \tag{17}$$

Given this two-step process, the net effect of imperfect communication and constrained search on the formulated equivalent measures is a priori not predictable. On one hand, the difficulty of anticipating a post-policy level of utility suggests that the individual would overestimate HE. On the other hand, the constrained search for minimum expenditure implies a downward effect on fHE. Without further restrictions, the net effect is ambiguous.

The value formulation process leads to qualitatively different results for the formulated Hicksian compensating and equivalent values. With the compensating measure, the difficulties of value formulation are mutually reinforcing and the formulated compensating measures do not overstate the ideal valuation. In addition, as respondents become more familiar with the proposed policy change, the formulated Hicksian compensating measure, fHC, approaches the ideal Hicksian measure, HC, from below. The formulated equivalent measure is less systematic and either understatement or overstatement is possible.

The Value Statement Problem

Having identified fHC (or fHE) the CVM respondent must now report a stated valuation, sHC (sHE), to the researcher. If the respondent perceives an advantage in misstatement, sHC (sHE) may diverge from fHC (fHE). Certain commonly stated, but perhaps not well-considered models of strategic misstatement suggest that optimizing individuals would pursue policies of extreme misstatement. However, empirical results provide very little evidence that extreme misstatement is widespread [25]. Perhaps the more simplistic models of strategic misstatement are misleading.

The decision context facing the CVM respondent influences the formulated valuation, the optimal stated valuation, and the deviation (if any) between the two. A respondent who likes increments in amenities but dislikes reductions in disposable income seeks to identify an individually optimal sHC (sHE) given fHC (fHE) and the rules governing policy implementation and individual payment.

Below, we consider five alternative configurations of the CVM decision context and examine the incentives for (or against) strategic misstatement. Optimal reporting strategies are independent of whether the value measure is compensating or equivalent. We therefore use the notation fH to denote fHC or fHE and sH to denote sHC or sHE. Since optimal reporting strategies may depend on whether the valuation is expressed as WTP or WTA—whether fH is, respectively, positive or negative—we discuss some of the more interesting results in these latter terms.[7] Proofs of the conclusions derived from models 1 and 2 follow from simple logic. Rigorous proofs to Models 3, 4, and 5 are discussed in the Appendix.

Model 1: A Naive Free-rider Model

The respondent perceives that the following policy decision rules are operative: (1) the change in q will be provided without regard to the outcomes of benefit cost (BC) analysis, and q is nonexclusive so that all have unrestricted access to it, and (2) each respondent pays (or receives) his/her own sH.

Extreme understatement is the optimal strategy. For fH > 0, stated WTP would approach zero. For fH < 0, sH would approach negative infinity (i.e., stated WTA would be indefinitely large).

Model 2: A Naive Overstatement Model

The respondent perceives the following policy decision rules: (1) the change in q will be provided if reported aggregate benefits exceed costs, and (2) no payment would ever be required of (or paid to) the respondent.

Optimizing respondents with fH > 0 would report very large values for WTP with resulting extreme overstatement of benefits. For decrements in q, respondents anticipating losses in utility would formulate fH < 0 and report sH approaching negative infinity (i.e., WTA indefinitely large). They would report large losses in order to forestall the policy change, given that they could not expect to be compensated in the event of change.

These two naive models lead to predictions of extreme misstatement. Model 1 is seldom invoked in discussions of CVM, since payments are seldom collected (nor compensation paid) during the research exercise. On the other hand, Model 2, in which payments are not collected and compensation is not paid, has a superficial resemblance to the CVM situation and is sometimes invoked by critics of CVM.

However, both models can immediately be dismissed, since they are quite false representations of the policy choice situation. In a contingent policy choice context, the individual seeks to simultaneously influence the amenity level and the level of disposable income available after payment for the policy. However, in Model 1, the

---

[7]The relationships between HC, HE, WTP, and WTA are defined in the following way [6]. For a compensating format that evaluates an increment in an amenity, HC > 0 and WTP^c = HC. For a compensating format and a decrement in an amenity, HC < 0, WTA^c = −HC. For the Hicksian equivalent measures, WTP^e = HE, where HE > 0 and WTA^e = −HE, where HE < 0.

amenity level is independent of the respondent's response and, in Model 2, disposable income is not at issue. The fact that sHC is not paid (or received) during the CVM exercise in no way validates Model 2. The respondent is a citizen and as such is aware that implementation of amenity increasing policies would surely decrease real purchasing power at the individual level, usually through some combination of taxes and higher prices for goods and services. Given the accumulated empirical evidence that systematic patterns of extreme misstatement do not dominate CVM data sets [25], it is perhaps unsurprising to find that the naive misstatement models simply do not capture the essentials of contingent policy choice.

We now consider three models in which the respondent attempts to influence amenity levels *and* real disposable income.

Model 3: A BC Criterion with per capita Costs

The respondent believes the following policy decision rules pertain: (1) the proposed policy is implemented if aggregate reported benefits exceed policy costs and (2) each citizen pays C/N, where C is the total cost of the policy change and N is the size of the affected population.

In this model, the size of a respondent's stated valuation has a direct impact on policy approval but influences eventual payment only by affecting anticipated per capita costs. In a similar per capita cost formulation developed by Brookshire et al. [5], each strategizing respondent selects an optimum strategy on the assumption that the other CVM respondents report sH equal to fH. We maintain this latter assumption but weaken the informational requirements of the Brookshire et al. model. We suppose that in a sample of size n, each strategizing respondent views the mean valuation, $\hat{b}$, of the other $n-1$ respondents as a random variable. We suppose only that, on average, individuals tend to guess correctly regarding $\hat{b}$ so that $E^*[E(\hat{b})] = E^*[\text{fH}]$, where E^* is an expectation operator across the sample.

Given the structure of this model, a strategizing respondent attempts to shift the sample mean valuation toward his/her own fH and therefore reports an sH based on the deviation between $\hat{b}$ and his/her own fH. Over the sample as a whole, the outcome of such strategic misstatement is an increase in the variance of the stated valuations and, assuming risk aversion, a shift downward in the sample mean valuation. Formally,

$$E^*[\text{sH}] \leqslant E^*[\text{fH}]. \tag{18}$$

Thus, while a specific individual may submit an sH greater than or less than his/her own fH, the sample mean valuation is not overstated.

In some CVM applications, the distribution of stated valuations may be truncated at zero with the result that misstatement may shift the sample mean upward. Nevertheless, under fairly general assumptions, statistical techniques are available to correct for any bias induced by truncation. One such method is described by Amemiya [1]. Thus, even in this case of truncation it is possible to construct a maximum likelihood estimator, denoted sH with asymptotic statistical properties such that $E^*[\text{sH}] \leqslant E^*[\text{fH}]$ [Hoehn (17)].

CVM data sets provide little support for the hypothesis that respondents follow strategies optimal for Model 3. For example, Brookshire et al. [5] find that instead of extreme variation, stated valuations are closely clustered. Rowe *et al.* [30] find only a single individual behaving in a manner remotely suggestive of the model's implications.

It is interesting to note that the Brookshire *et al.* [5] model of strategic behavior deviates from the structure of the standard CVM format in an important way. Respondents are frequently told they will have to pay their own sH, while instructions that they would pay C/N are, to our knowledge, never used in formats that elicit WTP. Thus, Brookshire *et al.* [5] must assume the strategizing respondent rejects the payment rule stated in the CVM format and substitutes the C/N payment rule. There seems to be little empirical support for this behavioral assumption.

Model 4: A BC Criterion with Payment Proportional to Own Bid

The respondent believes the following policy decision rules pertain: (1) the proposed policy is implemented if reported aggregate benefits exceed the costs and (2) each citizen pays in proportion to his/her stated valuation. However, the policy agency is assumed to use a balanced budget rule so that each individual would pay ksH where $k = C/B$ and B is reported aggregate benefits.

Since both C and B are unknown to the respondent, k is perceived as a random variable. The respondent can attempt to influence the policy outcome and his/her own payment by manipulating sH. As sH increases, the probability of implementation increases, but so do anticipated payments. With the incentives of Model 4, an individual does not overstate his/her formulated valuation and sH < fH (see the general proof in the Appendix).

To illustrate the case against overstatement, we analyze a simple case of an environmental improvement, $q^1 > q^0$, where all affected individuals are sampled and the valuation is elicited in a Hicksian compensating framework. Define $\hat{B}$ as the aggregate reported valuations of the other $n - 1$ persons. From the range of possible outcomes for $\hat{B}$, select an arbitrary, single value $\hat{B}^o$. If the respondent overstates fHC by some amount $\delta > 0$, his/her realized cost share would be

$$c(\delta) = C(\text{fHC} + \delta)/(\text{fHC} + \delta + \hat{B}^o), \qquad (19)$$

for any policy cost $C > 0$. Now consider the possible project outcomes. Policy costs are either greater than or less than fHC $+ \hat{B}^o$. Any policy with $C \leqslant \text{fHC} + \hat{B}^o$ would be obtained with $\delta = 0$. Therefore, for all policies with $C \leqslant \text{fHC} + \hat{B}^o$, overstatement of fHC increases a respondent's anticipated payment without affecting the probability of implementation. For policies with $C > \text{fHC} + \hat{B}^o$, a respondent stating $\delta > 0$ would increase his/her prospective payment and increase the probability of approving a policy with $C > \text{fHC} + \hat{B}^o$. If a project with $C > \text{fHC} + \hat{B}^o$ is actually approved when an individual states sH = fHC $+ \delta$ with $\delta > 0$, approval makes the individual worse off relative to u^0 since

$$c(\delta) = C(\text{fHC} + \delta)/(\text{fHC} + \delta + \hat{B}^o) > \text{fHC} \qquad (20)$$

for all $\delta > 0$ and $C > \text{fHC} + \hat{B}^o$.[8] Clearly, the above analysis can be repeated for

---

[8] To sketch the proof of line 21, note that $\hat{B}^o \delta > 0$. This can be used to show that $(\text{fHC} + \hat{B}^o)(\text{fHC} + \delta)/(\text{fHC} + \delta + \hat{B}^o) > \text{fHC}$. Line 21 follows since $C > \text{fHC} + \hat{B}^o$.

any possible value of $\hat{B}^\circ$. There is no incentive for overstatement of fHC. By understating fHC, $c(\delta)$ and the probability of policy implementation are both reduced. Thus, the strategizing respondent does not overstate his/her formulated valuation.

Model 5: A Policy Referendum with Individually Parametric Costs

The respondent believes the following policy decision rules pertain: (1) the policy is implemented if a plurality of citizens approves it, and (2) for each voting citizen, approval is conditional on a level of individual cost, c_j, which is specified in the question format.

The respondent is uncertain about how others will vote, which provides incentive for participation. The individual considers (q^1, c_j) pairs as if his/her vote were decisive. For $c_j < $ fH, the individual attains a surplus if the project is approved and it is thus optimal to report approval. For $c_j > $ fH, the individual suffers utility loss if the project is approved and it is optimal to report disapproval. Since approval is reported for all $c_j < $ fH and disapproval for all $c_j > $ fH, define sH as that c_j for which the voter is indifferent. At the indifference point, $c_j = $ sH $ = $ fH. *In a policy referendum model with individually parametric costs, truth-telling is the individually optimal strategy.*

Note that, unless c_j just happens to equal fH for the individual, respondents expressing approval are enjoying a surplus from their contingent choice. How, then, can a benefit estimate be derived from the contingent policy choice model? There are two possibilities. First, set c_j at different levels for different members of the sample. Then, with appropriate statistical analysis (e.g., a logit analysis [2, 15, 33]) benefit estimates can be obtained. Second, the iterative bidding routine that extracts a respondent's surplus [27] can be adapted to the policy referendum model. Since C is plausibly uncertain, it is quite plausible to repeat the referendum question for various levels of c_j. Since each vote is conditional on a stated level of individual cost, the favorable incentive properties of the referendum format are not destroyed and sH = fH can be determined by iteration.

Models 4 and 5 are consistent with the CVM formats used in many empirical applications. A valuation question of the form "tell me the highest amount that you would be willing to pay" would be consistent with Model 4. A valuation question "if a program to provide the policy change cost you $x, would you approve or disapprove the program?" would be consistent with Model 5. Existing empirical evidence is generally consistent with the predictions of Models 4 and 5. Rather than the extreme misstatement of Models 1, 2, and 3, we observe a "solid core" of observations [26]. With formats of the Model 4 type, empirical estimates of sWTP and sWTA diverge more than the theoretically predicted difference between WTP and WTA [2]. Formats of the Model 5 type yield larger mean bids than Model 4 formats [26]. These empirical findings are consistent with value statement Models 4 and 5.

Summary of the Analytical Results

A respondent's response to a CVM question requires solution of two problems, a value formation problem and a value statement problem. For formats designed to estimate Hicksian compensating measures of value, analysis of the value formation problem yields an unambiguous result: the expected value of fHC does not exceed the expected ideal HC.

Analysis of the value statement problem requires specification of models of the contingent policy choice context and their solution to identify optimal reporting strategies. Models 1 and 2 are consistent with certain off-hand dismissals of CVM. These two models, however, are unacceptable as a description of the contingent choice context since they fail to encompass both the prospect of a change in amenities and the prospect of a change in disposable income. Notably, of all the models considered, only Model 2 predicts a stated valuation larger than the formulated valuation and only in the case where the formulated valuation is positive.

Models 3, 4, and 5 are acceptable representations of contingent policy choice since each encompasses the prospects of both amenity and disposable income change. Importantly, several common CVM formats are structurally consistent with Models 4 and 5. Interestingly, data patterns consistent with Model 3 have not been observed [5, 30]. Should such patterns occur, the reporting behavior that is individually optimal under Model 3 would not distort the mean stated valuations (corrected for truncation) but may reduce the precision of value estimation.

With Models 3, 4, and 5, the mean stated valuation (corrected for trunction where necessary) does not exceed either the mean formulated valuation or, in the case of the compensating measures, the mean ideal compensating measure. Moreover, with a referendum model parametric in individual costs (Model 5), the stated valuation should be equal to the formulated valuation. Therefore, the Hicksian compensating measure stated in a willingness to pay/benefit cost format (Model 4) should not exceed the Hicksian compensating measure stated in a policy referendum format with individually parametric costs (Model 5). For Hicksian equivalent measures, ambiguous results at the value formulation stage preclude unambiguous conclusions about the relation between sHE and HE.

REFUTABLE CONSEQUENCES AND EMPIRICAL EVIDENCE

The theoretical analysis hinges on a fundamental assumption: respondents place some positive value on the opportunity provided by a CVM exercise for influencing policy and invest some positive effort in determining an individually desirable stated valuation. This assumption may be controversial. However, the analysis is rich in refutable consequences and empirical tests are possible.

In this section, we identify seven empirical consequences and reference the relevant empirical evidence. Future research is likely to extend the list of refutable consequences.

(C1) The stated compensating measure does not overstate the ideal, sHC $\leq$ HC.

(C1) is fundamental to the theoretical structure as described by Models 3, 4, and 5. Though HC may not be directly observable, an empirical test of (Cl) may be constructed by a comparison of the stated mean valuations with other, systematic benefit measurement techniques. For instance, Brookshire *et al.* [7] demonstrate conceptually that a hedonic benefit estimate tends to overstate the ideal Hicksian measure. Thus, if the mean sHC were found to be greater than the hedonic estimate,

(Cl) would be rejected. The Brookshire *et al.* [7] results, while they provide only a weak test, are consistent with (Cl).

(C2) Divergence of the compensating willingness to pay and willingness to accept.

The empirical divergence between the stated measures $sWTA^c$ and $sWTP^c$ will equal or exceed that predicted by the relationship (see [28]) between the ideal measures, WTA^c and WTP^c. This consequence is a corollary to (C1). The results of Bishop and Heberlein [2] are consistent with (C2).

(C3) Learning.

The mean sHC is non-decreasing with time or, by extension, other resources devoted to respondent decision-making. Recent experimental results [4] tend to corroborate this result.

(C4) Non-divergence over time of the elicited compensating willingness to pay and willingness to accept value measures.

The mean elicited compensating willingness to pay and willingness to accept measures do not diverge from their respective ideal measures as more time and decision resources are allocated to the contingent choice problem. This follows by the logic of consequences (C2) and (C3). The results of Hovis *et al.* [18], appear to be consistent with this consequence.

(C5) Compensating values elicited with a parametric cost referendum format weakly dominate the valuations obtained with a willingness to pay format.

By comparison of Models 4 and 5 results, we expect the valuations obtained with a one-shot "what is the maximum amount that you would be willing to pay?" format to be weakly dominated by the valuations elicited with a referendum format of the form "if a program to provide the policy change cost you $x, would you approve or disapprove that program?" Referendum formats may be iterated by repeating the valuation question to obtain responses conditional on alternative values of $x. Recent empirical results [4, 26] provide confirmation for this deduced consequence.

(C6) Dominance of the iterated form of the parametric cost referendum format.

Suppose that iteration increases the time used in value formulation. Then among the parametric cost referendum formats that elicit the Hicksian compensating measures, those that use iterative questioning do not generate smaller mean valuations than other parametric cost referendum formats. In the context of Model 5, this conclusion follows from the same logic as consequence (C3). Recent results [26, 36] tend to confirm this prediction.

(C7) Empirical relationship between the equivalent measure of willingness to pay ($sWTP^e$) and the compensating measure of willingness to accept ($sWTA^c$).

The relationship between $sWTA^c$ and $sWTP^e$ is unreliable and is not predicted by the relationship between the ideal measures, WTA^c and WTP^e (see [28]). This consequence is derived as follows. Since sHC $\leqslant$ HC, $WTA^c = -HC$, and $sWTA^c = -sHC$ for HC < 0, $sWTA^c \geqslant WTA^c$. In addition, fHE $\lessgtr$ HE and sHE $\leqslant$ fHE, so a $sWTP^e = sHE$ is unreliable. Thus, the difference between $sWTA^c$ and $sWTP^e$

cannot be predicted from the ideal relationship (see [28]) between WTA^c and WTP^c. Empirical evidence corroborating consequence (C5) is abundant [2, 6, 13, 30].

We do not claim that our theoretical model of the CVM respondent's value formulation and statement process is verified by the existing empirical evidence. First, verificationist logic is itself false [24] and, second, were it true, the empirical evidence we can bring to bear is sometimes sparse and some of the tests are weak. Rather, we claim the model has some unambiguous and refutable consequences and, for several such consequences, the existing evidence tends to be confirming rather than refuting.

In addition, the empirical consequences of the theory are consistent with a number of observations that have previously been considered anomalous. Larger than conventionally anticipated differences between WTP and WTA are now understood as consistent with consequences (C2), (C4), and (C7). Observations that the structure of the CVM format influences value results [4, 26] were problematic but may now be seen as consistent with consequences (C3), (C5), and (C6). Reports of information bias [9, 30] are now seen as entirely consistent with the contingent policy choice model. Changes in the policy implementation rule and/or the payment rule *should* be expected to change contingent policy choices.

A SATISFACTORY BENEFIT COST INDICATOR

A primary objective of benefit cost analysis (BCA) is to determine whether a given policy proposal would generate a potential Pareto-improvement (PPI). To do so, the sum across all policy components (benefit and cost items) and all affected individuals of the Hicksian compensating value measures must be positive [6, 21]. We define an *optimal benefit cost* (BC) *indicator* as one that identifies all proposals that offer PPIs as having positive net value and all non-PPI proposals as having negative net value. An optimal BC indicator is a perfect filter for PPI.

While an optimal BC indicator is the ideal, the inevitable imperfections of empirical work suggest that it is useful to recognize degrees of adequacy in applied BCA. With the actual policy environment typically characterized by constrained budgets and a large menu of proposals that are promoted as beneficial, a benefit indicator that is less than optimal but is still reliable as a filter for non-PPI proposals would be useful. To this end, we define a *satisfactory* BC *indicator* as one that identifies at least a portion of the true PPI proposals as having positive net value and all non-PPI proposals as having negative net value. Finally, an *unreliable* BC *indicator* is one that is simply not systematically related to the PPI criterion.

The theoretical analysis has shown that, generally, fHC $\leq$ HC and, for a set of CVM formats including those consistent with CVM Models 3, 4, and 5, sHC $\leq$ fHC. For this set of formats, we conclude on theoretical grounds that CVM in the Hicksian compensating framework is a satisfactory BC indicator. Stated benefits are no larger than the ideal measure of benefits and stated costs are no smaller than ideal measure of costs. With these formats, no non-PPI proposals would pass the BC filter. As the analysis of value statement makes clear, however, differences in CVM formats lead to predictable differences in performance. Thus, a general conclusion about satisfactoriness, applying to all conceivable formats, is impossible.

Value estimates constructed from contingent measures of sHE are unreliable BC indicators. First, HE is itself unreliable, since the well known income effect induces

a predictable divergence between HE and the correct HC indicator of PPI [28, 38].
Second, our theoretical analysis shows that the relationship between sHE and HE is
unreliable.

IMPLICATIONS FOR DESIGN OF CONTINGENT VALUATION FORMATS

The analysis of the value formulation and value statement problems makes one
thing abundantly clear: CVM designates a class of valuation methods and there is
considerable variety within that class. Not all CVM applications are created equal
and differences among formats are likely to influence CVM performance.

In this section, we review the theoretical results to extract implications for the
design of CVM formats. The performance objectives are (1) to ensure satisfactoriness and (2) within the satisfactory set of procedures, to reduce the divergence
between sHC and HC and thus reduce the number of PPI proposals which
incorrectly receive adverse BC evaluations. Below, we highlight a brief and nonex-
haustive list of implications.

(a) Wherever possible work with HC value measures. We have identified several
satisfactory CVM formats for estimating compensating measures. For these formats,
our theory predicts that $sWTP^c \leqslant WTP^c$ and $sWTA^c \geqslant WTA^c$, which, when combined with the results of Willig [38] and Randall and Stoll [28], provides a
considerable basis for interpreting empirical results obtained for these measures.
While the literature includes several reports of implausibly large estimates of WTA^c,
it is premature to abandon attempts to estimate WTA^c with CVM.

(b) The contingent policy choice situation posited by the CVM contains three
crucial elements: (1) a change in amenity levels associated with a proposed policy,
(2) a policy implementation decision rule, and (3) a rule determining individual
payments in the event of implementation. Each of these elements influences an
individual's contingent policy choice. Thus, an individual's valuation is conditioned
on the choice context. There is no unique valuation for a change in amenity levels
that is independent of the particular implementation and payment rule.

Two interpretations follow. First, the research task in applied CVM is not to find
the unique value of some change in amenities but to determine the value of the
change conditional upon an appropriate specification of the implementation and
payment rules. Second, criticism of CVM on the basis of a unique value postulate is
itself invalid. In particular, a change in a valuation following a change in the
payment or implementation rule cannot be interpreted meaningfully as information
bias.

(c) The structure of the implementation and payment rules determines the
incentives implicit in any particular CVM format. Since the referendum rule with
parametric individual costs (Model 5) is resistant to strategic bias, use of this format
to estimate sHC limits value estimation error to the value formulation stage of a
contingent choice process. This reduces the probability of falsely rejecting a PPI
proposal while retaining the satisfactory characteristics of compensating CVM
formats.

(d) Emphasis should be placed on increasing the incentives for careful value formulation when using a format based on a referendum with parametric individual costs (Model 5). This logic leads to what may otherwise seem a radical suggestion: emphasize to respondents the influence that their responses may have on public policy decisions. Some contingent valuation practitioners have recoiled from this, worried that if respondents believed that they would exert real policy influence strategic behavior would be rampant. The theoretical analysis shows that these worries are unfounded when an appropriate CVM format is used.

(e) Further reduction in value formulation errors may be pursued by seeking to reduce the costs to respondents of value formulation. In effect, the researcher could seek ways to subsidize the value formulation process. Graphic or computerized devices that provide decision-relevant information or perform pertinent calculations for the respondent may be helpful.

Taken together, the implications derived from the theoretical analysis provide a strong program of suggestions for increasing the precision of CVM while retaining satisfactoriness.

A CONCLUDING COMMENT

The economic-theoretic approach to predicting the influence of CVM design on respondent behavior has proven rich in several dimensions. The behavior of CVM respondents can, we have shown, be usefully analyzed with relatively standard microeconomic models of choice. These theoretical models have explicit empirical consequences. Further, the empirical findings that are consistent with our theoretical model include several that were previously thought anomalous. These findings subsume CVM respondent behavior under the established research program in microeconomics and expand the domain of CVM theory to explain anomalous empirical findings.

The possibility of constructing satisfactory benefit cost indicators from CVM data has been established. It has been shown that variations in CVM design influence performance in predictable ways. Not all CVM exercises are equally effective and the differences among them may be attributable to fundamental design features as well as to the care and attention paid to research procedures. Suggestions for increasing the precision of satisfactory BC indicators based on CVM emerge from our analysis. In these ways, the credibility of CVM may be enhanced and preconditions are established for further improvements in its performance and more insightful interpretation of results.

In research programs, progress occurs when any of the following occur: (1) the relationship between the program and some other, well-established, research program is strengthened, (2) the domain of the program is expanded as program shifts occur to explain anomalous findings without otherwise diminishing the generality of the program, (3) new evidence suggesting the validity of the program is generated, and (4), in the course of the above developments, novel hypotheses and/or insights are generated. We believe our analysis has established that CVM is a progressing research program in the sense of Lakatos [20], and has contributed a little to its progress.

APPENDIX

To complement the intuitive approach taken in the text, we formally examine the structure of incentives Models 3, 4, and 5. Model 3 is adapted from the per capita cost model developed in Brookshire *et al.* [5]. Models 4 and 5 are new to the literature on CVM. We demonstrate that the individually best value statement decisions can be summarized by simple and general first order rules. Additional discussion can be found in Hoehn [17].

The structure of the value statement problem is similar for both the compensating and equivalent measures. To take advantage of this similarity, we use a general Hicksian measure, fH, in the proofs. The measure fH is defined by

$$v(p, q^{1-i}, m - \text{fH}) = v(p, q^i, m) \tag{A1}$$

where $v(\cdot)$ represents a concave utility index that may be subject to either communication error or evaluation constraints. To indicate a Hicksian compensating format, $i = 0$. For a Hicksian equivalent form, $i = 1$. For instance, if $i = 0$, $v(p, q^0, m)$ is both the initial level of utility and the "reference level" [6]. The anticipated post-policy level of utility is $v(p, q^1, m - \text{fH})$ and fH = fHC. If $i = 1$, the format is the equivalent form and the reference level of utility is $v(p, q^1, m)$. With the equivalent form, fH = fHE would leave the individual indifferent between the initial level of q^0 and the reference level, q^1.

Each structure for the contingent policy choice requires somewhat different information. For instance, in Model 3, the size of the affected population, N, the sample size, n, and the anticipated sample mean valuation, $\hat{b} = \hat{B}/(n - 1)$ (where $\hat{B}$ is defined in the text), of the other $n - 1$ sampled citizens each play an explicit role. To allow for imperfect information, we assume that the respondent views $d(q^1)$ (defined in the text), N, n, $\hat{b}$, C, and r (defined below in the proof of Model 4) as random variables with well-defined probability density functions.

Depending upon the format type, C may represent one of two different concepts. In a compensating format, C denotes the costs of moving from the reference level, q^0, to the proposed alternative q^1 ($C > 0$ if $q^1 > q^0$ and $C < 0$ if $q^1 < q^0$). With an equivalent format, C represents the total cost savings associated with the reference level, q^1 ($C > 0$ if $q^0 > q^1$ and $C < 0$ if $q^0 < q^1$). Defined on an appropriate real domain (α, β), the probability density function of C is $g(C)$.

Models 4 and 5 require relatively few auxilliary assumptions and are therefore discussed first. A discussion of Model 3 concludes the Appendix.

Proof of Model 4. With this model the sampled individual's stated valuation, sH, represents a class of individuals of size r. In a compensating format, the policy proposal q^1 is accepted if

$$(N - r)\hat{b} + \text{rsH} > C \tag{A2}$$

and is rejected if the reverse inequality holds. The respondent expects to pay ksH if q^1 is accepted where

$$k = \{C/[(N - r)\hat{b} + \text{rsH}]\}. \tag{A3}$$

In an equivalent format, the proposal q^1 is rejected (accepted) if inequality (A2) holds (does not hold). With the equivalent format, if q^1 is rejected by the benefit cost rule, the individual sustains a cost of ksH.

By (A2), the probability that a policy is accepted depends upon the relation between aggregate benefits and aggregate costs. Thus, depending upon the response sH, a respondent's expected utility is

$$u = E \int_\alpha^{(N-r)\hat{b}+\text{rsH}} v\left(p, q^{1-i}, m - \text{ksH}\right) g(C)\, dC$$

$$+ E \int_{(N-r)\hat{b}+\text{rsH}}^\beta v\left(p, q^i, m\right) g(C)\, dC, \qquad (A4)$$

where E is a respondent's subjective expectation operator over the relevant random variables.

To find the choice of sH that maximizes expected utility, differentiate (A4) with respect to sH using Leibniz' rule [23] and set the result equal to zero. Simplifying, the best choice of sH satisfies a simple first order rule.

$$v\left(p, q^{1-i}, m - \text{sH}\right) = v\left(p, q^i, m\right) + a, \qquad (A5)$$

where

$$a = -\left\{E\left[g(\cdot) r\right]\right\}^{-1} E \int_\alpha^{(N-r)\hat{b}+\text{rsH}} D_{\text{sH}} v\left(p, q^{1-i}, m - \text{ksH}\right) g(C)\, dC > 0.$$

The optimal rule is clear: Since fH would equate $v(p, q^{1-i}, m - \text{fH})$ and $v(p, q^i, m)$ as in Eq. (A1), state an sH < fH.

Proof of Model 5.   The decision rule is a referendum with individually parametric costs. A respondent is asked to accept or reject a policy conditional given an individually specified cost share c_j. Across the sample, the respondent views cost shares as a set $\mathbf{C} = \{c_j\}$, $j \in \{1, \ldots, n\}$. If the project is approved by the group, realized individual costs are given by the rule $c_j = c_j(C)$ with inverse $C = c_j^{-1}(c_j)$ and $\mathbf{D}c_j^{-1} > 0$.

The respondent's subjective probability of either policy approval or rejection is conditioned on the anticipated cost shares, $\mathbf{C}$, and the respondent's own response. For a compensating format, let $P(\mathbf{C}, 1)$ be the subjective probability that the sample approves the policy proposal $(q^1, \mathbf{C})$ when the respondent accepts (q^1, c_j). Let $P(\mathbf{C}, 0)$ denote the subjective probability that the sample approves $(q^1, \mathbf{C})$ when the respondent rejects (q^1, c_j). Clearly, $P(\mathbf{C}, 1) > P(\mathbf{C}, 0)$.

For an equivalent format, let $P(\mathbf{C}, 1)$ represent the subjective probability that the sample approves $(q^0, \mathbf{C})$ when the respondent accepts (q^0, c_j). Let $P(\mathbf{C}, 0)$ denote the probability that the sample approves $(q^0, \mathbf{C})$ when the respondent rejects (q^0, c_j). Again, $P(\mathbf{C}, 1) > P(\mathbf{C}, 0)$.

Conditioned on a given cost share, $c_j = c_j(C)$, the respondent's expected utility is

$$u^1 = v\left[p, q^{1-i}, m - c_j(C)\right] P(\mathbf{C}, 1) + v\left(p, q^i, m\right)\left[1 - P(\mathbf{C}, 1)\right] \qquad (A6)$$

if he/she accepts $c_j = c_j(C)$. If the respondent rejects $c_j = c_j(C)$, expected utility is

$$u^0 = v\left[p, q^{1-i}, m - c_j(C)\right] P(\mathbf{C}, 0) + v\left(p, q^i, m\right)\left[1 - P(\mathbf{C}, 0)\right]. \qquad (A7)$$

For a given cost c_j and fH $> c_j$, $u^1 > u^0$ and the respondent is better off to accept (q^{1-i}, c_j). If $c_j > $ fH, the respondent is better off to reject (q^{1-i}, c_j). Therefore, viewed as a referendum or poll, a format that asks the respondent to accept or reject a given cost, c_j, encourages no misstatement.

An alternative format design may present the respondent with a (an iterated) schedule of costs. If he/she accepts costs up to c_j^*, expected utility is

$$u = E \int_\alpha^{c_j^{-1}(c_j^*)} \left\{ v\left[p, q^{1-i}, m - c_j(C) \right] P(\mathbb{C}, 1) \right.$$

$$\left. + v(p, q^i, m)[1 - P(\mathbb{C}, 1)] \right\} g(C) dC$$

$$+ E \int_{c_j^{-1}(c_j^*)}^\beta \left\{ v\left[p, q^{1-i}, m - c_j(C) \right] P(\mathbb{C}, 0) \right.$$

$$\left. + v(p, q^i, m)[1 - P(\mathbb{C}, 0)] \right\} g(C) dC, \qquad \text{(A8)}$$

where we note that $c_j = c_j(C)$ for all $c_j \in \mathbb{C}$. Using Leibniz' rule to differentiate (A8) and simplifying, the best choice of c_j^* is given by the first order rule,

$$v\left(p, q^{1-i}, m - c_j^* \right) = v(p, q^i, m). \qquad \text{(A9)}$$

Comparing Eqs. (A1) and (A9), it is clear that this variant of the referendum rule suggests no incentives for misstatement. A respondent accepts costs up to fH and rejects costs greater than fH.

Proof of Model 3. With this model the implementation criterion is the benefit cost rule using data from the CVM sample. With a compensating format, the CVM participant anticipates approval of the policy if

$$N\left[(n - 1)\hat{b} + sH \right] / n > C \qquad \text{(A10)}$$

and rejection of the policy if the reverse inequality holds. If the policy is approved, affected individuals pay C/N.

In an equivalent format, the proposal q^1 is rejected (accepted) if inequality (A10) holds (does not hold). With an equivalent format, the respondent pays C/N if q^1 is rejected by the benefit cost rule.

Relaxing the perfect information requirements of the Brookshire et al. [5] formulation, we suppose, as above, that the respondent views N, $\hat{b}$, and C as random variables. In this model, however, C is assumed to have a uniform probability distribution and the sample size is assumed to be known.

The respondent selects sH to maximize expected utility

$$u = E \int_\alpha^{N[(n-1)\hat{b}+sH]/n} v(p, q^{1-i}, m - C/N) g(C) dC$$

$$+ E \int_{N[(n-1)\hat{b}+sH]/n}^\beta v(p, q^i, m) g(C) dC. \qquad \text{(A11)}$$

Using Leibniz' rule and simplifying, the optimal choice of sH once again satisfies a simple first order rule,

$$Ev\left[p, q^{1-i}, m - \hat{b} - (1/n)(sH - \hat{b}) \right] = v(p, q^i, m). \qquad \text{(A12)}$$

By the concavity of v and (A1), it follows that

$$E(\hat{b}) + (1/n)[sH - E(\hat{b})] \leqslant fH \qquad (A13)$$

and, rearranging,

$$sH \leqslant E(\hat{b}) + n[fH - E(\hat{b})]. \qquad (A14)$$

Taking the expectation across the sample,

$$E^*[sH] \leqslant E^*[fH] \qquad (A15)$$

since, by assumption, $E^*[E(\hat{b})] = E^*[fH]$.

REFERENCES

1. T. Amemiya, Regression analysis when the dependent variable is truncated normal, *Econometrica* **41**, 997–1017 (1973).
2. R. C. Bishop AND T. A. Heberlein, Measuring values of extra-market goods, *Amer. Agri. Econom.* **61**, 925–930 (1979).
3. D. S. Brookshire and T. D. Crocker, The advantages of contingent valuation methods for benefit cost analysis, *Public Choice* **36**, 235–252 (1981).
4. D. S. Brookshire, R. E. Cummings, M. Rahmatian, W. A. Schulze, and M. A. Thayer, "Experimental Approaches for Valuing Environmental Commodities," Report (draft final), University of Wyoming for U.S.E.P.A. (1982).
5. D. S. Brookshire, B. Ives, and W. D. Schulze, The valuation of aesthetic preferences, *J. Environ. Econom. Management* **3**, 325–346 (1976).
6. D. S. Brookshire, A. Randall, and J. R. Stoll, Valuing increments and decrements in natural resource flows, *Amer. J. Agri. Econom.* **62**, 478–488 (1980).
7. D. S. Brookshire, M. A. Thayer, W. D. Schulze, and R. C. d'Arge, Valuing public goods: A comparison of survey and hedonic approaches, *Amer. Econom. Rev.* **72**, 165–177 (1982).
8. J. M. Buchanan, "Cost and Choice," Markham, Chicago (1969).
9. F. J. Cronin and K. Bersog, "Valuing Nonmarket Goods Through Contingent Markets," Pacific Northwest Laboratory, Richland, WA (1982).
10. J. T. Daubert and R. A. Young, Recreational demands for maintaining instream flows: A contingent valuation approach, *Amer. J. Agri. Econom.* **63**, 666–676 (1981).
11. R. K. Davis, Recreation planning as an economic problem, *Natur. Resources J.* **3**, 238–249 (1963).
12. D. Feenburg and E. S. Mills, "Measuring the Benefits of Water Pollution Abatement," Academic Press, New York (1980).
13. I. M. Gordon and J. L. Knetsch, Consumer surplus measures and the evaluation of resources, *Land Econom.* **55**, 1–10 (1979).
14. J. Hammack and G. M. Brown, "Waterfowl and Wetlands: Toward Bioeconomic Analysis," Johns Hopkins, Baltimore (1974).
15. W. M. Hanemann, Welfare evaluations in contingent valuation experiments with discrete responses, *Amer. J. Agri. Econom.* **66**, 332–341 (1984).
16. J. P. Hoehn, "Contingent Valuation and the Prospect of a Satisfactory Benefit Cost Indicator," First National Symposium on Social Science in Resource Management, Oregon State University, Corvallis, OR (1986).
17. J. P. Hoehn, "The Benefit Cost Evaluation of Multi-Part Public Policy: A Theoretical Framework and Critique of Estimation Methods," PhD. dissertation, Lexington, University of Kentucky (1983).
18. J. Hovis, D. Coursey, and W. D. Schulze, "A Comparison of Alternative Valuation Mechanisms for Non-Market Commodities," manuscript, University of Wyoming, Laramie (1983).
19. J. L. Knetsch and R. K. Davis, Comparisons of methods for recreation evaluation, *in* "Water Research" (A. V. Kneese and S. C. Smith, Eds.), John Hopkins, Baltimore (1966).

20. I. Lakatos, Falsification and the methodology of scientific research programs, *in* "Criticisms and the Growth of Knowledge" (I. Lakatos and A. Musgrave, Eds.), Cambridge Univ. Press, London (1970).

21. E. J. Mishan, "Cost Benefit Analysis," Unwin and Allen, London (1971).

22. R. C. Mitchell and R. T. Carson, "An Experiment in Determining Willingness to Pay for National Water Quality Improvements," Report (draft), Resources for the Future, Inc., Washington, D.C. (1981).

23. A. M. Mood, F. A. Graybill, and D. C. Boes, "Introduction to the Theory of Statistics," McGraw–Hill, New York (1974).

24. K. Popper, "The Logic of Scientific Discovery," Basic Books, New York (1959).

25. A. Randall, J. P. Hoehn, and D. S. Brookshire, Contingent valuation surveys for evaluating environmental assets, *Natur. Resources J.* **23**, 635–648 (1983).

26. A. Randall, J. P. Hoehn, and G. S. Tolley, "The Structure of Contingent Markets," Annual Meeting of the American Economic Association, Washington, D.C. (1981).

27. A. Randall, B. Ives, and C. Eastman, Bidding games for valuation of aesthetic environmental improvements, *J. Environ. Econom. Management* **1**, 132–149 (1974).

28. A. Randall and J. R. Stoll, Consumer's surplus in commodity space, *Amer. Econom. Rev.* **70**, 449–455 (1980).

29. S. Rosen, Hedonic prices and implicit markets: Product differentiation in perfect competition, *J. Polit. Econom.* **82**, 34–55 (1974).

30. R. D. Rowe, R. C. d'Arge, and D. S. Brookshire, An experiment on the economic value of visibility, *J. Environ. Econom. Management* **7**, 1–19 (1980).

31. P. A. Samuelson, The pure theory of public expenditure, *Rev. Econom. Statist.* **36**, 387–389 (1954).

32. W. D. Schulze, D. S. Brookshire, and M. A. Thayer, "National Parks and Beauty: A Test of Existence Values," Annual Meeting of American Economic Association, Washington, D.C. (1981).

33. C. Sellar, J. R. Stoll, and J. P. Chavis, "Validation of Empirical Measures of Welfare Change: A Comparison of Non-Market Techniques," Natural Resources Working Paper Series, Department of Agricultural Economics, Texas A & M University (1984).

34. V. L. Smith, Experiments with a decentralized mechanism for public goods decisions, *Amer. Econom. Rev.* **70**, 584–599 (1980).

35. C. F. Sorg and D. S. Brookshire, "Valuing Increments and Decrements of Wildlife Resources: Further Evidence," manuscript, University of Wyoming (1982).

36. M. A. Thayer, Contingent valuation techniques for assessing environmental impact: Further evidence, *J. Environ. Econom. Management* **8**, (1981).

37. G. S. Tolley *et al.*, "Establishing and Valuing the Effects or Improved Visibility in the Eastern United States," Report to the U.S. Environmental Protection Agency, Washington, D.C. (1984).

38. R. D. Willig, Consumer's surplus without apology, *Amer. Econom. Rev.* **66**, 589–597 (1976).

[10]

Measuring the Demand for Environmental Quality
John B. Braden & Charles D. Kolstad (Editors)
© Elsevier Science Publishers B.V. (North-Holland), 1991

TOTAL AND NONUSE VALUES

ALAN RANDALL

Ohio State University

10.1 Introduction

The idea of nonuse benefits is motivated by a concern that even after all of the various benefits associated with using an environmental amenity have been estimated and entered into the benefit calculation, something important might be missed. At first glance, the idea of benefits without explicit, observable use seems radical, just as did the earlier notion that use benefits could be unaccompanied by direct and observable commercial transactions. However, both of these ideas are well within the purview of the standard economic model of benefits. What counts as a benefit is delimited by neither the act of use nor the commercial transaction. Rather, an action has a *prima facie* economic benefits if an action increases the availability of something that is scarce at the margin and if that "something" is desired by someone; that is, if it is at least potentially a source of human utility.

As for what might be overlooked in a benefit account confined to use values, there has been no shortage of candidates. Those that are still frequently proposed include existence value, first suggested by Krutilla (1967), vicarious use value (Krutilla 1967), option value (Weisbrod 1964), and quasi-option value (Arrow and Fisher 1974; Henry 1974). Each of these nonuse value concepts was introduced to deal with a legitimate concern. *Existence value* addresses the idea that, in Krutilla's much-quoted example, there are people who value the existence of wilderness even though they would be appalled by the prospect of exposure to it. *Vicarious use value* addresses the possibility that people who cannot visit unusual environments nevertheless gain pleasure from pictures, broadcasts, written accounts, and so on, of these places. Although Randall and Stoll (1983) argued that vicarious use value is a form of use value, they conceded that it is difficult to distinguish by observation from existence values. *Option value* is applied to circumstances in which individuals may be willing to pay a premium to ensure the future availability of an amenity. This scenario, in which significant option value emerges for environmental amenities, is analogous to purchased options in real estate and financial instruments. *Quasi-option value* concerns unique natural terrain, species, and ecosystems, and their susceptibility to irreversible change. Some economists argue that a complete account of preservation benefits must include a benefit associated with the possibility that future discoveries may make fragile natural resources more or less valuable than they seem to be now.

The economic literature on nonuse benefits is almost a quarter-century old and has become quite voluminous. Unfortunately, from the practitioner's perspective, this literature was contentious almost from the beginning. New controversies flare-up faster than old issues are resolved. Economists debate the validity of important categories of nonuse value, as well as the relevance of others. They differ on how the various categories of use and nonuse value may add up to the total benefits of a resource service or amenity. Furthermore, their answer to a major question for practitioners — whether the analyst is better advised to estimate total value directly or by aggregating estimates of all the various components of use and nonuse value — depends on which side they take in the controversy about the merits of alternative estimation methods.

The intent of this chapter is first, to provide a theoretical basis for conceptualizing total economic value and its nonuse components, and second, to suggest some pragmatic methods for estimating benefits. Both objectives are essential because pragmatic strategies for benefit estimation must be built on valid conceptual foundations.

10.2 A Total Value Framework

The first step in laying this conceptual foundation is developing a simple model of total economic value in a deterministic framework. This model has important implications: total economic value is uniquely defined; it decomposes readily into existence value and several categories of use value; and in general, it misstates total value if the independently-estimated values for the benefit categories are simply summed. When uncertainty is introduced into the model, all benefit values become *ex ante*; that is, they represent the individual's expected benefits based on what is known at the time valuation takes place rather than in retrospect after she has experienced the consequences of her choice. A decomposition of *ex ante* total economic value reveals no new categories of value. Instead, *ex ante* existence value and various kinds of *ex ante* use value emerge. Furthermore, the concepts underlying *ex ante* use value, as a concept, adequately addresses the legitimate concerns that led to proposals that option value and quasi-option value be included in benefit accounts.

An illustration of the problem of valuation will be helpful before formally modeling total economic value. The Tongass National Forest covers approximately twenty-seven thousand square miles and accounts for more than 97 percent of the land area in southeastern Alaska. In and near Tongass the diversity of landscape, biota, and natural-resource-based human activities, both commercial and nonmarket, is unusually rich. Some sixty-five thousand residents and several hundred thousand annual visitors enjoy the services and amenities produced on Tongass. Due to its topography, southeastern Alaska has few roads connecting it with the rest of North America, and as a result, most visitors arrive by sea or air. Visits, therefore, typically are expensive, have several destinations, and include several activities.

To develop a total value framework for the environmental resources of such a place, it makes sense to consider three mutually exclusive classes of individuals who may value these resources: residents of southeastern Alaska, visitors to southeastern Alaska, and nonresident nonvisitors. All three classes of individuals would have nonuse values. For example, they all might value the continued existence of a nondegraded Tongass environment independently of any concern about actually using it. Residents and visitors would have, in addition, values deriving from prospective use.

It is customary for resource management agencies to conceptualize use values in terms of values derived from particular activities: for example, motorized water-based recreation and hunting are among the activities recognized in the Tongass National Forest. In addition to these specific activities in which both residents and visitors may participate, there is also a more amorphous kind of use. To give just two examples, every southeastern Alaska resident lives in an environment dominated by the Tongass National Forest in terms of scenery, wildlife, air and water quality, and so on. Therefore, they may well experience a positive residential value independent of participation in any specific activities. Similarly, visitors who arrive on the many cruise ships that travel the inner navigation passage can enjoy being immersed in an unusual environment, often without participating in any explicit activities within the forest. For a situation such as the Tongass National Forest, which is among the more complex valuation problems likely to be encountered, a total valuation framework should include existence values and two kinds of use values: site experience values and the values attributable to explicit activities.

10.2.1 Total Value in a Deterministic Context

Consider an individual with the utility function

$$u = u(x_e, x_s, x_1, x_2, Q, z) \tag{10.1}$$

where x is environmental services, Q is the state or condition of the environment, and z is a vector of ordinary goods and services. The subscripts denote, respectively: e, existence; s, site experience; 1, activity 1; and 2, activity 2. At this stage, x_e, x_s, x_1, and x_2 are each single elements; however, it would be simple to extend the analysis to consider a vector of existence services, a vector of site experience services, and n activities rather than just two.

The solution to the problem

$$\min\ (p_e x_e + p_s x_s + p_1 x_1 + p_2 x_2 + \boldsymbol{p}\boldsymbol{z}) \tag{10.2}$$
$$\text{s.t.}\quad u(\cdot) \geq u^o$$

is the expenditure function

$$e = e(p_e, p_s, p_1, p_2, Q, \boldsymbol{p}, u^o). \tag{10.3}$$

If one assumes, purely for notational convenience, that prices of ordinary goods and services are exogenous, the expenditure function can be written with $\boldsymbol{p}$ implicit: $e(p_e, p_s, p_1, p_2, Q, u^o)$.

The total value (TV) of environmental services is then defined, in terms of Hicksian compensating welfare change measures, as

$$TV = e(p_e^*, p_s^*, p_1^*, p_2^*, Q^o, u^o) - e(p_e^o, p_s^o, p_1^o, p_2^o, Q^o, u^o) \tag{10.4}$$

where p^* is a choke price (that is, a price so high that quantity demanded is zero), p^o is a baseline price, and Q^o is the baseline level of resource quality. Existence services generally are unpriced: thus, p_e is the virtual price of x_e. Virtual price, which is synonymous with shadow price, is defined as the price that would be efficient where efficient price is absent; that is, virtual price would clear efficient markets if they existed. The choke price p_e^* indicates a situation where existence services are not provided. When other kinds of environmental services are unpriced, for institutional or other reasons, the virtual price interpretation of price also applies.

Expression (10.4) suggest a one-shot, or holistic, measure of total value. However, it is possible to break down total value into its components, and to provide a common sense interpretation of each component.

$$
\begin{aligned}
TV = \quad & e(p_e^*, p_s^*, p_1^*, p_2^*, Q^o, u^o) - e(p_e^o, p_s^*, p_1^*, p_2^*, Q^o, u^o) && (10.5a)\\
+ & e(p_e^o, p_s^*, p_1^*, p_2^*, Q^o, u^o) - e(p_e^o, p_s^o, p_1^*, p_2^*, Q^o, u^o) && (10.5b)\\
+ & e(p_e^o, p_s^o, p_1^*, p_2^*, Q^o, u^o) - e(p_e^o, p_s^o, p_1^o, p_2^*, Q^o, u^o) && (10.5c)\\
+ & e(p_e^o, p_s^o, p_1^o, p_2^*, Q^o, u^o) - e(p_e^o, p_s^o, p_1^o, p_2^o, Q^o, u^o) && (10.5d)
\end{aligned}
$$

Equation (10.5) suggests a sequenced valuation that captures total value as the sum of various value components. Of the many possible valuation sequences, one particular sequence is chosen and elaborated here. Line (10.5a) defines existence value, (10.5b) defines site experience value, and (10.5c) and (10.5d) define the activity values for activities 1 and 2, respectively. Alternatively, line (10.5a) identifies existence value, while the subsequent lines define particular kinds of use value. Total value is, in a deterministic framework, the sum of existence and use values evaluated sequentially. The conventional wisdom, that nonuse value is the residual between total value and use value, is seen to be true but only with the proviso that all value components are evaluated in some valid sequence.

In contrast to the holistic or sequential TV frameworks, there is a common procedure that calculates total value by aggregating component values estimated independently. This procedure is denoted *independent valuation and summation* (IVS). The IVS value measure analogous to (10.5) is

$$
\begin{aligned}
\text{IVS} = \quad & e(p_e^*,p_s^*,p_1^*,p_2^*,Q^o,u^o) - e(p_e^o,p_s^*,p_1^*,p_2^*,Q^o,u^o) && (10.6a) \\
+ \ & e(p_e^*,p_s^*,p_1^*,p_2^*,Q^o,u^o) - e(p_e^*,p_s^o,p_1^*,p_2^*,Q^o,u^o) && (10.6b) \\
+ \ & e(p_e^*,p_s^*,p_1^*,p_2^*,Q^o,u^o) - e(p_e^*,p_s^*,p_1^o,p_2^*,Q^o,u^o) && (10.6c) \\
+ \ & e(p_e^*,p_s^*,p_1^*,p_2^*,Q^o,u^o) - e(p_e^*,p_s^*,p_1^*,p_2^o,Q^o,u^o) && (10.6d)
\end{aligned}
$$

Existence value and each of the use values is evaluated independently of the others, which is not consistent with (10.5).

Hoehn and Randall (1989) demonstrated that, in general, IVS $\neq$ TV; this result is not unexpected, given that the consumer surplus value of a bundle of goods is generally not the same as the sum of consumer surpluses for individual goods. Furthermore, they showed that TV is unique, whether defined in holistic (10.4) or sequential (10.5) terms; and each component value is not unique but depends on its position in the valuation sequence. As the number of components becomes large, the error in IVS becomes systematic: IVS overestimates the benefits of policy change, and non-net-beneficial policy changes may be misidentified as net beneficial.

Now, consider some proposed policy that would affect the condition of the environment, changing Q^o to Q^1. The total value for the policy change is

$$
\begin{aligned}
\text{TV}(Q^1;Q^o) &= e(p_e^*,p_s^*,p_1^*,p_2^*,Q^1,u^o) \ - e(p_e^o,p_s^o,p_1^o,p_2^o,Q^1,u^o) \\
&\quad - [e(p_e^*,p_s^*,p_1^*,p_2^*,Q^o,u^o) \ - e(p_e^o,p_s^o,p_1^o,p_2^o,Q^o,u^o)] && (10.7) \\
&= e(p_e^o,p_s^o,p_1^o,p_2^o,Q^o,u^o) \ - e(p_e^o,p_s^o,p_1^o,p_2^o,Q^1,u^o).
\end{aligned}
$$

This expression may be decomposed:

$$
\begin{aligned}
\text{TV}(Q^1;Q^o) = \quad & e(p_e^o,p_s^*,p_1^*,p_2^*,Q^o,u^o) \ - e(p_e^o,p_s^*,p_1^*,p_2^*,Q^1,u^o) && (10.8a) \\
+ \ & e(p_e^o,p_s^*,p_1^*,p_2^*,Q^1,u^o) \ - e(p_e^o,p_s^o,p_1^*,p_2^*,Q^1,u^o) && (10.8b) \\
- \ & [e(p_e^o,p_s^*,p_1^*,p_2^*,Q^o,u^o) \ - e(p_e^o,p_s^o,p_1^*,p_2^*,Q^o,u^o)] \\
+ \ & e(p_e^o,p_s^o,p_1^*,p_2^*,Q^1,u^o) \ - e(p_e^o,p_s^o,p_1^o,p_2^*,Q^1,u^o) && (10.8c) \\
- \ & [e(p_e^o,p_s^o,p_1^*,p_2^*,Q^o,u^o) \ - e(p_e^o,p_s^o,p_1^o,p_2^*,Q^o,u^o)] \\
+ \ & e(p_e^o,p_s^o,p_1^o,p_2^*,Q^1,u^o) \ - e(p_e^o,p_s^o,p_1^o,p_2^o,Q^1,u^o) && (10.8d) \\
- \ & [e(p_e^o,p_s^o,p_1^o,p_2^*,Q^o,u^o) \ - e(p_e^o,p_s^o,p_1^o,p_2^o,Q^o,u^o)]
\end{aligned}
$$

Expression (10.7) defines a holistic total valuation of the proposed policy change, whereas (10.8) defines a sequential total valuation. Again, total value is unique. Expression (10.8a) identifies the change in existence value attributable to the policy change, whereas (10.8b) through (10.8d) define, sequentially, the changes in various components of use value. It is, of course, possible also to define an IVS measure of the total value for the policy change, but such a measure would be misleading in general, and systematically upward biased for policies with many components (Hoehn and Randall 1989).

Most applied benefit-cost analyses evaluate proposed policy changes, and therefore expressions in (10.7) and (10.8) define the appropriate value measures. Nevertheless, for notational brevity and consistency, all further definitions and analyses will address the baseline valuation case as defined in (10.4) and (10.5).

10.2.2 *Total Valuation Under Uncertainty*

Uncertainty is introduced in two steps. First, define J possible states of the world, S_j, each independent of policy. Thus, S is a J-element vector, and S_j has probability π_j, such that $\Sigma_{j=1}^{J} \pi_j = 1$. Each category of environmental services is now a J-element vector of contingent commodities, each with its contingent price or virtual price. Thus, these are now J-element vectors: x_e, x_s, x_1, x_2, p_e, p_s, p_1, and p_2. This formulation permits policy-independent uncertainty that may affect the benefits of environmental services.

Second, uncertainty may pertain to baseline Q^o or to the effects of policy on Q^1. So, let q_k be the probability that the environment is in some condition Q_k. Thus, Q is a K-element vector of states of the environment and q is a K-element vector of probabilities, $\Sigma_{k=1}^{K} q_k = 1$. Uncertainty with respect to Q addresses what the standard literature calls *supply uncertainty*. In contrast to the tone of most of the option value and quasi-option value literature, neither the passage of time nor the introduction of policy necessarily decreases or eliminates uncertainty. New information emerging with time may increase uncertainty about states of the world, S, and a new policy may make Q^1 more uncertain than Q^o.

To define total value under uncertainty, economists use the *ex ante* or *planned expenditure function* (Helms 1985; Simmons 1984; Smith 1987a) *circa* equation (2.37): $\check{e} = \check{e}(p_e, p_s, p_1, p_2, \pi, q, EU)$, where π and q are independent and EU is expected utility.

Ex ante total value for the baseline policy (or environmental condition) is

$$\text{TV} = \check{e}(p_e^*, p_s^*, p_1^*, p_2^*, \pi^o, q^o, EU^o) - \check{e}(p_e^o, p_s^o, p_1^o, p_2^o, \pi^o, q^o, EU^o), \quad (10.9)$$

and

$$\text{TV} = \quad \check{e}(p_e^*, p_s^*, p_{1,2}^*, \pi^o, q^o, EU^o) \quad - \check{e}(p_e^o, p_s^*, p_1^*, p_2^*, \pi^o, q^o, EU^o) \quad (10.10a)$$
$$+ \; \check{e}(p_e^o, p_s^*, p_1^*, p_2^*, \pi^o, q^o, EU^o) \quad - \check{e}(p_e^o, p_s^o, p_1^*, p_2^*, \pi^o, q^o, EU^o) \quad (10.10b)$$
$$+ \; \check{e}(p_e^o, p_s^o, p_1^*, p_2^*, \pi^o, q^o, EU^o) \quad - \check{e}(p_e^o, p_s^o, p_1^o, p_2^*, \pi^o, q^o, EU^o) \quad (10.10c)$$
$$+ \; e(p_e^o, p_s^o, p_1^o, p_2^*, \pi^o, q^o, EU^o) \quad - \check{e}(p_e^o, p_s^o, p_1^o, p_2^o, \pi^o, q^o, EU^o) \quad (10.10d)$$

Observe how closely the total valuation framework under uncertainty parallels the framework for the deterministic situation. Either a holistic valuation (10.9) or a sequenced valuation (10.10) may be specified. Furthermore, the categories that emerge from the sequenced valuation under uncertainty (10.10) are the same as in the deterministic case: that is, existence value, site experience value, activity-1 value and activity-2 value. In this general total value formulation for the uncertainty case, no new categories of value emerge (see also Smith 1987a): there are no categories for demand-side option value, supply-side option value, or quasi-option value.

Uncertainty causes the emergence of no new components of value. Rather, it now permeates all of the value categories that were present in the deterministic case. Holistic total value and all of the value components are now *ex ante*, based on the planned expenditure function and dependent on the probabilities associated with the policy-independent states of the world (π) and the impacts of policy on the environment (q). Hicksian compensation tests are performed subject to maintaining the initial level of expected utility.

It is important to explain how the total value framework — which includes no terms for the traditional categories of supply-side option value, demand-side option value, and quasi-option value — nevertheless addresses the concerns that initiated the introduction of these terms into the standard literature.

Supply Uncertainty. Supply uncertainty is modeled by assuming that Q is a K-element vector of the states of the environment and q is a K-element vector of probabilities associated with these states. Uncertainty would be eliminated if one particular q_k were to be set equal to 1 and all q_h, if $h \neq k$, equal to 0. The earliest literature on supply uncertainty assumed that a policy action could be taken to change Q^o to Q^1_k; that is, to eliminate baseline uncertainty by taking action to ensure a unique post-policy environmental condition, Q^1_k. The model permits valuation of such a proposed policy.

More generally, both Q^o and Q^1 can be uncertain, and either can be "more uncertain" (that is, the probabilities associated with various elements of either the Q^o or Q^1 vector can be more dispersed) than the other. Policy may amplify rather than reduce uncertainty. The model permits empirical analysis of all the various possibilities.

Demand Uncertainty. One valid interpretation of S and π is that, independent of policy, demand for environmental services might be uncertain. Again, the uncertainty would be eliminated if one π_j took the value of 1 and all π_i, $i \neq j$, were set at 0. This appears to represent the traditional formulation of demand uncertainty, which states that if the potential user is required to enter into a use contract in advance, or if she can choose to enter into such a contract to reduce supply uncertainty, then uncertainty about what her demand will be when the time of use arrives may reduce her maximum offer for the advance contract. This uncertainty about future demand could arise from incomplete knowledge of one's own future consumption technology or income and from uncertainty about the value of demand shifters, such as the weather, when future use becomes available. The *ex ante* total value framework allows for these various forms of uncertainty.

Quasi-Option Value. Scenarios from which positive quasi-option value is said to emerge have something of a special-case quality. Within these scenarios there are two alternatives: development, $d = 1$, and preservation, $d = 0$; and two time periods: $t = 1$, and $t = 2$. Development is irreversible, such that $d_1 = 0$ permits d_2 to take either value, 0 or 1; whereas $d_1 = 1$ permits only $d_2 = 1$. If there is a chance that new information will emerge after $t = 1$ but before $t = 2$, information that will shift rightward the demand for services produced by $d_2 = 0$ but not by $d_2 = 1$, then this possibility generates a quasi-option value that should be counted as a benefit of choosing $d_1 = 0$. The typical example concerns period-1 species preservation, which might permit future benefits from as yet undiscovered uses of a species. The theoretical developments and numerical examples in the literature typically assume discrete time periods, discrete choices ($d = 1$ or $d = 0$), and strict irreversibility. Without these assumptions, the analysis becomes untidy and the theoretical results are more ambiguous (Fisher and Hanemann 1986).

A more general analysis of quasi-option value within this framework would allow: (1) reversion ($d_1 = 1$ and $d_2 = 0$) at some cost, which might range from quite small to very large, depending on the particular case; (2) d to be continuous in the range $0 \le d \le 1$; and (3) development (as well as preservation) to serve as a precondition for the usefulness of emerging information that might shift later-period demands rightward (or leftward).

What modifications would it take, for the total value framework to address quasi-option value? The only significant change necessary would be to extend the time frame to allow a time sequence of decision points, and to allow the earlier-period decisions to affect the costs attached to the later-period alternatives. Information emerging over time, independently of policy, would change π_t as t increases. However, prior policy decisions may render some kinds of new information less useful, by reducing the scope for later-period decisions that benefit from the new information. In concept, the necessary modifications to the *ex ante* total value framework are straightforward, but in execution they may be quite messy. That is the problem Fisher and Hanemann found when attempting to generalize their theory of quasi-option value.

10.3 Strategies for Estimating Total Value and Nonuse Values

For nonmarket valuation, the standard techniques are contingent valuation (chapter 5), the household production/travel cost method (chapter 3), and hedonic price analysis (chapter 4). In designing the research plan for any particular empirical study, the researchers must answer a number of questions.

First, do they want to start from scratch to design and execute a study that will estimate either total value holistically or total and component values in a valid piecewise sequential valuation framework? If so, they will be pushed toward contingent valuation. And, is it important to include in their research design some opportunities for using travel cost or hedonic methods to estimate use values? And last, as studies designed from scratch tend to be expensive, do they want to use at least some "typical" unit values that studies such as that of Sorg and Loomis (1984) have compiled? If their answer to either of the last two questions is positive, then they must resolve three additional problems.

The first concerns the forms of the values. Component values that are estimated by travel cost or hedonic methods or are gleaned from compilations of "typical" unit values, are usually in IVS form. That is, for the example of activity 1, such values usually conform to (10.6c) rather than (10.5c). To use them within a valid total value framework, the researchers would need to find a method of approximating a valid piecewise valuation using independent piecewise value estimates.

Second, an eclectic valuation strategy of using different methods (and perhaps even different teams of researchers) to estimate the various value components exposes the overall research effort to the problems of multiple-counting and its obverse, omissions. The discipline of the total value framework is absent and in its place the researcher must substitute painstaking examinations for consistency: for example, the researcher must determine if the existence value estimate includes some value that should be attributed to use value or option value, or if any important sources of value been omitted.

Third, when uncertainty is a concern, the total value framework calls for *ex ante* values (see equations 10.9 and 10.10), but travel cost, hedonic, and "typical" unit values are usually considered *ex post*; that is, values estimated from decisions made after the uncertainty has been resolved. An eclectic strategy for valuation under uncertainty seems to require procedures for translating between *ex ante* and *ex post* values.

The remainder of this section will elaborate on these issues, and so far as possible, resolve them.

10.3.1 Contingent Valuation Approaches

The total value framework developed in the previous section permits economists to measure total value either directly and holistically or piecewise and sequentially. Total value should be unique, whether measured holistically or sequentially. The components of total value will include existence value and various kinds of use value, and if estimates of particular component values are desired, a sequential piecewise estimation strategy may be used. The magnitudes of particular component values will depend on their places in the valuation sequence, which may be a problem when there is no reason to chose any particular sequence. If, instead of a piecewise sequential strategy, a piecewise independent estimation strategy was chosen, the estimates obtained would be misleading with respect to both total value and component values. The introduction of uncertainty changes none of these conclusions. Total value and its components are all defined in *ex ante* terms and measured with respect to a baseline level of expected utility. These modifications to the deterministic framework provide a valid response to the problem of uncertainty; it is unnecessary to introduce new components of value, such as option value and quasi-option value.

Total value and its components can be estimated *de novo* (for example, in an exercise that starts from scratch) via the contingent valuation method (CVM). Scenarios can be constructed to elicit total value holistically, or total value and component values in a valid piecewise sequence. The match between the total value framework and CVM is very close: the total value framework has a sound intuitive appeal; CVM is flexible in that it permits the valuation of a wide variety of plausible constructed policy scenarios, and CVM scenarios constructed to implement a total value approach, are as plausible and intuitive as the total value framework.

To implement CVM in a total value framework, all of the standard considerations and caveats pertinent to CVM (chapter 5) apply. The focus here is on constructing scenarios. For holistic total value, the scenario should follow the logic of equation (10.4) to estimate baseline value and equation (10.7) to evaluate a proposed policy change under certainty, and equation (10.9) to estimate baseline value under uncertainty. A CVM scenario based on equation (10.4) requires the respondent to compare two situations: $(p_e^o, p_s^o, p_1^o, p_2^o, Q^o)$, in which the particular environment exists, and site experience and the various activities are available at the current quality levels and prices; and $(p_e^*, p_s^*, p_1^*, p_2^*, Q^o)$, in which the environment does not exist and hence is unavailable for use. A Hicksian compensating approach to valuation would suggest questions designed to elicit — directly or by binary choice, perhaps in referendum format — willingness to accept compensation (WTA) to permit $(p_e^*, p_s^*, p_1^*, p_2^*, Q^o)$ given a reference situation of $(p_e^o, p_s^o, p_1^o, p_2^o, Q^o)$. A Hicksian equivalent approach would suggest eliciting WTP to avoid the less-desired situation.

Scenario construction for eliciting the holistic total value of a proposed policy (10.7), is even simpler because the environmental quality level changes, whereas the prices do not. The scenario must emphasize that existence and the opportunity for site experience and the various activities are to be valued simultaneously. If a proposed policy would change prices and quality levels, this would need to be reflected in the scenarios. To elicit *ex ante* holistic value under uncertainty (10.9), the basic scenarios for (10.4) must be modified to communicate the uncertainties that exist with respect to demand and to environmental quality. Recent developments in communicating risk and uncertainty in CVM are reviewed in chapter 5.

For valid piecewise total and component values, the researcher must develop scenarios that conform to, for example, equations (10.5), (10.8), and (10.10). As an example, consider (10.8). First, choose a valuation sequence. Intuition suggests that existence comes first since it is a prerequisite for any kind of use. (Previous studies have often treated existence value as an afterthought, perhaps worth considering after the use values have been estimated.) Similarly, intuition suggests that site experience has a claim to second position. The specialized use activities (hiking, boating, sightseeing, and so on) must also be sequenced, but there may be no intuitive reason to prefer any particular sequence.

Once a sequence has been chosen, as in (10.8), scenario construction proceeds according to the logic of sequential valuation. For $Q^1 > Q^o$, the first step is to elicit the value (again directly or via a binary choice) of the improvement from Q^o to Q^1 given that site experience and use activities are unavailable (Bennett 1984). The second step is to elicit the value of the Q^o to Q^1 upgrade in site experience given that the existence upgrade has already been secured and paid for. For example, a researcher might ask a respondent: Now, how much more would (the upgrade to Q^1) be worth to you if you were free to visit the site at a cost of p_e^o but not to engage in any special activities like hiking or boating? The third through nth steps (for an n-item valuation sequence) introduce an activity upgraded to Q^1 assuming all previous upgraded components have been secured and paid for. In general, a valid valuation requires that the respondent determine his or her valuation while considering fully the array of substitutes, complements, and alternatives, as well as budget constraints. For example, when he or she is considering existence values for particular species or for small areas with unusual ecosystems, a multitude of alternative potential projects may compete for (contingent) payments. CVM scenarios should communicate to the respondent that the proposed project or policy is just one of many potential efforts to preserve species or natural areas.

Clearly, researchers can obtain valid estimates of total value, existence value, and various kinds of use value (in a deterministic or uncertain context) by conducting, *de novo,* a CVM exercise. However, research sponsors and some analysts could object to a valuation research strategy that was confined to *de novo* CVM exercises. They could argue that a *de novo* effort is not always essential, and that there are circumstances in which they could adapt value data that had been assembled for some other valuation purpose. An insistence on *de novo* valuation efforts would unnecessarily increase the costs of routine benefit estimation. They could also argue that methods for obtaining value data other than CVM — for example, revealed preference methods, such as hedonics or travel cost — could be used in ways that approximate a valid piecewise sequential valuation framework. It is difficult, however, to see how these methods could capture existence value or total value holistically. To those practitioners who prefer revealed preference methods to CVM, and to those who believe that a sound benefit estimation strategy should include tests for cross-technique consistency in the estimates for at least some components of total value, it is important to find a legitimate role for the methods in a valid piecewise valuation strategy.

Are De Novo Value Estimates Essential? De novo valuation efforts can be designed to implement the valid holistic valuation framework (10.4) and the piecewise sequential framework (10.5). However, many agencies that routinely undertake benefit-cost analysis have invested substantial effort in assembling an inventory of "typical" unit values for various beneficial uses.[1] The idea is that the up-front costs of carefully assembling these "typical" unit values can be recouped by using them repeatedly in routine benefit-cost analysis.

The objection to this procedure is that it usually implies an IVS, or piecewise independent, valuation procedure (10.6) that Hoehn and Randall (1989) showed produces misleading estimates of total value and component values. The problem is that an IVS valuation procedure does not take proper account of resource scarcity and the interactions, such as substitution or complementarity among various kinds of environmental services. Still, given the considerable savings in research costs that might result from using "typical" unit value estimates taken "off the shelf," it is reasonable for researchers to try to devise methods that approximate the valid valuations using "shelf" data.

Randall, Hoehn, and Sorg Swanson (1990) and Hoehn (1989) have suggested methods for approximating the valid total and component values while economizing on the need for *de novo* value estimates. Hoehn started with a set of CVM values for a three-component policy in which each component could be implemented at one of three levels (the baseline and two alternative levels). He used this data to estimate a multidimensional value function, using quadratic and translog functional forms. He was able to test empirically for substitution relationships among policy components and to estimate the total value of any level or combination of policy impacts within the range of the sample data. Based on this result, one avenue of economizing on *de novo* value estimation may be to elicit values for a sample of policy combinations rather than for every relevant combination of policy components, and to econometrically estimate the values of other policy combinations within the range of the data.

If a large body of empirical results such as Hoehn's (1989) is assembled, it is conceivable that certain empirical patterns might emerge. Then, economists may start to get a feel for the magnitudes of the substitution relationships and the errors introduced by IVS procedures in various environmental valuation contexts. If this happened, the accumulated empirical experience

[1] Consider, for example, the work of Sorg and Loomis (1984) on recreation values, that was sponsored by U.S. Forest Service.

would provide correction factors that would enable economists to use "typical" unit values, such as those assembled by Sorg and Loomis (1984), to construct approximately valid total and component values for complex policies. This procedure could be justified only in relatively routine policy evaluations where economizing on research expense is an overriding consideration.

Opportunities for Using Revealed Preference Methods. Revealed preference methods, such as the travel cost method for estimating recreation benefits and hedonic price analysis for valuing various kinds of amenities that have spatial dimensions, are widely used in environmental benefit estimation (see chapters 3 and 4). Some practitioners prefer them to CVM because of their empirical basis in historical transactions. Others argue that as long as CVM and revealed preference methods remain roughly equal competitors, it is wise to make opportunities to use both kinds of methods in the same situation to check for cross-technique comparability of results.

However, the total value framework imposes some important impediments to the use of revealed preference methods. First, as mentioned above, revealed preference methods are generally inappropriate for measuring total value and its existence value component. So, incorporation of these methods in a benefit estimation strategy will force the practitioner into implementing some kind of procedure to approximate a valid piecewise sequential benefit estimate. (The present status of such procedures was discussed above.) Second, it can be argued that the long and tortuous controversy about option value, when benefits are uncertain, is an artifact of the use of revealed preference methods.

Revealed preference methods are typically used to estimate the amount of consumers' surplus implicit in a historical pattern of transactions. Using projections of future transactions, the analyst projects this surplus forward in *ex ante* benefit analysis and labels it the expected surplus (ES) from future use. Under uncertainty, it has long been argued that, in addition to expected surplus based on projections from historical experience, there is an option value (OV) representing the premium that prospective users would pay to reduce the risks associated with future supply. Therefore, option value emerges only as a result of a decision to estimate total value in piecewise fashion by applying revealed preference methods and historical transactions data to generate estimates of expected surplus for some kinds of use value.

There has been a long controversy about the sign and size of option value, and by the early 1980s a consensus emerged that, in general, sign is ambiguous while there is little evidence that size is typically substantial (see, e.g., Freeman 1984, 1985b). However, *option price — ex ante* willingness to pay to secure an option for future use — may be defined: option price (OP) = expected surplus (ES) + option value (OV), where $OV \gtreqless O$. Recently, several empirical studies have documented substantial option prices for various environmental resources (e.g., Brookshire, Eubanks, and Randall 1983; Desvousges, Smith, and Fisher 1987; Greenley, Walsh, and Young 1981; Walsh, Loomis, and Gillman 1984).

However, two recent developments have shattered this consensus. First, OP, ES, and OV are sure payments; that is, the amount paid is independent of which state of the world eventually emerges. Graham (1981) introduced the concept of an *ex ante* contract for an array of state-conditional payments. With perfect markets in contingent commodities, a researcher could define a fair bet point (FB), which is the set of state-conditional payments whose expected value (EF) is the maximum feasible, so that EF $\geq$ OP, and EF $\geq$ ES. This led some researchers, such as Cory and Saliba (1987), to question the relevance of OP and OV.

Second, Smith (1987a) introduced a formulation that combines the concepts of state-conditional payments and planned expenditures in order to define *ex ante* use values. As in the equation set (10.10), no separate category for option value emerges. Smith was adamant that *ex ante* use value, $\tilde{U}V$ is fundamentally noncomparable with ES because $\tilde{U}V$ is defined with respect to *ex ante* planned expenditures whereas ES is defined with respect to actual expenditures *ex post* (after the uncertainty has been resolved). It can be readily shown that OP is simply a restricted case of $\tilde{U}V$ (compare with Smith 1987a). Thus, it follows that OP is noncomparable with ES and that the traditional claim of OP = ES + OV is meaningless.

Given that *ex ante* benefit-cost analysis of proposed projects and policies requires *ex ante* measures of use value, such as $\tilde{U}V$ or OP, the noncomparability provides a powerful argument against using revealed preference methods to estimate ES and then adding in OV to estimate total use value. This argument clearly tilts the choice of method toward CVM, which is readily adaptable to measuring $\tilde{U}V$ and OP.

However, in response to an earlier version of Smith (1987a), Bishop (1986) argued that Smith overstated the distinction between *ex ante* and *ex post*. His point was that Smith's distinction was based on the relative timing of the value-revealing decision and the resolution of uncertainty. Smith stated that if the decision occurs while things are still uncertain, the valuation it reveals is *ex ante*; however, if the decision occurs after the uncertainty has been resolved, the valuation is *ex post*. Bishop argued that many revealed preference data sets are based on decisions that were made before all the uncertainties pertaining to use and enjoyment could possibly have been resolved. How, for example, can people be sure what the weather will be like during their vacation at the time they reserve their plane tickets and accommodations? Bishop believed that rather than overplaying the *ex ante/ex post* distinction, analysts should be alert to any differences among the information bases that underly the various value measures.

Obviously, several of the issues raised in this subsection await final resolution. In particular, the optimism engendered by Cory and Saliba that ES can serve validly as a lower-bound estimate of *ex ante* use value — and therefore that revealed preference methods have a valid role in a piecewise benefit evaluation strategy — has been questioned by Smith's analyses of the noncomparability of EF and OP to ES. For now, there seem to be serious impediments to incorporating benefit measures based on revealed preference methods into a valid measure of *ex ante* total value. However, there is little guidance as to the likely magnitude of the empirical errors that may be involved.

10.4 Empirical Estimates of Nonuse Values

During the 1980s, a number of empirical studies for estimating nonuse values were published. Yet, given that the conceptual understanding of nonuse values has been in a state of flux and (as has often been the case in environmental economics) that the earliest empirical applications preceded the systematic development of the relevant theory, several conceptual controversies remain unresolved. Thus, it is not surprising that the conceptual foundations of these various empirical studies are often inconsistent with one another. In some cases, there are — when examined from hindsight — clear conceptual errors (Greenley, Walsh, and Young 1981). Nevertheless, a body of literature has accumulated that shows, first, that estimation of nonuse values is often feasible, and second, that nonuse values are frequently substantial and sometimes exceed current use values by a considerable margin (Majid, Sinden, and Randall 1983; Schulze, Brookshire, et al. 1983).

Some general observations about the empirical literature may be helpful. First, all of the studies cited in this section used CVM. This is to be expected since existence value, option price, and option value are not readily accessible via revealed preference methods. Second, given that little more than a dozen empirical works are cited, the range of resources addressed is quite broad: air quality (Schulze, Brookshire, et al. 1983); water quality (Desvousges, Smith, and Fisher 1987; Edwards 1988; Greenley, Walsh, and Young 1981; Sutherland and Walsh 1985); wilderness and wildlands (Bennett 1984; Majid, Sinden, and Randall 1983; Walsh, Loomis, and Gillman 1984); hunting (Brookshire, Eubanks, and Randall 1983); fisheries (Bishop, Boyle, and Welsh 1987); and nonconsumptive wildlife use and existence (Bowker and Stoll 1988; Boyle and Bishop 1987; Samples, Dixon, and Gowen 1986; Stoll and Johnson 1984). Third, the studies vary with respect to the categories of value estimated. Some address total value or preservation value; and some of these attempt to break-out various components of value. Others are focused on OP. Still others are primarily concerned with existence value. Those cited in this paragraph and summarized in the table 10.1 include several of each type.

In an empirical experiment concerning existence values, Samples, Dixon, and Gowen (1986) specifically addressed the issue of how information provided before or in the course of the CVM exercise affects the value estimates obtained. Values were sensitive to the amount and kind of information provided. In one experiment, positive values were obtained for preserving

TABLE 10.1
A summary of published studies emphasizing nonuse values.

Publication	Range of value estimates ($/household/year)				
	Total[a]	Preservation[a]	Use[a]	Option[a]	Existence[a]
Bennett (1984) Preservation of Nadgee Nature Reserve, Australia	—	—	—	—	0-2.00
Bowker and Stoll (1988) Whooping cranes, Texas	5-149	—	—	—	—
Boyle and Bishop (1987) and Bishop, Boyle, and Welsh (1987)					
Bald eagles and	6.50-75.31	—	—	—	4.92-28.38
stripped shiners, Wisconsin	—	—	—	—	1.00-5.66
Brookshire, Eubanks, and Randall (1983)					
Grizzley Bear and	—	—	—	9.70-21.50	—
Bighorn Sheep, Wyoming	—	—	—	11.18-22.90	—
Desvousges, Smith, and Fisher (1987) Water quality for boating, fishing, swimming, Monongahela River	—	—	—	54.1-117.60	—
Edwards (1988) Potable groundwater protection, Cape Cod, Massachusetts	—	—	—	4,930-24,850[d]	—

TABLE 10.1 *Continued*

Publication	Range of value estimates ($/household/year)				
	Total[a]	Preservation[a]	Use[a]	Option[a]	Existence[a]
Majid, Sinden, and Randall (1983) Incremental value of additional parks, Australia	1.5-5.3[b]	—	—	—	—
Schulze and Brookshire, et al. (1983) Visibility preservation in S.W. parklands	—	2.89-4.50	3.16-4.93	—	—
Stoll and Johnson (1984) Whooping cranes, Texas	—	—	2.4-?15	28.90-41.96[e]	-0.29-39.48
Sutherland and Walsh (1985) Distance and water preservation values, Flathead Lake, Montana	—	8,183.70[c]	—	2,770.50[c]	5,413.20[c]
Walsh, Loomis, and Gillman (1984) Colorado wilderness levels, 10.0 million acres protected	93,200[c]	35,000[c]	58,000[c]	10,200[c]	24,800[c]

[a] Consult original for the definition employed.
[b] Increments to total value from addition of new parks to system.
[c] Aggregated annual values of all households x 1000.
[d] Present value of a 30-year stream of benefits.
[e] Option price *plus* existence value for households expecting to visit in future.

plausible but imaginary species. This study barely hints at the broad influences information might have on CVM-estimated existence values concerning resources about which the public, and even the specialists, have very incomplete knowledge. The issue of exactly how much and what kind of information to provide respondents is unresolved.

10.5 Conclusions

Despite several key developments in the 1980s — including the Hoehn-Randall work on valid holistic and piecewise sequential benefit estimation structures, Graham's theory of benefits under uncertainty in an environment of complete contingent markets, and Smith's elaboration of the distinction between *ex ante* and *ex post* value measures — the researcher is still faced with ambiguity about correct methods of evaluating nonuse benefits. What is known and not known about these methods is summarized below.

1. In either a deterministic framework or under uncertainty, total value is uniquely defined and can be decomposed into existence value and various kinds of use values. Under uncertainty, all value concepts are *ex ante*: ex ante total value, *ex ante* existence values, and *ex ante* use value.

2. Total value may be defined holistically or in a piecewise sequential framework. If a piecewise sequential framework is used, the value of a particular component is dependent on its place in the valuation sequence.

3. Piecewise independent valuation is a common procedure, and it has the virtue of permitting some economies in benefit estimation through the use of "typical" values for various kinds of use. Unfortunately, this procedure is misleading with respect to both total value and component values. Although some researchers are developing procedures that will use piecewise independent data for approximately valid benefit evaluation, as yet none exist. Furthermore, little is known about the magnitude of the errors due to piecewise independent valuation.

4. Contingent valuation methods are readily adaptable for measuring, *de novo,* all of the *ex ante* concepts of total, existence, and use value. Researchers are working on approximately valid methods that will economize on de novo benefit estimation by extending the scope of a sample of *de novo* benefit estimates.

5. Some researchers prefer revealed preference methods to CVM; others use both CVM and revealed preference methods to facilitate cross-technique comparisons. In a deterministic framework, revealed preference methods may be used to evaluate some kinds of use benefits, although care must be taken because of the piecewise independent framework in which these methods typically are used.

6. When uncertainty about future supply, demand, or knowledge is explicitly

recognized, CVM methods are readily adaptable to the benefit estimation task. However, theoretical developments in the 1980s have not resolved the option value controversy. Rather, additional complexities have emerged. These developments have tended to make it more, rather than less, difficult to define a valid role for revealed preference methods in benefit estimation under uncertainty.

10.5.1 Must the Practitioner Always Be Concerned with Existence Values and Uncertainty?

It seems clear that a concern with total value, existence value, and uncertainty tends to swing the balance, with respect to valuation techniques, toward CVM. On the other hand, an analyst who is satisfied to evaluate use benefits from a historical perspective will have much greater scope for reliance on revealed preference methods. Analysts who would prefer to reserve a substantial role for the latter methods have good reason to ask whether it is always necessary to be concerned with existence value and uncertainty.

It seems to be a truism that everything has an existence value; however, existence value at the margin approaches zero when existence is not scarce. Projects that modify small amounts of resources that are in large supply or have many substitutes are unlikely to cause substantial losses in existence value. This suggests that, in many routine benefit estimation contexts, existence values will be unimportant. Nevertheless, this conclusion should be approached cautiously; the burden of proof should always lie upon the analyst who claims existence value does not matter. Randall and Stoll (1983) have argued that, for environmental goods with a spatial dimension, important local and regional existence values may be at stake, even if existence at the global level is not threatened.

With respect to uncertainty and the concomitant obligation to estimate *ex ante* total (or existence and use) value, it is perhaps appropriate to observe that uncertainty is often recognized but treated as academic: often the analysis proceeds with scant attention to uncertainty. Where there is nothing especially unusual about the kinds and degrees of uncertainty involved, this may well be a justifiable strategy. However, where the uncertainties are great and it would be very costly to reverse a wrong decision or mitigate its damage, these uncertainties should be explicitly considered in the benefit analysis.

References

Arrow, K.J., and A.C. Fisher. 1974. Environmental preservation, uncertainty, and irreversibility. *Quarterly Journal of Economics* 88:313–319.

Bennett, J.W. 1984. Using direct questioning to value existence benefits of preserved natural areas. *Australian Journal of Agricultural Economics* 28:136–152.

Bishop, R.C. 1986. Resource valuation under uncertainty: theoretical principles of empirical research. In *Advances in applied micro-economics*, ed. V.K. Smith, vol. 4, pp. 133–152. Greenwich, CT: JAI Press.

Bishop, R.C., K.J. Boyle, and M.P. Welsh. 1987. Toward total economic valuation of Great Lakes fishery resources. *Transactions of the American Fisheries Society* 116:339–345.

Bowker, J.M., and J.R. Stoll. 1988. Use of dichotomous choice nonmarket methods to value the whooping crane resource. *American Journal of Agricultural Economics* 70:372–381.

Boyle, K.J., and R.C. Bishop. 1987. Valuing wildlife in benefit cost analysis: a case study involving endangered species. *Water Resources Research* 23:943–950.

Brookshire, D.S., L.S. Eubanks, and A. Randall. 1983. Estimating option prices and existence values for wildlife resources. *Land Economics* 59:1–15.

Cory, D.C., and B.C. Saliba. 1987. Requiem for option value. *Land Economics* 63:1–10.

Desvouges, W.H., V.K. Smith, and A. Fisher. 1987. Option price estimates for water quality improvements: a contingent valuation study for the Monongahela River. *Journal of Environmental Economics and Management* 14:248–267.

Edwards, S.F. 1988. Option prices for groundwater protection. *Journal of Environmental Economics and Management* 15:475–487.

Fisher, A.C., and W.M. Hanemann. 1986. Option value and the extinction of species. In *Advances in applied micro-economics*, ed. V.K. Smith, vol. 4, pp. 169–190. Greenwich: JAI Press.

Freeman, A.M. 1984. The sign and size of option value. *Land Economics* 60:1–13.

———. 1985b. Supply uncertainty, option price, and option value in project evaluation. *Land Economics* 61:176–181.

Graham, D.A. 1981. Cost benefit analysis under uncertainty. *American Economic Review* 71:715–725.

Greenley, D.A., R.G. Walsh, and R.A. Young. 1981. Option value: empirical evidence from a case study of recreation and water quality. *Quarterly Journal of Economics* 96:657–673.

Helms, L.J. 1985. Expected consumer's surplus and the welfare effects of price stabilization. *International Economic Review* 26:603–617.

Henry, C. 1974. Option values in the economics of irreplaceable assets. In *Symposium on the economics of exhaustible resources* 41(S):89–104.

Hoehn, J.P. 1989. *Valuing environmental policy alternatives in the presence of substitutes*. Staff paper, Department of Agricultural Economics, Michigan State University, East Lansing, MI.

Hoehn, J.P., and A. Randall. 1989. Too many proposals pass the benefit cost test. American Economic Review 79:544–551.

Krutilla, J.V. 1967. Conservation reconsidered. *American Economic Review* 57:777–786.

Majid, I., J.A. Sinden, and A. Randall. 1983. Benefit evaluation of increments to existing systems of public facilities. *Land Economics* 59:377–392.

Randall, A., J.P. Hoehn, and C. Sorg Swanson. 1990. *Estimating the recreational, visual, habitat and quality of life benefits of Tongass National Forest*. General Technical Report RM-192. Fort Collins, CO: USDA Forest Service.

———. 1983. Existence value in a total valuation framework. In *Managing air quality and scenic resources at national parks and wilderness areas*, eds. R.D. Rowe and L.G. Chestnut. Boulder, CO: Westview Press.

Samples, K.C., J.A. Dixon, and M.M. Gowen. 1986. Information disclosure and endangered species valuation. *Land Economics* 62:306–312.

Schulze, W.D., D.S. Brookshire, E.G. Walther, K.K. McFarland, M.A. Thayer, R.L. Whitworth, S. Ben-David, W. Malm, and J. Molenar. 1983. The economic benefits of preserving visibility in the national parklands of the southwest. *Natural Resources Journal* 23:149–173.

Simmons, P.J. 1984. Multivariate risk premia with a stochastic objective, *Economic Journal*, supplement 94:124–132.

Smith, V.K. 1987a. Nonuse values in benefit cost analysis. *Southern Economic Journal* 54:19–26.

Sorg, C., and J.B. Loomis. 1984. *Empirical estimates of amenity forest values: a comparative review.* General Technical Report RM-107. Rocky Mountain Forest and Range Experiment Station, U.S. Forest Service, Fort Collins, CO.

Stoll, J. R., and L.A. Johnson. 1984. Concepts of value, nonmarket valuation, and the case of the whooping crane. *Transactions of the forty-ninth North American wildlife and natural resources conference* 49:382–393.

Sutherland, R.J., and R.G. Walsh. 1985. Effect of distance on the preservation value of water quality. *Land Economics* 61:281–291.

Walsh, R.G., J.B. Loomis, and R.A. Gillman. 1984. Valuing option, existence, and bequest demands for wilderness. *Land Economics* 60:14–29.

Weisbrod, B.A. 1964. Collective-consumption services of individual-consumption goods. *Quarterly Journal of Economics* 78:471–477.

[11]

A Difficulty with the Travel Cost Method

Alan Randall

ABSTRACT. *Instead of observable prices of recreational visits, travel cost method (TCM) researchers are obliged to substitute researcher-assigned visitation cost estimates. I argue that visitation costs are inherently subjective, but are ordinally measurable so long as the cost increases with distance travelled. It follows that traditional TCM yields only ordinally measurable welfare estimates. The household production function formulation of TCM "resolves" this problem only by imposing severe and untestable analytical restrictions. TCM cannot serve as a stand-alone technique for estimating recreation benefits; rather, it must be calibrated using information generated with fundamentally different methods. (JEL Q26)*

I. INTRODUCTION

The research program to estimate recreation benefits via the travel cost method, TCM (Hotelling 1949; Clawson 1959; Bockstael, McConnell, and Strand 1991), has established an empirically robust result: site visitation and recreation participation rates decrease as the distance to be travelled increases. Assuming that travelling is costly and the cost increases with distance, then it follows that the visitation rate diminishes as the cost of visiting increases. Since the necessary assumption is so obviously plausible, this conclusion seems hard to challenge. Therefore it confirms an essentially economic explanation of recreation choice, a class of behavior that some observers had been tempted to claim lies beyond the reach of standard economic theorizing.

This is an important contribution. But the TCM research program, starting with Hotelling's (1949) initial suggestion, has always had larger ambitions. It seeks to measure the benefits of recreation facilities (e.g., site access); that is, to bring recreation under the scope of standard welfare change measurement theory and procedures.

It is a standard result that if recreation site quality and travel are weak comple-

ments, the compensated demand for travel contains all of the information necessary for welfare evaluation of recreation site quality. This result justifies a travel price method (TPM) of recreation benefit estimation. Unfortunately, travel is a nonhomogeneous good, and the demander typically plays a substantial role in its production. Thus, its price is typically unobservable. Instead, TCM depends upon substituting travel cost for the price of travel.

There are a number of persistent difficulties with TCM. I argue that many of these particular difficulties are symptoms of a general problem: travel cost is inherently unobservable. If travel cost is unobservable but is known to be an increasing function of distance travelled, it follows that travel cost is ordinally measurable. In this case, it is shown readily that TCM yields ordinally measurable benefit and welfare change measures. In modern household production formulations of TCM, the cost of travel depends, *inter alia*, on the household's opportunity cost of travel time and its activity production technology, both of which are unobservable. Again, ordinal measurability of welfare estimates is the best that can be expected. Nor do random utility (RUM) models resolve the measurability problem: these models are addressed to other, quite different, issues in the TCM research program.

Researchers using TCM, in its traditional or household production formula-

Professor, Department of Agricultural Economics and Rural Sociology, The Ohio State University.

This article is a contribution to regional project W-133, Benefits and Costs in Natural Resources Planning. Salaries and research support were provided by state and federal funds appropriated to the Ohio Agricultural Research and Development Center. Helpful comments from Thomas W. Blaine, Michael C. Farmer, John P. Hoehn, Charles E. Meier, Patrice Tagro and this journal's referees are gratefully acknowledged.

Land Economics • February 1994 • 70(1): 88–96

tions, report benefit and welfare change measures in money-denominated terms. This is accomplished—despite the inherent unobservability of the cost of travel—by the use of various cost accounting and analytic conventions. These conventions, however, do not resolve the measurability problem: any particular welfare estimate is in part an artifact of the particular conventions selected for imposition.

II. THE TRAVEL PRICE METHOD

Let q be the quality of a specified recreation site, and v be visits to the site. Let p_v be the price of v and $\bar{p}_v$ be its choke price, i.e., a price so high that no v is taken. General weak complementarity (Bradford and Hildebrandt 1977; Maler 1974) holds whenever

$$e(\bar{p}_v, q^0, u^*) = e(\bar{p}_v, q, u^*), \qquad [1]$$

where u is utility; $e(\cdot)$ is expenditure; and the superscripts ^{0} and * denote, respectively, the baseline level and any given level. In words, v and q are weak complements if, when no v is taken, the individual is indifferent to the level of q. Under these conditions, the demand for v contains all of the information about preferences for q that is needed for benefit estimation and welfare change measurement.

To value a household's economic surplus associated with a given level of q^0 (using, e.g., the Hicksian compensating value measure, HC), one needs to estimate

$$
\begin{aligned}
HC &= e(\bar{p}_v, q^0, u^0) - e(p_v^0, q^0, u^0) \\
&= \int_{p_v^0}^{\bar{p}_v} v(p_v, q^0, u^0) dp_v \\
&= \int_0^{v^0} p_v(v, q^0, u^0) dv - p_v^0 \cdot v^0, \qquad [2]
\end{aligned}
$$

where $v(\cdot)$ is the Hicksian compensated demand for v, and $p_v(\cdot)$ is the inverse Hicksian compensated demand. General weak complementarity permits welfare evaluation of q^0 by integrating under the compensated demand for v conditioned on q^0. A proposal to change from q^0 to q' may be evaluated by integrating between compensated de-

mands for v conditioned on q^0 and q' respectively.

The travel price method (TPM) of recreation benefit estimation would implement these welfare measures. So long as p_v is absolute-scale measurable (Boadway and Bruce 1984) and third-party observable—as, say, published prices or user-fees would be—these welfare measures have the standard properties of welfare measures (Chipman and Moore 1980). Most important for my purposes, if the compensated demands for v satisfy the standard requirements, HC will be a unique numerical welfare indicator. It will, of course, be conditioned on the prices of other goods, the availability of substitute and complement nonmarketed amenities, demander characteristics, etc., and on the reference level of utility.[1] But, *ceteris paribus*, the welfare measure will be single-valued.

Under the conditions described in this section, a researcher could produce welfare measures having the standard properties for recreation access, using the travel price method, TPM, a particular application of general weak complementarity. Let $p_v(d, \cdot)$ be an increasing function of d, distance to the site, and TPM would be an application of Hotelling's initial insight.

III. THE TRAVEL COST METHOD

Instead of TPM, we observe TCM in general use. Instead of using visit prices that are absolute-scale measurable and third-party observable, TCM practitioners attempt to apply weak complementarity principles using data on travel and access costs.[2] After some thirty years of methodological development and applica-

---

[1] These additional concerns are routinely included in attempts at detailed empirical estimation based on the simple general idea sketched here.

[2] Not all authors draw attention to this distinction. Two recent review essays provide a contrast. The conceptual development of the travel cost model in Bockstael, McConnell, and Strand (1991) refers only to travel price, p, variables. On the other hand, Anderson and Bishop (1986) base their model on variables identified explicitly as travel cost, TC.

tion of TCM, a number of stubborn methodological problems remain, and there is a considerable literature documenting that welfare estimates generated by TCM are sensitive—sometimes alarmingly so—to the discretionary analytical choices of researchers.

I plan to focus on a particular subset of these problems, those that concern the specification of the costs and opportunity costs of visiting a particular site:

(A) Recreationists vary considerably in their investment in durable equipment useful in travel and recreation. Such equipment may be more or less expensive, and more or less specialized. Allocation of the costs of owning and maintaining vehicles and other durable equipment to any particular trip proceeds, if at all, in arbitrary fashion.

(B) For multi-site recreational trips and multi-purpose trips, cost allocation to specific sites proceeds (if at all) without benefit of any acceptable theoretical basis.

(C) Lodging and subsistence expenditures have a large discretionary component. Should practitioners count all such expenditures as costs of visiting the site?

(D) There is ample empirical evidence that the treatment of substitute sites and/or activities influences the welfare estimates generated with TCM (e.g., Rosenthal 1987). And it is conceptually clear that substitutes should receive proper consideration because they help determine the opportunity costs of selecting the chosen site. However, no nonarbitrary procedure has emerged for delimiting the set of substitutes.

(E) Conventional TCM practice treats the distance from the home to the recreation site, and the cost per mile travelled as exogenously given. However, the disturbing possibility exists that recreational preferences may have influenced the choice of residential location and motor vehi-

cle. In such cases, recreational preferences would influence miles travelled and cost per mile, not just on recreation trips but year-round.

(F) There is general agreement that the opportunity cost of time spent traveling should be counted among the costs of travel. However, the cost of travel time remains an empirical mystery.

Economists are well aware of all these problems. Problems (A)–(C) are problems in the allocation of joint costs, involving joint production of: (A) multiple activities or attributes, both on-site and in-transit; (B) activities and visits to multiple sites; and (C) recreation, lodging, and cuisine experiences. However, as Hof et al. (1985) demonstrate, there exists no unique allocation to individual products of the costs in joint production.

Problem (D), the treatment of substitutes, is a standard problem in neoclassical demand modeling, while problem (E) is a problem in multi-stage budgeting. Standard TCM practice treats recreational choice as the final stage in a multi-stage budgeting process. After the residential location and the motor vehicle(s) have been chosen in previous budgeting stages, the number of trips to a recreational destination is chosen. If, however, this misspecifies the budget allocation process for at least some of the participants, costs are misspecified for those participants and standard aggregation conditions are violated (Deaton and Muellbauer 1980). Problem (F) is the familiar "time cost of travel" problem (e.g., Bockstael, Strand, and Hanemann 1987; Bockstael, McConnell, and Strand 1991).

These problems with TCM have proven rather intractable. Standard TCM practice, despite three decades of research, does not yet incorporate procedures to resolve these difficulties convincingly. Nevertheless, neoclassical economics holds out the hope that these problems may be resolved, one-by-one, with persistent effort by TCM researchers. To the contrary, I argue, they are manifestations of a common problem, one that can be expected to remain intractable. The common problem concerns specifying the "true" costs of participating in recreation at a particular site.

Neoclassical theory posits that cost is determined by technology and factor prices. Assuming that technology and all factor prices are observable, cost is claimed to be "objective." By that, the neoclassicals mean to claim that cost is absolute-scale measurable and third-party observable; in these senses, cost has the properties usually attributed to price. The Austrian school of economics takes a contrary view. Cost is opportunity cost and is therefore subjective. What counts as an opportunity is subjective, as is the sacrifice entailed in choosing one opportunity rather than another. Furthermore, opportunity cost is always *ex ante*; it is the subjective expectation of sacrifice that determines choice.

To clarify what is at issue, consider the empirical estimation of supply. The neoclassical position is that there are two alternative observational bases for supply estimation: one may observe either the response of quantity supplied to price offered, or the relationship between marginal cost and quantity produced. The Austrian position is that only the first-mentioned approach is available. Consider Buchanan's (1969) discussion of the prospects for an all-volunteer military force. He argued that it would be impossible to predict reliably the supply of volunteers by inferring their costs from observations of the wages paid in alternative occupations. Individuals may well have (unobservable) preferences that would influence their subjective opportunity costs of choosing the military line of work. If, however, one could observe the enlistments induced by an array of military wage-offers, one could estimate the supply of military labor.

The Austrians have much the better of the argument (e.g., Buchanan 1969, and Caldwell 1982). In principle, cost *is* subjective, as they claim. The neoclassical concept of cost survives not as a set of principles for understanding the nature of cost, but as a tractable approximation that is serviceable in certain empirical applications.

However, there are good reasons to believe that the neoclassical approximation to true subjective costs is rather poor, especially, perhaps, in the case of recreation. For any given trip, those variable factors purchased at observable prices are merely the tip of the iceberg. The household provides its stock of consumer durables (some of which have been accumulated in response to its recreational preferences), its recreational technology, its knowledge of alternative opportunities, its decision-making expertise, and its time. Nature, society, and policy determine q. Some elements of q—e.g., the weather, congestion, and state of maintenance—are *ex ante* uncertain to the household. The household may package its trip with some particular combination of en-route and on-site activities, visits to other attractions, and nonrecreational activities that serve business, work, and/or personal objectives. At every point the household may go "first-class" or "budget," which would produce distinctly different experiences. And all of the decisions that go into the making of the trip are based on the household's own subjective assessments of alternative prospects and their opportunity costs. The idea that third-party observers can define a typical trip and specify its cost is *prima facie* implausible.

The Traditional TCM

Imagine that v, d, x (purchased commodities), and p (their prices) could be observed for household h. If it were possible to vary d while holding the utility level constant, one could estimate $v(d, p, u^0)$, a function relating visits and distance, conditioned on commodity prices and baseline utility. Interpreting d as the "price" of visiting, $v(\cdot)$ is a compensated demand for visits. The household's willingness to pay for site access could be expressed, using the inverse compensated demand, as

$$\tilde{HC}_d = \int_0^{v^0} d(v, p, u^0)dv - d^0 \cdot v^0. \qquad [3]$$

$\tilde{HC}_d$ is denominated in distance units (miles of consumers' surplus—why not?).

The analyst, who prefers dollar-denominated welfare measures but cannot observe p_v, assigns a travel cost $c(d, \cdot)$ increasing in distance and estimates $v(c(d), p, u^0)$ using the same observable variables and rescaling d by the assigned travel cost. The household's willingness to pay for site access, now expressed in dollars, is

$$\check{H}\check{C}_c = \int_0^{v^0} c(d)[v, p, u^0]dv - c(d^0) \cdot v^0. \qquad [4]$$

Had the analyst assigned the travel cost $\psi[c(d)]$, where ψ is a monotone increasing transformation, household willingness to pay would be

$$\check{H}\check{C}_\psi = \int_0^{v^0} \psi[c(d)][v, p, u^0]dv - \psi[c(d^0)] \cdot v^0. \qquad [5]$$

The situation is illustrated in Figure 1, for the simple case where the visits-distance relationship is $v = a - b \cdot d$ (where a and b are estimated parameters) and c and ψ are scalars. Note that the inverse demands

$$d = \frac{a - v}{b}, \; c(d) = c\left(\frac{a - v}{b}\right)$$

and

$$\psi[c(d)] = \psi\left[c\left(\frac{a - v}{b}\right)\right]$$

are all consistent with the observation-based visits-distance relationship $v = a - b \cdot d$.

With unobservable travel costs, $c(d)$ and $\psi[c(d)]$ are equally plausible representations of the price of visits, yet the welfare measures $\check{H}\check{C}_c$ and $\check{H}\check{C}_\psi$ are not equal; one is a monotone increasing transformation of the other. It follows that if travel costs are ordinally measurable—while they are known to be increasing in d, there is no observational basis for determining whether they are $c(d)$ or $\psi[c(d)]$—the welfare estimates generated by traditional TCM are ordinally measurable. Ordinal-scale measures of household welfare change are noncomparable across households and violate the conditions for interhousehold aggregation. TCM analysts, of course, routinely produce

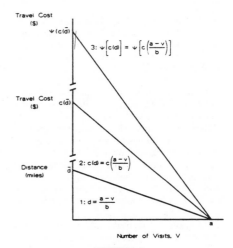

FIGURE 1

INVERSE DEMAND FOR VISITS, WITH ORDINALLY MEASURABLE TRAVEL COSTS

dollar-dominated aggregate welfare estimates for recreation projects and policies, but when these estimates are based on ordinally measurable travel costs, they are not comparable with welfare change measures for other kinds of projects and policies.

In practice, the TCM analyst proceeds by assigning dollar-denominated costs of participation. Assume that the cost for household h to visit site s can be specified

$$c_{hs} = c_h(d_{hs}, V_h, H_h, Y_h), \qquad [6]$$

where V is vehicle characteristics, H is household characteristics, and Y is some measure of annual household income. Note that [6] is not something to be estimated; we have no independent observation of c_{hs}. Rather, c_{hs} is something to be calculated. The analyst specifies some function for [6], observes d_{hs}, H_h, V_h, and Y_h and calculates c_{hs} in money units. In specifying [6], analysts may use all the economic and cost accounting intuition at their command, but given the third-party nonobservability of c_{hs}, they must ultimately impose some unique but arbitrarily chosen function for [6]. There will exist alternative specifications that are equally defensible, but because we have no independent observation of c_{hs}, we cannot conduct the customary formal and informal tests for misspecification of $c_h(\cdot)$.

The standard response to this situation is to seek, at least, to minimize the contribution of the TCM analysts to the noncomparability of travel cost calculations and welfare estimates. This is accomplished by establishing conventions for calculating travel costs. Those who abide by the same set of conventions impose the same unique function for [6]. The resulting travel costs and welfare estimates remain artifacts of the travel-cost accounting and specification conventions selected for imposition. The underlying subjectivity of travel costs—and the resulting ordinal measurability of TCM welfare measures—is not avoided, just masked.

Does the Household Production Function Formulation Solve the Problem?

Why, exactly, is $c(d)$ nonunique? First, because the budget is not directly observed. Define the budget as $m \equiv px + c(d) \cdot v$; i.e., the budget is equal to expenditures on things purchased plus the costs of visits taken. If it were possible to fix d, v, p, x, and m, $c(d)$ would be unique. But with unobservable $c(d)$, m cannot be fixed. The analyst who assigns the travel cost $c(d)$ to the household is implicitly assuming that the budget is $m_c = px + c(d) \cdot v$, whereas the analyst assigning the travel cost $\psi[c(d)]$ is assuming a budget of $m_\psi = px + \psi[c(d)]$ $\cdot v$. This interpretation is entirely consistent with ordinally measurable travel costs: if m cannot be fixed, there is an indefinitely large number of values for $c(d)$ that are consistent with known d, v, p, and x. Further, this interpretation of m is entirely plausible. The individual's endowment includes a nonmarket component including, but not limited to, access to recreation site s; and analysts assigning different costs (i.e., expenditures) for that nonmarket component would arrive at different accounts of the household's "full" income.

Second, it may be premature to fix v and

x independently; some x may be used in "producing" v. Most applications of TCM involve visits in which, at least, motor fuel is consumed. This possibility opens a window of opportunity: the analyst who can observe prices and quantities of purchased commodities used in "producing" a visit knows *something* about $c(d)$. However, the window soon begins to close: unless visits are nothing more than costlessly packaged combinations of commodities, the analyst does not know *everything* about $c(d)$.

The household production model is a reformulation of standard neoclassical consumption theory that addresses these two concerns: that the standard $m = px$ is an incomplete concept of the household's budget, and that the immediate sources of utility are not purchased commodities but activities that the household produces from purchased commodities and other inputs. Many TCM analysts have adopted the household production formulation (HPF) of TCM, in the hope that it would resolve persistent problems with traditional TCM.

In the HPF, utility is derived not from purchased commodities (x) directly, but from activities (z). For household h,

$$u_h = u_h(z_h). \tag{7}$$

Each activity z_j is produced in the household by combining commodities and time t, subject to environmental conditions q and the household's particular activity production technology $z_{hj}(\cdot)$:

$$z_{hj} = z_{hj}(x_{hj}, t_{hj}|q). \tag{8}$$

Money income constrains the purchase of commodities:

$$y_h = px_h. \tag{9}$$

Time is constrained at T, and must be allocated between working t_w and activity production:

$$T_h = t_{hw} + \sum_j t_{hj}. \tag{10}$$

This formulation tells a more appealing story about how households engage in recreation. However, for the task at hand—specifying the costs of recreation—it is not clear that the HPF permits much progress. We can derive an expression for the cost of recreation activity z_j. Let α_{hj} be the implicit cost of time spent producing z_j. Then c_{hj}, the cost to household h of activity z_j, is

$$c_{hj} = c_j[z_{hj}(\cdot), p, \alpha_{hj}|q]. \qquad [11]$$

The cost of the recreation activity depends on two things—α_{hj}, the implicit cost of household h's time when spent producing z_j and $z_{hj}(\cdot)$, the household's activity production technology for z_j—that are known subjectively to household h, but substantially if not completely hidden from third-party observers.

The general form of HPF-TCM does not resolve the measurability problems inherent in the standard TCM. Just as with traditional TCM, we can achieve a degree of regularity in HPF-TCM by imposing certain conventions on the analysis. Assume all income is earned by working at the hourly wage w_h, the demand for h's labor is perfectly elastic, and labor contracts are flexible. Then, we can write a single, linear budget constraint:

$$\begin{aligned} \bar{m}_h &= w_h \cdot T_h = w_h \cdot t_w + w_h \cdot \Sigma \, t_j \\ &= px + w_h \cdot \Sigma \, t_j, \end{aligned} \qquad [12]$$

where $\bar{m}_h$ is "full income."

Maximizing utility [7] subject to the household's activity production technology [8] and the full income constraint [12], the following first order condition is obtained:

$$\partial u_h / \partial z_{hj} = \lambda \left[\Sigma \, p_i \frac{\partial x_i}{\partial z_{hj}} + w_h \frac{\partial t_j}{\partial z_{hj}} \right], \qquad [13]$$

where x_i ($i = 1, \ldots, n$) is an element of x, and λ is the Lagrangian multiplier. Observe that, unless $\partial x_i / \partial z_{hj}$ and $\partial t_j / \partial z_{hj}$ are constants, $\partial u_h / \partial z_{hj}$ and hence the implicit price of activity z_{hj} are indeterminant. Remember that activity level z_{hj} is jointly determined by inputs of market goods and time, given the household's activity production technology $z_{hj}(\cdot)$.

If we assume that $z_{hi}(\cdot)$ is linear in all x_i

and t, the implicit price of z_{hj} is determined. A standard treatment imposes Leontief technology. Then, [8] can be replaced with

$$x_{hij} = a_{hij} z_{hj} \qquad [14]$$

and

$$t_{hj} = b_{hj} z_{hj}. \qquad [15]$$

The travel cost function [11] becomes

$$c_{hj} = \left(\sum_i p_i \cdot a_{hij} + w \cdot b_{hj} \right) z_j. \qquad [16]$$

Finally, assume $a_{hij} = a_{ij}$ and $b_{hj} = b_j$, $\forall h$, and we have

$$c_j = \left(\sum_i p_i \cdot a_{ij} + w \cdot b_j \right) z_j \qquad [17]$$

which is quite tractable. If a_{ij} and b_j can be estimated, c_j can be calculated in dollar-denominated terms. This accomplishment is an artifact of the conventions that the analyst imposes. Again, these conventions are nontrivial: flexible labor contracts[3] and identical Leontief activity production technology for all households. Because c_{hj} is not directly observable, these conventions are untestable.

So long as household production technology and the opportunity cost of time are known only subjectively, HPF-TCM welfare measures for site access are ordinally measurable at best, and therefore noncomparable with welfare measures for other kinds of goods and services.

Random Utility Models

Random utility models (RUMs) have been introduced, to deal more explicitly with the choice among substitute recreation sites. Regardless of their merits for that purpose, RUMs neither resolve nor circum-

---

[3]Bockstael, Strand, and Hanemann (1987) present a model that distinguishes between those recreationists who are able to adjust the number of hours worked and those who cannot.

vent the fundamental issue raised in the present article. For welfare measurement with RUMs, it is essential to specify a vector of visit prices for each site (Bockstael, McConnell, and Strand 1991). In practice, these prices are implicit and unobservable, and costs of travel and site access are substituted.

The Successes of the TCM Research Program

While TPM would generate absolute-scale welfare measures for recreation, it is much harder to make that claim for TCM. If we accept that the costs of travel are subjective to the recreationist household and thus hidden from the analyst, the best we can expect is ordinally measurable welfare estimates from the traditional TCM. More recent developments in TCM, including household production and random utility models, do not resolve this problem. What, then, about the various claims that the TCM research program has generated important successes? Smith's (1993) case that the TCM has worked well is based on three kinds of evidence:

(a) empirical trip demand models consistently support the properties implied by demand theory, e.g., negative own-price effects and elasticity properties consistent with the availability of substitutes;

(b) independent studies obtain roughly consistent demand characteristics and welfare measures for similar types of recreation sites; and

(c) differences in estimates of consumers surplus per unit of use and the price elasticity of demand can be explained by differences in (i) site characteristics and (ii) demand modeling practices.

Interestingly, none of this evidence in any way undermines the basic argument of this article. To the contrary, all of these successes for TCM are entirely consistent with ordinally measurable travel costs and TCM welfare estimates. All that is required for results (a) and (ci) is that own-price be an increasing function of distance, and will-

ingness to travel to a particular site decrease as own-distance and the availability and convenience of substitutes increase. Results (b) and (cii) are consistent with the need to impose conventions in cost-accounting and modeling in order to obtain money-valued cost and welfare measures. Conformity as to conventions used explains consistency in the results of independent studies; differences in conventions explains differences in results.

IV. CONCLUDING COMMENTS

A travel price method, TPM, based on reliable observations of (p_v, v) pairs, would be a strong contender for preferred status among methods of estimating recreation benefits. Preferred status is sometimes claimed for TCM, because it is based on observed v. But observed v is not enough, and observed (d, v) does not substitute adequately for (p_v, v). Frankly, we do not know—and cannot know—what recreational activity costs. With unobservable travel costs, recreation benefits are, at best, ordinally measurable and therefore unique only up to a monotonic transformation.[4]

A degree of standardization is attained, for travel costs and welfare measures, in the traditional TCM by observing particular cost-accounting conventions, and in the household production formulation of TCM by imposing arbitrary and simplistic specifications of household production technology and observing particular accounting or analytical conventions for the household's implicit cost of time. The level of money-valued welfare measures generated by these artifices depends on the particular cost-accounting conventions and the partic-

---

[4]This problem with TCM applies to other applications of weak complementarity and related methods in which crucial prices are unobservable. Consider the difficulties inherent in Larson's (1993) recent suggestion that nonuse values be estimated from information about nonusers' behavioral responses to changes in amenity levels. These behavioral responses might range from political activism to "just thinking about it;" reliable third-party observation of the costs of such activities is implausible.

ular specification of household production technology invoked. Since travel costs are unobservable, the customary specification tests are inapplicable.

The problem of obtaining valid absolute-valued welfare measures from TCM could conceivably be solved in two ways. One could *adjust the cost-accounting and analytical conventions* until TCM reliably generates welfare measures consistent with some benchmarks established using fundamentally different valuation methods. Alternatively, one could *calibrate the TCM estimates* using welfare information generated by fundamentally different methods.[5] Either way, TCM cannot stand alone.

References

Anderson, G. D., and R. C. Bishop. 1986. "The Valuation Problem." In *Natural Resource Economics: Policy Problems and Contemporary Analysis,* ed. D. W. Bromley. Boston: Kluwer Academic Publishers.

Boadway, R. W., and N. Bruce. 1984. *Welfare Economics.* Oxford: Blackwell.

Bockstael, N. W., K. E. McConnell, and I. Strand. 1991. "Recreation." In *Measuring the Demand for Environmental Quality,* eds. J. B. Braden and C. D. Kolstad. Amsterdam: North-Holland.

Bockstael, N. E., I. Strand, and W. M. Hanemann. 1987. "Time and the Recreational Demand Model." *American Journal of Agricultural Economics* 69 (Mar.):293–302.

Bradford, D. F., and G. C. Hildebrandt. 1977. "Observable Preferences for Public Goods." *Journal of Public Economics* 8 (Oct.):11–131.

Buchanan, J. M. 1969. *Cost and Choice.* Chicago: Markham.

Caldwell, B. 1982. *Beyond Positivism: Eco-nomic Methodology in the Twentieth Century.* London: Allen and Unwin.

Cameron, T. A. 1992. "Nonuser Resource Values." *American Journal of Agricultural Economics* 74 (Dec.):1133–37.

Chipman, J. S., and J. C. Moore. 1980. "Compensating Variation, Consumer's Surplus, and Welfare." *American Economic Review* 70 (Dec.):933–49.

Clawson, M. 1959. *Methods for Measuring the Demand For and Value of Outdoor Recreation.* Reprint No. 10. Washington, DC: Resources for the Future, Inc.

Deaton, A., and J. Muellbauer. 1980. *Economics and Consumer Behavior.* New York: Cambridge University Press.

Hof, J., R. Lee, A. Dyer, and B. Kent. 1985. "An Analysis of Joint Costs in a Managed Forest Ecosystem." *Journal of Environmental Economics and Management* 12 (Dec.): 338–52.

Hotelling, H. 1949. "Letter." In *An Economic Study of the Monetary Evaluation of Recreation in the National Parks.* Washington, DC: National Park Service.

Larson, D. 1993. "On Measuring Existence Value." *Land Economics* 69 (Nov.):377–88.

Maler, K. G. 1974. *Environmental Economics: A Theoretical Inquiry.* Baltimore: Johns Hopkins University Press.

Rosenthal, D. H. 1987. "The Necessity for Substitute Prices in Recreation Demand Analyses." *American Journal of Agricultural Economics* 69 (Nov.):828–37.

Smith, V. K. 1993. "Nonmarket Valuation of Environmental Resources: An Interpretive Appraisal." *Land Economics* 69 (Feb.):1–26.

---

[5]Cameron (1992) has some interesting suggestions as to how this might be done. However, her suggested methods, at their present stage of development, rely heavily on restrictive structural assumptions.

PART III

SUSTAINABILITY AND BIODIVERSITY

CHAPTER

25

WHAT MAINSTREAM ECONOMISTS HAVE TO SAY ABOUT THE VALUE OF BIODIVERSITY

ALAN RANDALL

Professor of Agricultural Economics, Department of Agricultural Economics and
Rural Sociology, Ohio State University, Columbus, Ohio

A wide variety of methodological and ideological perspectives has informed and directed economic inquiry. Nevertheless, in each of the topical areas where economists specialize, it seems that one or, at most, a few approaches are now recognized as mainstream. For evaluating proposed policies to influence the way resources are allocated, the welfare change measurement approach (which includes benefit-cost analysis, BCA) currently enjoys mainstream status. My purpose here is to explain what this approach can contribute to understanding the value of biodiversity. I will distill the basic message into a few simple propositions, stating them one by one and offering a few paragraphs of elaboration on each.

WELFARE CHANGE MEASUREMENT IMPLEMENTS AN EXPLICIT ETHICAL FRAMEWORK

Each human being is assumed to have a well-defined set of preferences. While the way these preferences are ordered should satisfy certain logical requirements, preferences may be *about* literally anything in the range of human concerns. Mainstream economists argue that preferences are seldom whimsical or capricious. Rather, people come by their preferences consciously, in a process that involves learning, acquisition of information, and introspection. The mainstream economic approach is doggedly nonjudgmental about people's preferences: what the individual wants is presumed to be good for that individual.

The ethical framework built on this foundation is *utilitarian, anthropocentric,* and *instrumentalist* in the way that it treats biodiversity. It is utilitarian, in that things count to the extent that people want them; anthropocentric, in that humans are assigning the values; and instrumentalist, in that biota is regarded as an instrument for human satisfaction.

There may be other views of the role of nonhuman life forms. For example, animals and plants may be seen as having a good of their own, possessing rights, or being the beneficiaries of duties and obligations arising from ethical principles incumbent on humans. Some people, including some economists, may subscribe to some of these views. Nevertheless, my purpose here is to confine myself to one particular instrumental, utilitarian, and anthropocentric formulation, exploring its implications for valuation. Implications of other approaches will, on their own merits, provide perspectives in addition to those offered here.

Having established preferences as a basis for valuation, any utilitarian formulation must come to grips with two additional issues: resource scarcity and interpersonal conflicts. The mainstream economic approach recognizes the role of ethical presumptions in resolving these conflicts and asserts two explicit ethical propositions. First, at the level of the individual, value emerges from the process in which each person maximizes satisfaction by choosing, on the bases of preference and relative cost, within a set of opportunities bounded by his or her own endowments (i.e., income, wealth, and rights). Thus, individuals with more expansive endowments have more to say about what is valued by society. Second, societal valuations are determined by simple algebraic summation of individual valuations. This means that from society's perspective, a harm to one person is cancelled by an equal-size benefit to someone else. By way of comparison with the ethics of welfare change measurement, note that individualism, as an ethic, accepts the first of these propositions, but explicitly rejects the second and instead, argues for protections against individual harm for the benefit of society as a whole. The classical market, in which all exchange is voluntary, institutionalizes (in principle) the individualist ethic.

Many economists are to some extent uncomfortable with the propositions that underlie welfare change measurement—and they are sympathetic with the discomfort of noneconomists—but these propositions have the virtue of explicitness: at least, one knows where mainstream economics stands.

THE ECONOMIC APPROACH IS NOT LIMITED TO THE COMMERCIAL DOMAIN

The explicit ethical framework of mainstream economics leads to the following definitions of value. To the individual, the value of gain (i.e., a change to a preferred state) is the amount he or she is willing to pay (WTP) for it, and the value of a loss is the amount he or she would be willing to accept (WTA) as sufficient compensation for the loss. For society, the net value of a proposed change in resource allocation is the interpersonal sum of WTP for those who stand to gain minus the interpersonal sum of WTA for those who stand to lose as a result of the change.

Because most laypersons have encountered the ideas that economics is concerned with markets and that since Adam Smith economists have believed that an invisible hand drives market behavior in socially useful directions, it is important for me to be precise about the relationship between economic values (WTP and WTA) and market prices. If everything people care about were private (in technical terms, rival and exclusive) and exchanged in small quantities in competitive markets, prices would reveal WTP and WTA for small changes. Conversely, prices are uninformative or positively misleading where any of the following is true: where people are concerned about goods and amenities that are in some sense public (i.e., nonexclusive or nonrival); where impediments to competitive markets are imposed (by governments or by private cartels and monopolies); and where the proposed change involves a big chunk rather than a marginal nibble of some good, amenity, or resource. The point is that market prices reveal value (in the main-stream economic sense of that term) not in general but only in a rather special and limiting case.

Most issues involved with biodiversity violate the special case where market price is a valid indicator of economic value. Nevertheless, the general theory of economic value encompasses these broader concerns. Here lies the distinction between economic values and commercial values; the essential premises for economic valuation are utility, function, and scarcity; organized markets are essential only to commerce. It is a fundamental mistake to assume that economics is concerned only with the commercial.

THERE IS AN (ALMOST) ADEQUATE CONCEPTUAL BASIS FOR ECONOMIC VALUATION OF BIODIVERSITY

The total value of a proposed reduction in biodiversity is the interpersonal sum of WTA. This total value has components that arise from *current use*, *expected future use*, and *existence*. Use values derive from any form of use, commercial or noncommercial, and including use as a source of raw materials, medicinal products, scientific and educational materials, aesthetic satisfaction, and adventure, personally experienced or vicarious. Future use values must take into account the aversion of humans to risks (e.g., the risk that the resource may no longer be available when some future demand arises) and the asymmetry between preservation and some kinds of uses (preservation now permits later conversion to other uses, whereas conversion now eliminates preservation as a later option). The concerns have encouraged the conceptualization of various kinds of option values, which are adjustments to total value to account for risk aversion and the irreversibility of some forms of development.

To keep the value of existence separate and distinct from the value of use, existence value must emerge independently of any kind of use, even vicarious use. That is a stringent requirement. Nevertheless, valid existence values can arise from human preference for the proper scheme of things. If some people derive satisfaction from just knowing that some particular ecosystem exists in a relatively undisturbed state, the resultant value of its existence is just as real as any other economic value.

For evaluating proposals that would have long-term effects, it is a fairly standard practice in economics to calculate present values by discounting future gains and losses. This procedure seems reasonable when evaluating alternative investments expected to last no more than one generation. When it is applied to potential disasters in the more distant future, it makes many people, including quite a few economists, uneasy. By discounting at standard rates, the inevitable collapse of the living systems on this planet several hundred years from now could be counterbalanced by relatively trivial economic gains in the immediate future. This unresolved issue of how to deal with long-range future impacts is what led me to insert the caveat "almost" in the heading of this section.

TECHNIQUES FOR EMPIRICAL VALUATION EXIST AND ARE APPLICABLE TO MANY BIODIVERSITY ISSUES, BUT LACK OF INFORMATION CAN BE DAUNTING

When price information is available and is informative about value, the analytics are relatively simple and familiar to most economists. The challenges in valuation arise where direct price information is unavailable and when price is not a valid indicator of value. For those situations, the valuation methods that have been developed and are considered reputable by economists fall into two broad classes: implicit pricing methods and contingent valuation.

The *implicit pricing methods* are applicable when the unpriced amenity of interest can be purchased as a complement to, or a characteristic of, some ordinary marketed goods. For example, travel services are purchased as a complement to outdoor recreation amenities, which permits valuation of outdoor recreation amenities by the travel cost method (Clawson and Knetsch, 1966). Hedonic analysis of the housing market may be used, for example, to estimate the value of such nonmarketed amenities as access that housing provides to open space or to a shoreline (Brown and Pollakowski, 1977).

Contingent valuation methods are implemented in survey or experimental situations (Cummings et al., 1986). Alternative policy scenarios are introduced and the choices made by citizen participants reveal WTP or WTA, directly or indirectly. Like other survey or experimental methods, the results may be sensitive to the design and conduct of the research. Nevertheless, there is growing theoretical and empirical evidence that contingent valuation yields results that are replicable and accurate within broad limits. The major advantage of this type of valuation is its broad applicability: it can determine WTP or WTA for any plausible scenario that can be effectively communicated to the sample of citizens. For estimating existence values, for instance, it may be the only feasible method.

With respect to biodiversity, the experts (i.e., ecologists and paleontologists) often have little confidence in their estimates of the impacts of ecosystem encroachment or disturbance. All too often the experts disagree. In these areas, contingent valuation cannot compensate for ignorance. If the experts cannot construct credible scenarios describing the effects of alternative policies on biodiversity, the WTP or WTA of citizens reacting to these scenarios will reflect that uncertainty and misinformation as well as any additional uncertainty they may have about their own preferences concerning biodiversity. More generally, the accuracy of any measure of value based on the preferences of ordinary citizens is limited by the reliability of citizen knowledge about the consequences of alternative actions for biodiversity. Some may regard this as an argument that policy should be based on the judgments of experts rather than of citizens. I disagree. It seems that public opinion quite rapidly reflects expert opinion when the latter is confidently held and expressed with convincing argument. On the other hand, confusion, ignorance, and apathy among the laity typically reflect incomplete and dissonant signals from the specialists.

POLICY DECISION CRITERIA HAVE BEEN PROPOSED

Mainstream economists have proposed two alternative criteria for deciding preservation issues. The *modified BCA* (benefit-cost analysis) approach attempts to implement the conceptual framework of welfare change measurement by identifying and measuring (insofar as possible) the benefits and costs of the alternative courses of action. This approach requires major efforts to measure the noncommercial components of economic value, including amenity, option, and existence values. The benefit-cost decision criterion itself is modified, however, by assigning any benefits of doubt to the preservation side of the ledger. The logic for this is that more is often known and can be documented about the benefits obtainable from commercial uses than is known about the benefits of preservation.

In another approach, the *safe minimum standard* (SMS) is defined as the level of preservation that ensures survival. Proponents of the SMS approach argue that although measuring the benefits of diversity in every instance is a daunting task, there is ample evidence that biodiversity is (in broad and general terms) massively beneficial to humanity.

Whereas the modified BCA approach starts each case with a clean slate and painstakingly builds from the ground up a body of evidence about the benefits and costs of preservation, the SMS approach starts with a presumption that the maintenance of the SMS for any species is a positive good. The empirical economic question is, "Can we afford it?" Or, more technically, "How high are the opportunity costs of satisfying the SMS?" The SMS decision rule is to maintain the SMS unless the opportunity costs of so doing are intolerably high. In other words, the SMS approach asks, how much will we lose in other domains of human concern by achieving a safe minimum standard of biodiversity? The burden of proof is assigned to the case against maintaining the SMS.

The SMS approach avoids some of the pitfalls of formal BCA, e.g., the treatment of gross uncertainty as mere risk, the false appearance of precision in benefit estimation, and the problem of discounting. In contrast to the procedure of discounting, the SMS approach simply accepts that the costs of preservation may fall disproportionately on present generations and the benefits on future generations. Its weakness is that it redefines the question rather than providing the answers. Nevertheless, an appealing argument can be made that "can we afford it?", with a presumption in favor of the SMS unless the answer is a resounding NO, is the proper question.

THE EMPIRICAL CUPBOARD IS NOT BARE

It is customary to draw attention to the scarcity of hard information about the economic value of biodiversity. But for each of the valuation methods discussed above, there has been a smattering of apparently successful empirical application. Fisher and Hanemann (1984) have used ordinary market data to estimate the potential value of the plant breeding that recently resulted in the discovery of perennial grass related to corn (see Iltis, Chapter 10 of this book). Literally dozens of economists have used implicit pricing methods to estimate the values of various environmental amenities. Stoll and Johnson (1984) used the contingent valuation method (CVM) to estimate the existence values for whooping cranes. Bishop (in press) used CVM to estimate the existence values for Wisconsin's bald eagles and striped shiners (a rather obscure freshwater fish). Bennett (1984) used CVM to estimate the existence value of a unique ecosystem that survives in a remote part of the coastline of southeastern Australia. Bishop (1980) has also completed some empirical analyses based on the SMS criterion. For several cases in the United States (the California condor, snail darter, and leopard lizard) and for mountain gorillas in low-income tropical Ruanda, he found the opportunity costs of pres- ervation to be reasonably low. In such cases, preservation decisions are not difficult.

Clearly, the empirical evidence is spotty at this stage, but these examples serve to counter the impression that high-quality empirical work on the value of diversity is not feasible.

FURTHER COMMENTS ON THE
MAINSTREAM ECONOMICS APPROACH

The mainstream economic approach has a built-in tendency to express the issues in terms of trade-offs. In that respect, it has much in common with the common law notion of balancing the interests. This makes the mainstream economic ap- proach potentially helpful in the resolution of conflicts. Perhaps it also makes the economic approach anathema to those who would brook no compromise.

Important problems in making decisions concerning biodiversity are seldom of the all-or-none variety. It is easy to provide the mainstream economic answer to the question, What is the value of all the nonhuman biota on the planet Earth? Its value is infinite based on the following logic: elimination of all nonhuman biota would lead to the elimination of human life, and a life-loving human would not voluntarily accept any finite amount of compensation for having his or her own life terminated. Earth's human population surely includes at least one such person. Thus, across the total population, the sum of WTA for elimination of all nonhuman biota is clearly infinite. Nonetheless, the question posed is not very useful. The meaningful questions concern the value lost by the disappearance of a chip of biodiversity here and a chunk there. For this smaller question, it is often possible to provide an economic answer that is useful and reasonably reliable.

The goal of the mainstream economic approach is to complete a particular form of utilitarian calculation. This calculation is expressed in money values and includes (in raw or modified form) the commercial values that are expressed in markets.

However, it expands the account to include things that enter human preference structures but are not exchanged in organized markets. This extension and completion of a utilitarian account, where preservation of biodiversity is at issue, is useful because it shows that commercial interests do not always prevail over economic arguments.

The claim that it is useful to complete this utilitarian account does not depend on any prior claim that the utilitarian framework is itself the preferred ethical system. Environmental goals that may be served by arguments that the biota has rights that should be considered, or that it is the beneficiary of duties and obligations deriving from ethical principles incumbent on humans, may also be served by completing a utilitarian account that demonstrates the value implications of human preferences that extend beyond commercial goods to include biodiversity. Some people would argue that a complete discussion of the value of biodiversity should extend beyond utilitarian concerns. Even these people would, presumably, prefer a reasonably complete and balanced utilitarian analysis to the truncated and distorted utilitarian analysis that emerges from commercial accounts.

REFERENCES

Bennett, J. 1984. Using direct questioning to value the existence benefits of preserved national areas. Aust. J. Agric. Econ. 28:136–152.

Bishop, R. 1980. Endangered species: An economic perspective. Trans. North Am. Wildl. Nat. Resour. Conf. 45:208–218.

Bishop, R. In press. Uncertainty and resource valuation: Theoretical principles for empirical research. In G. Peterson and C. Sorg., eds. Toward the Measurement of Total Value. USDA Forest Service, Rocky Mountain Forest and Range Experiment Station General Technical Report, Fort Collins, Colo.

Brown, G., and H. Pollakowski. 1977. Economic value of shoreline. Rev. Econ. Stat. 69:273–278.

Clawson, M., and J. Knetsch. 1966. Economics of Outdoor Recreation. Johns Hopkins University Press, Baltimore. 327 pp.

Cummings, R., D. Brookshire, and W. Schulze. 1986. Valuing Environmental Goods: A State of the Art Assessment of the Contingent Valuation Method. Rowman and Allenheld, Totowa, N.J. 270 pp.

Fisher, A., and M. Hanemann. 1984. Option Values and the Extinction of Species. Working Paper No. 269. Giannini Foundation of Agricultural Economics, Berkeley, Calif. 39 pp.

Stoll, J., and L. Johnson. 1984. Concepts of value, nonmarket valuation, and the case of the whooping crane. Trans. North Am. Wildl. Nat. Resour. Conf. 49:382–393.

[13]

Thinking about the value of biodiversity

ALAN RANDALL

The evidence seems strong that a mass extinction of species is underway and, this time, humankind bears most of the blame. The problem seems to be that the scale of human activity on the planet has grown so large that it is imposing unprecedented stress on the biota. The planet is supporting many more people than ever before, and the lifestyle that the affluent minority enjoys and most everyone else covets is increasingly intrusive on natural systems.

The interests of humanity and the rest of the biota are not in pure opposition. In some cases, the immediate threat to biodiversity comes more from simple human carelessness than from pressing human needs. Let me offer two kinds of examples. First, Bishop (1980) documents several cases in which the future of threatened species could be secured at quite small expense. In such cases, it does not require generous assumptions about preservation benefits to justify making the effort. Second, economists (e.g., Southgate, 1988) have argued persuasively that many deforestation and land-settlement movements around the Third World – major threats to biodiversity – are motivated by inefficient subsidies and incentives. Respect for traditional concepts of efficiency would be sufficient to rein in these threats; enlightened respect for biodiversity would be laudable but not strictly necessary. In both these examples, humans could accommodate the needs of biodiversity at very little real cost, if they would simply be a little more careful.

At the other end of the spectrum, humanity and the biota have a common interest in long-term survival. At some point, the survival prospects of people and other living things will become so intertwined that, given sufficient understanding of the urgency of the situation, human self-interest would demand action to preserve the biosystems that support human life.

Humans would do well to find ways to live in greater harmony with nature, whether by avoiding needless assaults on the environment for trivial gain or by recognizing the ultimate interdependence of life forms when survival is truly in the balance. In these cases, there are few difficult choices to make because, in the one instance, the gains from the probiodiversity option are not counter-balanced by significant costs and, in the other, because the absence of accept-able options precludes meaningful choice.

But these are not the situations I want to address here. At this point in human history, there are important choices to be made. On the one hand, there are plenty of cases in which the probiodiversity option carries real, if perhaps not insurmountable, costs. On the other, the kind of ecosystemic collapse that would threaten human survival is probably not yet at hand.

There is still scope for choice, and choice has real consequences. For one important example, many of the world's richest ecosystems and many of the world's poorest people can be found in the tropics. So, it is not surprising that the legitimate human aspiration for improved living conditions frequently clashes with biodiversity objectives in the tropics. We need to develop a rationale for choosing, when conflicts between biodiversity and other human goals cannot be circumvented.

Benefits of biodiversity

There is little doubt that we are presently embarking on a mass extinction that may well be worse than any since the last major ice age. This time, humans bear most of the blame and have it within their collective power to sharply reduce its severity if decisive action can be taken. Nevertheless, the fact that bio-diversity, worldwide, is under threat does not establish sufficient reason for concern. It is necessary to show also that biodiversity is worth caring about.

To many people, the most immediate reasons for caring about biodiversity are instrumental and utilitarian. A diversity of species in a variety of viable ecosystems serves as an instrument for people seeking to satisfy their needs and preferences. Many of the instrumental services that nature provides for people are obvious: food and fiber from domesticated plants and animals that were bred and selected from wild ancestors, and chemicals and pharmaceutical products with biotic origins.

Some attempts to develop a rationale for preserving biodiversity focus on these kinds of services. The argument proceeds as follows: there are many instances in which biotic resources have proven valuable to people and, to-gether, the total value of these services is enormous. However, the majority of species on this earth are yet to be catalogued and systematically evaluated for their commercial potential. But, since many of those species we know have proven useful, it is reasonable to expect that many of the presently unknown or poorly understood species will turn out to be useful, too (Bishop, 1978). In addition, it is reasonable to expect continued technological progress, although we cannot predict its direction (Fisher & Hanemann, 1986). So, new uses may be discovered for known species not currently thought useful. By standard statistical notions, the usefulness of many species under present technologies suggests a positive probability that literally any species, known or unknown, will eventually prove useful. Thus, we should approach the potential loss of any species with the presumption that its expected value to humans is positive; that is, its preservation is worth something to humans. Nevertheless, this appeal to current and expected future usefulness as commercial raw materials is only the beginning.

The knowledge arguments – that species represent a store of genetic information for future use – have been extended to include ethnobiological knowledge. Ecosystems and indigenous human cultures coevolved in considerable harmony, it is conjectured. This implies that disruption of indigenous cultures by colonists from elsewhere threatens destruction not only of the ecosystem but also the folk knowledge that enhances its value (Southgate, 1988; Norgaard, 1984, 1988).

In the 1970's, the rapidly growing field of environmental economics established that people have demand for natural systems not only as sources of raw materials, but also as amenities. Amenity values include use values and existence values. Use values include aesthetic and recreation values and, in this latter connection, it is suggestive to observe that travel is now the fastest growing industry worldwide and adventure travel is the fastest growing segment of the travel industry. Existence value arises from human satisfaction from simply knowing that some desirable thing or state of affairs exists.

The instrumental and utilitarian arguments for preserving biodiversity recognize not only raw material and amenity values, but also ecosystem support services. Natural ecosystems serve as effective assimilators of wastes. In this way, wetlands help purify water, and forests assimilate greenhouse gases and help restore the oxygen balance. Natural ecosystems contribute to water and air quality objectives. More generally, ecosystems are complex and fragile, and it is a tenet of ecology that everything has its place in the broader scheme of things. Thus, there is a presumption that species are not only useful directly as suppliers of raw materials and amenities but also indirectly for their contribution to ecosystem support. Thus, species that have no conceivable value in providing raw materials and amenities (if there are any) could still be valued for the ecosystem support services they provide to species that are more directly valued.

The ultimate instrumentalist argument – that all species must be preserved because the loss of any would initiate processes leading inexorably to the collapse of the whole ecosystem – seems clearly false. In its place, the Ehrlichs (1981) have introduced, by analogy, a statistical argument. Their much-cited rivet popper justifies his continued removal, one-by-one, of rivets from airplane wings by reasoning that the practice must be safe since no planes have been lost yet. There is an obvious logical fallacy in the rivet popper's claim: each successive inconsequential loss of a rivet does not serve to confirm the low probability of the practice causing a crash. Rather, since the initial numbers of rivets is finite and the number needed for safer operation is smaller yet, each inconsequential rivet removal increases the probability that the next one will be disastrous.

The point of the Ehrlich's analogy is that one may concede the redundancy that is built into the ecosystem without condoning a cavalier attitude to the piecemeal sacrifice of species. Each inconsequential loss of a species increases the probability that the next one will cause serious problems.

Taken together, these various considerations amount to a convincing argument, in the instrumentalist utilitarian tradition, that preserving biodiversity should be a serious consideration for a society of rational human beings pursuing what are essentially homocentric goals. At the very least, biotic resources are resources to be allocated carefully, rather than squandered or merely wasted. They are to be valued for their amenity services as well as their usefulness as raw materials; use and existence values count; the concept of value encompasses but goes beyond commercial values; ecosystem and environmental support services are recognized; and, where ignorance is rampant, statistical arguments are used to infer positive expected values.

This account of the reasons for valuing biodiversity is consistent with standard economic thinking about the benefits of biodiversity. This is scarcely surprising; after all, mainstream economics is a homocentric and utilitarian system of thought. The concept of benefits, however, is counterbalanced by the concept of costs, including opportunity costs. To recognize that biodiversity is beneficial does not, by itself, clinch the economic case for protecting biodiversity. What if the costs outweigh the benefits? Such an outcome is always possible, under benefit cost thinking, and would do little to promote the case for biodiversity.

In search of a failsafe case for biodiversity

I suspect Ehrenfeld (1988) speaks for many preservationists who "would like to see [conservation] find a sound footing outside the slick terrain of the economists and their philosophical allies" (p. 215). For these preservationists, the homocentric, instrumentalist and utilitarian rationale for conservation is

slick terrain, in that it provides a rationale for valuing biodiversity but its value
is always relative to the values attached to other things. Some of the preservationists and their philosophical allies have provided clues as to what is
needed, to develop a rationale for biodiversity that avoids the slick terrain. Such
a rationale should not depend on:

- The human utility function. Many conservationists suspect that any rationale
  for preservation that depends on human preferences provides less than iron-
  clad guarantees. Preferences for biodiversity may wane, or simply be overwhelmed by competing claims on behalf of other things that also give us
  pleasure.
- Instrumentalist arguments. Arguments that biodiversity is valued not so
  much for its own sake but because it serves as an instrument for various
  human purposes – e.g., as a storehouse of genetic information for agriculture
  and medicine – could be undermined by technological change. Ehrenfeld
  (1988, p. 213) claims that pharmaceutical researchers do not in fact tramp
  through the jungles searching for exotic species with medicinal prospects; a
  strategy of computer modeling, organic synthesis of promising molecular
  structures, and screening of the resultant synthetic compounds is more
  efficient. It is not yet clear whether the emerging technologies of bioengi-
  neering will enhance the value of naturally occurring genetic material or
  merely substitute for it.
- "Divide and conquer strategies." Norton (1988) argues that we should refuse
  even to try to answer questions about the value of the biodiversity losses
  associated with particular policy proposals considered one by one. The
  piecewise, or "divide and conquer," valuation strategy would inevitably
  trivialize the aggregate losses from human actions. The whole of the losses
  far exceeds the sum of its estimated pieces. Lovejoy (1986) makes a similar
  argument. Norton's solution is to deny the validity of any quantified values
  for piecemeal losses of biodiversity, while insisting that the value of biodiversity in toto "is the value of everything there is" (p. 205).
- Trade-offs. Norton (1988, p. 204) complains that the act of asking about the
  value of biodiversity is itself a measure of the unique arrogance of humankind. Ehrenfeld (1988) while citing the Old Testament, offers an argument
  that perhaps owes more to the concept of hubris in Greek tragedy: "Assigning
  value to that which we do not own and whose purpose we cannot understand
  except in the most superficial ways is the ultimate in presumptuous folly" (p.
  216). I interpret their arguments as not being opposed to the idea that
  biodiversity is valued in any absolute sense. Rather, what is being opposed
  is the idea that biodiversity can be valued in a relative sense; that one can

compare its value to that of other good things and adjust society's production and consumption for the better by making marginal trade-offs.

The kinds of rationales for biodiversity that would be developed by mainstream economists and homocentric utilitarian philosophers would surely fail the "slick terrain" test in every way: human preferences would count, instrumentalist arguments would have some force, choices would be conceptualized as typically piecemeal rather than all-or-none, and the interaction of technical possibilities and human preferences would often lead to trade-offs (although by no means always in favor of material goods at the expense of biodiversity). It is interesting to consider whether alternative philosophical approaches can avoid the slick terrain.

Consequentialist approaches

First, the homocentric, utilitarian approaches are a subset of a broader group of consequentialist theories that claim, loosely speaking, that the rightness of an action should be judged by the goodness of its consequences. Consequentialist theories do not have to be homocentric. Bentham was in principle open to the ideas that the utility of the animals could count; he just could not visualize any obvious way of incorporating it into the utilitarian calculus (1823, p. 311). More generally, utilitarianism evaluates all consequences in terms of their contribution toward preference satisfaction, whereas consequentialism is open to other ways of evaluating consequences.

Clearly, a consequentialist could accord preservation of biodiversity the status of the preeminent value. Then all proposed actions would be evaluated in terms of their effects on biodiversity, and those with the most favorable consequences for biodiversity would be chosen. Other objectives would be subordinated to biodiversity. Such a consequentialist scheme would avoid the slick terrain, but only at the cost of subordinating other worthy objectives such as enhancing the life prospects of the very worst-off people. Of course, according these other objectives the status of preeminent values too would return us to the slick terrain. The primacy of biodiversity cannot be assured in a clash of preeminent values.

Appeals to moral duty

Duty-based moral theories attempt to identify the moral obligations that bind humans, and the morally correct actions these obligations entail. Ehrenfeld (1988) offers a solution to the "slick terrain" problem: "If conservation is to succeed, the public must come to understand the inherent wrongness of the destruction of biological diversity" (p. 215). Clearly, Ehrenfeld's is a duty-based approach: right action is that which respects the moral obligation of human beings to preserve biodiversity.

When several considerations have moral forces (cannibalism is morally evil, while self-preservation is morally worthy), clashes among them (under what conditions, if any, would self-preservation justify cannibalism?) can be resolved only via deduction from higher moral principles. The slick terrain can be avoided only by asserting that preservation of biodiversity is a first principle, a trump among moral principles, that defeats all others. Without such an assertion, Ehrenfeld's "inherent wrongness" does not solve his problem. Surely, many would argue that enhancing the life prospects of the worst-off people has moral force at least powerful as that of protecting biodiversity. Again, biodiversity is on slick terrain.

Contractarian approaches

Contractarians argue that arrangements are justified if they respect the rights of all the affected parties. In duty-based reasoning, "rights" is often used to mean moral claims; one respects rights (in this sense) by observing moral obligations. In contractarian theories, rights are enforceable claims. Change occurs when all affected parties, endowed with enforceable rights, consent to it; without consent, the status quo prevails. While consent justifies change, the lack of consent for change is insufficient to justify the status quo. The starting point (or constitution) must itself be justified directly, typically by arguing that it was (or might have been) chosen by voluntary agreement among all concerned.

Contractarian approaches encounter great difficulties when taken literally. The burden of demonstrating that any existing starting point was actually chosen by consent, or that any proposed starting point might be endorsed unanimously by real choosers with diverse interests, seems insurmountable. Contractarians typical retreat to thought experiments, trying to deduce the characteristics of constitutions that might plausibly emerge from voluntary agreement under ideal conditions such as the "veil of ignorance" posited by Rawls (1971).

In serious discussion of the applied ethics of biodiversity, contractarian approaches have additional problems. Should all life-forms count equally or, at the other extreme, should the interests of the biota be represented by humans whose veil includes ignorance as to which generation they will be born into? Considering that rational choice is fundamental to contractarian approaches, should it be presumed (as it usually is, in western philosophy) that only humans are rational? Norton (1989) conducts a Rawlsian thought experiment where all potentially living things are represented behind the veil of ignorance, although it is recognized that all but those born humans will lose rationality at birth. The substantial probability of being born nonhuman would, in Norton's thought experiment, lead risk-averse participants to view with disfavor the extinction of any species. Thus, one would expect agreement on a constitution in which preservation of biodiversity is taken very seriously.

Nevertheless, it is unlikely that a contractarian thought experiment would yield iron-clad constitutional guarantees for biodiversity. It is individuals, not species, that are represented in the constitutional procedure, and there are many circumstances, other than extinction of one's designated species, that pose a real risk of an individual never being born (or being born into unrelievedly miserable circumstances). Thus, a contractarian thought experiment is likely to produce less than iron-clad commitments to biodiversity.

The consequentialist case for biodiversity is iron-clad if biodiversity is assigned preeminent value status. Similarly, the duty-based case is failsafe if conservation of biodiversity is the highest of all moral principles, and the contractarian case is secure if all participants in the constitutional process place the survival of all species above all other concerns. Recognition of other coequal or superior values, moral principles, or individual concerns returns us to the slick terrain. The case for biodiversity is always circumstantial, i.e., relative to the possibilities that are available and the strength of completing claims. Ehrenfeld (1988) claimed the high ground by resisting all the circumstantial approaches as mere manifestations of the moral repugnancy of homocentrism. But his victory is empty, since it depends on first-principle or preeminent value status for biodiversity, and such status is unlikely to survive scrutiny given the powerful appeal of many other candidates.

A strong, but circumstantial, case for biodiversity

We can do more than deny the viability of a failsafe case for biodiversity. It is possible to work, more affirmatively, toward constructing a strong but defensible circumstantial case.

First consider a duty-based approach. Assume that preserving biodiversity and enhancing the life prospects of the worst-off people are both moral goods. However, the claims of humans trump those of nonhumans. From these moral principles, it can be deduced that humans should make some, but not unlimited, sacrifices for biodiversity. This result endorses the basic idea of a safe minimum standard (SMS) rule: a sufficient area of habitat should be preserved to ensure the survival of each unique species, subspecies, or ecosystem, unless the costs of doing so are intolerably high (Ciriacy-Wantrup, 1968; Bishop, 1978). One could add an additional moral premise – marginal increments in the welfare of people count for less in the case of the already well-off than for those who are currently immiserated – and the implication is that one could identify situations in which the well-off have an obligation to subsidize the SMS in impoverished places.

The SMS rule places biodiversity beyond the reach of routine trade-offs, where to give up ninety cents worth of biodiversity to gain a dollar's worth of ground beef is to make a net gain. It also avoids claiming trump status for biodiversity, permitting some sacrifice of biodiversity in the face of intolerable costs. But it takes intolerable costs to justify relaxation of the SMS. The idea of intolerable costs, in a pluralistic society, invokes an extraordinary decision process that takes biodiversity seriously by trying to distinguish costs that are intolerable from those that are merely substantial.

At this point, consider a utilitarian approach. The benefit cost (BC) approach applies classical utilitarian principles with just one nod toward the value system of mainstream economics. The basic value data in BC analyses are those of economics – willingness to pay (WTP) for desired changes and willingness to accept (WTA) compensation for changes that are not desired – and as such reflect not only the preferences but also the endowments of the valuer. The rule that benefits and costs be aggregated anonymously – i.e., without regard to the identity and welfare status of the gainers and losers – is merely an economic operationalization of Bentham's classic rule of the greatest good for the greatest number. Thus, the BC approach is (at least) one rather direct and plausible approach of implementing a value system based on preference satisfaction. To the extent that humans value the services that biodiversity provides more than the services that would be foregone in pursuit of biodiversity, the BC approach would support biodiversity.

One of the more persistent arguments against the BC approach, and many alternative expressions of utilitarianism, is that preferences may be myopic and human understanding of the technical possibilities – in the Ehrlich analogy, the consequences of popping each and every possible combination of rivets on the airplane – may be incomplete or mistaken. Not that the BC approach does worse, in these respects, than other approaches that take citizen opinion seriously. As humans come to comprehend the technology of natural systems and how it limits the performance of anthropogenic technology, this understanding is reflected in a valid BC analysis. As human preferences extend to the amenity and existence services provided by diverse ecosystems, the valuations that emerge are fully reflected in a valid BC analysis.

Nevertheless, one must concede that human myopia is a valid concern. How can we be assured that the lure of immediate gratification will not induce us to make decisions that will surely have very unpleasant consequences later on? Elster (1979) has shown that "binding" behavior – Ulysses bound himself to the mast in advance to prevent himself from doing what he was quite sure he would do in the heat of the moment, i.e., steer his ship into the rocky waters separating it from the sirens – is consistent with both rational behavior and utilitarianism. Thus, one logically coherent utilitarian strategy would be to make policy choices on the basis of benefits and costs, but subject always to the constraint that actions we are reasonably sure we (or future generations of people we care about) will regret are forbidden. Biodiversity issues may be decided by consulting a BC analysis but subject to a safe minimum standard or similar constraint. Net benefits are maximized because benefits are good consequences, and the constraints are imposed because the consequences of not satisfying them are terrible. Again, the SMS constraint would not accord trump status to biodiversity, but would trigger a serious and searching decision process before it could be relaxed.

Let us return momentarily to the duty-based approach. We saw how the SMS could be derived from moral reasoning, but the decision rule was left incomplete. Upon what basis should people decide those many issues that do not threaten the SMS? It is hard to conceive of a plausible moral theory that does not, in the absence of overriding concerns, give a good deal of weight to the satisfaction of human preferences. Thus, we should take seriously a rule that policy issues be decided on the basis of benefits and costs, but always subject to constraints identified by moral reasoning. Net benefits are maximized because human preference satisfaction is morally worthy, and the constraints are imposed because they ensure that higher moral goods can trump preference satisfaction in the event of conflict.

Norton's (1989) contractarian thought experiment also identified the SMS constraint as a likely component of a just constitution. Preference satisfaction counts, also, in contractarian thought. However, many contractarians, naturally enough, pursue preference satisfaction via the individualistic routes of free exchange, voluntary taxation, and public decision by consent. The BC approach emerges from contractarian thinking as a kind of second-best result. If, as may well be the case, the pattern of compensating transfers to achieve voluntary agreement on policy is too complex to be feasible and the transactions costs too high, maximizing net benefits of policy becomes an attractive approach. At least it assures that the game is positive-sum. In the problem at hand, a plausible contractarian solution is to maximize net benefits (to satisfy preferences) subject to an SMS constraint (because participants in the "veil of ignorance" process would insist on it).

Interestingly, it seems that the same general kind of decision rule – maximize net benefits subject to an SMS constraint – is admissible under consequentialist, duty-based, and contractarian reasoning. If we accept that satisfaction of human preferences is at least a consideration, and that BC analysis can provide a method of systematically accounting for preference satisfaction, then estimated benefits and costs are at least a consideration when making choices about biodiversity. If environmental economists could be satisfied with claiming no more than this, and if preservationists could discipline themselves to eschew the grandstanding strategy of denouncing any and all moral theories that do not accord first-principle or preeminent value status to biodiversity, a harmonious collaboration ought to be possible.

The prospects for benefit evaluation of biodiversity

A sound argument for considering empirical estimates of benefits and costs when deciding policy with respect to biodiversity requires that these empirical estimates provide information, as opposed to misinformation or noise. In other words, the argument for considering the output of BC analysis depends on the possibility of producing estimates that reflect the underlying WTP and/or WTA with sufficient accuracy and precision that the results are informative rather than misleading or merely confusing. Those whose main line of attack is on the moral underpinnings of BC analysis in the context of biodiversity (Ehrenfeld, 1988; Norton, 1988; Sagoff, 1988) tend also to embellish their case with assertions about the inherent nonquantifiability of the benefits and costs of preserving biodiversity or the arbitrariness of the estimates obtained using the available methods. In contrast, Randall (1988) takes a relatively optimistic view of the feasibility of generating informative BC estimates.

There has been substantial progress in all aspects of environmental benefit estimation in the last quarter-century. The theory has been developed consistent with the economic theory of welfare-change measurement. Explicit concerns of environmental economics have been addressed: the benefits of complex policies and the relationship between total value and the value of policy components (Hoehn & Randall, 1989); the distinction between use values and existence values (Randall & Stoll, 1983); use value under uncertainty (Graham, 1981; Smith, 1987); a total value framework for benefit estimation (Randall, 1991); the concept of quasioption value to account for situations in which current decisions might forestall the opportunity to benefit from knowledge emerging in the future (Fisher & Hanemann, 1986); and development of the theory and methods for estimating values of nonrival, nonexclusive, and non-marketed environmental services and amenities, including contingent valuation

(Randall et al., 1974; Hoehn & Randall, 1987, Mitchell & Carson, 1989) and methods that use market observations for weak complements (Maler, 1974; Bradford & Hildebrandt, 1977). A very substantial body of empirical estimates of environmental benefits has been assembled. The practice of estimating environmental benefits has become routine in the United States policy process, encouraged by legislation, Presidential Executive Orders, and the Office of Management and Budget. There is no denying that challenging problems remain in environmental benefit estimation. However, there seems little doubt that environmental benefit estimation is a progressing research program (Lakatos, 1970) that has already achieved important successes.

Biodiversity is an especially challenging topic for environmental benefit estimation. In order to evaluate policies pertaining to biodiversity, it is necessary to develop scenarios that describe baseline conditions and project them into the future, and do the same for with-policy conditions. Yet scientific data bases and the understanding of the basic natural science relationships are often very incomplete. BC analysis will reflect this scientific uncertainty and ignorance (but, to be fair, so will any other process by which people try to come to terms with the policy issues surrounding biodiversity).

The basic economic data for BC analysis, WTP and WTA, are likely to be volatile, as new information is added to the very sparse information base that most people have about biodiversity issues. However, this volatility reflects the basic reality of decision processes that start with limited information and revise expectations as new information becomes available (Viscusi, 1985) and surely applies not only to WTP and WTA but also to any other measure of public preferences about biodiversity policy.

For several reasons – the relative importance of existence values, the importance of uncertainty and therefore of *ex ante* value (Smith, 1987; Randall, 1991), and the relative difficulty of identifying serviceable weak complements – contingent valuation seems destined to play a major role in benefit estimation for biodiversity. While contingent valuation is gaining respectability, it remains a controversial method (Mitchell & Carson, 1989). Nevertheless, a number of studies have successfully estimated existence or preservation values with contingent valuation (Bennett, 1987; Bowker & Stoll, 1988, Brookshire et al., 1983; Majid et al., 1983; Stoll & Johnson, 1984). The recent development of referendum methods of contingent valuation (Hoehn & Randall, 1987; Mitchell & Carson, 1989) will be especially important for evaluating biodiversity. These methods appeal to the public perception of public goods, such as biodiversity, and they rely on scenarios built around political rather than market institutions and should, therefore, be more readily adaptable to international contexts.

While contingent valuation will likely be the method most widely used in evaluating biodiversity benefits, there may be important opportunities to use weak complementary methods. The growing importance of adventure travel to, and vacation and retirement homes near, exotic environments suggests a limited but nontrivial role for travel cost and hedonic price methods.

In summary, biodiversity presents some of the most difficult challenges for the rapidly developing theory and methods of environmental BC analysis. Nevertheless, there are promising prospects for successful empirical applications.

Conclusions

Let me attempt to summarize the argument with a few succinct statements.

- Some preservationists and philosophers are contemptuous of any theory of value that treats the value of biodiversity as relative to the values of other concerns. Yet, it seems that any coherent duty-based or consequentialist theory will do that, unless the theory asserts that preservation of biodiversity is a first principle or a preeminent value that trumps all others. And there seems no overpowering reason to accord trump status to biodiversity. Finally, contractarian thought experiments seem unlikely to produce iron-clad guarantees for biodiversity.
- Without asserting first-principle or preeminent value status for preserving biodiversity, consequentialist, duty-based, and contractarian theories can be developed in which biodiversity counts.
- A sound argument can be made that human preference satisfaction counts morally. Thus, benefits and costs (as environmental economists conceptualize them) count in duty-based theories as well as consequentialist theories of value. This suggests that benefits and costs have a place in a more complete theory of the value of biodiversity.
- The idea that benefits and costs count in a more complete theory of biodiversity does not exclude other moral or consequential considerations. One admissible theory would be that policy should implement the strategy with the greatest net benefits, subject to the safe minimum standard (SMS) constraint. The SMS constraint could be derived from consequentialist, duty-based, or contractarian principles.
- Real and considerable difficulties exist in obtaining reliable empirical estimates of the benefits and costs of preserving biodiversity. Such estimates are likely to be volatile, reflecting the reality that the current information base is

Alan Randall

small and new information may change perceptions dramatically. Nevertheless, and in full awareness of the challenges, I believe the effort could be made and the results should be taken seriously.

Acknowledgments

The author wishes to thank Mike Farmer, Don Hubin, and Bryan Norton for helpful suggestions and comments, and the National Science Foundation for research support (grant number BBS 8710153).

References

Bennett, J. W. (1984). Using direct questioning to value existence benefits of preserved natural areas, *Australian Journal of Agricultural Economics*, **28**, 136–152.

Bentham, J. (1970). *An Introduction to the Principles and Morals and Legislation*. Darien, CT: Hafner. Originally published 1823.

Bishop, R. C. (1980). Endangered species: an economic perspective. *Transactions of the 45th North American Wildlife and Natural Resources Conference*, pp. 208–218. Washington, D.C.: Wildlife Management Institute.

Bishop, R. C. (1978). Economics of endangered species. *American Journal of Agricultural Economics*, 60, 10–18.

Bowker, J. M., & Stoll, J. R. (1988). Use of dichotomous choice nonmarket methods to value the whooping crane resource. *American Journal of Agricultural Economics*, **10**, 372–381.

Bradford, D. F., & Hildebrandt, G. G. (1977). Observable preferences for public goods. *Journal of Public Economics*, **8**, 111–131.

Brookshire, D. S., Eubanks, L. S., & Randall, A. (1983). Estimating option prices and existence values for wildlife resources. *Land Economics*, **59**, 1–15.

Ciriacy-Wantrup, S. von (1968). *Resource Conservation: Economics and Policies* (3rd ed.). Berkeley: University of California Division of Agricultural Sciences.

Ehrenfeld, D. (1988). Why put a value on biodiversity? In *Biodiversity*, ed. E. O. Wilson, pp. 212–216. Washington, D.C.: National Academy Press.

Ehrlich, P. R., & Ehrlich, A. (1981). *Extinction*. New York: Random House.

Elster, J. (1979). *Ulysses and the Sirens*. Cambridge, UK: Cambridge University Press.

Fisher, A. C., & W. M. Hanemann. (1986). Option value and the extinction of species. In *Advances in Applied Microeconomics*, vol. 4, ed. V. K. Smith, pp. 169–190. Greenwich, CT: JAI Press.

Graham, D. A. (1981). Cost–benefit analysis under uncertainty. *American Economic Review*, **71**, 715–725.

Hoehn, J. P., & Randall, A. (1987). A satisfactory benefit cost indicator from contingent valuation. *Journal of Environmental Economics and Management*, **14**, 226–247.

Hoehn, J. P., & Randall, A. (1989). Too many proposals pass the benefit cost test. *American Economic Review*, **79**, 544–551.

Lakatos, I. (1970). Falsification and the methodology of scientific research pro-

Thinking about the value of biodiversity 285

grams. In *Criticism and the Growth of Knowledge*, ed. I. Lakatos & A. Musgrave. London: Cambridge University Press.

Lovejoy, T. (1986). Species leave the ark one by one. In *The Preservation of Species*, ed. B. Norton, pp. 13–27. Princeton, NJ: Princeton University Press.

Majid, I., J. A. Sinden, & A. Randall. (1983). Benefit evaluation of increments to existing systems of public facilities. *Land Economics*, **59**, 377–392.

Maler, K-G. (1974). *Environmental Economics: A Theoretical Inquiry*. Baltimore: Johns Hopkins University Press.

Mitchell, R. C., & Carson, R. T. (1989). *Using Surveys to Value Public Goods: The Contingent Valuation Method*. Washington, D.C.: Resources for the Future.

Norgaard, R. B. (1984). Coevolutionary development potential. *Land Economics*, **60**, 160–173.

Norgaard, R. B. (1988). The rise of the global exchange economy and the loss of biological diversity. In *Biodiversity*, ed. E. O. Wilson, pp. 206–211. Washington, D.C.: National Academy Press.

Norton, B. (1988). Commodity, amenity, and morality: the limits of quantification in valuing biodiversity. In *Biodiversity*, ed. E. O. Wilson, pp. 200–205. Washington, D.C.: National Academy Press.

Norton, B. G. (1989). Intergenerational equity and environmental decisions: a model using Rawls' veil of ignorance. *Ecological Economics*, **1**, 137–159.

Randall, A. (1988). What mainstream economists have to say about the value of biodiversity. In *Biodiversity*, ed. E. O. Wilson, pp. 217–223. Washington, D.C.: National Academy Press.

Randall, A. (1991). Total and nonuse values. In *Measuring the Demand for Environmental Improvement*, ed. J. B. Braden & C. K. Kolsted, pp. 303–321. Amsterdam: North-Holland.

Randall, A., Ives, B. C., & Eastman, C. (1974). Bidding games for valuation of aesthetic environmental improvements. *Journal of Environmental Economics and Management*, **1**, 132–149.

Randall, A., & Stoll, J. R. (1983). Existence value in a total valuation framework. *Managing Air Quality and Scenic Resources at National Parks and Wilderness Areas*, ed. R. D. Rowe & L. G. Chestnut, pp. 265–274. Boulder: Westview Press.

Rawls, J. (1971). *A Theory of Justice*. Cambridge, MA: Harvard University Press.

Sagoff, M. (1988). *The Economy of the Earth*. New York: Cambridge University Press.

Smith, V. K. (1987). Nonuse values in benefit cost analysis. *Southern Economic Journal*, **54**, 19–26.

Southgate, D. (1988). *Efficient Management of Biologically Diverse Tropical Forests*. London: IIED/UCL, London Environmental Economics Centre.

Stoll, J. R., & Johnson, L. A. (1984). Concepts of value, nonmarket valuation, and the case of the whooping crane. *Transactions of the Forty-Ninth North American Wildlife and Natural Resources Conference*, **49**, 382–393.

Viscusi, W. K. (1985). Are individuals Bayesian decision makers? *American Economic Review*, **75**, 381–385.

[14]

The Rationality of a Safe Minimum Standard

Michael C. Farmer and Alan Randall

ABSTRACT. *The Safe Mimimum Standard (SMS) is a policy shift to safety defaults to forestall irreversible outcomes. Critics charge an inconsistency: what justifies "business as usual" cannot also justify switching to the SMS. Currently the SMS is only a procedural shift where economic optimality procedures are buttressed by extra-special focus on uncertainty. Yet social welfare function may not be complete enough, warranting a more fundamental SMS shift. Numerous moral positions support this SMS approach. This SMS also operationalizes the intolerable cost as a trigger point, noting societies with lower tolerance for sacrifice must trigger the SMS earlier.* (JEL Q20)

I. INTRODUCTION

If everyday practice provides inadequate defense against occasional threats of irreversible resource loss, the safe minimum standard (SMS) is an appealing mechanism to forestall those events. The SMS suspends standard arrangements under specific conditions and invokes defenses that provide society breathing room until the resource can recover and society can return to its "business as usual" arrangements. For this reason SMSs are best interpreted as strategic instruments within a larger policy context.

The appeal of such safety measures seems intuitive enough to most people, and current discussion reveals wide cross-disciplinary support for policy frameworks which utilize a safe minimum standard (Arrow et al. 1995). Yet while the support for the SMS is wide, it also seems shallow: without a more coherent development of the SMS and a more careful justification for it, it is hard to know the extent to which any real consensus exists.

The SMS understandably has been criticized for incompleteness and inconsistency (Norton 1995; Krutilla and Fisher 1975; Hohl and Tisdell 1993; Ready and Bishop 1991). Better, critics contend, to pursue objectives that are comprehensive enough to

manage the exceptional circumstance than to legitimize the SMS exception.

However, attempts to incorporate the SMS into a coherent policy rule have produced unsatisfactory results. Many economists, faithful to benefit-cost utilitarianism yet impressed by the pragmatic appeal of the SMS, reduce it to a simple safeguard. In the face of asymmetric uncertainties, analysts should take pains to avoid performing benefit-cost analyses badly. Special care should be taken to account for existence values and to impose risk aversion at every point in the analysis. Under such an interpretation, the SMS merely informs the application of the benefit-cost criterion, suggesting that somewhat greater costs than usual should be tolerated in order to avoid the risk of irreversible resource loss (Rolfe 1995). Other scholars argue that irreversible events narrow the alternative paths that future generations can pursue and, thereby, deprive these generations of their ability to pursue their own objectives. These advocates of the precautionary principle expand SMS protections into a comprehensive, strong sustainability objective (Daly and Cobb 1989; Norton 1995). Inconsistency and incompleteness is avoided by subsuming the SMS into the benefit-cost rule, on the one hand, and into strong sustainability objectives, on the other. Intuition suggests that the first-mentioned approach may provide too little protection for threatened resources, and the second too much. The SMS received from Ciriacy-Wantrup (1952) and Bishop (1978), however, postulates a break from the opti-

The authors are with, respectively, the Georgia Institute of Technology, Atlanta, and the Ohio State University, Columbus. The authors acknowledge helpful comments from Arild Vatn, Bryan Norton, and two anonymous reviewers. Also, the seminar series at the Agricultural University of Norway, Department of Social Sciences, and the University of New Mexico, Department of Economics, each provided valuable discussion.

Land Economics • August 1998 • 74 (3): 287–302

mizing criteria of economic efficiency when an irreversibility presents itself; yet the break is not so powerful that it cannot be overruled again if the embedded economic sacrifice is immoderate (Ciriacy-Wantrup 1952) or intolerable (Bishop 1978).

If the SMS is to retain its posture as a true policy regime shift, SMS advocates will have to respond to two challenges. First, there has to be a compelling reason for a discontinuity in standard practice. Irreversibility itself is not enough to warrant a discrete shift in the policy structure. To make a case for the SMS, there has to be a principled reason to expect that society will fail to articulate an appropriate response to some particular kinds of irreversible events, thus warranting a shift in policy toward the SMS. Second, the conditions that usher in an SMS defense must be specified. If conditions truly warrant a discrete policy regime shift, then the point at which standard operating rules no longer apply should be well marked. The SMS defenses familiar to most resource economists clearly presuppose a resolution to these problems. Yet satisfactory answers are not yet articulated.

Ciriacy-Wantrup (1952, 1968) and Bishop (1978, 1979) each offer a preservation SMS. Their constructions require preservation of the physical stock of a renewable resource at a level that assures existence (variously interpreted as ecosystem integrity or protection of a single species). If current practices appear to threaten the irreversible erosion of a renewable resource, then the SMS suspends existing procedures regulating resource use and imposes a resource preservation rule. In the absence of compelling reasons why the resource must be preserved at any cost, an escape clause is appended to the SMS rule: the rule itself may be suspended if the costs of preservation prove "immoderate" (Ciriacy-Wantrup) or "intolerably" too high (Bishop).

A compelling need for a policy shift, however, is perhaps difficult to motivate in the preservation context. The response to extinction threats is confused by uncertainty about the instrumental functions of the species. Concerns for valuing uncertain resource services, of course, are clearly consistent with a focus on option values, quasi-option values, and existence values, all of which fit into the benefit-cost framework. But the instrumental view of, say, species is itself rejected as inadequate by those who take intrinsic values seriously. Disagreement about society's ultimate values differs from uncertainty regarding the contribution that a resource may make to fulfilling particular objectives.

A cleaner example to showcase the SMS is needed to help illuminate the logic of a policy structure switch. It may be helpful to consider for demonstration an exhaustion event in which the useful features of the asset were already known and not subject to debate. To that end we introduce a conservation SMS. The conservation SMS seeks to avoid the possible exhaustion of a renewable resource whose harvest and use is widely considered essential to adequate human welfare. The conservation SMS is a useful exemplar to explore the SMS for two reasons. It retains the essential policy switch features of the more familiar preservation SMS. That is, if current practices threaten to permit a breach in a critical threshold stock level and lead irreversibly to erosion of a resource necessity, conservation defenses are invoked. Yet conservation defenses are sustained only in so far as the required sacrifice is not intolerably too burdensome. Because the harm that would arise from exhaustion of an essential resource is unambiguous, this case allows us to illustrate the relationship between the SMS trigger point and the magnitude of cost that would be intolerable.

II. OUTLINE OF THE ARGUMENT

First we review the structure of the SMS as presented in the literature. Section III emphasizes three structural elements. The SMS is activated as an exception to current efficiency practice; the SMS protection becomes the default management rule; and this protection can be overridden if the economic sacrifice is "immoderate" or "intolerable."

Section IV addresses the inconsistency critique of the SMS. Critics argue that the articulation of a consistent set of moral principles would obviate the need for any discrete switch (e.g., an SMS) in the order of moral concerns. The inconsistency objection emerges first from economists who argue that a comprehensive and careful benefit-cost analysis (BCA) already embeds safety concerns within a resource management program. Objections of incompleteness arise from ethicists who assert that the entire BCA framework and its substitution logic is wrong headed, and that a new, comprehensive ethic for the future is required. Both positions dispense entirely with the regime shift structure and the related requirement to define intolerable costs.

In Section V we argue that there are principled reasons preventing society from adopting a single, internally consistent moral framework to resolve intergenerational concerns. A moral society might require a dramatic policy shift to manage extreme events such as an irreversibility. A pluralistic society would find the SMS a pragmatic decision rule to complement a resource management program when issues of integenerational ethics are at stake.

Rebuttals by economists and ethicists to the traditional SMS are discussed in Section VI. The critiques of the SMS, we argue, discard the legitimate moral controversy surrounding obligations to the future. If we accept the current state of affairs in ethics for resolving questions of intergenerational justice, then SMS critiques themselves nest internal inconsistencies by espousing a single value position.

To illustrate the SMS consensus process, Section VII considers how a society of diverse moral agents would manage an extreme conservation crisis. It is shown that a society of diverse moral agents faced with a choice between crisis abatement and satisfying immediate needs would honor an SMS policy structure and would support nontrivial, material sacrifices for its defense. The appeal to consensus justifies the SMS; and that consensus also determines the limits to tolerable sacrifice. This defense of the SMS lifts the SMS framework into a substantive policy process in its own right.

III. THE SMS STRUCTURE

Ciriacy-Wantrup's depiction (Ciriacy-Wantrup 1952) of the role of economics in managing natural resources was addressed to a society struggling to define the proper role for economic analysis in resource management policy. A society must decide which types of public activities to manage by economic benefits and costs and which public activities to measure against some other valuation criteria. One can view *Resource Conservation: Economics and Policies* as an apology for economic analysis in natural resource management.

Ciriacy-Wantrup argues that the publically managed resources favor liberal governance according to efficiency principles. The pragmatic demands of national lands management, it was argued, lend itself to the utilitarian calculus of economic benefits and costs.

Nonetheless, within Ciriacy-Wantrup's defense of economic analysis is an acknowledgment that there are limits to the use of economic optimization in the policy process. A legitimate social decision process can recognize several different objective frameworks that can eclipse the role of stand-alone economic efficiency for many important decisions. Even processes already tapped to be administered by economic efficiency are subject to special circumstances under which decision making diverts to another social decision process.

It is within this context that the SMS is introduced. The SMS is defended as a responsible policy exception to questions otherwise administered according to efficiency principles. In the original conception, the SMS switch occurs whenever a decision process faces the extinction of a species. A manager confronting this irreversible event shifts focus from efficiency analysis to species protection. The Ciriacy-Wantrup discussion argues that a society is both reasonable and responsible for extending latitude over day-to-day decision making to economic efficiency analysis while insisting on treating differently questions in which a managed resource is irreversibly depleted.

The traditional SMS is not constructed as an absolute safety defense. As species preservation becomes more and more costly, a society overseeing resource management practices must decide at what point SMS defenses become immoderate or, sharpened by Bishop (1978), too expensive to tolerate.

The argument favoring the SMS, however, leaves several critical questions unanswered. First, it is unclear why irreversibility mandates a change in the decision rule. If a social consensus decides to manage natural resources by efficiency analysis as the best social practice, then there must exist some special reason to suspect that rules previously considered inferior to efficiency, such as strong preservation defense, are now superior to efficiency-guided policy when extinction is threatened. The SMS literature lacks an explicit articulation of the reasons grounding the policy shift.

The SMS structure appears incoherent. The decision to adopt one decision criteria, switch to another, and then maintain the SMS as long as the costs of safety defense remain tolerable begs the question regarding the type of appeals that necessitate such policy focus changes. In addition the criteria for tolerable (or moderate) sacrifice seems to be appended to the SMS structure without appeal to any consistent principle. Presumably some uniform guiding principle reconciles the various issues at stake without the ad hoc muddling through implied by the SMS. Policy switches expose an incomplete articulation of the moral intuitions motivating social practice.

IV. SMS CRITICS

A. Inconsistent and Incomplete Objectives

It is a current critique of SMS processes that they cannot be derived from a single direct objective statement that also derives the policy exception upon which they are superimposed (Ready and Bishop 1990; Rolfe 1995). For example, policies honoring benefits and costs can be interrupted by an SMS trigger requiring some explicit (if not "immoderate") sacrifice of net benefits in order to avert, say, a threatened extinction. The contingent policy nature of the SMS suggests

shifting fundamental management objectives: a discrete switch from expected welfare maximization to extreme risk aversion. The contingent policy switches have been widely interpreted as revealing the ad hoc theoretical foundations of the SMS itself: the SMS is either a muddle-through program for an ill-defined and unconsidered policy structure, or it is a simple procedural rule for implementing current practices as well as possible (Hohl and Tidsdell 1993). Rolfe (1995) adopts the second of these alternatives: maintaining a consistent utilitarian stance, he concludes that the SMS can be no more than a flagging device to tell us when normal day-to-day BCA estimation practices need to be suspended in favor of more complete and more risk-averse BCA estimation practices. We might call this a *procedural* SMS, shifting analytic practices rather than shifting objectives; and there are good reasons to honor this interpretation as a powerful conservation rule.

The umbrella of optimization under uncertainty is very broad. It admits concern for existence and options values under a known probability distribution (Krutilla and Fisher 1975; Coggins and Ramezani 1996) all the way to strong defenses constructed under Knightian uncertainty (Woodward and Bishop 1997)—the later used to reconcile the strong risk aversion of Rawlsian Difference (Rawls 1972) with efficiency (Gilboa and Schmeidler 1989).[1] A careful efficiency analysis mandates a detailed characterization of the uncertainty society faces to match up the diverse set of analytic tools to the problem at hand (Castle and Berrens 1993). These procedural SMS appeals are significant policy instruments, yet do not, in themselves, re-

---

[1] For particular specifications of the Rawlsian problem, the Rawlsian contract is a Pareto dominant outcome. If agents know everything in general (they can list all the possible outcomes and rank them from best to worst for each policy alternative) but know nothing in particular (agents cannot assign probabilities to those outcomes under the alternatives), then the most net beneficial policy choice is the alternative that maximizes the minimum (worst) outcome. This result from Gilboa and Schmeidler (1989) has been explored in the difficult applied resource management context by Woodward and Bishop (1997).

quire a principled shift from economic optimization.

It may be that when we carefully write down the sources of uncertainty under current institutional structures that an irreversibility is still admitted. This outcome of current practice may signal something fundamentally wrong with current practices. The appearance of an unacceptable, irreversible outcome unmanageable by current policy structures, even accounting for severe uncertainty, may provide the impetus for an institutional change that would, if implementable, still solve the problem without the appeal to the SMS.

The call for a comprehensive structural change invited by the appearance of an ecological threat opens the SMS to a more fundamental criticism. The dual objectives of efficiency and aversion to ecological risks and uncertainties that compete under certain initial allocations of rights might be reconciled by a coherent sustainability objective statement.

The policy inconsistency critique dovetails into recent discussions that endorse SMS-like practices (Toman [1994] echoing Norton [1986]). Irreversibility, the argument suggests, presents such a strong practical challenge that it forces an articulation of a powerful, new sustainability ethic that carves out an almost unchallenged respect for wholly irreversible outcomes. Respecting this more complete ethical position, SMS defenses may be activated often, approaching a strong sustainability policy. Here there is a complete moral posture that balances efficiency against other valued goals. The presence of such a deliberate resource defense program contrasts to the incomplete moral framework guiding the SMS policy process outlined. It is necessary, advocates contend, to ground the SMS in a basic, coherent ethic and to identify a complete ethical framework within which SMS defenses are activated as the best course of action to address an irreversible outcome. Only then is the SMS defense meaningful. Simply, the ethically undefended traditional SMS is a clumsy SMS. It risks being overridden too easily as the costs of defense are clearly articulated and stacked up against an unarticulated conserva-

tion principle. This critique of the traditional SMS in favor of a more comprehensive preservationist principle reduces to a warning that a society can't stage an effective ethical defense without discussing ethics (Norton 1995). The widely endorsed SMS that robustly switches the dominant moral concern from efficiency to future welfare under a critical threshold risk (Arrow et al. 1995), unsupported by moral reasons, amounts, in this critique, to self-subverting moral laziness.

All of this suggests that there may exist a number of competing moral theories that could offer a complete alternative to existing practices and ground an institutional reform. Adoption of any one will avoid the incompleteness of the SMS, suggesting the SMS is a clearly inferior policy choice. Yet each complete moral theory has implications for all facets of life, not just for sustainability policy, and therefore is complete only to the extent that society is prepared to adopt it *in toto*. Ultimately, inconsistency and incompleteness critiques of the SMS assume society can (or should) choose one comprehensive moral position to the exclusion of all others.

V. MORAL DIVERSITY

SMS critiques reduce to an observation that no clean objective statement will endogenously derive its own objective demise: an efficiency program cannot generate an SMS departure from the efficiency rule, just as strong sustainability clearly rejects the efficiency appeals to permit substitution in production and in consumption. Switches are inconsistent. This, of course, is true tautologically; but we think it is the wrong focus.

The inconsistency critique evaluates the social decision process at midstream. It demands that the range of legitimate social concerns reconcile to a single, coherent value statement. That value statement would value many things; but it is a retained assumption that there is one and only one valid moral system.

In the world of resource conservation, social objectives are neither obvious, well-defined, nor universal, and there are compelling reasons for this diversity (Randall and

Farmer 1995). Rawlsians, Lockeans, and utilitarians, for example, construct sustainability goals and obligations quite differently. It is not a retreat into moral relativism to admit that the set of well-considered moral theories entertained in philosophical discourse includes more than a single element (Norton 1991). In important ways, picking a single value statement to guide resource practice casts aside crudely the legitimacy of moral controversy. To accept the sweeping policy reversals required to adopt a single-value theory in response to inconsistencies exposed by a resource crisis arguably exceeds society's policy mandate for managing the resource. So, there is a prima facie case for seeking actions that respect a range of plausible ethical positions.

A. Incomplete Moral Theories of Obligation to the Future

The existence of numerous moral intuitions in a society generates critical doubt that a single value stance can competently regulate resource management. This recognition could, conceivably, justify case-by-case consensus rulings outside normal practice such as the SMS; but that move is still not assured. To construct an essential moral justification for the SMS, it needs to be shown that the SMS discontinuity to resource management is a robust component of any agreement. That an SMS-like result is observed in the management of some resource does not indicate that the SMS is a regular feature of management practices when resource exhaustion threats appear in the planning horizon. Negotiation among agents, each with their own coherent frame, might hammer out a complete, comprehensive, and continuous policy profile that involves no discrete shift in practice.

We take the position that the discrete, and seemingly inconsistent, regime switch of the SMS is justified directly because the largest share of individual moral agents participating in the consensus do not possess well-defined, fully articulated ethical positions for sustainability.

For issues of intergenerational justice, the responsibility to seek consensus among

moral theories is particularly acute. In this case we are not merely adjudicating among competing complete and coherent value theories to resolve our obligations to the future; but we contend that the field of ethics has work yet to do in defining objectively, subjectively, or even ontologically what constitutes an admissible agent for moral consideration. For moral issues concerning a given generation, the agents on whom we confer moral standing are, generally, those persons living. For sustainability, potential, but as yet non-existing, agents are necessarily part of the story. Yet standard moral theories of Western philosophy are constructed to define duties to immediate moral agents.

The real problem for moral philosophy concerning sustainability is that sustainability depends critically on the level of future human demands; but philosophy does not yet have a moral epistemology ready to specify obligations to create specific numbers of future agents and then provide specific standards of living (or ranges of life options) for them. This casts the consensus debate in a new light. Prior to resolving obligations to potential agents, we have trouble even defining the set of complete, coherent moral theories from which to choose that recognize direct obligations to the future and enjoy wide following (see, e.g., Sikora and Barry 1978; Hubin 1976; Parfit 1984; Farmer 1993).

Several prominent ethicists avoid the identification problem, as it is known, by rejecting any intrinsic respect for future generations. For example, Rawlsian contractors (Rawls 1972, 140–42) explicitly state that the Difference Principle is not well suited to the intergenerational question. Only the instrumental preferences to protect the future embedded in the preferences of existing agents, such as filial attachments, are epistemically motivated. Lockian contractors such as Gauthier (1983) and Hobbesian contractors such as Nozick (1974) seem to agree, finding contractarian protections for the future only in the instrumental values of existing contractors. This slippery slope protection for the future seems weak and competes with our moral intuitions regarding the future (Hubin 1976). So ethicists have sought other solutions to the identification problem that permit the moral agent to retain an intrinsic respect for the future.

One solution appears to exclude welfarist calculations from the values honored by a moral system (Weiss 1989). Yet it seems unlikely that a valid moral theory would wholly ignore the welfarist criteria as articulated by economists at least somewhere in a moral system (Hubin 1994). Also it is suggested to take future population levels as given, thus bypassing the identification problem. Yet if ethics is about making action choices that affect other agents, then noting that societies have chosen very different rates of reproduction through history suggests it is inconsistent to exclude these choices from moral dialogue when so many other features of human action fall within the purview of moral discourse.

Introducing these two obligations to potential persons (a duty to bring them into existence and then to provide for them) onto mainstream consequential, contractarian, or other deontological moral theories, challenges the discipline of moral philosophy and its classical, agent-centered ethical positions. A theory of sustainability must start with the question, What defines a moral agent to whom we have moral obligations? We are unlikely to derive an answer to that question (the origin of moral agency) inside traditional agent-centered frames that presume the answer to this question as a starting point to moral discourse.

The identification problem militates against proclaiming a favored value theory or single objective statement to capture our obligations to the future. For example, a strong non-declining consumption definition of sustainability is often used for discussion (Bishop and Woodward 1994; Pezzy 1994; Howarth 1995). If that principle is interpreted as a deontological obligation, society can meet that obligation by consuming everything over a few generations and ending the human experiment. Similarly, utilitarians can realize their maximization objective by a policy that would permit many persons across many generations to subsist barely or by one that would provide more fulfilling lives to fewer persons in each of fewer generations. Surely society wants to make these

moral distinctions to guide sustainability policy. In this state of affairs, consensus around basic moral intuitions gains a compelling moral relevance of its own, and the resulting pragmatic, consensus acts gain direct moral standing.

Though ethicists retain moral intuitions about sustainability, well-versed moral agents will find it difficult to articulate a complete sustainability profile within the strictures of existing deontological and consequentialist moral theories. This is not to say ethicists are mute on sustainability questions. Simply, single moral systems are not comprehensive enough to stand alone. In this environment, a responsible manager would approach a particular issue affecting sustainability by identifying the set of actions broadly consistent with the range of moral intuitions that come into play. Absent a single, coherent moral theory, ethics is not an invitation to moral relativism. It is both consistent and reasonable for managers to respond to sustainability questions by honoring robust moral intuitions regarding sustainability while resisting the imposition of a single, unique sustainability ethic.

VI. CONSENSUS FOR THE SMS

For issues involving sustainability, there is a compelling duty to avoid imposing a single-value theory onto the policy process. Rules for day-to-day resource management implement a range of objectives reflecting the different moral theories that enjoy support. Since many different social decisions need to be made, social coherence does not require consensus on each decision, just consensus that decisions in aggregate are being made decently well. The threat of an irreversible event, however, places a special burden on the policy process to seek consensus around a single decision. Irreversibility logically introduces new kinds of outcomes compared to those encountered in standard practice, and a legitimate policy consensus would account for that difference. Irreversibility demands greater confidence in policy implemention and, if one is not comfortable that the technical decision process fully reflects the concerns surrounding the question, warrants a different policy process to manage the resource than authority delegated to oversee day-to-day concerns.

This commonsense mandate to especially respect an irreversibility should not be understated. If our resource manager were equipped with a comprehensive value perspective, no fundamental policy shift would be required. Day-to-day measures could be employed with great care. The robustness of a policy switch is the product of a consensus among moral agents each of whom are still struggling with their own individual moral positions.

Incomplete moral orderings require special note of extreme outcomes, such as irreversibilities. Moral intuitions may justify one set of rules to guide day-to-day practices, comforted that the distance between an as yet unarticulated moral profile and the actions adopted is unlikely to be far apart. Yet the prospect of an irreversible decision demands more confidence, burdening the moral profile more. A rational moral thinker would build in defenses to forestall an irreversibility. The response to a particular exhaustion crisis will embed defenses inherently above and beyond those consistent with normal policy practice. This is a commonsense appeal. Moral agents are concerned that as their moral positions evolve, many current actions might later be viewed as immoral acts. If the original act is irreversible, of course, the agent may not be able to repair the offense. A whole society of such thinkers would typically demand that social practice adopt a discrete brake in standard operating procedures around resource exhaustion and adopt provisions that are fundamentally more conservative than the practice it replaces.

A. Objections to the Consensus Defense of the SMS

Economists and ethicists may argue that the SMS defense outlined oversimplifies their disciplinary response to resource exhaustion.

Economists possess an elegant method to address the ambiguities associated with managing an irreversible event. Exhaustion events can be analyzed by cataloging all of the different valued opportunities that resource exhaustion might reasonably sacrifice. Uncertainty regarding the potential uses of a resource does not eclipse the role of economics to inform the question; therefore, such uncertainty is an insufficient motive for shifting the principal focus of policy. However, grafting a "pricing under uncertainty" argument onto the discussion of moral ambiguity conflates outcome uncertainty, which economics may be able to manage, with preference or social welfare function incompleteness which economics manages much less well.

Economic efficiency analysis requires completeness of outcome orderings by actors in the system. It is a very different exercise to catalogue future outcomes and then assign economic values to those alternatives than it is to delineate the various ways agents may rank outcomes and then assign an expected utility value over those plausible orderings. Such a technical exercise to address moral ambiguity produces inconsistencies on its own. Violations to the independence of irrelevant alternatives, for example, are identified with choices made under incomplete preference orderings (Debreu 1959). If a moral society is uncertain how to order various future outcomes, such an artificial technical approach does not robustly generate a proper efficiency assessment of that ambiguity. It seems reasonable, from the neoclassical axioms of utility, that society may want to invoke another decision rule in such a circumstance.

Society could, consistently, trust efficiency rules to resolve issues around the reasonably well-defined domain encountered in day-to-day practice. Yet once that society faces an irreversible outcome, uncertain about how to completely articulate its sustainability obligations, it is not irrational for that society to desire a different objective framework to manage that event over an artificial technical adherence to day-to-day practices with ambiguous properties of its own. For the economist to pursue the inconsistency critique of the SMS in favor of very careful and meticulous economic analysis in exhaustion events, it is incumbent on the critic to affirm that the axiomatic conditions for defining a Potential Pareto Improvement hold, that preferences expressed by agents are approximately complete and well ordered, and that the economic decision framework is superior to competing vehicles to address the question.

Philosophers also may consider the SMS defense above unfair. We characterized the sustainability conundrum by the incapacity of traditional epistemology to manage the identification problem. Philosophers may object that this is an outdated concern. There exists today many well-respected post-epistemic (i.e., not deontological or consequential) philosophers. The appeal to democratic consensus values to resolve social questions is motivated largely by non-epistemic moral arguments found in Heidegger (1956), Habermas (1987), and Rorty (1988). It is now a strongly held proposition that the practical application of ethics is a largely extra-epistemic concern (Williams 1985)—a concern perhaps informed but not driven by traditional epistemology (Davidson 1969). Yet this begs the question regarding the practical rules society will adopt to manage sustainability concerns.

The existence of a complete process to construct moral consensus does not predetermine completeness of the content of that consensus. Individual democrats are still likely to possess an incomplete articulation of their own moral posture toward sustainability, and may rely on discussions with their fellow democrats to achieve a more coherent ethical position. An SMS structure seems just as credible an outcome from a democratic consensus as it is from a collection of moral thinkers motivated by traditional ethical concerns. If Taylor (1989) is even remotely correct, modern society is intensively locked into several robust contradictions in its intuitions regarding the good, or moral, life. A dialogue regarding social values will have to address these questions, suggesting that confusion among post-epistemic philosophers is equally likely. Eventually, democratic processes may produce an ontological, or extra-epistemic, statement that captures sustainability concerns; yet introducing the consensus process itself does not guarantee instant articulation of the moral map. Ambiguity and incompleteness in individual posi-

tions will remain. Therefore special caution to avert an irreversible outcome will also remain. If we argue that democratic consensus is a morally superior way to conduct practical ethical policy, then the emergence of the SMS as a consensus outcome from such a process only underscores the moral obligation to uphold the SMS structure.

VII. DERIVING CONSENSUS

To this point we have argued that moral ambiguity surrounding society's attitudes toward stewardship and sustainability justifies special, extra-economic optimization attention to irreversibilities. The argument, however, still doesn't give us an SMS. The SMS calls for a shift in the focus of moral objectives. The SMS structure also warns that the shift to an extra-procedural conservative stance is itself subject to reasonableness in the sacrifices required to support that posture. We need to map the SMS structure from moral ambiguity: a policy switch to extra-efficient conservation defense that can itself be overridden if the costs are too high. We still have to work a little harder to link the policy shift with considerations that allow society to override that concern.

The inability of society to act on a convincing and complete sustainability objective motivates the resource manager to act through more general and modest heuristics. On a case-by-case basis, threats of different irreversible events necessitate different SMS responses; yet in each case resource exhaustion obligates our resource manager to search for special exceptional practices likely agreeable to the diversity of agents who admit some sustainability concern as part of their objectives.

To illustrate how such a consensus may construct an SMS to address a sustainability question, first consider the types of moral intuitions our manager uses to guide resource management and then consider its application to an irreversible resource depletion.

There exists an enormous array of sustainability definitions, and different concerns will come into play for different questions; yet at minimum, we argue, each moral agent would recognize three heuristics, or principled intuitions—characteristics of the unarticulated constituate goods common to plausible moral positions:

1. The existence of future humans is valued.
2. The welfare of future humans is valued.
3. Moral agents have intra-generational obligations to each other (e.g, the welfare of the living).

It is important to recognize that these are heuristics, not direct value theory statements. The heuristics are features of a plausible moral theory. They are used to help the manager construct actions that retain a broad moral consensus for natural resource management policies.

It seems that nearly every plausible value theory will acknowledge intrinsically or instrumentally the moral relevance of heuristic (1). As noted, contractors with no intrinsic respect for future generations will recognize the existence of stewardship objectives in the attitudes of contractors. Consequentialists, such as utilitarians, will directly value the ongoing presence of humans as a value-increasing opportunity. Even Kantians, intrinsically motivated only by the exercise of human reason, could honor heuristic (1) as a means to maintain the exercise of human reason.

Support for heuristic (2) appears more controversial, particularly to Kantians. Nonetheless, Kantians could value heuristic (2) instrumentally as a means of sustaining society's well-being at a level high enough to afford the reflective stance they directly honor; or would respect welfarist concerns directly after all other obligatory processes have been honored. It is not required that human existence and welfare are directly the respected value principles for our manager to use these intuitions as robust moral guide posts. Rather the welfarist content in heuristic (2) admits acts that would be respected by more than consequentialist theories. Hubin (1994) argues this point in detail. Strict deontologists, he argues, would be persuaded decisively at times by welfare improvement: deontologists would respect future welfare as a heuristic even if not as a direct value statement. So in constructing supportable man-

agement acts, our manager could recognize heuristics (1) and (2).

Separating heuristic (2) from heuristic (3), however, does mark an important distinction for our manager. Some SMS alternatives in the literature intrinsically value only heuristic (3), disregarding heuristics (1) and (2). Rolfe's (1995) SMS, grounded only on potentials for regrettable mistakes in pursuing efficiency inherently places heuristic (3) in a dominant position relative to the future regarding heuristics (1) and (2). With no direct concern for the future[2] such an SMS cannot philosophically defend any conservation act that openly generates a real wealth loss for existing agents. That is, if we are sure that reducing risks of an ecological crisis is economically inefficient, even relatively inexpensive efficiency losses are (by the efficiency objective) directly unacceptable. A welfarist society could adapt a convention to tilt a little toward sustainability, by resolving empirical uncertainties in favor of conservation when confronting an exhaustion threat, and that is just what Rolfe's SMS does. Yet it is difficult to support such an arbitrary approach without some principled basis.

Sustainability policy, however, cannot accept the other extreme and ignore the needs of the present, challenging strict deontological positions. Heuristic (3) recognizes an obligation to enfranchise the present into the sustainability debate. In honoring heuristics (1) and (2) it is important to recognize that the implementation of ambitious reallocation schemes among generations has implications for all manner of social organization in achieving welfare targets. If implementation of sustainability objectives literally necessitates, for example, a strong central planner to control the management and allocation of all resources through the production and savings

---

[2] The mechanics of efficiency serve to maximize surplus among the agents currently acting in markets today. With productive land and capital and ideal intergenerational capital and asset markets, efficient actions taken by present generations can also maximize the prospects for future generations. Nevertheless, in implementing an efficiency criteria for the marginal project, the analyst is conducting an exercise to maximize surplus among existing agents within the existing structure.

cycle, then moral agents would be obliged to defend the merit of that process as inoffensive to intuitions guiding heuristic (3). Welfare sacrifices by the present to achieve a sustainability objective are not unbounded. If a sustainability objective valued expanding latitude (degrees of freedom) for the future (Norton 1995), presumably this would be tempered by a concern that maximizing alternative paths available to the future did not enslave the present to a singular choice path to achieve that end. In short, moral practice involves trade-offs between heuristics (1) and (2) with heuristic (3); yet society is unsure how to precisely affect that trade-off.

Once we accept all three heuristics above, true regime switches triggered by severe conditions are reasonable and pose no real conundrum for the manager. A society of moral thinkers, who each hold different ethical perspectives and who each admit to an ongoing search for a decisive moral theory to resolve and balance intergenerational obligations, will recognize heuristics (1) to (3). The *de facto*, perhaps fragile, consensus supporting the objectives of day-to-day operations is almost surely unwilling to tolerate potentially extreme violations to any one of the heuristics in support of another.

A. The Conservation SMS

To illustrate that a consensus process motivated by sustainability concerns would generate an SMS structure fundamentally different than an economic efficiency SMS (Rolfe 1995) or a strong sustainability policy (Daly and Cobb 1989), consider an economy whose trajectory of activity will generate a breach in the threshold of a resource considered vital to decent human survival.

The exhaustion of a resource necessity is surely an outcome that a sensible sustainability program would consider particularly noteworthy. It is reasonable that the highly diverse range of social concerns which hold *some* value for the welfare of the future would each recognize the special significance of a potential exhaustion of a renewable resource that might be essential for maintaining welfare at minimum acceptable levels. If standard practices could allow this

outcome, society has a special interest in safeguards to avert it.

The conservation SMS program is outlined in Figure 1. A society enters each period with a natural resource capacity, RC_t, from which it harvests resources, D_t, for use and saves resources, S_t, to regenerate resource capacity tomorrow, RC_{t+1}. A tangent slope to the renewal schedule at any point defines the marginal regeneration rate consistent with the resources saved, S_t, for tomorrow. The renewal process, $RC_{t+1} = g(S_t)$, is sigmoidal. Sigmoid g is more interesting, more general and, in the context of natural resource renewal, widely considered more representative (Hutchinson 1978). A line through the origin with slope $= 1$ is diagnostic: above the 45 degree line, net regeneration is positive; but, below it, a smaller stock is returned than had been deferred and, even with zero harvest, the resource is not viable. If D is critical for an adequate standard of living, then a breach of the threshold in deferring resources from immediate use where g crosses the 45 degree line initiates a conservation crisis. Although our purpose here is to simplify the issues for generating the SMS, this extreme outcome may not be unrealistic. Though no general demonstration has programmed the relevant non-convexities of the sigmoid shape within a full, Arrow-Debreu general equilibrium setting, neither does the counterclaim proof asserting the robust adequacy of markets exist. Concern that the exhaustion of essentials in economies with many resources might be vulnerable to the same exhaustion patterns found by Clark (1978) has been voiced by several prominent economists, including Arrow et al. (1995). Explicit concern has been raised by Dasgupta (1993), following the Russell and Wilkinson (1979) argument of exceptional corner solutions in critical contingent markets. Suggested solutions to avert threshold crises have been considered by Barbier and Markandya (1990).

In activating SMS defenses under conditions of generous information, a preservation SMS would safeguard against deferments of D below S_{min} (Figure 1). S_{min} may satisfy preservationists; but we have cast the sustainability question as the conservation of resources

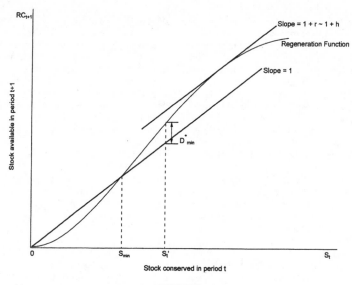

FIGURE 1
SETTING THE SMS

sufficient to support adequate production levels. Since some minimal amount of D, D_{min}, may be required to assure an adequate consumption level, a harvest of at least D_{min} must be sustained for all future periods. Suspending use below D_{min} is an intolerable burden to impose on agents whether they are today's SMS defenders or future victims of a failed SMS defense. So as society articulates what future outcome it wishes to avoid, it jointly articulates the tolerable limit to sacrifice it will accept to prevent that outcome. Accounting for this tolerable limit to sacrifice, the SMS trigger position can be established.

Delivering $S_{min} + D_{min}$ is not enough either. Once D_{min} is used, only S_{min} will remain for the period after, and inadequate harvestable surplus will then be produced. If agents are to use at least D_{min}, an SMS must set S_t at least where $g(S_t) = S_t + D_{min}$ to avoid breaching the viability of the resource. We label this level of deferment S_t^1 (Figure 1). Our sustainability SMS under conditions of perfect foresight is S_t^1. It is a very forward-

looking SMS as the distance $S_t^1 - S_{min}$ can be large and S_t^1 may be breached many periods before S_{min} is directly threatened.

The relation between the tolerable burden of sacrifice and the trigger point of the SMS is significant. If society were not prepared to vastly diminish its welfare opportunities to avert a future crisis, then the SMS would have to be triggered earlier. On Figure 1, this translates into a larger D_{min}, moving S_t^1 to the right. The inclusion of the tolerable level of sacrifice into the definition of the SMS trigger position avoids setting off the SMS alarm too late, when overruling the SMS is predetermined. If one were to add uncertainty to the regeneration process and to the economics dynamics in the decision environment, this strengthens even more the early warning trigger point of the SMS linked to the intolerable cost.

Endogenizing the intolerable cost into the SMS above can be illustrated in a standard species preservation context, showing the connection to be quite general. A productive activity, say development, may be conducted in two areas. One area is rich in natural resources and involves some chance of confronting a preservation crisis during the development activity. The other area is more costly to develop, but entails almost no risk of confronting such a crisis. If society recognizes up front a limited appetite to endure economic loss, then that society will logically back up the SMS from an alarm "as it happens" during the development process to the earlier choice position that determined where to allow development. If responding "as it happens" would occur only when the costs of turning around are terribly expensive, the SMS would surely be overridden. Whatever costs society tolerates to avert an extinction will be identified ahead of time— when society chooses between development sites. This avoids rendering the SMS toothless, initiated only when overriding its protections is a foregone conclusion. Generally, as our tolerable limit to sacrifice weakens (honoring heuristic 3), our desire to locate irreversible outcomes early strengthens (honoring heuristics 1 and 2).

The particular conservation SMS discussed structurally embeds respect for all three moral heuristics at the extremes, making it relatively easy to hypothesize the form of consensus in its support. The conservation SMS seeks directly to sustain for all time human welfare above a basic level, sustaining both humans and their welfare. It also bounds the obligation for sacrifice to defend the SMS at the same basic welfare level. This respects the basic needs of living agents while honoring their within-generation obligations to each other. So, a consensus supporting both normal practice and the SMS policy shift emerges. This generalizes to issues involving sustainability broadly as the trade-off between present and future concerns will enter numerous types of resource extinction scenarios. Other SMS structures that address other types of consequent outcomes will have to consult the individual social actors to define the tolerable level of sacrifice (and therefore the SMS trigger point) for that issue. They will differ from the conservation SMS in that they will be, in general, more sensitive to the mix of social agents than this less controversial case we used to illustrate

the process. Yet the basic conclusion is general: if a consensus is reached, that agreement will likely include SMS structures for all of the reasons argued. Day-to-day policy processes that favor current concerns (surplus maximization) can operate undisturbed as long as that practice generates no significant risks to heuristics (1) and (2). Yet, as present objectives begin to compete with obligations to the future, agents will desire to interrupt daily practice and to construct an inherently more defensive response to meet that circumstance.

A procedural safeguard against accepting the risk of irreversible damage to future welfare emerges as a very reasonable structure, acceptable to everyone with direct concerns for the future. The switch occurs because efficiency and ecological integrity may compete, but no clear single-value theory resolves this conflict a priori among a diverse society of moral persons.

The commonsense appeal of the SMS, on reflection, turns into a fairly compelling moral mandate. Failure to endorse SMS defenses until a comprehensive and consistent objective framework emerges is irresponsible; as it would needlessly hold the policy process hostage, stubbornly refusing to authorize social decisions for which there is broad and well-considered moral support. What emerges from this discussion is that adherence to standard practices when an irreversible event is threatened is itself an overly rigid, restrictive, and inconsistent policy program.

VIII. CONCLUSION

We have attempted to clarify several issues in the discussions about the Safe Minimum Standard. By focusing on a resource whose useful attributes are well recognized, the key question for managing an exhaustion threat is no longer centered on preserving options for potential uses that might emerge. In the case of a resource necessity, tinkering with ordinary benefit-cost procedures may be an inadequate defense; the need for a true shift in the order of social concerns, envisioned by the traditional SMS, is immediately plausible.

The rationale for a change in the order of social concerns is motivated by a society unsure how to balance future needs against present when they confront an irreversible decision affecting the future. These dual objectives may not be easily reconciled under a single, well-structured value theory. Ambiguity about our duties to the future compels a resource manager to regulate by consensus, derived from a set of widely held value heuristics for the question at hand. An economic efficiency rule, for example, might regulate resource use under standard conditions. Yet, there is no reason to presume that a decision about exhausting the resource will be determined by the same rules that prevail under normal conditions. Consensus will view day-to-day management and response to an exhaustion threat as calling for quite different policies.

A defense of the SMS on the grounds that serious moral thinking has yet to produce a complete, consistent, and compelling moral theory delineating the duties of present persons to each other and to the future is neither a retreat into moral relativism nor an abdication to untutored pluralism. If moral discourse reflects a sincere dialogue among reasonable yet diverse moral positions, it is enough to secure a consensus among thoughtful moral agents that future welfare counts.

Though our manager is obligated to avoid wasting economic wealth in an alarmist deference to strong sustainability, it is a significant development in the justification of the conservation SMS that deliberate sacrifice of economic surplus is warranted in irreversible circumstances. Conservation policy is no longer restricted to minimizing the market value of future regrets, which would be an overly rigid stance.

We have developed an argument to define the SMS in an internally consistent way and to defend it against some familiar criticisms of previous SMS proposals. This is illustrated in the explicit context of a particular case: a natural resource necessity whose regeneration is assured only if stocks are maintained above a critical threshold. In contrast, the initial SMS proposals (Ciriacy-Wantrup 1952, 1968; Bishop 1978) were addressed to

species and habitat preservation, as is much of the subsequent discussion. It is interesting to inquire to what extent our argument can be applied also to this case.

First, the good news: while the systematic relationship between the SMS trigger point and the magnitude of the intolerable cost is most readily demonstrated when some minimal level of harvest (D_{min}) is essential for human welfare, the essential point holds more generally. The primary concern of SMS designers always must be to specify a policy that each succeeding generation will honor: after all, what good comes from sacrifice today if some subsequent generation defects and the resource succumbs. If, as seems reasonable, the cost of interventions necessary to stabilize the resource is less when they are initiated well before the critical threshold is reached, the SMS must be triggered sooner for a society with a lower tolerance for sacrifice. Our notion of the SMS as the level of stocks that activates the defensive policy-switch, conditioned on the level of costs society is prepared to tolerate, holds generally.

Now, the bad news: our argument—that, in the absence of a single, consistent, and universally accepted moral theory, broad acceptance of a modest set of heuristics may be sufficient for consensus around a well-specified conservation SMS—is easier to establish given the premise of a resource essential for human welfare. When a possible extinction carries no plausible threat of welfare collapse, consensus on an SMS in principle (Randall 1991) does not necessarily extend to consensus on the level of sacrifice that can be supported. As Randall and Farmer (1995) suggest, utilitarians may be willing to tolerate only modest sacrifice of net benefits (see, also, Rolfe 1995), while those impressed with the intrinsic value of the threatened species may demand sacrifices as great as would be justified (we argue) to sustain a resource necessity. However such irreconcilable conflict, if it exists, would presumably interfere with the support of day-to-day practices as well.

Though the literature suggests room for confidence that sustainability policies can be reached by consensus (Norton 1991) and that open dialogue may commonly yield solutions (Habermas 1987), in part *because* agents possess no complete value stance on their own (Taylor 1989), there is no general assurance that a society will always succeed in reaching consensus around the tolerable level of sacrifice. Yet when a consensus is reached, SMS processes will be common features of that policy consensus.

References

Arrow, K., B. Bolin, R. Costanza, P. Dasgupta, C. Folke, C. S. Holling, B. Jansson, S. Levin, K.-G. Mäler, D. Perring, and D. Pimentel. 1995. "Economic Growth, Carrying Capacity and the Environment." *Science* 268:520–21.

Barbier, E. B., and A. Markandya. 1990. "The Conditions of Achieving Environmentally Sustainable Development." *European Economic Review* 34:659–69.

Bishop, R. C. 1978. "Endangered Species and Uncertainty: The Economics of a Safe Minimum Standard." *American Journal of Agricultural Economics* 60 (1):10–18.

———. 1979. "Endangered Species, Irreversibility, and Uncertainty: A Reply." *American Journal of Agricultural Economics* 61 (2): 376–79.

Bishop, R. C., and R. T. Woodward. 1994. "Intergenerational Welfare Economics and Environmental Policy." Presented at the AERE Workshop, "Integrating the Environment and the Economy: Sustainability Development and Economic/Ecological Modelling," Boulder, CO, June.

Castle, E. N., and R. P. Berrens. 1993. "Endangered Species, Economic Analysis and the Safe Minimum Standard." *Northwest Environmental Journal* 9 (1,2):108–30.

Ciriacy-Wantrup, S. V. 1952. *Resource Conservation: Economics and Policies*, 1st ed. Berkeley: University of California Division of Agricultural Science (3rd. ed. 1968).

Clark, C. W. 1976. *Mathematical Bioeconomics: The Optimal Management of Renewable Resources*. New York: Wiley-Interscience.

Coggins, J. S., and C. A. Ramezani. 1996. "An Arbitrage-free Approach to Quasi-option Value." Presented at the 1996 meetings of the Southern Regional Information Exchange Group: Available at the Department of Applied Economics, University of Minnesota.

Daly, H., and J. B. Cobb. 1989. *For the Common Good: Redirecting the Economy Toward Community, the Environment, and a Sustainable Future*. Boston: Beacon Press.

Dasgupta, P. 1993. *An Inquiry into Well-being and Destitution*. Oxford: Clarendon Press.

Davidson, D. 1969. "True to the Facts." *The Journal of Philosophy* 66:216–34.

Debreu, G. 1959. *Theory of Value*. New York: J. Wiley and Sons.

Farmer, M. 1993. *Can Markets Provide for Future Generations?* Ph.D. diss., The Ohio State University.

Gauthier, D. 1983. *Morals by Agreement*. Ann Arbor: University of Michigan Press.

Gilboa, I., and D. Schmeidler. 1989. "Maximin Expected Utility with a Non-unique Prior." *Journal of Mathematical Economics* 18 (2): 141.

Habermas, J. 1987. *The Philosophical Discourse of Modernity: Twelve Lectures*. Cambridge: MIT Press.

Heidegger, M. 1956. *An Introduction to Metaphysics*. New Haven: Yale University Press.

Hohl, A., and C. Tisdell. 1993. "How Useful Are Environmental Safety Standards in Economics—The Example of the Safe Minimum Standards for Protection of Species." *Biodiversity and Conservation* 2:168–81.

Howarth, R. B. 1995. "Sustainability under Uncertainty: A Deontological Approach." *Land Economics* 71 (Nov.): 237–52.

Hubin, D. C. 1976. "Justice and Future Generations." *Philosophy and Public Affairs* 6 (1): 70–83.

———. 1994. "The Moral Justification of Benefit/Cost Analysis." *Economics and Philosophy* 10 (2):169–94.

Hutchinson, G.E. 1978. *Introduction to Population Ecology*. New Haven: Yale University Press.

Krutilla, J., and A. C. Fisher. 1975. *The Economics of Natural Environments*. Baltimore, MD: John Hopkins University Press.

Norton, B. G. 1986. "On the Inherent Danger of Undervaluing Species." In *The Preservation of Species*, ed. B. G. Norton. Princeton: Princeton University Press.

———. 1991. *Toward Unity Among Environmentalists*. New York: Oxford University Press.

———. 1995. "Resilience and Options." *Ecological Economics* 15:133–36.

Norton, B. G., and M. Toman. 1995. "Sustainability: Ecological and Economic Perspectives." RFF Discussion Paper 95-34. Resources for the Future, Washington, DC, July.

Nozick, R. 1974. *Anarchy, State and Utopia*. Cambridge: Harvard University Press.

Parfit, D. 1984. *Reasons and Persons.* Oxford: Clarendon Press.

Pezzy, J. 1994. "The Optimal Sustainable Depletion of Non-Renewable Resources." London, CSERGE. Mimeo.

Randall, A. 1991. "The Value of Biodiversity." *AMBIO* 20 (2):64–68.

Randall, A., and M. Farmer. 1995. "Benefits, Costs, and the Safe Minimum Standard of Conservation." In *The Handbook of Environmental Economics,* ed. D. W. Bromley. Oxford: Blackwell Press.

Rawls, J. 1972. *A Theory of Justice.* Oxford: Oxford Press.

Ready, R., and R. C. Bishop. 1991. "Endangered Species and the SMS." *American Journal of Agricultural Economics* 72 (2): 309–12.

Rolfe, J. C. 1995. "Ulysses Revisited—A Closer Look at the Safe Minimum Standard Rule." *Australian Journal of Agricultural Economics* 39 (1):55–70.

Rorty, R. 1988. *Philosophy: Its End and Its New Hope.* Tokyo: Iwanami Shoten, chap. 5 ("The Priority of Democracy to Philosophy").

Russell, R., and M. Wilkinson. 1979. *Microeconomics: A Synthesis of Modern and Neoclassical Theory.* New York: J. Wiley and Sons.

Sikora, R. I., and B. Barry, eds. 1978. *Obligations to Future Generations.* Philadelphia: Temple University Press.

Taylor, C. 1989. *Sources of the Self: The Making of the Modern Identity.* Cambridge: Harvard University Press.

Toman, M. 1994. "Economics and 'Sustainability': Balancing Trade-offs and Imperatives." *Land Economics* 70 (Nov.):399–413.

Weiss, E. B. 1989. *In Fairness to Future Generations.* Dobbs Ferry, NY: Transnational Publishers.

Williams, B. 1985. *Ethics and the Limits of Philosophy.* London: Fontana Press.

Woodward, R. T., and R. C. Bishop. 1997. "How to Decide When Experts Disagree: Uncertainty-based Choice Rules in Environmental Policy." *Land Economics* 73 (Nov.):492–507.

PART IV

METHODOLOGY

Reprinted from
AMERICAN JOURNAL OF AGRICULTURAL ECONOMICS
Vol. 67, No. 5, December 1985

*Competing Systems of Knowledge in Natural Resource Economics
(Lawrence W. Libby, Michigan State University, presiding)*

Methodology, Ideology, and the Economics of Policy: Why Resource Economists Disagree

Alan Randall

It is evident that there is persistent disagreement among competent and articulate resource economists, disagreement not only about the appropriate analytical and prescriptive response to particular constellations of policy issues but also about the uses and limitations of economics as a thought system in the policy arena.[1] This must be disquieting and disappointing to many among us who would regard the emergence of an integrated and cohesive (as opposed to diverse and fractious) resource economics as evidence of its maturation.

It is my purpose here to argue that the disagreements among us go deeper than mere disputes about priorities and tactics for doing resource economics, where all participants share a common vision of what resource economics is and should be. Rather, these disagreements extend beyond alternative conceptions of resource economics to fundamentally opposing methodologies, i.e., conceptions of knowledge and how to get it. While the proximate foci of disagreement will shift over time, there is literally no good reason to expect an ultimate resolution of intradisciplinary conflict and convergence of viewpoints. Finally, I argue that persistent disagreement is not only a fact of life, it has its virtues!

Schools of Thought

While we each have our own preferred taxonomy, I would recognize four major schools

of thought influential in resource economics and label them institutionalist/land economics (I/LE), neoclassical/rational planning (N/RP), public choice/utilitarian (PC/U), and public choice/individualist (PC/I).

I would argue that there is a neoclassical mainstream in twentieth century thought about the economics of policy and that mainstream includes the N/RP and PC/U paradigms. Well-known economic works central to the N/RP paradigm, which flourished in the 1930s and 1940s, include those of Pigou on external diseconomies, Kaldor and Hicks (1939) on the compensation test for welfare improvements, Hicks (1943) on economic surplus, and Bergson and Samuelson on welfare maximization. Much of this work is summarized in Bator's pedagogical classics on welfare maximization (1957) and market failure (1958).

The neoclassical policy economics of that period was consistent with the then-dominant rational planning school of public administration. It was considered entirely plausible that government had the necessary equipment to make things better: the information base, the analytical technology, and the cadre of experts immune to self-interest and dedicated to professionalism in the public interest.

The "market failure/government fix" naivete of the N/RP paradigm, which attempted an intellectual justification for welfare state and regulated economy policies, is now clearly in eclipse. Arrow and Coase have shaken its economic foundations. With respect to public administration, there is little faith any more in the possibility of a rational and scientific process of policy formulation, choice, and implementation. Few believe in the decision maker with only the public interest at heart and his cadre of objective analysts who tirelessly assemble for his perusal all the facts and nothing but the facts.

Alan Randall is a professor of agricultural economics, formerly at the University of Kentucky, now at Ohio State University.

Stimulating comments on the initial draft were received from Terry Anderson, Olvar Bergland, Dan Bromley, Emery Castle, and Eldon Smith, who disagreed (but never disagreeably) with each other and/or the author.

[1] Anyone seeking confirmation of this proposition with minimal effort should consult the 1982 proceedings issue of *Amer. J. Agr. Econ.*, which includes papers by Anderson and Bromley espousing fundamentally divergent viewpoints on these matters.

With the advent of an economic literature on public choice (Downs, Buchanan and Tullock, Olson), the center of gravity of mainstream policy economics shifted in that direction. The PC/U model can be characterized as a "market failure/government failure" model. Participants at every level in the public decision process are seen as self-interested, utility-maximizing beings. It is as much a problem (no, even more of a problem) for public organizations to devise ways to keep the organization's interest in line with the public interest and its individual employees' interests in line with organizational interests, as it is for private firms to coordinate their work forces. Policy is not chosen by the planners but emerges from the interplay of myriad individuals and interest-group coalitions. This kind of policy process may well be wasteful in two ways: transactions costs may be exorbitant; and, for a constellation of reasons exemplified by the prisoner's dilemma, the wrong policy outcomes may emerge. However, the degree of waste depends on the design of institutions, the rules of the game.

The PC/U paradigm—taking cues from Coase, Buchanan and Tullock and Posner—applies utilitarian (e.g., benefit cost) criteria to identify the waste-minimizing configuration of imperfect markets and imperfect government institutions.

The methodology of the neoclassical mainstream is unabashedly reductionist,[2] which places it firmly in the mainsteam of postenlightenment western thought (Harre). In fact, reductionist methodology is so dominant that most nonspecialists, when asked to compare and contrast alternative philosophies of science, instinctively restrict themselves to philosophies that differ only to the extent that they are variations on the reductionist theme.

Reductionist thought is characterized by a preoccupation with the atomistic, the elemental, and the individualistic (wholes are seen as sets of individual units); the search for timeless and universal relationships (i.e., scientific laws); deductivism; and empiricism. Reductionism reached its zenith in logical positivism. That position being untenable, modern reductionists are inclined to believe

that the very best of science is represented by the hypothetico-deductive model (Hempel).

The reductionist neoclassical mainstream maintains the fiction that there exist a scientific realm (where the universal truth of propositions is at least a valid question), a metaphysical realm (where it is not), and a clear basis for distinguishing between the two. The establishment and maintenance of a science of economics is thus believed by the mainstream to require a sharp separation of science and ideology. Nevertheless, proponents of other points of view—be they from the other social sciences or from alternative schools of thought in economics—and introspective neoclassicists have little difficulty discerning ideological components deeply embedded in orthodox neoclassical economics. I/LEs and PC/Is tend to become irritable when confronted with mainstream insistence that its own work is conducted in an ideological vacuum.

The first thing to understand about the institutionalist/land economics (I/LE) and public choice/individualist (PC/I) schools of thought is that they are not merely alternative perspectives on how to go about doing reductionist economics. The I/LE school is clearly outside of the reductionist mainstream. The PC/I school is not quite so easy to categorize, as we shall see. but its claim of Austrian influence would seem to take it outside the reductionist mainstream.

The IL/E paradigm has its roots in the German historical school. Thus, its roots are not reductionist but romantic.[3] Modern institutionalists claim a methodology of pattern modeling, storytelling,[4] and holism[5] (Wilber and Harrison). In its I/LE applications, the holistic methodology starts with the premise that it is not the individual but society that is natural and organic. I/LEs have no difficulty seeing society as something beyond the mere aggregation of its individual members. Neoclassical textbooks, on the other hand, commonly treat the whole issue of the relationship between the individual and the collective

---

[2] Reductionism is the theory that complex phenomena ultimately can be understood completely in terms of regular relationships between simple, sense-observable entities. The importance of sense-observability links reductionism to materialism, objectivism, empiricism, and positivism. The insistence that the complex can be understood in terms of regular relationships among simple entities links reductionism to rationalism.

[3] Romanticism is an antireductionist philosophy that asserts the existence of organic realities that cannot be directly comprehended by analysis of relationships among their components. Further, romanticism asserts the validity of subjective experience and feelings, and treats values as having a kind of reality that a reductionist-materialist could never attribute to values.

[4] See Ward, who insists the storytelling is not a pejorative term but a meaningful methodology that is widely used in neoclassical as well as institutional economics.

[5] Holism is a theory that the universe is correctly seen in terms of interacting organic or unitary wholes that are more than a mere aggregation of elementary particles.

under the rubric of something called "the preference aggregation problem."

In the I/LE methodology, the particular, the concrete, and the historical are thought more important, and more real, than the universal and the timeless. The I/LE practitioner seeks understanding in terms of adaptive and evolutionary processes rather than in universal laws. The I/LE practitioner evaluates his/her work by pragmatic criteria rather than by tests for truth (or truth-likeness). The holism of the I/LE methodology makes it even more dependent than the mainstream on its observational base.[6] However, the imprecision of holist concepts often makes formal empirical hypothesis testing impossible (Wilber and Harrison, p. 83). Rather, holistic propositions more commonly confront the material world via the test of plausibility.

From romanticism, the I/LE methodology inherits a respect for the cognitive status of subjective thoughts, feelings, and values. The sharp separation of ideology from knowledge is not thought possible or especially desirable, and institutional analyses tend to meld descriptive and prescriptive components. There is a tendency to see values as operating within a domain of reality, blended and united with facts.

Ideologically, the romantic-holistic approach is compatible with well-developed collective institutions and strong government. However, there is no unique romantic-holistic party line about exactly what government should do. Edmund Burke and the economists of the German historical school followed politically conservative, inegalitarian, and somewhat authoritarian ideologies. On the other hand, the American institutionalists tended to be pragmatic social reformers.

The methodology of the public choice/individualistic (PC/I) paradigm is not so easy to categorize. The eighteenth-century English individualism of John Locke is clearly reductionist in methodology, and it is combined with a natural rights ideology. In addition, the PC/I school claims Austrian influence, and the Austrian methodology defies pigeonholing. In the famous "scientism" essays, Hayek called for the rejection of scientism,[7] objectivism, collectivism, and historicism, claiming that the last three members of this embattled quartet

are manifestations of the first. He takes the position that the only procedure by which wholes can be comprehended is their reconstruction from the parts (p. 73), and he combines this with methodological individualism. This much is standard reductionism. On the other hand, Hayek is uncompromising in his attacks on empiricism and objectivism, which are mainstays of modern reductionism.

The subjectivism of the Austrians leads them to reject, for a variety of reasons, the various reductionist-positivist doctrines on the testing and validation of theories. While logical positivists insisted that meaningful theories were necessarily constructed from sense-observable elements, Mises pronounced the basic axioms of economics to be self-evident facts of subjective experience and therefore true a priori. Empirical testing of the premises of theory is absurd, if one takes the a priorist position.

While the modern hypothetico-deductive/falsificationist methodology seeks to test theories by denying their predicted consequences, modern Austrians view the predictions of their theories as admittedly unfalsifiable. Because there are no constants in the social real world, empirical studies serve only to determine if a particular theory is applicable in a given situation. Falsification of universal theories about society is far too much to ask.[8] Combining the subjectivism of the Austrians with their skepticism about empirical testing, one arrives at a methodological position substantially removed from conventional reductionism-positivism.

Subjectivism makes it relatively unimportant for Austrians to distinguish among facts, feelings and ethics. There is no ambiguity as to the ideological leanings of the Austrian school: individualism is their ideology as well as their methodology, and many Austrians espouse an especially profound faith in the beneficence of markets and private property institutions.[9]

While the Austrian distrust of scientism may seem to imply some commonality with in-

---

[6] "Holism separated from its empirical base easily becomes loose, uncontrolled speculation" (Wilber and Harrison, p. 83).

[7] Scientism is an exaggerated trust in the methods of natural science to explain social and psychological phenomena.

[8] Hayek is often thought more of a falsificationist than other Austrians. However, Caldwell (1985 manuscript) shows that, while Hayek allowed that Popperian falsification has some methodological appeal, he believed it is a fundamentally unattainable ideal when applied to theories about complex social phenomena (i.e., the only really interesting kind of theories).

[9] Given its subjectivism, skepticism about empirical testing of theoretical propositions and clear ideological leanings, there is a persistent neoclassical claim that Austrian economics is primarily an ideological system. Caldwell (1982, chap. 6) evaluates this claim and reaches conclusions sympathetic to the Austrian position.

stitutionalism, the Austrian exaltation of individualism and contempt for collectivism immediately erodes that common ground. Against the N/RP and PC/U mainstream, the Austrians wield the clubs of individualism and subjectivism. The former denies utilitarian (e.g., benefit cost) public choice criteria because they are collectivist. The latter insists that benefits and costs can be known only subjectively and cannot be read from market-generated data.

The discussion of the I/LE and PC/I schools has first addressed methodology and ideology, rather than economics per se, because the former are the basic sources of the disagreements that are the initial premise of my argument. Contemporary resource economists of all four schools share a common core of neoclassical learnings which includes virtually the entire corpus of micro and welfare economics.

To absorb that core and to pass comprehensive examinations thereupon is not sufficient to ensure that all who have done so will arrive at a common world view. Many contemporary I/LEs and PC/Is can comprehend the neoclassical core and use it in constructive ways. The standard analyses of many problems in economics are neoclassical. It is nevertheless valid for I/LEs and PC/Is to quarrel with particular neoclassical analyses (consider the Austrian-PC/I complaint that neoclassicists do not understand the subjective nature of costs) and to disagree strongly about the interpretation and import of neoclassical analyses in the policy arena. Economic disputes among I/LEs, PC/Is, and mainstreamers are not confined to matters of correctness and incorrectness in analysis; more often at issue is not so much the accuracy of the answer as the validity of the question.

Consider the "preference aggregation problem" of the neoclassicists. It was a major blow to the N/RP mainstream, a major impetus for the transition to the emerging PC/U middle-of-the-road consensus, and a serious stumbling block to the practice of resource economics (Castle et al., p. 464) when Arrow promulgated his famous (Im)possibility Theorem. He showed that the attempt to deduce a coherent social decision rule by aggregating individual preferences was impossible under a particular set of conditions. There were various mainstream responses, but most involved the addition, removal, or substitution of conditions on individual preferences, the domain of alternatives, and/or the aggregation procedure, in the attempt to reverse or circumscribe Arrow's result. For the mainstream, the issue was the correctness and generality of Arrow's result.

Contrast this with the I/LE and PC/I reactions. I/LEs wre unconcerned about Arrow's result. Arrow's answer is uninteresting because he asked a foolish question. Of course, one cannot learn about the goals and imperatives of a society (an organic whole) by asking how individual preferences might be aggregated. That is a reductionist question, and its answer—whatever it may be—is of no interest to a romantic-holist. To PC/Is, Arrow's question was abhorrent. It presupposes the unthinkable, that it is ethically acceptable for a collectivist decision rule to be logically derived from diverse individual preferences and then imposed coercively on each of these same individuals. While mainstreamers worried about the correctness and generality of Arrow's result, I/LEs and PC/Is—each for reasons entirely consistent with their own methodologies—dismissed Arrow's question as foolish and abhorrent, respectively.

It is equally instructive to consider the mainstream, I/LE and PC/I positions with respect to economic efficiency. First, they all agree on certain basic propositions from contemporary neoclassical welfare economics. (*a*) From the rather simple premise of consumer sovereignty, it is possible to derive the conclusion that for any inefficient arrangement there exist efficient arrangements which are at least potentially attainable through trade and/or compensation. (*b*) General equilibrium solutions derived from fundamentally different initial distributions are Pareto-noncomparable. (*c*) Ideal competitive equilibrium is Pareto efficient, but real-world markets may for various reasons fail to achieve efficiency. On these basic propositions, the analytics are common to the mainstream, I/LE, and PC/I schools. But there is agreement on little else.

The N/RP mainstream—under forceful attack from PC/Us but, as Emery Castle (personal communication, 12 June 1985) points out, still enjoying the allegiance of many orthodox resource economists—treats efficiency as the primary social goal and a planning-oriented public sector as the way to get it. The efficiency/distribution relationship gets idiosyncratic treatment: N/RPs almost seem to argue that economic science justifies an efficiency goal and identifies the means to achieve it but does neither with respect to distribution. The "market failure/government

Amer. J. Agr. Econ.

fix" mentality is manifested in proposals for Pigovian taxation of external diseconomies and collective efficiency in providing public goods, elaborate efficiency-based planning models as guides to public sector resource allocation (the Forest Service's FORPLAN is a contemporary remnant of the N/RP era), promotion of benefit-cost analysis as a planning tool, and faith in market prices and shadow prices as information about the relative values of commodities and services.

The PC/U paradigm (the emerging contemporary mainstream) also treats efficiency as the primary goal but has little faith in the ability of government to directly impose it. Government is better advised to design and implement institutions that induce individuals in the private and public sectors to behave in ways consistent with global efficiency. Such institutions should maximize the opportunities for trade (both conventional commerce and political trades). Institutions should be chosen to maximize the excess of benefits over costs, and institutional change may be imposed in utilitarian (i.e., uncompensated) fashion. Benefit-cost analysis is essential to sound institutional design, and market prices and shadow prices serve as a totally acceptable information system about relative values of goods and amenities.

The PC/I school shares with the PC/Us the analytics of public choice, i.e., market failure/government failure. The primary social goal is to maximize the scope of individual choice and responsibility, and it is only secondary that global efficiency is consistent with that goal. If the scope of things that can be traded is maximized and some individual or group is entitled to claim the residual generated by each transaction, individual freedom will be enhanced and waste will be eliminated. It is especially important that institutions be privatized to the maximum feasible extent, since that would minimize the discretion of public employees to allocate that which they do not own. Major points at which the PC/I paradigm departs from the PC/U are the essentiality of Wicksellian compensation (because it is just and also serviceable in that it eliminates redistributive rent seeking) and the concomitant ethical unacceptability of utilitarian public decision rules; and the belief that benefits and costs are entirely subjective, so that markets permit efficient allocation but do not generate prices or shadow prices that are valid information for use in social planning or benefit cost analysis.

The I/LE school has its quarrels with each of the other schools. To I/LEs, exchange is a minor (albeit important) form of human interaction. It is a mistake to treat it as a model for all human interaction, a uniquely qualified generator of information about the relative values people place on things, and an ideologically preferred form of arrangements among people. Efficiency is a dubious social goal because efficiency is nonunique; alternative efficient equilibria are Pareto-noncomparable; and the public promotion of any particular efficient solution serves to validate a particular configuration of resource allocation, distribution, and prices for no good reason other than that it is one of many such configurations that could be efficient. While exchange is a valid form of social interaction, so is the constellation of interactions economists call political. Thus, political activities are valid ways of expressing one's values (not indefensible rent seeking), and political outcomes are valid sources of intelligence about what people value. Benefit-cost analysis is useful but should be kept in its place; were it to become dominant in the choice of social policies and programs, that would give prices (the outcomes of status-quo-based exchange) and their shadow-price counterparts undue influence on public policy.

Again, I reiterate that there is a core of analytical propositions about efficiency and markets that is shared by all schools. But fundamental differences in methodology and ideology lead the different schools to fundamentally different understandings of the issues as well as policy conjectures and proposals that differ in important ways.

Is Disagreement Irreconcilable?

As noted at the outset, there is a tendency among many of us to regard convergence of paradigm and methodology as an indicator of maturity for resource economics; persistent methodological diversity is therefore a little embarrassing. This reflects the Aristotelian tradition that resurfaced as post-Enlightenment rationalism. This tradition presupposes that there is one true theory of the universe waiting to be discovered; once the one true theory is found, all true "local" theories will be seen to be corollaries and special cases of the one true theory; and as the application of effort and ingenuity grows indefinitely large, human knowledge will converge toward the one true theory.

This tradition reached its zenith with logical positivism, which proposed to unify science and rid it of all metaphysical elements, with a program based on the following tenets: (*a*) all complex propositions can be derived logically from elemental propositions; (*b*) for every elemental proposition there corresponds a sense-observable elemental fact; (*c*) a statement is meaningful if a method of verifying it can be described; and (*d*) the difference between science and nonscience is identical to the distinction between meaningfulness and meaninglessness or sense and nonsense. Logical positivism foundered when its basic tenets—the perfect correspondence of propositions and sense-observable facts, and verification—were demolished.

The language of theory includes its elements and the axioms and rules of logic by which they are manipulated. In the logical sense, a theory can be entirely correct and yet have no point of contact with the real world. If a theory is to be about the real world, the elements of the theory need to be linked to real-world objects via an observation language, i.e., a dictionary (Harre) or a set of correspondence rules (Brown). However, there is no unique observation language (Brown, pp. 46–48). Thus, the choice of observation language becomes a convention, and theories based on different observation languages are fundamentally noncomparable. For any set of phenomena, there may coexist noncomparable theories that subsume language-based observations thereof within their overlapping but nonidentical domains. Coexistence may persist indefinitely because noncomparability precludes the climactic test in which rival theories are shown to be strictly contradictory in some respect and a confrontation with empirical evidence falsifies one of them. The coexistence thesis is dynamic: it does not preclude periods of ascendancy for particular theories, the consignment of some theories to obscurity, and the resuscitation and refurbishment of discarded theories. The preeminence of a single theory is neither the "normal" nor the ultimate state of science.[10]

The demolition of verificationism was devastating to the positivist ambition of a sharp demarcation of science and metaphysics, knowledge and ideology. Popper's (1935) falsificationism, while it resolved an important logical difficulty with verificationism, could not repair the damage. The Duhem irrefutability thesis denies the logical imperative of the falsification test: since an empirical test of a theoretical proposition requires auxiliary assumptions, it is always possible to preserve the theory by attributing an empirical anomaly to the failure of an auxiliary assumption. Among the important auxiliary assumptions are those that specify what counts as evidence (Gleymour), a point that links the Duhem thesis to the noncomparability thesis. More fundamentally, strict falsificationism does not provide for the growth of anything that can reasonably be called a body of knowledge. Note that, in his later years, Popper (1974) substantially amended his methodology, making less of falsification, attempting to allow for the growth of knowledge, and finding scientific merit in theories such as evolution, which is clearly nonscience under the tests of logical positivism and strict falsificationism.

All of this leads me to the following conclusions. Over the domain loosely called resource economics, rival but fundamentally noncomparable schools of thought can and will persist. The reductionist-positivist program to impose law and order on science has failed and, with it, the myth that social science can be strictly separated from ideology. Thus, the neoclassical reductionist mainstream is doomed to coexist with romantic-holistic and Austrian-subjectivist rivals that do not share its sense of urgency that knowledge and ideology be hermetically sealed, each from the other. The rival paradigms are noncomparable and, while they share some common territory, have nonidentical domains. Disagreement will per-

---

[10] The noncomparability of alternative theories is a recurring theme of recent literature in the philosophy of science. However, different authors treat it differently. Kuhn writes of paradigm switches in which, following a brief period of intellectual turmoil, a new paradigm achieves dominance in place of the former dominant paradigm. The new and the old are noncomparable. The views of Lakatos are more consistent with mine. He uses the notion of the scientific research program. Popperian testing of

rival, comparable, and contradictory theories may occur within the "protective belt" of a research program, and this process may lead to progress or degeneration of the research program. Lakatos' methodology permits the coexistence of rival research programs, fundamentally noncomparable but covering some common territory. These coexisting rivals may persist for a long time; the climactic test and final destruction of one of the rivals is impossible; there will be periods of progress and ascendancy and periods of degeneration and decline for various rival programs; and some declining research programs will eventually be abandoned. However, it is not necessarily foolish for a few stubborn souls to continue working on a declining research program, since there is always the possibility of a breakthrough that would reverse the decline. Feyerabend argues that Popperian falsification is fundamentally wrong, as history and as method: nothing is ever truly discarded in the search for knowledge, and a long-ignored concept is sometimes combined with a recent discovery to revive a moribund research program.

sist even though the common core of shared learnings will continue to expand as it has in the past. (Recently, the theory of the core and a considerable body of findings from game theory have been added.) The ultimate convergence of resource economists on the single true theory is an entirely false hope. Disagreement will be the norm, now and indefinitely, although the proximate foci of disagreement may change over time.

Since my argument has been complex, it may help to consider the question raised by a commentator (Terry L. Anderson, personal communication, 24 June 1985): do resource economists disagree because they have different goals, different ideologies, different methodologies, or different interpretations of the evidence? My response is that the fundamental sources of disagreement are ideological and methodological (and, at that level, it is hard to identify the chicken and the egg). Different methodologies lead to different interpretations of the evidence. Different goals emerge from different conjunctions of ideology and images of reality, where the latter depend on methodology and interpretation of the evidence.

Living with Persistent Disagreement

Given that persistent disagreement among competent and articulate resource economists is a fact of life, we could do more to prepare our students and our clientele to cope with it. The (false) premise of much scientific pedagogy—that disagreement about the nature of material reality means at least one party is wrong—serves us poorly. The premise of much teaching in the humanities, that different world views, each having its particular strengths, can be expected to persist without ultimate resolution, could usefully be introduced into the teaching of economics.

Finally, let me say a few kind words about persistent disagreement. It is entirely conventional to defend diversity but not disagreement. The idea seems to be that it ought to be possible to take what is best from each of the rival viewpoints and create a grand synthesis.[11] However, my whole argument is so structured that it must necessarily deny this possibility: it is possible for the practitioner to pluck various useful insights from the alterna-

tive paradigms, but the grand synthesis is a will-o'-the-wisp. I propose instead to defend persistent disagreement.

To deny the possibility of the grand synthesis or the universal true theory is not to deny the idea of progress in the search for knowledge. However, progress occurs mostly within the research program, and overt rivalry among research programs is an essential stimulus to that kind of progress.

To acknowledge the coexistence of noncomparable paradigms is not to undermine the goal of excellence in scholarship. However, excellence cannot be conceived of in terms of universal truth or error. Rather, excellence is multidimensional and, while some of its dimensions are universal (e.g., logical coherence), others are internal to the particular paradigm. The goal of excellence is common to all paradigms, but what counts as excellent may well differ across paradigms.

The key arguments for learning to live with persistent disagreement among resource economists are, first, the persistence of rivalry among noncomparable research programs is the reality to which we need become accustomed: second, cross-program disagreements are powerful stimuli for within-program progress and may occasionally lead to abandonment of hopelessly degenerating programs; and third (and to me, less compelling), the noncomparable observation languages and nonidentical domains of the rival paradigms do, as Castle et al. (p. 406) suggested, provide some limited basis for specialization along pragmatic lines.[12]

References

Anderson, Terry L. "The New Resource Economics: Old Ideas and New Applications." *Amer. J. Agr. Econ.* 64(1982):928–34.

Arrow, Kenneth J. *Social Choice and Individual Values,* 2nd ed. New York: John Wiley & Sons, 1976.

Bator, F. M. "The Anatomy of Market Failure." *Quart. J. Econ.* 72(1958):351–79.

---

[11] Our model protagonists genuflect in the direction of, respectively, an institutionalist-neoclassical synthesis (Bromley, 1982, p. 843) and a public-choice-Austrian-neoclassical synthesis (Anderson, p. 928).

[12] Nevertheless, competition and disagreement, rather than unchallenged dominance of a particular paradigm in its special area, remain the norm. It may be tempting to argue, for example, that the I/LE paradigm has a comparative advantage in the study of land tenure in the third world, while the property rights PC/I approach is well-adapted to studying the problems of the U.S. public lands. But no such special niches of single-paradigm dominance can be discerned. There is a PC/I alternative (Cheung) to the IL/E analysis of third world land tenure arrangements; and a trenchant I/LE criticism (Bromley 1985) of the PC/I program for U.S. public lands.

――――. "The Simple Analytics of Welfare Maximization." *Amer. Econ. Rev.* 47(1957):22–59.

Bergson, Abram. "A Reformulation of Certain Aspects of Welfare Economics." *Quart. J. Econ.* 52(1938): 311–34.

Bromley, Daniel W. "Land and Water Problems: An Institutional Perspective." *Amer. J. Agr. Econ.* 64 (1982):834–44.

――――. "Property Rights and Incentives in Resource and Environmental Economics." *The Political Economy of Natural Resource and Environmental Use,* ed. Gary D. Lynne and J. Walter Milon, SNREC No. 20. Mississippi State MS: Southern Rural Development Center, 1985.

Brown, H. I. *Perception, Theory and Commitment.* Chicago: University of Chicago Press, 1977.

Buchanan, J., and G. Tullock. *The Calculus of Consent: Logical Foundations of Constitutional Democracy.* Ann Arbor: University of Michigan Press, 1962.

Caldwell, Bruce. *Beyond Positivism: Economic Methodology in the Twentieth Century.* London: George Allen and Unwin, 1982.

――――. "Disentangling Hayek, Hutchinson, and Popper on the Methodology of Economics." University of North Carolina, Greensboro. Manuscript, 1985.

Castle, Emery N., M. M. Kelso, J. B. Stevens, and H. H. Stoevener. "Natural Resource Economics, 1946–75." *A Survey of Agriculture Economics Literature,* vol. 3, ed. Lee R. Martin. Minneapolis: University of Minnesota Press, 1981.

Cheung, Steven N. S. *The Theory of Share Tenancy.* Chicago: University of Chicago Press, 1969.

Coase, R. H. "The Problem of Social Cost." *J. Law and Econ.* 3(1960):1–44.

Downs, A. *An Economic Theory of Democracy.* New York: Harper & Bros., 1957.

Feyerabend, P. K. *Against Method: Outline of an Anarchistic Theory of Knowledge.* London: NLB, 1975.

Gleymour, Clark. *Theory and Evidence.* Princeton NJ: Princeton University Press, 1980.

Harre, R. "History of Philosophy of Science," *Encyclopedia of Philosophy,* vol. 7, ed. P. Edwards, pp. 289–96. London: Collier-Macmillan.

Hayek, F. A. "Scientism and the Study of Society." *The Counter-Revolution of Science,* pp. 11–102. Glencoe IL: Free Press, 1952.

Hempel, C. G. *Aspects of Scientific Explanation.* New York: Free Press, 1965.

Hicks, J. R. "The Foundations of Welfare Economics." *Econ. J.* 49(1939):696–712.

――――. "The Four Consumer's Surpluses." *Rev. Econ. Stud.* 11(1943):31–41.

Kaldor, N. "Welfare Propositions in Economics." *Econ. J.* 49(1939):549–52.

Kuhn, T. S. *The Structure of Scientific Revolutions,* 1st ed. Chicago: University of Chicago Press, 1962.

Lakatos, I. *The Methodology of Scientific Research Programmes: Philosophical Papers,* vols. 1, 2, ed. J. Worrall and G. Currie. Cambridge: Cambridge University Press, 1978.

Olson, M., Jr. *The Logic of Collective Action: Public Goods and the Theory of Groups.* Cambridge MA: Harvard University Press, 1965.

Pigou, A. C. *The Economics of Welfare.* London: Macmillan & Co., 1927.

Popper, K. R. "Autobiography of Karl Popper." *The Philosophy of Karl Popper,* vol. 1, ed. Paul Schilpp. La Salle IL: Open Court, 1974.

――――. *The Logic of Scientific Discovery.* New York: Harper Torchbooks, 1935. Translated 1959, 1968.

Posner, Richard A. *Economic Analysis of Law.* Boston: Little Brown & Co., 1972.

Samuelson, P. A. *Foundations of Economic Analysis.* Cambridge MA: Harvard University Press, 1947.

Ward, B. *What's Wrong with Economics?* London: Macmillan & Co., 1972.

Wilber, C. K., and R. S. Harrison. "The Methodological Basis of Institutional Economics: Pattern, Model, Storytelling and Holism." *J. Econ. Issues* 12 (1978):61–89.

[16]

What Practicing Agricultural Economists Really Need to Know About Methodology

Alan Randall

There has always been considerable methodological diversity among agricultural economists. Nevertheless, about a quarter century ago, a broad methodological consensus seemed to be emerging, especially among the younger members of our discipline. We sought to do positive economics, to apply the scientific method in pursuit of objective knowledge about the empirical phenomena in our domain. We believed that our discipline was on the right track when seeking to pose a refutable hypothesis and test it with empirical evidence, and at its very best when the hypothesis had been deduced from a well-articulated economic theory, so that the outcome of the empirical test could potentially challenge the theory itself.

Most agricultural economists made no claim to have read deeply in the philosophy of science or even in the specialized literature on economic methodology.[1] Our methodological views had been gleaned mostly from the introductory chapters of economics textbooks and the off-hand comments of our teachers and mentors. That, of course, is not a criticism of our profession: things would be fine, so long as the methodological orthodoxy that had trickled down to the practitioners reflected a well-articulated consensus among the specialists in philosophy of science and economic methodology.

The practitioners occasionally picked-up discordant signals. First, there were internal inconsistencies in the positivist-empiricist consensus. It became clear that the gurus of positive economics, Robbins and Friedman, had in mind methodologies very different from one another, and that neither methodology was consistent with

Alan Randall is a professor of agricultural economics at The Ohio State University. The author is grateful for continuing conversations with Michael Farmer and John Hoehn, and for detailed written comments from Thomas Blaine, Emery Castle, Gernot Klepper, and Eldon Smith.

[1] Among agricultural economists there have been and currently are honorable exceptions who read, write, and teach seriously about methodology.

logical positivism. Also, while many of us assumed Popper's falsificationism was a cornerstone of positivist methodology, Popper himself (1959) saw it as a devastating attack on logical positivism. Second, agricultural economists were sometimes disturbed by the inconsistencies between the orthodox methodology of economics that enshrined scientific objectivity and the pragmatic ideology of the land-grant college that emphasized science in the service of humankind.

Beginning in the 1960s, the orthodox methodology came under sustained attack from philosophers and historians of science. Kuhn challenged Popper's heroic model of science, with its bold conjectures and unflinching refutations. Kuhn's world of normal science is neither bold nor heroic, and the occasional scientific revolutions are not exactly rational processes. Lakatos leaves us facing only the prospect of long wars of attrition among rival but noncomparable research programs, each of which may pass through periods of amendment, advance, and degeneration. Feyerabend (1975) argued exuberantly that the acquisition and validation of knowledge is not a strictly rational process; therefore, it is a foolish project to develop a prescriptive methodology.

By this time, Popper himself was moving away from the falsificationist school that had formed around his earlier work. At the end of his long and productive career, Popper was willing to defend only critical rationalism, clearly a much less ambitious methodology than the strict falsificationism of his youth, or his mid-career scientific objectivity.

Recent writing on the methodology of economics reflects these trends in the broader philosophy of science literature. Caldwell (1982) considered the positivist-empiricist consensus and the various critiques thereof and concluded with a plea for methodological pluralism. No particular methodology has unchallengeable claim on our allegiance, and we would do well to remain

Amer. J. Agr. Econ. 75 (October 1993): 48–59
Copyright 1993 American Agricultural Economics Association

open to a diversity of methodological approaches. McCloskey's (1983) attack on the orthodox methodology was fundamental and sweeping. There is no scientific method, no prescription for acquiring warrantable knowledge. All we have is rhetoric, the art of argument. And there is no absolute standard for economic truth; the best economic ideas are simply those that are the most convincing.

McCloskey had expressed the hope that his concept of rhetoric would liberate economists from the artificial restraints of the orthodox methodology. Yet many practicing economists reacted with skepticism. Some worried that McCloskey had legitimized the kind of advocacy and propaganda from which scholarly economics had struggled so long and hard to separate itself. Even those who had some sympathy for McCloskey's project, e.g., Solow and Hoover (Choi), were obviously disappointed that McCloskey had not offered more specific instructions to guide the search for economic knowledge.

Some economic methodologists were similarly disturbed by the decline of prescriptive methodology. Redman dismisses Kuhn and Lakatos as offering little more than "science as consensus." Blaug reluctantly concedes that a strict positive-normative distinction is untenable. Nevertheless, he argues, it is best that economists behave as though they believe in such a distinction; such behavior would lead to the doing of better economics. Hausman and McPherson, in a brief article directed to agricultural economists, assert that there is (has to be) more to methodology than McCloskey's rhetoric.

Agricultural economists whose interests lie in more practical matters have been unable to escape the fallout of these developments. Where only two decades ago there seemed to be a growing majority backing some sort of positivist prescriptive methodology, that consensus is now in disarray. More threatening to some is that a strong contender in the current methodological disputes goes by the name "rhetoric"[2], ridicules the very idea of prescriptive methodology, and (in the eyes of some critics) is relativist to the core. A common reaction among the practitioners is that it is one thing to recognize the problems with the prescriptive standards that emerge

from positivism and scientific objectivity, but quite another to embrace a methodology that seems to impose no standards at all.

My objective is to examine the state of prescriptive methodology in a post-Popper, post-McCloskey world, focusing always on what practicing agricultural economists really need to know in order to go about their work. However, before getting to the heart of the argument, there are some preliminaries to take care of.

First, what do practicing agricultural economists hope to get from methodology? Hausman suggests that what economists want from methodology is theory appraisal: how can we tell whether a particular economic idea is good science? I think we want also appraisal of method and procedure: how can we tell whether a particular procedure will lead us to a clearer recognition and a better explanation of economic phenomena, i.e., is good method? In addition we want prescriptions, recipes for success, rules that will guide us in acquiring warrantable knowledge. Essentially, then, those practitioners who are neither serious scholars in methodology nor hobbyists therein make relatively narrow demands of methodology. They want appraisal and prescription.[3]

Second, what was the methodological consensus? McCloskey (1983) defines the methodological consensus as "modernism." He defines modernism in terms of eleven propositions (some of which contradict others in important ways), such that most modernists believe in most of these propositions.[4] Reductionism, empiricism, positivism, falsificationism, scientific objectivity, the belief that science is a human undertaking fundamentally different from all others, and the belief in a specifiable scientific method, are all elements of modernism.

The essence of the consensus methodology is its obsession with demarcation and prescription. Demarcation is the notion that there ought to be very clear and firm boundaries between science and other things that human beings do, and that it is the task of methodologists to define the things that make science different. This leads easily into prescription because if one can define what makes

---

[2] The word "rhetoric," while it has an honorable history, has accumulated some nasty baggage along the way. The dictionary on my desk gives equal billing to "the art and practice of argumentation," which is close to what McCloskey has in mind, and "inflated and grandiose oratory."

[3] While practitioners' demands may be narrow, the methodologist would need to conduct a broader enquiry to respond to those demands. Epistemology (what are facts, truth?) is necessary for methodology (how does one have the facts, the truth?). But it is not sufficient: claiming to know something about the nature of knowledge is not the same as knowing how to create new knowledge.

[4] As Backhouse points out, there are other definitions of modernism, clearer than McCloskey's, in the literature.

science different, then those things that make science different can be reformulated as imperatives: a set of rules by which new science ought to be done. Rationalism, empiricism, and the twentieth-century attempts to synthesize them (such as logical positivism, falsificationism, and logical empiricism) share the common objectives of demarcation and prescription. So I shall characterize the consensus methodology as demarcationist prescriptive methodology (DPM).

Third, what could a DPM do for practitioners? Assume that economists are confronted with arguments that take many forms—logic, mathematical models, empirical estimates of many kinds, calculations of efficiency and distributional outcomes, normative claims—and come in a wide variety of qualities. Assume, also, that we have the scholarly tools of rhetoric and criticism, as well as the specialized tools of economics and related disciplines, available to help us confront bad arguments and construct better ones. Then, what could a DPM do for us?

The useful service that a DPM could perform is to provide reliable shortcuts. After all, if every argument has to be taken seriously, at least at the outset—as rhetoricians seem to suggest—the rhetorical approach entails a lot of hard work. If it can be established that some things are settled in principle, then we can reliably resolve particulars by reference to these established principles. Incorrect or irrelevant arguments, failed theories, unfruitful methods, and unreliable results could be eliminated *a priori*. Historically, the search for a DPM has been a search for exclusionary principles: rules that eliminate certain kinds of arguments on principle. Without simple and robust exclusionary rules, it is much harder to identify "unscientific" practices or to claim that science is distinctly different from other forms of scholarship.

Can a Satisfactory DPM Be Developed?

Instead of asking what might be lost by abandoning DPM and relying on rhetoric or critical rationalism, consider the reverse question: starting with the standard intellectual tools of broad-based scholarship, would we want to add some kind of DPM to guide the doing of science? Let us consider the major DPMs as candidates for adoption.

Logical positivism

The most ambitious DPM developed thus far is logical positivism. The earlier rationalist and empiricist methodologies had sought to liberate the people from superstition and dogma. Rationalists would accomplish this by establishing the power of the mind to arrive at the truth through correct reasoning. Empiricists argue that warrantable knowledge about the material world is accessible to the human senses; thus, a scientific method based on systematic observation would lead people to the truth.

The logical positivists combined rationalism and empiricism to produce a methodology that, they hoped, would unify science and rid it of all metaphysical elements. Their program was based on four tenets: (*i*) all complex propositions can be derived from elemental propositions; (*ii*) for every elemental proposition, there corresponds a sense-observable elemental fact; (*iii*) a statement is meaningful if a method of verifying it can be described; and (*iv*) the difference between science and nonscience is identical to the distinction between meaningfulness and meaninglessness or between sense and nonsense. Tenet (*i*) introduces the rationalism and (*ii*) the empiricism, while (*iii*) and (iv) provide the demarcation between science and nonscientific thought, and place science on a pedestal. Tenets (*i*)–(*iii*) provide an unambiguous set of instructions for doing science.

While logical positivism promises a powerful DPM, it has three major problems. The first is the insistence that theories be constructed of observable elements. The body of science, at the time of the logical positivists, included the atomic theory of chemistry and the gene theory of inheritance. Both disciplines were making good progress with these theories, it seemed, although no one had yet seen an atom or a gene. The second problem is the insistence on empirical verification despite Hume's earlier critique of induction. The third problem is the insistence on a one-to-one correspondence between the elements of theory and observable facts. The language of theory includes its elements and axioms and the rules of logic by which they are manipulated. It is not logically essential that a theory be about the real world. But, if that is the objective, the elements of the theory need to be linked to real-world objects via an observation language, i.e., a dictionary (Campbell, Harre) or a set of correspondence rules (Brown). However, theories are necessarily simplified abstractions, while phenomena are complex and multifaceted. It follows that no unique observation language exists (Brown, pp. 46–48). It is characteristic of different theories—and different paradigms (Kuhn) and scientific research programs (Lakatos)—that they establish for their own good reasons different observation languages. Thus, the climactic test in which one theory is vindicated and its competitors are defeated is unavailable: if the competing theories are meaningfully different, their different observation languages will render them noncomparable (Feyerabend 1962).

Falsificationism and Scientific Objectivity

Popper solved the first and second problems of logical positivism. To resolve the first problem, Popper argued that it is not essential that theories be constructed of observable elements. It is enough that theories have observable consequences. This preserves the link between theory and observable evidence, and expands the set of theories to which it applies. This Popperian amendment extends, rather than shrinks, the scope of positivism.

Popper, most famously, resolved the problem of verification by replacing it with falsification. He showed rigorously that no finite series of confirming observations would verify a general statement. However, there is an asymmetry between verification and falsification: a single contrary observation is sufficient to falsify a general statement. Popper claimed that this totally destroyed logical positivism; and he thereafter refused to use the word "positivism" in any characterization of his own methodology.[5]

By mid-career, Popper (1957) had developed his concept of scientific objectivity, which he defined as a process involving (*i*) posing refutable hypotheses, (*ii*) testing them with relevant evidence, and (*iii*) reporting the hypotheses, the tests, and their results in a manner accessible to any interested person (Castle). This, too, is a strong DPM, offering a strict demarcation between science and nonscience[6] and a clear prescription for doing science. However, it too had major problems.

First, the Duhem-Quine thesis (which Popper recognized) denies the possibility of refuting a hypothesis unambiguously. Because an empirical test of a theoretical proposition requires auxiliary assumptions, it is always possible to preserve the theory by attributing an empirical anomaly to the failure of an auxiliary assumption.

Second, while strict falsificationism may serve to weed out false conjectures, it does not provide for the accumulation of warrantable knowledge. This problem worried Popper deeply. He worked for many years to establish the concept of verisimilitude—conjectures that had survived many attempts at falsification could be said, for that reason, to possess the property of verisimilitude, or truthlikeness—before eventually abandoning the project (Caldwell 1991). Falsificationism tells us what not to believe, but it does not tell us what to believe, even tentatively.

Third, falsificationism does not solve the problem of noncomparability. Among the important auxiliary assumptions for hypothesis testing are those that specify what counts as evidence (Gleymour). Competing theories, with their different dictionaries or observation languages, will have different evidentiary requirements and different interpretations of whatever evidence is brought to bear. The direct confrontation of competing theories, with the evidence as final arbiter, is denied.

The Methodology of Scientific Research Programs

Lakatos, a former student of Popper, attempted to salvage something of Popper's scientific objectivity—the concept of science as a rational process and the centrality of testing in that process—while recognizing the noncomparability problem and accommodating the growth of knowledge. He offered important amendments to the Popperian scheme: research programs consisting of a "hard core" of propositions that are untested (by convention) and perhaps inherently untestable, and a "protective belt" of derived propositions that are tested; criteria for amending refuted propositions (Popper had railed against any and all amendments as "immunizing stratagems"); criteria for judging whether a research program is advancing or degenerating; and contests, between rival but noncomparable research programs, viewed not as climactic battles but as wars of attrition. As with Kuhn before him, many practitioners found Lakatos quite plausible and congenial, and his methodology enjoyed a decade (beginning about 1976) of popularity among economists (Redman).

However, the bottom line is that Lakatos' attempt to find the middle ground failed to satisfy either the rationalists (Redman) or those who were most strongly opposed to the DPM project *per se* (Feyeraband 1975, McCloskey 1983).

---

[5] Others (Adorno et. al.) regard falsificationism as cleaning up a rather modest detail in a positivist agenda that Popper continued to pursue.

[6] Popper (1957) uses his demarcation criterion to question the scientific status of Adler's psychiatry and Darwin's theory of evolution.

We are left with the failure of the aggressive DPMs—logical positivism and strict falsificationism—and the unsatisfactory outcome of Lakatos' attempt to develop a DPM responsive to the criticisms of the aggressive DPMs. This, of course, is not sufficient to demonstrate the impossibility of a convincing DPM. Nevertheless, I am convinced that the noncomparability thesis is valid, and suspect strongly that it provides insurmountable obstacles for a DPM (Randall 1985).

Post-DPM Methodology

Given that we have no satisfactory candidate to adopt as a DPM, it makes sense to take another look at McCloskey's rhetoric and Popper's late-career critical rationalism. These methodologies are nondemarcationist—they appeal to intellectual and scholarly processes that apply not just to science but across the board—and both have been criticized for providing relatively little in the way of prescription. But, perhaps there is more to rhetoric and critical rationalism than has been recognized by the critics.

Rhetoric

In a nutshell, the rap on rhetoric is that, in the end, it offers little more than "good economic argumentation is whatever in fact persuades economists" (Hausman, p. 123). That is, persuasion is the test, and economists are those who have to be persuaded. By emphasizing that economists should be open to a wide variety of kinds of argument, McCloskey has attracted charges of relativism, i.e., the claim that any argument is as good as any other. By appealing to Rorty, McCloskey seemed to endorse the view that knowledge is socially constructed. By proposing literary criticism as a model for scientific discourse, McCloskey seemed to endorse the contention that meaning is provided neither by the text nor the reader but the interpretive community (Fish). If (*i*) knowledge is socially constructed, (*ii*) there are no general standards for argument except whatever persuades, and (*iii*) it is the interpretive community (or discourse community) that must be persuaded, what is to protect us from a proliferation of discourse communities, each proclaiming its version of knowledge secure from criticism from the outside, and demanding to be accepted by outsiders as a legitimate school of thought (Backhouse)?

McCloskey brought some of this upon himself by his refusal throughout the 1980s to say very much about what constitutes good argumentation. In 1990, he proposed what he called the rhetorical tetrad: fact, logic, metaphor, and story. He made much of the role of conflict: one learns something by opposing conflicting metaphors and stories. While few would deny this, it remains rather a broad-brush treatment that places McCloskey in an intellectual tent large enough to include Hegel and the late-career Popper.

Let me suggest a way to defend rhetoric from the charge of relativism. To make this case, it is necessary to deal with the role of appraisal in rhetoric, and the problems of persuasion and defining the discourse community.

To define rhetoric, McCloskey (1983) relied on Booth, who offered the art of discovering good reasons, of improving beliefs through shared discourse, and of finding what really warrants assent because reasonable people ought to be persuaded. There is ample room here for discovering and applying principles of appraising arguments.

The role of persuasion in rhetoric is worrisome to those who fear it might open the door to advocacy and propaganda. However, the problem of persuasion pervades all serious discussion of ideas in a liberal society. Assume the human mind demands a reasonable degree of autonomy; that is, assume that, in the end, people make up their own minds.[7] Then any argument, in order to be successful, must be persuasive. This applies even to methodological arguments; persuasion is not a special problem for rhetoric. In addition to the autonomy assumption, assume people have a tendency to listen to reason, sort through the arguments, and arrive at the right conclusion. Without this assumption, rhetoric would be a disaster; and without it, people would be likely to adopt false and unhelpful prescriptive methodologies. In a liberal society, both rhetoric and prescriptive methodology rely on the assumption of a human tendency to be persuaded by the better argument.[8]

---

[7] If this is problematic, consider assuming the contrary.

[8] But, it must be conceded, they rely on this tendency in different ways. It is true that in order for the DPM project to succeed, people must be persuaded, correctly, by a valid DPM. However, the purpose of DPM, once adopted, is to provide a small and coherent set of general principles by which to resolve particular questions of method, evidence, and inference. With a valid DPM in place, its prohibitions and exclusionary rules would serve a valuable legislative and policing function, to minimize error and deviance and to expose them when they occur.

The concern that narrow, self-selected discourse communities could establish themselves as arbiters of knowledge without scrutiny from the outside is overblown. We certainly observe small groups of scholars attempting to establish new paradigms. Recent examples include ecological economics and human values in agriculture. Nevertheless, these paradigms and discourse communities are permeable to stimuli from the outside (just as, to use another example, game theory has penetrated philosophy and most of the social sciences). To lapse into Lakatosian language, among these emerging research programs, those that are most successful at withstanding criticism and incorporating useful ideas from the outside will progress while the others degenerate. The ultimate discourse community is humankind.

Regardless of whether McCloskey has himself done it, one can develop a strong case that rhetoric is not inherently relativist. That is, one can adopt a stance of *a priori* openness to many different kinds of argument and evidence, without committing oneself to the belief that any argument is as good as another.

Critical Rationalism

While Popper's falsificationism is ultimately an untenable methodology, Popper has developed and promoted many useful ideas. Two, in particular, stand out. The mere search for confirmations of one's prior beliefs is a timid and unambitious kind of science; the unexpected observation and the unlikely explanation are the most interesting. Science is a social process, so that objectivity derives not so much from the commitment of individual scientists to be at all times objective and impartial as from the openness of the process to criticism from any interested person.

Popper's (1974, 1983) late-career critical rationalism backed away from strict falsificationism,[9] while retaining a central place for bold

conjectures, unflinching criticism, and science as a social process. However, critical rationalism prompted from many methodologists and practitioners much the same reaction as McCloskey's rhetoric: it doesn't say enough; surely there has to be more. Specifically, for those who had been nurtured on some version of DPM, it doesn't prohibit enough. As Caldwell (1991) observes, Popper would discard conjectures that cannot be criticized, but said relatively little about the critical process itself. His former student, Bartley, attempted to address this issue. He concluded that a theory is held rationally if (*i*) it contains no built-in devices for avoiding or deflecting critical arguments or contrary evidence, and its holder (*ii*) makes every attempt to expose the theory to criticism and (*iii*) does not maintain it in the face of cogent criticism. But this, still, provides little in the way of demarcation between science and nonscience (Redman). While critical rationalism remains disappointing to those seeking a DPM, it nevertheless provides a framework useful in appraising arguments.

Reasoned Discourse

From here on, I shall be less concerned with what McCloskey and Popper actually wrote, and more concerned with what one can make of their ideas. The best elements of rhetoric and critical rationalism can be combined in an approach that I propose to call reasoned discourse: reasoned, to emphasize the rational, critical, and appraisive aspects; and discourse, a term that is consistent with McCloskey's concept of rhetoric and Popper's notion that the search for knowledge is a fundamentally social process.

Meta-Methodology and the Tools of Reasoned Discourse

Reasoned discourse commits its adherents to evaluate a broad range of arguments and the evidence on their merits. However, not all arguments and not all evidence deserve to be taken equally seriously. To submit all statements to the same scrutiny would be unwarranted, and too costly. Not every exercise in appraisal needs to start from scratch. The failed search for a DPM has nevertheless generated some useful precepts to guide the task of appraisal. I propose to call this body of precepts "meta-methodology." Meta-methodology differs from DPM in that it forgoes the claim to have discovered universal rules

---

[9] Economic methodologists (Redman, Caldwell 1991) have drawn attention to Popper's one attempt to develop a methodology for economics (Popper 1974, 1985; Koertge). He calls it *situational analysis*, in which the objectives of actors are specified, as is the context or situation in which they find themselves, and the rationality principle is applied to predict the actor's choices. In the event the predictions are not realized, the rationality principle is maintained while the economist reconsiders whether the objectives and situation had been specified correctly. This sounds weakly Popperian at best. It seems to be confirmationist, especially with regard to the rationality principle; and it offers no bold conjecture about how economists do or should go about their science. Rather, it offers a readily recognizable picture of what mainstream microeconomists and the microfoundations school of macroeconomists already do.

of demarcation. It does claim, however, that there is a fairly well-developed scientific method that provides some instructions helpful in appraising scientific conjectures. There is no claim that each of these instructions is universally serviceable or that those who would be considered scientists are obliged to follow each. Furthermore, some inconsistencies among the components of meta-methodology are tolerated because meta-methodology is viewed as an inventory of potentially useful suggestions for researchers, not a single, coherent methodological system.

From the rationalists, we have learned that logical coherence is a highly desirable property of an argument, and we have some well-established principles of logic to guide us. From the empiricists we have learned to respect the evidence, and to develop procedures (both experimental and econometric) to impose *ceteris paribus* and to come to terms with stochastic phenomena. The logical positivists taught us to respect the distinction between empirical and metaphysical propositions, just as the disputes that led to the dismantling of their school taught us that this distinction is not quite as simple as it might seem. From falsificationism, we learned to cherish the opportunities to conduct a definitive test of an interesting, refutable hypothesis, on the rather rare occasions such opportunities are presented to us. These are among the ideas central to meta-methodology.[10]

In reasoned discourse, the tools of meta-methodology remain available and will be used on their merits. But reasoned discourse is not confined to meta-methodology; it also draws upon the whole body of precepts and methods of scholarship and rhetoric. The net effect of replacing DPM with reasoned discourse, it seems to me, is to unify scholarship by drawing science (however reluctantly) back into the fold.

The Prospect: Local Provisional Methodologies

There remains, nevertheless, merit in the idea that a prescriptive methodology might provide shortcuts for sorting out the evidence and the arguments. Rather than a universal scientific method or a DPM, it may be possible to develop local prescriptive methodologies, methodologies for solving the peculiar problems of partic-

ular fields. Much of this methodological work would need to be done by insiders, who are familiar with the details. But, in keeping with the idea that discourse communities are permeable and the ultimate discourse community is humankind, it would not be just an inside job. Local methodologies would be disciplined by the critical processes and reasoned discourse of society at large. Meta-methodology is both broader and narrower than any local methodology: broader because a local methodology will adopt some but not all of the precepts of meta-methodology, and narrower because local methodology will reach beyond meta-methodology to include the broader scholarly devices of reasoned discourse. Finally, at this level some things can be treated as settled for now, but one suspects that little is settled forever. So, instead of a universal scientific method, the realistic prospect is for local provisional methodologies (LPMs).

LPM: Illustration 1, Econometrics

The development of local provisional methodologies may be illustrated by the example of econometrics, a subject of concern to practitioners in all fields of agricultural economics. Haavelmo's synthesis of economic theory, probability theory, and classical hypothesis testing was adopted by the Cowles Commission. The Haavelmo program consisted of (*i*) specifying an economic model, (*ii*) specifying a probability model to capture the indeterminism of the data, (*iii*) using Neyman-Pearson testing theory to test pre-specified hypotheses, and (*iv*) applying probability theory to generate parameter estimates with good properties and forecasts with interpretable stochastic variability. This program quickly became the methodological standard for economics (Heckman) and agricultural economics (Judge).

This econometric methodology has several interesting characteristics. It focuses on model testing to the exclusion of model selection, and on theory testing rather than theory development. Theory and model come prior to data. Learning from data is denied; new data may be used only to test old models. The list of explanatory variables must be unique, complete, small in number, and observable. The theory and model to be tested must be completely specified and parsimonious: "quantity demanded is determined by prices, income, and who knows exactly what else; let's take a look" just will not

---

[10] A more complete account of the contents of meta-methodology could be compiled by reviewing several reputable textbooks on scientific methods.

do. Thus, the Cowles methodology makes exacting demands on economic theory. It has no patience with the approach of starting with a relatively permissive theory and amending it according to what is learned from the data. All of this is consistent with the strict falsificationism of the young Popper. It is also consistent with the idea of DPM, in that it makes an unambiguous claim to be the one right way to do (its particular) science. It is a local methodology for econometrics, but it displays the influence of (what were at the time) recent developments in probability theory and the philosophy of science.

In the intervening half-century, econometricians have come to accept that economic theory does not strictly forbid very much and it therefore makes little sense to prespecify a unique model and use data only to test that model. Such an approach takes the model too seriously and the data not seriously enough. During the same time, there has been an enormous improvement in computer capability, and new techniques useful in model selection have been developed. Defenders of the Cowles methodology were appalled by these developments in econometric practice, and terms such as data-dredging were used to suggest the unsavory nature of what was happening.

By now, many econometricians have become much more comfortable with model selection, specification search, and learning from the data. Nevertheless, there remains a variety of views, each enjoying the support of prominent individuals or schools. Leamer discusses the characteristics and validity of various kinds of specification searches and, in so doing, does much to relieve the phobia about specification searches.

Hendry and Hendry et al. argue that one should specify the most general model—general with respect to both functional form and the variables included—and "test down" to the best model. The Bayesian approach, with its concept of using the data to update one's expectations, has enjoyed a revival. There remain defenders of classical, Neyman-Pearson inference. Heckman finds it unfortunate that the Neyman-Pearson paradigm continues to be so influential when, by now, it should be viewed as just one of many competing views about how to do inference; points out that Hendry et al. have not demonstrated rigorously that a unified framework for model testing and model selection can be based on Neyman-Pearson methodology; and believes that Hendry and the Bayesians impose excessively rigid, although very different, procedures

for learning from the data. To Heckman, the development of econometric methodology is an ongoing process, and it should continue in the direction of learning from the data.

It is important to point out that these developments have not been a mere accommodation to model selection, specification search, and learning from the data. Along the way, methods have been developed, techniques have been improved, and errors have been eliminated. For example, testing procedures now recognize the jointness of sequential hypotheses when "testing down" from the most general model. It has, quite properly, become fashionable for economics journals to omit significance levels when publishing t-statistics, recognizing that joint hypotheses may invalidate the standard significance tables.

These developments in the LPM of econometrics did not occur in a vacuum. The current situation in econometrics is pluralistic, and the trend has been away from the idea that there are simple and universal standards for appraising econometric claims. Thus, econometric developments have reflected developments in the philosophy of science, the methodology of economics, and the theories of economics and statistics. While it is likely that econometricians write mostly for, and talk mostly to, each other, it seems true also that the econometrics discourse community has been penetrated by stimuli from a broader scholarly community.

Most of the hard work that underlies these developments was done by econometricians, theoretical and applied. While I have cited only a few of the most prominent authors, many more were involved in providing the vast body of empirical studies and technical innovations upon which the emerging interpretive generalizations are being built. Furthermore, while my account makes it all sound like a battle of the giants, these very same methodological issues were the subject of discussion in seminars, graduate examinations, and around the coffee pot, wherever people take an interest in econometric applications. At the local level, then, methodology is to some degree the work and the avocation of most practitioners. Finally, I would claim that—messy and uncertain as the process has been—econometrics is gradually getting it right.

Has econometrics developed local, provisional methodologies? Clearly, they are local; and, with several competing models of inference and Heckman's strong feeling that none of the current contenders is the final word on the subject, clearly they are provisional. But are they methodologies? Those for whom methodology means a DPM would worry that econometrics does not currently provide uniform and convincing rules. But an LPM is not required to provide uniform rules. It is required only to set some bounds on the discourse, to settle at least some issues (so that each argument does not have to start all over again, at the very beginning), and to improve the quality of discourse over time. The LPM of econometrics, it seems to me, is accomplishing these tasks.

LPM: Illustration 2, Contingent Valuation of Nonmarket Goods[11]

The contingent valuation (CV) method for evaluating gains and losses of nonmarketed goods and services relies on self-reports of value (e.g., maximum willingness to pay) or of value-revealing contingent choices (e.g., buy/not buy at a stated price; or vote yes/no at a stated policy cost). For this reason, it encountered immediate skepticism from economists who often distrust data about "what people say, rather than what they do," and from other social scientists who worry that the CV process imposes a welfare change measurement framework upon citizen-respondents who might more naturally invoke some other way of thinking about their preferences or values concerning public policies.

Nevertheless, the CV research program developed quite rapidly through the 1970s and 1980s. More and more scholars became involved; theory, methods, and techniques proliferated, and a fragile consensus began to emerge concerning what worked and what did not; refereed articles appeared in mainstream as well as specialized economics journals; and the CV discourse community established patterns of communication with researchers in incentive theory, econometrics, psychology, and survey research. CV researchers sought to test methods and validate results in a variety of ways. Tests were conducted for internal consistency, replicability, and the presence of various biases. External validation would be more convincing, but external validation is inherently elusive in nonmarket research. Nevertheless, various imperfect external tests were applied: e.g., consis-

tency of empirical results with theoretical expectations; and comparability of CV results with welfare estimates from alternative techniques such as hedonic price analysis and the travel cost method, techniques that have their own difficulties. While these tests generated some persistent results that seemed anomalous, the body of findings supportive of CV was impressive enough that applications continued to increase and government agencies began to accept CV as an appropriate technique for use in project evaluation.

In the 1980s, federal laws and regulations permitting public trustees to claim monetary compensation for environmental damage allowed claims for lost passive-use-values (e.g., existence values) and recognized CV as an acceptable valuation method. Private individuals and corporations could find themselves liable for compensation payments based on CV results. The *Exxon Valdez* oil spill of 1989 brought the issue into sharp focus: environmental damages can be enormous, and lost passive-use values may well dominate other categories of damage when distant and pristine environments are involved. CV had become too important to leave to a small discourse community of practitioners.

The Exxon Corporation put to work a group of scholars, mostly economists, to examine CV critically. The leading lights among this team were outstanding mid-career economic theorists and econometricians from elite economics departments, who had little prior involvement with CV. In April 1992, this group released their findings, trenchantly critical of CV, at a public meeting in Washington, DC (Cambridge Economics, Inc.). Soon afterward, the National Oceanic and Atmospheric Administration convened a "blue ribbon panel" of experts, co-chaired by Nobel Laureates Kenneth Arrow and Robert Solow, to report on the validity of the passive-use value concept and CV. In the panel report (Arrow et al.), CV was endorsed, a result disappointing to its opponents. However, some CV proponents thought the report gave too much credence to recent attacks on CV.

This sudden and dramatic expansion of the CV discourse community, before a backdrop of litigation and unaccustomedly large compensation claims for a newly-recognized category of compensable damages, provides an opportunity to observe the reasoned discourse process in upheaval, before the dust settles. Much of what we see is unappealing. In some cases, impressive credentials have been substituted for careful scholarship, and sweeping generalizations turn

---

[11] My objective here is to provide an introspective but nonpartisan commentary. Nevertheless, readers will recall that I have been, and remain, deeply involved in this research program.

out sometimes to hinge on special-case models and relatively arbitrary research decisions about data handling and statistical methods.

One would expect such problems to be mitigated as the process of reasoned discourse continues. However, appraising the reliability of CV is inherently difficult and it seems that some of the standard suggestions from meta-methodology have generated at least as many problems as solutions. For example, meta-methodology promotes the external test, the refutable hypothesis, and the crucial experiment. Yet, these ideas have proven problematic in the case of CV. External tests against expectations deduced from economic theory have remained controversial, because economic theory is generally rather permissive, and because the economic theory of ideal valuation of public and policy goods remains incompletely specified. Case study findings that CV values are relatively insensitive to the quantity of environmental protection offered have been presented as devastating evidence against CV (Cambridge Economics, Inc.).

However, other observers question the CV procedures used in these tests, and point out that theory is unclear about how quantity-sensitive such values should be. Given that policy is inherently multi-dimensional, there is no basis for identifying *a priori* the particular quantity dimension(s) that should elicit the most sensitivity. Empirical results showing that willingness to pay for a package of programs is typically much less than the sum of WTP for the same programs evaluated independently have been interpreted, alternatively, as the predictable consequence of limited budgets and substitutability among programs (Hoehn and Randall, Hoehn) and as evidence of "embedding," a pathology that is an artifact of CV itself (Kahneman and Knetsch). In both of these cases, the empirical test against theoretical expectations founders on the imprecision of the theory, leaving CV proponents to protest overblown conclusions from weak tests while the opponents complain that proponents seem determined to explain-away any inconvenient results.

More mischief than good has come from attempts to test the hypothesis that CV is a reliable welfare change measurement device, or to perform the crucial experiment that would validate or invalidate CV. Given present knowledge, the hypothesis that CV is reliable is untestable: we don't have precise notions of the performance characteristics of an ideal measure; and there is enough variety among CV procedures that no test using a particular CV exercise

would produce results applying to CV generically.[12] Generalizations based on experiments comparing contingent voluntary contributions and contingent purchases with their actual counterparts have received a very mixed reception: for both theoretical and evidentiary reasons, it is unclear if such experiments have anything at all to say about the performance of the contingent policy referendum (a preferred form of CV). More generally, the concept of the crucial experiment is fraught with Duhemian confusion; that is, the side-conditions required to reach a definitive conclusion about the generic reliability of CV are so demanding that the interpretation of the test results will likely remain contentious. There has been altogether too much posturing about "crucial experiments" that turn out to be much less than that.

The present situation regarding CV illustrates some characteristics of LPMs. First, a discourse community and the theories and methods that it develops cannot become influential without attracting scrutiny from "outsiders." Second, immediately following the recent and sudden expansion of the CV discourse community against a backdrop of big-money litigation, the quality of discourse and rhetoric is not comforting. Claims and counterclaims seem exaggerated, appeals to authority have been substituted for more reputable forms of argument, and a disturbing lack of both convincing argument and agreement among participants attends the crucial issue of what counts as evidence for or against the reliability of CV. And, this situation cannot be blamed entirely on the obtuseness or the ill-will of the participants: the questions are difficult, their answers are elusive, and insufficient time has elapsed to allow an informed consensus to emerge. Third, standard concepts from meta-methodology are insufficient to resolve all of the relevant issues. One must look instead to reasoned discourse to save the day, and one must hope that the controversies are eventually resolved by a preponderance of the evidence.

Concluding Comments

So, what do practicing agricultural economists really need to know about methodology? The

[12] The hypotheses that "attitude surveys are reliable" and "public opinion polls are reliable" are no longer taken seriously. Such hypotheses are recognized to be untestable and perhaps meaningless. Research programs about measuring attitudes and public opinion have moved on to mapping the performance characteristics of alternative approaches and techniques. The CV program should follow suit.

comforting certainties of the old methodological orthodoxy are gone and there is little hope that a new demarcationist prescriptive methodology will arise to replace them. There are those who worry that this development has made science and scholarship too easy, by weakening or repealing all of the rules. I believe that just the opposite is true: rhetoric, critical rationalism, and reasoned discourse are serious enterprises that imply a more painstaking form of scholarship.

Furthermore, prescriptive methodology is now largely a local enterprise for particular disciplines, schools of thought, paradigms, or research programs. Meta-methodology provides some principles and methods useful in appraising theories, methods, and empirical conjectures. However, it seldom provides ready-made solutions to local problems in applied economics; and the principles of meta-methodology, applied without subtlety, may serve only to restrict the scope of inquiry and increase the confusion. Local provisional methodologies draw upon all of the tools of scholarship (including meta-methodology), along with theories and procedures specific to the research program and its related disciplines. Despite the essentially local nature of methodology, the discourse community is and must be permeable to stimuli from the larger scholarly community. A research program that gains influence will assuredly attract scrutiny from the outside (perhaps rather abruptly, as was the case with contingent valuation of nonmarket goods and services).

Because researchers are the front-line methodologists for their own research programs, it follows that the serious study of methodology and rhetoric is desirable for researchers. Such study is unlikely to yield hard-and-fast rules for research, but is likely to yield a rich lode of insights that will raise the level of argument. Furthermore, it tends to make researchers more introspective about their own work, which is all to the good.

Finally, there is little reason to lament the demise of DPM. The failure of demarcationist methodology to establish a sharp boundary between science and nonscience tends to unify scholarship by bringing science into the fold. This is a blessing for agricultural economics, which was always an uncomfortable fit in the science box. Agricultural economics is at once a theory-based deductive exercise, an empirical science, an active contributor to the discourse on policy matters and ethical issues, and a learned profession offering analysis and advice to clients.

A framework of reasoned and critical discourse serves, among other things, to enlighten and improve our discussion of ethical and value questions. These issues pervade agricultural and resource economics; so, surely, it would be better for us to deal with them forthrightly. There is a great tradition of scholarship—which demarcationist methodology instructed us to ignore—that we can draw upon, and occasionally contribute to, in this quest.

References

Adorno, T. W. et al. *The Positivist Dispute in German Sociology*. New York: Harper and Row, 1976. (Original in German 1969).

Arrow, K., R. Solow, P. Portney, E. Leamer, R. Radner, and H. Schuman. *Report of the NOAA Panel on Contingent Valuation*. Washington, DC: National Oceanic and Atmospheric Administration.

Backhouse, R. E. "The Constructivist Critique of Economic Methodology." *Methodus* 4 (June 1992):65–82.

Bartley, W. W. "The Philosophy of Karl Popper: Part III. Rationality, Criticism and Logic." *Philosophia* 11 (1982):121–221.

Blaug, M. *The Methodology of Economics—or How Economists Explain*. Cambridge: Cambridge University Press, 1980.

Booth, W. C. *Modern Dogma and the Rhetoric of Assent*. Chicago: University of Chicago Press, 1974.

Brown, H. I. *Perception, Theory and Commitment*. Chicago: University of Chicago Press, 1977.

Caldwell, B. "Clarifying Popper." *J. Econ. Literature* 29 (March 1991):1–33.

Caldwell B. *Beyond Positivism: Economic Methodology in the Twentieth Century*. London: George Allen and Unwin, 1982.

Cambridge Economics, Inc., *Contingent Valuation: A Critical Assessment*. Cambridge, MA, 1992.

Campbell, N. R. *Physics: the Elements*. Cambridge: Cambridge University Press, 1920.

Castle, E. N. "On Scientific Objectivity." *Amer. J. Agr. Econ.* 50 (November 1968):809–14.

Choi, Y. B. "An Interview with Kevin Hoover." *Methodus* 3 (December 1991):118–27.

Feyerabend, P. K. *Against Method: Outline of an Anarchistic Theory of Knowledge*. London: NLB, 1975.

——. "Explanation, Reduction and Empiricism," in *Scientific Explanation, Space, and Time*, pp. 28–97, H. Feigl and G. Maxwell (eds.). Minnesota Studies in the Philosophy of Science, 3. Minneapolis: University of Minnesota Press, 1962.

Fish, S. *Is There a Text in this Class?* Cambridge: Harvard University Press, 1980.

Friedman, M. *Essays in Positive Economics*. Chicago: University of Chicago Press, 1953.

Gleymour, C., *Theory and Evidence*. Princeton: Princeton University Press, 1980.

Haavelmo, T. "The Probability Approach to Econometrics." *Econometrica*. Supplement, 12 (1944).

Harre, R. "History of Philosophy of Science." *Encyclo-*

pedia of Philosophy. vol. 7, ed. P. Edwards, pp. 289–96. London: Collier-Macmillan, 1967.

Hausman, D. M. "Economic Methodology in a Nutshell." *J. Econ. Perspectives* 3 (Spring 1989):115–28.

Hausman, D. M., and M. S. McPherson. "Agricultural Economics and the Chaos of Economic Methodology." *J. Agr. Econ. Res.* Supplement, (July 1991): 24–25.

Heckman, J. J. "Haavelmo and the Birth of Modern Econometrics:A Review of The History of Econometric Ideas" by Mary Morgan." *J. Econ. Literature* 30 (June 1992): 876–86.

Hendry, D. F. "Econometrics: Alchemy or Science?" *Econometrica* 47 (1980): 387–406.

Hendry, D. F., A. Pagan, and J. D. Sargan. "Dynamic Specification." Chapter 18 in Z. Griliches and M. Intrilligator (eds.) *Handbook of Econometrics.* Amsterdam: North-Holland, 1985.

Hoehn, J. P. "Valuing the Multidimensional Impacts of Environmental Policy: Theory and Methods." *Amer. J. Agr. Econ.* 73 (May 1991):289–99.

Hoehn, J. P., and A. Randall. "Too Many Proposals Pass the Benefit Cost Test." *Amer. Econ. Rev.* 79 (June 1989):544–51.

Judge, G. C. "Estimation and Statistical Inference in Economics." pp. 3–56 in G. C. Judge et al. (editors), *A Survey of Agricultural Economics Literature: Vol. 2, Quantitative Methods in Agricultural Economics, 1940s to 1970s.* Minneapolis: University of Minnesota Press, 1977.

Kahneman, D., and J. Knetsch. "Valuing Public Goods: The Purchase of Moral Satisfaction." *J. of Environ. Econ. and Manage.* 22 (Jan. 1992):57–70.

Koertge, M. "Popper's Metaphysical Research Program for the Human Sciences." *Inquiry* 18:437–62.

Kuhn, T. S. *The Structure of Scientific Revolutions.* 1st ed. Chicago: University of Chicago Press, 1962.

Lakatos, I. "Falsification and the Methodology of Scientific Research Programs." pp. 91–196 in I. Lakatos and A. Musgrave (eds.) *Criticism and the Growth of Knowledge.* Cambridge: Cambridge University Press, 1970.

Leamer, E. E., *Specification Searches: Ad Hoc Inference With Non-experimental Data.* New York: Wiley, 1978.

——. "Let's Take the Con Out of Econometrics." *Amer. Econ. Rev.* 73 (March 1983):31–43.

McCloskey, D. N., *If You're So Smart: The Narrative of Economic Experience.* Chicago: University of Chicago Press, 1990.

——. "The Rhetoric of Economics." *J. Econ. Lit.* 21: 481–517.

Popper, K. R. *Realism and the Aim of Science. The Postscript to the Logic of Scientific Discovery, 1.* Ed. W. W. Bartley. Totowa, NJ: Rowman and Littlefield, 1983.

——. "Autobiography of Karl Popper." *The Philosophy of Karl Popper.* vol. 1, ed. Paul Schilpp, La Salle, IL: Open Court, 1974.

——. "Philosophy of Science: A Personal Report, in *British Philosophy in the Mid-Century.* ed. C. H. Mace, London: George Allen and Unwin, Ltd., 1957, p. 155.

——. *"The Logic of Scientific Discovery.* New York: Harper Torchbooks, 1959 (Original in German, 1935).

Randall, A. "Methodology, Ideology and the Economics of Policy: Why Resource Economists Disagree." *Amer. J. Agr. Econ.* 67(1985):1022–29.

Redman, D. A. *Economics and the Philosophy of Science.* New York: Oxford University Press, 1991.

Robbins, L. *An Essay on the Nature and Significance of Economic Science.* London: Macmillan, 2nd ed. 1935.

Rorty, R. *Philosophy and the Mirror of Nature.* Oxford: Basil Blackwell, 1980.

Solow, R. M. "Comments From Inside Economics" in A. Klamer et al. (eds.) *The Consequences of Economic Rhetoric.* Cambridge: Cambridge University Press, 1988.

Name index

225

KILL THE INDIAN

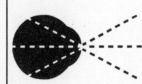

This Large Print Book carries the
Seal of Approval of N.A.V.H.

KILL THE INDIAN

A KILLSTRAIGHT STORY

JOHNNY D. BOGGS

THORNDIKE PRESS
A part of Gale, Cengage Learning

Detroit • New York • San Francisco • New Haven, Conn • Waterville, Maine • London

Copyright © 2012 by Johnny D. Boggs.
Thorndike Press, a part of Gale, Cengage Learning.

ALL RIGHTS RESERVED
The publisher bears no responsibility for the quality of information provided through author or third-party Web sites and does not have any control over, nor assume any responsibility for, information contained in these sites. Providing these sites should not be construed as an endorsement or approval by the publisher of these organizations or of the positions they may take on various issues.

Thorndike Press® Large Print Western.
The text of this Large Print edition is unabridged.
Other aspects of the book may vary from the original edition.
Set in 16 pt. Plantin.

LIBRARY OF CONGRESS CATALOGING-IN-PUBLICATION DATA

Boggs, Johnny D.
  Kill the Indian : a Killstraight story / by Johnny D. Boggs.
    pages ; cm. — (Thorndike Press large print western)
    ISBN 978-1-4104-5375-4 (hardcover) — ISBN 1-4104-5375-8 (hardcover) 1.
Comanche Indians—Fiction. 2. Murder—Investigation—Texas—Fiction. 3.
Large type books. I. Title.
PS3552.O4375K48 2012b
813'.54—dc23   2012032597

Published in 2012 by arrangement with Golden West Literary Agency.

Boggs, Johnny D.
Kill the Indian : a Killstraight story /

Eastern Branch
Jackson District Library

For Lucia St. Clair Robson,
fine friend, great writer, and a
Comanche at heart

CHAPTER ONE

Sweating profusely, Daniel pushes his way through the throng crowding the boardwalks of Hell's Half Acre.

Over the silk top hats, bowlers, Stetsons, and battered slouch hats, he can just make out Rain Shower, in her doeskin dress and moccasins, fighting through the multitude. She's maybe twenty yards ahead of him. He calls out her name. Screams it louder, but she can't hear him. He can't even hear his own voice.

The people — taibos, *all of them, white men without faces — grunt like pigs, pushing him backward. He turns sideways, letting some of these men rush past him. Now he can no longer see Rain Shower. He jumps, tries to catch only a glimpse of her. A boot steps on his own moccasin. A spur's rowel grazes his calf. Angrily he slams an elbow into the side of a passer-by, but doubts if the faceless man feels anything. He curses, in the language of*

The People and in the pale-eyes tongue, forces a path through the crush, jumps again, screams Rain Shower's name.

He spots her shiny black hair, but just briefly. She's too far ahead of him. He wants her closer. Needs her to be closer. Why does she keep walking? Why doesn't she wait for me? Why doesn't she turn back toward me?

"Rain Shower!" he cries. "Wait! Stop! Wait for me!"

Fort Worth, Texas, is no place for a Nermernuh *girl. Especially not in Hell's Half Acre.*

A white man in dirty vest and bandanna shoves him, and he stumbles, catches himself on a wooden column in front of a hitching rail. No horses tethered here, he notices, so he pulls himself onto the rail, gripping the column for support, finally able to see above the mass of people. They look like buffalo now, the way the buffalo used to look on the Llano Estacado, millions of them, so thick you could not see the ground.

Again, he yells Rain Shower's name, and this time she turns. His heart races, but he can breathe again. He almost slips on the rail; in fact, he swings off briefly, but somehow he manages to get his feet back on the wood. Recovered, he looks down the boardwalk.

Rain Shower laughs at him, and he smiles back at her.

8

"Wait for me," he says. Or starts to say. Before he can finish, he sees the hand reach around the corner. It grasps Rain Shower's arm.

Fear etches into her face. She stares at the man holding her — Daniel can't see the man, just his arm and hand, and the hand is covered in a bright red glove — then Rain Shower turns back toward Daniel and screams.

Only he can't hear her scream. The hand jerks her out of sight, around the corner of a false-fronted mercantile.

"No!" Daniel yells, losing his grip on the wooden column, feeling his moccasins slip off the rail. He falls onto the boardwalk, landing on his back, hard, forcing the air out of his lungs. He rolls to his side, opens his eyes, tries to catch his breath, and sees the stampeding buffalo, feels the first hoof crush his ribs, as thunder rumbles and the skies darken. . . .

Daniel Killstraight woke with a start.

His heart pounded, and his long black hair felt as if he had just been dunked in Cache Creek. He ripped the sweat-soaked sheet off his body, and stared at the darkened ceiling, trying to recall the dream. No, he decided. It would be better to forget that nightmare. It would be better to figure out

9

where he was.

Not home. Home, for Daniel Killstraight, was a cabin the Pale Eyes had built for Ben Buffalo Bone's late father, a wooden structure his friend's father, and now his uncle, used as a stable. For the past two years, those unshod ponies shared the house with Daniel Killstraight. Ben was Rain Shower's brother, and that started Daniel thinking about the nightmare that had awakened him.

He wasn't on the reservation near Fort Sill in Indian Territory, but at the Pickwick Hotel in Fort Worth. No, that wasn't right, either. When Daniel and his Comanche Indian friends had arrived in Fort Worth to meet a few Texas cattlemen, and attend a lecture by Captain Richard Pratt, the hotel manager had smiled like a weasel and stammered that no rooms were available in the hotel.

"No rooms for Indians, you mean," Daniel had said.

The hotel manager, a balding man with a waxed mustache, ran his finger underneath his paper collar, shaking his head, saying: "No, no, young man, no. That's not it at all. It's a busy weekend, you see. Lots of guests. But I have taken liberty to arrange for you to stay in the Taylor and Barr building. It is not far from her, gentlemen, just over on Houston Street. They have five modern and quite comfortable apartments upstairs." The man's small eyes shot from Daniel to Charles Flint to Yellow Bear and, finally, to Quanah Parker.

"Indoor plumbing," the man stammered. "Gas lamps. Much quieter, too."

This wasn't his first trip to Fort Worth, and Daniel let the manager know it.

"We stayed in the Texas Hotel last year," he said.

Quanah nodded. "Treat good. No ticks in bed. Ice cream."

"There are no ticks in our beds, either, Mister Parker." The manager sounded indignant. "I assure you." He trained his eyes on Daniel. "And you, young man, I'll have you know that a noble savage . . . I mean, a dignitary like Quanah Parker and his entourage, a friend to great cattlemen Dan Waggoner and Captain Lee Hall, both friends of the Pickwick Hotel, would be most welcome in any of our suites . . . if any happened to be available. We are full up, sirs."

Quanah Parker might be welcome here, Daniel figured, but not Daniel Killstraight. Not tonight. Not ever.

So here he was in the Taylor and Barr

building, sweating in a room that felt like a furnace. It was August, however, so no one could do anything about the heat. Charles Flint was just down and across the hall. Next door to Daniel were Quanah and Yellow Bear, who had insisted that they share the room. Isa-tai, Charles Flint's father, bunked with Nagwee, the *puhakat* of the Kotsoteka band who had come to counsel Quanah, in the room next to Flint's. As far as Daniel knew, the fifth room, directly across from Daniel's, remained vacant.

Sighing, he reached above his head, and turned up the gas lamp, before swinging his feet over the bed. Once his heartbeat had dropped to something more reasonable, he stood, and eased his way to the open window. Putting his hands on the sill, he leaned out into the Fort Worth night, hoping to catch a breeze, but the wind did not blow, and the air felt heavy with humidity. The thermometer outside the plate-glass window in front of Taylor & Barr's store had read one hundred and four degrees, and Daniel doubted if the mercury had fallen much.

Even at night, however, even in a miserable heat wave, Fort Worth's citizens remained active. A hack's carriage clopped down the street, and he could make out the noise of a piano, a banjo, laughter. A whistle blew. A horse snorted. A woman giggled.

Fort Worth, Daniel decided, never slept.

It reminded him of the cities he had seen back East. Philadelphia, Pittsburgh, and Carlisle, and while the latter seemed even smaller than Fort Worth, Daniel figured it couldn't be. Fort Worth, however, was certainly different than those Pennsylvania cities, and a long, long way from home.

The window overlooked an empty alley running between Houston and Main. With no street lamps in the alley, he could make out the dim outline of the walls of the Fakes & Company furniture warehouse. The three-story Pickwick Hotel was northwest, at the corner of Main and Third. He couldn't see that hotel, could barely make out anything in the darkness, although light shone from the windows and door at the saloon across the street, illuminating at least a part of Houston Street. Jinglebobs started singing a song beneath him, and Daniel looked down.

No, the alley wasn't empty. A cowhand was busy muttering something as he unbuttoned his pants, and soon began spraying the wall of the Taylor & Barr mercantile with urine, soaking the white-stenciled lettering on the brick walls.

WE OFFER OUR ENTIRE LINE OF CHILDREN'S, MISSES' and LADIES' CLOAKS AND DOLMANS, BOYS', YOUTHS' and MEN'S CLOTHING AT MANUFACTURRERS' PRICES.

Daniel wondered if he were the only person in Fort Worth who realized the painter had misspelled manufacturer.

Quanah had bought a cloak and a dolman earlier that afternoon, even though Charles Flint had told the Comanche chief that he could buy something cheaper at the agency near Fort Sill once they got back home.

Daniel could still picture the look Quanah gave Charles Flint. "But I ask you what dolman and you say you no know," Quanah had said as they stood on the boardwalk, staring at the wall advertisement.

"But . . . I . . . you . . . it's . . . I. . . ." Charles Flint could not think of anything else to say, and Daniel knew that rarely happened.

"Come," Quanah had announced, speaking in broken English for the Texians accompanying the Comanche delegation. "We find dolman. If like, me buy one for Tonarcy." Tonarcy was undoubtedly Quanah's favorite of his eight wives.

"Hell's bells, this alley stinks of piss!"

14

Daniel looked down at the cowboy again, heard him laugh at his joke, saw him stagger, those spurs chiming while he made a wandering path back toward Houston Street. As soon as he stepped out of the alley, he stopped. A police officer had grabbed the cowhand's shoulder, spun him around, and the tall, gangling man had toppled into the dust on his backside.

"Jesus, Mother Mary, and Joseph, what in the bloody hell were you doing in that alley, you drunken waddie?" The officer pointed something — nightstick, Daniel guessed, what he remembered both coppers and miners in Pennsylvania calling a billy club — at the cowhand.

It sounded like the cowhand answered: "Waterin' my mules."

The policeman said something Daniel couldn't understand, but a shout came from up the street, probably from the Occidental Saloon, and the policeman left the cowhand in the dust, and took off running toward the shouts, yelling something, and blowing his whistle.

After three clumsily failed attempts, the cowhand managed to push himself to his feet, and weave his way across Houston Street and through the batwing doors of Herman Kussatz's Tivoli Hall.

15

More whistles sounded, and he could make out shouts, curses. For seven years, Daniel had lived among the Pale Eyes in Pennsylvania. First as the lone Comanche student at Carlisle Industrial School — although Charles Flint would join him during Daniel's last year learning to be a *taibo*. Then in Franklin County, working for that hard-rock German until blisters covered his hands and feet. Finally, breathing coal dust and hardly seeing the sunshine at the Castle Shannon Mine near Pittsburgh. Yet he never really understood the Pale Eyes. For two years, he had been back among his people — if they were his people anymore — wearing the badge and uniform of The People's tribal police. Metal Shirts, The People called them. His own uniform showed the chevrons of a sergeant. At least it had, until Daniel, and all the other Metal Shirts, had cut off the sleeves of those scratchy, ill-fitting gray woolen blouses. Now they wore them like the pale-eyes vests.

More whistles blew. A window smashed. A horse whinnied.

He heard something else, and bumped his head against the open window. A door had shut down the hall. He rubbed his head, and walked to the dresser to pour a glass of water.

16

Tepid, tasting like iron, the water didn't cool him. He could barely even swallow it, but he made himself, then mopped his face and the back of his neck with a hand towel, and wiped his long black hair, sopping wet. He stared at the door, then at the clock, wondering who would be coming to his room so late. If that cheap little Progressor kept the right time, it was 3:17 A.M.

Daniel smiled then, remembering. He and Quanah had retired shortly after supper, and Charles Flint had said he would soon join them. Yellow Bear, however, had said he wanted to see the sights, so George Briggs, a pale-eyes cowhand who worked for the big *taibo* rancher Dan Waggoner, had promised that he and old Yellow Bear would "tree the town" — whatever that meant.

The shutting door he had heard must have been Yellow Bear, finally making his way back to the room after a night on the town. He couldn't wait to hear Yellow Bear's stories over breakfast.

Outside, a cow bawled, probably from those giant shipping pens at the stockyards.

Cattle reminded him of buffalo — *cuhtz* in The People's tongue — and that brought the final image from his nightmare to his mind. Daniel shook off the thought. Instead, he settled into the cushioned parlor chair,

17

remembering what had brought him to Fort Worth.

CHAPTER TWO

"You two are going to Texas," Joshua Biggers said with a smile.

Daniel and Charles Flint looked at each other, then stared at the young Baptist minister who had been appointed agent — the third in two years — for the Comanche, Kiowa, and Apache reservation, giving him the blank stares The People often gave Pale Eyes.

Hugh Gunter, Daniel's Cherokee friend and a member of the United States Indian Police with jurisdiction over the Five Civilized Tribes east of Comanche country, called it: "The dumb look."

The smile faded from the young agent's face. "Not permanently," he said, swallowed, and shuffled through the papers on his desk. Beads of sweat peppered his forehead. His Adam's apple bobbed, and at last he found the paper he wanted.

"This is a letter from Captain Pratt," he

said. "He's giving a talk in Fort Worth. He specifically requested that you two join him. . . ."

"Pratt." Charles Flint tested the name.

Daniel remembered Pratt. How could he ever forget him? A bluecoat, Richard Pratt had started the Carlisle Industrial School, teaching Indians to follow the white man's road. When Daniel was thirteen, he had been loaded onto a wagon with several Arapahoes and sent to the railroad station. In Pennsylvania, they had joined other frightened Indians — Lakotas, Cheyennes, Kiowas, even Pawnees, traditional enemies of The People. It was at school that School Father Pratt had given Daniel his new name.

Once, Daniel had been called His Arrows Fly Straight Into The Hearts Of His Enemies, the name his father had given him. Pale Eyes never could quite translate that name into their own tongue, so they had shortened it to Killstraight. At Carlisle, Pratt had made all the new students point to a Pale-Eyes *word* written on a blackboard — after white men and women had shorn the new students' long, black hair, forced them to bathe with smelly soap and steaming hot water, and made them wear itchy Pale-Eyes clothes. Reluctantly, almost defiantly, Daniel had pointed to one, and watched as

School Father Pratt nodded and scratched a white line through the *word,* the chalk screeching and making Daniel's skin crawl. "Now," School Father Pratt had said with a smile, "your name is Daniel."

Later, one of the School Mothers had demanded that Daniel take a new surname. Her word still rang in his ears. "Killstraight conjures simulacrums of depredations, of rapine, of the barbarous nature of these savage fiends. Strait. . . ." He could see her double chin wagging as her head bobbed with satisfaction. "Daniel Strait would fit him well. A noble Anglo-Saxon name. I knew many Straits in Hertshire."

"Perhaps," School Father Pratt had said with a smile, as he placed a hand on Daniel's shoulder and squeezed gently, "but, having taught this lad for these past few years, I think Killstraight fits him like a glove. Leave it Killstraight, Missus Hall. Daniel has earned that much, I warrant."

That might have been Daniel's only victory at Carlisle. He could remember the beatings, still feel the sharp sting of a switch against his back or one of the School Mother's rulers smashing his knuckles. Punishment for speaking his true tongue.

"You are no longer a savage!" School Mother Hall had admonished him. "You must speak English!"

They had made him pray to the pale-eyes god. Taught him to speak the pale-eyes tongue, taught him to learn the pale-eyes trades, taught him to eat like Pale Eyes, think like Pale Eyes, be a Pale Eyes.

Daniel had fought. Fought against all of them at first, and he was not alone. Lakota boys and girls fought. Kiowas resisted. Cheyennes argued. Some even died, not from the whippings, but of sickness, of broken hearts. They had been buried like Pale Eyes, in wooden boxes, buried deep in the smelly Pennsylvania earth far from their homes.

"Who are you?" School Father Pratt had once asked him, when School Mother Hall had brought Daniel into Pratt's office and told the bluecoat that Daniel would be better off sent to the prison in Florida, that he would never learn to follow the white man's road, that he would always be a savage. It was in his heart.

"Who are you?" Pratt had repeated.

"Nermernuh." He had answered in the language of The People.

"Comanche, eh?" That the School Father knew enough of The People's tongue surprised Daniel. Pratt rose from his chair, and moved around the desk. Daniel's fingers

22

balled into fists. He stared ahead, not looking at the School Father, just staring at the portrait of Abraham Lincoln hanging on the wall behind the desk. "I was commissioned a second lieutenant back in 'Sixty-Seven. My first station was at Fort Arbuckle in Indian Territory. I've been to Fort Marion, son. Three years there as a jailer. Trust me, Daniel. You don't want to go to Florida." Pratt had sighed, shaking his head. "Many white men and women would like to see your race exterminated. I don't believe that's right. It certainly isn't Christian. We must live and work together. But you're Comanche. Perhaps you think differently."

Abraham Lincoln had not moved. Daniel had not blinked.

"I wanted to bring Comanches," Pratt had continued. "More than just one. More Kiowas. More of the Indians I had gotten to know during my duty in the Territory, and there had already been schools established on the reservation. But Commissioner Hayt insisted that we start with primarily Sioux. Use the children there. They would be hostages, force the Sioux to stay on their best behavior. But you're Comanche."

Silence.

Daniel had kept staring at Abraham Lincoln.

Slowly School Father Pratt had stepped in front of him. "Wasn't your mother Mescalero?"

Daniel couldn't help it. His shoulders sagged, and he looked away from the Great White Father and into School Father Pratt's eyes. At that moment, Daniel knew the Pale Eyes had beaten him.

His father, who had taken the name Marsh Hawk, had been a Kwahadi warrior who had been shipped off to Florida. Soldiers had shot him when he had tried to escape from the train taking those prisoners to Fort Marion. Dying a fitting death for a warrior. Yet it was true. His mother was Mescalero Apache, and Daniel could remember boys his own age, some younger, and men much older often teasing him. "Your blood is not pure," they would say. "You are not whole." Or even worse: "You are not *Nermernuh*."

Years later, after Daniel had accepted the paper that said he had been graduated, School Father Pratt had smiled, shaken his head, and said: "You're one of the best students I have had, Daniel. Other Comanches, I hope, will follow the example you have set, son."

Charles Flint was one of those.

Flint had arrived the year Daniel had left

24

Carlisle, and had gone to work in those coal mines. After seven years of learning to be a white man, Daniel had returned to the Territory, to his home. Now he was a sergeant in the tribal police, a Metal Shirt, earning $8 a month. Charles Flint had returned from Pennsylvania a year earlier, and now worked for the Pale Eyes, George McEveety, who ran the trading post between the agency and Fort Sill.

"He's a crackerjack bookkeeper," Mr. McEveety said. "Got the best head for numbers I seen in any man, and I'm talkin' 'bout white men. Not just Injuns."

We are a lot alike, Daniel thought, *Flint and me. "White Comanches," Mr. McEveety would say.*

Glancing at Flint, Daniel realized *White Comanche* probably applied to Charles Flint more than himself. Two, maybe three, years younger than Daniel, Charles Flint kept his raven-dark hair closely shorn, and sat bolt upright in the chair in front of Agent Biggers's desk, hands folded neatly on his lap, a soft black fedora resting on his crossed knee. Despite the heat, he wore a double-breasted coat of gray wool, although he had unbuttoned it, matching trousers, and Congress gaiters that, if they weren't covered with so much dust after the walk from

25

the trading post, would have been as dark as his hair and eyes. A red satin tie clung tightly to his neck, dangling over the plaited-front, polka-dotted shirt of fine cotton. A silver-tipped mahogany walking cane rested against the arm of his chair, and Daniel could hear the ticking of Flint's gold watch. If Flint's skin had not been so copper, he could have passed for a Pale Eyes.

Yeah, School Father Pratt would definitely be proud of Charles Flint.

But proud of Daniel? No, Pratt would likely consider Daniel . . . what was the word he had heard Agent Biggers use once after a Sunday sermon?

Backslider.

Daniel's hair had grown long, and now hung in braids over his shoulders. His shirt, a flowery calico of red, green, yellow, and blue, came from the trading post, and his gray coat-turned-vest, an artifact from the Centennial Exposition, was pale-eyes clothing. Yet the bear-claw necklace, the buckskin leggings, and his comfortable moccasins were Comanche. And his hat, stiff-brimmed, high-crowned, caked with dust and made and sold by Pale Eyes, was the kind you'd find on just about every Comanche man on the reservation these days. Daniel had dressed his up by sticking a hawk feather in

26

the band.

A man cannot hide behind clothes, Daniel knew. Charles Flint dressed like a pale-eyes bookkeeper. Daniel wore the clothes of a Comanche Metal Shirt. After years at Carlisle, however, both struggled trying to accept who they were, what they had become. White? Comanche? Or, in Daniel's case, a pale-eyes-educated, Mescalero Apache-*Nermernuh* mongrel.

"Captain Platt thought this would be a great opportunity." Joshua Biggers was speaking again. Daniel looked up at the agent. "Captain Hall has requested that Quanah join him and the other stockmen in Fort Worth to negotiate a new lease on The Big Pasture."

Daniel only knew Captain Hall by name and reputation. For a while, Hall had commanded a Ranger company — a *taibo* Metal Shirt, Daniel mused — and before that had served as peace officer in a couple other North Texas towns, but had not worn a badge for several years now. He was president, Daniel remembered, of the Northern Texas Stock Growers' Association. Just before Daniel had returned to Indian Territory, however, Hall had served as an agent up at Anadarko, but had been removed. Daniel wasn't sure why, although he sus-

27

pected the captain had been charged with graft. Practically every agent on every reserve in the Territory had been charged with graft. He hoped Joshua Biggers would be an exception.

That tenure on the reservation, however, had led Captain Hall to meet and befriend Quanah Parker, which now came in handy since the captain operated a large ranch down in Texas.

Texas longhorns needed grass, and grass could be found aplenty on the Comanche reservation.

"Captain Platt says this would be a wonderful chance for you two young men, and Quanah, to show these Texians how much improvement has been made on the reservation," Joshua Biggers continued. "They have arranged speeches at the Wednesday Woman's Club and on the City Hall lawn. Captain Hall and Captain Pratt will pay all expenses for you. It will be a grand adventure, and an education to be sure."

To be sure. Daniel rubbed his crooked nose with two fingers. The last time — the only time — he had traveled to Fort Worth, he had damned near gotten himself beaten to death. The nose was a reminder. Well, actually, that had happened in Dallas, but Fort Worth hadn't been that much better.

With the exception of the Queen City Ice Cream Parlor, he remembered.

Texas cities were pretty much all the same. At least, that's what Hugh Gunter always told him. A "God-awful state" peopled with "fool Texians." On the other hand, Daniel wasn't sure his Cherokee friend and mentor had ever really set foot in Texas.

Charles Flint cleared his throat. "We would go to Fort Worth with Quanah?"

Not a trace of The People when he spoke, Daniel marveled. Half the time, Daniel still spoke in grunts and snorts, like most reservation Comanches. *What would School Father Pratt say when he hears me speak?* he wondered.

"Yes." Agent Biggers's head bobbed like a rocking horse. "Certainly."

Daniel studied Flint. He had removed the fedora from his kneecap, and was crushing the soft felt hat in his hands, staring directly at the young Baptist agent.

Daniel liked and admired Quanah, but not all of The People did. Daniel had been just a young boy, and Flint — in those years known only by the name his father had given him, Tetecae — had been even younger. Yet Daniel remembered the hunger, the pain. He could recall the cries of the young babies, the weariness everyone felt. Bluecoat Long Knives had killed their pony herds, burned their villages. Then there were the other *taibo* men, Pale Eyes who had killed buffalo by the thousands, more heartless than the bluecoat Long Knives. In the year Pale Eyes called 1875 but that The People sadly recalled as The Year The Kwahadis Quit Fighting, Quanah had been forced to lead the last of the Kwahadi band, the last of The People still resisting the Pale Eyes, to surrender at the bluecoat fort built near Cache Creek, in what not only once had been The People's homeland, but as sacred ground as The People had known.

Pale Eyes had made Quanah Parker the chief of all The People.

Some *Nermernuh* resented that.

Maybe Daniel saw much of himself in Quanah. Daniel's mother had been Mescalero; Quanah's was a white woman that had been captured on a raid in Texas. Daniel had heard some men complain that Quanah was not pure, was not truly of The People, but never to Quanah's face. As a warrior, he had been relentless in his fight to keep The People free. As the designated chief on the reservation, he now understood how hopeless fighting the Pale Eyes was.

So he took the white man's road. Lived in

a big, white-man house the Texas cattlemen had built for him. He encouraged the mothers to send their children to mission schools. He encouraged the men to eat beef, for there were no more buffalo. He wore pale-eyes clothes even better than what Charles Flint donned.

In his own way, however, Quanah resisted.

Every Indian agent assigned to the reservation — Joshua Biggers included — had tried to tell Quanah that he must have only one wife. Yet Quanah still had eight. When he spoke English, the words were broken, often butchered. Yet when he spoke the tongue of *Nermernuh,* it was pure, powerful, and forceful, and not lazy reservation talk.

Daniel waited to hear what Charles Flint would say.

"I must seek counsel with my father on this matter," he said, and rose, bowing, extending his hand to Agent Biggers. He reshaped his hat, set it atop his head, and walked outside.

Confused, Joshua Biggers turned to Daniel.

"I thought he'd jump at the chance to go to Fort Worth." Biggers's head shook slowly. "I hope he'll go. Or you. Else, I'll have to send Frank Striker to interpret, and I'd rather have Frank here to help me."

31

"I'll go," Daniel said. He remembered the peach ice cream at the Queen City Ice Cream Parlor, but he had also recalled hearing Deputy U.S. Marshal Harvey P. Noble say that butter pecan tasted even better.

Daniel tried to shake off this thought. Maybe he was becoming more Pale Eyes. But Charles Flint? Seeking out his father before making a decision? Tetecae was showing that he had not forgotten all the ways of The People.

CHAPTER THREE

Ration day came, as always, with much fanfare among The People. Men dressed in their best war shirts, shunning the open-crown pale-eyes hats for eagle feathers or dusty buffalo headdresses, smiles carved among the crevasses of the old women's wrinkled faces.

Toddlers stumbled. Dogs yipped, their tails wagging. Horses snorted. Young women sang, their eyes bright with joy. Boys acted like men. Men acted like boys.

By the corrals of the agency, Joshua Biggers, *taibo* cattlemen, missionaries from the schools, soldiers, and a half dozen laundresses from nearby Fort Sill watched. Daniel recognized the looks on the faces of those Pale Eyes. It was the same look he and his fellow miners had revealed when Adok Król had chided them into attending the Atkinson Dime Museum in Pittsburgh. Seeing the half-man, half-woman with the beard and arms thicker than Adok Król's had turned Daniel's eyes bulging. Watching a man swallow a sword had left Daniel's muscles tightening in his bowels. He knew those looks. Disgust. Fear. Amazement.

The corral gate swung open, and inside rode five boys, the tails of their painted ponies tied up, their small hands gripping huge lances. Spears carved from wood by old men, the way The People once hunted buffalo. No rifles. The People did not care to hunt that way, and this was as close to hunting buffalo as. . . . Daniel shook his head.

Yipping excitedly, mimicking coyotes, the boys kicked their horses into the midst of the bawling longhorns, got the beefs running, raising dust, and began thrusting lances into the sides of the cattle. Women sang louder. Older men, the fathers of these teenagers, laughed, pointed, called out encouragement.

A Negro laundress fainted. A white woman soon joined her.

When the slaughter was complete, the women came in, with skinning knives and buckets. Kneeling beside the revived laundress, Joshua Biggers mouthed a prayer, as he always did on ration day.

As a member of the tribal police, and

drawing his $8 in government script, Daniel was not eligible for rations. It was his job to keep the peace, make sure the lines moved as men and women stood in line to get their monthly rations: sugar and flour, both often not worth eating, corn that Mr. McEveety was decent enough to trade for coffee, barrels of salted pork, and sacks of bacon. Earlier that morning, Daniel and Ben Buffalo Bone, with Agent Biggers watching, had opened some of the barrels and sacks. Often, suppliers would put coal in the bottom of the barrel and fill the sacks with more rocks than rancid meat. But this time, the rations were fairly acceptable.

"My son remembers not the days of *cuhtz*," a voice said. "Do you?"

Daniel turned.

Isa-tai's shadow fell across Daniel's face. He was large, even for a man of The People, needing a neck like a bull to keep his huge head from sinking into his shoulders. A long strand of hair fell across his wide cheek. The strand was well-placed by the Kwahadi holy man. Isa-tai was just vain enough to try to hide the scar an angry Cheyenne had given him years earlier.

He had wrapped a trade blanket around his waist, and wore a calico shirt and gray woolen vest, a red silk bandanna secured

35

around his throat by a silver slide. A gold wedding band tightly gripped his left pinky, just between the fingernail and first knuckle, a ring he had taken off a pale-eyes woman killed during a raid up in Kansas, and a conch-shell hair-pipe breastplate, decorated with Russian blue beads and German silver, clung tightly to his broad chest, the buckskin neck strings wrapped with ermine skins.

"Yes, *Tsu Kuh Puah*," Daniel answered, using the term of respect for an older man. "I remember."

Isa-tai grunted. Standing slightly behind him, his son, Charles Flint, still dressed in suit, tie, and fedora, dropped his head.

Yes, Daniel remembered when The People ate buffalo, not cattle. *Cuhtz* was indispensable. Hide and hair, blood and bones, just about everything on the buffalo would be used by The People. He pictured his mother, holding his hand, singing from the top of a mesa, pointing out her husband, Daniel's father, down below as the Kwahadis chased a thundering herd of buffalo on the Llano Estacado of the Texas Panhandle. Dust soon swallowed everything below, and the hoofs of the great herd drowned out the shouts of the men.

He pictured his father, standing before him some time later, holding a liver in his bloody hand. He could taste the liver now, after his mother had emptied the contents of the buffalo's gall bladder onto the raw meat. His mother had laughed, and gone back to work, singing as she skinned and butchered the buffalo cow.

"All gone," Isa-tai said. His face showed no emotion. "I will tell you two the story of the time before *cuhtz.*"

Charles Flint lifted his head. Daniel nodded, waiting.

Isa-tai spoke.

"The People were playing games when a strange old man approached them, saying nothing, a quiver over his shoulder but he held no bow. He watched The People play, then said it was time for him to go shit. So he removed the quiver, laid it on the ground, and went down to the creek. One of The People decided to look into the quiver, and he pulled out a large piece of fat. 'This man has plenty of meat,' he announced.

"The old man came from the creek bed and changed into a bird. He flew over the mountain.

"Naturally The People were curious. They wanted to follow him. They wanted to fly over the mountain, to see what was there. So one man changed into an owl, because an owl flies quietly, and another became a quail, because a quail walks quietly. These two flew over the mountain as well. There, they saw a lone teepee, facing east, as is the custom of The People. At sunset, Owl flew to the teepee, but the old man knew that Owl was really one of The People, so Owl flew away and told Quail. Quail then walked softly to the teepee, and returned, telling Owl . . . 'There are three people inside . . . the old man, his wife, their daughter.' Both Owl and Quail returned to the teepee, and waited, listening.

" 'Mother, I am hungry,' the daughter said.

" 'Shush,' the mother said. 'Those Indians might be here.'

"But the old man said that he was hungry, too, so the woman opened a parfleche from which she pulled out much meat. The meat smelled good. Quail wanted to go in and snatch some, but Owl would not let him, whispering wisely . . . 'We must wait.'

"When their meal was finished, the woman brushed the remnants to the back of the teepee, and then they all went to sleep. When they were asleep, Quail entered the teepee, grabbed the crumbs, the suet, a few loose chunks, and brought them outside. Owl and Quail took all the meat they could carry and flew back to The People.

"There was much excitement in the village that night. The People loved the taste of the meat, and they were hungry. So they decided to move camp. They packed their stuff on ten horses, for ten horses represented each band of The People, and they rode around the mountain.

"The old man was not happy to see The People, who said they were just visiting. The old man drew a line from a tree to a stump, telling them that they must camp on this side of the line and never cross it. The old man visited The People each day for three days, but he always said that he knew not where to find any meat. But The People did not believe him.

"On the fourth morning, Kawus arrived, but the hero of The People came in the form of a coyote. He told The People that the old man would not give them any meat, would not tell them how to find it, but he would find it for them. He told The People that they must move their camp away from the old man's teepee. Then, Kawus changed himself into a puppy.

"The People moved their camp, but the old man followed them to make sure they were indeed returning to the other side of the mountain. Satisfied, he returned to his lodge, where he found his daughter calling to the puppy, who was whimpering under a juniper. She would approach, but the puppy would back into the brush that grew near the trunk of the juniper. 'Come here,' the girl said, 'you are mine now.' The puppy just whimpered.

" 'Do not be afraid,' she said. 'I will feed you.' And she held out a chunk of meat, and the puppy crawled out of the brush. It was suspicious, but it followed the girl into the teepee. Kawus saw a hole in the floor, and in the hole he saw a hundred thousand buffalo!

" 'Take that dog out or I will kill it!' the old man shouted. 'It is not a dog, but one of The People. You can tell by its eyes.'

"The girl obeyed her father. The old man walked out of the teepee and looked at the puppy, then went off to make sure The People were not coming back.

"When her father was gone, the girl picked up the puppy and brought him right back into the teepee. 'You will never go hungry again,' she said, and scratched the little dog's ears.

"Kawus jumped out of the girl's hands, and ran around the hole, shouting like one of The People. The buffalo stampeded. They crashed out of the teepee and took to the plains.

40

" 'You tricked me!' the girl yelled, and she picked up a club to brain the puppy, but by then Kawus had changed into the form of a man. He leaped onto the back of the last buffalo, and escaped the girl. Kawus rode straight to the new village of The People.

"They asked him what had happened. Kawus smiled and said . . . 'Tomorrow at sunrise those buffalo will be outside our door. The People will never go hungry. There will always be buffalo to eat.'

"That is how we got buffalo." Isa-tai, his face hardening, gestured toward the corrals with contempt. "And this is how we lost them!"

He was moving now, making a beeline toward a gathering of men beside a small fire outside the corrals. Daniel glanced at Flint, and both followed Isa-tai. *Keeping the peace today,* Daniel thought, *might not be so easy.*

Quanah Parker stood in front of the fire, stumping, as the Pale Eyes would say.

His long black braids, wrapped in otter skins, fell well past his shoulders, and beaded moccasins covered his feet. Yet he also wore black-striped britches of the finest wool, a matching Prince Albert coat, silver brocade vest, and a puffy silk tie with a diamond stickpin in its center. A black

41

bowler topped his head.

Tall, lean, especially for one of The People, he towered over the men who had gathered by the fire to hear him talk. Nagwee, the grizzled Kotsoteka *puhakat,* squatted, arms folded, eyes staring into the smoke. Yellow Bear sat in a folding Army camp chair, glancing every now and then through the corral slats to watch the butchering process. Across from Yellow Bear stood Cuhtz Bávi, Ben Buffalo Bone's uncle, another Kotsoteka, who had married Ben's mother after lung sickness had sent her husband on the journey to The Land Beyond The Sun. A young Kwahadi named Eka Huutsuu, meaning Red Bird, leaned against the corral, while a gray-haired Penateka, whose name Daniel could not remember, squatted by the fire, looking up as Quanah talked.

Whatever words Quanah had now died on his tongue as Isa-tai positioned himself between Yellow Bear and Quanah.

Quanah nodded, his face hard, eyes angry.

Flint stepped behind his father, and Daniel walked to the corral, put his hand on the top rail, and turned.

He knew what this conversation was about. It had to be about one of two things, or maybe both.

A year ago sometime during the Sleet

Month, *Positsu mua,* the Congress of the United States had enacted the Dawes General Allotment Act. Daniel had met Henry L. Dawes when the Massachusetts senator had been doing some stumping of his own before Quanah Parker at the Comanche chief's Star House.

The way Daniel understood it, the new law would allow the President, whenever he so pleased, to give up their reservation. The land the government had placed The People on would be surveyed by *taibos* and divided into . . . what was that word? Yes, allotments. The land would be owned by individual Indians.

Which was foreign to Daniel as it was incomprehensible to all of The People. Land belonged to everyone, or at least everyone strong enough to hold onto it. Individuals did not own land. Land was not the same as horses, as wives.

So far, the President had not yet decided it was time for The People to relinquish their reservation. That time, Daniel knew, would come soon. He had learned that much about Pale Eyes. They wanted to own all the land on the earth.

Or, it was about the lease. Quanah had made a tidy profit, and so had The People, by leasing pastures to the *taibo* cattlemen to feed their longhorns.

At first, Quanah had opposed both Senator Dawes and Texas cattle barons, yet he had been won over by their arguments. Or maybe Quanah was wise enough to know that Pale Eyes would get whatever it was they wanted. Hadn't they already stolen the land that once belonged to The People? One had to follow the white man's road, it seemed, for at least a little bit, or be squashed like a bug. Quanah, Daniel knew in his heart, would do what he thought best for The People.

Isa-tai, on the other hand, was not so certain.

"You speak like you dress," Isa-tai said, nodding at Quanah. "Like a *taibo*."

"I speak for The People." Surprisingly Quanah spoke in a reserved voice that belied the expression etched in his face.

Isa-tai spit into the fire. "The People." He grunted, shaking his massive head. "Pale Eyes say you are our chief, but that is not our way."

"This I know," Quanah said. "But I also know we must bend. For the benefit of our loved ones, our children, our wives. If not, The People will disappear like the buffalo."

Yellow Bear grunted and nodded. That didn't surprise Daniel. After all, Yellow Bear was the father of Quanah's favorite wife.

Cuhtz Bávi looked from Quanah to Isa-tai, as if he expected a fight to commence. That didn't surprise Daniel, either.

"Hear me," Isa-tai announced, loud enough for the women and children inside the corral with the dead cattle to hear. "Quanah has his own herd of *taibo* beef. The white cattle rancher named Hall pays him in the paper money of the Pale Eyes. These same liars built Quanah that fancy pale-eyes house." Isa-tai's eyes found Cuhtz Bávi. "Quanah is not like your brother, Cuhtz Bávi."

Ben Buffalo Bone arrived, thumbs hooked in the belt that held his ancient Remington revolver, and stopped beside Daniel.

Isa-tai smiled at Ben, a fellow Metal Shirt and probably the best friend Daniel had on the reservation.

"I remember your father," he said, his head bobbing, and spoke the name Ben had known before the Pale Eyes gave him a *taibo* name. "The Pale Eyes built a home for Naro Toneetsi, too, but Naro Toneetsi never lived in it. He stayed in the teepee. That big house, ha! He put his best horses in it."

And now I live there with those horses, Daniel thought.

"He was truly of The People," Isa-tai said.

"But Quanah? I say he has forgotten the ways of The People."

Realizing he was holding his breath, Daniel slowly exhaled. Waiting. The only sound now came from yipping dogs and bawling babies.

Slowly Yellow Bear looked away from the corral. His eyes landed on a smoldering stick in the gray ash, and he deftly pushed it closer to the flames with the toe of his moccasin. Still staring at the fire, he said: "It is you who have forgotten the ways of The People. It is impolite to speak the name of those who have traveled to The Land Beyond The Sun, Isa-tai."

Men's heads bobbed around the fire, and Isa-tai stiffened at the rebuke.

"I meant no harm," he told Ben Buffalo Bone and Cuhtz Bávi.

The two Kotsotekas nodded their acceptance in return.

"It is hard to say what is right." The holy man, Nagwee, had spoken, although he still stared into the white smoke. "My teeth are gone. I barely taste the *taibo* meat. That is good. I like not the taste. But Quanah speaks with wisdom. Once The People were strong as the limb of an oak. Now we have grown weak. But if we are not careful" — he reached over and picked up a handful of ash, lifted it, and, opening his hand, let the wind carry the ashes away — "The People will become what this once strong oak limb has become."

Silence. Even the dogs had stopped barking.

"Soon," Quanah said, "I go to meet with Captain Hall, with the other *Tejano* ranchers. Nagwee will travel with me, for he speaks with much wisdom. Yellow Bear will come with me, for he wishes to see this city called Fort Worth, and his counsel is strong and wise." Quanah's eyes locked on Isa-tai's. "Anyone is welcome to come with me, and make sure that the decision I make is what is best for The People."

Isa-tai straightened. "I will go with you."

Quanah nodded. "It is done." He turned, and walked away.

"Bávi, why are you smiling?"

He turned, embarrassed, seeing Ben Buffalo Bone staring at him, laughter in Ben's bottomless eyes, found himself almost falling into the traps of the Pale Eyes with a lie — "Brother, I am not. . . ." — before stopping himself.

"I go to Fort Worth, too, bávi," Daniel told his friend.

"Fort Worth." Ben Buffalo Bone's head shook. "Very far. The agent has asked me to

47

go to The Big Pasture. Longhorn cattle are there."

That stopped Daniel. Quanah had been holding that pasture for reserve, to strike up a better deal for The People when he negotiated a new lease agreement with the *taibo* ranchers.

"Would you like me to ride with you?"

Ben's head shook. "I go alone. My sister, Rain Shower, she saw the cattle. She saw no Pale Eyes. They probably . . . what Pale Eyes call them . . . strays?"

"Probably," Daniel agreed.

"I go alone," his friend repeated. "And you?"

Daniel smiled. "I will not be alone when School Father Pratt gives his talk." He wasn't looking at Ben Buffalo Bone any more. He watched Charles Flint, walking behind his father.

CHAPTER FOUR

Above the belching and hissing of the greasy black locomotive rose the crowd's roar. Daniel, who had just helped Yellow Bear out of the passenger car, turned and stared, amazed at all the spectators. The throng must have stretched half a block, with city constables in their black-visored navy caps forming a human fence to keep them from crushing the newcomers. The band struck up "Johnny Get Your Gun" as Quanah stepped onto the depot platform. It hurt Daniel's ears.

He felt a breath on his ear, turned, saw Yellow Bear but couldn't hear him. Daniel leaned closer.

"Ice cream," the ancient Kwahadi grunted.

Beside him, Charles Flint laughed.

"We must wait a while, *Tsu Kuh Puah,*" Daniel said with a smile, again using the term of respect for an older man.

49

Quanah was shaking hands with some red-headed *taibo,* his curly hair neatly combed and parted, a flowing handlebar mustache bending in the breeze, dressed in a brown suit with a red ribbon tie. He wore no gun, no badge, no epaulets, but over the din of music, applause, and modern mechanics, Daniel heard Quanah introduce the tall *Tejano* to Nagwee as a captain. He couldn't make out the man's last name.

"This is crazy!" Charles Flint had to shout in Daniel's ear.

"Haa," Daniel said, nodding, but did not take his eyes off Quanah and the tall man.

Quanah's mouth moved, and the *taibo* extended his hand toward Isa-tai. Frowning, Isa-tai folded his arms across his chest and glowered. The tall redhead, however, did not seem offended. He merely nodded at the holy man and moved with Quanah down the depot platform until both tall men stood in front of Daniel.

"His Arrows Fly Straight Into The Hearts Of His Enemies," Quanah said, speaking in the language of The People, and Daniel straightened. Rarely did people call him by that name any more. "Metal Shirt," Quanah said in English. "Ser-geant. Good Co-manch'." As Quanah smiled, Daniel's pride soared.

50

"This Captain Hall."

Lee Hall extended his hand, and Daniel shook it. The *taibo*'s grip felt like a vise. His pale eyes, however, were soft, almost sad.

"Metal Shirt, eh?" Hall's voice sounded like hominy, not the harsh twang of most *Tejanos,* but something far more genteel, from deeper in the South. "Then we, sir, have much in common. Once I wore the cinco peso star of the Texas Rangers."

They slid down the rough pine planks of the depot, and Quanah introduced Captain Hall to Yellow Bear.

"It is an honor to make your acquaintance," Captain Hall said.

"Ice cream," Yellow Bear demanded.

"And this," Quanah said, "Tetecae. Charles . . . Flint. Work at post. He . . ." — Quanah took a moment to think of the right word — "cipher."

"That is a handsome suit, sir," the former Ranger said. "Better than anything one should find at Taylor and Barr's, I would dare say."

"Thank you." Charles Flint cast a nervous glance at his father, who still stood there, unmoving, his face a mask of copper granite, arms still folded.

The band paused, the applause died down, and mutely women in their bonnets

51

and parasols and men with their cigars, pipes, and city hats stared, gawking at the Indians at the depot, some of them dressed in suits, others, Daniel included, in buckskins and leggings. The silence lasted only a moment before a tuba bellowed, a cymbal clashed, and some song Daniel had never heard wailed over the whistle of another Texas & Pacific locomotive.

"Hello, Daniel."

He turned, swallowed, stared into the eyes of School Father Pratt.

"It has been a while."

Those few years had aged him. Oh, although heavier, Pratt still stood erect, shoulders square, and wore the spotless uniform he had worn at the Carlisle Industrial School. His hair seemed thinner, however, more gray than brown, his eyes held a weariness, his nose had reddened like a whiskey drinker's (though, as far as Daniel could recall, Pratt did not imbibe), and his earlobes had grown.

"School Father." Out of the corner of his eye, Daniel saw Charles Flint snap to attention. Pratt saw it, too, and his smile seemed to reduce his age.

"Mister Flint," Pratt said, nodding. "I hear many great things about you." Looking back at Daniel: "And you, as well, Mister Kill-

52

straight. Do you enjoy being a peace-keeper?"

Did he? Daniel wasn't sure. "It is. . . ." He tripped over an answer.

It sets me apart from The People. Many do not trust me. Afraid that I will arrest them, take them to The Lodges That Are Always In Darkness, put them in chains. Whiskey runners fear me, and well they should. I can count my friends on one hand. But that has been the path the Creator must have laid out for me. Nothing has changed.

He was amazed those words ran through his mind. That he did not speak them did not surprise him.

School Father Pratt had turned to Charles Flint, shaking his hand, asking about book-keeping, admiring his clothes.

At the far end of the depot platform, Captain Hall spoke to a slight man with a neatly trimmed salt-and-pepper beard. The man pointed a walking cane, its gold curved top reflecting sunlight, toward three canopy-topped surreys. Captain Hall's head bobbed, and he called over the last notes of the band: "Captain Pratt, we should go!"

"Ice cream," Yellow Bear said.

The Wednesday Woman's Club engagement had proved uneventful. Ladies who smelled

53

of lilac powder waving their handheld fans to fight off the oppressive heat, and afterward offering gloved white hands to shake with slight curtsies while serving punch and, to Yellow Bear's delight, ice cream — vanilla, however, and not, to Daniel's disappointment, peach or butter pecan — and lemon cookies.

An hour later, Daniel couldn't remember anything about School Father Pratt's speech to those women other than a few quotations from the Bible.

City Hall was different.

Men and women crowded the lawn as they had at the train station. Even more. They covered every blade of grass, no one could move up or down Weatherford Street, and people pushed for perhaps a full block down Houston Street and maybe halfway down Main. Far in the back, others stood in the stirrups of their horses or in the back of buckboards. Down Weatherford and Houston Streets, men and women leaned out of second-story windows. More than a few even sat on rooftops.

"Once," School Father Pratt began, "and not that long ago, you wonderful, gracious citizens of this magnificent city would be barring your doors and filling musket barrels with blue whistlers at the very thought

54

of Comanche Indians inside the city limits. And now . . . this!"

Laughter.

Daniel looked at his lap, saw his thumbs twiddling. Tried to stop. Started again.

"Ladies and gentlemen, when it comes to Indian civilization, I am a Baptist."

Fitting, Daniel thought. Just moments earlier, the minister from the First Baptist Church had given the invocation.

"I strongly believe in immersing the Indian in our civilization. Hold them under. . . ." Here, Pratt raised both fists, then pretended to be holding a head under the water.

Daniel straightened, a memory from ages ago coming to the forefront. He could picture old Isa Nanaka, now traveling to The Land Beyond The Sun, holding a buffalo hunter's head under the water of the river the *Tejanos* called the Pease, could see the man's boots thrashing in the mud until Isa Nanaka had drowned the fool.

". . . until they are soaked thoroughly." School Father Pratt's hands fell to his side. "This task would be impossible to do on the reservations of old. It could be done only at boarding schools. That is why I created the Industrial School in Carlisle, Pennsylvania. And rest assured, ladies and

55

gentlemen, that we did not teach these Indians to be . . . *ahem* . . . Yankees!"

More laughter. To the left of the lectern, Captain Lee Hall slapped his thigh, leaned over, and said something to Fort Worth's mayor whose name Daniel had already forgotten.

"Good citizens of Texas, you know all too well the savagery of war, the butchery of barbarians. The rivers once flowed red through this country."

Now Daniel recalled Isa Nanaka dragging the man's lifeless body from the muddy water. Saw him unsheathing his knife. Remembered the warrior taking the *taibo*'s scalp.

"I served in the Army. I saw the carnage. I know what brave settlers went through. Indeed, I can understand the hatred you felt for Indians such as these that now share this stage with me. Wipe out the Indians, you once said. Nay, you demanded it. Send them the way of the buffalo."

He paused, letting the words take hold.

"But is this the way of a Christian?" His head shook. "My way is better, ladies and gentlemen. It is as I have long championed. Kill the Indian, not the man."

Applause built to a crescendo, echoed by a roar of approval. No one challenged Pratt.

56

No heckles. That, Daniel found hard to comprehend. Most *Tejanos* he had met likely still wanted to kill both Indian and man, with relish. Especially Comanches.

"My good friends, my fellow citizens of Our Lord Jesus Christ, I want to introduce you to two prime examples of how Carlisle works. These two young gentlemen came to Pennsylvania as heathens, as raw, wild savages, but through dedication . . . on their part, indeed, as well as on the part of my excellent tutors . . . they have proved themselves as champions for the Comanche race. They are no longer savages, but are men among the best of their fields."

Sand caked Daniel's throat.

"Texas, allow me to introduce you to Charles Flint, a clerk and accountant for George McEveety's trading post in Indian Territory." Applause. "And Daniel Kill-straight, the head police officer for the tribal police on the federal reserve near Fort Sill."

Something grazed Daniel's moccasin. He looked down at a shiny black shoe, followed the trail up the dark pants and coat until he stared up into Charles Flint's coal eyes. He realized Flint was standing, no longer sitting, and although he couldn't hear Flint's words, he could read his lips, and that urgent expression on his face.

"Stand up!"

Daniel looked out into the crowd. He wondered if he could rise, and was surprised when he did not collapse and roll down the steps of the courthouse.

His prayer was answered. School Father Pratt did not ask either to make a speech. Still clapping his hands, his face beaming, Pratt nodded at the two, and Daniel dropped into his chair. Sweat poured down his face and neck. His heart pounded.

"Their education would not have been possible without the co-operation of tribal elders." Pratt gestured behind him. "This is Yellow Bear. His savage heart has been tamed by the love, thanks to the gracious ladies of the Wednesday Woman's Club . . ." — laughter — "for ice cream. And let me just say that ice cream tastes far better, and has better results, than bullets and powder."

Daniel mopped his brow.

"And here is Nagwee." He butchered the name, but no one seemed to notice. "Among the Comanches, he is a medicine man. He is wise beyond his years.

"On Nagwee's left is another medicine man. This, folks, is not Isa-tai's first trip to Texas. He led that fateful attack in the year of Our Lord Eighteen Seventy-Four at Adobe Walls. Only the keen eye and true

58

shots of those stalwart white buffalo hunters prevented the Comanches from setting civilization back thirty or forty years. Isa-tai's name means Coyote Droppings. Imagine, my friends, if your parent had named you Coyote Droppings."

Laughter swept across Fort Worth. Someone on the platform stopped his boots and howled like a coyote. "Coyote Droppings! Don't that beat all!"

Daniel shook his head at the pale-eyes translation. Isa-tai meant no such thing.

"Charles Flint over here came to Pennsylvania with a savage name, but he has followed the white man's road. Isa-tai is also the father of Charles Flint. Look at father and son, my friends. Cannot you see how much the Carlisle Industrial School has, can, and will accomplish!"

The roar sounded deafening. Charles Flint muttered a pale-eyes oath. Daniel fought the urge to look at Isa-tai.

When the noise at last subsided, Pratt stopped to mop his forehead with a handkerchief. "Lastly, this tall man sitting behind me is a warrior and leader, a man of war, a man of peace. He fought hard to keep his people free, but now works hard to hold peace. He is more respected, more honored, more cherished than Crazy Horse or Sitting

Bull or Cochise or Osceola. He is a judge. He is the chief of the Comanches. He is the Abraham Lincoln and George Washington and Robert E. Lee of the Comanche people. And, as many of you know, he is a native Texan."

Roars. Someone even fired a pistol shot into the air. A horse whinnied, and cymbals clashed. The band's trumpeter sounded the charge. More laughter.

Pratt even snickered. He wiped his face again, then slid the handkerchief into his vest pocket. "His mother was the dearly departed Cynthia Ann Parker, taken captive by the Comanches from Parker's Fort 'way back during the dark days of Texas in Eighteen Thirty-Six. Ladies and gentlemen, I give you . . . Quanah Parker."

Daniel found himself clapping, watching Quanah rise, bowing, moving uncomfortably as School Father Pratt beckoned him to the lectern. Everyone was clapping. Everyone, that is, except Isa-tai.

Gradually the crowd hushed.

A camera flashed, belching smoke and bad smells. Reporters scribbled on their note pads, which reminded Daniel that he probably should buy some Old Glory writing tablets, a Columbus lead sharpener, and two or three packs of Faber's No. 2 pencils.

Ever superstitious, Daniel practically refused to use anything but those brands for his police work, and they were hard to find on the reservation. Even McEveety didn't carry those. In fact, the trading post stocked few writing utensils.

"Ladies, gentlemen." Quanah's soft voice carried over the crowd. "Me once bad man. Now me citizen of United States. Me work for Comanche. Me work for you. Good friends here. Captain Pratt. Captain Hall. This used to be hunting ground for Comanche. Many rattlesnakes here."

"Still are!" someone shouted from Main Street.

"Hush up, Horace!" countered a feminine voice.

"I see many faces here. Good faces. White faces. I work for my people. Government say . . . 'Put Indians in school. Make Indians do like white man.' This I do. Me proud. Tet-*uh* Flint . . . Charles Flint. Daniel Killstraight. Make proud. Make you proud. They good. But some Indians no good."

Daniel found enough nerve to shoot a quick glance at Isa-tai, but the large Kwahadi seemed to be asleep in his chair.

"But me say some white man no good. Bring whiskey. Get Comanche drunk. Steal souls of men. Women, too. Others bring

61

cattle. But pay not. This wrong. This, Killstraight, he try stop. Good lawman. I come here to talk with friend Captain Hall. Come see friend Waggoner. Friend Burnett. Good to see many faces. See friends. I miss my mother. She good woman. Good mother. She white woman. I go now."

As he turned, Daniel saw Quanah wipe a tear before it rolled down his cheek. Daniel thought of his own mother.

CHAPTER FIVE

Like red ants, reporters swarmed. Most of them came from Fort Worth and Dallas publications, but Daniel heard a bald man mention Austin and a man with Dundreary whiskers say San Antonio. A tall gentleman in a silk hat and peculiar accent said he hailed from London, and Daniel also heard names like *Frank Leslie's Illustrated, Scribner's Monthly, Harper's Weekly,* and *National Police Gazette,* the last of which Daniel had not only heard of, he had even read a few issues. A woman, her hair neatly in a bun, stood sketching page after page. Photographers scurried about, setting up their huge boxes on tripods. One man with a sweaty hand pulled Charles Flint from his chair, urging him to pose for a photograph with his father. "Good Injun and bad," the photographer said through a nasal twang. "It'll sell like Bohemian suds."

Daniel stepped aside as the photographer

pulled a laughing Charles Flint toward Isa-
tai.

"Come on, old-timer," another photographer called, trying to coax Yellow Bear from
his chair. "It won't take but a moment for
me to capture your likeness. Your grandchildren will love it, yes, sir, indeed they
will."

Yellow Bear jerked his arm from the
photographer's grasp, and barked in his native tongue.

The photographer straightened, turned,
searching for help, and found Daniel.

"Hey, boy. Can you talk this old chief into
posing for a photograph?"

"He says he will not let you steal his
shadow," Daniel said, translating Yellow
Bear's words.

"Huh?"

Then the photographer saw Quanah, surrounded by reporters, and quickly grabbed
his camera and tripod.

Daniel filled his lungs with hot air, and
slowly exhaled. A few newspapermen left
Quanah, and hurried to join the throng that
surrounded Isa-tai. Charles Flint sat in a
chair, his photograph already taken, con-
versing with a reporter who furiously
scribbled with his pencil, while the lady art-
ist knelt, working her pens to capture

Charles Flint's likeness. A moment later, a reporter tugged on Flint's coat sleeve, urging him to translate what his father was saying. A woman brought Yellow Bear some ice cream, and the *puhakat* smiled a toothless grin, and took the cone greedily. Other artists and photographers knelt beside Nagwee.

Nobody would be leaving for a spell, so Daniel sat in the chair Flint had abandoned. He picked up one of the paper fans the ladies from the Wednesday Woman's Club had handed out to their guests. There was a quote from Proverbs stenciled on the yellow paper, but Daniel was too tired, too hot to read. He waved the fan in front of his face, closed his eyes.

"Hello, Daniel. We have not had much of an opportunity to talk. It's been rather a whirlwind since you arrived."

Eyes opened, fan lowered, Daniel started to rise, but School Father Pratt raised a hand to stop him, and settled into the nearest chair.

Daniel tried to think of words. "I thought . . . you would . . . newspapermen . . . why don't they talk to you?"

"They've talked to me for ages." Checking his pocket watch, he added: "Though I have an interview with Mister Etheridge at

the *Standard* in a little more than an hour."
Pratt smiled, took the fan Daniel had
dropped, and waved it so that it would send
warm air toward him and Daniel both.
"These are the celebrities. Quanah. Isa-tai.
You should go up there, make yourself
known."

Daniel's head shook strongly.

"I'm surprised they haven't circled around
you like vultures. Maybe I should not have
said all that about Isa-tai. No, there's no
maybe. That was stupid of me. Those ink-
spillers can't get enough of that old tyrant."
He lowered the fan, let it fall, and pointed.
"Look at him, Daniel."

Daniel glanced, shrugged, turned back to
his former educator.

With a smile, Pratt turned in his chair,
reached over, and tapped the shield pinned
on Daniel's vest. "You've done well, Daniel.
But, of course, I knew you would. You're a
good peace officer from all that I hear."

No, Daniel thought. He remembered
something Hugh Gunter had once said.
They were camping in the Nations, one, no,
two years ago, bringing the body of Jimmy
Comes Last from Fort Smith to the reservation. Having breakfast, or maybe it had been
supper. Daniel couldn't remember exactly,
but he knew they had been sitting around a

fire, and the Cherokee had been sipping coffee. Daniel had asked if Gunter liked being a policeman. "Sometimes," Gunter had answered, before motioning toward the coffin in the wagon. "Not always." And moments later, Gunter had added: "I am good at it."

Daniel wasn't good at it. Oh, sure, he had been promoted to sergeant of the Tribal Police, but that was because he could speak English and Comanche, and understood a little bit of Kiowa. What he couldn't speak, he could usually sign with his hands. He was no detective, and not much of a peace officer. The law? What did he understand of white man's law? People — red and white — said he had solved crimes, had stopped whiskey-running operations, had sent murderers and thieves to prison, but Daniel knew better. He had bungled his way through any investigation. Good at it? Not hardly.

"I knew you were a leader when you first arrived at Carlisle." Laughing, Pratt shook his head. "You were quite the rebellious little red devil. Our School Mothers must have cracked three score rulers on your knuckles. Yet, eventually, you saw the light, realized that the Comanche . . . and all other Indian tribes . . . must learn to adapt

67

to the white man's ways. It is the only way for you people to survive. We must stop the butchery, the violence." He was sounding like the speechmaker again. Daniel bit his bottom lip. "You are the one to lead the Comanches to a better way of life, a better living. You and Quanah."

He could feel the School Father's eyes boring into him, knew Pratt wanted a verbal response. Daniel tilted his head toward Isa-tai. "He is a leader," he said. "Not me."

"Do you know what a chameleon is, Daniel?"

"No. That is a word I do not know." *One of many,* he thought but did not say.

"It's . . . never mind. Suffice to say that Isa-tai is not the right leader," Pratt answered immediately. "He proved that at Adobe Walls."

On that, Daniel had to agree.

Memories, clear as spring run-off in the Wichita Mountains, came flooding before his face: Isa-tai claiming his *puha,* telling The People he could heal the sick, he could even raise the dead. Saying that no bullets would hurt him. None of this was new. Though just a young boy, Daniel had heard other prophets. False prophets, the old *puhakats* would say. Yet many of The People claimed to have seen Isa-tai travel to The

Land Beyond The Sun, remaining there all night, then coming down from the sky on the following morning. Others had seen him belch out cases and cases of cartridges. Once, a comet had appeared in the night sky, and Isa-tai had told The People that the light would disappear in five days. Daniel had heard that prediction himself. Daniel himself had seen the comet. And five days later, as Isa-tai had concluded, the white light in the night sky had vanished, never to return.

The Kwahadis believed him. So did Daniel, for he was a child. The Cheyennes came to hear his words, as did the Kiowas and Arapahos. Isa-tai came to Quanah, asked him to help him destroy the *taibos* who were waging their war against the buffalo, which The People needed desperately. It would be a revenge raid. Quanah would avenge the death of his uncle, killed by the Pale Eyes. First, they would hold a Sun Dance, and The People had never held a Sun Dance.

They would attack the killers of the buffalo at their camp at the place called Adobe Walls. Bad medicine, Yellow Bear had warned. Years ago, The People had attacked a pale-eyes force led by the great white scout Kit Carson near those same grounds, and death songs were sung, and women,

69

children, and men left mourning. Isa-tai had not listened. Nor had Quanah. Thus, they had attacked Adobe Walls.

Again, death songs were sung, and women, children, and men left mourning. The Pale Eyes had far-shooting guns. Guns that would shoot today and kill tomorrow. One bullet fired from the *taibo* camp had struck and killed a warrior more than a mile away. Infuriated, a Cheyenne had lashed at Isa-tai with his quirt, but Isa-tai had blamed the Cheyennes for the defeat. One had killed a skunk before the battle, Isa-tai had claimed. It had ruined his *puha.*

"I hear," School Father Pratt said, "that Isa-tai wasn't known as Isa-tai back then. The Comanches gave him that name only after the battle. It means Coyote Droppings. Right?"

Daniel smiled. "No. He has always been known as Isa-tai. At least, as long as I can remember. And it does not mean Coyote Droppings, or Rear End Of A Wolf, or anything like that."

"What does it mean?"

Daniel tightened his lips. He could not tell School Father that in the language of The People Isa-tai meant Coyote Vagina.

"Pa-cha-na-quar-hip did not mean Buffalo Hump."

70

Daniel looked up, wondering how long Charles Flint had been standing there. "But that's how you white men always translate it?"

"Is that so?" Pratt stood up and shook Flint's hand. "And what was Buffalo Hump's real name?"

Flint grinned, and when he answered — "Erection That Won't Go Down." — Pratt guffawed.

"Well, I can understand why that name got changed." Pratt's eyes beamed. "Lord have mercy, can you imagine how the Wednesday's Women's Club would have reacted?" He slapped his knee, leaving Daniel wondering how the School Mothers would have behaved if they could see School Father Pratt's amusement over such a profane joke.

Yet the name was no joke, and Daniel could not hide his frown, his disappointment in Charles Flint. Oh, it wasn't like the true name of Buffalo Hump, a legendary leader of the Penateka band who had been dead for years, among The People had been some secret. Still, Flint had disappointed Daniel. Like his father, the bookkeeper seemed to have forgotten the ways of *Nermernuh*. He did not remember, or maybe care, that for any of The People to speak the

71

name of someone who had journeyed to The Land Beyond The Sun showed much disrespect.

"And what of your father's name?" Pratt said.

"His name?" Flint's grin widened. "My father? He is called Isa-tai."

Names. Isa-tai refused to call his son by the name he had been given by the Pale Eyes. To Isa-tai, his son was only Tetecae.

They had moved from the Tarrant County Courthouse across Weatherford Street to the office of the Fort Worth *Standard,* where Pratt gave an interview to the newspaper editor, who then proceeded to discuss the grazing situation with Quanah, and finally turned his attention to Isa-tai, with Charles Flint again handling the translations. Daniel sat listening in silence, while Yellow Bear's stomach growled, and the old *puhakat* shifted his feet impatiently. By the time the *Standard* editor had filled his notebook, the cattlemen had arrived — Dan Waggoner, Captain Lee Hall, and a gangling man with a weather-beaten face named Burk Burnett who wore a silver-plated Colt revolver holstered over his stomach, the numbers *6666* engraved on the .45's ivory grip and tooled in the rich leather.

The air inside the stifling newspaper office began to fill with thick smoke from cigars these cattlemen fired up. It stank of *taibos,* of lies the *Tejanos* told with laughter.

"It's about time, Red," the one named Burnett told the former Texas Ranger.

The Mansion House Hotel was only four blocks down Rusk Street, but Captain Hall had summoned several hacks to drive the cattlemen and Comanche guests to the hotel for supper. School Father Pratt, however, did not attend. "I will see you gentlemen for breakfast," he announced, tipped his hat, and walked down Weatherford Street toward the courthouse, followed by the newspaper editor.

Elegant. That's the only word Daniel could think of to describe the Mansion House. He felt uncomfortable as soon as he entered the building, his moccasins gliding noiselessly across the rich velvet carpet.

A tall man with a gray silk tie and well-groomed mustache that looked as if it had been drawn on with a pencil nodded courteously at Captain Hall. "The dining room is all yours, sir," he said, and held open the door to let the men, red and white, pass.

This was not like the Pickwick Hotel. Oh, Daniel could feel the stares of the waiters, bartender, clerks, and hotel guests, even from the *maitre d'* after leading them to the table — the same as he had felt at the Pickwick. Yet soon he forgot those angry looks as cattlemen and Comanches found their seats around a long table, covered with white lace cloth, decorated by long, skinny candles in a spotless silver candelabra. He wondered why Quanah's group was not staying at this hotel, but imagined the rates probably had something to do with that.

When Daniel pulled out a chair next to Charles Flint, a firm hand gripped his arm, and Quanah said: "You sit by me." As Quanah led him around the table, he whispered: "Make sure I understand what these men say."

Soup came first. Well, first, actually was wine for the Texians, water, coffee, or tea for the Comanches. Daniel dipped his spoon into the creamy soup, tasted it, then found a napkin to wipe his tongue. Some sort of fish, and The People rarely ate fish. Naturally the *Tejanos* did not notice that they were the only ones slurping their bowls. The waiters came quickly, picked up the empty bowls and the full ones, disappeared, only to return with thick steaks, mounds of biscuits, ears of corn, boiled potatoes, and slices of watermelon. These, both Texians and The People enjoyed.

"Dessert, gentlemen?" the head waiter asked. "Brandy? Port? Coffee?"

Faces of the cattlemen turned toward Quanah, who wiped his fingers on his trousers, and said: "Full."

"Just brandy for us," Captain Hall said.

"I'll have a port, if you don't mind," Dan Waggoner interrupted.

The waiter snapped his fingers, and looked at Quanah. "Anything for you gentlemen? We have a wonderful strawberry rhubarb pie."

No answer.

"Very well," the man said, and turned.

"Ice cream."

Daniel looked across the table at Yellow Bear. "Ice cream," he repeated, and when the cattlemen began to laugh, the waiter joined them.

"Do you have ice cream, Stephen?" Captain Hall asked.

"I'm afraid not, sir."

"Run on over to the Queen City and fetch a gallon," Burk Burnett ordered, and the waiter nodded before scurrying back to the kitchen.

"Well, Quanah," Captain Hall said. "I guess we should get down to business."

"We need all of The Big Pasture," Captain

75

Hall was saying. "All of it. Every blade of grass."

Quanah spoke, and Daniel translated. "He asks if you know the size of The Big Pasture."

"Three hundred thousand acres," the red-headed *taibo* said immediately. "I know exactly how big it is. And how much we need. Burk here has ten thousand head of Durhams and Herefords alone. I have half that, longhorns, and Dan here a little less than half. We've had some dry years. Your pasture can support our beef, and we'll pay you handsomely for it."

Daniel translated. He felt uncomfortable, seeing the eyes of Isa-tai, Charles Flint, and Nagwee boring into him. Only Yellow Bear seemed to have no interest, working his spoon like a shovel in the gallon container of butter pecan ice cream.

Quanah leaned toward Daniel, whispering, although Daniel felt certain that none of the ranchers could speak a smidgen of Comanche.

"It is much land."

"Yes, *Tsu Kuh Puah,* it is."

"They have never requested so much land."

"They are Texians. It was only a matter of time."

76

Quanah smiled, started to straighten, then leaned back. "What is this Dur-ham and . . . ?" He could not form the word on his tongue.

"Some kind of *taibo* cattle," Daniel answered. "Not the ones with the long horns."

Quanah grunted. Now he sat straight, looked across the table at Captain Hall, and asked in English: "How much?"

"The board of directors has authorized me to pay you and your tribe three cents an acre."

Burk Burnett put in: "At three hundred thousand acres, that's. . . ."

Charles Flint cut him off: "Nine thousand dollars."

"Nine thou-sand dol-lars." Quanah's head bobbed. "Much money."

"Much money indeed," Captain Hall said, and pulled out several papers from the inside pocket of his coat. "Now, if you'll. . . ."

"But not enough," Quanah said.

Daniel grinned.

Captain Hall's face tightened. The papers were shoved back inside the pocket. "How much were you thinking?" Hall's voice no longer sounded smooth.

"Twelve cents."

"Christ!" Dan Waggoner's glass hit the

77

table so hard that the stem broke, and red wine stained the white lace cloth.

Quanah spoke again, and Daniel translated. "Twelve cents for only half The Big Pasture. The People have many horses that need grass, too."

"Unacceptable."

Silence — except for Yellow Bear's slurping of the now-melted ice cream.

"Give them four cents, Red," Burk Burnett said.

"Daniel," Charles Flint said, "that's twelve thousand dollars. That'll buy a lot of food and stores for our people."

Captain Hall's eyes locked on Daniel's, not Quanah's. "You heard the man."

So had Quanah. He held up both hands, extending all fingers.

Hall's head shook. "Ten cents! I'm not a fool, nor am I as rich as the Grand Duke of Prussia. I'm a cow-poor Texian. Four and a half."

"We go now." Quanah pushed out of his chair.

CHAPTER SIX

"Wait!" His face ashen, Burk Burnett gripped the table, as if he needed support. While Quanah remained standing, his face unreadable, Burnett turned to Captain Hall. "I need that grass, Red. Hell's fire, we all do."

Daniel hid his smile. These cattlemen weren't the first *taibos* who had underestimated Quanah Parker.

"Six cents. But we need all of The Big Pasture." A bead of sweat rolled down the captain's forehead. Hall and Burnett looked nervous. Still holding his broken wine glass, Dan Waggoner appeared angry.

"Seven." Quanah remained standing.

Burnett let out a heavy sigh. Waggoner released the wine glass, and clenched his fists. Captain Hall ran his fingers across his mustache, smoothing it, eyes studying Quanah.

"I can't go that high, Quanah." Despera-

79

tion accented the Ranger's voice. "And that's the God's honest truth. It would bust Burk, bust me, bust the entire association."

"Then how you say . . . ?" Quanah looked again to Daniel for help.

"Six and a half?" Daniel asked.

The Texans glanced at each other. "No," Dan Waggoner said, but Daniel read something else in the eyes of Captain Hall and Burk Burnett.

Turning back to Quanah, Burnett asked hopefully: "For all of the pasture?"

Daniel didn't need to translate. "Big Pasture only."

Quanah's head bobbed. "Other pastures need for Comanche ponies."

The captain's facial muscles relaxed, and he found a handkerchief in his vest pocket, and wiped perspiration off his forehead. Once he had returned the white square of cotton, he lifted his brandy, took a sip, and started to say something, but what came out was: "Aw, hell."

His gaze went past Quanah and Daniel, and Dan Waggoner rose, mumbling: "What the hell is he doing here?"

Hearing the footsteps, Daniel turned in his chair.

A powerfully built *Tejano* strode toward the dining table, spurs chiming as his big feet clopped on the floor. Thick beard stubble and a giant, unkempt mustache hid much of his face, but Daniel could see the glare in the man's dark eyes, the crooked nose, the missing tip of his left ear. His jaw worked like a piston on the thick wad of tobacco in one of his cheeks, and, when he stopped, he spit out a river of tobacco juice that landed between Captain Hall's polished boots, ignoring the cuspidor next to the table.

The former Ranger's face flushed, but Burnett cautioned him: "Easy does it, Red."

Satisfaction replaced the anger in the newcomer's eyes.

"What are you doing here, Carmody?" Captain Hall asked, his voice unpleasant.

"I got me an invitation." The big man hooked his thumbs in the belt of his battered, dust-caked, cow-hide leggings, between grimy leather work gloves he had shoved behind the leather. He wore a wide-brimmed, beaten-all-to-hell hat, maybe gray, maybe white, maybe darker and just caked with dirt, dust, and sweat stains. A frayed, green calico bandanna hung around his neck, and huge muscles strained against the thin blue cotton of his shirt. His chest resembled a rain barrel, his neck, the back blistered red, might have been larger than

Daniel's own head.

"You are not a member of the Northern Texas Stock Growers' Association," Burk Burnett told him.

That, Daniel could believe. He didn't look much like a wealthy pale-eyes cattleman, but a working cowhand, though bigger than any thirty-a-month cowboy Daniel had ever seen.

"Get the hell out of here, Sol," Dan Waggoner said. "We've rented this dining room and are conducting business."

Sol Carmody shifted the tobacco into the other cheek. "Told y'all I got me an invite. And I got business here, too. Ain't that right, Chief?"

He was looking between Quanah, still standing, and Daniel. Daniel turned as Isa-tai rose from his chair, and began speaking in the language of The People. Out of the corner of his eye, Daniel saw Quanah's fingers ball into fists.

"This *taibo*," Isa-tai said, tilting his jaw at Sol Carmody, "already feeds his *pimoró* on the grass of The People, on what you call The Big Pasture."

"That he cannot do!" Quanah barked. "Tell him to remove his longhorns."

That's when the memory struck Daniel. Ben Buffalo Bone saying, around ration day,

82

that Agent Biggers was sending him to The Big Pasture, that someone had seen long-horn cattle eating grass there. Merely strays, they had figured, and Daniel, busy with the work of cleaning up the pens after rations had been issued and cattle butchered, and his mind preoccupied with thoughts of his trip to Fort Worth, had not thought to ask Ben Buffalo Bone about the matter. Following the ways of The People, Ben Buffalo Bone had not volunteered any information.

"No." Isa-tai grinned.

"He cannot feed his cattle on *Nermernuh* grass. Not without permission."

"He has my permission." Isa-tai leaned forward. "You said the grass belongs to The People, Quanah. You are just angry that you will not get rich."

"I do not do this for my own profit. I do this for the good of The People."

"Bah." Isa-tai waved his hand in dismissal. "Look at you and your shiny stickpin, your *taibo* clothes. You are the one who travels by the iron horse to Washington City. To Texas. You are the one these men . . ." — he spit on the table — "built that fancy *taibo* house for. I live in a teepee, not a pale-eyes contraption. You are the one the Pale Eyes have proclaimed the chief of The People, when you very well know that among *Nerm-*

83

ernuh, there is no one leader. You are greedy, Quanah. Greedy for power and the riches you think these *taibo* snakes will give you."

Quanah took a step, stopped himself, and Daniel knew why. He would not let any *Tejanos* see two leaders of The People fight each other.

"These *taibos* cannot lease till Car-mo-dy is gone." Isa-tai put his hands on his hips. "And he will not leave. This is my victory, Quanah Parker."

"Killstraight?"

Daniel faced Captain Hall.

"What's this all about? What are they saying?"

The big Texian answered before Daniel could think of the right words. "Ol' Isa-tai here's been tellin' Chief Parker the way things is." Sol Carmody spit again, this time into the brass cuspidor, then wiped his lips and mustache with the sleeve of his stained shirt. "I got three thousand head eatin' that fine green grass on the reservation, boys. All that grass, nigh a half-million acres, for my little ol' herd. And you boys say I ain't fit to belong to your cattle king's association."

"We need that grass, Carmody!" Dan Waggoner shouted.

"Well, so do I!" Sol Carmody's voice thundered across the practically empty dining room. "And I got it."

"We'll have the Army drive you off, you son-of-a- . . . ."

"Watch it, Waggoner. I'm bigger than you, and ain't one to abide no insults. You think you can drive me off, you try it. I'll have forty cowhands and gun hands up on the pasture by the week's end, and Isa-tai has agreed to send some of his Comanche boys out to help me protect my herd. It ain't Quanah's pasture, boys. It's all of the Comanches, and Isa-tai, he's Comanch'. I got me a deal with Isa-tai. Ain't that the way y'all work, Kill . . . what the hell did he call you, boy?"

"Killstraight," Daniel answered without meaning to.

Carmody sniggered at the name. "Well, I reckon my business here is complete." He tipped his hat, and walked out of the dining room, whistling.

Voices exploded from every direction. Daniel couldn't catch what Nagwee was telling Quanah, who pointed a finger across the table at Isa-tai and spit out words, most of them unintelligible. Captain Hall was saying something about a judge named Starr, Burnett had bellowed the name of the commanding officer at Fort Still, and Waggoner sang curses at both the now-departed Sol Carmody and the grinning Isa-tai. Yellow Bear told Quanah and Isa-tai to settle down. Only Daniel and Charles Flint remained silent.

"Killstraight!"

Again Daniel faced Captain Hall.

"We need that grass. All of it. You get Carmody's tick-infested cows off our range."

Not your range, Daniel thought, but held his temper.

Suddenly Charles Flint spoke: "Isn't it possible that you could share the pasture with that man, Carmody? He has three thousand head, but we have much grass."

Isa-tai glared at his son, although Daniel was certain the *puhakat* did not understand much English.

"We won't share one blade of grass with the likes of Sol Carmody," Burnett said.

Which was the answer Daniel expected from a Texian. They were all crazy, and all greedy.

Waggoner roared: "My beefs'll starve if we don't get that pasture, boy!"

"Shut up, Dan!" Hall was sweating again. He started to say something, but Daniel raised his hand.

"Let us talk among ourselves," he quietly requested.

Once the ranchers had retired into the hotel's saloon next door to the dining room, Daniel found his place in a circle on the floor. No teepee, not even a council fire, but Nagwee had brought his pipe, tamped down the tobacco, and Yellow Bear lighted it with a candle. Behind him, Daniel heard the whispers, could feel the stares of the restaurant's wait staff and cooks.

When the pipe came to Daniel, he offered it to the directions, lifted it to his mouth, and drew in the acrid smoke. The pipe, he saw, was old, fashioned from a bone from an antelope shank, then wrapped with the ligament from the back of a buffalo bull's neck, its bowl made from soapstone. No feathers. No ornamentation. It smoked quite well. As Daniel passed the pipe to Charles Flint, he remembered the story his father had told him and his mother. On the way to Adobe Walls, Isa-tai had carried his sacred pipe with him, letting each society dance every night as the warriors made their way across the Staked Plains. That pipe had been a war axe, an engraved steel bowl on top, and an ugly, killing weapon on the bottom.

Another difference struck Daniel. The pipe he had just smoked was simple yet elegant. Nagwee had likely killed the antelope himself, punched out the marrow, smoothed and pared the end. He would have gathered the white soapstone, fashioned it, dying it red with pokeberry and grease. The pipe Daniel's father had told him about, the one that had belonged to Isa-tai, had not been traditional. Oh, Isa-tai had probably carved out the wood, but the pipe-axe end had undoubtedly been bought from a Comanchero, or stolen from a trader.

As the pipe passed from Comanche to Comanche, Nagwee prayed until the pipe returned to him.

After a respectful silence, Yellow Bear rose. "This is a hard thing," he said. "I do not like the taste of pale-eyes beef, but, with the buffalo all gone, it is better than the pig meat. Pigs are not clean. I would rather eat grasshopper. I do not understand the ways of the Pale Eyes. But they want to pay us money for grass. Grass that grows free. In the old days, which were not that long ago, we would not pay for grass. If there was grass, and it belonged to our enemy, we would take it." He pounded a fist into his open palm. "I do not need pale-eyes money. I have two wives, thirty-nine horses, but

88

four are mares and will foal in two, three moons. I have many grandchildren. Quanah is a good husband to one of my daughters. He was a great warrior, a leader of the Kwahadi. My eyes are no good. His are strong. He sees far. He sees what we must do to work with, and live with, those who once were our enemies. I do not like the Pale Eyes. Except their ice cream. I like Quanah. He does what is best for The People. We should listen to him."

He sat. Daniel nodded in agreement, saw Isa-tai's black eyes boring into him, could feel the *puhakat*'s anger, then realized that Isa-tai was not looking at him, but at his son Charles Flint.

In the tradition of The People, the men remained silent, considering the words Yellow Bear had spoken. Nagwee looked at Daniel, who realized it was his turn to speak. He shook his head. Charles Flint also declined to speak.

It was Quanah's turn. He stood.

"Yellow Bear is a wise man," he said. "I have always listened to him, respected his opinion, even when we disagree. I am glad we do not disagree now. This paying for grass for pale-eyes beef is a subject as foreign to us as the god the Black Robes pray to, as trying to understand the ways of the Mexicans. I am *Nermernuh.* We are all *Nermernuh.* But we live with *taibos.* We must understand *taibos.* The Pale Eyes, these *Te-janos* with their many heads of cattle, they believe in money. Money is what buys our shirts. It buys our hats. Yes, these are clothes of the Pale Eyes, the *Tejanos,* but it also buys us coffee and sugar and blankets for when the north wind blows angrily. These ranchers have offered us six and a half cents an acre for three hundred thousand acres. I must ask the son of Isa-tai to tell us how much money that would mean."

Charles Flint cleared his throat. Avoiding the stare of his father, he withdrew a pencil and note pad from his coat pocket. "I have. . . ." He smiled shyly. "I can't do that ciphering in my head." He worked, scratched the eraser in his hair, pressed the lead point, nodded, said: "Nineteen thousand five hundred dollars."

A snort sounded, and Isa-tai turned his head to spit. His head shook, and he mumbled something that Daniel could not catch. Rude. Daniel could not believe a *pu-hakat* like Isa-tai would be so disrespectful. One did not interrupt any speaker during a council. Ever.

After thanking Daniel, Quanah continued. "Nineteen thousand five hundred. That is

90

much." He removed his hat and held it toward the others. "This I bought at the store where Tetecae works for the *taibos*." He used Flint's *Nermernuh* name. "It cost me one dollar and fifty cents, and it is a fine hat. Imagine how much nineteen thousand five hundred dollars could buy for all of The People. It could fill the bellies of our children, our grandchildren. It could keep our wives warm. That is how much the cattlemen I have spoken to will pay. I have not heard from Isa-tai how much his friend will give The People."

There was no time to consider Quanah's words. Isa-tai shot to his feet the moment Quanah sat and crossed his legs.

CHAPTER SEVEN

"What I have done, what I will do, what I do now, I do to protect The People," Isa-tai said. "My people. This Pale Eyes, Car-mo-dy, he will not pay as much as those friends of Quanah *Par-ker.*"

Charles Flint's father stressed the name Quanah had adopted, the *taibo* surname name that had been his mother's, a white girl taken captive during The People's raid in the pale-eyes year of 1836. Daniel looked into the faces of the older men, wondering how they would react, but trying to read any emotion in the face of a *puhakat,* or any Comanche, for that matter, always proved fruitless.

"That is true," Isa-tai continued. "I, however, do not believe that we should let any *taibo* feed any of his poor cows on grass that belongs to The People. It is not right. That is why I let Car-mo-dy bring his cows. To stop Quanah *Par-ker.*"

Daniel's head already hurt, and he decided against trying to figure out Isa-tai's logic. Instead, he just watched and listened as the *puhakat* paced around the circle as he spoke, waving his arms, his voice rising, his face animated. When he stopped in front of his son, Isa-tai extended his right arm and pointed directly at Quanah.

"See this man. He has become a *taibo*. Look at him. Look at his fancy clothes, his pale-eyes hat. He has even taken the name of a Pale Eyes. No longer do we know him as Fragrance. He has become Quanah *Parker*. He lives in a pale-eyes house built for him by Pale Eyes. He has learned to speak some of the tongue of the Pale Eyes. On this very afternoon, he goes into that big house and buys those Pale-Eyes clothes. That cloak, and what they call that dol-man. Bah!"

Now his left arm pointed at Charles Flint, then swept toward Daniel.

"They give my son and this son of a brave warrior the names of Pale Eyes, and this was done with the blessing of Quanah Parker. I do not call them by those names. My son is Tetecae, and this one will always be His Arrows Fly Straight Into The Hearts Of His Enemies. Good *Nermernuh* names." He touched the front of his buckskin shirt, and let his fingers stream through the blue-dyed fringe. "I do not wear the clothes of the Pale Eyes. I am *Nermernuh*. I will always be *Nermernuh*."

Walking again, flailing his arms, his voice reverberating across the practically empty dining room.

"This Car-mo-dy will pay me two hundred and fifty dollars to let his cattle eat The People's grass. I do not know how much money that is. I do not care. I care not for pale-eyes paper. I judge my wealth by the number of my horses, by the scalps I have taken in battle, by the coup I have counted. This Car-mo-dy, he will also pay *Nermernuh* boys to help guard his cattle. This will put ten dollars a moon into the hands of those who wish to work for this Car-mo-dy."

Now he stopped. "But this is not the way of The People. Once, we stole horses from the Mexicans, and *Tejanos,* and the foolish travelers to the north of us. We stole horses from all of our enemies. This was the way of The People. It was a good way. We will steal this man's Car-mo-dy's cattle for ourselves. They are not fit to eat grass that belongs to The People. I am like Yellow Bear. I do not care for the taste of *pimoró. Cuhtz* is what a warrior, a *puhakat,* should eat, but the Pale

94

Eyes do not let us hunt the buffalo any more. They treat us like women. Like children. I will show these Pale Eyes that we are men. We are men who will not be tamed, that we will not become Pale Eyes."

He sat down, folded his arms, glared across the room at Quanah, who bowed his head, considering the words Isa-tai had spoken, but waiting for someone else to speak.

The words came from Nagwee: "If you steal or kill the *taibo* cattle, the Long Knives will arrest you."

"They will try," Isa-tai said, still looking at Quanah.

"I," Yellow Bear said, "would like to hear words from that one."

Daniel swallowed. The father-in-law of Quanah was pointing at him.

"I. . . ." Daniel could not summon any words.

"Rise and speak, His Arrows Fly Straight Into The Hearts Of His Enemies," Nagwee said. "Yellow Bear is right. We are old men. We do not understand the ways of the Pale Eyes. You have lived among them. You speak their tongue. Yet you also protect The People. You are a good Metal Shirt. This I know. You once arrested my son after he had drunk too much of the bad whiskey the

Creeks bring to our land. That was a good thing. My son could have hurt someone, could have hurt himself. Rise. Speak. We will not bite you, at least, not too hard. As for me, I cannot bite you at all." He pulled back his lips to reveal his missing teeth.

Laughter made its rounds across the circle. Only Isa-tai found no mirth in Nagwee's joke. Neither was Daniel exactly bemused.

That his legs supported him came as a surprise. Daniel did not attempt to walk around the circle. He cleared his throat, wet his lips, and tried to think.

"We are The People, yet we act like Pale Eyes."

Those words surprised him; indeed, they surprised everyone in the circle.

"Go on," Nagwee said.

Daniel took a deep breath, slowly exhaled, and found his courage.

"We argue over land. Land, that as we know, none of us owns. How does one own grass? It belongs to all. We fight over money. This is not something we would have done ten summers ago. I was sent, as was Tetecae, to follow the white man's road, and this was something I did not wish to do. But it is done. I am back. I try to find the right path. Sometimes I see that The Peo-

96

ple's path is the best. Yet there are times when I believe that we can learn from the road the Pale Eyes take. In this day, we must learn the white man's road, for the road of The People is becoming shorter, arduous, more difficult to travel."

He nodded respectfully at Isa-tai. "I have heard the words of Isa-tai, and know he believes in his heart" — Daniel tapped the center of his chest — "what he does is best for The People." Facing Quanah, he said softly: "Quanah has led The People in war and now in peace. His way would bring in more money for The People, not for himself. What Isa-tai proposes would lead to much trouble. I respect Isa-tai, but I do not think his plan is something The People should consider. He invites this rancher named Carmody to graze his cattle in The Big Pasture, yet at the same time he plans to steal those cattle? A lie? This is something I would expect from a *taibo*."

Shit, he thought, and even silently mouthed the pale-eyes curse he had picked up working in the coal mines in Pittsburgh. It was, he had always thought, a good word. Yet he knew comparing Isa-tai to a *taibo* was wrong. There's no worse insult to a man like Isa-tai.

He couldn't look at Isa-tai, nor could he

apologize. So he stood there, trying to think of something else to say, but his tongue had swollen, and his brain refused to give him any words. Feeling the stares, he slowly sat down and crossed his knees.

"Good." Yellow Bear's head bobbed. "He speaks well."

"And we did not have to bite him," Nag-wee added, then looked at Charles Flint. "Would you like to speak?"

With a shrug, the young bookkeeper said: "I have nothing to say."

Grunting, Isa-tai stood, pointing at Daniel. "He Whose Arrows Fly Straight Into The Hearts Of His Enemies has become a *taibo,* too. He is no different than Quanah *Par-ker.* I no longer call him by the name his father gave him. I call him by the name he is known among the *taibo. Kill-straight.*" He spit, and sat down, but wasn't finished talking. "He disgraces The People with his words, and with his actions. Metal Shirt. *Bah!*"

Anger flushed Daniel's face. When he glanced at his hands, he realized his fists were clenched so tightly they shook. After sucking in air, he slowly exhaled, did it again, and again, waiting for the temper, that strong Comanche temper, to subside. Looking up, he saw Yellow Bear pushing

98

himself to his feet.

"You speak of disgrace, Isa-tai," the old man said. "You say Quanah and this young one have disgraced us. You say they have betrayed The People." His voice was steady, but Daniel could feel the temper, the tension. "Should I bring up your disgrace, Isa-tai?"

The *puhakat* did not wait for Yellow Bear to finish. Shooting lithely to his feet, Isa-tai roared in defiance: "I have heard those insults since that day. I do not have to defend myself, old man. It was that fool warrior of the *Paganavo*." Meaning the Cheyenne, who The People knew as Striped Arrows. "When that idiot killed a skunk, he destroyed my *puha* for the entire raid. If that Cheyenne had listened, had followed my instructions, we would not have been defeated by those *Tejanos* with the far-killing rifles."

Yellow Bear simply stared, his black eyes like buckshot. "That is not the disgrace I refer to," he said bluntly, and sat down again.

"*Puha?*" Nagwee, still sitting, suddenly sniggered. "What *puha?*"

"You are old men," Isa-tai said. "I do not stand here to be insulted by old men, one whose belly is full not of buffalo, but a pale-

99

eyes sweet thing that is so cold it hurts one's teeth." Now, he sat down, and the floor was open.

It stayed that way, too, for five minutes, maybe longer, until Quanah rose one more time.

"We should not quarrel amongst ourselves. Not when the Pale Eyes can see us, hear us. On this matter, we will speak no more while in the land of the *Tejanos.* When we return to our country, then we will hold a council. Yet I have heard enough. Carmody will remove his cattle from The Big Pasture, and even if The People say that I am wrong, that Carmody's cattle should stay, we will not steal those cows." He glared at Isa-tai. "Not if you have invited him, Isa-tai. We do not lie. Not to ourselves. Not to *Tejanos.* We have not become that much like Pale Eyes."

No one else spoke, and, of that, Daniel was glad.

They gathered their belongings, and left the dining room, letting the waiters and cooks and the tall one with the thin mustache who Captain Hall had called a maître d' stare at their backs as they went through the door and stepped into the hotel's immaculate lobby.

More stares found them there, and all of

the Comanches stopped except for Isa-tai, who strode through the doors and stepped outside onto the boardwalk in front of Rusk Street.

Charles Flint started after his father, but Yellow Bear stopped him.

"Let him go."

Flint turned. "He is my father," he said, "and cannot find the Pickwick, I mean, the apartments near that hotel."

"Go, Tetecae," Quanah said. "Go with your father."

Charles Flint walked out the door.

"Well, Quanah?" The question came from Captain Hall, backed by the ranchers Waggoner and Burnett, and some other *Tejano* wearing a dusty, high-brimmed hat, wiry mustache, and goatee.

"We sign no papers," Quanah said in English. "We talk more on reservation. But I think your beef will eat our grass."

None of the cattlemen cared much for that answer.

"We can't wait long, Quanah," Burnett said.

Quanah's head bobbed, but he said nothing.

"Red," Burk Burnett said, suddenly grinning, "I'm a man of faith, and I believe in Quanah Parker. Everything'll work out.

We'll put Carmody in his place, our beefs'll get fat on Comanche grass, and the Comanches will have a lot of our coin to spend."

"I hope you're right, Burk," Waggoner said.

"I'm always right, Dan."

The smiles looked as forced as the silence, but when Yellow Bear said — "Ice cream." — the laughter that followed was real.

"All right, Chief," Captain Hall said, putting his right arm around Yellow Bear's shoulder. "Let's get you over to the Queen City. I don't think Missus Connor would have closed up yet, not as hot as tonight is."

So Captain Hall and Burk Burnett led the procession to the Queen City Ice Cream Parlor, where they were soon joined by Charles Flint, who said his father had retired to the room for the night at the Taylor & Barr building. Daniel, Flint, Yellow Bear, and the cowboy — who Dan Waggoner introduced as his *segundo,* George Briggs — were the only ones to partake in Mrs. Connor's butter pecan ice cream. The ranchers, Nagwee, and Quanah smoked cigars, with Burnett and Hall sipping coffee.

Yellow Bear lifted his bowl to his mouth, tilted it, and slurped, producing more grins on the faces of the *Tejanos.* Even Quanah, lowering his cigar, shook his head and laughed.

"Is it that good?" he asked in Comanche.

Yellow Bear nodded, and the bowl rattled on the table.

A loud ticking drew Daniel's attention, and he saw that Captain Hall had drawn a gold watch on a heavy chain from his vest pocket. "It's getting late. Been a long day."

Quanah nodded. "We go," he said in English.

Which suited Daniel, but not Yellow Bear.

"I want to see more of this *taibo* city," he said. "I am an old man. I want to see what else these Pale Eyes offer."

After Daniel translated, the cowhand, George Briggs, slapped his thigh. "Hell's bells, I'd be right proud to tree this town with a man like you." He glanced at his boss. "Be able to tell my grandkids that I once treed Cowtown with a renegade Comanch'."

More laughter, and Quanah rose. "I go my way. To bed. You go yours. Don't wake me up."

"I'm going with you," Daniel said, and stood beside Quanah.

"We'll meet you tomorrow in the lobby of the Pickwick Hotel and go eat some breakfast," Captain Hall said. "Say, seven o'clock?"

Quanah grunted.

"My stomach hurts," Nagwee said. "I will go with you. Sleep. Feel better."

Daniel looked at Flint.

"I've got to get the post books in order. I promised Mister McEveety I'd get that done while I was here. So I guess. . . ."

Yellow Bear grunted. "My *Nermernuh* friends are women."

Daniel tried to fight down his smile, and Charles Flint shook his head. "All right, *Tsu Kuh Puah,*" he said. "I will go with you. But just for a little while."

Chapter Eight

Church bells, chiming in the distance, woke him. Daniel swung out of bed, and rubbed his stiff, aching neck. He remembered waking up in the parlor chair, stumbling back to bed, still sweating. Even now, he felt damp and hot.

"This time of year, Fort Worth," he remembered overhearing someone say last night, "would make a good hell."

Again, he moved to the open window, sticking his head out, hoping to catch a cool breeze, only to feel no wind at all, just rank dampness and morning heat. With a sigh, he went back to the dresser, poured the last of the water from the pitcher into a bowl, and washed his face, his neck, under his armpits, and across his chest.

Already 7:00 A.M., the Progressor told him. He had overslept, if he could call how he had spent the night "sleeping." After drying his body, he opened the valise.

Who should I dress like today? he thought. *Nermernuh or Pale Eyes?* He grinned. *Or Mescalero?*

In the end, he went as he usually dressed, part The People (from the waist down), part *taibo* (waist up): moccasins and buckskin britches, red calico shirt, and the gray coat he had turned into a vest. He grabbed the wide-brimmed, open-crowned black hat and his room key, and hurried out the door.

What he saw across the hall stopped him. The door was cracked open, but the clerk at the Pickwick Hotel had said nobody was staying there. Curious, maybe even suspicious, Daniel stepped to the door and listened. The hinges creaked as he pushed it open. The covers were pushed back, the window open, and the room smelled of pipe smoke, but nobody was in. No grip. Nothing.

Feeling silly, he shook his head. Likely somebody checked in late in the night, and the clerk had sent him here. A drummer, already gone. Up early to make his sales.

Up early, Daniel thought, *and I'm late.*

He raced to the stairwell.

"I thought you Comanches got up with the sun," Burk Burnett said lightly, and extended his hand to Daniel.

"Only during a raidin' moon," the cow-hand, George Briggs, said, chuckling, then spit tobacco juice into the street as Daniel shook hands with the rancher.

They had gathered in front of a coffee house on Houston Street — Burnett, Briggs, Waggoner, Charles Flint, and Nagwee. Isatai sat cross-legged near a hitching rail, away from the others. Moments later School Father Pratt and Captain Hall stepped through the doorway of the coffee house, holding steaming cups.

After Daniel shook hands with Pratt, he stepped off the boardwalk, and looked toward the Taylor & Barr building.

"Nobody gets up early in Hell's Half Acre," Pratt said.

He was right. Last night, or rather early this morning, the streets had been bustling with activity. Daniel remembered the drunken cowboy stumbling out of the alley toward the Tivoli Hall. He could still hear the cacophony of voices, the music, the laughter, the horses, the curses of the policeman. Now, as he looked across the street, the Tivoli looked worn-out, deserted. The hitching rails were all empty. So was Houston Street, except for a lone man with a broom, sweeping up broken glass in front of some beer hall far down the street.

"What's keeping Quanah?" Flint asked in English.

"Maybe ol' Yellow Bear," George Briggs said, shifting the quid from his left cheek to his right.

"Y'all tree the town, George?" Captain Hall blew over the rim of his coffee mug.

"Just wandered from the Club Room to the Bismarck to the El Paso and Occidental."

"You didn't get him roostered?" Waggoner asked facetiously.

"They don't serve Injuns, boss," Briggs said, and took off his hat. "And this morn', I wish they hadn't served me."

Every Pale Eyes chuckled.

"What time did you finish?" Daniel asked.

Briggs pushed his hat back. "Midnight. Early night for this ol' hoss."

Charles Flint laughed. "I was in bed long before that."

"I know," Briggs said. "You flew the coop about ten."

An hour and change after I left with Quanah, Daniel remembered. He thought again, remembering last night. He had heard a door shut down the hall, what sounded like the one to the room Quanah shared with his father-in-law, yet that had been 3:17 A.M. It had not been midnight. He studied

108

George Briggs and decided that, from the look of the *taibo*'s eyes, his memory, his concept of time, might not be trusted.

"Well, I had work to do," Flint was saying, and Daniel cut him off.

"Are you sure it was midnight?"

Briggs pushed his hat back. His bloodshot eyes locked hard on Daniel, and he reached into his vest, and withdrew a silver watch. "You see this here thing?" he said. He pressed on the stem, and the case opened. The hands were large enough that Daniel could read the time, 7:48, and the second hand was moving. "This here's an Illinois railroad watch. Ain't but ten years old, if that. It wasn't quite midnight when I taken Yellow Bear to that buildin' yonder and bid him a fine fare-thee-well. Then I wandered over to the Empress" — jutting his jaw down the street toward the man with the saloon — "for me nightcap."

"How many nightcaps, George?" Waggoner asked lightly.

"Daniel, Charles," School Father Pratt said, changing the subject, "would either of you care for coffee?"

That sounded good, but Nagwee spoke in the language of The People. "It is not like Quanah or Yellow Bear to sleep after the sun has risen."

"No, it isn't," Daniel said in English, and moved down the boardwalk, back toward the Taylor & Barr mercantile. Charles Flint caught up with him, and boot steps told Daniel they had pale-eyes company.

"You don't think anything's wrong?" Flint asked.

Daniel's head shook. He didn't. Oh, maybe Yellow Bear had eaten too much ice cream, or he was plumb tuckered out from wandering the saloons with George Briggs. Yesterday had been a tiring day. Maybe Quanah was exhausted, too. Daniel could have slept another three or four hours himself.

He looked back, found School Father Pratt and Burk Burnett walking behind them, concern disfiguring their faces. Back down the boardwalk, Dan Waggoner stood talking to George Briggs, while Nagwee was standing, arms folded across his chest, staring. Isa-tai remained sitting, face hard, not moving. He hadn't moved since Daniel had arrived, had barely even blinked.

Daniel and the others reached the outside staircase of the Taylor & Barr building. He took the steps two at a time until he reached the second landing, opened the outer door, and ran down the hallway. Once he had stopped, he could hear footsteps following

110

him up. He knocked gently on the frame.

"Ahó," he called softly, then louder. His knuckles struck the door, harder. *"Ahó! Tsu Kuh Puah!"* Now, he struck the door with his fist, and shouted the names of Quanah and Yellow Bear.

Charles Flint stood beside him, echoing his shouts. Gripping the handle, he turned the knob, pressed his weight against the door, pushed. "It is locked," he said.

He struck the door again.

"Quiet!" Pratt tried the door, but Flint was right. The door was locked. The School Father pressed his ear against the door, and spoke: "Quanah? Yellow Bear."

Sounds drew his attention. Daniel looked, saw that Briggs, Waggoner, and Nagwee had decided to come, too. Another figure came through the doorway, and Daniel straightened. Isa-tai.

"Could they have gone somewhere?" Pratt asked.

"Where would they go?" Flint replied. He hit the door with his fist.

George Briggs was rolling a cigarette — the chaw of tobacco gone from his cheek.

The men stopped when Pratt kicked the door, screaming Quanah's name.

"The clerk." Flint whirled. "The clerk. He will have another key. I will go."

"No time for that." Pratt stepped back.

"For the love of God, man," Burk Burnett said. "What are you doing?"

The School Father did not answer. Bending his leg, he slammed his boot just under the doorknob. Wood splintered and cracked.

"Jesus!" Dan Waggoner shouted down the hallway. "What the hell's up?"

The door swung into the room, banged against the wall.

Daniel stepped inside, tripped, landed on the rug. He rolled over, and gasped. Next to the bed, Quanah lay face down on the hardwood floor, his head turned toward the door. When School Father Pratt had kicked open the door, the door had just missed striking Quanah's face. Daniel had tripped over the great warrior's outstretched left arm.

Already Pratt was kneeling beside Quanah, lifting his wrist, feeling for a pulse. Charles Flint ran to the bed, yelling Yellow Bear's name. Gripping the footboard of the bed, Daniel pulled himself to his feet.

"Yellow Bear. . . ." Flint tugged at the sleeping *puhakat*'s sleeve. "It is I, Tetecae. Wake up, *Tsu Kuh Puah*." Flint turned his head to the side, coughed, turned back, started to say something, but coughed again.

Daniel coughed, too. Suddenly light-

112

headed, he gripped the footboard for support, tried to lean over, tried to say something. He filled his lungs, and the cough doubled him over.

"Criminy." School Father Pratt went to his feet, whirled. "Burk," he cried, "tell that cowhand to put out that damned cigarette!"

"What?"

"Now!"

That's when Daniel understood. Pratt lurched for the lamp on one side of the bed. Putting an arm over his nose, Daniel moved to the other. He found the knob, turned it down, stopping the flow of gas. Across the bed, School Father Pratt nodded, then pointed across the apartment room.

"The window," Pratt said, then coughed, shook his head. "Open the window. Get some fresh air in here."

Daniel hurried, almost tripped again on the rug. He found the latch, pulled it, shoved the window open, leaned out, filled his lungs with fresh air. Below, on the streets, he saw Captain Hall chatting with a man in a plaid suit and gray hat. Unaware of what was happening upstairs.

He turned back, saw the other rancher, Waggoner, grabbing Quanah's bare feet. Burnett had long arms. They lifted, took Quanah. Nagwee barked something in the language of The People, but the two *Tejanos* could not understand.

"Take him to his room," Daniel translated. "Across the hall."

Pratt waved a pillow over the bed, circulating the air, forcing the poisonous gas out. He looked up, found Waggoner's *segundo*, George Briggs. Isa-tai was in the room now, too, standing beside the torn door, arms folded, staring, his face a mask of indifference.

"Briggs," Pratt said. "Fetch a doctor. Quick."

"What happened?" the cowhand asked.

"Must have. . . ." Pratt had to stop for a breath of air. "Must have blown out the lamps." He turned back to Yellow Bear.

"Holy Mother of God." The cowboy took off, running at an awkward gait, spurs singing a song as he raced down the hallway.

"We must get out of this room. Till that gas has cleared." Pratt sounded like a School Father again.

"Help me then," Flint said. "Help me with Yellow Bear."

"There's no need, son."

Fifteen minutes had passed, and they had returned to the room Quanah had shared with Yellow Bear. Nagwee remained across

114

the hall with Quanah, and the Pale Eyes waited for their own doctor.

"What's keeping that damned sawbones?" Pratt said angrily. Daniel could not ever remember hearing the School Father curse.

A song filled the room. Charles Flint looked over at his father, who had closed his eyes, raised his arms to the sky, and began singing.

Daniel looked at Yellow Bear. The old man's eyes were closed as if sleeping, and Daniel turned away. Again, he leaned out the window, closing his own eyes, trying to shake the image of Yellow Bear. As he ducked back inside, something on the window caught his eye. He peered closer at a reddish smudge on the glass below the latch. Like blood. Saw the lines. Like part of a man's finger. No, thumb.

Isa-tai sang.

Daniel turned, took a step, stopped, looked back at the window. Something was wrong. But what?

"Yellow Bear! Wake up!" Flint's voice cracked. Tears streamed down his face. The bookkeeper refused to believe the School Father's statement that Yellow Bear was dead.

Daniel started for the bed, only to stop again. He looked beyond Isa-tai and at the door, then to the small table next to a parlor chair. Quanah's coat draped the chair, and the table overflowed with Yellow Bear's clothes. Quanah's tie, even his diamond stickpin, lay on the dresser beside the water pitcher. He looked again at the table. There was the brass room key, on top of Yellow Bear's bone breastplate. Again, he looked at the door, then turned back toward the window.

Isa-tai sang, and soon his voice was answered by the song from across the hall. Nagwee's voice.

Both *puhakats* singing a song for the dead.

After shaking his head clear, Daniel walked to the bed, sitting on the edge, avoiding Charles Flint's face. He reached down until his fingers rested on Yellow Bear's forehead.

He looked strange, long silver braids matted from sweat, not dressed as *Nermernuh,* but in a long, bleached muslin nightshirt, the front unbuttoned, damp with sweat. Quanah wasn't the only one to have bought something downstairs in the mercantile the previous afternoon. Yellow Bear had traded an elk-horn knife for this nightshirt. A *taibo* shirt of coarse material, now stinking with sweat. It was not what a powerful *puhakat* of The People should be

116

wearing when he died.

Daniel murmured his farewell.

"What's going on here?"

Daniel looked up to see a bald, sweating man holding a black hat. Behind him stood a panting George Briggs and a grim-faced Captain Hall.

"Yellow Bear's dead," Waggoner said. "Gas killed him."

"How's Quanah?" Captain Hall asked.

"I don't know," School Father Pratt said softly. "I couldn't even tell if his heart was beating. He is in the room across the hall with those two Comanche medicine men."

From the sound of Nagwee's song, Quanah was also preparing to begin his journey to The Land Beyond The Sun.

CHAPTER NINE

Asphyxiation.

A *taibo* word that held no meaning for Daniel, but that is what they said had killed Yellow Bear.

"So, the old medicine man . . . ," said a man in an ill-fitting, frayed, plaid suit, a reporter for Dallas *Herald.* "Let me get this straight. He comes to the room, in his cups, thinks the lamps are coal oil as they'd likely have up on the reservation. Not knowing they're gas, he blows them out. Goes to sleep, and the gas does its dirty work. Poor bastard just never woke up."

"That's what it looks like," Captain Hall said.

"Except," School Father Pratt added, "Yellow Bear definitely was not in his cups."

The man in the plaid suit winked. "He will be in our newspaper, Capt'n. Anything the Dallas press can do to make Fort Worth look bad, we'll do it, sir." He laughed, but, when nobody joined in, he grimaced, swallowed, and said meekly: " 'Course, Yellow Bear just made an honest mistake. Pity. I liked the ol' boy."

Their talk continued, but Daniel did not, would not listen. They had taken hacks to a restaurant on Bluff Street — Pratt and Hall, Daniel and Flint — to get away from the horde of newspaper reporters who had gathered at the Pickwick Hotel and Taylor & Barr mercantile.

"Gathered," Burk Burnett had said, "for the deathwatch."

Burnett had stayed behind. Isa-tai and Nagwee remained upstairs in the Taylor & Barr apartment, attending to Quanah with the Fort Worth doctor, an old man named Stallings whose breath, even at 8:00 A.M., reeked of rye whiskey. Daniel wished the pale-eyes sawbones was Major Becker — he trusted that bluecoat — but Becker was up at Fort Sill in Indian Territory. This reporter — Daniel glanced at the Old Glory writing tablet he had bought at the mercantile, saw where he had scribbled the ink-slinger's name, Kyne — had been enterprising enough to follow them to the café near the Trinity River.

The food smelled like the river, too.

"Best eat, Daniel." School Father Pratt's

119

voice was soothing, not scolding. "You too, Charles. You'll need your strength."

Glancing at the bowl of chili, Daniel lifted his spoon, and dug into the bowl of brown meat and grease, which reminded him of the mud on the streets at the edge of town. He left the spoon in the bowl, and stared out the window.

That was something he could never get used to, the way these Pale Eyes ate. The People were not used to having a noon meal. They would serve food on the flesh side of a dried hide, eating in the morning, in the evening. Rarely would they eat what the Pale Eyes called dinner. Oh, sure, if one got hungry, he could help himself to food in the day, pemmican maybe, or some dried beef. On the other hand, Daniel had not had breakfast that morning, not even coffee. Yet he couldn't eat. Not now. Not with Quanah back in that stifling room above the mercantile. Likely dying.

"Doc Stallings said Quanah Parker was in a coma?" the reporter, Kyne, asked.

No one answered, but that's what the frowning Dr. Stallings had said. When asked by reporters about Quanah's chances of recovery, the doctor had slowly, grimly said: "It is not good. Not good at all."

"What a shame." Kyne shook his head,

pulled a nickel flask from his coat pocket, and began to unscrew the top. "I liked that ol' boy, too."

Back in his room above the Taylor & Barr mercantile, Daniel leaned out the window, and drew in a lungful of fresh air. Well, as fresh as air could be in a dirty, cramped, and now noisy *taibo* city. The Progressor clock told him it was 4:37, and Hell's Half Acre had begun to come alive again. Above the sonance of Cowtown — clopping of hoofs, jingle of traces, plodding of feet down the boardwalk, the voices, laughter, and beginnings of music — the sound from across the hallway reached Daniel.

A song from Isa-tai. The shaking of a gourd rattle by Nagwee.

Stallings, the drunken doctor, had announced to the newspapermen in the lobby of the Pickwick Hotel that he had done all he could for Quanah Parker, that his recovery or demise lay in the hands of God, not medicine. The *taibos* had accepted that, but the two *puhakats* of The People would not give up so easily.

Daniel stepped back toward the pitcher and basin on the dresser, stopped, turned, looked back at the window.

Quickly he picked up his hat, strode

through the door, and walked down the hall to the room Quanah and Yellow Bear had shared. He pushed open the door, still broken from School Father Pratt's kick, and stepped inside.

Pratt and Burk Burnett had arranged for Yellow Bear's body to be taken to a funeral parlor to be prepared for burial. Daniel hadn't liked that at all, but he had kept his mouth shut. The Pale Eyes would put Yellow Bear in a wooden box, plant him in a cemetery. Burnett had promised it would be a fine funeral, with the best preacher Fort Worth had to offer. He had said a crowd of mourners would fill the church. They'd give Yellow Bear a great send-off.

Pale Eyes could not or would not understand the ways of The People. They would not sit Yellow Bear down so that he was facing east, to begin the journey to join his ancestors. Back home, along Cache Creek, Yellow Bear's belongings would be burned. Daniel regretted that they had traveled by train. Else, they could have killed one of Yellow Bear's best ponies to carry him to The Land Beyond The Sun.

Besides, what did these Pale Eyes know about mourning?

The thought stopped Daniel, and he glanced at his hands, his arms. He had forgotten, too. He should draw blood, cut a gash down his forearms. Maybe chop off his hair, or the tip of a finger. Anything to show how much he had loved Yellow Bear. That was how The People mourned. And they would never speak the name of Yellow Bear again.

Mourning would have to wait.

Refusing to look at the bed where Yellow Bear had died, or at the gas lamps that had killed him, and maybe would finally kill Quanah Parker, Daniel walked across the room. He stopped at the table. The belongings of both Yellow Bear and Quanah had been moved to the room shared by Isa-tai and Nagwee, but the brass key remained on the table. He picked it up, looked back at the door, and laid it on the table, then moved to the window.

It remained open, but Daniel pushed it shut. That's how he had found it. He knelt and studied the reddish print on the glass.

"What are you doing, kid?"

When Daniel turned, he saw Captain Lee Hall standing in the doorway, hat in one hand at his side, the other with a thumb hooked in his waistband.

Daniel closed the window all the way, and stood.

"It's a little hot, isn't it?" Captain Hall

said. "Don't you think you'd better leave that open?"

"Exactly," Daniel said, but walked away from the closed window. He stopped beside the table.

Lee Hall stepped through the doorway. His face had been curious, friendly, but the expression quickly changed. "I asked you a question. What are you doing in here?"

Daniel's fingers climbed up his vest, and he tapped the shield badge pinned on the lapel. "I am what they call a Metal Shirt. You, too, were once one."

"Meaning a Texas Ranger, that's right. I told you that already. But you best speak straight to me, Killstraight."

Daniel pointed to the lamps. "This was no accident."

Lee Hall's mouth dropped open. He started to say something, shook his head, and leaned against the wall next to the open door. He ran fingers through his red hair, swallowed, and inhaled deeply. After holding the breath, he let it out slowly, and once more shook his head.

"Son," he said, sounding much like a School Father who did not wish to scold an ignorant child, "I know this has been a terrible shock. But here's what happened . . . Quanah was asleep. Yellow Bear came back.

He dressed for bed, went to the lamps, and, tragically, thinking they were coal oil, blew them out. He went to sleep, and the gas killed him. The gas would have killed Quanah, but it looks like Yellow Bear, maybe in his death throes, kicked Quanah out of bed. Quanah must have tried for the door, but couldn't make it. The fact that his head was close to the crack between the door and floor likely saved him. Maybe. We'll see."

Daniel nodded. Yes, this Texas Ranger was a good detective. Perhaps as good as Hugh Gunter or Deputy U.S. Marshal Harvey P. Noble.

"So you see," Captain Hall said, "it was an accident."

Now Daniel shook his head. "No accident." He pointed to the window. "That's how the window was when we entered the room this morning. Only it was latched shut, too."

The former Ranger pulled on his hat. "So?"

"It was hot. Very hot. The newspaper this morning said the temperature reached one hundred and seven. Hot. It did not cool down much at night. Even the body of the one who is no more" — he wondered if Lee Hall would understand this need not to speak Yellow Bear's name — "was wet with

125

sweat when we discovered him."

"So they got hot."

"Hotter upstairs here than even downstairs. So hot I woke up in the middle of the night. After three o'clock. My window was open. Everybody's window was open. Everybody's but in this room."

Outside, a horse whinnied, followed by loud curses, and a whistle. Inside, Isa-tai sang, and Nagwee shook his gourd.

"I don't know, Killstraight. Maybe Yellow Bear had so much ice cream last night, he felt cold. He came in, closed the window, blew out the lamps. And died. An accident. Not murder."

Only now Lee Hall sounded as if he were trying to convince himself of it.

"Shortly after I woke," Daniel said, "I was leaning out the window, trying to cool off, and I heard a door open and close. This door." He pointed at the broken one the manager of the Pickwick had said he'd have to hire a carpenter to repair.

Captain Hall pointed out: "Yellow Bear coming back from his night on the town."

"According to the cowboy, Briggs," Daniel countered, "Yellow Bear was back here at midnight." He pointed at the dresser. "That clock put the time at between three-fifteen and three-thirty."

Glancing at the Progressor, Captain Hall pulled a gold watch from his vest pocket. "Then that clock's. . . ." He didn't finish. Instead, after looking at his timepiece, he slid the watch back into the pocket. "George Briggs could have been mistaken. Yellow Bear might not have been in his cups, but Briggs most definitely was."

That was one point Daniel could not dismiss.

"And another thing." Lee Hall had gathered up some steam. He pointed at the brass key. "The door was locked, wasn't it? That's why Richard had to kick open the door."

Daniel gave him a Comanche stare and let the *Tejano* Metal Shirt continue.

"Locked." Hall nodded. "That means Yellow Bear got here, locked the door, closed the window. Blew out the lamps. And died."

Daniel said nothing.

Captain Hall let out a mirthless chuckle. "I suppose you think the killer came in, locked the door behind him, blew out the lamps, crawled through the window, closed the window behind him, somehow managed to latch it shut, too. And drop, what, twenty, thirty feet, into the alley? Something like that?"

Shaking his head, Daniel picked up the key, tossed it, caught it, and held it between his fingers.

"The one who has joined his ancestors would not know what to do with this. Even I do not lock my door. Even Quanah, who lives in the Star House that you and other ranchers had built for him, he does not lock his doors. It is not the way of The People." He let the key fall back to the table.

"Then how did the door get locked?"

Daniel had been thinking about this. After they had found the door locked this morning, Flint had suggested that there would have been another key at the Pickwick Hotel, which managed the rental of the rooms above the Taylor & Barr mercantile. Daniel had stayed in enough hotels to understand that getting a key from behind the registration desk at night was not that difficult. The killer could have stolen the key, unlocked the door, blown out the gas lamps, locked the door behind him, and left the key back in its proper place.

Or there could have been another key.

Or. . . .

"One of us could have put the key on the table when we came into the room this morning? Is that right, Daniel?"

Charles Flint stepped inside, wiping his hands with a handkerchief. His tone had been far from friendly, but Daniel could not

128

deny that was his thinking.

"Everybody was in the room," Daniel said evenly. "Everybody but you, Captain Hall."

Hall straightened. "I was in here, too."

"Yes, but I had seen the key before. You had remained outside, did not come until the cowboy, Briggs, told you what was going on when he ran to get the doctor."

Hall blinked. "I could have stolen the key from the clerk at the Pickwick," he said. "Nobody really needed that key." He pointed at the one on the table.

Daniel smiled. Yes, this *taibo* was a good detective.

"Daniel," Charles Flint said as he slid the handkerchief into his trousers pocket, "who would have wanted to see Yellow Bear dead?"

Daniel grimaced. Flint had traveled the white man's road far too long, had forgotten that The People respected those who had joined their ancestors too much to speak their names among the living.

"Not him," Daniel said. He jutted his jaw toward the room across the hall where Nagwee and Isa-tai tried to bring Quanah back from death.

"Quanah?" Charles Flint stared out the door.

"Sure." Lee Hall's head bobbed in agree-

129

ment. "Yeah, we treat Quanah like royalty now, but I warrant there are plenty of folks in Fort Worth who'd like to see Quanah dead. Or any Comanch'. Your people made things rough on our settlers for a number of years. And what you did to our women. . . ."

Charles Flint bristled. "Your people made things rough on us Comanches, too."

"I won't argue that." Hall sighed. "All right. I still think this was a terrible accident. How do you prove it was murder and attempted murder?"

To that question, Daniel had no answer. He wasn't even sure where to begin.

"Who are your suspects?" Hall continued. "I think you're wrong about the killer leaving the key here this morning. None of us had reason to kill either Quanah or Yellow Bear."

Daniel tried to put this delicately. "There is the matter of The Big Pasture."

"Quanah was going to sign the lease agreement, Killstraight," Hall said. The *Tejano* did not like the accusation. "The association had no reason. . . ."

"The agreement was not signed," Daniel pointed out. "It might not have been signed. Might not be signed. And there is the other one."

"Sol Carmody? That rapscallion?" Hall

130

started to shake his head, but stopped. He whispered the name again: "Carmody."

"It is not Carmody that Daniel means," Charles Flint said. "Is it?"

Silence. Even the singing and rattling of the gourd across the hallway had stopped.

"He means my father," Flint said. "*Bávi,* you are wrong!"

Maybe. Daniel said nothing, but he intended to ask Nagwee not to leave Quanah alone with Isa-tai.

CHAPTER TEN

He had filled three pages of the Old Glory tablet, but as he reread his notes, Daniel decided what he had written added up to nothing.

The Progressor said it was 10:18. Yawning, Daniel pushed himself up, decided to check on Quanah. He opened the door, and stopped.

The door across the hall was shut. He stepped to it, put his ear against the wood, listening. Nothing from inside, though the sound from Hell's Half Acre echoed through the open windows.

"I am stupid," he said aloud, and returned to his room, grabbed his hat, two pencils, and the writing tablet, and hurried down the hall.

"If you do not leave, you will force me to call a constable and have you arrested."

The Pickwick Hotel manager's beady eyes

132

looked past Daniel toward the main door, as if hoping to summon a police officer.

"My request is not unreasonable," Daniel said again, not angrily, not pleadingly, but firmly.

"You will leave here." The manager wiped his waxed mustache, then ran a hand over his sweating pate. "I will call the police."

Daniel could feel the stares of patrons, but would not waver. "There are five rooms at the Taylor and Barr building," he said for the umpteenth time. Umpteenth. Another fine *taibo* word. One of the School Mothers at Carlisle had used it often: "Daniel, I've told you for the umpteenth time. . . ."

"Boy. . . ."

Daniel silenced him with a finger. "Five rooms. Four you let to us. Who was registered to the fifth room? That is all I need to know."

"For one thing, boy, it is not the policy of this hotel to give just anyone personal information about our guests." His tone had turned nasal and nasty. "Carlos, go fetch a copper."

Again, Daniel tapped his badge. "I am a peace officer."

"Peace officer my ass," the manager said. "Injun copper. What a joke." He shook his fist at Daniel's face. "You get out this moment. This is a respectable hotel."

Feeling his face flush, Daniel stepped back. Had School Father Pratt and those other teachers not taught him the white man's way, he would have struck the manager right then and there. Yet what honor could be found in counting coup on a worthless specimen like this sweating knave who did not even have enough hair to scalp?

"What's the problem here, Andy?"

Daniel sighed, resigned to the fact that he was about to be arrested. That would bring shame to School Father Pratt, to Agent Joshua Biggers, but he knew he had been in the right. All he wanted was an answer to an important question.

"This red devil's just being a nuisance, Billy. I've asked Carlos to bring in a policeman."

Turning just enough to see the newcomer, Daniel recognized him. He wasn't a peace officer at all, but the newspaper reporter from the Dallas *Herald.* Kyne. William J. Kyne, who extended his right hand toward Daniel.

"It's Killstraight, right?"

He stared at the hand, but did not accept it, expecting some ruse from this *taibo.*

The reporter didn't seem to be offended. Maybe newspaper reporters were used to such treatment. Instead, the right hand reached for a pencil tucked above his ear, and the left brought up a writing tablet. An Old Glory, with pages filled with indecipherable scratch marks.

"Billy," the Pickwick's manager began, "don't give this heathen. . . ."

"Quiet, Andy. Just give me a minute here. What's troubling you, Killstraight?"

Daniel remained mute.

The reporter returned the pencil to his ear, and set the Old Glory tablet on the registration desk. "All right. This ain't for the record. But I remember you at Norma's Café this afternoon when we were having dinner. I could tell something troubled you. Something about what happened to Quanah and that other ol' bird." He looked at the Pickwick manager. "Yes, sir, I could see why you wouldn't want to help out this detective, Andy. One guest dead. Another in a coma and likely not long for this world. It would be a shame if the Pickwick Hotel got sued by the Comanche nation. And it sure won't look good when all those Indian-loving Eastern papers like the Boston *Tribune* and *Harper's Weekly* start running articles about how the Pickwick killed Quanah Parker, chief of the Comanches."

"We are not responsible. . . ."

"You didn't tell the Comanches that those lamps were gas."

"Those rooms are owned by the Taylor and Barr. . . ."

"But they're managed by you boys." Kyne picked up the Old Glory, thumbed to a blank page. "Your mother was raped, killed, scalped, and mutilated by the Comanches, ain't that right, Andy?"

"My mother's alive and well in Mobile, Alabama."

"She won't be in the Dallas *Herald.* She'll be a motive that led to the death of Quanah Parker. That's the story that'll go out on the wires, that's the story all those Eastern papers'll pick up, and by the time you see a retraction, you'll be out of a job, my friend."

Daniel's head spun. He didn't know what to make of this conversation at all. The manager swore, and both hands dropped below the counter, returning with a leather-bound book, which he opened, then he flipped to a page, turned the book around, and shoved it toward the *Herald* reporter.

"There, you son-of-a-bitch. See for yourself. Nobody. *Nobody* stayed in Room Four last night. Or tonight. Or the night before."

Billy Kyne leaned forward. He wet his lips, and turned the book toward Daniel. "Can you read, Killstraight?"

The date marked under *Checked In* was yesterday. Rooms 1, 2, 3, and 5 were marked *N. Texas Stock Grw Assn,* and he could make out the handsome, almost feminine scroll of Lee Hall. No one had registered for Room 4. Daniel flipped back a page, then another. No one had stayed in Room 4 since July 2nd, and that was a man whose name, from what Daniel could make out, was Carmichael and who lived in Chicago.

"Satisfied?" The manager slammed the register shut, and drew it sharply off the desk, shoving it back onto a shelf underneath.

"The bed had been slept in," Daniel said. "The door was open."

"Get out of here!" the manager snapped. "Both of you. Especially you, Billy. You've worn out your welcome with me, you callous bastard."

Billy Kyne grinned. Putting his arm around Daniel's shoulder, he steered a path through the crowded lobby until they stepped outside onto the Third Street boardwalk.

"A copper's coming, lad," Kyne muttered. "Let's go back to your room before we both get hauled to the calaboose."

Daniel stopped in front of Room 4, and

gripped the knob. He turned it, pushed, and the door opened.

A match flared, and Billy Kyne stepped inside. He wasn't in the room long, before he shook it out, tossed the Lucifer into a cuspidor, and walked back into the lighted hallway.

"I tell you," Daniel said, reading the doubt in the reporter's face, "when I woke this morning, the door was open, the bed unmade."

"I don't disbelieve you a moment, Kill-straight." He pointed across the hall. "That your room? Let's sit in there for a few minutes and figure out where you're headed."

A carpenter had repaired the door to Room 3, but to Daniel's surprise it was unlocked, too. Billy Kyne stepped through, and stared at the door.

"So you say Comanches don't lock their doors?"

Daniel nodded. "It is not our way."

"That's interesting," the reporter said, "but it doesn't mean much. A fellow, even an Indian, would be a fool to keep his door unlocked in this part of town. It's called Hell's Half Acre for a reason, you know."

Kyne moved to the wall lamp closest to

the door. He turned the knob, bathing the room in yellow light. Daniel moved to the window, and felt some measure of relief.

If he had imagined the open door and unmade bed, at least he had not dreamed this. He pointed to the smudge, and Billy Kyne joined him.

"What's this mean?" Kyne asked.

"I don't know," Daniel answered honestly. "But the window was shut."

Kneeling, Kyne squinted, pursed his lips, and looked at Daniel. "You reckon it's blood?"

Daniel shook his head. "Blood would have dried brown. That's still reddish."

"Uhn-huh. Ink, by my guess."

Ink. Daniel had not thought of that. Red ink.

"I use a pencil myself." Straightening, Kyne said: "But be that as it may, this thumb print . . . that's sure what it looks like . . . could have been here a day, a month, a year. Figure this. If they don't bother locking their doors at this place, then it isn't likely the chambermaids clean any window frequently, either."

"She made the bed," Daniel pointed out.

Smiling, Kyne reached into a pocket of his plaid sack suit, and withdrew a flask. "Sure you don't want a snort, Killstraight?"

139

Without waiting for a reply, he unscrewed the lid, and tossed his head back as he drank. "Was your bed made?"

Daniel had to think. "Yes, it was."

"Really. Even with all the commotion going on around here all day? That's impressive. All right, tomorrow, you wait on the maid. With luck, it'll be the same gal who cleaned your room today. You ask her if she made up the room across from yours."

He nodded. He had planned on doing that already.

"Why would they leave the door unlocked?" Daniel asked.

Billy Kyne shrugged. "Honest mistake, maybe."

Daniel threw Kyne's earlier argument back in his face. " 'But one would be foolish to keep his door unlocked in this part of town.' "

The reporter, however, wasn't listening. He was moving back to the globes of the lamps, looking at the one that was lit, then at the other. "Well, looky here." His grin revealed tobacco-stained teeth.

Daniel moved from the window to the bed. He didn't see it until Kyne tapped the smudge with his pencil.

Another red mark. Fainter, but clear enough.

"Don't expect no medal yet, Killstraight. Did you check ol' Yellow Bear's thumbs and fingers?"

His shoulders sagged, and he sighed. As a detective, he had much to learn. Billy Kyne read the answer on Daniel's face. "Too bad. Likely the undertaker's already cleaned up the ol' bird for his trip to the hereafter." He sipped again from his flask.

An idea struck Daniel, and his face brightened. "But the one who died here . . . he would not have used an ink pen."

Perplexed, Kyne lowered the flask. " 'The one who died here'?"

Daniel had to explain Comanche etiquette, and for the first time William J. Kyne scribbled something in his notebook. While he was writing, he said: "Well, you're forgetting the power of a celebrity, kid. And 'the one who died here' reminded me of ol' Sitting Bull, the Sioux."

"Lakota," Daniel corrected. At Carlisle, the Lakotas he had known hated being called Sioux.

Kyne didn't seem to hear.

"Before I landed in this dump of a town working at this dump of a newspaper, I was working in Saginaw, Michigan, when Buffalo Bill Cody brought his Wild West to town. Sitting Bull, the very red bastard who killed Custer, was touring with Cody, and let me tell you he was the star of that spectacle. Signed autographs for scores of children, men, and women. Even soldiers, mind you. Dumb son-of-a-bitch that I was, I didn't get one. Mainly on account I didn't have a buck to spend on his John Hancock. That ol' boy made more money on autographs in one night than I'd make in a month, and that's on top of the fifty a month he was pulling from Cody."

Daniel frowned. "Then I must ask the cowboy, Briggs, if the one who is no more signed" — he tested the word — ". . . autographs . . . while he was wandering from saloon to saloon."

The pencil Kyne held waved in front of Daniel's face. "There's one other thing you need to consider."

Without speaking, Daniel waited.

"Quanah Parker, he who isn't dead yet, was signing scores of autographs yesterday. He could have blown out the lamp. And he could have closed the window."

That would be easy enough to check, but something else troubled Daniel. He kept thinking back to earlier that day, visualizing Charles Flint wiping his hands with a handkerchief. Charles Flint, the bookkeeper. A bookkeeper wrote in ink, right?

He did not want to think that. He liked Flint. Flint's father, on the other hand. . . .

"I like your theory, kid." The reporter filed away pencil, notebook, and flask. "But even my idiotic editor, who plumb loves to give Fort Worth hell, wouldn't print what we have. That's because what we have, Killstraight, is a bunch of nothing. Now you get some evidence, and that'll be a whale of a story. 'Indian policeman suspects foul play in Cowtown.' That would be our headline. Or something a hell of a lot stronger. You said you told Capt'n Hall what you thought, and he didn't really believe it, right? You tell anybody else?"

Daniel shook his head.

"You trust me, don't you, kid?"

His lips just turned up a tad, not enough to be called a smile, but as close as Daniel could muster. Again he shook his head.

Kyne tilted his head back, and laughed. "That's good, boy. Don't trust the press. Especially the Dallas *Herald.* Especially Billy Kyne. You probably don't trust any white man, do you, Killstraight?"

No answer, although Daniel was thinking how much he wished Deputy U.S. Marshal Harvey P. Noble was in Fort Worth right now. Kyne opened the door, and stepped into the hall. After Daniel had joined him,

Kyne closed the door.

"Too bad we don't have a witness. Streets were full of people last night. Maybe somebody saw something."

Daniel was already ahead of Kyne on that front. He remembered the drunken cowboy in the alley, the police officer who had scolded him, almost arrested him. He didn't tell Kyne this, decided it would be better to keep that to himself. Although he had smiled when he had let Kyne know he didn't trust him, the truth was he didn't trust him.

"I'll have to do some checking," Kyne was saying. "Digging, rather. This won't be easy, not since I wore out my welcome with Andy at the hotel. And Tom Bode, that skinflint of an editor at the *Herald,* he sure won't cotton to the idea of me trotting back and forth from Dallas to this ol' burg every day. But I warrant I can talk him into it, for a couple days, anyhow. Anything to bring scandal to Fort Worth. First thing we need to do, though, is prove that Quanah didn't blow out those lamps, close that window."

He tilted his head to the door across the hall.

Daniel went to the room where Nagwee and Isa-tai tended to Quanah. Billy Kyne followed, but Daniel turned, raising his

144

hand. "Not you," he said. "I will check."

"Now, kid. . . ." Daniel's stare ended Kyne's begging.

Turning, Daniel tried the knob — unlocked — and pushed open the door. He stopped, staring, not believing.

"Criminy." Billy Kyne quickly drew out both pencil and notebook. "Where the hell is everybody?"

CHAPTER ELEVEN

His heart sank, and he trembled, knowing that Quanah had died, that Isa-tai and Nag-wee had sneaked the body out of the Taylor & Barr building. Having learned what the Pale Eyes would do to Yellow Bear, they would not allow Quanah to be subjected to such sacrilege. Even Isa-tai, who despised Quanah, was too much *Nermernuh* to let Quanah receive a *taibo* burial.

Turning, bumping so hard into Kyne that he knocked the reporter against the wall, Daniel stepped into the hallway. *Where? How?* He started toward the stairs, stopped, turned.

"Damnation!" Kyne had hurried out of the room, slamming the door behind him. "I told Jason to let me know if that chief bought the farm." He shot Daniel a glance, saying — "I'll check the funeral parlor." — and ran toward the exit.

Daniel waited until he heard Kyne's feet

pounding the stairs out front, then he moved down the hall and entered Room 4. For the first time since arriving in Fort Worth, he felt a breeze. He walked to the open window, and leaned out.

Isa-tai and Nagwee would have known better than to take Quanah down the stairs, onto the crowded streets. It would have been difficult, but he could picture Nagwee nudging his way out of the window, stepping down onto the roof of the neighboring building that butted against the mercantile, grabbing Quanah's shoulders and carefully backing up until Isa-tai was outside, gripping Quanah's feet.

Daniel slipped through the window, and moved across the flat roof. Yes, he said to himself, nodding when he spotted the crates stacked against the alley wall. That's how they had done it. The wooden boxes would have been like stairs, and Daniel followed them until his moccasins touched dirt.

Although the alley was empty, noise echoed across the wooden and brick façades. A gunshot boomed. A whistle screeched. Hell's Half Acre was turning lively tonight.

"Where would they have taken him?" Daniel asked himself aloud, and looked north and west toward the Trinity River. Maybe. Not Main Street, not Houston. Too

147

crowded this time of night. He hurried past Rusk Street, across Calhoun, all the way to Jones, and stopped.

Which way? Down toward Fort Worth's "Bloody Third Ward", toward the Texas and Pacific depot, the railroad? Or to the banks of the Trinity, heading north, trying to get Quanah closer to the land of The People? Perhaps East, toward the rising sun, out of town?

A nighthawk sounded, its cry carrying above the ruction from Houston Street, and Daniel walked toward it, moving down the dark, deserted street. After two blocks, doubt crept into his mind. He even wondered if he had actually heard a hawk, or was that just his imagination? He often thought of the marsh hawk as his *puha* — it had certainly been his father's — but now he wondered if he should just turn around, go back to the room, wait for Isa-tai and Nagwee to return. If they ever would.

The streets became more alive with glowing yellow light shining out of the windows of brothels and saloons. The breeze carried a mixture of smells: horse manure, stale beer, dust, vomit.

A drunken cowboy brushed Daniel's shoulder, muttered something he could not understand. A horse whinnied in front of a hitching rail. Daniel found more people on the streets as he moved southeast, and the tintamarre of laughter, words, and a strumming banjo echoed inside his head. When he reached the Waco Tap Saloon at Seventh Street, he stopped.

"Hey, sugar," a woman called from the corner, her words a slurred Texas drawl, "come on over here, hon'!"

Ignoring her, he bit his lip.

A horse raced from Calhoun Street, its rider pulling so hard on the reins the horse skidded to a stop in front of the saloon. The rider turned in the saddle, and yelled through the open doors: "Billy! Billy! Get your arse out of here, kid!"

That was pointless. Billy could not have heard the man's shouts unless he were standing outside the Waco Tap Saloon.

Swearing slightly, the cowboy leaped from the saddle, tripped on the boardwalk, and flew into the saloon.

"C'mon, sugar!" the woman called again. "Cleopatra will show you a good time."

Daniel sighed, crossed the street, and moved back toward Rusk.

"Two dollars!" the woman yelled with desperation. "And I got some mescal that won't cost you nothin'!"

A moment later, he stopped and turned.

The cowboy and his companion had burst through the saloon's doorway, and Daniel thought he had heard the one called Billy say something about a teepee.

The cowboy swung into the saddle, while Billy moved down the hitching post until he came to a small bay.

"I tell you, Billy," the first one said, "there's a damned teepee in the middle of the wagon yard."

"You're drunk." Billy backed the bay onto the street, tipped his hat at the woman on the corner, and spurred his horse.

They galloped past Daniel, wheeling their horses at the next intersection, disappearing as they rode north on Rusk. Billy was likely right. His friend must be drunk, yet what were the odds? Daniel took off running, crossing the street, leaping over a cowhand sleeping off a drunk in the middle of the boardwalk. The cowboys had vanished, and there were two wagon yards just up the block, the Texas and the City, but Daniel knew the one he wanted.

A crowd was already gathered, fighting for a better look inside the Texas Wagon Yard on the corner of Rusk and Sixth.

"Excuse me," he said, and slipped between a man in a bell crown hat and a snuff-dipping woman leaning on a cane before being stopped by a *taibo* wall. He tapped a shoulder, asked for a path, but nobody listened until the snuff-dipping woman spit into a coffee can she clutched with the hand not holding the cane yelled: "Hey, let this Injun through. Maybe he knows what's goin' on here!"

Shoulders parted, eyes stared, voices whispered.

Something resembling a path appeared, and Daniel meandered through, trying to ignore the stares. One person even ran his fingers through his long hair, then told a companion: "I touched me a red savage."

"Should have taken his scalp, Lou," another voice said, answered by a chorus of sniggers.

The last two people, a blacksmith in his work apron rubbing rough hands through an even rougher beard, and a one-eyed Negro with thumbs hooked in his waistband, stepped aside, and Daniel stepped clear, halting beside a wheel-less phaeton, its axles propped up on thick blocks of wood.

By The People's standards, it would not be much of a lodge. Lacking the needed ten to twenty buffalo hides, Isa-tai and Nagwee had fashioned canvas they must have borrowed from the wagons parked along the

151

Sixth Street side of the sprawling yard, and fetched cedar poles out of two black birch farm wagons parked in the middle of the yard.

A *Nermernuh* teepee could be raised in fifteen minutes, but The People considered that women's work. He could not imagine Nagwee and Isa-tai getting this set up, especially since they had to improvise, yet there stood a teepee, the entrance facing east, smoke wafting through the hole, and a loud roaring coming from inside.

"What's that noise?" someone asked.

"I ain't goin' in to find out."

In front of the teepee, a two-foot deep ditch had been dug running north and south for roughly six feet. Floating in the breeze was an eagle feather attached to the top of an iron lantern rod at the edge of the corner closest to the teepee's doorway.

Taking a deep breath and slowly exhaling, Daniel walked to the split in the canvas. He removed his badge and coins, leaving them at the edge of the pit, for metal was not allowed inside a curing lodge, leaped into the ditch, jumped out, and entered the teepee.

Anyone could enter a curing lodge, though usually only other sick ones would come in except for the *puhakat*'s singers and helpers. Daniel moved clockwise around the fire, and sat cross-legged on the north side.

Quanah lay on a blanket along the west-facing side of the teepee. *At least he's still alive,* Daniel thought.

Above Quanah stood Nagwee, draped in a heavy buffalo robe, sweating profusely, whipping his *yuane,* the bull-roarer known among The People as "warm wind", over his head. When Nagwee whirled the thin piece of wood attached by a long string, the roar of wind made Daniel's head throb. Isatai had stopped singing and sat beside a drum. He gave four beats, then stopped, arched back his head, and yelled.

Outside, the crowd's voices grew louder.

This was *pianahuwait,* the Big Doctoring of the Beaver Ceremony. The People were never much for group dances. They had performed the Sun Dance only once, at Isatai's urging, and that was right before the disastrous raid at Adobe Walls. Daniel had performed the Eagle Dance, but never had he actually seen a Beaver Ceremony. Usually a loved one would request a great *puhakat* to perform the ritual for someone suffering from the lung sickness or maybe after a witch's hex.

He held his breath, observing. From what he understood, there should be a cottonwood trunk in the center and rising all the

153

way to the top of the teepee, but, undoubtedly, that would have been too hard for Isa-
tai and Nagwee to find in the middle of Fort
Worth. Yet they had managed to secure a
thick wagon tongue where the tree trunk
should have been. The *puhakats* had taken
time to dig ponds on the north and south,
edging the rims with willows that they had
likely found along the riverbank. They had
filled each pond with water, undoubtedly
from the troughs outside. Mud had been
used to form effigies shaped in the form of
beavers just outside each pond, facing west.

The roaring fire told Daniel that the
ceremony was just beginning.

Isa-tai unwrapped deerskin, revealing a
pipe. As he tamped tobacco into the bowl,
Daniel remembered enough to move to the
fire, pull out a stick, and offer the glowing
red end to Isa-tai. With a nod, Isa-tai accepted the gesture, and lit the pipe.

Daniel stared. Isa-tai had to grunt angry
guttural words before Daniel realized that
Charles Flint's father was offering him the
pipe.

He accepted it, shamed, took three puffs,
and handed it back to Isa-tai, but the *puhakat* sternly shook his head.

"Ayarocueté," Isa-tai said in a hoarse
whisper, and held up four fingers.

154

Of course. Now Daniel remembered. Four puffs. Four was the mystical number. Four beats of the drums. Four songs. Four puffs. He took another drag, and Isa-tai nodded and accepted the pipe this time.

Daniel stared as Isa-tai smoked. He had donned a buffalo skull headdress and ceremonial clothes, but what struck Daniel was Isa-tai's face. Two lines had been painted across his cheek under his eyes, and four smaller vertical lines ran from his bottom lip to his chin. All of the lines were the color of vermillion.

Red ink . . . red paint . . . like what he had seen on the windowpane and lamp's globe in Quanah's room.

Isa-tai drew four times, and handed the pipe to Nagwee. After the healer's puffs, the pipe returned to Daniel, who suddenly remembered that it was a woman's job to clean the pipe. He wished Rain Shower were here.

After Nagwee prayed, he grabbed feathers and strode to the north beaver pond, dipping them into the muddy water, before heading, still singing his prayers, to the south pond to repeat the process. He moved clockwise, always clockwise and, hovering over Quanah, began fanning the Kwahadi leader with the feathers, water dripping off

155

them onto Quanah's face, his chest, his arms.

Isa-tai spoke, and Daniel turned away from Nagwee. Isa-tai pointed at the pipe, made the sign to refill its bowl, and Daniel did as instructed. After Nagwee had finished his prayers, the three men smoked again.

As Daniel cleaned the pipe, Nagwee moved back to Quanah. Now he knelt, and began rubbing herbs — Daniel did not know what kind — on the comatose man's chest, over his forehead, his eyelids, his throat.

At last, Nagwee straightened, and let the heavy buffalo robe slide off his body, which glistened with sweat. Suddenly he darted to the upright wagon tongue, and began shimmying up the pole. Daniel held his breath. The wooden tongue leaned slightly, and, for a moment, Daniel thought it might break or at least collapse under Nagwee's weight.

Isa-tail barked something, and hurried to the pole, motioning for Daniel to help him. They pressed both hands against the wagon tongue, putting their weight into it, grunting, straining, sweating. Daniel wanted to look up, but couldn't, wouldn't.

Outside, a woman screamed, echoed by the shocked voices of men and women.

"Look at that!"

156

"My God!"

"It's a head!"

"What the hell's that buck doin'?"

Nagwee had reached the top, had stuck his head through the opening. Now he announced that he was coming down, and Daniel and Isa-tai backed away. The holy man's feet hit the sand, the wagon tongue quivered and tilted to one side, but did not fall.

Daniel backed away, watching Nagwee as he ran around the fire before stepping, from the east, into the bed of coals. Daniel bit his lip. Tears welled in his eyes. He smelled the burning of moccasins, of flesh. He could feel the pain, yet Nagwee's face showed nothing while he moved his arms like a burrowing owl flitting its wings. At last, Nagwee backed out of the fire, moccasins smoldering, and walked to the south, stopping at the western edge of the curing lodge.

Nagwee moved to the south pond, where he chewed bark from the willow sticks. Tilting his head back, the *puhakat* let out a gush of air. The smell, Daniel remembered, reminded him of beaver.

He looked at Quanah, who still breathed, still slept, but did not look any better.

The crowd parted as Isa-tai and Nagwee

walked out of the Texas Wagon Yard. Daniel stopped outside the ditch as School Father Pratt, Captain Hall, and other men in fancy duds and worried expressions approached him. Kyne, the newspaper reporter, came with them.

"What's going on, Daniel?" Pratt asked.

"It is what we call *pianahuwait*," he said, and explained the Beaver Ceremony as best he could.

"The singing?" Hall asked.

Daniel had joined Isa-tai and Nagwee in the final song, as was custom for The People, then Nagwee had extinguished the fire inside the lodge, and, after each had left the teepee, they had jumped into the ditch and climbed out on the east side.

"It is how we close the ceremony."

Church bells chimed. It was midnight. Nagwee had timed this perfectly.

"Let me get this straight," Kyne said. "Those two medicine men fetched Quanah out of the hotel, rigged all this up?"

Daniel nodded.

"Damn!" The reporter slapped his notebook against his thigh. "Wait till my editor hears about this. Comanche Indians are so discouraged with Fort Worth's doctors, they decide to heal their chief themselves. That'll make that ol' miser Bode happy! Damn!"

He tilted his head back and howled.

Others were not amused.

"How's Quanah?" Captain Hall asked.

"Better?" Kyne added hopefully.

"It is just the first night," Daniel explained with a shrug of his shoulders.

"You mean," said a man wearing a fancy badge, "this Beaver thing isn't over?"

CHAPTER TWELVE

"It lasts three days," Daniel said, hoping he remembered correctly.

"Three days!" The badge-wearer shook his head. "There's no way this circus can stay here for two more nights."

"Hold on, Charley," said a man in duck trousers and a sweat-soaked muslin shirt. "This here's my property, and, if they want to work on their chief in my wagon yard, I sure ain't complainin'."

The city lawman and wagon yard owner stared at each other.

"Daniel," School Father Pratt said suggestively, "Quanah needs a doctor's care. He needs to be in his bed in the apartment." He gestured behind him. "Look around. This is no place for a sick man."

"I will stay with him," Daniel announced. He hated the look on Pratt's face, felt the School Father's disappointment.

"This is going to be a nightmare, Zeke,"

the city policeman said.

"You tell Mayor Broiles that I'll pay for a permit if that's what it takes, but this is gonna be good for my business, Charley, and I say this is my property, and that teepee stays put."

"Good for you. Not me." The marshal spit. "I'll have to put two officers here all day, all night. You know what my force consists of? Two mounted officers, two patrolmen, a jailer, and two sanitary officers. Now how in hell can the city afford this? We've already blown our year's budget just because of these red niggers!" He hooked a thumb angrily, just missing Daniel's nose.

"Marshal," School Father Pratt said, "watch your tongue, sir."

There was no breeze, and tension hung in the air like humidity.

Captain Hall stared at the teepee. "I'll have some of my men help you police the wagon yard, too, Marshal. You can make them special deputies if you like, and the association will foot the bill."

When most, but certainly nowhere near all, of the crowd had scattered across Hell's Half Acre, Daniel returned to the teepee, stopping to pick up the metal he had left

161

near the ditch. He found the badge. Some son-of-a-bitch had taken the coins he'd left. Sighing, he pinned the shield on the lapel of his vest, knowing he should feel some relief. Most thieves would have taken the tin badge, too, if for nothing more than a souvenir.

"You held out on me, Killstraight. I thought we were pals."

He turned to find William J. Kyne standing on the other side of the ditch, dribbling his fingers on the Old Glory writing tablet.

Daniel felt no need to explain, to tell this reporter that he had not known what had become of Quanah.

Kyne tilted his jaw toward the lodge. "Be all right if I took a look-see in there?"

Daniel answered with surprising venom, but Kyne appeared to take the rejection. To Daniel's surprise, the *Herald* journalist smiled.

"What would it take to show you that I'm not the typical white man? I don't hate Indians, not even you Comanches. Hell, I don't even hate Fort Worth. I'm just practicing what my paper preaches, and that's that Dallas is a hell of a finer city than this cow town."

Daniel had been to Dallas. In fact, some roughnecks had beaten the hell out of him there. He didn't care much for either Texas town.

"What do you need? For Quanah? For your witch doctors? You tell me, and ol' Billy Kyne'll produce. Won't cost you a thing."

Except my soul.

Ignoring Kyne, he ducked inside the lodge. He could still smell the scent of beaver, over the last wisps of smoke from the fire. He scanned the teepee, then quickly pulled himself back outside.

Kyne was walking away.

"Are you serious?" Daniel called out.

The reporter turned. Several long seconds passed. "You name it, kid. The *Herald* will get it."

Daniel pursed his lips, thinking, finally deciding to chance it. "I need the trunk of a cottonwood tree."

Kyne blinked. He found his flask, drained it, shoved it back into his coat pocket. "A cottonwood tree?"

"Just the trunk," Daniel said. "But . . ." — he glanced at the teepee — "it should be fifteen feet high or thereabouts."

"How big?"

Big enough to hold up Nagwee, Daniel thought, and could not hide his smile. He held out his arms in a circle. "About like that?" he requested. "And I need it by early

163

morning."

With a chuckle, Kyne turned toward Rusk Street. "I'll see what I can do, Killstraight."

He jerked awake to the bells of St. Stanislaus Catholic Church. Groggily he stumbled out of the healing lodge, and headed for the water trough. Whispers reached him before he even realized he had an audience, and, after splashing water on his face and wetting back his hair, he saw the crowd. A few school-age boys, black men and women, white women and men, a family of Chinese, nowhere near the size of the throng last night, but plenty considering if the church bells were right, it was just 6:00 A.M.

After filling the gourd, he returned to the teepee, squatted beside Quanah, lifting his head into his arms, pouring water down his throat.

The canvas flap flew open. Charles Flint stepped inside. "How is he?" Flint asked.

Daniel shrugged, and lowered Quanah's head onto the blankets.

Flint looked around, his face masked with a curiosity. "What . . . ?" He shook his head. "What is this?"

Of course, Daniel realized. Having come of age on the reservation and at Carlisle, Charles Flint would not know about the

164

Beaver Ceremony. Daniel barely comprehended it himself. Before he could explain,
wagon traces sang out, accompanied by a
squeaky wheel, braying mules, and a string
of cuss words that left the God-fearing
women in the Texas Wagon Yard gasping.

Daniel followed Flint outside to see a
gray-bearded Mexican in a battered straw
hat snapping a blacksnake whip over the
left mule's ear. The crowd quickly moved to
the Sixth Street side, and let the wagon ease
past the wheelless phaeton and come to a
halt near the ditch. A figure leaped off the
back of the market wagon, and Daniel
recognized Billy Kyne's voice.

"You fellas, lend a hand. *Pronto,* boys.
Pronto."

Daniel moved around the ditch, and
stared, unbelieving, as black and white men,
under the supervision of Billy Kyne, pulled
a huge cottonwood trunk out of the wagon.

"Where you want this piece of fine furniture, Killstraight?" Kyne asked.

Nagwee grunted as he walked around the
cottonwood, putting his hand against it,
nodding, eying Flint and Daniel with suspicion, and finally looking at Isa-tai and asking something too low for Daniel to understand.

165

Isa-tai snorted and spat.

"It is better than that skinny thing that felt as slippery as a fish," Nagwee said, and nodded his final approval at Daniel. "We will begin the *pianahuwait* soon," Nagwee said. "When the bells ring again."

Flint struggled for words. "I do not know what to do."

"Then go do books," Isa-tai said harshly in English, and his son's head dropped.

"I will tell him what he needs to do," Daniel said, eyes angry, staring at the *puhakat.* Isa-tai wore the same red paint on his face.

The Kwahadi spit. "How? You do not know the way yourself?"

Daniel couldn't deny that.

A train's whistle cut across the morning air.

"They will do fine," Nagwee said. "We must prepare for the Big Doctoring."

"You're a real bastard, Daniel."

Daniel dumped water from an oaken bucket into the pond, and stared at Flint.

"You think my father did this." Flint switched to the language of The People.

"I do not think anything." Daniel rose. "Yet," he added, and he exited the lodge and walked back to the water trough. Flint caught up with him.

166

"My father would not harm one of The People." And in English: "No Indian would harm a member of his tribe."

Daniel shook his head, and dropped the bucket into the trough. "You have not been back from the East very long, my friend. Everything has changed on the reservation. And I remember the story of a powerful *dohate* of our friends the Kiowas. When the one that was chosen to speak for all the Kiowas told the Pale Eyes to send this *dohate* to the prison at Fort Marion, the *dohate* placed a spell on the peace chief. The peace chief died."

"I know that story," Flint said. "Kicking Bird died, then Maman-ti went to Fort Marion, where he died. Of malaria. Or dysentery. But not because he had killed another Kiowa."

Angrily Flint sent his bucket splashing into the trough, jerking it up, letting water slosh over the sides as they returned to the healing lodge.

"This was an accident," Flint said after dumping water into the pond. He jutted his jaw toward Quanah. "Yellow Bear paid for his mistake, but that's all it was, Daniel, a mistake."

Daniel glared at the bookkeeper. "It was no mistake," he said flatly. "It was murder.

Attempted murder."

An angry wail exploded from Flint's lungs. "Do you hate my father that much?"

"I do not know that it was your father," Daniel said again, silently adding to himself: *But he is certainly . . . what was it he had heard the* taibo *judge named Parker say in Fort Smith? A man of interest.*

Remembering seeing the bookkeeper wiping his hands, Daniel's eyes dropped to Flint's hands. *And I would like to see your fingers, too.*

"I will prove to you that my father committed no crime," Flint said.

"Tzat." Daniel nodded. Good. "I can use much help."

"Bávi, then it is a good thing we are here."

Daniel stepped back, his jaw dropping as Ben Buffalo Bone stepped inside the lodge. His best friend's uncle, Cuhtz Bávi, followed, stopping and staring grimly at the unconscious Quanah. The flap moved yet again.

"The former bluecoat called Pratt and the *taibo* Metal Shirt named Hall," Ben Buffalo Bone explained. "They used the talking wires to tell the agent, Biggers, what has happened here."

Ben's uncle looked around. "What has become of the one who journeys to The

Land Beyond The Sun?"

Daniel's head dropped. How could he tell a man like Cuhtz Bávi that Yellow Bear had been given a white man's burial? The undertaker had planted the corpse in some potter's field the same day, had not even let The People attend the funeral.

"Biggers gave us all passes to come to Texas," Ben Buffalo Bone said. "Frank Striker came with us as he speaks English good."

Striker was the agency interpreter, a big Texian who was married to a Kiowa. Daniel was glad Ben had changed the subject from Yellow Bear.

"Striker is outside. He talks to a *Tejano* Metal Shirt." Suddenly Ben announced excitedly: "We took the iron horse."

"It stinks," said Cuhtz Bávi. "Smells nothing like a good pony, and I do not like the places where they make us sit. It is not as comfortable, or as cool, as my brush arbor."

Daniel barely heard Ben Buffalo Bone's uncle's complaints. He stared at the woman who had followed Cuhtz Bávi into the healing lodge.

Her hair, shining with grease, looked blacker than midnight, parted in the middle in the fashion of The People. Her face was round, and she wore copper bracelets

169

adorned with bright stones, a bone necklace strung with sinew that held three German silver crosses. Her dress was made of doeskin. She looked away from Quanah, tears welling, and stared at Daniel.

"You should not be here!" Daniel shouted.

Immediately he regretted his sharpness, saw the hurt in her face, replaced almost immediately by anger.

"I am here!" she barked back at him.

Which she always was. Here. For Daniel.

Rain Shower, perhaps with assistance from her mother and sister Oajuicauojué, who had just reached puberty, had made his britches. She had sewn the stripes — chevrons, they were called — on his jacket's sleeve to show that he was a sergeant. After he had cut off the sleeves, she had stitched the stripes onto the front of what was now his vest. She had helped him find his way, his path, his medicine, since he had returned from Pennsylvania.

If the government had paid him more than $8 a month, he would have bought many horses and brought them to her uncle. He would marry her. He. . . .

His lips tightened. And he remembered the nightmare. The hand grabbing Rain Shower, jerking her out of Daniel's sight.

Before he could speak, Nagwee returned

to the lodge. "We will begin," the *puhakat* announced. "It is time."

By noon, the second day of the curing ceremony was complete. It had pretty much been a repeat of last night, but this time Rain Shower had cleaned Nagwee's pipe, while Daniel, Ben Buffalo Bone, and Flint had sung while Ben's uncle and Isa-tai had beaten drums.

"So what happens next?" a reporter from some newspaper in Austin asked.

Daniel felt uncomfortable talking to so many reporters, yet Nagwee had told Daniel that they must pacify the Pale Eyes, else they might take Quanah out of the healing lodge before it was time. Daniel would speak for The People. He would make the Pale Eyes happy, let them understand the ways of *Nermernuh*.

But there are so many!

A cacophony of questions assaulted Daniel's ears. There must be more ink-slingers in this wagon yard than breast collars and buggy harnesses combined.

"We will start again tonight," Daniel said. "The ceremony will be over by tomorrow at noon."

Pencils scratched. Every reporter but Billy Kyne scribbled furiously.

"Is it helpful to have more Comanches here?" a reporter asked.

Daniel nodded.

"So what happens at noon tomorrow?"

A shrug. He would not tell them.

"Will Quanah die?" a Fort Worth reporter asked.

"I do not know."

"You must be thankful," said a woman reporter from some Eastern paper, "to have so many of your own kind here to assist you."

"I am thankful," Daniel said, "that a white man brought a cottonwood trunk this morning."

Leaning against the Sixth Street stone wall, Billy Kyne gave Daniel a mock salute.

By six o'clock that evening, the crowd at the Texas Wagon Yard had tripled. An hour later, that number had doubled. Now Daniel could see why the city marshal had been so worried, and he did not see any cowboys helping the police officers as Captain Hall had promised.

Holding their Chicago nightsticks, two policemen forced some of the onlookers back. One of the peace officers cursed as Daniel entered the healing lodge. He watched the policeman for two or three

172

seconds, no longer, and stepped through the flap.

"Tsu Kuh Puah," he whispered to Nagwee. "There is a man outside that I must talk to."

Nagwee's face hardened.

"If you say I must stay, I will," Daniel said. "But I need to speak to this man."

"A *taibo?*"

Daniel nodded.

Nagwee shot a glance toward Quanah, then shook his head, and waved his hand in Daniel's face. "Go. Do what you must."

He wanted to apologize, thought better of it, and stepped through the flap. Billy Kyne was not in the crowd, which Daniel considered lucky. The *Herald* reporter, likely in one of the saloons, would have been almost impossible to sneak past. The newspaper horde, however, had divided into groups with a handful of reporters agreeing to alert the others of any new news. Billy Kyne would right now be in one of the saloons, drinking. Maybe with Frank Striker. Daniel didn't see the interpreter, either.

He looked through the opening, saw Rain Shower's questioning glare, then faced the newspaper men.

"It is about to begin?" one bespectacled reporter asked.

"Soon," Daniel said. "It will be over by noon tomorrow." He moved toward Sixth Street.

"Well, where the Sam Hill are you going?" the reporter said.

Daniel forced a smile. "The Comanche have bodily functions same as white men."

That got several chuckles, and the newspaper reporters turned away, rolling cigarettes or pulling bottles of beer from an ice-filled bucket resting on the ground.

Daniel moved past some of the younger employees of the wagon yard and railroads, and walked away from the lodge, the ditch, the smoke, and the smell of beaver. He made a beeline for the policeman with the Irish brogue.

CHAPTER THIRTEEN

He had not seen anyone resembling the cowboy he had glimpsed in the alley, but he knew this Pale Eyes was the same one Daniel had spotted on the streets. Maybe the Metal Shirt had seen somebody enter the Taylor & Barr's upstairs apartments.

Once he reached Rusk Street, Daniel stopped, caught a glimpse of the policeman as he turned east onto Eighth Street. Daniel broke into a sprint, weaving past men and women, careful not to knock anyone over. He took the corner, and spotted the officer passing a two-story structure on the corner of Calhoun. Twirling a nightstick in his right hand, the man moved at a lively clip, and Daniel, already out of breath, wished he had that copper's gait. The cop turned south onto Calhoun, heading toward the Third Ward.

Sucking in air, Daniel chased after him.

He didn't catch up with him until the officer had heard his footsteps, and stopped, turning, raising his nightstick while reaching for a holstered pistol. Sensing the policeman's alarm, Daniel stopped, held out his empty hands, and tried to catch his breath.

"My name . . . is Daniel . . . Killstraight," he said. "I would like . . . to talk to . . . you."

The police officer didn't move, didn't speak. He was almost to Eleventh Street.

Laughter echoed across the Third Ward, someone sawed a fiddle, terribly, and Daniel could hear the clinking of glasses, the curses and catcalls.

"Step into the bloody light." The policeman had finally spoken.

Daniel moved until he stood under a gas lamp next to the City Gas Works building.

"That's good. Just keep your bloody hands where they are."

The officer moved closer to him, hands nervously, but determinedly, clutching the club and the butt of a Smith & Wesson revolver.

"You're one of those Comanches," the man spoke.

Daniel nodded, and tapped his badge. "I, too, am a peace officer."

The policeman let out a mirthless chuckle and spit onto the street. A tall, angular man

176

in the navy blue uniform of the Fort Worth Police Department, he had deep-seated blue eyes that never seemed to blink, a crooked nose, dark walrus mustache flecked with gray, thin lips, and a cleft in his chin. A scar ran from the corner of his right eye, then up to his temple like a check mark. Two items hung from his neck: a whistle, part of the police force's equipment, and a golden medallion that Daniel had seen worn by many of the miners in Pennsylvania who followed the Pale Eyes religion of the Black Robes.

"Peace officer. There's no peace in the bloody Third Ward, boy. Best get your arse back to the wagon yard."

Often, Daniel felt that way about the Comanche, Kiowa and Apache reserve near Fort Sill.

"On Wednesday night," Daniel said, "early Thursday morning, actually, you were patrolling on Houston Street."

The police officer released his grip on the revolver, and lowered the billy club just a little. "Aye. And what of it?"

"That was the night Quanah Parker, our chief, was poisoned by the gas and another was killed."

"So?"

A grunt, curse, and thud sounded behind

him, and the officer turned, gripping the Smith & Wesson again, flattening himself against the wall. He saw a cowboy pushing himself up from the boardwalk, slipping again, trying to pick up a bottle he had dropped, but unable to make his right hand co-operate.

"Jesus, Mother Mary, and Joseph," the policeman said, shaking his head, glancing at Daniel before moving down Calhoun Street toward the buffoon.

Upon reaching the drunkard, the officer reached down, grabbed the cowhand by the collar and waistband, jerked him to his feet, and slammed him against the picket wall of a ramshackle building. "You've had a wee too many tonight, you dumb bloke," the officer said.

The cowboy slurred words Daniel could not understand.

"Aye, and your breath reeks of a brewery."

Daniel eased down the boardwalk. "There was another drunk on that night," he said. "He had relieved himself in the alley, was trying to make his way back to the Tivoli." Hoping he pronounced that right. "Do you remember this?"

The officer had fished metal bracelets from his belt, had slapped one on the drunk's right wrist, was trying to get the

178

other hand secured.

"What are you talking about? Can't you see I'm busy here."

"I just wish to know if you saw anyone entering the Taylor and Barr building around this time. Or coming out of it."

No answer. Having managed to get the handcuffs on, the copper jerked the drunk around. The cowboy tilted toward the officer, but the billy club caught him in the sternum and forced him back against the wall.

"It is important," Daniel said. "Do you remember?"

The policeman whirled, his blue eyes fierce. "Here's what I remember, you bloody red heathen. I remember that tonight is me daughter's birthday, but I'm patrolling this hell-hole instead of celebrating with my family on account of you Comanch'. I remem—"

Like water from an artesian well, vomit hurled from the cowboy's mouth.

"Damnation!" The officer tried to turn to his side, but the stinking wretchedness caught the right side of his uniform, his arm, his nightstick. His boot heel fell into a hole in the warped pine planks, and he turned, twisting, cursing as he crashed into the fine dirt and horse droppings. The

179

cowboy slid down the wall.

Daniel moved for the officer, who rolled over, and sat up, lifting his billy club, snapping: "Get the bloody hell back to the wagon yard, you stupid son-of-a-bitch."

"But. . . ."

"Bugger off! Or I'll run you into the jail with this cad!"

Well, he thought while walking dejectedly back up Calhoun Street, *that's probably what I should have expected. He hadn't even gotten the officer's name, but Daniel refused to give up. My fault. Policing the Third Ward has to be more stressful than policing the reservation. I caught this Metal Shirt in a foul mood. But he has not seen the last of me.*

He remembered the conversation he had overhead with the city marshal. How many officers? Two on horseback, two patrolmen, a jailer, and two sanitary officers. Something like that. All Daniel had to do was go to the jail, wait for the patrolman to return. Offer to buy him a cup of coffee — providing Charles Flint would loan him money. Meet this Irishman on friendlier surroundings. But not tonight. Better to let the man cool off, and clean his uniform.

Turning left onto Eighth Street, he saw her.

180

At the same time Rain Shower spotted him, and halted in front of the two-story building.

Two men walking west angled around her, ignoring her, but another man, leaning against the building between a window and batwing doors, smoking a cigarette, pushed himself off the wall, flicking the cigarette into the street, and approached her from behind.

Like in Daniel's nightmare.

Rain Shower smiled, started again toward him. Daniel wanted to shout a warning, but he couldn't quite comprehend what was happening. She stopped, sensing the presence behind her. Daniel found his voice, roared out a warning in the language of The People, knowing he was too late.

As she started to turn, the cowboy wrapped a massive hand around Rain Shower's mouth, while his left arm wrapped around her waist. Her eyes showed fright. The man was a giant. Laughing, he dragged her through the doors, and they disappeared inside the two-story building.

The two men who had passed Rain Shower on the boardwalk stopped, turned, but did nothing else, other than to grin. The one on the left elbowed the other.

Daniel ran, watching the two men turn

back around to continue their journey as if they had not seen the abduction.

A laughing man staggered into Daniel as he made his way toward the batwing doors. "Watch where the hell. . . ."

The man never finished. Daniel slammed a left fist into the man's temple, and he crashed into the trash can, pulling it over as he slammed onto the boardwalk.

Daniel pushed his way through the batwing doors. Light from the chandeliers and wall sconces made him squint, yet his vision soon adjusted. He wasn't aware that the musician had stopped playing, lowering his fiddle. Wasn't aware that the rough-looking men lining the bar had stopped, turning, staring. Wasn't aware of the meaty woman in the corner, tossing a cigar into a spittoon and hefting a bung starter.

He moved to his right, toward the table. Two giggling men stood in front of it, one of them with his arm around a red-headed woman wearing nothing but calf-length drawers and a camisole.

The redhead saw him first. She started to utter a warning, then pulled herself away from the snickering man's grip, and leaped away.

"What's wrong, Cynthy?" He saw Daniel. His partner didn't.

Daniel grabbed the man's shoulder, jerked, sending him sprawling to the floor. He ignored the one who had been holding Cynthy.

The big man had thrown Rain Shower on a table, his left knee between her legs, hat on the floor, his face pressing against her neck, moving up to her face, her lips. He jerked back suddenly, spitting out blood from where Rain Shower had bit his bottom lip.

"You little . . . !"

Daniel grabbed him by the collar and waistband — just as he had seen the Irish policeman handle the drunk earlier. He threw the man, off-balance, to the floor. Rain Shower rolled off the table, black eyes malevolent — but not as angry as Daniel's.

The one who had taken Rain Shower off the street had to be taller than six-foot-two, and likely weighed better than two hundred pounds, with muscles tearing at the sleeves of his calico shirt, and a face covered with scars. Like most Comanches, Daniel was short, stocky — no match for this man who began pushing himself off the floor. No match under London prize ring rules, that is.

"Well, well, well," the man said. "Reckon I get you first, her second. Suits me to a T."

Daniel kicked him in the face.

The man crashed back to the floor, and Daniel was on top of him, slamming a knee into the man's groin, left hand wrapping around the man's throat, right hand smashing into his nose, his mouth, feeling the teeth break, carve into his knuckles. Blood splattered his face. He stopped hitting, grabbed a fistful of hair, jerked the man's head off the floor, slammed it onto the hardwood. Again. Again.

Behind him, the giggling man suddenly wailed. Daniel turned, saw the man writhing on the ground, his left leg drenched in blood. Rain Shower held a broken beer bottle.

The redhead screamed.

Cowboys, muleskinners, and railroad men left the bar, moving toward Daniel.

He didn't care. He turned back to the man, kneed him again in the groin, slammed a right, then a left into the man's face. The nose gave way. The jaw bone broke. Daniel locked both hands on the man's throat, pressed harder, harder.

Suddenly his head rocked with fire.

He shook off the pain, turned away from the unconscious giant's unrecognizable face, spotted the fat woman, her face plastered with rouge like mud on a Mexican's *jacal.* The woman raised the bung starter over her head again, started to bring it down a second time.

Daniel swung his right arm, catching the woman just below her knees. She yipped as her feet flew out from under her, and fell hard onto the floor.

"Get that sum-bitch!" one of the men cried out.

"*Aiiiyeeeeee!*" Rain Shower leaped in front of him, and the men suddenly stopped, watching her warily as she waved the bloody end of the broken bottle. She taunted them as women, as worthless as Pawnees, afraid of one warrior and one woman. She said they had no honor, that they were dogs. They could not savvy her words, but they certainly understood her meaning.

Daniel pushed himself to his feet, took one step toward Rain Shower, then fell.

The first cowboy he had thrown to the ground had jerked Daniel's ankle. Daniel rolled over, felt the cowboy jumping on top of him. He saw Rain Shower turn, and tried to warn her. . . .

Too late. A wiry man in buckskins took advantage, whipping out his right hand, locking on Rain Shower's wrist, wrenching the beer bottle from her hand. Daniel swung his fist upward, a glancing blow, but the man holding him did not budge.

Rain Shower screamed.

A boot crashed into Daniel's shoulder. Another struck his ribs. Something smashed his face. He tasted blood.

Something roared, but Daniel couldn't see. Vaguely he was aware that the pressure was off his chest, and that nobody was hitting or kicking him.

Words reached him.

"Stop him!"

"He'll kill him!"

"Mickey, for the love of God!"

He heard Rain Shower. Opened his eyes. Saw her face. He shook his head, trying to shake off the fog, pulled himself up.

The policeman came into view. He had struck the man in the buckskin britches with the barrel of his pistol. He struck him again. The man lay on the floor.

"Mickey!" the fat woman cried. "Stop!" She turned. "Find another marshal!"

The Irish officer muttered something about his daughter, brought the pistol down on the man again, missing his head, but clipping his ear and smashing the collarbone. He spoke again, raising the pistol, using words Daniel did not understand. Not English. Something else.

"Stop!" the woman named Cynthy yelled.

"Stop him, in God's name! He'll kill Petey!"

None of the men moved, either intimidated by the Irishman's badge, his Smith & Wesson, or his savagery.

The copper was about to strike the man again, when Daniel — who didn't even remember climbing to his feet — grabbed his arm, pulled him back, spun him away.

Blood pooled on the floor underneath the buckskin-clad man's face, but his lungs still worked. Cynthy ran to him, turning his battered head upward, looking up at the crowd, uttering a plea: "Get a doctor. Somebody get a doctor!"

There were plenty of volunteers, for the room quickly emptied.

A metallic click brought Daniel's attention back to the Irish patrolman.

The Smith & Wesson's hammer was cocked, and the barrel trained on Daniel's heaving stomach.

Daniel wiped the blood off his face. His eyes locked on the policeman's. "It is over," he said.

CHAPTER FOURTEEN

"I don't know what came over me." A sigh escaped the police officer, and he shook his head, and lifted his coffee cup. "That wasn't you I saw in that disorderly house, but me daughter." He sipped, set the cup back on the table, and leaned back, clenching his fists. "I hate this bloody town. It ought to be in England, not Texas."

The waitress brought another ice-filled rag, swapping it out for the one Daniel had been pressing to the side of his face.

"You need anything else, Mickey?" she asked.

The patrolman's head shook, and the woman left.

They sat in the Queen City Ice Cream Parlor, leaving the blood, carnage, and confusion behind at the sporting house on Eighth Street. Daniel did not know what had become of the man the policeman had buffaloed, the one Daniel had almost beaten to death, or the one Rain Shower had stabbed with a broken beer bottle. He didn't even know what had happened to the drunk the patrolman had been carting off to jail. They had left the bawdy house together, backing out of the saloon, the officer warning the big woman he called Loretta that, if he heard a peep from her house or a complaint, this place would go up like Chicago in '72.

"Will the woman make things difficult for you?" Daniel asked.

Sergeant Mickey O'Doherty shook his head. "Loretta? She knows to keep her bloody mouth shut. That was no idle threat I gave her. Me name in the old language is Dochartaigh. It means hurtful, and that I can be, laddie, lassie. That I can be. Now, what do your names mean?"

Rain Shower answered for both, then Daniel said: "But I am called Daniel Killstraight." His fingers lifted the bottom of his vest, and he pointed to the chevrons. "I, too, am a sergeant."

"Sergeant Killstraight." O'Doherty let out a chuckle. "That's an apt name, laddie, seeing how you almost killed that one fellow." He looked across the table. "But I don't know if Rain Shower fits you, lassie. Not after that ruction. You fight mighty well. I

189

warrant you could give John Sullivan, the Boston Strong Boy himself, a run for his money."

Rain Shower's eyes dropped to the bowl of butter pecan in front of her, but Daniel could tell she was smiling.

"I should not have been curt with you earlier, Sergeant." The patrolman's tone turned professional. "This is not a pleasant town, however, and it can be quite stressful. What is it you wish to know?"

After Daniel explained, the patrolman sadly shook his head, and Daniel's heart sank.

"Even by Fort Worth standards, that was a wild night for a Wednesday eve," O'Doherty said. "I remember the lad. Drunk he was. I was about to run him in, but some b'hoys started a row over at the Occidental. I had to run over there and keep that bucket of blood from being dismantled."

He drained his coffee, and shook his head again. "But, sorry to say, I can't say I saw anything that drew me attention to the Taylor and Barr, or the Pickwick Hotel. Usually I'm watching the rowdier places, the saloons, the . . . *ahem, ladies boarding houses.* No, I just don't remember seeing anyone around those stairs that lead to those apartments. How's your chief doing, by the way?"

"He lives." That was all Daniel could think to say.

"Well, I should be on me way." Once he pushed himself to his feet, he brought out some coins, gestured to the waitress, and set them on the table. "My treat. Can you make it back to the wagon yard safely? Or, better yet, the Taylor and Barr?"

"We can," Rain Shower answered.

O'Doherty tipped his cap, and turned to leave, stopping at the door to call back: "If I remember anything, I'll let you know."

The bell rang as the officer opened the door.

"That *taibo*," Rain Shower blurted out, and the patrolman stopped.

"Excuse me?"

Daniel stared at Rain Shower blankly.

"The one who had lost his reason to whiskey. The cowboy. On that night. Did you recognize him?"

"Just a drunken saddle tramp," O'Doherty said flatly. "I've seem him around, but I can't put a name on him." Another tip of his hat, and the police officer was gone.

Daniel adjusted his bundle of ice, looking at Rain Shower. The ice cream shop was empty again, except for them and the waitress.

"You should find this *Tejano,*" Rain Shower instructed.

"The drunken cowboy?" Daniel shook his head. "Even had he seen something, the whiskey would rob him of his memory."

Silence. Rain Shower focused on the ice cream. Mad. At him. Daniel shook his head, and lowered the ice.

"I would not know where to begin to look for this cowboy." The alley had been so dark, Daniel had never gotten a good look at the man's face.

"The place you mentioned," she said, not bothering to look up.

Herman Kussatz's Tivoli Hall. He considered this, and shook his head.

"They would not let me in that place. I am *Nermernuh.*"

Another spoonful of ice cream. Still not looking at Daniel, she said: "They let in the one who has gone to The Land Beyond The Sun."

"But he was with a *taibo.*"

Now Rain Shower raised her spoon, pointing the handle toward the door. "The Metal Shirt, he is a *taibo.* He would assist you. Striker, who has traveled from our country with us, he, too, is a Pale Eyes. He likes you.

He would help."

This he had to consider.

Rain Shower spoke again. "There is another thing you should investigate, Daniel." He flinched. Whenever she called him by the name the Carlisle teachers had given him, it meant she was angry with him.

"This cowboy. He was drunk on whiskey. Could he have entered the building? Could he have gone into the room where Quanah and the other one slept? Could he have accidentally, or purposefully, blown out the lamps?"

For a long moment, Daniel thought about this, but finally shook his head.

"No." The door to Quanah's room. He had heard it being closed after he had seen the drunken cowhand's encounter with Sergeant O'Doherty. He explained this to Rain Shower.

"And after this, did you hear footsteps down the hall?"

This took him longer to remember. "No," he said at last.

"So maybe all the others are right. The other one comes in. He blows out the lamps. It is an accident. He dies, and Quanah fights to stay with the living. But that is all it is. An accident."

His head throbbed. He sat there, feeling

the ice melt in the rag he held, looking at Rain Shower but not really seeing her.

She dipped her spoon in the ice cream again, began eating. "You do not want to believe," she said. "Your head is hard."

Harder than a bung starter. Harder than the boot that had kicked him.

"The door was locked," he explained. "The People have no use for keys."

Focused on the food, she answered: "You do not want to believe." She swallowed, and looked up at him, her black eyes firm. "You want to think Isa-tai is responsible. You hate him, and it clouds your reason."

"That is not true."

"Bah." The ice cream was all but gone, but she scooped up the soupy melt.

He found another argument. "The *Tejano* who accompanied the other one. The one named Briggs, who works for the rancher, Waggoner. I asked him. He said he sent Quanah's companion upstairs at midnight. When I saw the cowboy and the Metal Shirt, it was three seventeen."

"That *Tejano* had been drinking whiskey, too. You cannot believe him."

"I do believe him." Flatly.

"I do not believe it is Isa-tai," she said. "He uses his *puha* now to save Quanah."

"What *puha?*" Daniel said, remembering

194

Nagwee's insult.

The spoon clattered in her bowl, and she stared defiantly across the table at Daniel. "Tell me this . . . was not Isa-tai sharing a room with Nagwee?"

Daniel nodded.

"Nagwee does not sleep well. Would he not have heard Isa-tai had he sneaked out of the room to commit murder?"

He had not thought of that. He hadn't even asked Nagwee.

"Isa-tai would not kill another *Nermernuh*," Rain Shower said. "Nor would Nagwee. Or Tetecae. It is not done among The People."

"You should not be here." Daniel had heard enough of this. He thought back to his nightmare that had almost come true tonight. Rain Shower had almost been killed, and Daniel would have had no one else to blame but himself.

"I am here," she said. "Agent Biggers thought that I should go."

"You were almost killed." He felt tears welling in his eyes.

"*Bah*. I would have killed that Pale Eyes. He was nothing. He was no warrior."

His head fell. A small hand reached out and touched his, and Daniel looked up.

Rain Shower smiled. "A *taibo* cannot harm

195

me, my precious one. But I have forgotten my place. I should have thanked you. You counted many coup tonight. We will sing songs of your bravery upon our return to Cache Creek."

He liked her touch, and felt more pain when she returned her hand to grip the spoon.

"So if you still think this was . . . what is it the Pale Eyes say . . . a crime? Yes, crime. If that is what your heart tells you, then you must seek out that *Tejano*."

He repeated his excuse. "I cannot go into the Tivoli by myself."

She shook her head, and Daniel wondered if she thought that he was revealing coward-ice. "Then ask the Metal Shirt. Ask Striker, who speaks true." The bell above the door rang. Rain Shower looked up and pointed the spoon. "Or ask that *taibo*. He is your friend. He would help you."

As Daniel turned around toward the door, he heard Rain Shower's voice drop. "He would do anything to drink the Pale-Eyes whiskey."

Hat in hand, smile creeping across his face, Billy Kyne walked toward their table, and sat down in the seat that the patrolman had recently abandoned.

■ ■ ■ ■

"You been holding out on your old pard, Billy Kyne," the reporter said after ordering a cup of coffee from the waitress. "I'm cutting the dust with some of the boys at the watering hole at the Commercial Hotel, and come back to the Texas Wagon Yard only to find that Daniel Killstraight has up and flown the coop. And this pretty Comanche squaw has taken off after him. Sounds peculiar to me, so, with my nose smelling a story, I roam across Hell's Half Acre. And what do I find? Besides a waddie sleeping off a drunk with his hands manacled behind his back down on Calhoun Street? I discover a hell of a lot of commotion at a sporting house."

He paused as the waitress placed a steaming cup of coffee on the table, then scooped up the coins Sergeant O'Doherty had left behind, and handed them to the waitress. "Will this cover everything, darling?"

She rolled her eyes, muttered a sarcastic thanks, and left for the cash box.

Kyne brought the flask from his pocket, sweetened the black coffee, and held out the flask. "Care for a snort?"

Comanche eyes glared back at him.

197

"I admit, it's an acquired taste, but, once you get used to it, there's few things better than Manhattan rye."

"I could get used to eating dirt," Rain Shower said, "but why should I want to?"

His eyebrows arched as Billy Kyne shook his head, screwed the lid on tight, and dropped the flask back into his coat pocket.

"Well, I do have to say my editor will be pleased as punch at the story I'll file when I get back to Dallas. Comanches on warpath in Cowtown. According to my findings, a Comanche buck and his squaw. . . ."

"I do not care for that word . . . *squaw.*"

Kyne stopped, studied Daniel, and took another sip. "All right, this Comanche princess and her warrior left one gent with his jaw broken, nose flattened, and he won't be able to go back to work at the Texas Express Company for nigh a month. Two other blokes didn't make out good, either. One got his brains almost beaten out of him." He drank more rye-spiced coffee. "Not quite sure I've got all the particulars on that. There might have been another red savage in the mix." The cup sank below the table onto Kyne's lap. "And the third victim, his end is a heartbreaker. Got a bottle shoved into him. Doc says he'll likely loose that limb for sure. Poor Leo Barton. Never

198

again will he dance with a pretty gal unless he can learn to do the Virginia reel on a peg leg."

Rain Shower leaned forward, eyes wide. "It is true? The one will lose his leg?"

Kyne winked. "He will in the Dallas *Herald,* pretty warrior. Till Leo Barton demands a retraction."

The cup returned to his lips, and Kyne drank heartily, ignoring the black brew's heat. He put the cup on the table, and brought out his Old Glory tablet and a pencil. "So set the record straight, folks. What happened tonight?"

Daniel and Rain Shower exchanged glances, but did not answer.

Kyne sighed, and emptied his coffee cup. "And after I've done your work for you," he said. "I found that maid, Killstraight, and talked to her about Room Four. Good thing I've learned some Spanish living in Texas. Not that she knew anything, but, yes, she made the bed that morning. Says they never lock the doors. Got tired of drunks busting them down to break into empty rooms, but that they warn lodgers to lock their doors, it being Hell's Half Acre. So anybody could have slept there. Anybody."

The bell rang above the door, and Daniel turned, surprised to find O'Doherty making his way back inside the ice cream parlor. He stopped at the table, studying Kyne with a mixture of suspicion and contempt, then looked at Daniel.

"A word in private, Sergeant Killstraight?" O'Doherty said stiffly.

When Daniel started to rise, Kyne said good-naturedly: "Oh, whatever you can say to Daniel, you can certainly share with me, Sergeant. We're pards, me and Daniel. Share and share alike. Ain't that right, Daniel?"

Daniel planned on ignoring Kyne, until the newspaper reporter added something in a less friendly tone. "Or have you forgotten that cottonwood trunk ol' Billy Kyne fetched for you Comanch' to help with poor, sickly Quanah Parker?"

He sank back into his chair, suddenly ashamed. When he found his voice, he nodded toward Kyne and told the Fort Worth policeman: "You can speak in front of this man."

O'Doherty didn't like it, but he cleared his throat. "Something came to mind," he said. "The drunk from Kussatz's dram shop. I remember him. Not his name, but I know the brand he rides for. He's *segundo* for Sol Carmody's outfit on the Elm Fork, and that's fitting, that he'd ride for Carmody. They're two of the hardest rocks in Texas."

200

CHAPTER FIFTEEN

After the police sergeant left the Queen City Ice Cream Parlor, Billy Kyne pushed back his hat with the end of his pencil, whistled, and began writing furiously in his notebook. Finished, he tucked the pencil over his ear and looked at Rain Shower, then at Daniel, his face beaming.

"That theory you have about foul play is perking up something considerable, Danny, my boy. Sol Carmody. That copper was right, kids, when he said Carmody's hard. Hard and mean. And if my memory hasn't been clouded by Manhattan rye, I'd say he's got as good a motive as anyone hereabouts to see Quanah . . . or any Comanch' . . . done in." He let out a chuckle, and shook his head. "You two Indians are going to get Billy Kyne back on staff in New York City for the *Tribune,* and that'll sure have Horace Greeley spinning in his grave."

He leaned forward, elbows on the table,

head held by his hands, and whispered: "Carmody's wife and two sons were massacred by Comanches in 'Seventy-Two. The newspapers hereabouts wouldn't even print what you-all had done to Missus Carmody."

Daniel pushed himself up. "Come," he said. "We must go to the saloon."

"That's an offer Billy Kyne would never turn down." He stood, too, but Rain Shower stopped them.

"No."

They looked down at her. Her face was rigid.

"Have you forgotten *pianahuwait?*" she asked. "We must return to the Beaver Ceremony. Nagwee needs us. As does Quanah."

The sun rose, the church bells pealed, yet they continued to dance, drum, and sing. Fighting exhaustion, they went on until shortly before noon, when, as they sang the closing song four times, Nagwee loosened the ropes securing the teepee to the stakes. Still singing, they rose, and ran out of the curing lodge in all directions.

The Big Doctoring was over. The People would have to wait and see how strong Nagwee's *puha* would prove to be.

From the size of the crowd, Daniel figured

Fort Worth's curiosity had dwindled. He could count the spectators — including five hymn-singing women led by a Bible-clutching man with a long black beard and flat-brimmed black hat shouting that the city should not condone such sacrilege, that Fort Worth was a Sodom for allowing this heathen practice. The only newspaper reporters there were Billy Kyne, a Negro from a Dallas newspaper, and four Fort Worth reporters. *Harper's Weekly, Scribner's,* and the *Police Gazette* were gone. So were the journalists from Kansas City, Jacksboro, Austin, London, and San Antonio.

"I must help take Quanah back to his room," Daniel whispered to Charles Flint. "Can you answer their questions?" He hoped Flint's anger at him had subsided.

It must have, because Flint stammered before finally nodding. "I will try. But what if I'm wrong?"

Smiling, Daniel put his arm on the book-keeper's shoulder, and squeezed. Lowering his voice, he whispered: "They won't ever know."

Following the two *puhakats,* Ben Buffalo Bone and Daniel carried Quanah on a litter provided by the city fire department back upstairs above the Taylor & Barr mercantile.

Rain Shower, Cuhtz Bávi, and Frank Striker trailed them, as Flint went to the reporters, already firing questions at him. Nagwee opened the door to the room he shared with Isa-tai, and they laid Quanah on a buffalo robe on the floor near the window.

Frank Striker said he would retire to his room, and headed downstairs for the Pickwick Hotel.

The window was open, and a surprisingly cool breeze filled the room. Daniel hadn't noticed until now that the skies had darkened. Thunder rumbled. Rain Shower prepared a pipe, and Nagwee accepted it and sat, the other men joining him in a circle.

As always, the first puff of smoke was offered to the Great Spirit, and the next to the sun. They smoked, and, when the pipe returned to Nagwee, he nodded.

"It was a good ceremony," he said. "Considering."

"Not so good," Isa-tai said with bitterness. "Polluted by *taibo* hands. *Taibo* cloth instead of buffalo hides for the lodge. Not even a cottonwood trunk on that first night of prayer." He looked at Quanah with contempt, then stared directly at Daniel. "He will die."

Rage boiled inside Daniel, but Nagwee spoke calmly. "Not if my *puha* is strong."

204

Isa-tai started to comment, but stopped.

After a moment of silence, Ben Buffalo Bone said: "I thought the Pale Eyes were helpful. Not all of them. But many."

"This is true." Nagwee's head bobbed.

"They helped kill him," Isa-tai said.

Cuhtz Bávi looked from face to face, but said nothing.

Lightning flashed. Several seconds later, thunder rolled. No one spoke, and Daniel sensed a presence. They had left the door open, and, when he turned, he saw Billy Kyne leaning against the frame, nodding his head politely, then tilted it in a gesture that it was time to go.

Daniel looked back at Nagwee, who frowned and said: "I suppose you must go again, He Whose Arrows Fly Straight Into The Hearts Of His Enemies."

Daniel dropped his head.

"Go. This is not a pleasant smoke." He glared at Isa-tai, then painted on a smile, and lifted his hands toward Rain Shower. "Help an old holy man to his feet, dearest one."

Rain Shower was staying in Room 4, while Ben Buffalo Bone had thrown his gear in Daniel's apartment, and Cuhtz Bávi was rooming with Charles Flint. Since Frank Striker had a room in the Pickwick Hotel, obviously the management did not realize he had married a Kiowa. The room where Yellow Bear had died remained unoccupied.

"Give me one minute," Daniel told Kyne, and gestured at Ben Buffalo Bone. They walked down the hall to Daniel's room, went inside, where Daniel grabbed two pencils and his Old Glory tablet. *"Bávi,"* he said, "I ask you to do a huge favor for me."

"It will be done, *bávi.*"

Daniel ran his tongue across his lips. "Watch Quanah. Make sure he is not left alone with Isa-tai."

Ben Buffalo Bone frowned. "Isa-tai . . . do you think . . . ?"

He silenced his friend by holding up his hand. "I am not sure of anything. That is why I go with this *taibo.* Just keep your eyes and ears open."

"Bávi, it will be done." Ben Buffalo Bone nodded.

He left Ben Buffalo Bone, saying — *"Pbah vee."* Take care. — and followed Billy Kyne down the hall. They met Charles Flint on the stairs outside, and Daniel stopped.

"How did it go?"

Flint's eyes were glassy, but he nodded. "Well . . . I guess."

Daniel gave him a thankful nod, took a few steps down, and stopped. "Will you do me one other favor?"

"Yes."

"Watch over Rain Shower. This place can be unpleasant."

"It will be done," Flint said, and Daniel joined Billy Kyne, who was waiting at the bottom of the stairs.

The beer-jerker at Tivoli Hall wiped down the edge of the bar with a damp towel, started to answer Kyne's question, but a shout from the other end commanded his attention, and he moved down the bar, drawing a foamy beer from a tap, and slid a pewter stein down to a waiting customer. Seconds later, he stood in front of Daniel and Kyne.

It was not much after 1:00 P.M., and Herman Kussatz's saloon was crowded with men in suits, farmers in denim, cowhands wearing big hats. Various languages rang out, most of which Daniel recognized from his mining days as German. He could understand the saloon's popularity. Kussatz offered a free lunch all day long, and it was dinnertime. Even Kyne had ordered a draft beer and was spreading something yellow on the thick slice of bread he was about to use to cover a chunk of ham.

"Vednesday night?" The barkeep snorted.

"Ja, I vork dat night. You expect me to remember Vednesday? *Nein.*"

Daniel had known this would be a long shot.

The bartender pointed down the bar at a big box labeled Gurley's Patented Refrigerator. "Kussatz buy that. Keeps beer colder than ice, vill hold one hundred fifty kegs. Place is very busy. *Nein, nein,* I don't know the cowboy."

Kyne bit into the sandwich, chewed, chased it down with a long pull from his stein, while the bartender went back to draw three more beers and pour a shot of bourbon.

"The Hun's right," Kyne said with a mouthful of beer and sandwich. "I wouldn't let that miser I work for in Dallas know my true feelings, but this beer hall is finer than anything in Dallas, that's for certain. Ranchers, mayors, newspapermen, cowboys, cattle buyers. Everybody drinks here. Probably the best dram shop in all of Texas."

When the German returned, the bartender asked: "Vot does the cowboy look like?"

"He wore spurs," Daniel answered.

The beer-jerker laughed, and Kyne joined him. "Most do in this city," Kyne said. "You need more of a description than that."

Daniel tried to remember. He could not

remember anything about the man's face, wasn't even sure he had seen the face. The hat the cowboy had worn was indistinguishable. Even the spurs sounded as did most he had heard in Fort Worth, Dallas, Wichita Falls, Fort Smith, and on the reservation pastures.

Kyne drained his beer, and addressed the German: "He's *segundo* for Sol Carmody. You know Carmody, don't you?"

The bartender tossed the rag into a tin pail behind the bar. "Ja. Most do."

Kyne pushed the empty stein toward the German, who scooped it into a huge hand, and moved back to the line of taps. When he returned, and set the beer in front of the newspaperman, Kyne said: "All we want is the *segundo*'s name?"

"*Nein.* I don't know the cowboy." He took the empty plate, and moved back down the bar.

After sipping his second beer, Kyne looked at Daniel and shrugged. "Well, it was a long shot, Killstraight. But if that copper was right, and it was Carmody's ramrod, I should be able to find his name directly. Or you and I could ride out north to the Elm Fork, pay a visit to Sol. I take it you want to question this fellow yourself?"

Daniel stared at his full glass of water and

the bowl of beans he had not touched. Deep in thought, he did not answer Kyne, who finished his beer, and fished out three coins, which he slapped on the bar. "Come on, Killstraight. I need to get to the depot and hop a train back to Dallas."

The bartender was back, staring at Daniel's bowl, swiping the coins into the deep pocket of his apron. When he turned to leave, Daniel spoke. "*Herr* Bartender." He remembered the miners calling the beer-jerkers that back in Pennsylvania. When the big German looked at him, Daniel asked: "Was Sol Carmody here on Wednesday night?"

"*Ja.*" He nodded, and hooked a thumb toward a table facing the Houston Street window. "Sit there. Vit your Injun."

Kyne's shoe slipped on the brass rail. He bumped into the well-dressed man standing next to him, excused himself, and pulled the pencil from his ear. "Carmody was drinking with Yellow Bear?"

"*Ja.*" The bartender nodded. "*Ja.* Now I remember. The cowboy. He sit vit them, too. Vear spurs, ja. Dark hair. Mustache. But his name?" He shrugged apologetically. "*Nein.*"

Daniel and Kyne exchanged a quick glance, then Daniel asked: "How many were sitting at that table?"

"Injun chief vit feathers. Carmody." He held up two fingers. "Zwei cowboys." Another shrug. "Others come, go, sit, talk."

The bartender went back, this time carrying Daniel's untouched bowl of beans.

Daniel thumbed back three or four pages of his Old Glory tablet. He found the name. "George Briggs," he said.

"Right." Kyne scratched something on a blank page. "Foreman for Dan Waggoner."

"I thought Waggoner and Carmody did not like each other," Daniel said.

Kyne wrote something else. "That's an understatement, Killstraight. Nobody in the Northern Texas Stock Growers' Association cares for Sol Carmody, and he hates everybody."

Daniel chewed on the end of his Faber's pencil for a moment, then removed the pencil. "But could Briggs and Carmody . . . could they be friends?"

" 'Misery acquaints a man with strange bedfellows,' Shakespeare wrote in *The Tempest.* Or as Charles Dudley Warner, who gave me my first newspaper job at the Hartford *Courant,* put it . . . 'politics makes strange bedfellows.' And to quote William J. Kyne . . . 'Cold draft beer and a free lunch can absolutely make the bitterest of enemies temporary pals.' "

The beer-jerker was back, bringing a plate of smelly beef and a tumbler of whiskey to the gent standing beside Kyne, and placing a stein of beer into the hand of a tall, blond man.

"On the other hand," Kyne continued, "Briggs might hoist some beers with Sol Carmody's ramrod, but share a table with Carmody himself? Not a chance in hell, Killstraight. Not if he wanted to keep his job riding for Dan Waggoner."

"*Ja, ja.* Vagner," the German said. "He come, too. Sit for a few minutes." He looked at Daniel and Kyne. "You finished?"

Kyne stared at Daniel, who leaned on the bar and asked: "Dan Waggoner sat down with Sol Carmody?"

"*Ja.* Not long. Five minutes maybe. Then he left."

"What time did everybody leave?"

He shook his head. "*Nein.* I can't say."

"Horse apples, you damned Hun!" Kyne straightened, tried to look bigger, but no matter how much he sucked in his stomach, he would not be a noon shadow to the bruising German. "You might not remember when those two cowhands left, or even Sol Carmody or Dan Waggoner, but a Comanche all decked out like Yellow Bear. You wouldn't forget him. You'd be watching

212

him on account you're curious as everybody else, and you'd never seen a Comanche back on the Rhine or the Danube or wherever you come from. You know. Put that little brain to moil and give us an answer."

It was not the approach Daniel would have chosen, but it worked. The beer-jerker frowned, but answered. "The chief left vit von cowboy at midnight." Shrugging. "Near midnight. Before, after, I can't say."

So George Briggs had been telling the truth.

"Just Yellow Bear and Waggoner's cowhand, George Briggs?" Kyne spoke with urgency. "Not them other two? Or Waggoner. Yellow Bear walked out with just one man?"

"Don't know the name of the cowboy, but *ja,* von left vit the chief. Vagner, he vas gone long time before."

"And Carmody," Daniel asked, "and the other?"

"Nein." Another shake of his head. "I don't remember." Glaring at Kyne. "Dat is so."

Again, a customer called, and the barkeep moved down the bar.

"That's something," Kyne said, gathering his tablet and pencils. "I don't have a farthing what it means, but it must mean something." They headed for the batwing doors. "I'll find out that gent's name. You want to ride out to Carmody's ranch? I can rent a buggy. Take us all day to get there."

Daniel shook his head. There was no guarantee Carmody or his foreman would be at the ranch, and, besides, Kyne was right. Maybe they had something, but what?

"And when I see Dan Waggoner, I'll nail his hide to the barn. What's he doing, meeting with Sol Carmody?"

They pushed through the batwing doors, and Daniel ran straight into Ben Buffalo Bone.

His Kotsoteka friend's face looked troubled.

"It is Quanah," Ben said. "Come quick."

CHAPTER SIXTEEN

Large, hard drops of rain pelted them as they ran across the street and up the stairs. Daniel was soaked and cold by the time he reached Nagwee's room. The door was open, the window now closed to keep out the dampness, and Rain Shower and Charles Flint knelt over Quanah.

His heart sank as he entered the room, squeezing past Nagwee and Isa-tai. Cuhtz Bávi sat on the floor, tamping tobacco into a pipe bowl.

Rain Shower looked up, smiling, and Quanah turned his head. His eyes focused, and he worked his lips before calling out in a weak voice: *"Maruaweeka."*

A grin exploded, and Daniel sank onto the blanket, reaching down, grabbing Quanah's extended hand — "Hello yourself." — he said in English.

Behind him, Billy Kyne's voice thundered: "Damnation. No other reporters here?

Excellent. Just excellent. Is he going to live?"

Turning around, Nagwee spoke in his native tongue. "My *puha* is strong." He was speaking, not to the *Herald* reporter, but Isa-tai, and he was smiling with satisfaction when he said it. Isa-tai's face grew harder, his frown deeper, and he folded his arms across his chest, and turned away from Nagwee, staring at the wall.

"What's that mean?" Kyne wiped his notebook on his coat, which was dripping wet. "What did he say?"

"He said his power is strong," Daniel said.

Quanah added, summoning strength from somewhere deep within, in English: *"I will live."*

Kyne wrote, tried harder, gave up, flipped his notebook to another page, and tried again, before cursing and sending the pencil flying across the room, where it bounced off the wall and landed in Nagwee's bed.

"Wet pencil. Wet pages. Damn, I gotta get this in now." Thunder drowned out Kyne's farewell. Lightning flashed, more thunder rolled, and Billy Kyne was gone.

"It is good to see you," Quanah told Daniel.

Tears rolled down his cheeks. "My friend, it is great to see you."

Flint lifted Quanah's head, and Rain

216

Shower gave him water from a tumbler. Some dribbled down Quanah's chin, but, when the glass was empty, he said: "More."

Flint rose, and, as he poured from a pitcher, Quanah's eyes wandered around the room.

"Where is Yellow Bear?" he asked.

Charles Flint held up Quanah's arm, letting Daniel wrap clean linen strips around the cuts the Kwahadi leader had carved down his forearm with Cuhtz Bávi's knife. Personally Daniel had not thought this had been a good idea, weak as Quanah was, but Quanah had insisted, and Nagwee had grunted that it was good, that the one who had gone to The Land Beyond The Sun should be mourned by his daughter's husband.

"There." Gently Flint lowered Quanah's arm.

Releasing a heavy sigh, Quanah sadly shook his head. Tears streamed down his face, shaming Daniel as he remembered he had not properly mourned Yellow Bear.

"It is hard to believe he is gone," Quanah said. "I have lost too many wise men whose counsel I often needed."

Daniel bit his bottom lip. Isa Nanaka and now Yellow Bear had died. Teepee That Stands Alone was broken, shattered, living

217

alone, hardly seeing anyone, south of Saddle Mountain. Others had fallen victim to the pale-eyes whiskey, no longer caring for The People, for their families, living for nothing except another drink. Other than Nagwee and Cuhtz Bávi, who was left? Isa-tai? The thought made Daniel shudder.

"You are cold," Quanah said. "Tetecae, close the window."

"I am all right," Daniel said.

"But something troubles you. Speak, He Whose Arrows Fly Straight Into The Hearts Of His Enemies."

Daniel glanced at Charles Flint, but, when his eyes met the bookkeeper's, he quickly looked away.

"Go ahead," Flint said. "Ask him."

"Ask me what?"

"You are weak," Daniel said. "You should rest."

Quanah reached over, grabbed Daniel's forearm, and squeezed tightly. *Ask me what?*"

Daniel swallowed. Lightning flashed, followed by a deafening roar of thunder. The rain, which had been falling off and on all afternoon, had turned into a downpour. He wondered about Isa-tai, Nagwee, Rain Shower, and the others. School Father Pratt and Captain Hall had come upstairs, paid

Quanah their respects, then taken the others to a steakhouse to eat supper. How long had they been gone? Thirty minutes? An hour?

"Speak, my friend. What is on your mind? What troubles you?"

He looked into Quanah's eyes. His lips moved as he tried to find the words.

"What do you remember about the night?" It was Charles Flint who had spoken.

"The night?" Quanah blinked.

"The night you were almost called to The Land Beyond The Sun?" Flint explained.

Quanah's eyes closed, and his brow furrowed. "I went to sleep," he said. "I was very tired for it had been a long day." He motioned for a drink, and Daniel filled the tumbler and handed it to him as Flint helped raise his head.

"I have a vague memory of falling onto the floor. My head was spinning. My lungs did not wish to work. I pulled myself toward the light."

"The light?" Daniel asked.

"*Haa*, the light. It marked the door."

Light . . . shining through the crack between the door and the floor. Which meant the lamps were off in their room. Well, Daniel had known that already.

"Yellow Bear had kicked you out of bed,"

Flint said, and Daniel saw Quanah cringe. Flint had done it again, dishonoring the dead by speaking their names. "He saved your life, undoubtedly."

"He who is traveling to The Land Beyond The Sun saved my life more than once."

No one spoke for a long while. Rain pounded the windowpanes. The breeze felt almost cold.

"That is not all you wish to know," Quanah said.

Daniel ran his fingers through his hair, nodding. "The *kupl-ta.*" He pointed to the lamp, turned off, on the wall over Nagwee's bed, then decided to explain. "Did you turn it off?"

"Haa." His head bobbed. "After I came in and prepared myself to sleep."

Flint cleared his throat. "Blow it out, or turn it down?"

Quanah's answer made Daniel's heartbeat increase. "Turn it down. The kupl-ta was gas. This, Captain Hall explained to me."

"This was explained to you," Flint said, "and what of . . ." — this time he remembered — "the one who is no more?"

"I told him." His eyes narrowed, and he looked first at Flint, then at Daniel. "What are you trying to say?"

Daniel pointed to the window, where rain

dribbled on the sill and splattered against the glass. "Did you open the window when you came back from our supper?"

Quanah's head shook. "No."

Daniel frowned, and Flint shook his head.

"I had no need to open it, for it was already open. You two young Kwahadis have short memories. It was not always so cool. It was stifling when we first arrived in this place. We always left the window open."

"The father of your favorite wife?" Flint asked. "Do you remember when he came back? Did he wake you?"

Shaking his head, Quanah said: "I remember nothing, except falling to the floor and crawling toward the light, and I am not certain I even remember that. It seemed more like a dream."

"Could he who is gone," Flint asked, "could he have blown out the lamp by mistake?"

Quanah stared.

"Could he have closed the window?" Daniel asked.

First, Quanah wet his lips, then he clenched his fists. Lightning flashed, and the rain seemed to slacken as the thunder pealed somewhere to the east. "Why would he have done either of those things? You two are foolish boys. He who has traveled to The

Land Beyond The Sun was no fool, which you two seem to think he was."

Daniel started to protest, but Quanah would not let him.

"He was a *puhakat,* and a very wise man. I always listened to what he had to say, for he was a man who spoke with great wisdom. He never touched the *taibo* spirits that rob our young and old of their tact, their reason, their souls. If I told him that these lamps were not coal oil but gas . . . and this I did tell him . . . and that he should not blow them out, he would have remembered. He was very wise." Angrily he rose one arm to lean on his elbow and hooked a thumb toward the window. "Nor would he have closed the window. As I once heard a Pale Eyes say . . . 'One does not make hell any hotter.' "

Daniel hung his head, and tried to explain. "We did not mean to insult a great *puhakat.* He was a man Tetecae and I always respected and admired. We just had to know these things."

"Why?"

Again, Daniel pointed to the gas lamps on the wall. "When we found you the next morning, the lamps were on, but the fire had been put out." He pointed to the window. "And the window was shut and

222

even latched shut."

Flint cleared his throat, then added: "The door was locked. We found a key on the table."

"School Father Pratt kicked the door open," Daniel added. "We barely got you out before you began the great journey."

His eyes closed tightly, Quanah lay there, not moving except for the slight shaking of his head, as he tried to comprehend everything.

"Could . . . ?" Flint hesitated, tried again. "Could that *puhakat* . . . could he have made a mistake?"

Eyes still closed, head still moving, Quanah said tightly: "No."

"He was tired," Flint said. "As you were. He had been up till midnight with the *Tejanos*. Is it possible . . . ?"

"He would not have blown out those lamps," Quanah said, his eyes open, blazing. "And what kind of fool would have closed the window. The windows in my Star House are always open during the summer. Otherwise my wives and I would not be able to live in such a place."

"Then it is settled," Daniel said. He did not want to upset the great Kwahadi any more.

"I meant you no disrespect," Flint added.

"We just need to know for certain," Daniel said.

"The key?" Flint said cautiously. "What of the key? Did you lock the door?"

This time Quanah thought for a minute or two, recalling details from a memory clouded by a coma.

"We had one key. The man gave it to us in the hotel." His Adam's apple bobbed. He pressed his lips together. "I do not believe in locking doors. If anyone wants to visit me, my door is open. At my home. At the many hotels I have stayed in pale-eyes cities." Another pause to remember. "When we got to our room, I put the key on the table by the bed. It was always there."

Daniel straightened. "The night table?"

"*Haa.* I put the key by the Jesus book."

Flint looked at Daniel, then back at Quanah. "Not on the dresser? The wooden tower with boxes where Pale Eyes keep their clothes."

"The table by the bed. It was there when I went to bed. I know this because I thought to pick up the Jesus book, but I do not understand all of those marks."

Again, Daniel and Flint stared at each other.

"Why do you ask me these questions?" Quanah said. "What does this mean?"

224

Daniel looked at the sick chief of The People. "*Tsu Kuh Puah,* I do not believe this was an accident," he said. "The window was found shut, locked. The key was found on the dresser, not on the table by the bed. The lamps were on, the flames blown out, filling the room with poisoned air. We found red markings, prints from someone's thumb, on the lamp's globe, and on the glass of the window. I believe that someone was trying to kill you."

"And the father of my favorite wife?"

"His death was an accident," Flint said. "You were the one he meant to kill."

Far off in the distance, thunder rolled across the night sky. The rain had stopped, and the streets of Hell's Half Acre became alive again.

Quanah's tears resumed their flow. "Who would want to kill me?" he asked, and choked back a sob for Yellow Bear.

"That is the question we must answer," Flint said.

The sobs ceased, and Daniel saw that Quanah was asleep. Good. He needed more strength, and Daniel felt guilty for draining Quanah so. He should have waited, asked Quanah these questions later. On the other hand, he had read in the *National Police Gazette* that it is best to interview witnesses immediately, and not wait until their memories are clouded by ideas of what they thought they had seen, thought they remembered. A detective should, he recalled, have all his questions written out before him. A good detective must know what to ask. His Old Glory tablet was in his room down the hall. He hadn't even thought to bring it to the Tivoli Hall.

Some detective I am.

"I have told you," Charles Flint said, "that you think my father did this, but I say he did not. I will prove to you that he did not."

"We must work together," Daniel said.

Flint stared, eyes as black and as untrusting as Isa-tai's.

"Do you know what an alibi is?"

"It is. . . ." Flint finally flashed a rare smile. "It is something one needs not know to keep books for a trading post."

Daniel grinned back. "It is something that proves one did not, could not commit a crime."

"My father could not have committed this crime."

"So he must have an alibi. He has motive, and this you cannot deny. He had opportunity."

"Then his alibi is that he was asleep in the same room with Nagwee."

226

"We will ask Nagwee about that night. My friend Hugh Gunter, a Cherokee policeman, says that one must investigate a crime with an open mind." Actually Hugh Gunter hadn't said that at all. Hugh Gunter's philosophy was often: *If I think the sum-bitch did it, he did it, and I'll prove he did it, and see the bastard gets what's coming to him.* "I have an open mind. I do not wish ill upon Isa-tai. I hope he did not have any hand in this. And he is not the only person who is what Deputy Marshal Harvey P. Noble calls a suspect."

He let Flint digest this. Maybe he could make Charles Flint a Metal Shirt. As sergeant, he could always use someone willing to risk his life and hair for $8 a month, someone who didn't mind the taunts from The People. Someone who could be spit on in the afternoon by a grandmother for arresting her son or grandson.

"We eliminate the suspects," Daniel explained. "We find who has an alibi that says they did not commit the crime. But first we must find out why the crime was committed." He posed the question to Flint. "So who would want to see Quanah dead?"

While Flint chewed on that, Daniel was already thinking: *Who was in the room when I saw the key on the dresser? Nagwee and*

Isa-tai. Flint and School Father Pratt. George Briggs. Burk Burnett. Dan Waggoner.

He frowned.

Or there could have been another key. That gave him more suspects. Sol Carmody. The thousands of Pale Eyes who hate The People and were in Fort Worth. And what do I really know of this Pale Eyes newspaperman, Kyne? Why is he so curious about what happened?

Still, another thought struck him.

Or Quanah could be wrong, and Flint right. Yellow Bear might have moved the key. No matter how intelligent he was . . . and in my heart I know he was a great, wise man . . . this is not the land of The People. He could have locked the door, closed the window, blown out the lamps.

Daniel sighed. Tonight, he would fill up his Old Glory tablet. He'd have to buy another at the Taylor & Barr mercantile tomorrow morning.

Chapter Seventeen

He studied the list:

Isa-tai
Nagwee
Pratt
G. Briggs
Burnett
Waggoner
Carmody
Kyne
Capt. Hall
Cowboy in alley?
Tetecae Tetecae

Nagwee would not have tried to kill Quanah. Never. Nor could Daniel suspect School Father, even though both the holy man and Pratt had been in the room, and could easily have placed the key on the dresser. Captain Hall was the only one who hadn't been upstairs in the room. So Daniel had scratched their names off his list of suspects. He thought about the cowboy he had seen in the alley, and while Daniel knew the drunken man who worked for Sol Carmody was in the alley when he heard the door close, he had put a question mark beside that entry.

Kyne had been right. Daniel needed to find this cowboy who worked for the Comanche-hating Sol Carmody. Needed to ask him some questions.

He looked at Flint's name. At first, he had scratched through it, but then he had to reconsider. He liked Tetecae well enough, wanted to like him even more if only for no other reason than he needed someone to trust.

"I do not understand those bird-track marks," Ben Buffalo Bone said from over Daniel's shoulder.

Which made Daniel smile. He was glad that his Kotsoteka friend had joined him in Fort Worth. He could trust Ben Buffalo Bone.

"Do you remember how we used to steal the chickens from the coop at the missionary school after I first arrived on the reservation?" Daniel asked.

Ben Buffalo Bone had a hearty, rich laugh.

"My father would say that The People

230

have fallen on hard times," Ben said, "when their young braves must go on raids for stupid birds that cannot even fly, and not horses or Mexicans to turn into slaves."

Tears welled in Daniel's eyes. "My mother would just shake her head, when I showed her our plunder. But she would glare at the Black Robes when they came to tell her that we must be punished, that stealing was wrong in the eyes of their Lord."

"What does a *taibo* god know about The People?"

School Father Pratt's words echoed in Daniel's mind: *Kill the Indian, not the man.*

Ben's broad hand slapped his shoulder. "Those were fine days, *bávi*. Not as fine as when the Kotsotekas, and you, the Kwahadis, roamed free to hunt, free to do as we pleased, but we made the best of those days, did we not?"

"Surely, we did."

A fat finger pointed to one of the words. Tetecae's name.

Daniel frowned. He just could not get around the fact that Charles Flint had been in the room. He could have slipped the key onto the dresser.

"But I do not understand why the Pale Eyes have to put down stories on paper. Some of them speak well, and there is noth-

231

ing better than sitting around a circle, smoking, telling stories. The People do not tell stories this way."

Daniel wrote another line — *Accident?* — and flipped to a new page in his new Old Glory writing tablet.

"But we do," he told Ben Buffalo Bone. "We draw pictures on our hides to tell the stories of what happened during a year. We tell stories in pictures on our war shields."

"*Haa,* but when we paint a *chimal,* this paper is only good for stuffing the insides so that a *chimal* might turn away the arrow of an enemy. And pictures make more sense than these marks."

Ben Buffalo Bone walked around the writing table, and sat in the chair across from Daniel.

"Nagwee and Isa-tai say that Quanah is no longer in danger, and the Pale Eyes doctor agrees. Soon, we will return home. So what is it that troubles you, my brother?"

What troubled him was Rain Shower, and the nightmare. Maybe that had been not a dream, but a vision, foretelling of the ruction at the sporting house when Daniel had almost killed a *taibo* with his bare hands. He raised a finger, and gently touched the bruise between his eye and hair, just above the temple.

He left out his concerns about Ben's sister, and told him instead about what he suspected had been an attempt to kill Quanah Parker.

Typical of The People, Ben Buffalo Bone's face betrayed no emotion, and he never interrupted Daniel to ask questions. When Daniel had finished, his friend just sat there, staring, thinking.

"One *Nermernuh* would not kill another *Nermernuh*," he said at last. "I will not believe that."

"Even Isa-tai?" Daniel said.

"Especially Isa-tai. It is true that Isa-tai and Quanah do not often agree on what is best for The People, but Isa-tai is a powerful *puhakat*. It was not his fault for what happened all those years ago. The stupid Striped Arrows brave killed a skunk and destroyed Isa-tai's *puha* during the raid. Isa-tai vomited up thousands of cartridges for our fast-shooting rifles. My own father saw this with his very eyes."

Daniel glanced at his list. "Then one of the Pale Eyes cattlemen. This Sol Carmody, he despises The People for what they did to his family."

Daniel's mind flashed to another cattleman, a *Tejano* named J.C.C. McBride who had hated The People. Immediately Daniel tried to block out that memory. He had killed the rancher, and had done it in a way that The People of old — especially his father, and old Isa Nanaka, Quanah, too — would have appreciated, except that he had not taken the *taibo*'s scalp.

"I do not know this Pale Eyes that you call Sol Car-mo-dy." Ben Buffalo Bone shook his head.

Daniel stood and walked toward his bed, found the original Old Glory tablet in his valise, and returned with it to the desk. He flipped through some pages, read a few notes, and looked up at Ben Buffalo Bone.

"His cattle graze at The Big Pasture. Weeks ago, you rode there when we learned that there were longhorns eating The People's grass. Do you recall this?"

Ben Buffalo Bone's head bobbed. "*Haa,* I rode there. There were cattle. Twice Bent Nose came with me. Many cattle. Three *Tejanos.*"

"But they had no right to be in The Big Pasture."

"No, *bávi,* they did. One of the Pale Eyes shows me a piece of paper with the scratch marks. He says it gives him the right. I do not know about this. Nor does Twice Bent Nose. But the *Tejano* says that I can take it to show Biggers. This I do."

"And what did Agent Biggers say?"

"He reads the markings and says that the paper seems to be . . . I do not remember the *taibo* word. . . . But that the cattle should stay in The Big Pasture for now."

"What did Quanah say?"

"I did not tell Quanah."

Daniel pressed his lips tight. "Why did you not speak of this with Quanah?"

Ben Buffalo Bone could only shrug, but now his face showed emotion.

Smiling, Daniel reached across the table and put his hand on Ben Buffalo Bone's shoulder. "It is all right, my friend. You did nothing wrong. Did Agent Biggers keep the paper?"

The young Kotsoteka nodded.

Daniel found his new writing tablet, flipped back a page, and studied the list. George Briggs . . . Burk Burnett . . . Dan Waggoner.

He made a mark through Burnett's name. Like Captain Lee Hall, Burk Burnett needed Quanah. So did the Northern Texas Stock Growers' Association. Quanah supported these cattlemen, and they, in turn, supported Quanah. Quanah's death would have complicated any future lease on The Big Pasture or the other grazing areas controlled by The People.

235

That brought him to the names of Briggs and Waggoner.

Waggoner needed grass, or his ranch might be ruined. He had said so himself, but, then, if he could trust his memory, so had Burk Burnett. Yet Waggoner's words had been the sharpest, and Waggoner had been seen with his foreman in the Tivoli Hall, sharing drinks with Sol Carmody and his *segundo*. On the other hand, Dan Waggoner hated Sol Carmody. Or had that been an act? Or maybe . . . if Waggoner were desperate enough, would he have aligned himself with Carmody?

The ways of the Pale Eyes Daniel had learned. Quanah had signed one agreement, or was about to, that would lease The Big Pasture to Captain Lee Hall and his organization. Isa-tai had signed an agreement with Sol Carmody. They would fight this out for months, maybe even years, in courts. He thought of Greer County, a section of land north of the Red River that bordered the federal reservation of The People, the Apaches, and the Kiowas. Texians claimed that land belonged to the state of Texas. The government in Washington City said it was part of Indian Territory. Nothing had been decided, and this argument had been going on since before Daniel had been born.

So if two men said they had rights to The Big Pasture, what would happen? Lawyers would get rich. Eventually somebody would win, but by then many cattle might be dead from starvation. The Northern Texas Stock Growers' Association had no cattle on the land of The People. Sol Carmody did, and removing those cattle might take forever under the pale-eyes law. When you considered that, Daniel thought, it would make practical business sense for Dan Waggoner to agree to a truce with Sol Carmody.

"Would a truce be enough to commit murder?"

He hadn't realized he had said those words aloud, until Ben Buffalo Bone asked what did he mean.

"Bávi. . . ." Daniel gave him a weary smile. "I don't know what I mean."

It was a whole lot easier trying to solve disputes in the Nations, even if The People looked down on Metal Shirts. Judging a horse race would not cause Daniel's head to ache as it did now. Putting his elbows on the table, he reached up and massaged both temples.

If Quanah were dead, who would become leader of The People? Nagwee? Maybe, but he was no leader, just a holy man. Isa-tai? The Pale Eyes did not like him much, but they could not ignore his influence with The People. They might think that by naming him chief — which The People always considered silly for no one man led all the bands — it would make him easier to control.

Of course, they had thought that about Quanah, too.

He dropped his arms, staring at the names, thinking something else. Nagwee would not replace Quanah. Nor would Isatai. The Pale Eyes would first look to Yellow Bear. He was not only Quanah's father-in-law, but perhaps the most powerful *puhakat* on the reservation, even more powerful than Nagwee. Yellow Bear was a man much respected by both The People and the government of the Pale Eyes. Agent Biggers had once told Yellow Bear how much he enjoyed the old man's company, despite the fact that Yellow Bear spoke hardly any English and Biggers understood only a few *Nermernuh* words, despite their different opinions on religion.

Yellow Bear would have replaced Quanah.

Charles Flint had said that Yellow Bear's death had been an accident — probably not the correct *taibo* word — and that Quanah had been the intended victim. Maybe the man who had blown out the lamps, closed

238

the window, and locked the door had wanted both men to die. The more he thought about that, the more it seemed so reasonable.

Why haven't I considered this before?

"Tell me what you are thinking, my brother," Ben Buffalo Bone said. "I am no holy man, so I cannot read what is in your mind."

After Daniel had explained, Ben Buffalo Bone shook his head. "I will never understand the ways of the *Tejanos.* Or the Long Knives. You think this *taibo,* or *taibos,* they wanted to kill both Quanah and the father of his favorite wife? That sounds crazy to me, bávi."

Daniel shrugged. "I have known many *po-sa taibos.*"

Ben Buffalo Bone finally managed a smile. "That is true. And I have known many crazy *Nermernuh.* Maybe you should show this paper to Tetecae. He is smart, and understands both the *taibo* and The People."

Daniel shook his head. "I can talk to Tetecae, but I don't think I should show him this." Not with Flint's name on the list. Not with his father at the very top. He thought of something else. "Do you think Tetecae would make a good Metal Shirt?"

Doubt creased Ben Buffalo Bone's round

face. "When he works at the big store, which is full of the hard candy and coffee that I like so, and dresses better than many *Tejanos,* why would he want to be spit on, to have rocks thrown at him? To be shot at?"

Why do we? Daniel thought, but did not say.

"You should ask Rain Shower."

Daniel looked amused. "To be a Metal Shirt?"

"No, *bávi.* But she knows much. You have often talked to her about matters that trouble you. This I know. And you should take her for your wife, have many *Nermernuh* babies. You should do this soon, my brother."

The smile had faded instantly. Daniel shook his head.

"You do not like my sister?"

He shook his head violently. "No, I like her very much. I have no ponies to give your uncle."

"Cuhtz Bávi would not want many. Rain Shower is not as pretty as Oajuicauojué. Some brave will pay many ponies for my younger sister, but Rain Shower?" He snorted.

Daniel stared at the writing tablet.

"*Bávi,* I am not as smart as you. Nor as brave. But I do know one thing, for my eyes

240

see very well. You should speak to Cuhtz
Bávi about Rain Shower. Before Tetecae
steals her away from you."

CHAPTER EIGHTEEN

It did not surprise Daniel.

When the Pale Eyes doctor insisted that Quanah sit in the wheelchair and be rolled down the hall, carried down the steps, wheeled to the hack, driven to the depot, and pushed to the train, Quanah said: "No."

"But. . . ."

"Damn no."

The doctor started to protest again, but School Father Pratt cut him off. "Leave your contraption here, Doctor. Quanah will walk."

"He is too weak. He cannot make it down those steps. I dare say he will collapse before he even reaches the door."

"My money's on Quanah." Captain Hall smiled.

As for Quanah? He was already standing, ramrod straight, face pale, lips chapped, and arms still bandaged, but his eyes a firm, unblinking black. The doctor began shaking his head, and Quanah started walking.

He led the procession, followed by Nagwee and Cuhtz Bávi, then the doctor, Captain Hall, School Father Pratt. Isa-tai gave them a good lead before he stepped through the door with Frank Striker, carrying both his and Quanah's grips, trailing. Ledger in one hand and valise in the other, Charles Flint let Rain Shower go ahead of him. Daniel brought up the rear, a few feet behind Ben Buffalo Bone. Most of the luggage had been taken to the depot already by two Negroes. Daniel carried only his grip, and one of his Old Glory tablets.

He kept his eyes on Rain Shower as they made their way down the stairs and into the waiting cabs on Houston Street. School Father Pratt helped Rain Shower into the last hack, and Flint climbed in beside her, with Ben Buffalo Bone sitting next to the bookkeeper. Daniel had to sit in the driver's box, and School Father Pratt ran to climb into his vehicle. While waiting for the cabs to begin their journey, Daniel glanced at Tivoli Hall, but, from all appearances, it was closed. It was, after all, 8:00 A.M.

They rode down Houston Street, past the sporting houses, gambling halls, the saloons, hotels, into the Third Ward, and finally arrived at the depot for the Texas & Pacific. A

243

big, greasy, black 2-8-0 locomotive belched thick smoke, as eager to get out of Cowtown as Daniel was.

Captain Hall stood on the platform, talking to Quanah. Daniel only made out a few of the rancher's words, but knew the former Ranger's concern was more on leasing The Big Pasture than on Quanah's recovery. They shook hands, and Quanah headed to the car, stopping to sign an autograph for a freckle-faced red-headed boy whose father hid nervously in the shadows.

"Daniel."

He turned, finding School Father Pratt extending his right hand, using his left to tip the old military hat he wore at Rain Shower. "Charles."

The former bluecoat shook hands with his two students, who had to lay ledger and writing tablet on the platform to free their hands. "I wish to express my sympathy over the loss of Yellow Bear. It was a terrible accident." His eyes looked questioningly at Daniel, as if he wanted a confirmation that it was an accident. Looking away quickly, Daniel saw Captain Hall taking to Frank Striker. Hall must have relayed Daniel's suspicions to Pratt.

Daniel looked back at Pratt, but said nothing.

"You two Comanches are excellent representations of what the Industrial Boarding School is all about," Pratt said, giving up on prying any information out of Daniel. "You are traveling the white man's road and leading your people into a new era." He tilted his head toward the train. "Like Quanah Parker."

"Thank you," Flint said.

Daniel could only nod.

"Kill the Indian, not the man. That's what I preach and teach. When you get back to the reservation, do what is right. Help Quanah lead your people. We have accomplished much, but there is much left to accomplish. It will be a long journey."

Another handshake, another tip of his hat and a polite farewell to Rain Shower, and Pratt walked back to one of the waiting hacks.

"Come, let us board the train." Flint's voice. When Daniel turned, he saw the bookkeeper had already picked up his ledger and was escorting Rain Shower up the platform, following Nagwee and Cuhtz Bávi aboard.

"I warned you," Ben Buffalo Bone muttered, and headed to the train.

Always too much going on, Daniel thought. *Metal Shirt work, much of it nothing more than drudgery, but now more. Yellow Bear dead. Quanah had barely survived. A fight among Tejanos over The Big Pasture. A fight among The People over that same grazing land. One and a half Old Glory tablets filled with mostly nonsensical notes. Theories and superstitions, but nothing solid. And now Rain Shower is laughing at something Charles Flint had said.*

Spitting onto the dirty planks, he picked up his tablet, and headed for the train.

"Killstraight!"

Turning, he straightened, tensing, as William J. Kyne ran down the boardwalk. Kyne's Congress gaiters slid to a stop, and he caught his breath, looking around. "Damn. I just made it. Take it everybody else's on that train?"

Daniel's head bobbed.

"No chance I can get a fare-the-well quote from Chief Quanah, eh?"

A conductor yelled the answer: "All aboard!"

Kyne sniggered, and shook his head, and, when Daniel resumed his walk to the train, Kyne walked alongside him.

"We're still partners, aren't we, Killstraight? We're still working on this story together, right?"

No answer.

"Listen, I'll work on the Sol Carmody end

246

down here, but I'm going to need your help when you get back to the reservation."

Daniel slowed his pace, and shot the *Herald* reporter a glance.

"I got the name of the cowboy, Carmody's *segundo,* the one you likely saw drunker than Hooter's goat in the alley on the night ol' Yellow Bear up and went to the happy hunting ground. Vince Christensen. Word is . . . and this isn't from the Dallas *Herald,* so it's likely accurate . . . that Vince spent three years in Huntsville for manslaughter. The way I see it, it's not hard to get someone who has already killed one person to murder another. Especially if all you're asking him to do is to kill one or two Indians."

Daniel walked on, but knew he would write the name of the cowboy in the tablet as soon as he settled into his seat.

"You need to talk to Vince. Wire me what you find out. The *Herald* will pick up the charges."

Sticking the Old Glory underneath his arm, Daniel grabbed the handle, and pulled himself onto the step. The train lunged, started to pull away. He looked down and back at Kyne.

"Me talk to Vince?" he called out.

Kyne nodded. "Carmody sent him up to the reservation. To make sure his herd of longhorns stays on The Big Pasture." He blinked. Smiling, Kyne waved his hat over his head, yelling: "Don't be surprised, Killstraight, to find old Billy Kyne paying you a visit in Indian Territory in a couple of weeks. But find Vince Christensen! Talk to him!"

He longed to sit close to Rain Shower, but Quanah motioned for him to sit across from him and Nagwee, so Daniel obliged. The car rocked without rhythm, and the smell of smoke and cinders lay heavy in the late morning air. Fort Worth became a distant memory, and the rolling hills stunted with trees replaced the landscape, gradually losing the trees, soon flattening.

The train increased speed.

"This Iron Horse breathes much fire," Nagwee said, staring out the window. "Not good."

Daniel knew what the holy man meant. Even despite the recent rains, the land here was brown, the coarse, dry grass nowhere near as high as Daniel had seen it in previous years.

Quanah agreed. "The grass is not as green as it is in our land."

"That is why the Pale Eyes want it so."

Quanah grunted. "Of this we will speak

among the elders when we return to the land of The People."

"It will be good to be home again."

"*Haa.*" Quanah nodded.

Turning, Nagwee revealed a mischievous grin. "You will be happy to be no longer where you can hear my snores."

"Snores? I thought those were pale-eyes cannon roaring in my ears."

Daniel smiled, then fetched a pencil and hurriedly opened his tablet. He had almost forgotten to write down Vince Christensen's name. He looked back at some of his notes, put the end of the pencil in his mouth, and chewed. The train whistle blew. Ahead of him, Rain Shower laughed at something Charles Flint had said. At the rear of the car, Ben Buffalo Bone began playing a song on his flute.

He barely heard the words, wasn't quite sure he understood, and, removing the pencil from his mouth, he looked at Nagwee.

"I am sorry," Daniel said, "*Tsu Kuh Puah,* what did you say of Isa-tai?"

Nagwee and Quanah stared. With a frown, Nagwee answered: "I said that Isa-tai liked not my snores, either." Flashing another grin at Quanah, he added: "My wife minds not, though."

249

"Your wife is deaf," Quanah said.

"No. She just cut off her ears because I snore."

This was something Pale Eyes did not understand about The People, that they had a wicked sense of humor, that they were devoted to their family. *Taibos* found Comanches to be solemn, heartless, cruel. Yet Daniel knew The People laughed often, loved with all their heart, only he was not in a mood to hear Nagwee and Quanah's jovial banter.

"But did you say Isa-tai left because of your snoring?"

Nagwee grunted. Quanah frowned. Nagwee crossed his arms over his chest and glared at Daniel. "I said that. You were not listening. Isa-tai got up in the middle of the night. He opens the door. I wake up. 'Where do you go?' I ask him, and he says . . . 'To get away from this racket where I can sleep.' "

"So he went down the hall?"

"I did not ask him the next morning. He did not say."

"Was that the . . . ?" No, he would not bring up that night, especially not spoil the fine spirits Nagwee and Quanah were in. Daniel thanked Nagwee, and filled the page of the Old Glory tablet.

Isa-tai left room. No alibi from Nagwee.
Took Room 4. Had to be. Where else?
But what time? Nagwee would not know.
He could not read a clock, and the roof
hides the stars.
Could that have been the door I heard
shut? No. I would have heard footsteps
pass my door. Or would I, had he been
quiet?
Red paint on Isa-tai's face. Red marks on
window, globe.
Theory: Isa-tai leaves. Nagwee wakens.
Isa-tai lies. Shuts door. Waits for Nagwee
to fall to sleep.
Enters Quanah's room. Shuts window.
Blows out lamps. Grabs key off table.
Locks door. Sneaks to Room 4. Sleeps
there. Next morning returns key when no
one is looking after Quanah discovered.
?????????
Shit!

Quickly he looked up and flipped the page
as Charles Flint passed by on the way to
the water bucket at the end of the car. The
notes from Ben Buffalo Bone's flute wailed
sadly, and Daniel looked down the aisle and
found Rain Shower. Her face seemed happy,
but he noticed that she was watching
Charles Flint. She must have felt his stare,

251

because she turned, but by then Daniel had avoided her eyes, and looked out the window, watching the burned, ugly land pass by.

The train took them to Wichita Falls. From there, they boarded wagons, filled with corn bound for Fort Sill, and traveled on. After crossing the Red River at Hill's Ferry, they wove along the trail through gullies and over tree-lined hills, and toward the Wichita Mountains.

Past Crater Creek . . . to Blue Beaver Creek. Sage shined across the land.

"This is holy place," Cuhtz Bávi said.

"Once it was," Nagwee said, "but no more. It is owned by the Long Knives."

Daniel knew what the *puhakat* meant. Among The People, wherever one found natural sage, the land was holy. Once, this had been The People's domain; now the bluecoats controlled it. In the year the Pale Eyes called 1875, Quanah had camped at Crater Creek before riding on to Blue Beaver Creek to meet Bad Hand Mackenzie to surrender the Kwahadis.

"Is that not right, Isa-tai?" Nagwee said. "Was this not once the land of The People? Our most holy land?"

Isa-tai did not move. Legs buried by corn,

he sat with his back against the hard side of the wagon, arms folded, black eyes unblinking.

Frank Striker changed the subject. "You want to get off at your home, Quanah?" The trail led just past Quanah's Star House. Isatai lived near there, too. In fact, Daniel could have gotten off here along with Cuhtz Bávi, Ben Buffalo Bone, and Rain Shower. Despite wanting to meet with the Indian agent, he now realized that's what he should do. He would have been alone with Rain Shower. Most likely Charles Flint would have to journey on to the trading post with his ledger books.

"No. I must meet with Biggers. With the bluecoat chief."

Besides, the bearded Pale Eyes driver yelled back: "Striker, my orders is to get all of these bucks to Fort Sill!"

So it was settled.

A kernel hit him on the nose, and Rain Shower exploded with giddiness. Daniel found her, saw he picking another kernel, tossing it, but laughter spoiled her aim. This one bounced off the crown of his hat.

Ben Buffalo Bone played his flute. Rain Shower threw a handful of corn. Daniel loved the way she looked, how she laughed.

He shielded the cannonade of corn, plucked a kernel from between his legs, and fired a salvo that sailed over Rain Shower's head.

The corn fight was on.

Cuhtz Bávi hit Frank Striker. Quanah buried the toe of Nagwee's moccasins. Nagwee dumped a handful on Quanah's bowler. Corn and laughter flew with the musical notes. Only Ben Buffalo Bone, who played a merry tune, and Isa-tai and Charles Flint did not participate. Ben would have, Daniel felt, had he not been enjoying the flute. But Isa-tai and his son? They just did not seem to know how to laugh.

"Cut out that damned foolishness!" the driver of the wagon called out, and sprayed tobacco juice onto the road. "Cut it out, I say! We're almost to the fort!"

They did not listen. The war went on until Ben Buffalo Bone lowered the flute. He raised his head, and then they all heard.

Strains of music from the bluecoat band reached them, and they pulled themselves to their feet, corn spilling off their bodies into the wagon or down their clothes. Daniel reached up, grabbed the top of the side, and pulled himself up.

They drove into the parade ground at Fort Sill. It looked as if the entire Army was out there, standing at attention in the hot, humid afternoon, in dress uniforms, brass buttons reflecting the sunlight, brass horns of the regimental band wailing, drums rolling like thunder.

Metal Shirts were there, too. Daniel recognized Agent Joshua Biggers, Bible in hand, and Twice Bent Nose. Other Indians — not just The People, but Kiowas and Apaches — stood. They were singing songs, welcoming Quanah back.

Daniel dropped back down. Tears streamed down Quanah's face. Ben Buffalo Bone tried to match the band's melody with his flute.

It was a happy time, and, when Rain Shower reached up and took Daniel's hand, he knew he had not felt this way in months. Everyone in the wagon sang.

Except for Isa-tai and Charles Flint. Isa-tai's sharp eyes locked on Nagwee. Flint stared acidly at Daniel. But holding Rain Shower's hand, seeing the laughter in her face, hearing the music in her voice, Daniel scarcely noticed.

CHAPTER NINETEEN

"I prayed for Quanah. I will continue to pray for him. He looks weak."

Agent Joshua Biggers, the Baptist minister from North Carolina, ducked behind his desk, and opened a drawer filled with papers.

"Don't you think so, Daniel?"

Weak? That's what Isa-tai had been telling several *Nermernuh* men outside by the corrals. Quanah felt so weary from his near-death that his wives had returned him to that pale-eyes-built Star House so they could care for him. He lacked the strength, Isa-tai railed, to guide The People. The blue-coats and the agent should appoint a new leader. Isa-tai should be that leader.

Said Daniel: "Quanah is strong."

"Yes, that he is." The young preacher returned his attention to the papers. "We also held a memorial service for Yellow Bear. A great number of Indians and whites attended. A fine turnout. I'm sure Yellow Bear would have been glad." Biggers's head shook. "What a tragic accident."

Daniel did not respond. *Tragic? Yes. Accident? Hardly.*

Not far from Cache Creek, headquarters for the Comanche, Kiowa, and Apache reservation was a small cabin, hotter than Hades except during the bitterest winter. A drawing of the Easter resurrection, done by a Kiowa girl on ledger paper, had been tacked to the wall, book-ended by portraits of Grover Cleveland and Jesus. Unlike his predecessors, Joshua Biggers kept his desk relatively free of filth, unless you considered the dust that spread across everything. The only thing not coated with the fine powder was the Bible in the center of the desk.

"Ah, here it is." Biggers rose, turned, and slid the yellow envelope across the desk. "This came for you the day before yesterday."

The last thing Daniel expected was a telegram. Especially one from William J. Kyne less than a week since they had left Fort Worth.

THINGS ABOUT TO BOIL OVER HERE
STOP CARMODY HAS NO NEED FOR
COMANCHE GRASS STOP LEASES

*WITH CHEROKEE FOR HIS HERDS
STOP TELLS ASSN HE WILL SELL HIS
COMANCHE LEASE STOP NOW WE
KNOW REASON STOP BLACKMAIL
STOP HAVE YOU TALKED TO CHRIS-
TENSEN YET STOP*

"I trust this is not bad news, Sergeant."

Daniel shook his head. Not bad news, but what did it mean? If what Kyne said were true, blackmail was an obvious deduction. Sol Carmody had bought rights for a full year to lease The Big Pasture for $250. The Northern Texas Stock Growers' Association had offered . . . what? Daniel wished he had his Old Glory tablet with him to check. His memory said it had been $17,000, $18,000 . . . no, $19,000 or thereabouts.

"Christ Almighty!" Immediately he felt shamed. He looked up, saw the ashen look on Joshua Biggers's face, and apologized for taking the Lord's name in vain. For breaking one of the Ten Commandments back in Carlisle, the School Mothers would have pounded his knuckles with their rulers until he bled.

He studied the wire.

The People would get $250 under the agreement Isa-tai had signed with Carmody. That *Tejano* would net $19,000. Men,

258

women, and children — red, white, all colors — had been murdered for a much smaller sum than that. Carmody would have a big reason to silence any protest from Quanah, or Yellow Bear.

He shoved the telegram into his vest pocket, and looked back at the agent. "Before we left for Fort Worth, you were brought a paper. An agreement to lease The Big Pasture. Signed by Isa-tai."

"Yes, that's true."

"Do you still have it? May I see it?"

Biggers returned to the drawer. A minute later, Daniel had stepped into the doorway for better light.

To who this konserns

this leter is a agrement Btwen Sol Carmody, Elm Fork of trenety Rver, Tex, and Kiyota Dropins, reeprezentin the Comanch nation

in xchang for $250 per anum, the Comanch nation aagres 2 let "The biG pastir" to the S-C𝛿, Ω5, ††† and .45-70 brands — all reg- estred Dallas, Tex, Sol Carmody OwNer.

no Othr Brands wil be allwed 2 Share grazin leese withot Carmodys apruval

This leter is Legaly bindin 2 all parteys.

Signed on this 12th day off jewLie in year of our Lourd 18 and 88

Solomon R. Carmody

X [Kiyota Dropins]
Witnesd by
V. Christensen
X [Tony johnsoN]
George McEveety

Daniel reread the letter. Carmody's *segundo,* Vince Christensen, had been one of the witnesses. He didn't know any Tony Johnson, but suspected that he could be found riding for one of Carmody's brands. George McEveety's signature, however, surprised him. Maybe that would give the document more of a legal standing in the pale-eyes courts. Daniel just didn't know.

"I didn't do anything wrong, did I, Sergeant?"

Shaking his head, Daniel returned the letter to Joshua Biggers. That was something new. Previous agents would have told Daniel to shut up, warning him that this was none of his affair, and that the letter was legal, valid, and nonnegotiable.

"The handwriting is atrocious, the spelling a comedy of errors," Biggers said. "Immediately I took it to the trading post, and Mister McEveety confirmed that he had signed it. I found Charles, and asked him to take me to see his father, just to make sure. I knew Quanah had something in mind for

260

The Big Pasture, but Isa-tai himself said he signed it. I decided that if anything were wrong, Quanah would let me know, take it directly to the colonel at Fort Sill, or, knowing Quanah's connections, all the way to Washington City. I guess I should have asked you about it, Sergeant."

Daniel shook his head, thinking: *No, I should have asked Ben Buffalo Bone.*

"I will speak to Mister McEveety about this," Daniel said. "Thank you, Reverend Biggers."

Once the trading post had been a brilliant red building that stood out on the prairie for miles, but an unrelenting sun and constant wind had faded the paint to more pink than red, and dust and dirt made it look more brown than pink. Still, by reservation standards, it remained impressive — a two-story building of wood planks with a fancy façade and plenty of windows on the top floor. The awning over the front porch sagged a little, as did the porch, and one of the steps was missing, and chickens squawked and pecked in the coyote-fenced coop to the side. Two Kiowa women sat cross-legged in the shade by the door, and a burly black man stood on the other side of the porch, broom in one hand, cigarette in the other. Dogs yipped as Daniel rode up, but it was too hot to be barking, so the ugly, bone-thin mongrels quickly retired under the porch, growling steadily to inform the newcomer that they weren't too tuckered out to take a chunk out of his leg if provoked.

Daniel expected to find George McEveety upstairs, where he lived in a small room in the back — the rest of the floor a warehouse, stockroom, something like that. Rumors around Fort Sill said the upstairs were also used for something more stimulating than the chicory he sold, but less sanitary. Instead of sweating in his quarters, the gray-bearded merchant sat on an overturned barrel, fanning himself with a newspaper, and slaking his thirst with a bottle of root beer.

"Well, if it ain't Gen'ral Metal Shirt hisself," McEveety said. "Step off your high horse, Killstraight." He held out the bottle. "Want some firewater, chief?"

The Negro exhaled smoke as he laughed at his boss' joke.

After swinging from his horse, Daniel wrapped the hackamore around the hitching rail, carefully climbed the steps, and greeted the two stone-faced Kiowa women who ignored him.

He stopped and leaned against a sun-rotted column, as much as he dared, and looked through the open door to see Charles Flint showing off a bolt of yellow calico to one of Twice Bent Nose's daughters. When he returned his attention to George McEveety, the trader was gulping down the rest of his root beer, and had stuffed the newspaper into a knothole. His face was pasty, hair matted with sweat, and the armpits of his shirt dark and stained. From where Daniel stood, he could smell McEveety's stink.

"I wish to ask you some questions, Mister McEveety," he said.

With a burp, McEveety leaned forward on his makeshift chair and pitched the empty bottle over the porch railing. "If it's them Old Glory writin' books you want, I still don't carry none. Ream paper and envelopes. That's all I got, and not much of them. Not much of a market, or a profit, for writin' when most of the customers is ignorant savages. Ain't that right, Buck?"

The black man laughed again.

"This is about an agreement you witnessed for the Texas rancher named Carmody."

McEveety's smile vanished instantly, and he shot from his chair. "Don't you. . . ." He stopped, turning, half smiling as Twice Bent

Nose's daughter — Daniel couldn't recollect her name — passed through the door, holding three yards of the calico in her hand. She sang out a hello to Daniel, bid the merchant and his helper good day, but did not speak to the two Kiowa women.

No one spoke until she was out of earshot.

The merchant waved a railroad spike of a finger in Daniel's face. "That tin shield don't give you no right to question me, boy. I might call you a white Comanch', but you ain't no white man. Best know your place, Killstraight. Don't get uppity like some Yankee nigger. I tol' that Bible-thumper I signed it, and I signed it. That's the end of the story, boy. End of the story."

Buck, the black man, no longer laughed.

Daniel met McEveety's glare for ten full seconds. No one spoke. Even the dogs had quit growling. Footsteps on the hardwood floors turned his attention to the doorway, and there stood Charles Flint, wearing sleeve garters and wiping ink off his fingers with a handkerchief.

Suddenly Daniel remembered, and he couldn't help but stare at the bookkeeper's hands. The ink, he found with relief, was black. Flint shoved the handkerchief into the pocket of his trousers, and said: "If it's referring to that letter my father signed,

Daniel, I can answer any questions."

"That's right," McEveety said. "You two bucks hash things out. I got a store to run." He spit between the cracks in the porch, and stormed inside.

The black man stepped off the porch, and walked around the post. The Kiowa women remained silent.

"You never mentioned this in Fort Worth," Daniel said after a long silence.

Flint sighed. "I did not think it was important. My father said he signed the paper. The rancher also said so." He shrugged, and leaned against the door frame. "I am sorry, *bávi*. I did not know this was important. I am no detective. I am a bookkeeper."

It was Daniel's turn to sigh. He crossed the porch until he found a comfortable, shadier spot on the wall to lean on. "It is not important," he told Flint. "I just wonder why he" — motioning inside the store toward McEveety — "would witness it."

"He is a white man. A man of property. People would not question his word."

Daniel wasn't quite so sure about that. George McEveety was not Lee Hall or Burk Burnett. Still, he nodded as if in agreement with Flint. "This Carmody," Daniel said. "I have not seen him on our land before. Did he know McEveety? Has he traded here before?"

Flint shook his head. "The only time I ever saw the *Tejano* was in Fort Worth at the restaurant. I swear this is true." His eyes said he wasn't lying, and Daniel felt remorse for having doubted another *Nermernuh,* no matter who his father happened to be.

"Your father signed the agreement?"

"*Haa.* This he has never denied. You know that as well as I do. When Agent Biggers brought the agreement to the post, Mister McEveety said he had signed it, and then we took it to my father. He said the words were what he and Carmody agreed to."

"The other witnesses," Daniel continued. "Vince Christensen works for Carmody. The other is someone named Tony Johnson. Do you know them? Have they ever . . . ?"

"Their names mean nothing, *bávi.* But that does not mean I have never seen them here or anywhere."

Hoofs clopped down the road, but Daniel ignored them. He stood there, staring at his moccasins, trying to decide where he should go next. Well, that seemed obvious.

"I must go back to Fort Sill," he said.

"Why?"

"To send a telegram to Hugh Gunter." Stupid. He should have thought about that before leaving the agency, after Biggers had shown him the wire from Kyne. It was out of the way, but Deputy Marshal Harvey Noble had taught Daniel not to believe everything you read. He would need to confirm with Gunter that Carmody did lease Cherokee range. "Then I must find this Vince Christensen. He was in Fort Worth, near the hotel, the night. . . ." He stopped short.

"I hope both help you better than I have done, *bávi*. I am sorry to have failed you."

Daniel looked up, started to tell Flint that he was not to blame, but the bookkeeper was gazing at the steps, a smile replacing his frown, and that's when Daniel heard the giggling of girls' voices. He straightened, turned, and saw Oajuicauojué's laughing face as she slid off her pony, and climbed the steps. Behind her strode her older sister, Rain Shower.

"We have come to trade," Oajuicauojué announced. She treated Daniel to a coquettish grin, and slipped inside the door.

"I must go," Flint said, and followed.

Rain Shower passed through the threshold without a word, without a glance at Daniel.

Angrily Daniel stormed off the porch, swung into the saddle, and kicked his buckskin mare into a gallop.

267

CHAPTER TWENTY

When he reached The Big Pasture the following morning, his heart felt lighter, and he regretted his jealousy. He should not be angry at Rain Shower, or at Tetecae. This land, perhaps the most holy that belonged to The People, often affected him so. It made him happy, let him forget whatever troubled him.

Surrounding The Big Pasture, the Wichita Mountains stood bold, powerful, the trees so verdant that even the rocks looked green. In the pasture, the tall grass was lush, almost reaching his saddle, waving in the refreshing breeze.

The mare's hoofs splashed across a creek, and, somewhere to the north, a longhorn bawled. Daniel couldn't see the cow, however, for the grass was too high.

What struck him as odd, though, was the fact that he couldn't see any cattle. Oh, he knew they were there, but finding three thousand head of dumb *Tejano* beef in three hundred thousand acres could take forever. Usually, at this time of year, it was impossible not to stumble over cattle the Pale Eyes shipped north to graze during the summer. Of course, Daniel didn't need to find the cattle. He just rode toward the smoke rising from the edge of the woods at the foot of a hill. The wind carried not only the smell of smoke, but the aroma of coffee, and bacon. That, he knew, would lead him to Vince Christensen.

The mare snorted, stopped, and Daniel heard the dung splatter beneath the grass. He waited, then let his mount graze on some of the grass. *Why let Carmody hog it all?* he asked himself.

Ahead of him, in the rocks above the smoke, sunlight glinted. Daniel leaned forward, wondering. The mare lifted her head — and saved Daniel's life.

He never heard the shot until the echo reached him after the mare lay in the grass, kicking spasmodically though already dead. He had pitched out of the saddle, rolled through the grass, and now started to push himself up. The second shot tore through the grass far from him. On his knees, Daniel reached for the revolver, spotted something brown through the tall grass, came to his feet, and sprinted toward it.

The second shot he heard, and felt, instantly. It dug a ditch across his left side, and knocked him into the mound of manure the buckskin had just deposited, ricocheting off the boulder in front of him. Rolling over, he felt tears stream down his face, and he cursed himself for crying, but, son-of-a-bitch, his side hurt. The next shot kicked up mud into his cheeks, and he raised the Remington, shakily, and snapped a shot.

"Damned *taibo* gun!" he said through clenched teeth. The percussion cap had misfired.

He turned over, crawled, leaped the final feet, and pulled himself into a ball behind the boulder a second before the next bullet clipped off the side of the big rock. Daniel moved to his right, aimed, pulled the trigger. This time the Remington bucked in his hand, and he slid back behind the boulder.

"Stupid." He lowered the smoking revolver. The shooter had to be a good two hundred yards, probably more, from where he squatted — far out of range for the antiquated cap-and-ball revolver the agency provided him with. From the thundering echo that bounced off the Wichitas, from how hard his horse had dropped, from the way his side bled and throbbed, he was up against one of those far-shooting Sharps rifles the *Tejanos* had used to whip The People at Adobe Walls.

Daniel had no chance, and he knew it. Now would be a good time to begin his death song.

A fly buzzed. Next came the sound of hoofs on hard rock. Daniel picked up the Remington, thumbed back the hammer, and leaned to his left. Cautiously he pushed back the grass with the long barrel. Sweat burned his eyes, clouded his vision, but he spotted a horse — brown, maybe a bay — trotting up the hill, away from the snaking smoke. He couldn't make out much about the rider, other than he wore a light-colored hat and a duster that billowed behind him in the wind. Still, he wasn't truly certain that he wasn't hallucinating. Horse and rider vanished behind the hill, and Daniel slid back behind the rock. He tore a strip of cloth from his calico shirt, pressed it against his side, and pulled himself up.

Dizziness and nausea almost knocked him onto his back, but somehow he managed to keep his feet. Salty sweat poured into the wound, and he bit his bottom lip. Cattle bawled, and more hoofs sounded, but these came from the east. Still, Daniel fumbled for his revolver, felt it slip from his fingers and off the boulder, and felt himself sliding back to the ground.

"Vince! Vince!" A shot rang out.

"Get up!" Rough hands dragged Daniel to his feet. A hand slapped his face. Fingers gripped his black hair, and pulled it until Daniel screamed. His eyes opened.

Another shot roared. Daniel managed to glimpse a Pale Eyes cowboy on a side-stepping horse cock a Colt, send another bullet toward the sky. "Vince!" the rider yelled.

"Damn it, Joe," the man pulling Daniel's hair snapped, "lope over yonder. See what the hell's going on. See if Vince is wounded or what. Now! We'll bring this buck along."

"Bet these Comanch' was tryin' to steal our herd," another voice said. "And Vince stopped 'em."

He neither heard nor saw the rider leave. The next thing he knew, his face was mashed against the flank of a horse. He thought he saw the brand, †††, but wasn't sure. Someone jerked him by his vest into the saddle, and then the rider swung up behind him, the saddle's big horn jamming into Daniel's bleeding side. Spurs chimed, and the horse exploded.

Daniel vomited.

A sledge-hammer jarred his head. "Do that again . . . I kill you here."

Air rushed out of his lungs. The cowhand had thrown him to the ground. He reached for his bleeding side, but, before he made it, a boot rocked his ribs. What the buffalo gun's bullet had failed to do, the boot succeeded. Three ribs cracked, and Daniel felt his bladder release.

"Bastard. This red bastard. . . ."

"Put that gun away."

"But he murdered Vince. Slit his throat!"

"We ain't shootin' him."

"But. . . ."

"We're hangin' the red nigger."

Someone jerked his head off the gravel. Hemp slid over his head, tightened against his throat. They jerked him to his feet. The rope choked off his air. When he fell, they dragged him.

"To that blackjack yonder."

He wouldn't live to make it to the tree. He'd choke to death right here, or bleed to death.

Another cannon roared, and a *taibo* screamed.

A pistol roared over Daniel's face. He forced his eyes open, found out he could breathe again, saw a gloved hand cock a

273

revolver. Another bullet screamed, and the man holding the gun fell back, crying out in pain.

"It's the whole damned Comanche nation!"

"Injuns! God A'mighty, they'll butcher us all!"

"Shut up, Joe!"

Then, guttural English: "Guns down! Now! Else die!"

Shadows crossed his face. How cool it suddenly felt, and he opened his eyes. Twice Bent Nose's ugly face hovered above him. His mangled hands reached down to Daniel's side, and Daniel flinched, tightened his eyes, remembered how he had wet himself, and felt shame. He was no warrior, but a frightened child.

"Just stand back there." This was in English. A voice he recognized.

"You speak English? This bastard killed our foreman. Slit his throat."

"Look at him. Look at him. Look at what he done to Vince!"

"Just shut up. Don't move. We don't want to kill anyone."

He turned his head. Did not believe what he saw. Charles Flint stood, rifle in both hands, standing in front of three or four *Te-*

janos, yelling at them. One more Pale Eyes sat against a rock, blood soaking through his blue shirt at the left shoulder.

Another voice reached his ears, this one speaking the language of The People, saying that coup had been counted, that now it was time to kill these thieves, or turn them over to The People's women for torture. Horses snorted all around him, and Daniel made his head turn the other way.

"No, Father!" Charles Flint's voice again. "We will not kill anyone!"

Daniel swallowed. Isa-tai swung around on his horse, face defiant, holding a rifle over his head. Then he began to sing. To Daniel's surprise, he did not argue with Flint or Twice Bent Nose. Instead, he sang a song of pride.

Look at my son
Look at my son
Look at my son
See how brave he is
See how brave he is
He has taken his first coup
He has saved the life of a warrior of The
    People
We will sing songs in his honor
Look at my son
Look at my son

Look at my son
Tetecae
Tetecae
Tetecae
See how brave he is

The words held no meaning for Daniel. Not now. What he wanted to focus on, what he had to remember, was the rifle Isa-tai held. It was a Sharps, one of those far-killing weapons of the buffalo hunters. And Isa-tai's face. He must remember that, too. Painted red.

CHAPTER TWENTY-ONE

He woke into a world of darkness.

Cold. Damp. The smell of rot.

As his eyes grew accustomed to the darkness, smoky gray light sneaked between iron bars on a window above him. Shivering, he brought his hand to his forehead. Even that slight exertion exhausted him, and his hand slid off his head and struck hard rock, wet rock, skinning his knuckles. His throat felt parched, and fire blazed across his side every time he drew a breath. He ran his tongue over cracked, bleeding lips. He touched his chest, realized he lay on a blanket, shirtless, though his ribs were bandaged. Turning his head, he could just barely make out the thick door. Dripping water was the only sound, almost deafening, maddening, until he began to make out voices carrying beyond the barred windows.

He called out, but no one could hear a whisper he barely heard himself. He was alone, but Daniel knew where he was. He had sent his share of men here himself.

Bluecoats called it the dungeon. The People knew it as The Lodges That Are Always In Darkness.

The post guardhouse at Fort Sill.

Daniel closed his eyes, letting sleep overtake him again.

The song brought him back to life. A gourd rattled over his head, then his chest, and he felt the cloth being pulled away, small fingers gently applying a salve to the wound in his side.

The rattling and the chant stopped, and a strong voice called out: "You are awake, my son!"

His eyes fluttered, focused, and a mostly toothless smile greeted him.

Tears filled his eyes, and he tried to reach up to Nagwee. The *puhakat*'s fat hand swallowed his, and pressed it against his cheek.

"We feared for you, He Whose Arrows Fly Straight Into The Hearts Of His Enemies. I wanted to perform another *pianahuwait,* but the Long Knives would not allow it. They will not even allow you into the big doctor house at the soldier fort. But my *puha* remains strong. You will live, and that is good for The People."

"Tsu Kuh Puah," Daniel whispered. "I shamed The People. I disgraced myself. When the Pale Eyes wounded me, I cried from the pain. When one kicked me in the ribs, I wet myself."

Nagwee lowered Daniel's hand, and patted his shoulder. "There is no disgrace. You performed bravely. The Pale Eyes say you killed a *taibo.* You would have killed the others, but there were too many. It is good that Twice Bent Nose arrived when he did, or we would speak your name no more. Instead, now, we will sing songs of your bravery, in your honor. For you. And for Twice Bent Nose, Tetecae, and Isa-tai, who stopped the other *Tejanos* from killing you."

Hands began wrapping a new bandage across his side and chest, but Daniel tried to comprehend what Nagwee had just told him. He wet his lips, blinked, shook his head slightly.

"Tsu Kuh Puah." Speaking hurt. He wanted to ask for water, but felt he needed to explain first. "I killed no one."

"Hush." The sharp, feminine voice brought his attention to his chest, and he flinched as those delicate, once gentle, hands tightened as they knotted the bandage. Daniel looked away from Nagwee and met Rain Shower's stare.

"Don't talk," she said. "You are still weak."

His lips parted, but she raised a warning right fist. His lips closed. His Adam's apple bobbed.

As Nagwee disappeared in a dark corner, Rain Shower suddenly broke out in laughter. Briefly Daniel joined her, but his ribs ached too much, and he shook his head, fighting off the pain. The medicine man returned, sat, gently lifted Daniel's head, and he tasted sweet, cool water. He drank greedily, wanted more, but this Nagwee would not allow.

The old holy man then gathered his belongings, and walked away. Daniel heard Nagwee's fist hitting the door. Keys rattled, metal turned, and the door dragged heavily against the rock floor as it opened.

"You done?" a bluecoat voice called out.

With a grunt, Nagwee stepped into the hall.

"Hey, woman. You done?"

"No!" Rain Shower answered in English.

Tobacco spit splattered into the slop bucket in the corner, and the door slowly shut.

"I did not kill that *taibo*," Daniel told her.

"This I know. The Pale Eyes are such fools. The agent, Biggers, he yelled at the big bluecoat chief, but they say you must stay here. For now. One *taibo* is dead. Another, in the soldier fort, might die."

She slid down the blanket, and touched his hand. Daniel shuddered.

"I hear Tetecae was very brave." He stumbled over the words.

"*Bah.* He is not as brave as you. Twice Bent Nose was even braver. He stopped them from. . . ." She couldn't finish, forced a smile, and tried again. "And Isa-tai, his *puha* was very strong. He shot the one the Pale Eyes say might die. But you were the bravest. One *Nermernuh* against a dozen Pale Eyes." She leaned forward, and pressed her lips to his.

"It was not that many," Daniel said after they had kissed. He knew he sounded unconvincing.

"Twice Bent Nose says there were even more Pale Eyes."

"He. . . ." Daniel shrugged, and gave up on trying to translate the pale-eyes phrase "stretches the truth" into the language of The People.

She kissed him again, though this time on his forehead, and stood. "I must go. The bluecoat will be impatient."

"I. . . ."

He didn't know what to say, so she said it for him: "I love you, He Whose Arrows Fly

281

Straight Into The Hearts Of His Enemies. I have always loved you. I will always love you."

He runs in the morning sun, side no longer throbbing, legs no longer weak, wearing not the uniform of a Metal Shirt, but buckskins and moccasins, no shirt, a lone hawk feather hanging behind his left ear. He carries a magnificent shield that would have impressed even old Isa Nanaka.

Stopping, he reaches down and plucks the leaves from a bush, crumpling them in his hand, bringing them to his nostrils. The scent is stimulating. It makes him free. Sage. Holy sage. He stands in a field of sage that stretches across the prairie. Nothing to see but blue sky and green sage.

The marsh hawk lands on a nearby clump.

Daniel sees it, and greets the raptor politely.

"This is holy land." The marsh hawk speaks in the voice Daniel remembers as his father's.

"It is." Daniel nods. "The People will always cherish it."

"No," the hawk tells him. "The People will not have it for long. That is to their disgrace."

"I do not understand."

"You will, my son. In time, you will."

Silence. The wind blows. Daniel and the hawk fill their lungs with sage-sweet air.

"Your side has healed?" the hawk asks.

"It hurts no more."

"Because of this holy ground."

"Haa. And because of Nagwee's puha."

"Haa. His puha has always been strong."

Another voice whispers behind him: "Should I bring up your disgrace, Isa-tai?"

"Yellow Bear?" he asks, whipping his head around, but discovers nothing but sage.

Daniel's head falls, and he cannot look back at the marsh hawk. Tears stream down his cheeks.

"What is the matter, Oá?"

He looks up. The hawk called him Horn, the name Daniel had been given before his father presented him with his own name, He Whose Arrows Fly Straight Into The Hearts Of His Enemies.

"I spoke the name of a brave Nermernuh who has traveled to The Land Beyond The Sun." Daniel's voice cracks as he confesses, and bitter tears flood the ground.

The hawk shakes his head. "He was not dead when you spoke his name."

He forces his head up, sniffs, wipes the last tears from his eyes, and says: "I do not understand."

The hawk spreads its wings. "This is holy land."

Silence. The wind still blows.

"What else troubles you?" the hawk asks.

He touches his side. Now it hurts. "Father," Daniel says, "I disgraced myself. I cried when those Pale Eyes shot me. I wet myself when they broke my ribs."

"Nagwee said there was no shame, and I am not one who would argue with Nagwee. Pain is no disgrace, Oá. Nor is fear. Neither means cowardice, and you are no coward, my son. No, pain and fear are part of life. And death."

Yellow Bear's voice comes from another direction. "Should I bring up your disgrace, Isa-tai?"

When Daniel looks, however, again, he sees nothing but sage, so he turns back to his father.

"What does he mean?"

"Who?"

"The one who has traveled to The Land Beyond The Sun."

"I did not hear him, my son. He was speaking to you. Not to me."

"Why have you come?"

"Because I love you."

Tears well again. His voice chokes. "I love you, too, Father."

"The marsh hawk is your puha, as it was mine," his father says. "You will always find strength in the hawk. That is why you wear my feather on your hat."

He reaches up, surprised. He is wearing the battered, dusty black hat he had bought at McEveety's post a year earlier. But hadn't he been wearing just a ribbon and a lone feather dangling behind his ear? He turns the hat around by the brim, the feather floating in the breeze.

Sage remains pungent.

When he hears Yellow Bear's voice again, now coming from the north, he does not bother to look. His tears stain the sage leaves, which turn into blood.

"It is hard for you, Daniel," the marsh hawk says. "It will always be hard for you."

"I am not Daniel," he says.

"You are Daniel. And you are Killstraight. And you are Sergeant. And you are He Whose Arrows Fly Straight Into The Hearts Of His Enemies. You are Oá."

Adds a feminine voice: "And you are Huuma."

He pivots, heart aching, and gazes at his mother, the way she looked before the Kwahadis surrendered. Young, beautiful. She has not come to him in the form of an animal, but as a Mescalero captive who became one of The People.

Smiling, he asks: "I am With The Stick? This I do not understand."

"When you were but a child, just learning to walk, wherever you went, you would be carrying a twig." His mother's voice is musical, relaxing, as refreshing as the sage. "Perhaps it gave you balance. Perhaps you just wanted it to chew on, for often that is what you did. Always, however, you grasped a stick. So your father and I called you With The Stick."

"I do not remember this."

"Of course not," the hawk tells him, "for you were too young."

He closes his eyes, trying to summon the memory of this childhood story, but can't. When he opens his eyes, his mother has gone.

"Mother!" He turns, desperate. The hawk has flown away. Daniel stands alone in a wilderness of sage. His side begins to throb. He wears the uniform of a Metal Shirt.

"One thing lasts forever," the familiar voice says, and, when he turns to the west, he knows he will see Yellow Bear this time.

Sitting cross-legged, the old man prepares a pipe, which he offers to the directions before breathing fire into the bowl. Yellow Bear smokes, then offers the pipe to Daniel.

"What lasts forever, *Tsu Kuh Puah*?" Daniel asks. He smokes, and passes the pipe back to the elder.

"Not you," Yellow Bear replies. "Nor I.

286

Certainly not the buffalo. Sadly not even this."
He gestures toward the sage. "Perhaps not
The People as we know The People. Certainly
not the taibos, *ignorant and as unclean as*
they are. Not the Mescalero. Not the marsh
hawks."

"Then what?"

"Love." Yellow Bear nods. "Some day, the
taibos, *especially the* Tejanos, *will say that*
The People fought them the hardest, and why
did we do this? For the love of our family. Our
ways. Our land. Love endures."

"I do not understand."

"I think you do." The pipe has disappeared.
"Isa Nanaka remains with you. As does Marsh
Hawk. And your mother. I will always be here
for you, my son. Quanah and Nagwee will
always be here for you. Rain Shower will
always be here for you. Don't forget us. We
shall not forget you. For we love you. And we
know that you love us. You love all The
People. That is why you are a Metal Shirt."

Yellow Bear's body is becoming translucent.

Desperation fills Daniel's voice. "Don't leave
me! Tsu Kuh Puah!"

The old man smiles. "I said I will never leave
you, my son."

"But there is something you said." Yellow
Bear is fading into the sage. " 'Should I bring
up your disgrace, Isa-tai?' You said that. But

what does it mean?" He shouts to only sage. "What does it mean? Please, Tsu Kuh Puah. *What does that mean?"*

From the east echoes Yellow Bear's fading voice. "I think you know the answer to that question, too."

Alone, sweating, he closes his eyes, trying to dam back the tears. When his eyes open, he no longer sees a never-ending field of sage. Something flaps above his head, and he looks up, finds the bluecoat flag of red and white stripes, of stars in a night sky, flapping in the wind.

Daniel stands in the center of the parade ground at Fort Sill.

CHAPTER TWENTY-TWO

Now he knew how Quanah had felt when the Fort Worth doctor insisted he take a wheelchair to the T&P depot. Defiantly pushing aside the curved walnut cane Major Becker had offered him, Daniel stood, taking a deep breath. That was a mistake. Pain rifled up his side, making him grimace, but Daniel tried not to show how much he hurt.

"Are you ready?" Rain Shower asked.

"I am ready." He took a tentative step toward the open door.

"You're as mule-headed as Quanah Parker," Major Becker said, causing Daniel to smile.

Light almost blinded him when he stepped into the tiny hallway, and he was still inside the guardhouse. He fumbled along, feeling Rain Shower beside him, hearing the footsteps of Major Becker, the post surgeon, behind him. From outside, came angry voices, muffled by the prison's thick stone walls. A bluecoat snapped to attention, and pulled open the outer door.

Even more light. Daniel had to stop, squeeze his eyelids closed.

"Are you sure you don't want this cane, Daniel?" Major Becker asked.

He wasn't quite sure of anything, but he forced his eyes open, waited for the dots to disappear, and stepped into clean air for the first time in a week.

"There's the murderin' savage!"

"We should have lynched that sum-bitch when we had the chance!"

"What kind a law is this, Marshal?" a voice thundered. "Lettin' a murderin' red devil out?"

"Reckon that's the kind of law a Texian should expect from a damyankee."

"Carmody." The drawl eased Daniel's tension just a tad. "You're the biggest damned fool I've had the displeasure of meetin' in a month of Sundays."

The big *Tejano* rancher straightened, face turning scarlet, and started to raise a fist, but Deputy U.S. Marshal Harvey P. Noble stopped him with words.

"That's right, Carmody. Add assaultin' a federal peace officer to the charges I might file against your ornery hide. Hell, I might even call it attempted murder." Noble's big, gloved hand rested on the butt of his revolver. "Or maybe, with my luck, I won't have to file no charges, just a report on how come I killed a worthless cur at Fort Sill."

Another cowhand said: "Why aren't you chargin' that buck with murder? He killed Vince Christensen. Slit his throat like you'd do a deer."

"Daniel Killstraight didn't kill anyone." That was another familiar voice. Turning, Daniel spotted the Cherokee policeman, Hugh Gunter, sitting at the edge of the guardhouse's porch, his long legs dangling toward the ground. Gunter was whittling a stick, but now he stopped and pointed the blade of a Barlow knife at one of Carmody's cowhands.

Daniel looked around. Carmody stood in front of the steps to the guardhouse, facing Harvey Noble. Behind the big rancher waited four cowhands, holding the reins to their mounts in their left hands, their right palms balancing precariously over the butts of their own weapons. Carmody's big dun grazed on Army grass. A buckboard was parked beside the dun. In the back, Daniel saw, were two pine coffins.

Hugh Gunter was still speaking. "Your man got his throat slit. Daniel yonder didn't even have a knife on him. Plus, you idiots

291

yourselves said you found Daniel shot in the side, his horse killed, three hundred yards from where your ramrod's body was found. Now how in the hell do you figure Daniel killed him?"

Before one of the cowhands could speak, Gunter cut him off: "Maybe you reckon that Daniel is a big medicine man among the Comanches. Maybe he used some redskin magic to slit this Christensen gent's throat. Then changed that knife into a Forty-Four Remington. Then managed to shoot his own horse in the head. 'Course, that must have been more Comanche magic 'cause the bullet we dug out of that horse's head was a chunk of lead that had to be Fifty caliber. About the same caliber that likely cut Daniel's side."

"Who the hell are you?" another cowboy demanded.

Gunter closed the blade. "I'm your better."

The reins dropped to the grass. The cowhand made a beeline, but stopped at the click of the hammer of a Colt now held in Harvey Noble's right hand.

"How many bodies you want to haul back to Texas, Carmody?"

"Whit," Carmody said, "let it lie."

The cowboy's fist clenched. His body

shook. But he stayed put.

A blond-haired cowboy with a freckled face — likely still in his teens — cleared his throat. "Well, Vince sure didn't shoot this Indian, neither. Not if you say it was a Fifty caliber. Vince had a Forty-caliber Bullard."

Another cowboy snickered. "And he couldn't hit the backside of a barn, let alone a movin' target three hundred yards away."

"We never said your cowhand shot anybody, either," Hugh Gunter said. "Hard to shoot anybody, with your throat slit ear to ear. But you Texians'll believe anything."

"Hugh. . . ." Noble's voice revealed tension. "Let's behave like gentlemen."

"Gentlemen!" Carmody spat. "Damyankees. Damned prairie niggers."

"I didn't come here to start a ruction, Carmody," Noble said, his voice powerful and steady once again. "Came this way to stop one. And I'm no Yank. Born, bred, and baptized in Arkansas." He reached into his jacket, and pulled out a folded set of papers. "This here is a court order that says you are to get your Texas longhorns off The Big Pasture. Forthwith. That means no dilly-dallyin'. If you don't, Carmody, I'll just say it's ration day and the Comanches, Kiowas, and Apaches'll have three thousand head to slaughter."

293

Carmody made a start for the marshal, but the Colt stopped him, too. "I got it legal," Carmody stammered. "Isa-tai . . . he signed."

"Carmody" — Noble shook his head pathetically — "you must be an idiot. After you come up here and got an ignorant Comanche to sign three copies of a letter you wrote out, Quanah Parker and the Northern Texas Stock Growers' Association were having their lawyers file writs in courts. You gave one copy of that thing you wrote to your cowhands to give to any Indian or agent, kept the other to yourself, gave another one to Dan Waggoner. Figured that made everything legal, especially since you had witnesses sign it, too."

"Witnesses." Hugh Gunter chuckled.

"Yeah." Noble's head shook. "Vince Christensen served time in Huntsville for manslaughter. He also rode for you. So did that other cowhand, can't rightly recollect his name. And then you got George McEveety. He left two wives behind in Mississippi. A bigamist. Also, the way I understand it, a liar, cheat, whoremonger, whiskey peddler, and genuine rapscallion. Yes, sir, that's a fine band of witnesses you got."

Sol Carmody stood, flexing his fingers. Noble paused to give him time to speak, but, when the rancher said nothing, Noble kept talking. "You didn't even file the *agreement* you got with any court. Didn't have it notarized. This ain't the old days, Carmody. It's Eighteen Eighty-Eight. We're civilized. Mostly."

"That paper. . . ."

"Is as worthless as you are, Carmody. Hell, you might be facin' criminal charges of extortion. Judge Parker and me'll have to talk that over with the commissioner. You didn't need that grass. You got plenty in the Cherokee Nation. Ain't that right, Hugh?"

Gunter nodded. "He did. But that agreement is being reconsidered after what all's come up hereabouts. Sol Carmody ain't the type any of us Five Civilized Tribes want to associate with."

The rancher's mouth hung open.

"You just thought you could take advantage of these poor Indians and make a handsome profit for yourself," Noble told him. "What was that we figured he'd make out with, Hugh?"

Gunter answered: "Nineteen thousand two hundred and fifty dollars."

Noble smiled. "Sounds like grand larceny. Yes, sir, a real handsome profit . . . if it worked."

"It didn't," Gunter said. "Stupid Texians."

Daniel fought off dizziness. Comprehending all this was proving too hard.

"A Comanch' killed Tony Johnson, Marshal," another cowboy said. "Witnesses will swear to that."

"And I got witnesses who'll say they was part of a tribal police posse stoppin' a bunch of trespassin' Texians from lynchin' a Comanche peace officer." Noble shook his head in disgust.

"That's for a jury to decide, ain't it?" yelled another cowboy, his head bandaged, left eye blackened. Apparently he was the one upon whom Charles Flint had counted coup.

"I ain't wastin' Judge Parker's time on something as picayune as this." Noble waved his Colt at all the cowhands. "Your Johnson boy was killed by Isa-tai, but that was self-defense. Criminy, I should run the lot of you in for tryin' to lynch a bona-fide peace officer. But then them ticky mossyhorns would still be eatin' Comanche grass that rightfully belongs to Capt'n Hall and his outfit."

Noble's tone changed. "The other one, your top hand, well, you're damned right. That was murder. Cold-blooded. But Killstraight didn't do it. I'm certain sure of that. You rest easy, Carmody. All of you Texas

296

brush poppers. I'll find the son-of-a-bitch, and that son-of-a-bitch'll hang."

"Even if it was an Injun?" the man named Whit asked. " 'Cause you seem to like a lot of Injuns, Marshal." The cowboy glared at Gunter, who pushed his silk top hat back with the stick he had been whittling, and smiled.

Another rider came loping toward the guardhouse.

"It was not an Indian," said Daniel, who suddenly faced better than a half-dozen stunned men.

He took a step down. Gently. Another. His side seared, but he made it to the bottom without falling. Rain Shower stood behind him, her face worried. He wet his lips and said: "I saw a man. White man. On a dark horse. He rode over the hill, away from camp. He must have seen your riders coming across The Big Pasture."

"Could you recognize him, Daniel?" Gunter asked.

His head shook. "Too far away. He wore a hat. Tan, I think, but it could have been covered with dirt. And. . . ."

The rider reined in on a blood bay gelding. Daniel swallowed. The man slid off the saddle, grabbing his back with one hand, while fetching a note pad with the other.

"Damnation," he said. "Looks like I've got another story that'll get me a job back in the East. Showdown at Fort Sill! What's going on here? I'm Billy Kyne. Dallas *Herald.*"

The ends of Kyne's duster flapped in the wind.

"So, Marshal, let me get all this down straight. Factual, for once in the *Herald*'s short, fruitless life." Billy Kyne took a swig from his flask, which he passed to the federal deputy.

They sat in Noble's and Gunter's camp in the sage west of Fort Sill near Cache Creek, the Cherokee poking the fire under the coffee pot, and Noble, looking worn out and pale, rubbing a foot with one hand while sitting on a rock.

Daniel sat beside Rain Shower. She held his hand.

"You read the *Herald* story. We telegraphed that to all the Fort Worth papers, even to the federal marshal. I'm sure you saw it. Heard about it in the dram shops and all."

"All I saw was the writ the marshal give me. All I heard was what he told me." Noble took a drink, and passed the flask to Gunter, who pitched it back to Kyne without taking a sip.

"Well, the *Herald* . . . well, actually me . . .

broke the story. It'll be in *Harper's Weekly* soon, I assure you. Don't know how many papers in the East. Carmody's scheme has been foiled. He attempted to blackmail the Northern Texas Stock Growers' Association, wanted to deprive the great Comanche nation" — winking at Daniel and Rain Shower — "of wealth the tribe desperately needs. But justice, thanks to the Dallas *Herald,* prevails. Can I quote you, Marshal?"

Noble drank again from the flask Kyne had tossed him. "All I saw was the writ the marshal give me," the deputy repeated. "All I heard was what he told me."

"Excellent. This case is closed." Kyne waited for the flask to come back his way.

It was Gunter who spoke. "Hell, it ain't over. Who the hell killed that Texas waddie? Who the hell shot Daniel?"

Kyne looked perplexed. "I thought the cowhand shot Daniel."

"Uhn-huh." Gunter flung the stick into the sage. "Then cut his own throat out of remorse."

The end of the pencil went into Kyne's mouth. He turned it, biting, several rotations before removing it and writing something in his tablet. "Well, this is excellent to be sure. Another mystery. Another article for the *Herald,* or better yet, the New York

Tribune." He wrote again, then looked at Daniel. "And who tried to murder Quanah? Right, Daniel?"

That got both Noble's and Gunter's attention.

"What are you talkin' about?" Noble asked. "From what I read, that was an accident."

The eyes bore into Daniel, who took a deep breath, slowly exhaled and said: "It was no accident."

They waited for his explanation.

"You say it was a white man, eh, Killstraight?" Kyne was talking again, talking and scribbling, scribbling and talking. "The one who shot you? The one who slit the cowboy's throat?"

Instead of answering, Daniel asked: "When did you get here, Mister Kyne?"

"I arrived at Fort Sill when they carried you into. . . ." He dropped the pencil, and smiled weakly. "Killstraight. Surely. . . ." His eyes darted to Noble's, then Gunter's, to Rain Shower's, and back to Daniel's. "Killstraight. We're pards. You don't think I'd. . . ." He wet his lips.

Undeterred, Kyne scooped up his pencil, slid it over his ear, and thumbed back several pages in his tablet. "This is interesting, gentlemen. Most interesting. Three men witnessed the document Carmody signed with Isa-tai. Two of those are dead. The third is George McEveety, a wretched man who runs the foul trading post in these godless parts. I think it's time for me to interview that cad and get to the bottom of this. If you'll excuse me, gentlemen." He tipped his hat at Rain Shower. "And you, dear squaw, as beautiful and as lovely as Hera, daughter of Kronos, wife of Zeus, I bid *adieu.*"

Even before Billy Kyne was on his horse, Gunter had filled a tin mug with coffee. "Daniel," the Cherokee asked angrily, "how in hell did you hook up with that insufferable son-of-a-bitch?"

Daniel smiled. "Actually," he said, "he reminded me of you."

CHAPTER TWENTY-THREE

In the cabin the Pale Eyes had built for Ben Buffalo Bone's father, Daniel ducked under the pinto's neck, his right hand gently rubbing the coarse hair. He came up on the other side of the horse, walking over straw, speaking softly, his hand never leaving the pinto's body. The stallion's tail swished. "Good boy," Daniel said, and stepped away, admiring the animal.

"Cuhtz Bávi is too generous," Daniel said. "I should not accept such a gift, for I have nothing of value to return to your uncle."

Rain Shower grabbed Daniel's hand and squeezed it. "Cuhtz Bávi," she said, "thinks he will get the horse back."

She giggled.

It was a Mexican Hat pinto, and Daniel knew what The People said of a horse like this: ride it, and you are invincible. That Rain Shower's uncle, the head of the household since her father's death, would give such a gift overwhelmed him.

"Do you . . . ?" He stopped. Saying — *Do you think you would be worth such a pony?* — did not strike him as a smart thing to say, especially considering how much he enjoyed her hand in his.

"What will you call him?" she asked.

He shrugged. "What would you?"

She held her chin, considering. The white cotton dress she wore highlighted her round face and raven hair. Ben Buffalo Bone, Daniel decided, was wrong. Rain Shower was far more beautiful than her younger sister. She would be worth twenty horses like the Mexican Hat pinto.

"I would call him Kwihnai."

"Eagle." Daniel nodded. "It is a good name. I will call him that."

Leaving the horse to graze on hay, Daniel led Rain Shower around the makeshift stall and into the portion of the house where Daniel lived. Gingerly Daniel bent down and picked up the saddle, a wood and deerhorn frame covered with rawhide and a Navajo saddle blanket.

"You are leaving?" Rain Shower sounded hurt.

"I must try out my new pony," he said lightly, forcing a smile.

"Your wounds have not completely healed.

303

You should not ride hard."

"I will go no faster than a trot."

"You should not go far."

"I won't go far."

"How far?"

He stopped his work, and grinned at her. "Crater Creek."

After gathering his hackamore along with the saddle, Daniel went back to Eagle. Rain Shower followed him.

"That is where Nagwee has his lodge," she said.

"That is who I must see."

She did not speak again until Daniel had saddled his new horse, and returned to his living area to gather his holster and revolver. Her face turned hard as her frown.

"I am not going there to arrest Nagwee," he said lightly.

Silence. Then: "You think Isa-tai is responsible for all of this."

He did not answer. Instead, he checked the caps on the Remington.

"Isa-tai would not. . . ."

"Isa-tai despises Quanah," he said. The jovial banter was gone, and he regretted that, but he knew what he had to do. "He would have given away The Big Pasture and The People would have nothing."

"He did not shoot you."

Daniel holstered the Remington. "He carries a rifle like the one the Pale Eyes used to hunt buffalo with."

"Which he took off a Pale Eyes he himself killed." She raised a finger. "You said it was a *taibo* who shot you."

"I saw a man in *taibo* clothes riding over the hill. Having thought more of this, I now realize that person did not have to be the one who shot me." It could have been Billy Kyne, riding away upon hearing the shots for the reporter was, at heart, a coward. It could have been anyone. Hell, it could have been Isa-tai, dressed up in pale-eyes clothes. Even had Daniel been able to identify the man, he could never prove that rider had shot at him. Not in a *taibo* courtroom.

"Isa-tai saved Quanah's life," Rain Shower argued. "He and Nagwee performed the Big Doctoring."

"And Isa-tai painted his face red."

"That is his *puha*. And what does it mean? The paint he wears does not make him a murderer."

Sighing, Daniel explained the red prints that had been found on the windowpane and lamp globes at the room above the Fort Worth mercantile. "Billy Kyne said it was red ink."

"Ink." Rain Shower shook her head. "A

Nermernuh uses vermillion, not ink."

"Perhaps it was vermillion." He led Eagle out of the cabin and into the sunlight.

"If he had meant to kill you," Rain Shower said, "you would be dead. Isa-tai has the best eyes of any of The People when it comes to shooting a long gun. Tetecae told me that himself."

Daniel swung into the saddle.

"He saved your life," Rain Shower said. "He killed one of the Pale Eyes who was trying to kill you. He saved the life of Quanah."

He wanted to explain, but found no words. Rain Shower started to argue more, but her expression changed, and she stiffened.

"I must see Nagwee," he said. "I will speak to you later."

"I must see someone, too," she said.

He pressed the paint horse's sides with his moccasins, and felt Eagle take flight.

In the blistering heat of the day, with no clouds to block the sun's rays, Daniel found Nagwee sitting in his brush arbor. Three dogs barked as he rode Eagle across Crater Creek, and Daniel greeted the old *puhakat,* and swung from the saddle.

"Maruaweeka!" Nagwee called out, and

began gathering his pipe and tobacco. "That is a fine horse you ride, my son."

"Thank you. It was a gift from Cuhtz Bávi."

The old man laughed. "You should be giving Cuhtz Bávi horses, not the other way around."

Daniel stepped inside the arbor, and Nagwee motioned for him to sit. Hot as the afternoon was, Nagwee had a small fire going in the brush arbor, as if he had expected someone would join him for a smoke.

"What do you call that horse?" the old man said as his thick fingers and thumb packed the bowl with tobacco.

"Kwihnai."

"A good name. You want to trade?"

Smiling, Daniel shook his head.

"I could run him in many races against the Long Knives. I could win much money."

"I could race him myself."

"Then I will bet on you. Let us smoke."

"Two nights ago," Daniel said carefully, "I had a . . . dream."

Nagwee lowered the pipe. "A vision?"

He shook his head. "I said a dream, *Tsu Kuh Puah.*"

The old man's belly bounced as he laughed. "Sum-bitch," he said, using one of

307

the few pale-eyes words he knew and liked, "He Whose Arrows Fly Straight Into The Hearts Of His Enemies had a vision."

Again Daniel started to protest, but Nagwee held up his thick right hand. "Tell me of this dream."

They smoked again after Daniel had told the *puhakat* all he could remember of the dream, or vision, or whatever one called it. One of the dogs had fallen asleep in front of Nagwee's teepee, and snored. This was the only sound.

"Why do you come to me?" Nagwee asked.

"You are a man of great *puha*. You are the wisest *puhakat* among The People. My father once went to you when he had a . . . dream. You explained to him his purpose, you told him what he needed to do, what the vis- . . . what the spirits told him he should do. You have helped Quanah. You have helped many. I hoped that you might help me."

Nagwee looked up. His smile became lost in the crevasses of his large face.

"You don't need me, my son. You already know."

"I. . . ."

"Tell me. Tell Nagwee what you think this vision means."

Daniel swallowed, looked away. After inhaling deeply, he faced the *puhakat* again. "First, will you tell me about Medicine Bluff Creek?" he asked.

Nagwee grunted. "The People knew it to have much healing powers. It was the most priceless thing The People had."

"Sage grows there," Daniel said.

The old man nodded. "Where sage grows, the land is holy."

Daniel waited, trying to find the right words, and finally said: "Major Becker. He is the doctor at the soldier fort where the Long Knives stay. He tells me that Fort Sill was established in Eighteen Sixty-Nine. Um . . . nineteen winters ago."

Nagwee looked at the roof of the arbor, chewing on his lips, tapping his fingers, then faced Daniel again. "That would be just about right."

"The People were powerful then, stronger than we are now. We would not have let the Pale Eyes just take this land from us. We would have fought them."

Nagwee's thick fingers began tamping the pipe bowl again. "We are lucky," he said. "Many of the Apaches, they were sent from their homeland to Florida, as were many of our own warriors. But now our men . . . those who have not traveled to The Land

Beyond The Sun . . . have returned to this country. The Apaches stay here, too, far from their home. The Cherokees, the Creeks, those other inferior Indian peoples who live toward the rising sun, they are many miles . . . too many for an old man like me to count . . . from their homes. The Pale Eyes drove them out. We live near Medicine Bluff Creek. That is good."

Daniel made his voice stern as he repeated: "Fort Sill stands on The People's holiest ground. That soldier fort has stood there almost as long as I have breathed. We would not have let the Pale Eyes just take this land from us. We would have fought them."

Setting the pipe down, Nagwee looked solemn. A tear fell down his cheek. "We could not fight them," he said. "They did not steal the land. It was given to them."

Tears welled in Daniel's own eyes, and he looked away, shaking his head, mumbling: "And that is Isa-tai's disgrace."

Nagwee cleared his throat. "Isa-tai was a young *puhakat* then. He trusted the Pale Eyes. He loved them. When the bluecoats came, it was Isa-tai who led them to Medicine Bluff Creek. He thought if he gave the Long Knives The People's most precious thing, they would love The People. They

310

would let us alone. He did not know or understand the true nature of all Pale Eyes. Later" — Nagwee had to stop to wipe away the tears, to swallow down the bile — "later . . . when he saw what was in the pale-eyes hearts, he became bitter. That is why he wanted to wipe out the killers of the buffalo. Maybe he would have, had not the Cheyenne brave destroyed his *puha.*"

Daniel tried to shake his head clear. "Did Quanah know this?"

"I think not. When Isa-tai gave the Long Knives our land, Quanah would not have been much older than you are now. He was a warrior, a fine, brave warrior, but he was not the great leader of The People that he has become. Besides, Quanah, your family, and most of the Kwahadis lived in the land of the *Tejanos,* on the Staked Plains, not along Medicine Bluff Creek. Quanah would not come here until more than a handful of winters later."

Daniel stared at Nagwee. "Who knew what Isa-tai had done?"

Nagwee shrugged. "Most are names we must never speak again."

"But the father of Quanah's favorite wife. The one who traveled to The Land Beyond The Sun when we were in the *Tejano* town called Fort Worth . . . he knew."

311

The nod was solemn, final. "Yes, he knew."

He had been awake for more than an hour, but still lay on the blanket, one arm over his head, the other gently holding his aching side. Cuhtz Bávi's dogs barked in the morning light, and Eagle stamped his hoofs, demanding breakfast. Daniel tried to block all of that out. The dogs barked louder. Ben Buffalo Bone yelled.

A horse snorted, and Daniel realized someone had ridden to Cuhtz Bávi's lodge.

Back in Fort Worth, Tetecae had said Yellow Bear's death had been an accident, and Daniel had believed that. Quanah had been the intended victim. Why would anyone want an old *puhakat* like Yellow Bear dead? Now, Daniel realized how wrong he had been. If Quanah had died, Isa-tai would not have grieved, but it was Yellow Bear who he had to silence.

Yellow Bear.

A piercing wail, almost inhuman, lifted Daniel out of his bed. Next came shrieks. Shouts. The sound of confused dogs running away. Cuhtz Bávi's voice began a death song, and Daniel was up, holding his ribs, running through the door.

He saw the horse, a blue roan pulling a travois, recognizing the rider as an Apache named Netdahe, head hanging down. Sitting beside the travois, Ben Buffalo Bone's mother lifted her head to the sky, and screamed.

"No!" Daniel yelled.

Tears blinding him, he stumbled, falling to his knees beside the travois. His vision returned, though he wished it hadn't, and he reached down, and lifted Rain Shower into his arms. He hugged her tightly, kissed her cold forehead, rocked her, rocked her.

Ben Buffalo Bone was sawing off his braids. Cuhtz Bávi mourned his niece and adopted daughter in song. Daniel felt as if he had been kicked in the stomach. He laid Rain Shower's head back on the travois, kissed her lips, stroked her hair, saw the bruises around her throat.

He also spotted a smudge of red ink on the collar of her new white dress.

Savagely he shot to his feet, found the Apache, and demanded: "Where did you find her?"

Netdahe did not understand the language of The People. Daniel had to sign his question, and the Apache answered. Netdahe had not been in this country long, but Daniel knew where he meant.

Blue Beaver Creek. Along the sage. Where Isa-tai lived.

He headed toward his lodge, which seemed to become farther from him, not closer, weaving now, heart shattered, trying to find a way to make it to Eagle.

Then he was lying on the ground, curling up like an infant, crying . . . wishing he were dead . . . wondering how he could ever go on . . . alone.

CHAPTER TWENTY-FOUR

"Daniel. . . ." Closing his Bible, Agent Joshua Biggers pushed himself to his feet. His mouth opened, and his face showed shock and repulsion, which the young minister tried to hide.

His hair had been shorn, shorter now than even the Pale Eyes had cut it at Carlisle. He had carved gashes on both forearms, his calves, thighs. The arm wounds had clotted, but the legs bled again after his ride to the agency headquarters. Biggers would likely never understand how The People grieved. Ben Buffalo Bone had chopped off not only his braids, but his left pinky. Daniel had considered removing fingers himself, but then he remembered how Rain Shower had held his hands, and he could not bring himself to do that.

Standing in front of Biggers's desk, he looked at the ring he had braided from Rain Shower's black hair. He tried to find courage, tried to stop the tears from overflowing again.

"Daniel," Biggers tried again. "I know this is hard. But you must believe me, my son, when I say that she's in a far better place now. Matthew said blessed are they that mourn, blessed are the meek, blessed are the merciful, blessed are the peacemakers, blessed are the pure in heart. Rain Shower was all of those, and much, much more."

Daniel looked at the wall. " 'Blessed are they which are persecuted for righteousness's sake,' " he said, " 'for theirs is the kingdom of heaven.' "

"That's right." Biggers followed Daniel's gaze. He tapped on the drawing tacked to the wall. "A Kiowa girl drew this. I just think it's beautiful. Because of what happened at Calvary, Daniel, Rain Shower won't really die. She lives now, with Jesus. She'll be there waiting for you. But she'll also always be with you."

Daniel stepped around the desk. He studied the picture. Reached up, touched it, and with a curse, snatched it from the wall, and stormed outside.

"Jesus, look what the cats drug up." George McEveety laughed as he pushed himself off the overturned keg, and blocked the door-

316

way to the entrance path. He was alone outside this day. The Negro named Buck was nowhere to be seen. Nor were the two silent Kiowa women. "Hold on, Killstraight. You ain't bleedin' all over my merchandise, boy. You just turn. . . ."

Daniel hit him, feeling the pain shoot through his ribs, feeling the gashes in his arms open again. From underneath the porch, the dogs barked. McEveety bounced into the wall, and Daniel struck him again, again, once more as the trader slid to the porch. Then he kicked McEveety in the head, and moved to the counter.

Dogs growled, but none dared climb the steps.

"My God, Daniel!" Charles Flint said. "What . . . ?"

"I was at the agency just now," Daniel said. Somehow he reached the counter, and leaned against it. He had to catch his breath. Blood ran down his arms and into his fingers, dripping onto the dust that coated the store's floor. His side screamed in pain. His legs ached, throbbed, bled.

Flint remained quiet. When Daniel could breathe again, he said: "I was requesting permission to arrest your father."

The bookkeeper straightened. "Daniel, my father did not kill anyone . . . except the Te-

317

jano who he shot to save your life."

Daniel reached to the ledger. He turned a page.

"He gave away Medicine Bluff Creek," he said, and turned another page, then looked at Tetecae to see his expression. "The People's land. Holy land. Gave it to the bluecoats." He turned another page. "Just as he would have given away The Big Pasture." Another page. "For nothing."

"You're wrong, Daniel. My father saved Quanah's life. Your life. My father is a great man. A powerful *puhakat*."

"He shoots a big buffalo rifle."

"Which he took from a dead *taibo*. Along with the scalp he also took from that Pale Eyes when we were children. Look!" He pointed to the rack of weapons, most of them worthless old muskets, chained behind the counter. "Even on the reservation, it is easy to find a rifle."

Turning another page in the ledger, Daniel said: "Isa-tai wears red paint."

"For his *puha*."

Daniel looked up. "Why was he wearing red paint when he saved me?"

Flint shook his head. "He didn't go there to save you. We . . . Twice Bent Nose and I . . . we ran into him and a party of young braves he was leading. He was planning on stealing cattle from the *Tejanos,* as he said he would."

Daniel flipped the page.

"My father did not kill Yellow Bear," Flint said. "He did not kill the *Tejano* cowboy. He did not try to kill Quanah. He would never have harmed. . . ." He looked down.

"Can you say her name?" Daniel asked.

Flint's head shook.

"I know your father is innocent," Daniel said, his heart breaking as he tapped on the page of the ledger. "You did it."

Flint's head jerked up, and he took a step back. His eyes fell to the ledger.

"Bávi. . . ."

Flint rocked back, his lips bleeding. Daniel didn't even realize he had backhanded the bookkeeper until he saw the blood, saw his own hand shaking over the counter.

"Don't call me brother!" Daniel roared. "I saw the Kiowa girl's drawing on ledger paper on Agent Biggers's wall. Red ink. Black ink. I remember the phrases now from Carlisle. 'In the red' and 'in the black.' Never did understand what they really meant."

Daniel's breath had the taste of gall. He shook his head with disgust. "The girl I loved once said Isa-tai was a great shot with a rifle, and she spoke the truth. Your father taught you how to shoot. I had forgotten that. You obviously hadn't and, as you say, finding a weapon was easy."

Before Flint could protest, Daniel added: "I thought I saw a *taibo* riding away after I was shot. But it was you . . . wearing your pale-eyes clothes."

"I rode there with Twice Bent Nose. . . ."

"You rode into Twice Bent Nose. He told me that at the agency. You had no choice but to ride back with him. And then your father and his raiding party joined up. Saving my life was an accident, Tetecae."

Flint shook his head, touching his lips with trembling fingers.

"And here's something else," Daniel said. "The only person who knew I was going to see the pale-eyes cowboy was you. I told you that right here. You weren't sure what Vince Christensen had seen in the alley in Fort Worth, so you rode there, slit his throat, and tried to kill me."

Flint shook his head, tried to laugh, and said: "Daniel, you are way, way. . . ." But Daniel's eyes told the bookkeeper something else, and Flint threw the inkwell into Daniel's face.

Turning, trying to shield his eyes, Daniel slipped, hit the floor hard. His chest cried out in pain. He saw Flint leap over the

320

counter, saw something flash in his hand. As Flint ran for the door, Daniel drew his Remington.

Hearing the hammer click, Flint turned quickly, bringing up his arm, a pepperbox pistol in his right hand. Daniel's Remington roared first. The bullet smashed the wall, startling Flint. He never fired his pistol. Instead, he turned away, ran for the door.

Daniel's second shot struck Flint in the back, and the bookkeeper tripped over George McEveety's boots, crashed onto the porch, tumbled down the steps.

The dogs wailed, yipped, barked, but remained hiding under the porch.

Stepping over the unconscious trader, Daniel had to lean against the warped column for support. He still held the pistol, but hadn't cocked it. Charles Flint was sitting, one hand stanching the flow of blood from his lower back, not looking at Daniel, but at a *puhakat* mounted on a fine buckskin stallion.

Isa-tai frowned at his son.

"Father," Flint groaned. "You have to understand. . . . Father . . . I did it for you . . . Yellow Bear . . . he would have told everyone about Medicine Bluff Creek. You remember? The cowboy . . . he might . . . I don't know . . . I had to make sure. . . ."

321

"And what of her?" Daniel barely recognized his own voice.

Flint shook his head. "She . . . saw. . . ." Speaking in English now, pleading to Daniel: "I didn't mean to hurt her, Daniel. I swear to God I didn't mean it."

He flung his head back to Isa-tai. "Father," he said in the language of The People. "I had to protect you. You remember, Father. You said giving away our most precious land was your biggest disgrace . . . *until they sent me to Carlisle!*"

Isa-tai said nothing. Straightening his shoulders, he spit, turned the buckskin away, and eased the horse down the trail, back toward Blue Beaver Creek.

"Father!"

Daniel came down the steps.

"Father!"

He didn't remember walking, but now he stood over Flint. Daniel cocked the .44's hammer.

Flint turned, face streaked with tears, with pain. "Kill me, Daniel!" he begged. "For God's sake, kill me. Kill me. Kill me. Please, please, please, just kill me."

Daniel raised the revolver.

CHAPTER TWENTY-FIVE

He remembered Isa-tai's song.

My son is dead to me
My son is dead to me
My son is dead to me
He is dead to all The People
Hear me now
Tetecae
It is the last time
You will hear his name
He is dead
Speak his name no more
He is dead to me
He is dead to me
He is dead to me
He is dead to us all
He forgot the ways of The People
The People's ways are good
The People's ways are good
The People's ways are good
I have no son

Do not mourn him
Do not speak his name
He is not worthy
My son is dead to me
My son is dead to me
My son is dead to me
He is dead to all The People
Hear me now

Then the rest of Isa-tai's song haunted
Daniel as the song had done for the past
eight months.

I am dead to The People
I am dead to The People
I am dead to The People
I am dead to all The People
Hear me now
Isa-tai
Do not speak my name
You will not hear my name
I am dead
Speak my name no more
I am dead to you
I am dead to you
I am dead to you
I am dead to you all
I forgot the ways of The People
The People's ways are good
The People's ways are good

The People's ways are good
I gave away our most holy land
Do not mourn me
Do not speak my name
I am not worthy
I am dead to you
I am dead to you
I am dead to you
I am dead to all The People
Hear me now

He hadn't planned on being here, yet here he stood on a cool spring morning in Fort Smith, Arkansas, having delivered seven prisoners to the cold, dark dungeon to await their trial. Most of his wounds had healed, and his hair was growing back, but now those wounds felt raw again, and he thought that maybe he should just leave. Turn back.

Deputy U.S. Marshal Harvey P. Noble, dressed in the uniform Judge Parker made all his volunteers wear for this special duty, put a hand on Daniel's shoulder. "You sure you're all right, Daniel?"

He nodded.

"All right. If you need anything, I'll be" — Noble frowned — "up there."

Daniel watched the tall, aging deputy climb the steps, and take his place beside George Maledon.

"Here he comes!" a reporter called out, and a melody of voices rang out.

Two, almost three years earlier, Daniel had watched three men hanged on these same gallows, but on this April morning, Charles Flint, also wearing a new suit, stepped onto the platform to die alone. A man in a dark suit began reading from a paper, but Daniel did not care to listen to the words.

"Hello, Killstraight," a voice sounded behind him. Daniel glanced over his shoulder, then turned away from the gallows.

William J. Kyne had lost weight. His clothes looked more expensive, and he sported a well-groomed beard. His breath smelled of coffee, not rye. The reporter even looked sober.

"The *Herald* send you up here?" Daniel asked.

With a wry smile, Kyne reached into his vest pocket and withdrew a card, which he passed on to Daniel. "The Cincinnati *Commercial*. It isn't the *Tribune*, isn't New York, isn't even the East Coast. But it's a start."

Daniel returned the card, and started to look back. Off in a shady corner, six elderly women began singing as a Black Robe prayed for Charles Flint's soul.

"I hate to do this, partner," Kyne said,

"but it's my job."

Daniel looked back. Kyne withdrew a folded piece of paper from his pocket. "Captain Pratt wired this to the newspaper reporters here. Wonder if you'd care to comment?"

Daniel took the paper, unfolded it, read:

FIRST, I WISH TO EXPRESS MY DEEP-EST SYMPATHY TO THE PARENTS, FAMILY, AND FRIENDS OF VINCE CHRISTENSEN STOP

Only the Pale Eyes, Daniel thought bitterly. *Not Yellow Bear. Not Rain Shower. But, then, Charles Flint wouldn't be hanging if he had killed only an old Comanche man and a young Comanche girl.*

JUSTICE HAS BEEN SERVED AND I HOPE THIS ENDS THE UNCALLED FOR ASSAULT THAT HAS BOMBARDED THE CARLISLE INDUSTRIAL SCHOOL STOP WE DO NOT TEACH MURDER STOP FOR ALL THOSE NAYSAYERS I AGAIN POINT OUT THAT IT WAS A COMANCHE INDIAN AND A FORMER STUDENT AT THIS SAME SCHOOL WHO SOLVED THIS EVIL CRIME AND BROUGHT THE PERPETRATOR TO JUSTICE STOP I

HAVE ALWAYS PREACHED THAT WE MUST KILL THE INDIAN AND NOT THE MAN BUT IN THIS CASE WE MUST EXECUTE BOTH MAN AND INDIAN STOP MAY OUR LORD IN HEAVEN HAVE MERCY ON CHARLES FLINT'S SOUL

Behind him, the trap door thudded, the choir gasped. Daniel heard everything — and felt relief that he had not seen Charles Flint die.

Daniel returned the telegram to Kyne, who wrote something in his notebook, then asked: "Well?"

Daniel shook his head. "I have nothing to say."

Kyne's smile was truly sad, but not from disappointment. "That's what I figured. Don't worry. I won't make up something and attribute it to you. Unlike the Dallas *Herald,* the *Commercial* has real journalistic standards." He offered his hand. "I am sorry, Killstraight, about that girl. Can't remember her name, but I know she was sweet on you, and I reckon you liked her a lot, too." He shook his head. "She was pretty. It was a damned shame, Killstraight. I mean that."

To his surprise, Daniel accepted the handshake, then watched Billy Kyne excuse himself, and hurry over with the rest of the newspaper reporters to talk to the marshals, Flint's court-appointed attorney, and the hangman, Maledon.

Daniel stared at the ring he had made from Rain Shower's hair. Birds began to sing again.

He had wanted to say something, to let Billy Kyne quote him, but knew he couldn't. Kyne couldn't have understood. Nor would have School Father Pratt. Even the agent, Joshua Biggers, who tried to understand, couldn't. Without glancing back at the gallows, Daniel stepped with the crowd through the gates and into the throng of curious Pale Eyes waiting outside the execution yard's walls.

As he walked to Eagle, he thought again of what he had wanted to tell Kyne, but what no Pale Eyes could ever comprehend.

When you kill the Indian, you kill the man.

AUTHOR'S NOTE

Most biographies of Quanah Parker mention his near-death escape from asphyxiation in Fort Worth, Texas. He was sharing a room with Yellow Bear, his father-in-law or uncle (depending on which account) at the Pickwick Hotel or, as Richard F. Selcer notes in *Fort Worth Characters,* in the second-floor apartment of an adjacent building. In all accounts, a gas lamp was left on, Yellow Bear died, and Quanah barely escaped with his own life.

Murder conspiracy? Highly unlikely, but the story seemed too good an opportunity to pass up, so I turned it into a murder mystery. The incident happened in December 1885, but I moved it to the summer of 1888.

Sources for Fort Worth included the aforementioned *Fort Worth Characters* by Richard F. Selcer (University of North Texas Press, 2009) as well as Selcer's *Hell's*

Half Acre (Texas Christian University Press, 1991) and Oliver Knight's *Fort Worth: Outpost on the Trinity* (Texas Christian University Press, 1990).

For the Comanche language, I relied on *Comanche Vocabulary: Trilingual Edition,* compiled by Manuel García Rejón and translated and edited by Daniel J. Gelo (University of Texas Press, 1995), *Comanche Dictionary and Grammar* by Lila Wistrand-Robinson and James Armagost (SIL International, 1990), and the Comanche National Museum & Cultural Center in Lawton, Oklahoma.

As always with my Killstraight novels, William T. Hagan's *Indian Police and Judges* (Yale University Press, 1966) and *United States-Comanche Relations: The Reservation Years* (University of Oklahoma Press, 1990) proved valuable, as did *The Comanches: Lords of the South Plains* by Ernest Wallace and E. Adamson Hoebel (University of Oklahoma Press, 1952, 1986). Other sources include *The Comanches* by Joseph H. Cash and Gerald W. Wolff (Indian Tribal Series, 1974); *Comanches: The Destruction of a People* by T.R. Fehrenbach (Alfred A. Knopf, 1974); *Los Comanches: The Horse People, 1751–1845* (University of New

Mexico Press, 1993); *Encyclopedia of Religion and Ethics, Part 22* by James Hastings and John A. Selbie (Kessinger Publishing, 2003); and *The Comanches: A History, 1706–1875* by Thomas W. Kavanagh (University of Nebraska Press, 1996).

I also made a new friend in fellow Comanche enthusiast and historian, S.C. Gwynne, whose *Empire of the Summer Moon: Quanah Parker and the Rise and Fall of the Comanches, the Most Powerful Indian Tribe in American History* (Scribner, 2010) was a *New York Times* bestseller. I gathered a lot of new information and ideas from Gwynne's powerful book. And, no, Gwynne, a reporter for the Dallas *Morning News,* wasn't the inspiration for Billy Kyne.

Richard Henry Pratt's autobiography *Battlefield & Classroom,* edited by Robert M. Utley (University of Oklahoma Press, 2003), provided background on the Carlisle boarding school, as did *The Indian Industrial School: Carlisle, Pennsylvania 1879–1918* by Linda F. Witmer (Cumberland County Historical Society, 1993). *Quanah Parker, Comanche Chief* by William T. Hagan (University of Oklahoma Press, 1993), and *The Last Comanche Chief: The Life and Times of Quanah Parker* by Bill Neeley (John

Wiley & Sons, 1995) were also frequently consulted.

The Eagle Park Trading Post near Cache, Oklahoma gave me an extended tour of Quanah's Star House and the Wichita Mountains, and an excellent history lesson. The Star House could definitely use some restoration work, but it's still standing, and the post deserves much praise for doing its best to keep this part of Comanche history alive.

Finally I owe my Comanche friends (and Quanah Parker descendants) Nocona and Quanah Burgess, their father, Ronald "Chief Tachaco", and their families many thanks for their help, support, friendship — and their amazing art.

Johnny D. Boggs
Santa Fe, New Mexico

ABOUT THE AUTHOR

Johnny D. Boggs has worked cattle, shot rapids in a canoe, hiked across mountains and deserts, traipsed around ghost towns, and spent hours poring over microfilm in library archives — all in the name of finding a good story. He's also one of the few Western writers to have won four Spur Awards from Western Writers of America (for his novels, *Camp Ford,* in 2006, *Doubtful Cañon,* in 2008, and *Hard Winter* in 2010, and his short story, "A Piano at Dead Man's Crossing", in 2002) and the Western Heritage Wrangler Award from the National Cowboy and Western Heritage Museum (for his novel, *Spark on the Prairie: The Trial of the Kiowa Chiefs,* in 2004). A native of South Carolina, Boggs spent almost fifteen years in Texas as a journalist at the Dallas *Times Herald* and Fort Worth *Star-Telegram* before moving to New Mexico in 1998 to concentrate full time on his novels. Author of dozens of published short stories, he has also written for more than fifty newspapers and magazines, and is a frequent contributor to *Boys' Life, New Mexico Magazine, Persimmon Hill,* and *True West.* His Western novels cover a wide range. *The Lonesome Chisholm Trail* (Five Star Westerns, 2000) is an authentic cattle-drive story, while *Lonely Trumpet* (Five Star Westerns, 2002) is an historical novel about the first black graduate of West Point. *The Despoilers* (Five Star Westerns, 2002) and *Ghost Legion* (Five Star Westerns, 2005) are set in the Carolina backcountry during the Revolutionary War. *The Big Fifty* (Five Star Westerns, 2003) chronicles the slaughter of buffalo on the southern plains in the 1870s, while *East of the Border* (Five Star Westerns, 2004) is a comedy about the theatrical offerings of Buffalo Bill Cody, Wild Bill Hickok, and Texas Jack Omohundro, and *Camp Ford* (Five Star Westerns, 2005) tells about a Civil War baseball game between Union prisoners of war and Confederate guards. "Boggs's narrative voice captures the old-fashioned style of the past," *Publishers Weekly* said, and *Booklist* called him "among the best Western writers at work today." Boggs lives with his wife Lisa and son Jack

in Santa Fe. His website is www.johnnyd
boggs.com.

The employees of Thorndike Press hope you have enjoyed this Large Print book. All our Thorndike, Wheeler, and Kennebec Large Print titles are designed for easy reading, and all our books are made to last. Other Thorndike Press Large Print books are available at your library, through selected bookstores, or directly from us.

For information about titles, please call:
  (800) 223-1244

or visit our Web site at:
  http://gale.cengage.com/thorndike

To share your comments, please write:
  Publisher
  Thorndike Press
  10 Water St., Suite 310
  Waterville, ME 04901

Boggs, Johnny D.
Kill the Indian : a Killstraight story /

Eastern Branch
Jackson District Library   3/20/2014

WITHDRAWN

W9-CGV-544